THE LANGUAGE LIBRARY
Series Editor: David Crystal

The Language Library was created in 1952 by Eric Partridge, the great etymologist and lexicographer, who from 1966 to 1976 was assisted by his co-editor Simeon Potter. Together they commissioned volumes on the traditional themes of language study, with particular emphasis on the history of the English language and on the individual linguistic styles of major English authors. In 1977 David Crystal took over as editor, and *The Language Library* now includes titles in many areas of linguistic enquiry.

A History of English Words

Geoffrey Hughes

Blackwell
Publishing

BLACKWELL PUBLISHING
350 Main Street, Malden, MA 02148-5020, USA
9600 Garsington Road, Oxford OX4 2DQ, UK
550 Swanston Street, Carlton, Victoria 3053, Australia

First published 2000

5   2005

Library of Congress Cataloging-in-Publication Data

Hughes, Geoffrey, 1939–
   A history of English words / Geoffrey Hughes.
      p.   cm. – (The language library)
      Includes bibliographical references and index.
      ISBN 0-631-18854-1 (hbk. : alk. paper). – ISBN 0-631-18855-X (pbk. : alk. paper)
         1. English language – Lexicology. 2. English language – History.
      I. Title. II. Series.
      PE1571.H83 2000
      423'.028–dc21   99–34523
                                                                    CIP

ISBN-13: 978-0-631-18854-4 (hbk. : alk. paper). – ISBN-13: 978-0-631-18855-1 (pbk. : alk. paper)

A catalogue record for this title is available from the British Library.

The publisher's policy is to use permanent paper from mills that operate a sustainable forestry policy, and which has been manufactured from pulp processed using acid-free and elementary chlorine-free practices. Furthermore, the publisher ensures that the text paper and cover board used have met acceptable environmental accreditation standards.

For further information on
Blackwell Publishing, visit our website:
www.blackwellpublishing.com

CONTENTS

To Otto Jespersen,
who revealed to so many
English speakers
the treasure of their own tongue

LIST OF FIGURES

LIST OF TABLES

PREFACE

Why has English so many words? Where have they all come from? How does it come about that we have different vocabularies for love, for illness, for food and for the manifold branches of knowledge? This book is designed as a guide for students and lovers of the English language, more especially to introduce them to its absorbing past and complex present through a study of the lexical evolution of this fascinating and extraordinary tongue. In it will be traced the demographic and social features which constitute the sequence of what is termed 'the external history' of the language. These form the main stages of the remarkable growth of a vocabulary initially brought to England some 1500 years ago by some belligerent Germanic tribes in what probably seemed an accidental and minor turbulence of the times. Subsequently it will trace the phases of how English survived being displaced as the official language of the land for 300 years of Norman hegemony, how it was enriched by Norman-French and classical elements, and how in the last four centuries it has expanded through colonialism, trade and prestige to become the most spoken language in the world.

The rehearsal of these main historical features shows that English has played a number of social roles: conquering, subordinate, colonizing and global. This also prompts certain questions of definition. We speak and write of 'the English language', yet from the beginning 'English has existed in regional varieties which remain robustly apparent to anyone travelling through the British Isles. Today the world varieties of English are so obvious and marked that the question is increasingly asked whether there is an 'English language' or rather a variety of 'Englishes', the notional language having split and spread as did the previous world language, Latin, to become the Romance languages. Certainly the situation is now too complex and the language is on too many tongues for the use of such previous appropriating titles as *Our Language* or *The Treasure of Our Tongue*, fine though those studies are. Thus the latter part of this work deals with these new, interesting and challenging developments. More especially, the concluding chapters address the global question of how these changes have affected the core of the vocabulary.

There are other motivations for this study. Scholarship of the past few decades has emphasized the role of language as a fundamentally formative social factor affecting world-view and ideology, virtually on a subliminal basis. Lexical structure is increasingly perceived as reflecting a society's values. People who are otherwise placid will die for a word, or what they conceive as being the meaning of that word. What are the implications of these perceptions for the history of English? Furthermore, most histories stop at a conveniently safe distance in time, avoiding the controversies of modern times. However, the exploitation of particular sectors of the lexis as motivating resources in advertising, politics and propaganda – aspects not usually dealt with under the traditional rubric of 'history' and trenchantly described by George Steiner as 'the hypnotic mendacities of the mass media' (1969, p. 261) – these too require some coverage.

Less fashionable than these sociolinguistic emphases are the stylistic or literary approaches. These remind us that great writers have forged their own original medium of expression out of the potentialities of the language of their times, and that their contributions have become part of our inheritance. Anthony Burgess reminded us, by means of a Yeatsian quotation, that literature, no less than language, is 'a mouthful of air', that spoken language is 'the primary reality, while writing and printing are of a secondary order' (1992, p. x). This is true, but it is also an overstatement: *OK* has acquired a huge gobal currency as a spoken form since its confused origins in the 1840s. But it started life in print. Similarly, seminal formulations like Jefferson's 'life, liberty and the pursuit of happiness' (in the American Declaration of Independence) or the wealth of Shakespearean quotations in current idiom, derive their original potency from written documents which are not as evanescent and transient as air. While we might not all agree with Shelley that 'Poets are the unacknowledged legislators of mankind,' we cannot deny that many major authors have moulded for us forms of received expression which have become part of our mental and emotional make-up. Thus the literary contribution to the lexical mosaic of English is also significant.

Some fifty years ago a great medievalist, the Reverend Professor Walter W. Skeat observed: 'The history of the English language is one of the most fascinating and inexhaustible subjects, yet the number of students who have even an elementary knowledge of it is extremely small' (1941, p. 1). Skeat, like his great contemporaries, was a philologist *par excellence* and he was probably dismayed principally by ignorance and a lack of love for words. Today, when we are more aware of the intertwining of language and culture, the key to understanding our individual and collective pasts still lies in this 'most fascinating and inexhaustible subject'.

Any book on the English vocabulary is necessarily indebted to a great tradition of preceding scholarship. This includes the lexicographers from Cawdrey to Murray and beyond, with intervening figures as diverse as Johnson, Grose and Webster, and the historians from Jespersen onwards.

In addition to these figures from the past, I owe a special debt of gratitude to David Crystal, who saw the potential of this study in an amorphous and rambling first draft, and who has been consistently generous with his wisdom, advice and guidance. I should also like to thank my friend and colleague, Professor Anthony Woodward, for reading the whole typescript and giving me his sage assessment.

I was fortunate to have in Sandra Raphael a copy-editor who has been punctilious, learned and judiciously helpful. At Blackwell, Philip Carpenter supported the project decisively as the word-hoard accumulated, while Lisa Eaton gave the book its excellent design.

Finally I must mention my trusty old Amstrad word-processor. It lacks the modern accoutrements of bells and whistles, hard drive and laser (with their wonderful capacities for instantaneously disappearing text). But it saw me through.

Geoffrey Hughes
Johannesburg
February 1999

ACKNOWLEDGEMENTS

The author and publisher wish to thank the following for permission to use copyright material: David Lodge and Curtis Brown Ltd for an extract from *Nice Work*; Seumas Heaney and Faber and Faber Ltd for an excerpt from 'Bone Dreams', from *Opened Ground: Selected Poems 1966–96*, copyright Seumas Heaney 1998, reprinted by permission of Farrar, Straus and Giroux, LLC; Derek Walcott and Faber and Faber Ltd for 'Wales', from *Collected Poems 1966–96*, copyright 1986 by Derek Walcott, reprinted by permission of Farrar, Straus and Giroux, LLC; David Hill and Blackwell Publishers for the map on p. 96 (from *An Atlas of Anglo-Saxon England*, 1981); Harold Orton, Nathalie Wright and Academic Press Ltd for the map on p. 98 (from *A Word Geography of England*, 1974); Peter Trudgill and Blackwell Publishers for the map on p. 8 (from *The Dialects of England*, 1990); Tilgher-Genova for 'A Short History of the Dictionary', previously published in *Textus* X (1997); ASLA, the Swedish Association of Applied Linguistics, for 'The Historical Development of the Register Barrier in Professional Language', previously published in *ASLA Skriftserie* 6 (1994); Cambridge University Press for 'Words of War', previously published in *English Today* 17 (1989).

Every effort has been made to trace the copyright holders of material included in this book, but in some cases this has not proved possible at the time of going to press. The author and publisher therefore wish to thank copyright holders of material included without acknowledgement, and would be pleased to rectify at the earliest opportunity any omissions brought to their attention.

LIST OF SOURCES AND ABBREVIATIONS

This study is, of necessity, heavily dependent on the essential source-work on historical change in English, the *Oxford English Dictionary (OED)* (1884–1928), the collaboration of Murray (pre-eminently), Bradley, Craigie, Onions and Furnivall 'with the assistance of many scholars and men of science', and the *Supplement* (1972–86) produced by Dr Robert Burchfield and his research team at Oxford. The two sequences were consolidated into the second edition in 1989. The obligation to this wonderfully comprehensive source led Owen Barfield to this acknowledgement, which I endorse: 'In case the fear of wearisome repetition has induced me to mislead, the *OED* is the authority for practically all the etymological and semantic material on which my book is based' (1962, p. 216). Quotations from the *OED* are thus not acknowledged other than by this statement.

Abbreviations used are:

OE Old English
A-S Anglo-Saxon
ME Middle English
OF Old French
ON Old Norse

COD Concise Oxford Dictionary
EDD English Dialect Dictionary
EETS Early English Text Society
LDOCE Longmans Dictionary of Contemporary English
OCEL Oxford Companion to the English Language
SOED Shorter Oxford English Dictionary
TLS Times Literary Supplement

A CHRONOLOGY OF ENGLISH

410	Departure of the Roman legions
c.449	The Invasion of the Angles, Saxons, Jutes and Frisians
597	The Coming of Christianity
731	Bede's *Ecclesiastical History of the English People*
787	The first recorded Scandinavian raids
871–99	Alfred King of Wessex
900–1000	Approximate date of Anglo-Saxon poetry collections
1016–42	Canute King of England, Scotland and Denmark
1066	The Norman Conquest
c.1150	Earliest Middle English texts
1204	Loss of Calais
1362	English restored as language of Parliament and the law
1370–1400	The works of Chaucer, Langland and the *Gawain* poet
1384	Wycliffite translation of the Bible
1476	Caxton sets up his press at Westminster
1525	Tyndale's translation of the Bible
1549	The Book of Common Prayer
1552	Early canting dictionaries
1584	Roanoke settlement of America (abortive)
1590–1610	Shakespeare's main creative period
1603	Act of Union between England and Scotland
1604	Robert Cawdrey's *Table Alphabeticall*
1607	Jamestown settlement in America
1609	English settlement of Jamaica
1611	Authorized Version of the Bible
1619	First Arrival of slaves in America
1620	Arrival of Pilgrim fathers in America
1623	Shakespeare's *First Folio* published
1649–60	Puritan Commonwealth: closure of the theatres

1660	Restoration of the monarchy
1667	Milton's *Paradise Lost*
1721	Nathaniel Bailey's *Universal Etymological English Dictionary*
1755	Samuel Johnson's *Dictionary of the English Language*
1762–94	Grammars published by Lowth, Murray, etc.
1765	Beginning of the English Raj in India
1776	Declaration of American Independence
1788	Establishment of the first penal colony in Australia
1820	Arrival of the 1820 Settlers in South Africa
1828	Noah Webster's *American Dictionary of the English Language*
1884–1928	Publication of the *Oxford English Dictionary*
1903	*Daily Mirror* published as the first tabloid
1922	Establishment of the BBC
1947	Independence of India
1957–72	Independence of various African, Asian and Caribbean states
1961	Third Edition of *Webster's Dictionary*
1968	Abolition of the post of Lord Chancellor
1989	Second edition of the *Oxford English Dictionary*

1

HISTORY IN THE LANGUAGE: THE VOCABULARY AS A HISTORICAL REPOSITORY

Here, therefore, is the first distemper [imbalance] of learning, when men study words and not matter.

Francis Bacon, *The Advancement of Learning* (1605)

It has only just begun to dawn on us that in our own language alone, not to speak of its many companions, the past history of humanity is spread out in an imperishable map, just as the history of the mineral earth lies embedded in the layers of its outer crust.

Owen Barfield, *History in English Words* (1926)

Today we find Bacon's downright rejection of the study of language extra-ordinary, coming as it does from one of the greatest minds of the Renaissance. Barfield's archaeological model of language is entirely in tune with our way of thinking, despite being written over seventy years ago. We find recent echoes in George Steiner's dictum that 'History in the human sense, is a language net cast backwards' (1975, p. 70) and in Roger Fowler's observation that 'Quite simply, the vocabulary of a language, or of a variety of a language, is a map of the objects, concepts, processes and relationships about which the culture needs to communicate' (1991, p. 80). Has this lexical 'map' changed, and if so how? In exploring the evolution of the English vocabulary, we shall find that words are both fossils in which the culture of the past is stored and vital organ-isms responsive to the pressures of the present.

Words surround us in their myriad multiplicity, the common and the rare, the local and the alien, the ancient and the new, the philosophical and the technical, the private and the political, the sacred and the profane. Where have they all come from? How have they arrived in these categories? How does one analyse, how make sense of this lexicon, so vast, eccentric and copious, which at the last count amounted to more than half a million words?

A valuable starting-point was achieved by the great pioneering editor of the monumental *Oxford English Dictionary on Historical Principles*, the indefatigable and scholarly Sir James Murray, who articulated the problem with admirable clarity in his preface a little over a hundred years ago. Introducing this huge work of historical reconstruction, Murray used the memorable image of the vocabulary being like a galaxy:

> That vast aggregate of words and phrases which constitutes the Vocabulary of English-speaking men presents, to the mind that endeavours to grasp it as a definite whole, the aspect of one of those nebulous masses familiar to the astronomer, in which a clear and unmistakable nucleus shades off on all sides, through zones of decreasing brightness, to a dim marginal film that seems to end nowhere, but lose itself imperceptibly in the surrounding darkness. (1884, p. xvii)

Murray's astronomical image is arresting, but also daunting. It gives us the big picture, but we seem to be lost in it. Given that lexis is generally taken to mean the aggregate of words, phrases, idioms and meaningful units in the vocabulary, how do we divide up this 'nebulous mass'? The dictionary format, being based on the arbitrary sequence of the alphabet, not on the logical connections of associated meaning, encourages us to consider words as atoms or individuals, like disparate people in the telephone directory, with their special place, function and use. This format also imposes on words a misleading equality, since every word, no matter how central, rare or insignificant, has its entry. The comprehensive dictionary also complicates things by bringing in the historical dimension, showing that individual words have biographies or semantic histories which are long and complicated, and sometimes quite bizarre. But, as with individuals, words also belong to families and nations, though their family resemblances and national affiliations may in time become obscured by assimilation.

Developing his image, Murray starts to focus on what distinguishes the core of the galaxy from the perimeter:

> the English Vocabulary contains a nucleus or central mass of many thousand words whose 'Anglicity' ['Englishness'] is unquestioned . . . they are the *Common Words* of the language. But they are linked on every side with other words which are less and less entitled to this appellation, and which pertain ever more and more distinctly to the domain of local dialect, of the slang and cant of 'sets' and classes, of the peculiar technicalities of trade and processes, of the scientific terminology common to all civilized nations, of the actual languages of other lands and peoples. And there is absolutely no defining line in any direction: the circle of the English language has a well-defined centre but no discernible circumference. (1884, p. xvii)

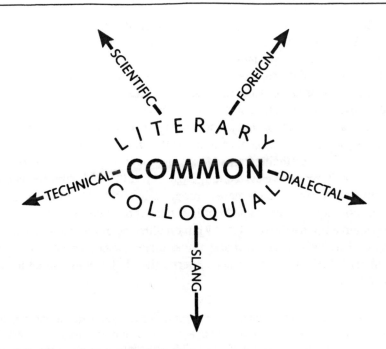

Figure 1.1   Murray's lexical configuration

Murray illustrated the structural relationship between the core and the diversity of other words by means of a diagram (figure 1.1).

Murray's diagram or plan of the constellation is profoundly valuable and illuminating. (It was also an innovation in its time.) It gives us a framework within which to categorize different kinds of words, and it makes the point with simple clarity (by means of the arrows) that words are 'in' the language to differing degrees. It also establishes a fundamental hierarchy of usage, with 'Literary', 'Common', 'Colloquial' and 'Slang' categorized in descending order. In discussing it we shall develop the main lexical concepts and categories and also introduce the principal periods in the time-frame of the development of English.

Register

Murray's diagram or word-map depicts in essence an important linguistic concept, that of register, namely a particular variety of diction or choice of word appropriate to a given social situation or literary context. The term **register** is traditionally associated with music and is comparatively recent in its application to linguistic usage (being first recorded in this sense by T. B. W. Reid in 1956). However, the core concept of a particular choice of diction is deeply traditional. We are familiar from the earliest stages of our language acquisition of the difference between the personal terms *pa* or *dad* as against the more formal *father*, or *kitty* and *pussy* as against *cat*, and so on. Register is based on the classical notion of decorum, whereby certain levels of usage are considered appropriate (or inappropriate) to particular topics and social situations. Register is typically conceived of (as it is in Murray's configuration) on a hierarchical scale, ranging from high words to low, so that in literature a high action properly requires elevated language (typically producing the genre of the epic) while a low action is more appropriately couched in humbler or even obscene language (typically apparent in the farce or 'dirty story').

The main emphasis is traditionally put on differing degrees of formality (for example, *chuck* as against *throw* and *row* as against *disagreement* or *confrontation*). A useful set of criteria which governs the choice is explained in these observations:

> This degree of formality/informality depends upon four variable factors, in increasing order of importance: sex, age, status and intimacy . . . Students talking among themselves would use a different type of vocabulary and even different grammatical structures from those they would use in addressing their teacher, or when being interviewed for a job, or when talking to a young child – or a dog. (Batchelor and Offord, 1982, pp. 1, 3)

This gives an important different emphasis, namely that register reflects the role of a speaker in a particular context. Words may be 'out there' in large numbers, but there is not a completely free choice between them. On this point Shakespeare's friend, the dramatist Ben Jonson, observed in his *Discoveries* (1641) that words

> are to be chose[n] according to the persons wee make speake, or the things wee speake of. Some are of the Campe, some of the Councell-board, some of the Shop, some of the Sheep-coat, some of the Barre, &c. (1923, p. 73)

However, register is rich and variegated in its manifestations. It can also be demonstrated in a variety of alternatives in word-choice: old or new; concrete or abstract; blunt or polite; coarse or refined; direct or euphemistic; common or recherché. The motives behind the choice of different registers can be equally various, such as social, literary, professional, commercial and political.

The noted scholar M. A. K. Halliday refined the concept further by distinguishing between the language variety of the user (termed *dialects*) and the

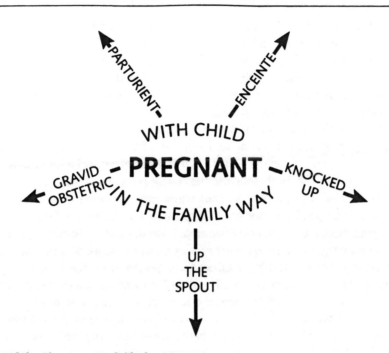

Figure 1.2   The semantic field of pregnancy

variety required by the situation (termed *registers*). He further distinguished between registers according to *field* (subject matter), *mode* (speech, writing, format) and *manner* (the social relations we have just been discussing). Of these categories, *field* is perhaps the most important, since it introduces a diversity of word-fields, for example, those of morality, law, business, politics and sport. These all have their various vocabularies, but a common word like *right* will be found in the first four categories, albeit in different senses, *goal* will be found in the last three, and so on.

We shall be returning to the central concept of register, but let us now illustrate it by applying Murray's diagram to a particular notion. In so doing we shall be constructing a semantic field, or a set of synonyms which applies to a particular notion. We shall start with a slighty unusual topic, that of being pregnant, since it contains a few highly diverse terms, which are set out in figure 1.2.

Most of us would find it difficult to construct a complete semantic field on the basis of our own knowledge. We shall gain useful assistance from a major work built on this principle, namely Roget's *Thesaurus*, first published in 1852 and updated in many editions since. Roget's enterprise was revolutionary in that it worked from concepts to words and phrases, collected into semantic fields. Roget was truly the pioneer in English **lexicology**, meaning 'the study of the structure of the vocabulary', a term coined in 1828 by Noah Webster. Murray, on the other hand was part of the great tradition of **lexicography**, the writing of dictionaries, which goes back to the late sixteenth century.

When we distribute or allocate the various terms and phrases referring to pregnancy, we discover that there is little difficulty in matching Murray's categories, since the field is fairly rich and varied. We have, indeed, other terms which might be used: *expecting* and *expectant*, for example, would be placed slightly above *pregnant*, while *having a bun in the oven* would be lower down the scale, between *in the family way* and the coarse phrase *up the spout*.

This exercise is valuable in various ways. First, it shows us that although **synonym** is a useful term for practical purposes, there are, in fact, few exact synonyms, especially in this sensitive area. Indeed, most authorities agree that, strictly speaking, there are no exact synonyms in the sense of terms which are semantically interchangeable in all contexts. See, in this respect, David Crystal (1995, p. 164), John Lyons (1968, pp. 447–8) and Leonhard Lipka (1990, p. 142). Rather, in this field there are marked differences of directness and nuance: some words are blunt, some more discreet, others slightly mystifying. *Enceinte*, for example, from French, where it means literally 'unbound', is quite rarefied and delicate. *Parturient* and *obstetric*, both from Latin, are technical and used by specialists, but are unfamiliar to the layman. As is generally the case with technical terms, they are quite specific and cannot be used in any other sense, as *pregnant* can be in, say, the phrase *a pregnant pause*.

Secondly, the exercise makes us focus in greater detail on the categories. What is the real difference between 'scientific' and 'technical'? Where, for example, would we place *impregnated*? It is more of a 'written' word than a 'spoken' word, so on that basis it would go under 'scientific'. Furthermore, what is really meant by 'literary'? The example chosen here is the archaic biblical phrase *with child*. Many languages have areas of the lexis which are chiefly literary: as we shall see, a considerable portion of the Anglo-Saxon vocabulary was exclusively poetic. This is still true of a small sample of Modern English: witness the use of *isle* (as against *island*), *mount* (as against *mountain*), *weeds* (as against *clothes*), *dulcet* (as against *sweet*), *fount* (as against *fountain*), *steed* (as against *horse*) and *serpent* (as against *snake*). As these examples show, there is commonly an overlap between 'literary' and 'archaic', a category which, curiously, does not figure in Murray's configuration: words such as *henceforth, foe, sans, multitude* and *damsel* are examples. In Murray's time the euphemistic phrase *in an interesting condition* was current and would then apply: now it seems old-fashioned and prissy.

Writing a hundred years ago, Murray did not find it necessary to define 'literary' language. It meant, self-evidently, the language used by the authors who made up the 'canon' of English literature, including the great Victorian novelists and poets of his own time. While this was a largely unproblematic concept, some might have pointed out that there are difficulties of obscenity in Chaucer and Rochester, and of **idiolect** or individual dialect and features of personal expression in Dickens. But these objections were not raised. Today 'literary' definitely is a problematic concept, in that many books are 'literary' in the traditional sense of being 'well written' in a formal fashion, while others are classed as literature but use a great deal of slang and obscenity. We shall return to this topic in our concluding chapter.

Finally, when we come to 'dialectal', we can see that this category is illuminating because it depends on where the centre of the word-field is conceived as being. This in turn depends on the definition of the speech-community. Murray would probably have confined the field to the British Isles, so that 'dialectal' would have yielded terms like *wi bairn* or *boukun*, the Scots equivalents of 'with child' or 'pregnant'. (These are found in *The New Testament in Scots*, translated by W. L. Lorimer at St Matthew 1:5 and St Luke 2:5.) The phrase chosen at present for the category (*knocked up*) is, however, an American colloquialism.

Dialect in its modern academic usage includes both the traditional meaning of a regional form of speech as well as a class usage. In this word-field the form *preggers* could be used, since it is a distinctively upper-class usage, marked by its suffix, as is *champers* for 'champagne'. *Dialect* as a category has also risen in status since Murray's time, when it implied 'back-woods', 'rustic' or 'outlandish' speech. The first comprehensive study of English dialects was carried out by Joseph Wright about a century ago and published in six volumes between 1898 and 1905. Today, with regional forms of speech under threat, they are regarded with more sympathy and respect. However, because of these traditional negative connotations, *dialect* is often replaced by the more neutral term *variety*. Nevertheless, a comment in a recent study on English dialects is noteworthy:

> The subject which Wright did so much to make popular and academically respectable, now has followers studying, for example, 'traditional' regional dialects . . . the dialects of the cities, the dialects of ethnic minorities, occupational dialects and the relationship between dialect and social class or gender. (Upton and Widdowson, 1995, p. ix)

In leaving 'dialect' as a category, it is important to stress that the distinction between spoken and written varieties carries many implications. Although we can state that *pregnant* is the central or general term in the semantic field and *boukun* is a 'dialect' word, this is a perception which comes largely from the

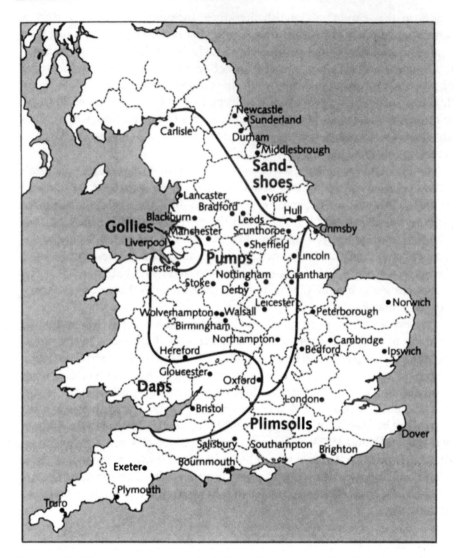

Figure 1.3 Dialect terms for gym-shoes (from Peter Trudgill, *The Dialects of England,* Blackwell, 1990, p. 102)

written language. In oral usage there are many cases where a whole range of regional forms are the norm for speakers on the ground. Thus a basic word like *grandfather* has the regional variants of *granda, granfer* and *gramp,* while *scarecrow* has the surprising range of *flay-crow* in the north, *mawkin* in the Midlands and East Anglia, *gally-bagger* in Hampshire and *mommet* (from Mohamet) in Somerset and adjoining counties. Figure 1.3 shows a similar regional range of words for gym-shoes. A sense of the extraordinary diversity of dialect words, some of which we would not regard as being obviously English, is shown in figure 1.4, a page from Joseph Wright's *English Dialect Dictionary*.

Before we leave Murray's diagram, we should note that a slightly modified version was used in the preface to the *Shorter Oxford English Dictionary* (*SOED*), first published in 1933 (p. viii). The two substantial changes were that 'archaic' was now admitted as one of the sub-categories of 'literary' usage, and 'vulgar' was introduced as part of 'colloquial'. Also noteworthy is the point that 'slang' had a meaning for both Murray and the editors of the *SOED* which differs from ours. Murray, we recall, referred to the 'slang and cant of "sets" and classes', and elaborated: ' "Slang" touches the technical terminology of trades and occupations, as in "nautical slang", "Public School Slang", "the slang of the Stock Exchange".' (Eric Partridge's excellent study *Slang* (1933 and later editions) uses similar categories.) In other words 'slang' was then closer to what we would now call 'jargon', as well as to other 'in-group' languages, categorized by the *SOED* as 'of lower or less dignified status'. We can thus see that some categories which were clearly defined and stable for Murray and his immediate successors subsequently turn out to be fairly fluid.

The word-field of pregnancy is a fruitful example, since it consists of a few, clearly differentiated terms from a diversity of origins. Other word-fields show a different balance of registers and concentration of terms. Those for madness, for example, set out in figure 1.5 show a remarkable range and size. That for drunkenness, like that for money, shows a distinctly 'bottom heavy' imbalance, with hundreds of slang terms.[1] A discussion of 'Words of War' is to be found in chapter 8. Other fields, such as those covering economics, politics and xeno-phobia, are contained in my *Words in Time*, while euphemisms and the cate-gorization of women and homosexuals are discussed in my *Swearing*.

We shall be returning at intervals to Murray's constellation. It is a most valuable word-map and a remarkable innovation, considering that it was devised over a hundred years ago. We must now return to the core of the galaxy, the 'well-defined centre' of common words.

The Three Word-Stocks

As we have already gathered from our word-fields, the English vocabulary does not originate in one language, but is a fascinatingly hybrid conglomeration, as we shall see in the course of this book. In essence and in detail, the structure of the vocabulary reflects the history of the English-speaking peoples. But even fairly common words do not all come from the same source. This point is exemplified even in the words which make up the title of this book. They

YICKIE-YAWKIE, *sb.* Sc. Also in form yeekie-yakie. A wooden tool, blunted like a wedge, with which shoemakers polish the edges and bottoms of soles.
Dmf. (JAM.) Gall. MACTAGGART *Encycl.* (1824). Kcb. Tam ... gathered up his knife, 'yeekie yakie,' lap stone and rags, ARMSTRONG *Kirkiebras* (1896) 12.

YIELD, *sb.*[1] Ags. (JAM.) See below.
When the ice melts, although there be no proper thaw, it is said to be owing to the yield of the day.

YIELD, *v.* and *sb.*[2] Sc. Nhb. Yks. Chs. Brks. Suf. Ken. Sus. Also in forms eeld Nhb.[1]; yeild Chs. Sus.[1]; yeld Ken.[1]; yelt Suf.[1]; *pret.* yald Sc.; *pp.* youden Sc. (JAM.) [jīld.] 1. *v.* To reward.
w.Yks. THORESBY *Lett.* (1703). Chs. God yeild you (K.); Chs.[123] 2. To produce a crop; to be fruitful. See Eald, Ild.
Sc. (A.W.) n.Yks. T'cooarn yields weel(I.W.). Chs.[1] Thus we speak of a good crop of wheat as 'yielding well,' or peas which have many seeds in a pod as 'yielding well'; Chs.[2] Suf.[1] Ta yelt a matter a' tew coom an acre. Ken.[1] 'Tis a very good yelding field though it is so cledgy.
3. Of a cow: to give milk.
Sc. (A.W.) Nhb.[1] Hoo much is the coo celdin? w.Yks. (J.W.) 4. To give up; to relinquish. Sc. (JAM.), s.Cy. (HALL.), Sus.[1] 5. To give way.
Fif. The kirk-yard's coffins yald and broke Aneath the press o' livin' fock, TENNANT *Papistry* (1827) 168. Abd. When the effects of a thaw begin to be felt, it is common to say 'the ice is yowden'; i.e. it has begun to give way (JAM.). 6. To admit, confess.
Rnf. Priests may preach and scribes may jaw—And sodgers shoot ... Or [ere] ye wad shrink or yield a flaw, WEBSTER *Rhymes* (1835) 8.
7. In *comb.* Yield-yow, a violent pressure of the thumb under the lobe of the ear. S. & Ork.[1] 8. *sb.* Produce.
Brks.[1] Whate maaykes poor yield this crap.
[1. God yelde thee, freend, CHAUCER *Tr. & Cr.* i. 1055.]

YIELD, see Geld, *adj.*, Yeld.

YIELDY, *adj.* Sc. [jī·ldi.] Yielding, giving way.
Gall. Time's shingly sands I see Turn dry an' yieldy 'neath my feet, SCOTT *Gleanings* (1881) 31.

YIFFER, see Yewfir.

YIFF-YAFF, *sb.* Obs. Rxb. (JAM.) A small person who talks a great deal to little purpose.

YIGGA, *sb.* Cum. [ji·ga] A dial. form of 'ague.' Cum.[1] (s.v. Ayga), Cum.[4]

YIGLET, YIK, see Aglet, Oak.

YIKE, *sb.* Sur. Hmp. [jaik.] The call of the woodpecker.
Sur. Here you could listen to the yike, yike, yike of the green woodpecker, and watch him at his work, SON of MARSHES *On Sur. Hills* (1891) 136; Then he [the yaffle] yells his loudest, making the woods ring with his maniacal yikes, *ib. London Town* (ed. 1894) 193.
Hence **Yikeing,** *ppl. adj.* making the sound of 'yike.'
Sur. The yikeing laugh of the yaffle, *Forest Tithes* (1893) 30. Hmp. *Cornh. Mag.* (June 1893) 595.

YIKKA, *v.* Sh.I. [ji·ka.] To snarl.
He yikkas an growls, BURGESS *Rasmie* (1892) 17.

YILL, *sb.* and *v.* Sc. n.Cy. Also in forms yeill N.Cy.[1]; yuill Ayr. [jil.] 1. *sb.* A dial. form of 'ale.'
Sc. Send down for bread and for yill, tobacco, &c., SCOTT *Bride of Lam.* (1819) xxiii. Frf. [She] loot them pree her yill an' kebbuck, WATT *Poet. Sketches* (1880) 108. w.Sc., s.Sc. (JAM.) Ayr. A howff ... whaur you get your yuill oot of fine auld siller communion caps, SERVICE *Dr. Duguid* (ed. 1887) 108. N.Cy.[1]
Hence **Heather-yill,** *sb.*, see below.
Wgt. They say that the Picts brewed some awful grand kind of drink they ca't Heather Yill, out of heather and some unknown kind of fogg; but they kept the secret of making of it to themselves, and it is now lost, SAXON *Gall. Gossip* (1878) 995.
2. *Comb.* (1) Yill-boat, an ale-barrel; see Boat, *sb.* 3; (2) -cap or -cup, a horn or wooden vessel from which ale is drunk; (3) -cup eye, a large or 'saucer' eye; (4) -house, a house where ale is sold; (5) -seasoned, seasoned with ale; (6) -seller, a person who sells ale; (7) -shop, see (4); (8) -wife, a woman who brews or sells ale.
(1) Bwk. (JAM.) (2) Sc. (JAM.) Ayr. The Change-house fills.

Wi' yill-caup commentators, BURNS *Holy Fair* (1785) st. 18. Gall. MACTAGGART *Encycl.* (1824). (3) Gall. (JAM.) Kcb. Chiels wi' sooty skins, and yill-caup een, DAVIDSON *Seasons* (1789) 13 (*ib.*). (4) Sc. (JAM.); I never gang to the yillhouse—that is unless ony neighbour was to gie me a pint, SCOTT *Rob Roy* (1817) xiv. Edb. The coarsest night that cou'd hae blawn, I at the yill-house door bid staun', A' shiverin', R. WILSON *Poems* (1822) 35. N.Cy.[1] (5) Ayr. Yill-season'd haivers Are no worth a plack, WHITE *Jottings* (1879) 290. (6) Ayr. Yuill-sellers shouldna be story tellers, ye ken, SERVICE *Dr. Duguid* (ed. 1887) 235. (7) Lnk. Oot an' intil yill-shops they gaed, COGHILL *Poems* (1890) 77. (8) Sc., Cld. (JAM.) Ayr. Ye're welcome, neighbour jill wives, here, FISHER *Poems* (1790) 59. Edb. Yill-wives licker brisk decantet For drinkers' food, CRAWFORD *Poems* (1798) 46. Gall. MACTAGGART *Encycl.* (1824) 166, ed. 1876. N.Cy.[1]
3. *v.* To treat to alc.
w.Sc. (JAM.) Ayr. Langsyne it was the fashion ... for lads tae tak their lasses intae the public hoose on the Sabbath day, at twull-oors, tae get a bake an' a hue o' porter, or like tat ye ken, an' that was ca'd 'yuillin', SERVICE *Dr. Duguid* (ed. 1887) 206.

YILL, YILLOCH, see Yeld, Yelloch.

YILLYART, *adj.* Sc. Stubborn; ill-conditioned; 'thrawn.'
Per. Then ye can get, ye yillyart tyke, Home rule or ony rule ye like, FERGUSSON *Vill. Poet* (1897) 72.

YILP, YILT, YILV(E, see Yelp, *v.*, Gilt, *sb.*[1], Yelve.

YIM, *sb.* and *v.* Sc. [jim.] 1. *sb.* A particle; an atom; the smallest portion of anything. See Nyim.
Ags. (JAM.) Rxb. Nor leaves in creation a yim to afford A bite to a beast or a bield to a bird, RIDDELL *Poet. Wks.* (1871) II. 204. Gall. MACTAGGART *Encycl.* (1824) 500, ed. 1876.
2. A very thin film of condensed vapour or fat. Bnff.[1] 3. *v.* To break into fragments. Kcd. (JAM.) 4. To become covered with a thin film. Bnff.[1]

YIMMER, see Yammer.

YIMMET, *sb.* Obs. Sc. A lunch; a 'piece.' Gall. MACTAGGART *Encycl.* (1824). See Yim.

YIMOST, YIN, see Eemost, One, Yon.

YINDER, see Yonder.

YINK, *sb.*[1] Sh.I. [jiŋk.] An indefinite quantity.
A yink o' sheep (J.S.).

YINK, *sb.*[2] Sh.I. [jiŋk.] A lover; a sweetheart. (A.W.); S. & Ork.[1]

YINK, *v.* Sh.I. [jiŋk.] To set aside.
Whin hit wis lamb'd we haed da midder o' hit hame, an' Girzzie ... yinkit hit ta wir Gibbie, as shûne as shû saw hit, *Sh. News* (Aug. 7, 1897); S. & Ork.[1]

YINST, see Once.

YIP, see Gip, *v.*[2], Yap, *sb.*[2]

YIPPER, *adj.* e.An. Sc. Also in form yepper Suf. [ji·pə.] Brisk, active; in good spirits. Cf. yap, *adj.*
e.An.[1] Nrf. She is right yipper, COZENS-HARDY *Broad Nrf.* (1893) 60. Suf. (HALL., s.v. Yep).

YIP-YAP, *sb.* Chs. Also in form yip-yop s.Chs.[1] [ji·p·jap, ·jop.] An upstart; a young, scatterbrained person. See Yap, *sb.*[2]
Chs.[12] s.Chs.[1] Wo)ddo ahy ky'ae'r fūr ū li·t·l akwuu·rtin yip·yop lahyk dhée? Wot aat'·ji bûr ū gau·ki wop·strau ūv ū laad', wen au·ji sed?

YIRB, YIRD, see Herb, Earth, *sb.*[1]

YIRDIE-BEE, *sb.* Obs. Sc. A bee which burrows in the ground.
Slg. No honey dug from yirdie bees, WRBA *Poems* (1869) 19.

YIRDLINS, YIRK, see Earthlins, Yark, *v.*[1]

YIRKIN, *sb.*[1] Irel. [jə·rkin.] The place where a shoe is tied. Ant. *Ballymena Obs.* (1892).

YIRKIN, *sb.*[2] N.I.[1] [jə·rkin.] The side of a boat.

YIRLICH, *adj.* Obs. Sc. Also in form yirlisch. Wild, unnatural. Cf. eldritch.
Slk. (JAM.); Sett up sic ane yirlich skrighe, HOGG *Tales* (1838) 110, ed. 1866.
Hence **Yirlischly,** *adv.* wildly.
They yellit and youtit soe yirlischly, *ib. Poems* (ed. 1865) 315.

YIRLIN, see Yoldring.

YIRLING, *sb.* Not. [jə·lin.] A thatcher's handful of straw. MORTON *Cyclo. Agric.* (1863).

YIRM, *v.* Sc. Irel. Also written yerm Sc.; yurm Sc.

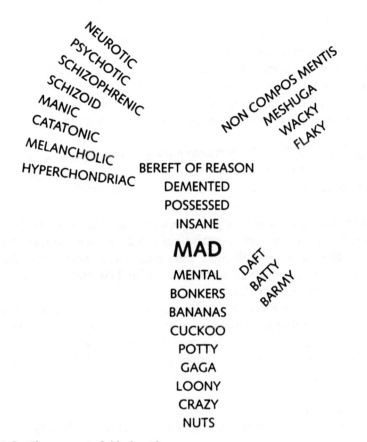

NEUROTIC
PSYCHOTIC
SCHIZOTIC
SCHIZOPHRENIC
SCHIZOID
MANIC
CATATONIC
MELANCHOLIC
HYPERCHONDRIAC

NON COMPOS MENTIS
MESHUGA
WACKY
FLAKY

BEREFT OF REASON
DEMENTED
POSSESSED
INSANE

MAD

DAFT
BATTY
BARMY

MENTAL
BONKERS
BANANAS
CUCKOO
POTTY
GAGA
LOONY
CRAZY
NUTS

Figure 1.5   The semantic field of madness

encapsulate its theme, but they also embody it in a miniature fashion, for they come from the three seminal languages which, over some fifteen centuries, have amalgamated into English. The basic roots and core vocabulary of our language are Anglo-Saxon (also known as Old English), deriving from the ancient Germanic word-hoard brought to England by the Angles, Saxons and Jutes in the fifth century. To this skeleton or foundation there have been two further additions from the continent of Europe. The first is a Romance element, the legacy of the conquering Norman-French elite who took control of the land after the Battle of Hastings in 1066. The second element is classical, taking the form of a more bookish, learned, abstract and technical vocabulary of Latin and Greek terms steadily accumulated by authors and scholars from late medieval times and given increasing impetus by the development of printing from the late fifteenth century.

There have been thousands of subsequent borrowings, from virtually every language in the world. Those from the continental languages are especially numerous, but the tripartite character of the lexical core remains the dominant feature of the vocabulary. If we were to assign and organize the component terms of this volume's 'working' title on the basis of their origins in a scheme of linguistic archaeology, with the oldest terms at the most remote level, we would arrive at the following diagrammatic representation of the 'dig':

Latin and Greek: lexical history
Norman French: guide   language
Anglo-Saxon: a   to the   of the English

We can see here a separation of registers, as we did in the word-field for being pregnant. The common words are to be found in the Anglo-Saxon and Norman French origins, as were 'with child' and 'in the family way', while the Latin and Greek are less familiar, as were *parturient* and *obstetric*. This is a pattern we shall see repeated many times.

If, however, we were to translate our title back into the ancient terms used by scholars of Anglo-Saxon times, such as Bede or Aldhelm or Ælfric, then it would be very different. The title would then be on the same level because other, native words would be needed for *guide*, *lexical*, *history* and *language*. It would then read:

an handboc ealdgesegena wordhordes tunge angelcynnes
('a handbook of the ancient traditions of the vocabulary of the tongue of the English race')

Viewed across the mists of time and the accidents of linguistic change, the Anglo-Saxon does not now seem to us at first sight even recognizable as English, appearing as alien as the markings on some primitive heathen stone. It seems wise, therefore, to defer the deciphering of the ancient forms of the language until the following chapter.

Historical Overview: A Road Map through the Past

The language itself contains evidence of the major demographic movements which occurred in the first millennium of what we may call the English-speaking peoples. It may therefore be useful at the outset to trace in an overview a broad outline of these waves of invaders who have left parts of their language, large and small, in the linguistic amalgam of English.

The 'original' inhabitants of Britain (within the historical period) were the Celts, who some 2000 years ago occupied most of Western Europe. From them are derived the ancient languages of Britain, namely Welsh, Irish Gaelic, Scots Gaelic, Manx and Cornish (both now extinct), as well as Breton, still spoken in Brittany in France. Having been sufficiently dominant to threaten Rome in 390 BC, the Celts thereafter found themselves retreating before that expanding Empire. Within a century of Julius Caesar's assassination in 44 BC, Britain, also known as Albion, had suffered a full-scale Roman invasion by an army of 40,000 men. However, when the Roman legions were in turn withdrawn in 410 Britain became a power vacuum, into which came the Angles, Saxons and Jutes.

What must have seemed a minor turbulence of the times turned out to be the most significant event in British history. Unlike the previous Roman occupation, which had made Britain a colonial outpost of Rome, this was the permanent settlement of a whole people who were not going to be dislodged if the natives got restless. The Celts were subjected to servitude and driven into the mountain fastnesses of Wales and Cornwall, where their language retained a precarious foothold. The next influx of this early period was the dissemination of Christianity, brought initially by St Augustine, who landed in Kent in 597. The linguistic significance of this diaspora was the introduction of Latin scholarship.

From the late eighth century the Anglo-Saxons became in turn the victims of slaughter and rapine, fire and the sword, at the hands of their northern relatives, the Vikings. The depredations of the *Dene*, as they were generically called, became so devastating and so widespread that when they were eventually defeated, King Alfred was able to sue for peace only by ceding to them about half of England, to the north-east, an area which was appropriately called the Danelaw. Old Norse (ON), the language of the Vikings, was a Germanic language related to Old English (OE), but as different as are, say, Modern Dutch and German. These early developments are treated more fully in chapter 2.

The Norman Conquest of 1066 was fundamentally different in nature from the preceding invasions in that the ruling caste spoke an entirely alien language, Norman French, by which they defined themselves and imposed their rule. Consequently Norman French became the language of power and prestige, reinforcing social distance between the elite and the masses. These distinctive qualities lasted for centuries, creating a stratified linguistic separation between the rulers and the ruled. To a certain extent this linguistic class-division has continued between 'us' and 'them', 'upstairs' and 'downstairs', 'U' and 'non-U'. Looking back, what is in many ways more remarkable, is that English not only survived, but re-established itself as the national tongue in the fourteenth century after ceasing to be the official language of the land for three centuries. This major influx of a dominant, foreign language was the basic cause for the emergence of what historians of the language term Middle English, which is thought of as extending from *c.*1100 to *c.*1500, by which time the more standardized form of Early Modern English was developing.

In the course of the Middle English period, as scholars once more absorbed the fruits of classical learning, so the third major strand of the English vocabulary was slowly intertwined with the Germanic and French. This Latin and Greek influx was also different in character from the previous one in that it came more directly from the source, linguistically speaking. The Celts and the Germanic tribes had, of course, encountered Roman merchants and legions on the continent, and had borrowed from them basic terms of food and measurement; the missionaries from Rome had brought their special religious vocabulary; the Normans had established their rule in their Romance dialect; now literary Latin came 'direct' in the form of manuscripts and charters. So it comes about that many a basic word may be borrowed more than once: Latin *discus* was first absorbed as a trading borrowing as A-S *disc*, yielding Modern *dish*; it acquired a Late Latin sense of 'table', which developed as Medieval Latin *desca*, borrowed as Middle English *deske*, Modern *desk*; the sense of 'table' also emerged in Old and Middle French as *deis*, which has become Modern *dais*; it generated *disc* in its various senses, including the compact computer device; finally, *discus* in the athletic sense was borrowed 'direct' in the sevententh century. The lexical developments of the Norman Conquest and Middle English are dealt with in chapter 3.

Thus, in the millennium and a half between the coming of the Roman legions and the absorption of Classical Latin, a whole series of linguistic and lexical layers had been brought to England. In terms of our archaeological metaphor they would appear thus:

Late Middle English ⇒	**Classical: Latin and Greek**
1066 ⇒	**Norman French**
787 ⇒	**Scandinavian**
597 ⇒	**Religious Latin**
455 ⇒	**Anglo-Saxon**
55 AD ⇒	**Colonial Latin**
2000 BC ⇒	**Celtic**

By the end of the Middle English period the vocabulary was heterogeneous and diversified, having acquired three registers, reflecting the differing status of the component elements, namely a Germanic base of common, basic words,

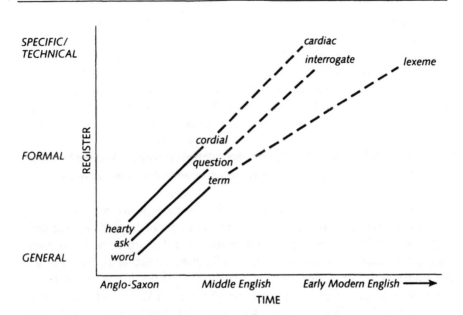

Figure 1.6   The correlation between lexical origin and register

a courtly, formal register from Norman French and an intellectual, abstract and bookish register from Latin and Greek. As a cursory study of the thesaurus will show, virtually any word-field reflects this structure. For example, in the following lists, the differing registers are clearly apparent:

Anglo-Saxon	Norman French	Latin/Greek
ask	question	interrogate
hearty	cordial	cardiac
folk	people	population
go	depart	exit
holy	sacred	consecrated
lively	vivacious	animated
guts	entrails	intestines
gift	present	donation
word-hoard	vocabulary	lexicon
word	term	lexeme

(In this study, the general terms *word* or *term* are preferred to *lexeme*,[2] the comparatively recent term used in linguistics for a lexical unit.) The relationship between lexical origin and register is shown in figure 1.6.

The invention of printing in the late fifteenth century had two contrary influences on the language. Although the press acted as a stabilizing force on spelling, it accelerated the rate of lexical change. Words no longer travelled at the rate of a migrating community; they sped across continents in the new editions of the Renaissance. As the ancient works of the classics were translated into the vernaculars, so the influx of borrowings became a flood. Some scholars saw the process as an enrichment and embellishment of English, others as a corruption of the 'purity' of the language. These opposing attitudes, one endorsing the high status of the foreign, recherché word, the other showing chauvinist hostility to the alien interloper, consolidated into what was known as the Inkhorn Controversy. Although historically it proved to be something of a storm in an inkwell, the underlying attitudes have proved surprisingly resilient, as we shall see.

The Renaissance, which is discussed fully in chapter 4, saw a great efflorescence in the growth of the language as a fine literary and dramatic instrument. In this respect Shakespeare stands pre-eminent as the author who has made the greatest single-handed contribution to English. Furthermore, the resonant yet simple use of the language in the Book of Common Prayer (1549) and the translation of the Bible, especially the Authorized Version of 1611 (commissioned by King James) clearly gave the language increasing authority. Surprisingly, this was also the period when the argot of the underworld first appeared in the published form of canting dictionaries, which gave permanence to a whole lower register.

The period of Early Modern English (1500–1700) also saw an important change in the global status of the language as England became a major colonial and trading power. This remarkable change occurred in a mere two centuries: around 1400 English was still in the process of re-establishing itself as the official language of England, whereas around 1600 it was starting to be transplanted across the world. The early explorers and colonists also brought back with them increasing numbers of exotic words which were steadily absorbed in the language. Thus from the so-called New World came *potato, tomato, barbecue, buccaneer, cannibal, canoe, hammock, hurricane, maize, tobacco* and *chocolate*. This process has steadily continued as a consequence of colonialism and the spread of English. More significantly, colonial outposts were established in the Carolinas (1584), Virginia (1607) and New England (1620) which were to grow into the largest English-speaking community in the world, with distinctive features of pronunciation, lexis and idiom which have increasingly differentiated the offspring from its parent stock. The same is true of Indian English, Australian English, West Indian English, and those varieties which make up the mosaic of modern world English. The borrowings from colonialism and imperialism supply the material for chapter 6.

Words as Mobile Forms

Up to now we have been considering the general expansion of English lexis mainly as a consequence of demographic change. But there were important developments going on within the language itself which accelerated lexical change. In order to understand them we need to consider briefly the relationship between grammatical form and function.

The fundamental change in the development of English grammar has been in the direction of simplicity of form. Put more technically, there has been a **reduction of inflections**, an **inflection** being a word-ending or **suffix** which has a grammatical function, such as -*s* to indicate plurality in nouns or -*ed* to indicate the past tense in verbs. For various reasons the English inflectional system has become simpler over time, as the number of forms has been reduced. Consequently increased flexibility of function has been acquired by the individual form of a word, since the reduced number of forms has been required to take on a greater range of functions. If we ask the question 'What part of speech is *love?*' the answer now depends not on the form, but on the context, as we can see from the following statements:

I *love* you. (verb)
Love is a many-splendoured thing. (noun)
Isolde drank the *love* potion. (adjective)

Such flexibility was not possible in the earlier stages of the language, since different functions were indicated by specific inflections. In Anglo-Saxon the forms required for the contexts listed above would be quite distinct, namely *lufie*, *lufa* and *lufe* respectively. Though we do not spend much time thinking about it, our present **conjugation** of the verb *love* consists of but four forms: *love*, *loves*, *loved* and *loving*. These are the 'survivors', so to speak, of eleven different forms in Anglo-Saxon.

The major point of all this is that from late Middle English, words had largely shed their grammatical inflections and were thus no longer limited to particular functions. Words were set free, becoming what is called in modern grammar 'free forms'. This meant that they could be used in all sorts of new ways which had not been possible before. For instance, *dog*, an ancient noun (originally OE *docga*) was used as a verb for the first time (meaning 'to follow like a dog') in *c.*1519. Likewise, *hound* first developed a verbal capacity *c.*1518, *fox c.*1567 and *ape c.*1632. Simeon Potter points out that 'Names of many parts of the human body – *eye, nose, mouth, arm, breast, shoulder, elbow, hand, knuckle, thumb, stomach, leg, foot, heel* and *toe* – have come to be used as verbs'

(1975, p. 169). This process, called **conversion**, applied both to native words and to classical borrowings (which we shall discuss in chapter 4).

It became possible for individuals to exploit this new flexibility in a creative fashion. Shakespeare, for example, frequently extended the grammatical functions of words in new ways. Cleopatra, one of his most poetically liberated characters, says of Antony: 'He words me, girls' (i.e. he's 'chatting me up'), using *word* as a verb for the first recorded time in 1608 (V. ii. 190). After her final defeat, she anticipates the humiliation of being *windowed* ('shown off') in Rome and of being made the topic of theatrical spectacle in which some youth will '*boy* my greatness' (V. ii. 219). Here we can see very ancient words being given a new grammatical and lexical lease of life.

It is hard to overstate the significance of this development, since there was and continues to be a great semantic expansion from the same lexical base. Thus *tough*, originally an adjective, has expanded to being a noun ('a tough') and (in US usage) a verb, as in 'to tough it out'. Similarly, *clock*, originally a noun, has acquired at least three senses as a verb: to hit, to measure in time and 'to clock in' for work. In contemporary English this has become commonplace, with nouns like *showcase, mothball, host, flight, fuel, target* and *mushroom* being increasingly used as verbs. This theme is taken up in chapter 7.

Modern English: establishing the lexicon

The seventeenth and eighteenth centuries saw the steady coalescence of a notional Standard English. The desire of the Enlightenment for the imposition of rational order was apparent in attempts to 'fix' the language, i.e. formalize it on a rational and scientific basis. This took the form of a number of proposals for an English Academy to regulate the language, and more concretely, the first major attempts at comprehensive dictionaries by Nathaniel Bailey (in 1721 and 1730) and, most famously, by Samuel Johnson (in 1755). These established the word-stock more authoritatively, giving rise to the influential notion that for a word properly to exist, it should be 'in the dictionary'.

As we shall see in chapter 5, which deals with the evolution of the dictionary, the latter part of the nineteenth century was a period of intense lexicographical activity. This was evidenced principally by the compilation of the great *Oxford English Dictionary* or *OED* (1884–1928), with a first Supplement (1933), the major source-work for the reconstruction of the lexical history of the language. Other remarkable lexicographical achievements focusing on less central areas of the lexis were Joseph Wright's *English Dialect Dictionary* (six volumes, 1898–1905), Bosworth and Toller's *Anglo-Saxon Dictionary* (1894) and J. S. Farmer and W. E. Henley's *Slang and its Analogues: Past and Present* (seven volumes, 1890–1904).

Recent decades have seen the publication of the four-volume *Supplement* to the *OED* (1972–86). In 1989 the two sequences were integrated, producing the second edition, consisting of twenty volumes. In addition to the third edition of *Webster* (1961), definitive works on Australian, South African and New Zealand English have been produced, in 1988, 1995 and 1998 respectively. For a variety of reasons, contemporary English shows a diminution of previous attitudes of suspicion or haughtiness about borrowings, and has become omnivorously receptive of words of all varieties, new words, exotic words, 'buzz' words. Consequently, the major dictionaries have difficulty keeping up, and compilations of new words appear almost on an annual basis. Dictionaries on historical principles are giving way to those based on corpora or collections of quotations showing written or spoken language. New lexical varieties are discussed in chapter 7, while the concluding chapter considers changes in the lexical structure, as well as the implications of these developments for the future of the language as English or Englishes.

Semantics and Lexis:
Synonyms, Antonyms and Hyponyms

As we can see from this overview, there are many kinds of words, or lexical varieties. Apart from the variations of register, there are terms for geographical features or place-name elements, such as *fell*, *cwm* and *by*. These are, in the nature of things, often regional or dialectal. However, as we shall see, place-names are also reflective of social dominance in various ways: originally they reflect demographic movement (*Denby*, for example, meaning 'the town of the Danes'); subsequently they reflect political dominance, as in the use of *Victoria* and *Wellington* all over the former British Empire.[3] There are general names for things, such as *book* and *guts*, and specific terms, such as *lexicon* and *intestine*. There are names for qualities, such as *hearty* and *cordial*, and for abstractions, such as *beauty* and *idea*, as well as for whole areas of study, such as *philosophy* and *physics*. There are terms for political ideologies, such as *democracy* and *communism*. There are even words for imaginary beings like *unicorn*, *elf*, *banshee* and *gnome*. We can see here a range from basic words for everyday communication to crucial keywords by which a whole nation's values may be defined or altered. These may extend to phrases, such as *for king and country*, *it's not cricket* and *free enterprise*, which encapsulate certain ethical notions. In a useful phrase, the literary critic William Empson called them 'compacted doctrines' (1977, p. 21).

Most languages contain such key cultural terms: *cunha* in Portuguese defines a sense of obligation to respond to a call for help; Spanish *mañana* conveys an unhurried, lackadaisical attitude; *Deutsche ordnung* sums up a German passion for efficiency; *noblesse oblige* is a Gallic formulation of upper-class obligations to behave nobly. This said, it would be naive to assume that these terms define national characteristics in any strict sense. Still more erroneous is it to construct supposed national characteristics on the basis of vocabulary. Consider these chauvinist sentiments on the German word *Schadenfreude* ('malicious pleasure at the misfortune of others') in the *Spectator* of 24 July 1926: 'There is no English word for *Schadenfreude*, because there is no such feeling here.' Leaving aside the highly questionable assumption that Germans are more guilty of *Schadenfreude* than other nations, the word English *gloat* conveys, albeit in a broader sense, the essential meaning of *Schadenfreude*.

Leaving these broad cultural matters of language, the essential point is that the lexical richness of English makes it possible to articulate a great variety of shades of meaning or semantic nuances, and it is to the general interrelationship between semantics and lexis that we now turn.

Semantics is the study of meaning, which is a complex matter in that it involves the relationship between words, ideas and things as well as the relationship between words of similar meaning. A distinction is often made in this respect between **reference**, or the relations between language and the world, and **sense**, or the relationship between words of similar meaning. Semantics also examines how sets of words are used to divide up experience: thus in English *black* and *blue* designate different colours, whereas in Old Norse the term *blá* served for both; in Russian, however, there are two distinct terms for blue, *goluboy* for light blue and *siniy* for dark blue, like *azure* and *violet*. The prism of colour terms tends to open up with time and cultural contact: historically *black*, *white*, *red*, *yellow* and *green* are Anglo-Saxon in origin, but *blue*, *brown* and *orange* entered the vocabulary via Norman French (as did *azure* and *violet*).[4]

Up to now we have been discussing words and meanings largely in terms of **synonyms** in particular word-fields, showing how these reflect in their structure the evolution of the language. And we have noted that exact synonyms are seldom to be found, even in a multitude of similar terms. However, meaning is also conceived of in terms of opposites and negations, generating the category of **antonyms**. We note, as a prime example, that Roget's *Thesaurus* is fundamentally structured by means of synonymic and antonymic categories. Some of these derive from the physical world, for example:

light/darkness
heat/cold
summer/winter

These we may think of as being mutually exclusive, i.e. one category denies the other, or as the classical grammarians put it, *tertium non datur*, i.e. there is no third possibility (Lipka, 1990, p. 146). Others may derive from the physical world or nature, but are more complex:

> male/female
> human/animal

The male/female categorization seems absolute, but is complicated by *hermaphrodite* (having characteristics of both sexes) and *neuter* (having neither). Likewise, the human/animal dichotomy, thought of as absolute by medieval philosophers, is complicated by terms like *brutal* and *bestial*, which mean broadly having the characteristics of an animal, but can be applied only to humans.

Other antonyms derive from social categories, for example:

> single/married

Once again, this pair has traditionally been regarded as mutually exclusive, but is complicated by the modern categories of *separated* and *living together* or being *a common law husband/wife*. One can refer, somewhat unkindly, to a person as being 'much married'. Other examples, philosophical or moral, are:

> good/evil
> physical/spiritual
> kind/unkind
> fair/unfair

Most of these are categorized by authorities under the heading of 'complementarity' (Lipka, 1990, p. 145). It is perhaps a sad reflection on human nature that the 'negative' word-fields in the thesaurus are so much larger than the 'positive'.

English has developed the simple category of the antonym in a variety of nuanced ways, mainly by the subtle use of complex negatives. Thus the plain antonymic pair of *talented/untalented* is complemented by the double negative *not untalented* which, despite its literal formulation, implies 'having considerable talent'. Similarly *able* and *lacking in ability* are complemented by *not without ability*, and so on. These *not un-* categories show the fallacy of applying to semantics the simple arithmetical or logical notion that 'two negatives make a positive.' They indicate a more guarded, noncommittal assessment on the part of the speaker or writer, who avoids the baldly negative or positive.

Although negative forms like *uninterested, disinterested, unmake, non-intervention* and the like have been growing by the thousand as the language has developed, new kinds of negatives have grown up in recent decades. Thus a positive term like *charming* has acquired a whole variety of antonyms ranging from *unattractive* to *repulsive*; to these has been added the equally critical coinage of *uncharming*, first used by Dryden in 1687 but currently fashionable. On the same model are the modern formations *unchic* (1960), *unglamorous* (1960), *unprestigious* (1968), *unsexy* (1959), *un-with-it* (1965) and many more. Bram Stoker resuscitated the form *undead* (recorded in Anglo-Saxon) in his *Dracula* (1897), while *ungreen* has similarly been revived to mean 'environmentally unacceptable'. As we shall see in chapter 2, Anglo-Saxon had an interesting lexical category, the 'intensive antonym'.

One of the curiosities of the field is the category of **pseudo-antonyms**, the considerable number of negative forms which either lack a positive or use a negative form in a way unrelated to the positive. In the first category are *inclement, uncouth* and *disgruntled*, which lack a positive *clement, couth* and *gruntled* (although D. G. Wodehome used 'gruntled' (facetiously in 1938). Similar 'negative half-pairs' are *unspeakable* and *malcontent*. The second category includes forms like *disaffected, disagreeable* and *indifferent*, the last of which has developed *two* senses ('mediocre' and 'unconcerned'), which are quite unrelated to *different*. 'New' negatives coined in recent years include *unbundle, unban, unpick*. Less numerous are the new **pseudo-positives** like *forgettable*, used ironically of books, films and events to which *unforgettable* has been too commonly applied.

The **hyponym** is a generally less well-known term, having been coined only in 1963 by John Lyons (Lipka, 1990, p. 141). It describes an important notion which is central to the way we define meanings in terms of lexical structures. Thus we would define *crimson* as 'a brilliant red colour', i.e. it is a particular variety of the categories 'colour' and 'red', and *camembert* as 'a kind of cheese'. In other words, even though we may not be aware of it, we construct meaning in terms of a hierarchy of categories, ranging from the generic, technically called the **hypernym** (literally 'the word above') to the subsidiary or **hyponym** (literally 'the word below').

Roget's *Thesaurus* works on this lexicological structure, dividing the world and the map of human knowledge into six vast general categories, namely Abstract Relations, Space, Matter, Intellect, Volition and Emotion, into which are subsumed Religion and Morality. Each category has numerous subdivisions, ranged hierarchically through hypernyms to hyponyms. The great merit of Roget's scheme is its flexibility and its capacity to accommodate new terms and concepts as the speech community using English has evolved. Each revision (and there have been over thirty since 1852) shows further expansion. As civilization and technology have developed (not always in concert) so previous hyponyms have become hypernyms. For example, *atom* in the age of Newtonian physics was a hyponym, meaning the smallest indivisible form of matter, from its Greek etymology 'that which cannot be cut'; with the growth of modern atomic physics and the splitting of the atom, it has become a hypernym. A contrary example would be *soul*, which in the Middle Ages was a crucial spiritual hypernym, but which has largely fallen out of use in modern secularized society, having developed a sense in modern music as a hyponym. A useful discussion of schematic arrangements of knowledge is to be found in Tom McArthur's *Worlds of Reference* (1986).

In a profound observation, George Santayana perceived that a split in the register of the English vocabulary between the Germanic and the Classical induces a parallel division of consciousness:

> In French, Italian and Spanish, as in Latin itself . . . the reader passes without any sense of incongruity or anti-climax from passion to reflection, from sentiment to satire, from flights of fancy to homely details. . . . As the Latin Languages are not composed of two diverse elements, as English is of Latin and German, so the Latin mind does not have two spheres of sentiment, one vulgar, the other sublime. All changes are variations on a single key, the key of intelligence. (1916, pp. 131–2)

Before we proceed further with our discussion of semantics and lexical variation, in which Santayana's observation can be assayed, let us consider the essential problems of definition and the role of the dictionary.

Agreed Meanings: Usage and the Dictionary

How do we learn or know what a word means? Essentially we rely on two models, namely usage and dictionary definitions, both of which have their strengths and limitations. In chapter 5 the main focus will be on the evolution of the dictionary as a form, starting in the late sixteenth century. But at this stage we need some discussion showing that words do not have absolute values like numbers, and that meanings are conventional, according to global, regional and social contexts.

As the early users of the language were for the most part illiterate, and as we are all illiterate at the first stages of our acquisition of language, usage has been the predominant force, historically speaking. Isolated speech-communities, such as those of Tristan da Cunha and some boarding schools, have their own vocabulary.[5] But most groups use words current in global English in their own quite distinctive ways. Thus soldiers in the US Army prefer the euphemism *wasted* to the blunt 'killed', the Sloane Ranger set in London uses the term *wrinkly* for a 'middle-aged person', while in Black American teenage street talk *bad* means 'good' and *vicious* means 'excellent'. The users of Valspeak, in the vicinity of the San Fernando valley of Los Angeles, use *radical* positively and unpolitically to mean 'good', 'wonderful' or 'challenging', while *satisfactory* will have very different meanings in a school report and in a medical bulletin. Likewise, a basic word like *grass* has the special meaning of 'informer' in the criminal underworld and 'cannabis' or 'marijuana' in the drug culture. Several of these meanings are, of course, unfamiliar to outsiders and, like most 'in-group' language, prone to fashion. Outsiders can make considerable gaffes when venturing into unfamiliar semantic terrain: perhaps the most hilarious was that of Robert Browning, who wrote innocently of 'cowls and twats' in *Pippa Passes* (IV. ii. 96) 'under the impression that it [twat] denoted some part of a nun's attire'. It is usually only when one travels outside one's community, either physically or via the written word, that one becomes aware of the same word covering different semantic areas. Thus *pond, vest, trailer* and *pants* have different meanings in American and British English, while *bagarap* is the general word for 'destroy' in Pidgin English, being an erosion of *bugger up*, but lacking any sense of impropriety. *Bastard* has a strongly critical sense in America, a broad range of tones in Britain, ranging from hostility to sympathy, but is a fairly mild term in Australia, where it is often preceded by the adjective 'good'.

To the members of these various speech-communities, their particular usage is predominant, and if they are illiterate, their meaning is for them the only meaning. It is worth observing here that *speech-community* can be a slightly misleading term, since it implies an unrealistically circumscribed area of relationship. It may have been a valid notion in the past, when society was comparatively static, and can still be applied meaningfully to isolated and 'primitive' communities, but in modern, commuting, socially mobile, mass-mediated society, most people belong to more than one speech-community. They will consequently use different language conventions at work, at home, and with the various professional and social sets to which they may belong. Therefore, in a profound sense, 'learning the language' involves becoming aware of, and discriminating between, the usage of these different speech-communities. As the editor of the *Oxford English Dictionary*, Sir James Murray, observed in the preface to the great work, 'No one man's English is *all* English' (1884, p. vii).

The Uses and Abuses of Etymology

Etymology is the study of the root or origin of a word: it derives from the Greek root *etymos*, meaning 'true'. The importance and the implications of etymology are considerable, as we shall see. Generally speaking, there are two contradictory processes at work in the relation between etymology and meaning. The first is a gradual erosion of the original link, discussed more fully in the following section on semantic change: words tend to move steadily away from their original meanings. Contrary to this is a desire to revive the link, to get words 'to make sense' with their past, an attitude which has various consequences, affecting not just semantic change, but almost everything to do with semantics. First, people prefer memorable or logical origins for words, and even invent them if they do not exist. Some words do indeed have such striking origins. Few of us ever forget (once we are told) that the *sandwich* derives from the Earl of Sandwich, a compulsive gambler who, in order not to leave the gaming table during a twenty-four-hour bout, sustained himself in part with slices of cold beef between slices of toast. Thus was born the *sandwich*, first recorded in 1762. Similarly engaging origins are discussed later in this chapter.

The two basic words used in greeting and parting provide a useful pair of examples demonstrating the erosion of the link between etymology and meaning. *Hello* is a later form of *hallo, halloo* and *hollo*. In these earlier forms it was not a greeting but a shout to call attention or to express surprise, which was still the sense up to about a century ago. (Interestingly, this was the original sense of *Hi!*, which has now adopted a less challenging meaning and is a standard greeting, especially in the USA.) In the forms *halloo* and *hollo* it was a hunting cry used to urge the hounds on in the chase, recorded as far back as the sixteenth century. *Goodbye* shows more dramatic erosion from its origins, which were in the phrase *God be with you*. Many intermediary forms such as *God be wi ye* and *God bye* are recorded from the sixteenth century. The change from *God* to *good* started around 1700, possibly as a result of confusion with the other formulas of parting, such as *good morrow, good day, good evening* and so on.

But most words have dull, obvious or unclear origins. Nevertheless, plausible, colourful explanations are proffered. In my own experience, I recall over a dozen people informing me that the word *fuck* (which has complex and uncertain roots) 'in fact' originates in a coded acronym: one group insisted that the term derived from the words 'fornicate under command of the King', supposedly a royal edict issued during the time of plague. Another group insisted (with equal certainty) that the word was a police acronym for the phrase 'for unlawful carnal knowledge'. These are examples of **folk etymology**, the positing of plausible but inaccurate explanations for the origin of a word.

Folk etymologies, as their name suggests, are collective and spontaneous. The origin of the word *woman*, for example, lies in A-S *wifmann*, which transliterates as 'wife-man', since A-S *mann* meant both 'man' and 'mankind' and *wif* meant 'woman'. However, as the *OED* notes, the word was used 'in the 16th

25

and 17th centuries frequently with play on a pseudo-etymological association with *woe*'. The first instance is given as *c.*1500 from the Chester plays, while even that noted humanist Sir Thomas More could write in 1534: 'Man him-selfe borne of a woman is in deede a wo man, that is full of wo and miserie.' Simeon Potter records Ruskin's preference for another pseudo-etymology of the same word: he 'found pleasure in reminding the married women in his audience that since *wife* means "she who weaves", their place was in the home' (Potter, 1961, p. 106). In recent times pressure groups have taken to invent-ing origins for ideological purposes: the form 'wimmin' has been created by some feminists who stated: 'We want to spell women in a way which does not spell men' (*Observer*, 13 March 1983). This remains a minority and specialist use. In other cases the speech community as a whole will bend the shape of a word to suit the meaning: thus the fanciful form *sparrowgrass* was created in the seventeenth century from *asparagus* (which has been in the language since Anglo-Saxon times). (Dr Johnson lists only *sparrowgrass*.) There are many cases of innocent misnomers: thus the 'white' rhinoceros is so called, not from its colour, but from a corruption of '*wide*', referring to the distinctive shape of its mouth. Once the misnomer was established, it became logically necessary to extend the confusion by referring to the other variety as 'black', although it is indistinguishable in colour.

Instances of folk etymology affecting spelling (to suggest the origin of the word) are surprisingly numerous. For example in *bridegroom*, the second element turns out to be a confusion of A-S *guma*, 'a man'. The Anglo-Saxon form *bryd-guma* survived up to the fourteenth century as *bride-gome*, but is later superseded by *bridegroom*, probably because *gome* had become obsolete. The *Jerusalem artichoke* has nothing to do with Jerusalem, but is so called through a distortion of Italian *girasole* meaning 'sun flower' (both plants belong to the same botanical genus).

In similar fashion *humble pie* derives from the *numbles*, originally a loin of veal, but subsequently downgraded to 'certain inward parts of an animal as used for food'. *Belfry* comes from OF *berfroi*, 'a watch-tower' before the form changed from popular associations with *bell* in the fifteenth century. In the phrase 'to *curry favour*', the second element derives from Favel, the name of a famous medieval French horse. *Crayfish* derives from OF *crevice*, Modern French *écrevisse*, more related (etymologically) to the crab than the fish. In similar fashion *penthouse* is an understandable distortion of ME *pentice*, 'a small sacred building dependent upon a larger church', while *shamefaced* comes from the OE form *sceamfæst*, meaning 'bashful or modest'. The *cellar* in a *salt-cellar* is a corruption of OF *saler*, meaning a container for salt.[6] The oddly named *Welsh rarebit* comes about from an etymologizing alteration of what was originally and facetiously called *Welsh rabbit*. Two foreign terms showing the same process are *mongoose* (from Marathi *mangus*) and *cockroach* (from Spanish *cucuracha*). In all these cases we can see that as the original form ceases to be understood (through time or foreignness), so it is changed to something recognizable or probable.

The study of semantic change necessarily shows us that the *etymology* or original root meaning of a word has little subsequent status, despite the etymology of *etymology*. Nevertheless the 'argument from etymology' is often resorted to, in forms such as this: 'The word *aggravate* is derived from Latin *gravis*, "heavy or serious" and therefore means "to make worse"; it should not be used to mean "to annoy".' On such a basis one could supposedly insist that a *climax* is a 'ladder', that a *marshal* is 'a boy who looks after horses' and that a *candidate* is a person dressed in white.[7] Manifestly this is not so; one cannot turn back the semantic clock so drastically. Nevertheless, this kind of argument tends to be used by older, usually more educated people to resist the development of a new meaning. The shrewd comments of C. S. Lewis are apposite here:

> Statements that *honour*, or *freedom*, or *humour*, or *wealth* 'do not mean' this or that are proof that it was beginning to mean, or even had long meant, precisely this or that. We tell our pupils that *deprecate* does not mean *depreciate* or that *immorality* does not mean simply *lechery* because these words are beginning to mean just those things. We are in fact resisting the growth of a new sense. (1960, p. 18)

The 'argument from etymology' can also be shown to be fallacious through the study of **doublets** or words which derive from a common origin, some of these are quite remarkably diverse. For example, *lobster* and *locust* are doublets, as are *glamour* and *grammar*, *cretin* and *Christian*, as well as *zero* and *cypher*. In other cases the root word can ramify and mutate to the point that the descendants no longer resemble the parent. Thus Latin *panis*, meaning 'bread' is the root of words as diverse as *pannier*, *companion*, *pantry*, *pastille* and *marzipan*. Similarly, salt used to be a valuable commodity, as is evidenced in such phrases as 'the salt of the earth' or to be 'worth one's salt', and so on. Yet the root notion is no longer obvious in such derivatives as *salary*, *salad*, *sauce*, *saucer*, *sausage*, *silt* and the verb to *souse*.

Yet etymological roots often reveal obscure and tantalizing connections which words retain through their semantic changes. Thus *custom* and *habit*, now essentially mental in their senses, are both rooted in the concept of clothes; likewise the verbs *flounce* and *bustle*, both meaning to move with agitation, derive from parts of a woman's dress.

The importance of etymology, for all its fascination, should not be overrated. In the eighteenth century, when serious lexicography started to evolve, the assumption developed that 'proper' words, like people of 'good' family, came from clearly defined origins, namely Latin, Greek and Germanic (or 'Teutonic', to use the contemporary term). If they did not, then they were regarded as linguistic bastards. Dr Johnson was particularly vexed by contemporary slang terms, which seemed to have come from nowhere. He could not ignore them; neither could he explain them. So he cast them into outer linguistic darkness. He thus denounced *to banter* as 'a barbarous word, without etymology'; nevertheless, the word had been in use for nearly a century, having been recorded by Samuel Pepys in his *Diary* on 24 December 1667. It has continued to thrive, despite Johnson's stricture. More significantly, we do not know the origins of basic words like *boy*, *bird*, *child*, *dog* and *smell*, but ignorance of their origins casts no aspersions on their legitimacy.

The Problems of Definition

While the dictionary will obviously seek to give a clear meaning for a term or a quality, much of life remains semantically elusive. As a character in Tom Stoppard's play, *Jumpers*, pronounces, 'Language is a finite instrument crudely applied to an infinity of ideas' (1972, p. 63). Persuasive though this view undoubtedly is, the dictionary contains an astonishing diversity of notions and terms. For example, a *gammerstang* is a tall awkward person, usually a woman, a *battologist* is 'one who needlessly repeats the same thing', to *slonk* is 'to swallow greedily', to *yamph* is 'to bark, especially of a small dog', a *taisch* is in Gaelic folklore 'the apparition of a living person who is about to die', while to *digitate* means 'to speak with the fingers', an activity which is becoming increasingly common, when people gesture that a particular word should be put into inverted commas or what are called 'scare quotes'. All of these are to be found in the *OED*. However, there are words in the dictionary like *unicorn* and *mermaid* for which there are no factual referents. The odd word *muggle* the *OED* classifies perplexingly as having 'origin and meaning obscure', while the odder entry *sooterkin* is defined with equal sobriety as 'an imaginary kind of afterbirth formerly attributed to Dutch women'.

Even in defining the physical world the dictionary is not entirely satisfactory. An Eskimo looking up *fallow* (adj.) in the *OED* would not be much helped: 'Of a pale brownish or reddish yellow colour, as withered grass or leaves'. In Anglo-Saxon times the meaning was even more unspecific, *fealwe* being applied, variously, to the colours of gold, the sea and horses, in which last sense it is still used of *fallow* deer. We may ascribe this lack of clarity quite fairly to the basic instability of colour terms. For example, 'A gem of a sky-blue to apple-green colour' is the *OED*'s definition of *turquoise*, while *azure* (from lapis lazuli) is 'a bright blue pigment or dye . . . Prussian blue'. How many people would recognize the definition 'a very pale blue with a trace of red' as describing the colour of *lavender*? Emotive terms also present problems. The *COD* (sixth and seventh editions) defines *chuffed* as 'Pleased; displeased', while the simple ejaculation *shit!* covers a range of emotions from anger, disappointment, surprise, pleasure and exasperation. The context will usually determine which meaning is appropriate.

The simplest matters are often the most difficult to define. It takes most of us some time to decode this: 'A perennial plant with single woody self-supporting stem, usually unbranched for some distance above ground'. It is the *COD*'s definition of *tree*. Dr Johnson's *tree* has, for a modern reader, some affinities with science fiction: 'A large vegetable rising, with one woody stem, to a considerable height'. Here our difficulty arises from his use of *vegetable* in its old broad sense. Sometimes words may retain in certain contexts an anachronistic disguise. Consider the following statement: 'A rocket, having more thrust than a jet engine, is the ideal mechanism for launching a satellite.' To us, this has the appearance of an unmistakably modern passage. But this notion derives solely from the technology it describes. On a strictly lexical basis, the passage could have been written as far back as *c.*1700, since by that time the key words *rocket, jet, engine, launch* and *satellite*, had all acquired meanings which would make broad technical sense in this context, even though most of them started with quite different meanings.

We may briefly consider the problems posed by old words used in some special technical sense which is no longer clear. For example, the noun *stole* carried a number of senses, from 'robe', to 'vestment or narrow strip of silk or linen worn by an ecclesiastic', before developing (about a century ago) the present meaning of 'a woman's fur or feather garment' of a similar shape. However, there is a second sense, *stole*^{2}, which the *OED* notes:

> Commonly identified with *stole*^{1}, to which the unauthenticated sense of 'royal robe' is commonly assigned. But there seems to be little doubt that the 'stole chamber', served by the Groom or Yeoman of the Stole was originally the room containing the king's close-stool [privy or lavatory] and that the word is properly a variant of STOOL.

This amusing example records a process which is reasonably common, whereby an erroneous meaning may become institutionalized, often aided by misleading spelling.

An apparently comprehensive definition may, on the other hand, be equally inadequate, as Dickens shows in his bitter satire on utilitarian education in *Hard Times* (1854). When the classroom tyrant, Thomas Gradgrind, demands of his class the definition of 'horse', his lackey Bitzer responds with a tissue of opaque equine information in the bloodless style of an encyclopaedic dictionary:

Quadruped. Graminivorous. Forty teeth, namely twenty-four grinders, four eye-teeth, and twelve incisive. Sheds coat in the spring; in marshy countries, sheds hoofs too. Hoofs hard but requiring to be shod with iron. Age known by marks in mouth. (chapter 2)

Dr Johnson was more succinct and practical: 'A neighing quadruped, used in war, and draught and carriage'. Often dictionary definitions depend on other dictionary definitions: the horse, according to the *OED* is 'A solid-hoofed peris-sodactyl quadruped (*Equus caballus*), having a flowing mane and tail, whose voice is a neigh'. (*Perissodactyl* is defined as 'having an odd number of toes on each foot'; for *Equus caballus* one would need a Latin dictionary or a guide to zoological nomenclature.)

Most people get through life without needing a definition of a horse. They use the dictionary to discover or to verify and, in fairness, the best definitions capture the essence of what are often very subtle qualities, as in Dr Johnson's definition of *pedant* 'A man vain of low knowledge, a man awkwardly ostenta-tious of his reading' and *to sit*: 'to rest upon the buttocks'.

One essential problem which compilers of dictionaries increasingly face is what level of usage is to be assumed. The older dictionaries tended to assume a written standard; the more recent, being increasingly based on corpora of usage, incorporate spoken idioms and a great variety of oral usage. These issues are discussed more fully in chapter 5.

Semantics

A historical study such as this necessarily involves some coverage of semantic change, namely the remarkable and fascinating changes of meaning under-gone by words over time. The *OED* supplies copious details of such changes, showing that few words have maintained a stable meaning through their his-tories. Here are some examples:

wan	A-S *wann*, 'dark'
worm	A-S *wyrm*, 'dragon'
free	A-S *freo*, 'noble'
fiend	A-S *feond*, 'enemy'
silly	A-S *sælig*, 'blessed'[8]

This process differs from lexical change, which concerns changes in the struc-ture of the vocabulary. As a consequence of the Norman Conquest, many Anglo-Saxon words were replaced by French equivalents. Some were central terms, such as *uncle*, which displaced A-S *sweostorsunu* 'sister's son' and *vegetable*, which displaced A-S *wyrt*. However, the two processes are often related, since the arrival of new words through lexical change necessarily affects existing word-fields, causing semantic changes. Thus the modern verb *starve* used to mean' to die' in the form of A-S *steorfan*; our word *die* derives from Old Norse *deyja*, which displaced it. *Starve* has survived, but in a different sense. We shall see, especially in chapters 2 and 3, how this process is repeated many times.

In studying the changing structure of the vocabulary, a valuable lexicological distinction was made by the French scholar Georges Matoré between 'witness words' (*mots témoins*), reflecting material progress, and 'key words' (*mots clés*), reflecting ethical change (1953, pp. 65–8). Matoré's own example of the first category was *coke*, the by-product of coal, developed in the eighteenth century, and first recorded in 1669. We can usefully apply Matoré's distinction to more modern developments, where there are many examples. Witness words from recent decades are *sputnik* (1957), *video* (1958), *laser* (1960) and hundreds more reflecting technical advances. *Mots clés* are generally fewer in number and less easy to detect, but Matoré chose the emergence of *gentilhomme* in the course of the nineteenth century. From the English past there are the terms for such social types as the *rake*, 'a man of loose habits and immoral character; an idle, dissipated man of fashion', recorded from *c.*1653, the *beau*, 'a man who attends excessively to dress, mien, and social etiquette, a fop, a dandy', recorded from *c.*1687, and the *scab*, 'a strike-breaker, from *c.*1777. From recent times we can point to similar terms for such types as the *yuppie* (*c.*1982) and the *couch potato* (*c.*1976). A general term in this category is *weekend*, recorded from 1879 and clearly affecting the lifestyles of whole populations.

One must be cautious in assuming too direct a correlation between lexical change and social change. Not even all technical words are reliable winesses: thus *railway* is first recorded in 1776 (in Act 16 of George III), but the first railway (from Stockton to Darlington in the English Midlands) opened nearly fifty years later in 1825. *Helicopter* is first recorded in 1872, but the first helicopter flight took place only in 1907. *Baseball* is mentioned in chapter I of Jane Austen's novel, *Northanger Abbey* (1818), but it is obviously not the modern American game. Sometimes a word formulates an ancient practice: *contraception* is recorded from 1886, but there are oblique references to the practice as far back as the *Ancrene Riwle* ('The Rule for Nuns') in the twelfth century. A similar time-lag may be assumed to apply in terms such as *sadism* (1880), *masochism* (1893) and *security blanket* (1956).

Semantics itself is a comparatively new term, having been coined around the turn of the last century, derived from the Greek roots *sema*, 'a sign' and *semaino*, 'to mean', which have also yielded *semaphore* and *semiotics*. The term was given

31

special prominence when the French scholar, Michel Bréal, produced his classic study, the *Essai de Sémantique* in 1897, translated into English as *Semantics: Studies in the Science of Meaning* in 1900. However, the study of meaning obviously preceded the emergence of the term *semantics* by centuries, major contributions having been made by many philosophers and poets. Although the word originally carried the prestige of its classical origins, it has, regrettably, acquired increasingly negative overtones (outside professional use) in recent decades, becoming virtually a 'dirty word' implying linguistic obfuscation or dishonesty. An early recorded instance of this debased usage dates from 1944: 'The technique of character-assassination instead of argument is . . . standard totalitarian semantics.' Even within the profession, several major studies, such as those by Ogden and Richards (1923), Stern (1931), Lewis (1960), Waldron (1967) and Williams (1976), prefer the general term *meaning*.

Meaning is a highly complex subject, since it involves tacit understandings between users as well as overtly defined relationships between words and referents, and a symbiotic contract between individuals and groups within a given speech community. In the case of a world language like English, this relationship becomes more complex, involving a global community of users with regional conventions. Thus a term like *fanny* has quite different meanings and degrees of taboo in the United Kingdom, where it is an impolite slang term for a woman's genitals, whereas in America it is a fairly common slang term for the buttocks.

Despite these problems, it is remarkable how precisely speakers and listeners are able to isolate the intended meaning out of hundreds of available options, for instance, those attaching to the word *lost* in the following statements: 'He *lost* his pen'; 'He *lost* his life'; 'England *lost* the match'; 'He *lost* his temper and his way'; 'She *lost* her mind'. To these can be added the more American idioms 'He *lost* his cool', 'He's just *lost* it' and 'Tell him to get *lost*'. Just as diverse are the meanings of *just* in 'He's a *just* man'; 'He's *just* a man'; 'He's *just* the man'; '*just* as I was leaving, it started to rain'; '*just* listen to him!'; 'wouldn't you *just* like to give it all up?' Quantifying the meanings of common words, the American scholar G. K. Zipf arrived at the alarming statistic that 'Different meanings of a word will tend to be equal to the square root of its relative frequency' (1945, p. 255).

The examples just given are comparatively straightforward, but communication often seeks more indirect modes of euphemism or vagueness: people are described as 'financially embarrassed' rather than 'poor'; or 'experiencing some discomfort' rather than 'in pain', and so on. (We notice in both examples a marked change in lexis.) Delicacy and vagueness are often used of romantic or sexual matters, e.g. *affair, understanding, courtship, scene*, sometimes with disastrous results. In L. P. Hartley's novel *The Go-Between* (1953), the meaning of *spooning* is withheld from the sexually innocent central character until the traumatic dénouement. Sometimes deliberate ambiguity is resorted to: when Benjamin Disraeli, a notable combination of Prime Minister and novelist, was sent unsolicited manuscripts, he allegedly replied: 'I shall waste no time in reading your manuscript.' This had one meaning for him but another for the would-be novelist.

The argument that meaning is not absolute or eternal, but simply conventional (philosophically termed *nominalism*) is highly plausible, particularly in an age such as ours in which semantic engineering by oligarchies is widely manifest. It has a long tradition, especially among philosophers. Ferdinand de Saussure, the great Swiss scholar, regarded as the founder of linguistics, made an axiomatic statement on 'the arbitrary nature of the sign' (1966, p. 67). However, there are semantic areas where the need for agreed and stable meanings is vital. Matters of law, especially those concerning constitutions and treaties, come immediately to mind. The same is true of scientific or technical language. These semantic areas require what is termed **referential** language, i.e. that which is neutral, factual and primarily **denotative**, the **denotation** of a word being its central or essential area of meaning.

In other domains, such as, say, political rhetoric and advertising copy, a higher degree of semantic licence, even of 'legitimate puffery', is condoned. Here a far more **emotive** kind of language is common, exploiting the favourable or negative **connotations** of words. **Connotations** are the associations, overtones and implications which exist in addition to a word's primary meaning. For example, among the synomyms for *thin* are *skinny* and *scrawny*, which have unfavourable connotations, as opposed to *slim* and *svelte*, which are favourable alternatives. Commenting on the current use of *gay*, Kingsley Amis observes: 'The word *gay* is cheerful and hopeful, half a world away from the dismal clinical and punitive associations of *homosexual*' (1997, p. 84). Connotations are commonly exploited for particular purposes. Thus a government report may note 'a shortage of *houses* and *electricity*', using referential and denotative language, whereas a bank or building society will prefer emotive language in persuading the public to purchase connotatively attractive *homes*. Likewise, an electricity company will claim to be selling, not referentially neutral *watts* and *ampères*, but favourable qualities such as *warmth*, *efficiency* and *comfort*.

The Historical Perspective

Looked at from a historical point of view, there emerges a clear relationship between parts of the word-stock and their denotations and connotations. A notable feature of the English vocabulary is that the native register has a more emotive quality than does the borrowed classical element, which is more referential. Thus the following piece of enticing copy is pure Anglo-Saxon: 'Warm, rich and full of golden-goodness, Fido dog food will give your furry friend health, strength and get-up-and-go.' However, marketing aimed at giving a more scientific 'image' to a product uses more referential vocabulary, most of which came into the language after the Renaissance. In the following example, from a packet of breakfast cereal, the classical terms are in bold type:

> **Nutritionists estimate** that the body needs 30 **grams** of **fibre** each day to **assist** the **normal** working of the **intestine** by speeding up the **passage** of **waste** so that harmful **materials** are **eliminated** quickly. **Fibre** plays a **definite role** in the **prevention** of **obesity. Fibre** can also be **instrumental** in the **prevention** of heart **disease**.

In this example 20 words out of 55, or 36 per cent, are of classical derivation. Technical matters have the highest concentration of classical vocabulary, as is seen in the following definition of *plastic* (taken from the *OED*):

> Any of a **large** and **varied class** of **substances** which are **polymers** of a high **molecular** weight **based** on **synthetic resins** or **modified natural polymers** and may be **obtained** in a **permanent** or **rigid form** following **moulding, extrusion** or **similar treatment** at a **stage during manufacture** or pro-**cessing** when they are **mouldable** or **liquid**.

Here 26 words out of 54, or 48 per cent, are of classical derivation. These 'content analyses' show how clearly the native core makes up the basic 'nuts and bolts' of the language.

The distinction between referential and emotive language is valuable and illuminating. However, it is not absolute, but a matter of degree, since no variety of the language can be completely referential nor entirely emotive. The context of usage is often a primary defining factor. It is even possible for the same form of words to be referential or emotive: hence the statements 'Mr Jones is a bastard' or 'Mr Smith is a bugger' would be referential when used by a judge, but emotive when used by a layman. Contrariwise, classical terms which were originally neutral and academic, such as *phenomenal, sensational, categorical* and *absolute*, continue to be used in this fashion in philosophical textbooks, but can also be effectively exploited in an emotive fashion: 'Jones must be categorically condemned as a phenomenal liar and an absolute fraud.' The same word can have different denotations in the same statement: 'Granny and Grandpa used to have a beautiful home down in Sussex, but after Grandpa died, Granny couldn't cope, so she's now moved into a very comfortable home not far from here.' The second 'home' is obviously a retirement or old folks' 'home'.

As has partly become apparent, the difference between native and classical terms is also shown in their degree of comprehensibility. Native terms are, generally speaking, semantically *transparent*. If one focuses on the core of the vocabulary, on words like *light, darkness, good, evil, strong, weak, hand* and *heart*, the basic meanings are obvious, even though they may be greatly diversified by metaphorical extension. Native terms form the language of first resort. In Spoken Word Counts, or analyses of natural conversation, the native content is very high. One such analysis (Jones and Wepman, 1961) yielded the following results: of the 200 most commonly used words, 83.5 per cent were Anglo-Saxon, 4.5 per cent were Old Norse (the closest Germanic relative), 10 per cent were from Latin via Old French and the remaining 1.5 per cent were from post-medieval Latin borrowings. As Dickens remarked fulsomely in an essay called 'Saxon English' in *Household Words*: 'When a man has anything of his own to say, and is really in earnest that it should be understood, he does not usually make cavalry regiments of his sentences, and seek abroad for sesquipedalian words' (1858, vol. 18). (*Sesquipedalian* is an example of itself, a ponderous polysyllabic alien formation. It was used by the Roman poet Horace to refer to words which were 'a foot and a half long', metrically speaking.)

The essentiality of the simple but flexible roots of the language was demonstrated artificially but dramatically through the invention of Basic English by C. K. Ogden in 1928. Using only the condensed core of the language, Ogden showed that with only eighteen verbs (curiously called 'operators') suitably combined with prepositions, a great diversity of meanings could be conveyed. Thus the simple combination *give up* can cover the meanings of a whole range of classical terms, such as *abandon, abdicate, abjure, cease, cede, desert, desist, discontinue, relinquish, renounce, resign, sacrifice, succumb, surrender, vacate, yield* and others. Without labouring the point, let us consider the remarkable range of common phrases which can be generated from the simple verb *do*, such as *do away with, do down, do for, do-gooder, do in, do-it-yourself, do or die, do up, do with* and *do without* (We should note, even-handedly, that while native terms have the advantage of flexibility, the classical have that of precision). The eighteen verbs of Basic English were: *come, get, give, go, keep, let, make, put, seem, take, be, do, have, say, see, send, may* and *will*. Of these all are Anglo-Saxon, except for *take*, from Old Norse.

The resonant clarity of the native word stock is apparent in many contexts, notably in the marriage service, formulated in the sixteenth century:

I take thee to my wedded wife/husband, to have and to hold, from this day forward, for better for worse, for richer for poorer, in sickness and in health, to love and to cherish, till death us do part, according to God's holy ordinance, and thereto I plight thee my troth.

Here the words which stand out as being not native are the Latin *ordinance* and *according*; poorer, *part* and *cherish* are actually from Norman French, but have become part of the core.

The only unfamiliar native terms are those which have become archaic or regional. Thus *housecarle, folkmoot* and *wapentake*, originally central terms concerning the social structure of Saxon times, are now obsolete, as is *swain*. Similarly, *thole* 'suffer', *bairn* 'child', *urchin* 'hedgehog' and *ken* 'know' are now regional survivals of what were originally central words.[9]

As we have seen, historically the varieties of register clearly reflect the class distinctions of their origins: the Anglo-Saxon terms tend to be those of the common people; the Norman-French overlay came from the Norman overlord, while the Latin and Greek terminology derived from a scholarly elite. The native terms tend to be short, blunt, emotive and direct; the Norman French tend to be imbued with courtliness and refinement, while the Latin or Greek are abstract and bookish, or technical and precise.

Although this broad categorization is sound, there are interesting historical complications, whereby words may change register over time, especially if they change shape or spelling. Consider the following high register terms *vis-à-vis* their subsequent *déclassé* descendants:

physiognomy (ME)	phiz (1688) ⇒ fizz (face)
lunatic (ME)	looney (1872)
fanatic (1553)	fan (1889)
obstreperous (1600)	stroppy (1951)
perquisites (1565)	perks (1869)
acute (1570)	cute (1868)
demonstration (1668)	demo (1963)
pornography (1864)	porno (1970)

Furthermore, the relationship between register and class is complex in its historical development. The amusing distinction that 'Horses sweat, men perspire, but ladies only glow' rests on a prescriptive decorum of style, rather than fact. The notion that the upper classes use exclusively high-register language is simplistic. Queen Elizabeth I 'swore like a man', we are told, and there is a great tradition of aristocratic swearing, vituperation and insult: this mode has even been developed into the art form of ritual insult known as flyting.[10]

The distinction between 'U' and 'Non-U', initially formulated by A. S. C. Ross in a scholarly journal in Finland in 1954, is an aspect of register which has received much publicity in the past few decades.[11] Ross demonstrated, albeit in a tellingly impressionistic fashion rather than one based on documented academic research, that 'U' (upper-class speakers) prefer plain low register rather the supposedly genteel evasions or euphemisms preferred by the bourgeoisie. Among the examples he gave ('U' terms first) were: *bog/toilet, mad/insane, rich/wealthy, false teeth/dentures, die/pass on, sweat/perspire* and *what?/pardon*. Others are simply conventional, namely *vegetables/greens, salt and pepper/cruet, napkin/serviette* and the naming of meals. Only *breakfast* is shared by all classes: thereafter the sequence for 'U' eaters is lunch ⇒ tea ⇒ dinner, while for the non-'U' it is dinner ⇒ tea/supper ⇒ high tea.

Ross's insights were popularized in a humorous collection of essays edited by Nancy Mitford under the title of *Noblesse Oblige* in 1956 and Ross himself edited a simiar symposium called *What are U?* in 1969. In a subsequent collection *U and Non-U Revisited*, edited by Richard Buckle, he observed that 'the antitheses between U and Non-U have *not* changed' (1980, p. 28). Linguistic class-consciousness was a necessary aspect of *The Official Sloane Ranger Handbook* (1982), by Ann Barr and Peter York. This glossary indicates the same preference in this upper-class type for the blunt or direct word in preference to the vaguer euphemism, commonly derived from the higher registers. They listed *bumph* for 'paper', *fuck-up* for 'organizational disaster', *pissed* for 'drunk', *bollock* for 'ball or social gathering', *poncy* for 'effeminate or aesthetic', *thunder box* for 'lavatory', *pong* for 'an unpleasant smell', *spastic* or *thick* for 'stupid' and *bin* for 'mental hospital'. In this milieu there is also a tendency for baby language to be used, as in: 'Mummy is dotty about this silly old colonel: he's a real sweetie, but he's always losing lolly on the geegees.'

It is a notable feature of sub-culture languages that they are made up of specialized use of low-register general terms rather than specific words. For instance, underworld argot includes *pig, mole, mule, hit, pinch (vb), lift (vb), shop (vb)* and *heat*, used in specialized senses. Similarly, the drug 'scene' uses *coke, pot, acid* and *high*. A single word may be used in both milieux: thus *grass* means both 'an informer' and 'cannabis', while *crack* means both 'to break in' and 'cocaine'. Among homosexuals a special currency of the words *gay, pink, cottage, drag, cruise* and *queen* is prevalent. In Black street slang in the United States, *bad, mean* and *wicked* have precisely opposite meanings.

We must distinguish between what is the natural evolution of registers within semantic fields through social conventions on the one hand, and the exploitation of particular registers for various motives. Variation in register is frequently manipulated to establish authority. 'If you do that again, I shall hit you' is an example of low-register, direct personal style. A public warning, on the other hand, would not normally be framed in such terms, but would employ high-register abstractions and an impersonal mode: 'Infringement of these regulations will result in prosecution.' In recent times much has been written, notably by George Orwell, on the deliberate exploitation of opaque, high-register Latinization for the purposes of evasion, deceit and propaganda. Terms like *liquidation, operation, incident* and *elements* are useful as 'anaesthetic' variants of *murder, invasion, riot* and *people*. C. S. Lewis appositely observed in 1942 'Once we killed bad men; now we liquidate undesirable social elements.' This theme forms a substantial part of chapter 7.

Register and Specialization

In various technical fields, there is a division of register clearly reflected between the general and the specialist term. Even in what we may call the general vocabulary, the base-term will commonly be Saxon, but the descriptive adjective will be classical:

finger	digital
ear	aural
mouth	oral
hand	manual
tooth	dental

Professional language is especially marked by the use of the higher register. For instance, in legal language:

theft	larceny
beat	assault
burn down	arson
crime	felony/delict

Thus the demotic idiom of being 'caught red-handed' is translated in legal jargon as *in flagrante delicto*. The same division applies in the fields of science:

hole	orifice/cavity
speed	velocity
force	intensity
size	volume

It is particularly apparent in medicine:

bleeding	haemorrhage
wound	laceration
skull	cranium

Anglo-Saxon		Middle English		Renaissance		Augustan	Victorian	Modern
shit(n)	turd	**ordure**		**excrement**			crap*	**defecation**
	piss (v)			**urinate**		**micturate**[1]		pee
sleep with	swive	fuck*		**copulate**	screw	make love	shag	bonk
	pollution	frig[2]		onanism **digitation**				wank
				self-abuse masturbation				
arse	bum*	buttocks	**fundament anus**		bottom			
			posterior(s)					
	cunt	thing[3]		**coney pudendum**	twat*	**vagina**	quim*	
weapon[4]	cock	yard	tool	prick	**penis**	(privy) member		

Notes: **Bold** type indicates Romance origin
* Origin uncertain
1 'The sense is incorrect as well as the form' (*OED*)
2 *Frig* overlapped with *fuck* in the seventeenth and eighteenth centuries
3 *Thing* has served for both male and female genitalia since Middle English
4 OE *wæpened* ('weaponed' or 'armed') has the basic sense of 'male' in many compounds including gender in children and plants

Figure 1.7   The semantic field of 'rude' words

sweat	perspiration
heart attack	cardiac arrest

Thus in medical jargon the opaque, high-register statement that 'The patient is experiencing a potentially fatal haemorrhaging episode' means basically: 'The patient is bleeding to death.'

In essence, we now have two vocabularies for our bodies, flora and fauna: an 'outer' vocabulary made up of common words, and 'inner' semantic fields comprising classical anatomical and botanical terminology. The development of medical and legal professional language is discussed in more detail in chapter 4.

In the area of sexual vocabulary, the separation of registers is so strong that there are no neutral, generally acceptable terms in English for the genital organs and sexual activity. As C. S. Lewis put it trenchantly, 'as soon as you deal with [sex] explicitly, you have to choose between the language of the nursery, the gutter and the anatomy class' (in Tynan, 1975, p. 154). Figure 1.7 depicting 'the semantic field of rude words' shows the evolution of the different registers. The field shows two important shifts over time, first a move from plain native terms such as *shit* and *arse* (from Anglo-Saxon) to abstract classicism in the Renaissance and Augustan periods, and then a reversion to plain terms like *bonk* and *wank* in recent times. However, the notion that terms now regarded as grossly impolite, coarse or obscene have always been taboo is not valid. The first recorded usage of the word *cunt* is in a medieval London street-name, *Gropecuntlane*, which would not pass muster in a modern borough. Many ancient proverbs are full of racy, naughty terms, to be discussed in chapter 3.

Today, the general division between Saxon and Classical is not absolute. In many semantic fields both options are available. Thus we have *equine* for horses, but *horsey* for people, *catty* for people but *feline* for cats; but both *piggish* and *porcine* are for people. The context is paramount, a point made in a memorable moment in W. H. Auden's poem, 'Musée des Beaux Arts', on a classic painting of the fall of Icarus by Brueghel. Commenting on the irony that Icarus drowns close to land but quite unnoticed, Auden writes:

> The dogs go on with their doggy life

deliberately using the low-register word, so unphilosophical and untragic, evocative of their purely physical existence of dozing, sniffing and scratching for fleas. Obviously *canine* would be unsuitably scientific. A wonderful contrary instance is the use of *liquefaction*, an apparently scientific term, in a sensual lyric by Robert Herrick ('Upon Julia's clothes', 1648):

> Whenas in silks my Julia goes,
> Then, then, how sweetly flows
> The liquefaction of her clothes.

Herrick uses *liquefaction* in a literal sense of 'flowing like water'.

Registers can be exploited or transposed for humorous or facetious effects. Thus the familiar nursery rhyme 'Twinkle, Twinkle, Little Star' is, expectedly, in almost pure native register, with *diamond* the sole classical term in this simple ditty. However, when facetiously transposed into an artificial classical idiom, the text comes out as:

> Scintillate, scintillate, globule vivific
> Fain would I fathom thy nature specific
> Loftily poised in the ether capacious
> Greatly resembling a gem carbonaceous

Now fourteen out of twenty-two words are of classical origin, making the piece abstract and opaque. The alien quality is also accentuated by the inversions and the contrast between the archaic idiom of 'Fain would I fathom thy' and the scientific terminology of 'nature specific'. In similar vein, Sir Arthur Quiller-Couch wrote a fine parody of Hamlet's soliloquy 'To be or not to be' in ponderous officialese:

To be or the contrary? Whether the former or the latter would be preferable would seem to admit of some difference of opinion; the answer in the present case being of an affirmative or of a negative character according as to whether one elects on the one hand to mentally suffer the disfavour of fortune, albeit in an extreme degree, or on the other to boldly envisage adverse conditions in the prospect of bringing them to a conclusion. (In Nash, 1993, p. 94)

Turning to more familiar publicly mediated language, the registers employed in modern journalism vary according to the sector of the market a particular publication is aiming to reach. The popular and tabloid press tends to use short, highly emotive, low-register terms like *slam, slate, blast* and *ban*, while the 'quality' press, the serious or responsible press, uses a more sober style. Curiously, even the popular sector occasionally resorts to archaisms such as *slain, yule, agog* and *scribe*.

Classical terms are often semantically *opaque* to native speakers, especially to those unfamiliar with their roots. Thus *otorhinolaryngology* is meaningless to a person who does not perceive that it is made up of four Greek elements, namely *ot-*, 'ear', *rhin-*'nose', *laryng-*'throat' and *logos* 'word' used in the sense of 'the study of'. The point of opacity in classical terms is easily demonstrated by their concentration in that area of comic semantic error called **malapropism**. This term derives from French *mal à propos* ('inappropriate'), but became part of the language through a humorous stage character created by Sheridan in his play *The Rivals* (1775). Mrs Malaprop blundered into such verbal gaffes as '*allegories* on the banks of the Nile' (for *alligators*) and *hydrostatics* (for *hysterics*). However, this mistaken use of classical terms had been previously exploited centuries earlier by Chaucer, Langland and Shakespeare.[12] While their malapropisms are often contrived as a comic device, there is a genuine core of incomprehension at the heart of the phenomenon. This has been explored in studies such as *The Lexical Bar* (1985) by David Corson and 'Elaborate and Restricted Codes' (1971) by Basil Bernstein.

Because of their alien and often mystifying quality, classically derived terms have invoked hostility from writers and commentators on the language. We shall see in chapter 4 that one such period of opposition was the Inkhorn Controversy in the sixteenth century, when classical borrowings were seen by some as bankrupting and weakening the healthy native stock of the language. However, in the eighteenth century, classical borrowings were regarded more favourably, and figure largely in the vocabularies of Gibbon and Dr Johnson, who showed such a penchant for them that he included in his *Dictionary* such oddities as *excubation* ('the act of watching all night'), *ebriosity* ('habitual drunkenness'), *effosion* ('the act of digging up from the ground') and *enecate* ('to kill; to destroy'). Others can be seen in figure 5.2. In recent decades the old hostility has revived. It is well exemplified in George Orwell's much-quoted prescriptions: 'Never use a long word where a short one will do; never use a foreign phrase, a scientific word or a jargon word if you can think of an everyday English equivalent' (1958, p. 88).

Amidst lexical diversity, the concentration of Anglo-Saxon in the core vocabulary is equally dramatic, bearing out Murray's observation quoted earlier. It is this central core 'whose Anglicity is unquestioned' which forms the nucleus of everyday speech, as is demonstrated in analyses such as the Spoken Word Count, previously mentioned. More remarkably, a similar analysis applied to the diverse vocabulary of literary authors (by Professor O. F. Emerson about a century ago) yields similar results:

King James Bible	–	94%	Pope –	80%
Shakespeare	–	90%	Johnson –	72%
Spenser	– –	86%	Hume – –	73%
Milton	– –	81%	Gibbon –	70%
Addison	– –	82%	Macaulay –	75%
Swift	– –	75%	Tennyson –	88%

(In Wood, 1969, p. 47)

The percentages are remarkably high, especially in writers like Milton, Gibbon and Dr Johnson, who had a penchant for the recherché or esoteric term. Of course, there will be variations within an author's work depending on theme or topic. But the durability, indeed the tenacity of the Anglo-Saxon core thus remains a permanent feature of the language, written as well as spoken, no doubt because it is the register of immediate recourse. The concluding chapter contains further discussion and more recent analysis of this aspect.

However, as we have already seen, classically derived words have their place, notably in technical and abstract semantic areas. Where would we be without words like *quantity, quality, procrastination, maturity?* Native equivalents, like *muchness, suchness* and *ripeness* are either quaint, unmeaningful or already bespoken. *Procrastination* has no true native synonym and requires a cumbersome paraphrase or translation such as: 'the deferment of action'. The same is true of *simultaneous, synchronize* and *atmosphere.* One thinks, too, of the power of the classical register evidenced in Disraeli's devastating denunciation of his rival, Gladstone as 'a sophistical rhetorician inebriated with the exuberance of his own verbosity'. A translation into the native equivalents, 'A dishonest public speaker drunk with the sound of his own longwindedness' manifestly does not have the same effect. A high proportion of classical terms occurs in recently coined scientific vocabulary, which has generated terms such as *spectrophotometer, teleroentgenography, transpepidation, tropomyosin,*

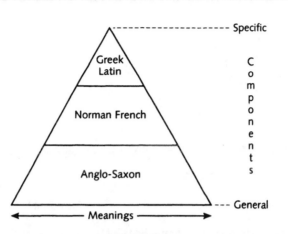

Figure 1.8   Lexical origins and range of meaning

zoochlorella and thousands more. The most most astonishingly gargantuan specimen is *pneumonoultramicroscopicsilicovolcanoconiosis,* a facetious word coined by F. Scully in 1936. While these are undoubtedly opaque and alien to the non-specialist, we should see them not simply as strangers, but as extensions of a classical word-stock of basic technical terms, such as *theory, method, pressure, motion* and *reaction.* The inestimable advantage that English has gained is its lexical richness, evidenced in virtually every word field. Consider the amazingly diverse (if morbid) possibilities of this range: *deadly, killing, lethal, mortal, fatal, deathly,* recently joined by *life-threatening.*

We may sum up the relationship between lexical origin, range of meaning and comprehensibility by means of two schematic figures, namely figure 1.8 'Lexical origins and range of meaning' and figure 1.9 'Lexical categories and comprehensibility'.

Taboos and Euphemisms

We have noted many examples of the perennially close relationship between social and lexical change. A large, complex and changing field concerns **taboos** and **euphemisms.** *Taboo* is a fairly recent borrowing, having been brought back from Polynesia by Captain Cook in 1777. It originally concerned areas of human experience which were sacred and therefore prohibited; it now refers to that which is unmentionable because it is ineffably sacred or unspeakably vile. **Euphemism** refers to the use of deliberately indirect, conventionally imprecise or 'comfortable' ways of referring to taboo or unpleasant topics.

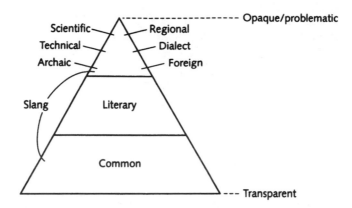

Figure 1.9   Lexical categories and comprehensibility

Euphemism shows that interference in the semantic market is not always deliberate, since taboo is frequently unconscious and collective in its effects.

In origin euphemism is profoundly concerned with word-magic, that primitive belief that there is a mystical relationship between words and things. The essential mode of euphemistic expression is thus indirect, and as the etymology of the term in Greek *eu* ('well) and *pheme* ('to speak') suggests, the motive is to describe the situation as better than it is, or to avoid the taboo area, thereby pacifying some dreaded force by managing not to offend it. Interestingly, one of the most striking examples is the ancient Greek use of the term *Eumenides*, meaning literally 'the friendly ones', to refer to the Furies. In many European languages the weasel, a bloodthirsty and ferocious creature, is called by a variety of pacifying names, such as 'little beauty' or 'little lady' (Ullmann, 1951, p. 77). Within the Christian frame of things one notes similar titles of respect for the Devil, such as *Old Nick, the Prince of Darkness, Lord of the Flies* and so on.

Despite the exotic origins of the word *taboo*, the notion of things sacred and unmentionable occurs at every level of civilization and in all kinds of environments. Feared or prohibited semantic areas vary greatly, including the name of God, reference to death, disease, madness, being crippled, as well as such common aspects of physicality as copulation, the genitalia and the varieties of excretion, even the most trivial of embarrassments, which in some societies include references to underclothes and humble occupations.

In order to avoid these areas of taboo it becomes necessary to adopt a disguise mechanism. In extreme cases the subject is avoided entirely. Thus no major English dictionary included the two most egregious 'four-letter' words, *fuck* and *cunt* between 1728 and 1963, a point which is taken up in chapter

5. The more common mode is less conscious and involves using a euphemism. Some of these allude explictly to the inexpressible quality of the taboo object. Thus in Victorian times it was taboo to mention *trousers*, with the consequence that terms such as *inexpressibles, indescribables, inexplicables* and other comic evasions were forced into service.

One mode of avoiding the embarrassingly direct is via a metaphorical route. Death and sex, being universal areas of euphemism, provide many examples. Death is referred to, not as a final shocking or peaceful state, but as a metaphorical journey, in comforting variants and traditional forms such as *passing away, passing on, going to one's Maker, in Abraham's bosom, joining the majority* and the speciality of the Salvation Army, *promoted to glory*. Similarly, we note that to *sleep with, go to bed with, make love, make out* are socially accept-able allusions in modern times to sexual intercourse. Of course, the degree of explicitness of these formulas has not remained constant historically. Until the early part of this century to *make love* meant roughly the same as 'to flirt'. In earlier times *lover* could mean 'friend': in Shakespeare's *Julius Caesar* (1599) Brutus refers to Caesar as 'my best lover' (III. ii. 45), with no sexual sense implied, but such an allusion has a very different meaning today.

These metaphorical modes existed as far back as Anglo-Saxon times. Thus the *Anglo-Saxon Chronicle* annal for the year 588 records: 'In þissum 3eare King Ælle forþeode' ('In this year King Ælle died,' literally 'passed on, went forth'). Similarly, the attempted seduction of Joseph by Potiphar's wife in Genesis 39:7, translated in the King James Bible (1611) as 'his master's wife cast her eyes upon Joseph and said "Lie with me",' was rendered by Ælfric in the year 1000 in a more modern idiom: 'His hlæfdige lufode hine and cwæþ to him Slap mid me' ('His lady loved him and said to him "Sleep with me"'). Incidentally, in the King James version, instead of the direct verb 'loved' we find the phrase 'cast her eyes upon Joseph', and note the similarity to the modern idiom of seduction 'to make eyes at', one of several suggestive but imprecise phrases, such as 'to make a pass at'.

Metaphors, it should be noted, can all too easily lead to the opposite of euphemism, namely **dysphemism**, which is the startlingly direct, low-register and shockingly coarse violation of the taboo. Thus dysphemisms for death include *pushing up daisies, snuff it* and *croak* which allude, with a large measure of black humour, to the physicality of dying, including the death-rattle and reincorporation into the cycle of nature. In similar vein, in Ameri-can underground slang, a corpse is a *stiff*, while to go to the electric chair is jauntily translated as 'to take a hot squat', and in Army parlance comrades may jokingly say that they will be 'back in a jiffy' i.e. in a body bag.

The major alternative euphemistic strategy is to use a high-register, abstract term. Thus in the vocabulary of death *undertaker* took on its funereal function around 1700, but has since lost its euphemistic sense and become the standard term in British English, whereas in American English the high-register equivalent *mortician* has been established for over a century. Similarly *coffin*, which originally meant in French a small basket, has become the direct term in British English, being replaced by the more elegant and precious euphemism *casket* in American English. Referring to the dead person remains problematic in British English, since *corpse* and *body* are uncomfortably direct; the American equivalent, *the loved one*, is ideally vague and comforting, if a little sentimental. In the sexual area, terms like *intercourse* and *intimacy* have lost their original euphemistic quality; similarly, *assault* is often preferred to *rape* despite its lack of precision, and *interfere with* often does service for *molest* or *abuse sexually*.

As we have noted in the discussion on semantics, the strong, direct and emotive terms in English are predominantly drawn from the Anglo-Saxon base register: among them are *murder, kill, steal* and *lie*, terms which would not be acceptable in diplomatic language. By far the most common register of recourse for euphemisms is the classical component, well described by Edward Gibbon in the eighteenth century as supplying 'the decent obscurity of a learned language' (1854, p. 212). From this source we derive *perspiration, urination, micturition, expectoration, defecation, copulation* in the area of 'bodily functions' (itself something of a euphemism) and *elimination, extermination* and *liquidation* in the semantic disguise of death. Some areas are surprisingly well-stocked in classical variants: *bad breath*, for example, is supplemented by *halitosis* and *pyorrhea*. As the explicit terms for sexual activity became unacceptable and then taboo, so numerous Latinized variants were drawn in to the semantic vacuum. Among them were *rape* (1482), *consummation* (1530), *seduce* (1560), *erection* (1594), *copulation* (1632), *orgasm* (1684), *intercourse* (1798), *climax* (1918) and *ejaculation* (1927). In other cases the classical term does not have a socially acceptable native equivalent: hence *fellatio* and *cunnilingus*. French supplies a useful array of euphemisms in *accouchement* for 'being brought to the labour bed' and *derrière* for 'backside'.

Classically taboos lead to another kind of disguise-mechanism, the use of what are called 'minced forms' of taboo words. We are familiar with self-conscious forms such as 'the f-word' for *fuck* and *bleeding* for *bloody*. However, many historical forms no longer reveal the original link with the taboo terms to the majority of users. Among them are *gosh, golly* and *gad* for *God, Jiminy, Jeez* and *Jeepers* for *Jesus* and *effing* and *frigging* for *fucking*. Figure 1.10 deals with the astonishing variety of euphemistic mutilations of the name of God, showing that the process has been fairly continuous since the Middle Ages, but received a marked boost in the period 1598–1602, when Puritan injunctions against profanity on the stage produced such forms as *'snails* for *God's nails* and

Term	Date	Euphemism
God	1350s	gog
	1386	cokk
	1569	cod
	1570	Jove
	1598	'sblood
	1598	'slid (God's eyelid)
	1598	'slight
	1599	'snails (God's nails)
	1600	zounds (God's wounds)
	1601	'sbody
	1602	sfoot (God's foot)
	1602	gods bodykins
	1611	gad
	1621	odsbobs
	1650s	gadzooks (God's hooks)
	1672	godsookers
	1673	egad
	1695	od
	1695	odso
	1706	ounds
	1709	odsbodikins (God's little body)
	1728	agad
	1733	ecod
	1734	goles
	1743	gosh
	1743	golly
	1749	odrabbit it
	1760s	gracious
	1820s	ye gods!
	1842	by George
	1842	s'elpe me Bob
	1844	Drat! (God rot!)
	1851	Doggone (God-damn)
	1884	Great Scott
	1900	Good grief
	1909	by Godfrey!

Figure 1.10   Euphemisms for the name of God

zounds for *God's wounds*. One of the linguistic ironies of life is that these euphemisms often become fashionable.

One of the curiosities of euphemism, indeed of the English language, is the development in the eighteenth century of the code language known as Cockney Rhyming Slang. This exemplifies a highly developed 'disguise mechanism' in witty and ingenious coded formulas where the last term rhymes with the intended word: thus *trouble and strife* alludes to *wife*, *brass tacks* to *facts* and *loaf of bread* to *head*. These are, of course, not especially euphemistic and have passed into general usage, so that their origin is often not realized. But in the grosser provenance there are such established forms as *Richard the Third* for *turd, Bristol Cities* for *titties, Hampton Wick* for *prick, Khyber Pass* for *arse, cobbler's awls* for *balls* and *Berkshire Hunt* for *cunt*. Of these the abbreviated forms *wick* and *berk* have passed into common slang, while *bristols* and *cobblers* are commonly used in the original speech community. Indeed, *cobblers* is often used in the broad sense of 'rubbish'. In the television series 'Porridge' (a slang term for 'prison'), a character says 'I sees through all that Home Office cobblers' (1990, p. 19). A rarer variety of slang is back slang, of which *yob* for *boy* is the only commonly used term.

Even more interesting historically are the substitute terms which have no obvious relationship with the taboo word. For example, *donkey*, which one would expect to be a common word found in the earliest stages of the language, is actually first recorded only in 1785. The traditional synonym, *ass*, had been in the language since Celtic times, and was the natural term in Scripture, proverb and folklore. However, in the eighteenth century the word started to fall into disrepute through an uncomfortable proximity to *arse*, so that the lexicographer Francis Grose observed that 'a lady who affected to be extremely polite and modest would not say *ass* because it was indecent.' Thus *donkey*, a dialect word, moved into the lexical gap.

Similarly *rabbit*, recorded from the fourteenth century, replaced the old word *coney* when it started to develop too close a relationship with *cunny*, meaning *cunt*, illustrated in jaunty verses such as 'All my Delight is a Cunny in the Night' (1720). A similar syndrome is apparent in American English, where *cock* has traditionally been replaced by euphemisms and substitutions: hence *rooster* for the famyard fowl, *faucet* for *cock* in the sense of 'tap', and the emasculated form *roach* for *cockroach*. (By contrast, in British English *cock* has never been a taboo term and is found in dozens of compounds, notably *cock-horse*.) The essential distinguishing point about all these substitutions is that they were collective, and presumably unconscious developments within the speech communities, not deliberate interventions by individuals.

There is, of course, an important distinction between those euphemisms which appear to be natural, unconscious and universal currency in most cultures, and those which are contrived (usually by oligarchies) to conceal politically unpalatable truths. George Orwell is especially associated with the trenchant exposure of such cynical evasions, now captured in his enduring coinages Newspeak and Doubletalk, discussed further in chapter 7. Although we tend to think of this last category as being an aspect of modern propaganda, the Roman historian Tacitus succinctly exposed the process in the first century in the sardonic quotation: 'They make a wilderness and call it peace' (*solitudinem faciunt pacem appellant; Agricola*, chapter 30).

However, these particular instances have proved surprisingly enduring, since it is generally the fate of euphemisms to become too closely associated with the taboo area, to become tainted and thus to require replacement. The considerable turnover of euphemisms naturally causes imbalance in various semantic fields as new replacements are brought in. In their classic slang thesaurus, *Slang and its Analogues* (1890–1904), Farmer and Henley show that no less than 600 bawdy phrases have been coined over the centuries for the sexual act. A small sample is given in figure 1.11, under the odd headword *Greens*. The dynamic between the taboo term *fucking* and related euphemisms, with dates of their first recorded usages, is shown in figure 1.12. As can be seen, the process has been going on for centuries.

In the underground slang of two centuries ago *commodity* was defined in an amusingly trenchant fashion as 'the private parts of a modest woman and the public parts of a prostitute'; *corinthians* were 'frequenters of bawdy houses', and a *commons* was 'a necessary house', i.e. a lavatory. These have all passed away, as euphemisms tend to do. Others prove surprisingly resilient: in the same period *hump* was 'a fashionable word for copulation' while *screw* was a plainer term for the same activity.

Western society has since added other areas of taboo, such as matters of race, financial collapse, poverty, going to prison, even trivialities which include fatness and shortness. Hence terms like *ethnic* for *racial, coloured folk* for *blacks, technical correction* for *crash, recession* for *slump, financially underprivileged* for *poor, choky, clink, slammer* and *nick* for *prison, dustman* for *rubbish collector, vegetable executive* for *greengrocer, vertically challenged* for *short, possessing an alternative body image* for *fat* and *substance abuse* for *drug addiction*. These are clearly more conscious, indeed highly contrived, part of the explicit agendas of political correctness, discussed in chapter 8.

Word-Formation

Most native speakers of a language are not consciously aware of word-formation. It would probably have to be pointed out to them that in the previous sentence the form *native* has a Latin root *nat-* which comes from the verb 'to be born' and a suffix *-ive* which indicates an adjective function (as in *adjective* itself); that *speakers* comes from a root *speak*, an agent suffix *-er* and a plural inflexion *-s*; that *consciously* has a Latin verbal root *scio* 'I know', with a collective prefix *con-* and an adverbial suffix *-ly*, and that *word-formation* is a compound. We are more aware of new formations like *disinformation, malfunction, unbundle* and *animatronics* than the well-worn, familiar words which we use every day. Since part of chapter 7 will deal with the more recent varieties of word-formation, this section will cover the more traditional.

GREENS, *subs.* (old).—1. Chlorosis: *i.e.*, the green sickness.

1719. DURFEY, *Pills*, etc., i., 313. The maiden takes five, too, that's vexed with her GREENS.

2. *in. pl.* (printers').—Bad or worn out rollers.

TO HAVE, GET, or GIVE ONE'S GREENS, *verb phr.* (venery).—To enjoy, procure, or confer the sexual favour. Said indifferently of both sexes.

Hence, also, ON FOR ONE'S GREENS=amorous and willing; AFTER ONE'S GREENS=in quest of the favour; GREEN-GROVE=the pubes; GREEN-GROCERY ⇒ the female *pudendum*; THE PRICE OF GREENS = the cost of an embrace; FRESH GREENS=a new PIECE (*q.v.*). [Derived by some from the old Scots' *grene*=to pine, to long for, to desire with insistence: whence GREENS=longings, desires; which words may in their turn be referred, perhaps, to Mid. Eng., *zernen*, A.S., *gyrnan*, Icelandic, *girna*=to desire, and Gothic, *gairns*=desirous. Mod. Ger., *begehren*=to desire. *See* DALZIEL, *Darker Superstitions of Scotland*, 1835, p. 106:—'He answered that he wald gif the sum Spanyie fleis callit cantarides, quhilk, gif thou suld move the said Elizabeth to drynk of, it wold mak hir out of all question to GRENE eftir the.' *Trial of Peter Hay, of Kirklands, and others, for Witchcraft, 25th May, 1601.* But in truth, the expression is a late and vulgar coinage. It would seem, indeed, to be a reminiscence of GARDEN (*q.v.*), and the set of metaphors—as KAIL, CAULIFLOWER, PARSLEY BED, and so forth (all which *see*) —suggested thereby.]

ENGLISH SYNONYMS.—TO BE all there but the most of you; in Abraham's bosom; up one's petticoats (or among one's frills); there; on the spot; into; up; up to one's balls; where uncle's doodle goes; among the cabbages.

To DANCE the blanket hornpipe; the buttock jig; the cushion dance (*see* MONOSYLLABLE); the goat's jig; the mattress jig; the married man's cotillion; the matrimonial polka; the reels o' Bogie (Scots'); the reels of Stumpie (Scots'); to the tune of THE SHAKING OF THE SHEETS; with your arse to the ceiling, or the kipples (Scots').

To GO ballocking; beard-splitting; bed-pressing (Marston); belly-bumping (Urquhart); bitching (Marston); bum-fighting; bum-working; bum-tickling; bum-faking; bush-ranging; buttock-stirring (Urquhart); bird's-nesting; buttocking; cock-fighting; cunny-catching; doodling; drabbing; fleshing it; flesh-mongering; goosing: to Hairy-fordshire; jock-hunting; jottling; jumming (Urquhart); leather-stretching; on the loose; motting; molrowing; pile-driving; prick-scouring; quim-sticking; rumping; rump-splitting; strumming; twatting; twat-faking; vaulting (Marston, etc.); wenching; womanizing; working the dumb (or double, or hairy) oracle. twat-raking; tummy-tickling; tromboning; quim-wedging; tail-twitching; button-hole working; under-petticoating.

TO HAVE, or DO, A BIT OF beef (of women); business

Figure 1.11 The profusion of copulatory synonyms: a page from Farmer and Henley's *Slang and its Analogues* (1890–1904)

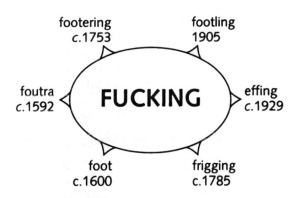

footering
c.1753

footling
1905

foutra
c.1592

FUCKING

effing
c.1929

foot
c.1600

frigging
c.1785

Figure 1.12 The dynamic between a taboo term and related euphemisms

As we have seen in the previous survey, English has a hybrid vocabulary. This applies not just to the individual words, but to the elements which are used in word-formation. Thus a basic word like *beautiful* is French + English; *musical* is Greek + Latin; *bureaucracy* is French + Greek and *tarmacadamization* is really polyglot, English + Celtic + Hebrew + Greek + Latin. In earlier times there was a purist view that linguistic hybrids of this sort should be avoided: thus *sociology*, coined in French by Auguste Comte, was condemned as being 'barbarously termed' shortly after its appearance in English in 1843 (Potter, 1975, p. 92). Today it is entirely acceptable, as are hybrids like *unscientific, doable, antifreeze* and so on.[13]

It may be of use to supply the student with a concise guide of the more common elements which indicate these etymological origins (Table 1.1). They are arranged alphabetically, with the less familiar elements being glossed.

As was stressed, this is a concise guide. When the Revd Walter W. Skeat, a great Victorian philologist, produced his *Concise Etymological Dictionary of the English Language* in 1882, he listed five pages of prefixes, but declined to do the same for suffixes, saying that 'The number of suffixes in Modern English is so great, and the forms of several, especially the words derived through the French from Latin, are so variable, that an attempt to exhibit them all would tend to confusion' (p. 630). Laurence Urdang has published a useful collection, *Suffixes* (1982), over 250 pages long.

The most obvious feature of the list is the great proportion which come from Latin and Greek, an aspect studied by Donald M. Ayers (1986) and Richard M. Krill (1990). These elements feature largely in new words like *semi-conductor, microchip, sociopath, superhighway* and *synergy*. A number of these prefixes have developed their own new senses as individual words, such as *retro, techno,*

Table 1.1 Prefixes and suffixes

Prefixes/beginnings	Suffixes/endings
acc- Latin/French	*-able*, *-ability* Latin/French
aero- Latin	*-age* French
ante- Latin (before)	*-ance* French
anthrop- Greek (mankind)	*-ant* Latin
anti- Latin (against)	*-archy* Greek (rule)
arch- Greek (chief)	*-arian* Latin
astro- Greek (star)	*-ary* Latin
audio- Latin	*-centric* Latin
auto- Greek	*-cide* Latin (kill)
be- English	*-craft* English
bi- Greek	*-cy* Greek/Latin
bio- Greek	*-dom* English
cardi- Greek (heart)	*-ectomy* Greek (cutting)
cent- Latin	*-ed* English
circum- Latin	*-ee* French
col- com- con- Latin	*-en* English
contra- Latin	*-ese* French
counter- French	*-esque* French
cross- English	*-ess* French
crypto- Greek (secret)	*-est* English
deca- Greek (ten)	*-fold* English
dys- Greek (abnormal)	*-ful* English
eco- Greek (home)	*-gon* Greek (angle)
em- en French	*-gram* Greek (written)
ex- Latin	*-graph* Greek (pictured)
for- English	*-hand* English
fore- English	*-hood* English
geo- Greek (earth)	*-ian* Latin
haem- Greek (blood)	*-iana* Latin (associated with a person)
half- English	*-ible* Latin/French
hand- English	*-ic* Latin/Greek
hetero- Greek (different)	*-ics* Greek
homo- Greek (same)	*-ing* English
home- English	*-ion* Latin
hydr- Greek (water)	*-ish* English
hyper- Greek (over)	*-ism* Greek (doctrine)
infra- Latin (below)	*-ist* Greek (follower)
inter- Latin	*-itis* Greek (illness)
kilo- Greek (thousand)	*-ity* Latin
macro- Greek (great)	*-ive* Latin
mal- Latin (bad)	*-kind* English
man- Latin (hand)	*-less* Englsih

Table 1.1 (*Continued*)

Prefixes/beginnings	Suffixes/endings
matri- Latin (mother)	*-let* French
mega- Greek (great)	*-like* English
micro- Greek (small)	*-logue* Greek (speech)
mid- English	*-ly* English
mille- Latin	*-made* English
mini- Latin	*-man* English
mis- English	*-mania* Latin (madness)
mono- Latin	*-ment* Latin/French
multi- Latin	*-metre* Latin
neo- Latin (new)	*-naut* Latin (sailor or ship)
neuro- Latin	*-ness* English
non- Latin	*-ocracy, -ocrat* Greek (rule)
octo- Latin	*-ology* Greek (field of study)
omni- Latin	*-osis* Greek (process or state)
out- English	*-phobia* Greek (morbid fear)
over- English	*-phone* Greek (sound)
pan- Latin (all)	*-ship* English
para- Greek (beyond)	*-side* English
photo- Greek (light)	*-some* English
physio- Greek	*-type* Greek
post- Latin	*-ular* Latin
pre- Latin	*-ure* French
pro- Latin	*-ward* English
proto- Greek (first)	*-ware* English
pseudo- Greek	*-wide* English
psycho- Greek (soul)	*-wise* English
quasi- Latin	*-woman* English
re- Latin	*-work* English
retro- Latin (back)	*-worthy* English
self- English	*-wright* English
semi- Latin	*-y* English
socio- Latin	
sub- Latin	
super- Latin (above)	
sym-, syn- Greek	
techn- Greek	
tele- Greek (distance)	
theo- Greek (god)	
thermo- Greek (heat)	
trans- Latin	
ultra- Greek (beyond)	
un- English	

physio, psycho, ex and *mega*. But although the classical variety is very great, the native forms are highly productive, albeit fewer in number. Thus the *un-* prefix made up about 4 per cent of the words in Anglo-Saxon and can still be used with great flexibility, as was shown in the section on antonyms. Similarly, consider the semantic range which can be derived from suffixes added to a basic word like *wood*, namely *woody, wooded, wooden* and *woodsy*.

Word-formation operates not only by using prefixes, suffixes and roots as building blocks on the model of *antidisestablishmentarianism*, a slightly absurd nineteenth-century formation. As we have already seen, with the reduction of grammatical inflections, new verbs could be derived from existing nouns by conversion. New verbal forms can also be derived from relatives. Thus the verb *edit* was formed about a hundred years after *editor*, a seventeenth-century agent noun, while the verb *peddle* occurs about 200 years after *pedlar*. This process is called **back formation** or **back derivation** since, as Simeon Potter puts it, 'New words are created by analogy from existing words that are assumed to be derivatives' (1975, p. 83). In a similar fashion *greed* and *difficult* are back formations from *greedy* and *difficulty*. The process is steadily on the increase, with verbs like *enthuse, commute* and *electrocute* already over a hundred years old, and being joined by annual harvests, like *bulldoze, televise, escalate* and *babysit*.

Lexical Varieties

Moving to more formal lexical categories, we find a considerable range of varieties. Our treatment of them, which concludes this introductory chapter, will discuss those types which are found throughout the history of English. These are **borrowings** or **loan words, neologisms, archaisms, eponyms, toponyms** and **compounds**. In chapter 7 we shall return to the topic to discuss those lexical varieties which are more a feature of Modern English, namely **portmanteaux, abbreviations, conflations, acronyms** and **diminutives**, as well as newer kinds of **compounding**.

Loan words

The many thousands of examples in the English vocabulary, from a great diversity of sources, form one of the major focuses of this study. (Latterly, with the growth of English as a global language, there has been the widespread converse development of 'Anglicisms', borrowings from English into other languages.) Both **borrowing** and **loan word** are misleading terms in that words are not really borrowed, since they remain in the parent language and are not returned by the borrower.

A threefold distinction derived from German is applied by scholars to loan words on the basis of their degree of assimilation in the new host language. A **Gastwort** ('guest word') retains its original pronunciation, spelling and meaning. Examples are *passé* from French, *diva* from Italian and *leitmotiv* from German. A **Fremdwort** ('foreign word') has undergone partial assimilation, as have French *garage* and *hotel*. *Garage* has developed a secondary Anglicized pronunciation ('garrij') and can be used as a verb; *hotel*, originally pronounced with a silent 'h', as the older formulation *an hotel* shows, has for some time been pronounced like an English word, with the 'h' being sounded. Finally, a **Lehnwort** ('loan word') has become a virtual 'native' in the new language with no distinguishing characteristics. *Loan word* is thus an example of itself. Other examples abound in the earlier borrowings, such as *bishop* from Greek *episcopos* 'an overseer' and *cheese*, from Latin *caseus*, has developed the forms *cheesy*, *cheesed off* and so on. A more recent example is *waltz*, puritanically defined in 1825 as 'a riotous and indecent German dance', but now accommodated in various phrases, such as *waltz in*, *waltz off with* and *waltz up to*, which suggest impropriety but have nothing to do with the original dance.

A **calque** is a loan translation from another language. Examples are *superman*, the creation of George Bernard Shaw from the German original *Übermensch*, coined by Nietzsche in 1883, and English 'world-view', derived from German *Weltanschauung*. We may note the difference that whereas *superman* now seems to us a natural English formation, partly because of the character in popular fiction, 'world-view' still seems slightly unfamiliar. Calques (loan translations) were more common in the earlier stages of the language (see Crystal, 1996, p. 27). One of the most notable from the Anglo-Saxon period was *godspell*, literally 'good news', from Latin *evangelium*; although *evangelist* and *evangelical* have since become established, in recent decades *good news* has become part of religious parlance.

Neologisms and archaisms

As the language develops through time, so new words or **neologisms** make their appearance and old words or **archaisms** become obsolescent and then fall out of use. The Roman poet Horace used the charming image of a tree dropping its leaves and replacing them to illustrate the point in his *Poetics*. Historically this process is not continuous and constant. The Renaissance was a period of great lexical expansion. Of the hundreds of words which are first recorded in the plays of Shakespeare, we may confine the list (for the time being) to ten: *assassination, obscene, critic, lonely, pedant, barefaced, puke, perusal, prodigious* and *mutiny*. By contrast, verbal innovation was less common in the eighteenth century.

There are degrees of neologism, differing extents of originality, which in turn affect the acceptability of a new term. For example, *weird*, now a common term virtually indispensable in American spoken English, was an ancient word which died out after the Anglo-Saxon period. It owes its modern currency to Shakespeare's resuscitation in the phrase 'the weird sisters' for the Witches in *Macbeth* (III. iv. 133). Other extremely original new words do not develop a life in the general lexicon. For example, in Shakespeare's *Macbeth*, consider the extraordinary use of *incarnadine* in Macbeth's terrified soliloquy (II. ii. 62–4):

> ... this my hand will rather
> The multitudinous seas incarnadine
> Making the green one red.

Incarnadine is never encountered again, apart from some rare literary uses in the nineteenth century, unlike the ten words previously listed, which are now common. Another example would be *Amansstrength*, the unique creation of the Victorian priest-poet Gerard Manley Hopkins in his poem 'Harry Ploughman'. Such words are termed nonce words, meaning words found only once. (The term is derived from the archaic phrase *for the nonce*, meaning 'for the occasion', from Anglo-Saxon *for þæm anes*.)

Most neologisms are not literary, but witness words reflecting technical change. Examples from the past decade are: *walkman, teflon, daisy wheel* and *skateboard*. But they may derive from many sources. The word *blurb* was coined by the American journalist and wordsmith Frank Gelett Burgess in 1907, originally as a fictional name (Belinda Blurb) for a 'pulchritudinous young lady' on a book cover he had designed. The word obviously 'caught on' because it filled a semantic gap. *Serendipity*, meaning 'the capacity for making unplanned but fortunate discoveries', was coined by Horace Walpole in 1754. A rarer instance derives from the American mathematician Edward Kasner, who asked his son to coin a word for the number 1 followed by a hundred zeros: his son came up with the memorably symbolic form *googol*, which has become a standard term in the profession. In modern times neologisms have become very fashionable, especially in journalism: hence such recent forms as *airhead, brat-pack, toyboy, bonk, wannabe, lookalike* and *bimbo*. We shall return to the varieties of neologisms in chapters 7 and 8.

Archaisms are generally less in favour today, but one still encounters *sans* ('without'), *smitten* ('to be seriously in love') and *woo*, meaning 'to court', itself becoming obsolescent. In recent years *wondrous* has been resuscitated as something of a vogue word. Archaisms continue to exist in traditional phrases, like extinct insects in amber. For example, the formula in the death penalty runs 'You shall be hanged [not hung] by the neck until dead.' The old sense of *fond* was 'foolish', still preserved in the phrase 'fondly imagine'.

Eponyms and toponyms

Two lexical categories which tend to excite philologists particularly are words derived from the names of people, or **eponyms**, and those originating in place-names, or **toponyms**. As with other areas of the vocabulary, we should distinguish between common words like *guy* (from Guy Fawkes), *pander* (from Pandarus), *tantalize* (from Tantalus), *nicotine* (from Jean Nicot), *panic* (from Pan) and the more rarefied, such as *pompadour* 'a shade of purple and an elaborate, usually high, coiffure' (from Madame de Pompadour, the mistress of Louis XV of France) and *mithridatize*, from Mithridates, meaning 'to achieve immunity from poison by taking small doses'. A suprisingly large number of common words are eponyms in origin, as the five italicized terms in the following brief extract show:

> As it was bitterly cold and wet, I wore a *cardigan*, a *mackintosh* and *wellington boots*. An hour after trekking up the muddy path we reached the *tarmac* road and stopped to have a makeshift picnic of pork pies and *greengages*.

The *cardigan* is named after the seventh Earl of Cardigan, who led the disastrous charge of the Light Brigade in 1854 during the Crimean War, when the garment was first worn by British soldiers. Charles Mackintosh invented the waterproof material from which the *mackintosh* is made, while *wellington boots* derive from the high leather boots made fashionable by the great British general, the first Duke of Wellington. John McAdam developed the process of producing *tarmac* roads, while the *greengage* is partly named after Sir William Gage, who introduced the fruit into England from France in 1725.

Certain notable individuals have left their names in a variety of forms: thus the *caesarian* operation derives from Julius Caesar, who was delivered in this way, while his political pre-eminence is commemorated in the titles *Kaiser*, *Czar* and *Tsar*, as well as in 'Caesar's wife', meaning the consort of a great man, who should be above suspicion.

The depth of the classical tradition is apparent in many eponymous terms, such as *cereal* (from Ceres, the Roman goddess of fertility), *volcano* (from

Vulcan), *siren* (dangerously seductive mythological women), *meander* (from the river near Troy) and the more literary terms *draconian, procrustean* and *laconic*. The panoply of pagan gods lives on in the adjectives *jovial, martial, mercurial, saturnine* and *venereal* (from Jove/Jupiter, Mars, Mercury, Saturn and Venus respectively), while *Aphrodite* survives in *aphrodisiac*.

Toponyms similarly range from everyday names like *jeans* (from Genoa) *alsatian* and *spaniel* (dogs originating in Alsace and Spain respectively) to curiosities like *balaclava, antimacassar* and *solecism*. The first is a woollen head-covering, named after a battle in the Crimean War in 1854; the second is a covering on the back of a tall chair, originally to prevent soiling by macassar oil, used to lubricate gentlemen's hair (though there is some dispute about the actual origin of the oil) and the third is a linguistic mistake, deriving from the inhabitants of Soloi in Greece. Toponyms are also surprisingly common, being found in the following six italicized words:

> Brigitte Bardot created *bedlam* in the fashion show when she removed her plain *denims* and *paisley jersey* on stage, revealing a stylish *turqouise bikini* beneath.

Bedlam, meaning 'pandemonium' or 'confusion', comes from the name of a medieval lunatic asylum in London, the Hospital of St Mary of Bethlehem. *Denim* was originally called *serge de Nîmes*, after the city in France. The *paisley* pattern takes its name from a town in Scotland, although the design originated in India. *Jersey* originates from the Channel Island of that name, while *turqouise*, meaning 'Turkish', refers to the bluish-purple gemstone, associated with Turkey. The *bikini* derives from the name of an atoll in the Pacific where the USA exploded an atom bomb in 1946. However, the two-piece swimsuit has no direct link with the place, being a clever opportunistic fashion-launch term trading on the associations of sun, heat and powerful impact.

As these examples partly show, eponyms and toponyms frequently relate to certain categories: items of clothing, cloths or materials, inventions, wines and spirits are prominent. Thus *muslin* comes from Mosul, *worsted* from *Worthstead* in Norfolk, *gauze* from Gaza, *calico* from Calicut, while *aran, duffle* and *jodhpurs* similarly derive from place-names. Likewise, the hats variously known as the *trilby*, the *bowler* and the *stetson* are named after those who made them fashionable. So are *bloomers*, the *teddy bear* and the *Windsor knot*. Sometimes the names become confused in the process: *sideburns*, for example, were made fashionable by Ambrose Everett Burnside, a Union general in the American Civil War. *Tawdry*, meaning an item of clothing or jewellery which is bright, arresting but cheap, comes from a fair named after St Awdrey. The enquiring student will make many surprising discoveries in words which do not seem personal or exotic: thus the common *tabby* cat derives its name from silk with a waved pattern, with the pedigree of fifteenth-century French *tabis*, from Spanish *tabi*, from Arabic *utabi*, the name of the quarter in Baghdad where the silk was made.

Most wines are named after their grape cultivars, such as *chardonnay* and *riesling*, or their area of original production: hence *champagne, burgundy, bordeaux, alsace* and *sherry*, from Jerez in Spain. Spirits, on the other hand, have more interestingly complex origins. Thus *whisky*, previously spelt *whiskybae* and *usquebaugh*, derives from Gaelic *Uisgebeath*, meaning 'water of life'. This emphasis on the supposed medicinal benefits of the alcoholic beverage is, of course, a standard euphemism paralleled by *aqua vitae* and its continental variations, *akvavit* and *eau de vie*. In a similar fashion Russian *vodka* means 'little water'. *Gin*, the demon of eighteenth-century England, is an abbreviated form of *geneva*, via Dutch *genever* and Old French *genevre*, ultimately from Latin *juniperus*, 'juniper', the main flavouring agent. *Brandy* also has a Dutch origin in *brandewijn*, meaning 'burnt wine', since it is distilled in oak barrels which have been lightly burnt inside to impart the distinctive flavour of the spirit. *Rum* is a truly curious term, and a more spectacular abbreviation, being known in the eighteenth century as *rumbo*, short for *rumbowling*, properly *Rumbullion* in Barbados, named from a Devonshire word meaning 'uproar'.

Understandably, many eponyms commemorate inventors. Amongst them are: *ampère, biro, braille, bunsen, Celsius, derrick, diesel, Fahrenheit, galvanize, guillotine, joule, morse, ohm, pasteurize, pavlovian, richter, salmonella, saxophone, silhouette, volt, watt, zeppelin*. A sub-category here is the naming of guns, including *colt, gatling, kalashnikov, mauser, maxim gun, tommy gun* and *winchester*.

The diversity of human types, of what Alexander Pope called 'the glory, jest and riddle of the world' is commemorated in the names of those famous for extremes of behaviour, notably: *casanova, chauvinist, dunce, martinet, masochist, maverick* and *sadist*. Particular individuals remembered as criminals, victims or eccentrics are: Fanny Adams, Heath Robinson, Hobson's choice, Ned Kelly, Namby Pamby, Peeping Tom, Robin Hood, Uncle Tom, Smart Aleck, Boycott and Hooligan.

A whole vocabulary of literary eponyms has filtered into daily usage. Amongst them are: *bowdlerize, don juan, Falstaffian, gargantuan, kafkaesque, lilliputian, odyssey, pander, romeo, quixotic, rabelaisian, jekyll* and *hyde, malapropism, stentorian, yahoo, shylock* and *scrooge*. Some are now unrecognizable offspring of their distant parents: *zany*, meaning a buffoon or something bizarrely comical, comes from *Giovanni*, a comic character in the Italian *commedia dell'arte*.

Eponyms and toponyms provide a stock of roots which are often interesting in their own right. Most people respond with simple philological pleasure to the information they provide about human behaviour and enterprise. But students must be cautious and sceptical not to be seduced into accepting folk etymologies. Examples abound, but let us consider the case of *crap* in a standard work of eponyms:

> To *crap* is to defecate and derives from Crapper's Valveless Water Waste Preventor which was the name under which the first flush lavatory was sold in England. The inventor, Thomas Crapper, who was born in Thorne, near Doncaster, in 1837, delivered England from the miserable inconvenience of the chamber pot and the garderobe. (Boycott, 1982, p. 35)

Unfortunately, the connection between the name and the object is not supported by any major reference work. Although it is difficult to distinguish between the various senses of 'rubbish' and 'waste' which accumulate around *crap*, they seem to have solidified into the main low sense of 'excrement' by the late eighteenth century, at least fifty years before Crapper was born.

Folk etymology is an interesting phenomenon, since it shows, not so much that people are gullible, but that they expect words to have intelligible origins, as many eponyms and toponyms in fact do. This particular lexical area has attracted a number of studies, but students and philologists should be warned against taking James Cochrane's amusing study, *Stipple, Wink & Gusset* (1992) in any spirit other than that intended. *Wink* is very much the key term in the title, appearing last, and facetiously etymologized by Cochrane as follows:

> Wink, Friedrich von 1755–1811 German nobleman . . . As Bavarian ambassador to the court of George III he introduced into London society his native custom of closing one eye to indicate that a witty or ironic remark was being made.

Compounding

As **compound** forms such as *barefaced, weekend, superman* and *brat-pack,* already encountered in the discussion, show, English has considerable capacities for making up new words from its own resources. In fact compounding is one of the earliest and most extensive kinds of word-formation, and continues to be so. It is a general feature of the Germanic languages, and we shall find many examples in the sections of chapter 2 which deal with Anglo-Saxon.

There are literally hundreds of ways of making up compounds. Two nouns are commonly combined, as in *handbook* and *workshop*; some are very ancient, such as Old Norse *wind-auga* ('eye of the wind') which has yielded modern *window*. Thousands, like *cupboard* and *saucepan*, *holiday* and *eyelid*, no longer immediately strike us as being compounds. Two adjectives may be used, as in *bitter-sweet* and *deaf-mute*. Adjectives and verbs combine in older formations, such as *blindfold*, while more recent formations, such as *see-through*, combine a verb and a preposition making a new compound adjective, alternative to *transparent*. Nouns and verbs make up *shoplift* and *babysit*, while adjectives and nouns combine in *eyesore* and *black market*. More rarely, two verbs are used, as in *hitch-hike* and *has-been*. More complex formations are *man in the street*, *dog in the manger*, *lackadaisical*, *dryasdust*, *ne'erdowell* and *good for nothing*. As we have seen in the previous section, great numbers of prefixes and suffixes, which may be native or classical, create further possibilities. The great efflorescence of compounding in Modern English will be discussed in chapter 7.

A curious mode of compounding consists of **reduplicating forms**, such as *shilly-shally*, *hugger-mugger*, *rugger bugger* and *walky-talky*. Although they seem like baby-talk, many of these formations have interesting formal origins and extensive histories. The first derives from Middle English *shill I shall I*, 'shall I do it or not?' before it took on the meaning of to vacillate around 1700. The second is much associated with the secrecy, skulduggery and intrigue of the Elizabethan stage; the third is a humorous modern description of the sport-obsessed philistine type, while the last is a piece of portable radio equipment, although the form is first recorded in Jamaica in 1774. Another enduring example is *namby-pamby*, applied to someone insipid or feeble, originally the eponymous nickname given to a minor poet of the eighteenth century, Ambrose Philips. *Hocus-pocus* is a corruption of the sacred phrase *hoc est corpus*, used in the Eucharist; it became a juggling phrase before the first word degenerated further into *hoax*. The reduplicating type thrives creatively, with hundreds of forms deriving from a great diversity of sources, such as *lovey-dovey*, *mumbo-jumbo* (from West Africa) and *Oedipus-schmoedipus* from Yiddish.

Conclusion: Words and Power

Looking back over the evolution of the English vocabulary which we have traced in this introductory outline, we can isolate and analyse the main factors affecting stability or change in lexical development. In the period up to Early Modern English the main factor was demographic change, with waves of invaders producing what Daniel Defoe amusingly described as 'Your Roman-Saxon-Danish-Norman-English' in his poem, *The True-Born Englishman* (1701,

l. 139). The main social, political and economic changes of this earlier period are reflected symbiotically in lexical changes.

As we have partly seen, these lexical elements exist in different proportions and are found in different registers. We shall be tracing their incorporation in more detail in the course of the following chapters, showing that words are the signs and markers of cultural dominance in the process of social change. We shall focus in detail on the foundations of the word-stock in Anglo-Saxon and trace the survivals from Celtic, the subsequent additions from Norse, Norman French, Latin, Greek and various foreign languages as reflections of different social structures and dynamics within the English speech-community. These social dynamics may be categorized as annihilation, cohabitation, dominance, prestige and colonialism.

Thus the sparse remnants of Celtic exemplify the annihilation mode: apart from place-names only a few words such as *ass, bin, dad* and *brock* have survived. The grass-roots infiltration of Norse exemplifies the cohabitation mode: although the Vikings were territorially constrained to the Danelaw in the north-east, they interacted with the Anglo-Saxons on the same social level, so that a surprising number of common words deriving from Old Norse have penetrated the core vocabulary. These include the central grammatical forms *they, their, them* and *are*, as well as such everyday words as *law, egg, sky, leg, ugly, rotten* and *husband*. The dominance mode is seen in the exercise of a new language of power in Norman French. The Norman influx in fact affected every lexical field, from basic words like *face* and *vegetables* to cultural words like *art, paint, picture* and *music*, but revealingly our vocabulary of power is still largely derived from them, as is attested to by words like *power, reign, realm, court, state* and *govern*. Latin and Greek terms represent the prestige mode, and (looking further ahead) the slow absorption of foreign and exotic words signals the mode of imperialism. Finally, the growth of a large and powerful speech-community in the 'New World' can be plotted in the shift in the balance of linguistic power between British and American varieties of English.

Other social changes had lexical consequences. With the coming of printing, semantic fields became more responsive to literary and academic interventions and influences through the various forms of the print media, as new words were brought into the language by individuals rather than peoples. Furthermore, technological changes brought about by noted innovators have created many new terms or witness words. Some of these are semantic recyclings of older words, such as *satellite* (which originally meant 'a servant') and *plastic* (originally an adjective meaning 'mouldable'); others are entirely new words like *wireless, radio, transistor* and *railway*.

Perhaps the most significant change between Early Modern English and Contemporary English from a lexical point of view has been one of attitude. This is shown in two ways. First, there has been a far greater acceptance of innovation. Secondly, there has been a diminution of the earlier chauvinism and suspicion towards alien terms, regarding them as interlopers, and an increasing acceptance of the foreign and the exotic. This change, part of the recognition that English has attained the status of a global language, in which norms are no longer determined by standards within the British Isles, has brought about the tremendous lexical growth of recent decades, which we shall discuss further in chapters 7 and 8.

Notes

1   The richness of the field of slang terms for drunkenness can be gauged just from the words beginning with the letter 's', namely *sloshed, slammed, slewed, smashed, stewed* and *sozzled*. Similar terms for money are more recent, historically speaking, but include *loot, bread, moosh, dough, duff, lolly* and *spondulix*.

2   *Lexeme* appears to have been coined by that remarkable researcher, Benjamn Lee Whorf. He distinguished between 'lexemes (stems) and other morphemes (formatives)' (1940, p. 160).

3   St Petersburg provides the most extreme case of a place-name being changed for ideological reasons. It was renamed Petrograd (1914–24), then Leningrad from 1924 to 1995, when it resumed its original name.

4   Berlin and Kay (1969) have shown the sequence of colour terms in lexical history. The basic sequence is black and white ⇒ red ⇒ yellow and green ⇒ blue ⇒ brown, grey, orange, purple and pink.

5   Winchester College, the oldest of the English public schools (founded 1382), has a very extensive dialect called 'Notions' which every new boy is expected to learn.

6   *Salt-cellar* is thus etymologically a tautology: so is *greyhound*, in which the first element is derived from ON *grey*, 'a dog', not from OE *græg*, 'grey'.

7   Students will enjoy Kingsley Amis's retailing of the hilariously implausible explanation (in Liddell and Scott's *Greek-English Lexicon*) of the etymology of *sycophant* as 'fig-shewer' from GK *sukon* 'a fig' and *phaino* 'to show' (1997, p. 221).

8   Other notable semantic changes are *garble* from 'separate' to 'confuse', *anon* and *presently* from their original sense of 'immediately' to 'in a while', *aristocracy* from its literal sense of 'rule by the best' to its modern 'unpopular' meaning, and *purchase* from 'to acquire by force' to the modern monetary sense. Many other examples are covered in my study, *Words in Time*.

9   Studies of dialect terms, such as those by Orton and Wright (1974), Upton and Widdowson (1996) and Trudgill (1990), give further examples of regional survivals of ancient terms.

10 The curious history of flyting is discussed in more detail in my study *Swearing* (1991).

11 Ross's seminal article, which started with the premise that the aristocracy was distinguished solely by its language, was originally entitled 'Linguistic class-indicators in present-day English' in *Neuphilologische Mitteilungen*, 1954.

12 The term *malapropism* dates only from 1849, but Grose's *Dictionary of the Vulgar Tongue* (1785) includes *slip-slopping* for 'misnaming and misapplying any hard word' (from the character of Mrs Slipslop, in Fielding's *Joseph Andrews* (1742)).

13 Although hybrids are increasingly the order of the day, there are limits. While Latin and English elements can be mixed quite freely (as in *earth science*), Greek requires more harmony. Hence *bibliophile* not 'bookphile', *philanthropy*, not 'philperson'. Similarly, words ending with *-archy* or *-ocracy* require first elements from Greek, making up combinations such as *oligarchy* and *ochlocracy*.

2

THE FOUNDATIONS OF ENGLISH AND THE FORMATION OF THE BASE REGISTER

The 'origin of language' is not to be sought in far-off Indo-European antiquity, or in a still earlier pre-Aryan yore-time; it is still in perennial process around us.
James Murray, preface to volume II of the *Oxford English Dictionary* (1893)

This chapter will be largely concerned with what Murray called 'the common words' of the language, those which make up the core of the lexis. Although the central mass of this core is drawn from Anglo-Saxon, there are significant elements derived from Norse, Roman and Celtic origins, in diminishing proportions. We shall discover that, despite obvious differences, all these languages have a common ancestral origin. But before we start to delve amongst these remote lexical roots, perhaps we should focus on one illuminating central word-field which reflects the whole picture of these various invasions, namely the landscape, language on the ground.

The land is the silent witness of these changes, bearing in its primary features the names given by its inhabitants and conquerors. Thus *land* and *sea*, *earth* and *water*, *hill* and *dale*, *field* and *stream*, *moor* and *mere*, *upland* and *down*, *heath* and *wood*, indeed the majority of terms denoting the landscape, are Anglo-Saxon. So are the most widely dispersed, seminal place-name elements, as we shall see. Similar in origin are the basic words for routes between these places like *path*, *way* and *road*, from A-S *rad*, originally the 'place of riding'.

The decimation of the Celts is apparent in the paucity of terms derived from them: apart from regional terms like *cwm*, 'valley', the first element in *Cumbria* and *Cumberland*, *aber*, 'estuary' and *tor*, 'tower', the main record of these lost voices is found in the river names *Avon*, *Dee* and *Tees*. However, some scholars take the view that since these names cannot be etymologized, some are probably even pre-Celtic (Lockwood, 1975, p. 17).

The Roman contribution is, revealingly, more reflective of their constructions and military artefacts imposed on the land than of terms for the landscape proper. Their skill in road-building has left us *street*, from Latin *strata*, describing the layered construction. The term was in earlier times used of the major arterial conduits like the Watling Street, which extended 180 miles from London to Chester, not to the common urban thoroughfare of our times. We still see this aspect in names like Oxford Street in London. Chester is itself derived from the basic term of Roman fortification, Latin *castra*, 'a camp', widely dispersed as a name and reshaped in *Cirencester, Worcester, Lancaster, Chichester* and so on. In the demarcation of territory, Latin *vallum*, 'a rampart', has come down to us as *wall*, originally a military and propagandist term, as in Hadrian's Wall and the Antonine Wall, but now common and domesticated, except for the Great Wall of China and the erstwhile Berlin Wall.

While the Vikings might be thought of as having contributed little on the planes of social and cultural affairs, their influence in the north-east is apparent in the concentrations of regional terms, as we shall see. In parts of Yorkshire 75 per cent of the place-names are of Norse origin. Of general terms the most central is *sky*, but there are also a number of basic words like *dale, bank, flat* and *rugged*.

Ancestral Origins

The name *English* derives from *Anglisc*, the dialect spoken by the *Angles* or *Anglii*, one of the Germanic tribes which invaded Britain in the fifth century, together with the Saxons and Jutes. However, the ancestral origins of both the language and its speakers lie in remote antiquity in a region which has not been positively identified, although Mesopotamia, the Steppes of the Ukraine and the Danube valley have been proposed. The peoples and languages deriving from this matrix are given the broad names Indo-European or Aryan, though this latter name has been out of favour since the propagandist use of the term by the Nazis to identify the supposedly 'pure' stock of pristine Nordic *Übermenschen* or 'supermen'. The language which most closely corresponds to the source is Sanskrit, which was standardized about 300 BC and has survived as the learned language of India (rather as Latin did in Europe).

As the Indo-Europeans started to migrate, so they split into two great streams, one current spreading west across the Middle East and the Levant into the European mainland, eventually crossing the English Channel, the Irish Sea and the North Sea, while the other moved east across the Caucasus and the great steppes of central Asia. As the western branch (with which we are primarily concerned) expanded and divided, so it generated the Hellenic, the

Latin, the Germanic and the Celtic language families. As the Eastern branch spread, so it mutated into the Slavonic, the Baltic, the Indian and the Iranian languages, among others. These two branches were traditionally termed by scholars of language the *centum* and the *satem* languages, so called from the respective terms for 'hundred' in the language families. (English and Latin are *centum* languages, while Sanskrit and Russian are *satem* languages.) However, the validity of these keywords was questioned by the transcription earlier this century of Tokharian, an eastern Asiatic language, since it proved to be – against expectation – a *centum* language.

Thus it comes about that all these languages, which English speakers often think of as being quite different and even alien, grew from this single source. Put another way, this huge Indo-European family, which constitutes the most extensively spoken group of languages in the world, comprises all the languages which have amalgamated into English, that is to say, the Germanic base as well as the elements derived from Celtic, French, Latin and Greek. In this chapter we shall be concerned with the Anglo-Saxon core of the language, the closely related Norse element, the remote Latin borrowings and the vestiges of Celtic as they interacted during a period of over a thousand years. The time-span, as well as the geographical extent of the whole evolution, is correspondingly enormous. Proto Indo-European is considered to have come to an end around 2000 BC, leaving no written records. Consequently the details of the subsequent diaspora continue to be the subject of debate, summarized by C. L. Barber (1993, pp. 62–80).

Since all this happened so very long ago, how can we prove this familial relationship? One broad characteristic of the Indo-European group is the binary division of syntactic structures into subject and predicate. The grammatical categories of nouns, verbs, adjectives, adverbs and so on forms another common feature. However, the most illuminating way is by comparing base-words in the **cognate** languages, i.e. those deriving from a common ancestor, a cognate root, such as those in table 2.1.

The words are set out in their mutations, first in the Germanic group and then in the Romance and Hellenic forms closer to Sanskrit. We immediately perceive how the various languages supply stocks for word-fields in Modern English. As we noticed in chapter 1, there are marked differences in register between the categories of common, formal and technical terms:

English:	*mother*	⇒	mother tongue; mothering
Latin:	*mater*	⇒	maternal; maternity
English:	*father*	⇒	father-figure; fatherland
Latin:	*pater*	⇒	paternal; paternity; paternalism; patrician
English:	*hand*	⇒	handy; handiwork; handbook; handcuff
Latin:	*manus*	⇒	manual; manipulate; manacle; emancipate

Table 2.1 Cognate roots

Modern English:	mother	father	hand	fish	sun	moon	star
Middle English:	moder	fader	hand	fish	sunne	moone	sterre
Old English:	modor	fæder	hond	fisc	sunne	mona	steorra
German:	mutter	vater	hand	fisch	sonne	mond	stern
Swedish:	moder	fader	hand	fisk	zon/sol	måne	stjärna
French:	mère	père	main	poisson	soleil	lune	étoile
Latin:	mater	pater	manus	pisces	sol	luna	stella
Greek:	meter	patēr	cheiros	psaros	hēlios	selēnē	astron
Sanskrit:	matār	pitar	hasta	mina	sūrya	māsa	tārā

Greek:	*cheiros*	⇒	chiropodist; chiropractor; chirology
English:	*star*	⇒	star-struck; star-gazer
Latin:	*stella*	⇒	constellation; stellar
Greek:	*astron*	⇒	astronomy; astrology; astrophysics.

We also note how the native Anglo-Saxon roots tend to extend themselves by metaphor and by simple compounding (as in *father-figure* and *fatherland*, in which the root *father* remains intact) whereas the Latin and Greek forms show greater flexibility in their formations and precision in their meanings. Thus the Latin root *manus*, 'a hand', appears variously in the formations above as *manu*, *mani*, *mana* and *man*. Generally, the classical terms supply the technical and scientific registers.[1]

Even this small sample shows that the interrelation between these languages is not self-evident, since obviously words change in shape and sound over the centuries. One might think of them in terms of the analogy of rocks and stones which have been weathered and eroded into different shapes through time and climatic variation. Most people would not recognize English *mother* and French *mère* as cognate terms without some persuasion or training in phonetics. However, a little analysis shows that virtually all the 'mother' words conform to a formula of *m + vowel + dental [d or t] + r*. (It is often claimed that all words for 'mother' begin with the sound [m] as an onomatopoeic rendition of the action of the child suckling its mother's breast.)

But even a rudimentary examination of the other terms shows that significant familial differences are also apparent. There is a clear division, for example, between Germanic *hand* and Romance *manus*, Germanic *moon* and Romance *luna*, which suggests something more drastic than phonetic erosion, indeed points to different origins. The same would appear to be true of *father* against *pater*, *père*, etc., *fish* against *poisson*, *pisces*, etc. We shall find this pattern repeated many times.

Sound-Shifts

These fundamental differences in base-words obstructed the view of a common ancestry for centuries, until a number of scholars realized that there was a missing link between the Germanic and the Romance languages. This was not a mysteriously lost language, but took the form of a phonetic mutation or sound-shift which affected certain consonants in their evolution from Indo European to Germanic. One such shift involved Indo-European p_1 subsequently Romance **p**, becoming Germanic **f**. As one can deduce from simple experiment, the sounds are not actually so different in character, both being made by the air being expelled through the lips (technically called **bilabial**); **p** is technically termed a **plosive**, describing the sound of the air being stopped and then released, while **f** is called a **fricative**, describing the friction as the air is forced through a narrow constricted space. Once one recognizes this sound shift, *father* and *pater*, *fish* and *pisces* turned out to be related, indeed the same word in different stages of phonetic development.

The recognition of this sound-shift was an intellectual breakthrough of Darwinian proportions, since it explained continuity through apparent difference and pointed to a common linguistic ancestry.[2] Though the phenomenon was originally called Grimm's Law, after the great German philologist, Jacob Grimm, it was in fact an aperçu arrived at independently by a number of scholars, including a Welshman, Sir William Jones, a Hungarian, Franz Bopp and a Dane, Rasmus Rask, who formulated the crucial phonetic shift in 1818. However, in an address to the Asiatick Society in Calcutta in 1786, Jones, a judge stationed in India, pronounced that there existed between Sanskrit, Greek and Latin 'a stronger affinity . . . than could possibly have been produced by accident; so strong, indeed, that no philologer could examine them all three, without believing them to have sprung from some common source which, perhaps, no longer exists' (McCrum et al., 1986, p. 52).

Furthermore, the significance of the sound-shift was not a limited insight, but introduced the realization that other, related consonants might also be involved and affect a word's permutations over time. These are **b** and **v**, which are phonetically termed the **voiced** versions of **p** and **f**, since they are enunciated in the same basic fashion, but with the vibration of the vocal cords also being employed. This wider family of related consonants links words which are by no means obviously cognate, as can be seen from the following lists:

Modern English:	soap	seven	bishop	devil	brother
Middle English:	sope	sevene	bishope	devile	brother
Old English:	sāpe	seofon	biscop	dēofol	brōthor
German:	seife	sieben	bischof	teufel	bruder

Swedish:	tvål	sju	biskop	djävul	broder
French:	savon	sept	évêque	diable	frère
Latin:	sapo	septem	episcopus	diabolus	frater
Greek:	sapon	hepta	episkopos	diabolos	phrater
Sanskrit:	*seib	saptan	——	——	bhrātri

Once again, we note common semantic derivatives from different sources:

English:	bishop	⇒	bishopric
Latin:	episcopus	⇒	episcopal; episcopate
English:	devil	⇒	devil-worship; devilry; devilish
Latin:	diabolus	⇒	diabolical; diabolism
English:	brother	⇒	brotherhood; brotherly
Latin:	frater	⇒	fraternity; fraternize; fratricide
French:	frère	⇒	confrère

Grimm's Law, which is now more neutrally termed the First Consonant Shift, also affected the sounds represented by the letters *g*, *k* and *h*, which are phonetically termed **velar**, since they are enunciated by the use of the **velum**, a soft flap to the rear of the palate which, together with the tongue, can be used to stop or constrict the passage of air.

Modern English:	knee	hundred	heart	hound	know
Middle English:	knee	hundred	herte	hound	knowen
Old English:	cnēo	hund	heorte	hund	cnāwan/cunnan
German:	knie	hundert	herz	hund	kennen
Swedish:	knä	hundra	hjärta	hund	känna
French:	genou	cent	coeur	chien	connaître
Latin:	genu	centum	cordis	canis	gnoscere
Greek:	gonu	hekaton	kardia	kyne	gnoskein
Sanskrit:	jānu	satam	hrid	cwan	jnā-

Once again, the cognates of these basic words prove to be surprisingly fruitful:

English:	heart	⇒	hearty; heartfelt; heartache
Latin:	cordis	⇒	cordial; discord
Greek:	kardia	⇒	cardiac; cardiology
English:	knee	⇒	kneel; knee-deep; knee-jerk
Latin:	genu	⇒	genuflect
English:	hundred	⇒	hundredth; hundredfold
Latin:	centum	⇒	century; centenary; centipede
English:	hound	⇒	wolfhound; greyhound
Fench:	chien	⇒	kennel

Table 2.2 Different roots in base words

Modern English:	woman	meat	cheese	leg	horse	rabbit	money
Middle English:	woman	mete	cheese	legge	hors	cony	monnaie
Old English:	wīfmann	mete	cēse	scæanca	hors	smygel	fēoh
German:	frau	fleisch	käse	bein	pferd	kaninchen	geld
Swedish:	kvinna	kött	ost	ben	häst	kanin	pengar
French:	femme	viande	fromage	jambe	cheval	lapin	argent
Latin:	femina	caro	caseus	crus	caballus	cuniculus	argentum
Greek:	gyne	kreas	turos	skelos	hippos	konikos	argurio

Latin:	*canis*	⇒	canine;
Greek:	*kyne*	⇒	cynic; cynical; cynosure

The last example, *cynic*, seems to have no semantic connection with its cognates: the explanation is that the philosophical school in ancient Greece was called the Cynics, some say because they were 'the snarlers', others because like ill-trained dogs, they lifted their leg against everything. Similarly *canary*, now meaning a song-bird or its yellow colour, derives from *canis*, since the Canary Islands were noted from Roman times for their large dogs.

These insights give the lie to the cynical observation of Voltaire that 'etymology is the science in which the consonants count for little and the vowels count for nothing.' (We should recall, in fairness, that he came before the discovery of the First Consonant Shift.) Indeed, once one grasps the correlation, all sorts of fascinating family resemblances between words which have hitherto appeared unrelated become apparent. For instance, we notice that the main root of the word *root* is Latin *radix*, which has yielded us such diverse forms and meanings as *radish*, *radical*, *radicle*, *eradicate* and *race* in its special sense of a root, especially ginger, which in turn yields *deracinate*.

Up to now we have been focusing on the differences which obscured similarity. Using the insights of the First Consonant Shift, we can see that forms as diverse as *heart* and *cardiac*, *knee* and *genou*, *bishop* and *episcopus* are indeed related. But it would be a mistake to suppose that these consonant shifts are some magic key to all etymologies. For, as we have partly seen, even base words in related languages can be derived from quite different stocks. For example, the English words *dog*, *bird* and *pig* have no cognate equivalents in related languages. (They have also managed to displace the terms which originally occupied the centre of their semantic fields, namely *hound*, *fowl* and *swine*.) Table 2.2 illustrates other instances of different roots in base words.

Nevertheless, these examples do not call into question the fundamental relationship between the Indo-European languages and the growth of the

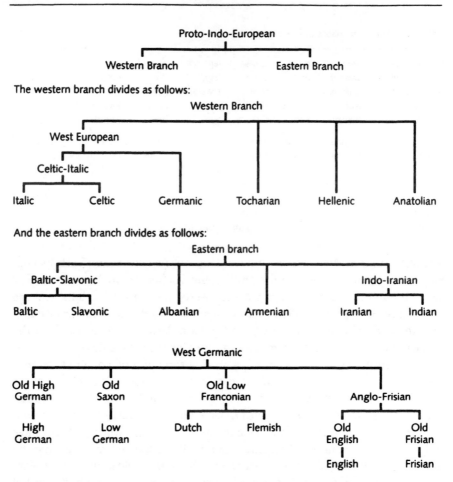

Figure 2.1 and Figure 2.2 The development of the Indo-European languages

various branches within the structure of the 'family tree'. The growth of the branches is shown in figures 2.1 and 2.2.

Lexical evidence for the origins of Indo-European

Since the identity and location of the original Indo-Europeans have not been positively identified, the structure of the base vocabulary has been analysed for its emphases and omissions, in order to deduce the environment and lifestyle of the original speakers. This method is not without its dangers, particularly when applied over vast aeons of time, during which words may be borrowed or lost. The assumption is that the values or concerns of a culture can often be deduced from the structure of its vocabulary. Concentrations and gaps in the vocabulary are also significant. Anglo-Saxon had some thirty-six terms for 'warrior'; indeed at that stage of the culture the semantic fields of 'man' and 'warrior' overlapped. Malay has three words for rice, depending on its stage of development: it is *padi* in the paddy field, *berasin* in the storehouse or in the shop and *nasi* on the table. Although the Inuit or Eskimo people have been credited with having seven words for snow to describe its varying depth and consistency, this attribution has been refuted.[3]

Closer to our own civilization, we note semantic concentrations which reflect cultural emphases: medieval English contained a collection of detailed terms such as *vambraces, rerebraces, chamfrons, crinets, peytrals* and *cuisses*, denoting different parts of armour. All are now largely extinct. In the nineteenth century there were various terms to define different carriages, such as *chariot, brougham, post-chaise, landau* and *phaeton*. With the advent of the 'horseless carriage' we now have another variety, including *saloon, sedan, limousine, convertible, station wagon, sports car, hatchback, compact* and so on.

The common terms of the Indo-European vocabulary suggest a nomadic or semi-nomadic pastoral people with cattle, sheep, horses, pigs, cheese, butter, mead (but not beer) and the means of transport which used wheels and axles. They also knew how to work leather, weave wool, plough the land and plant grain. The lexical evidence used to identify the ancestral climatic environment includes terms for snow and such wild animals as frequent cool temperate climates as wolves, bears, beavers and otters, but none for those animals which live in hot zones, such as elephants, lions, tigers or camels. As we have seen, there was a common term for 'fish', but there was no equivalent for 'sea'. The presence of the terms *salmon* and *eel* has been used to exclude the rivers which flow into the Black Sea, which do not bear these varieties. The common term for the beech tree is similarly used to exclude north-eastern Europe or anywhere east of the Caspian Sea, in which regions the tree does not grow.

The Celts

The earliest of the Indo-European migrations to the British Isles within the range of recorded history was that of the Celts, whose descendants still live in in a broad crescent extending from Brittany in north-western France through Cornwall, Wales, the Isle of Man, Ireland to the Highlands of Scotland. The Celtic languages, namely Breton, Welsh, Manx, Scottish Gaelic, Irish Gaelic and Cornish (now extinct) are of such antiquity as not to be immediately

Table 2.3 Base words in Celtic languages

English:	mother	father	fish	heart	foot	sun	water	moon
Welsh:	mam	tad	pysgodyn	calon	troed	haul	dyn/gwr	loer
Cornish:	mam	tas	pesc	colon	tros	houl	den/gur	lor
Breton:	mamm	tad	pesk	kalon	troad	heol	dan	loar
Gaelic:	mathair	athair	iasg	cridhe	cas	grian	duine	gealach/re

Table 2.4 Divergences in Celtic languages

English:	nose	ice	north	marsh	stream	field	hazel	world
Welsh:	trwyn	rhew	gogledd	cors	nant	cae	collen	daear
Cornish:	tron	rew	cleth	kersek	gover	kew	knofen	dor
Breton:	fri	skourn	hanternoz	palud	gwaz	park	gwezenn	bed
Gaelic:	sron	eigh	tuath	lon/boglach	allt	machair	calltuinn	cruinne

identifiable as belonging to the Indo-European group. This is apparent from applying the test of base words to a Celtic sample (table 2.3).

We can see relationships in the first three examples (especially when we spot the link between *tad* and informal English *dad*) and apply Grimm's Law to *pesc/k*, linking them with *fish*, but thereafter differences are more obvious than similarities. In some words Celtic has Romance echoes. For instance, the common word for 'bridge' is *pont*, that for 'honey' is *mel*, that for 'ox' is *tarow*, that for 'arm' is *braich*; these are related to the Latin roots *pons*, *mel*, *taurus* and *braccus* respectively. In other areas Germanic roots are still visible: for instance, the common word for 'horse' is *march*, cognate with *mare*, and the common word for 'young' is *ieuanc*. But in many instances the Celtic term is quite unlike any geographical neighbour or historical ancestor in the family. Examples are *du*, the common term for 'black', *glas* and *gwer*, the common terms for 'green', *pen*, the common term for 'head', *amser*, the common term for 'time', *dall*, the common term for 'blind', *tan*, the common term for 'fire', *mab* or *mac*, the common terms for 'son', and so on.

It should also be noted that even within the Celtic family there are wide divergences among common words, chiefly as a result of the languages being so greatly separated geographically. Consider the dissimilarities in table 2.4.

These differences explain the division of the Celtic languages into two groups, the Brythonic (or British), which includes Breton, Cornish and Welsh, and the Goidelic (or Gaelic) which includes Irish and Scottish Gaelic and Manx.

The term *Celt* derives from *Keltoi*, the name given them by the Greek historian Herodotus, though the Roman writers referred to them as *Galli* or *Gauls*, while those who settled in Britain were called the *Britanni*. The earliest archaeological evidence places them in France and western Germany around 1200 BC. The historical overview in chapter 1 explains the circumstances which led to the decline of the Celts in the face of the expanding Roman Empire, which colonized them, and the Germanic tribes, who dominated them. Their displacement westwards from the rich arable land of England to the mountain fastnesses of Wales, the bleak promontory of Cornwall, across the Irish sea to Man and Ireland, northwards to the Highlands of Scotland and southwards to Brittany is reflected most obviously in the precarious survival of the Celtic languages in these areas.

There is no surviving evidence of the Celtic language as it was used in the fifth century. However, a revealing semantic change in the Anglo-Saxon period is to be seen in *wealh*, the term used by the Anglo-Saxon settlers to describe the Celtic inhabitants. (It is the root form of *Wales*, the second element of *Cornwall* and the first element of *walnut*.) Its earlier sense was, simply, 'foreigner', which reflects an ironic reversal of roles as well as the dominance of the invaders. However, as the Celts lost status, so the term started to acquire the sense of 'slave' or 'servant'. Finally, as the term deteriorated to mean 'a shameless person', a variety of disreputable compounds developed, such as *wealh-word*, 'a wanton word', and *wealian*, 'to be impudent, bold or wanton'. Usages often have sexual associations, as in 'he used impudent language [*wealode*] and said that he intended to enjoy his wife during the (?) forbidden period.' The details of this deterioration are of interest since they reveal a pattern of stereotypic decline which is paralleled in a great number of similar sociolinguistic circumstances.[4]

Place-names also tell their tale, signally in the transfer of the capital from the Celtic Camelot, identified with Winchester, to the Roman Londinium, subsequently London. Celtic vestiges are still apparent in Lincoln, previously Lindum Colonia, ultimately derived from Welsh *llyn*, meaning a lake, and in Dover, in Roman times called Dubris, rooted in Welsh *dwfr*, 'water'. But outside their areas of refuge, the Celtic terms which have survived are generally not place-names but those of rivers, such as *Avon*, *Exe* and *Wye*, or those terms (already mentioned) denoting geographical features, such as *crag*, *tor* and *combe/cwm*.

The paucity of Celtic terms which have survived in the English vocabulary is also a stark witness. Among the handful of survivors are *bragget*, a drink similar to mead, *ass*, *brock*, a badger, *coracle*, a light wicker boat, and the more central terms *flannel*, *clan* and *whisky* in its older forms, *whiskybae uisgebugh*, which means 'water of life'. Other Celtic terms which are either regional or

Table 2.5 Basic terms borrowed from Latin

Latin	(meaning)	⇒	Anglo-Saxon	⇒	Modern English
caupo	a trader		ceap		cheap, chap
butyrum	butter		butere		butter
vinum	wine		wine		wine
caseus	cheese		cese		cheese
prunus	plum		plume		plum
piper	pepper		pipor		pepper
cucina	kitchen		cycene		kitchen
discus	dish		disc		dish
cuppa	cup		cuppe		cup
calx	chalk		cealc		chalk
pondo	weight		punde		pound
millia	a thousand (paces)		mil		mile
uncia	one-twelfth		unce/ince		ounce/inch

may not be of such antiquity are *slogan*, originally a Gaelic war-cry, *eisteddfod*, *loch*, *colleen*, *claymore* and *plaid* (*tartan* is disputed).

Early Latin borrowings

We have noted several terms of Latin origin in the Celtic word-stock, clear evidence of the contact between the Celts and Roman legionaries and traders. Similar evidence of Latin borrowing is apparent in Anglo-Saxon as a consequence of relations between the Romans and the Germanic tribes on the continent. At the outset of this chapter we traced the development of Latin *vallum*, *strata* and *castra* into English *wall*, *street* and the place-name element *-chester* respectively. Other basic terms which were borrowed early had to do with trade, cooking and measurement, and included those in table 2.5.

The last example in table 2.5 is especially interesting in that it yields the doublets *ounce* and *inch*: the sense of a division into one-twelfth is still current in *inch* and in *ounce* in the scale of troy weight, used by jewellers. Our modern form *mint*, on the other hand, has two unrelated senses (the herb and the place where money is coined); the first derives from Latin *mentha* and the second from Latin *Moneta*, a surname of Juno, in whose temple in Rome money was coined. From this name we subsequently get the terms *money* and *monetary*. In all some 175 basic terms reflect the interaction of the Roman colonists and the Germanic tribes.

The Coming of the English

The Roman occupation of Britain extended for some four and a half centuries, from 55 BC to AD 410, when the legions were withdrawn to protect the mother city from the invading Goths, Vandals and Burgundians. Although one-tenth of the Roman army was stationed on the island, the occupation was essentially military in character rather than settler-colonial. Towards the end of the Roman era England was subject to raids by the Picts and the Scots from the north and by the Saxons from the east. (The Picts were so called because they painted their bodies; the Scots were then Irish Celts.) The Roman military commander appointed to organize the defence of the eastern seaboard from the Wash to the Isle of Wight against the Saxon raids was called, appropriately, *Comes litoris Saxonici*, 'The Count of the Saxon Shore'.

Into the power-vacuum left by the retreating Roman legions came the Anglo-Saxons, first as contracted mercenaries, then as belligerent settlers impressed by 'the worthlessness of the Britons and the excellence of the land', as the annal for 449 in the *Anglo-Saxon Chronicle* trenchantly puts it. This source is unique and remarkable in that it was not written in Latin, but is the first history of a western people in its own vernacular. The *Chronicle* is fragmentary, a thread of knowledge in the void known as the 'lost centuries', but its terse entries give us a moving account of the state of a nation catastrophically transformed.

We have no detailed contemporary account of the invasions. Our main source is the Venerable Bede's *Historia Ecclesiastica Gentis Anglorum*, a history of England in Latin from the Roman occupation until 731, the year of its completion. It is translated as *The Ecclesiastical History of the English People* and contains a description of the invasions which has become virtually traditional:

> They were from three very powerful races of the Germans, namely the Saxons, the Angles and the Jutes. From the Jutes are descended the people of Kent and the Victuarii (that is, the race which lives in the Isle of Wight, and in those parts of Wessex opposite the Isle of Wight, who are still called Jutes). From the Saxons (that is, from the land now called Old Saxony) came the East Saxons, the South Saxons, and the West Saxons. From the Angles (that is, the country called Angulus, between the countries of the Jutes and the Saxons, which is said to have remained unpopulated to the present day) are sprung the Middle Anglians, the Mercians, all the Northumbrian peoples (that is, those to the north of the River Humber), and the other Anglian peoples. (Chapter 15)

Bede's account may, of course, be simplified, being written nearly three centuries after the event. Although he lived as a monk in the monastery at Jarrow from the age of seven. Bede was a painstaking scholar who assessed the available evidence, both documentary and oral.

Bede's version is corroborated by two major lexical features: it explains the distribution of dialects caused by the dispersal of the various peoples, and it is supported by the English county names such as *Essex* from the East Saxons, *Sussex* from the South Saxons, and *Wessex* from the West Saxons, as well as the regional name *East Anglia*, from the Angles. Other philological links would relate the ancient *Jutes* to modern *Jutland* and *Saxony* to *the Saxon shore*.

However, there are various areas of dispute. These concern the origin, identity, even the presence of the Jutes, and the role of the Frisians, whom Bede does not mention, but who figure in a more contemporary account, *On the Fall of Britain* written *c.* 550 by Gildas, a British priest, which describes the invaders as Saxons, while the sixth-century Byzantine historian Procopius terms them Angles and Frisians. Neither of them mentions the Jutes at all.

Perhaps the more significant fact is not the origins of the invaders, but their diversity. Bede stresses that the invaders were not one people, as the Romans had been and as the Normans were to be, but consisted of three main groups. This in turn explains the linguistic diversity which is apparent from the earliest Anglo-Saxon manuscripts and is a feature of England to this day. Figure 2.3 translates this account into diagrammatic form, while Figure 2.4 represents the disposition of Anglo-Saxon dialects, which largely supports Bede.[5]

As their former clients became their victors, the Celts were reduced from the comparatively mild indignity of Roman colonization to the miseries of deprivation, destitution and virtual extermination under the harrying of the Saxons. The devastating impact of the invasion is unquestionable: 'Never was there such slaughter in this island,' wrote the chronicler, adding that the Welsh fled from the Saxons 'as from fire' (annal 473).

The extent and thoroughness of the invasion is revealed in a number of ways, most obviously by the concentration of place-names, and by the fact that Anglo-Saxon comprehensively displaced Celtic and still forms the core of the language, despite the subsequent Norman Conquest and the copious infiltration of thousands of Latin and Greek words. Typically the ancient names of places changed from Celtic roots which were then Romanized and Saxonized (table 2.6).

As Figure 2.5 demonstrates, Anglo-Saxon place-names flooded the land, engulfing the previous Celtic strongholds. The point becomes clearer on the map when one recognizes the ubiquitous key elements in these names (table 2.7).

The element-*ing* ties a place-name to the Saxon founder in what is known as a patronymic fashion: *Buckingham* breaks down to 'the home of the sons of Bucca'. Less palatably, *Nottingham* has its roots in 'the home of the sons of

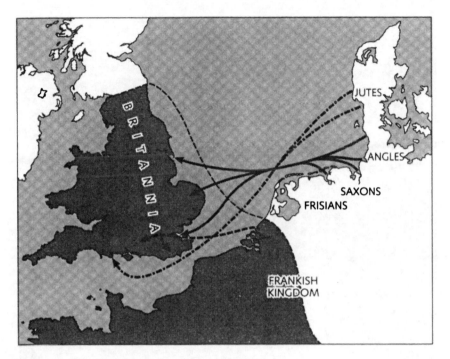

Figure 2.3   The Anglo-Saxon invasions of Britain

Snot'. Unsurprisingly, these -*ing* names are found in great concentration all over the south-east of England, especially in Sussex and Kent. The terms commemorating the Saxons are found predominantly in the same areas, in *Sussex*, *Essex* and *Middlesex*, now the names of English counties, but initially, together with *Wessex*, the names of separate kingdoms. The *shire* remains a fundamental term for county administration.

The early names of the English

The invaders were originally called the *Saxons* ('Saxones'), but later Latin writers began to term them the *Angles* ('Angli'), probably because of their expansion into the northern and north-western areas. (*Saxon* is appropriately derived from *seax* meaning 'a sword', and *Angle* less obviously from the angular shape of the original *Angulus* in Holstein.) The title *rex Anglorum* ('King of the Angles') was that used by Pope Gregory in 601 to address Æthelbert, King of Kent. Prior to the Norman Conquest the name *Angelcynn* ('the nation of the Angles') was commonly applied to both the people and the land; *Englalond* ('the land of the Angles') emerged around the period of the Danish invasions, some-

Figure 2.4 The Anglo-Saxon dialects

times spelt as one word, more aften as two. *Anglo-Saxon* was used from the eighth century both in Latin and Old English to distinguish the Saxons of England from those in Old Saxony. However, from the earliest times the term applied to the variety of dialects was *Englisc*. Thus *English* turns out to be older as a name for the language than for the people.

Table 2.6   Place-names from Celtic roots

Celtic	Roman	Anglo-Saxon	Modern
Londinos	Londinium	Londene	London
Verulamium	Verulamium	St Albanestow	St Albans
Glevum	Glevensis	Gloyceaster	Gloucester
Corinion	Corinium	Cirenceaster	Cirencester
Camulodunum	Camulodunum	Colceaster	Colchester
Eboracon	Eboracum	Eoforwic	York
Durobrivis	Hrofibrevie	Hrofesceaster	Rochester

These unified terms disguised very clear regional differences, both political and linguistic. An initial medley of petty Saxon realms in time consolidated into seven kingdoms or the *heptarchy*, consisting of Northumbria, Mercia, East Anglia, Essex, Sussex, Kent and Wessex. As might be expected, there was a close correlation between region and dialect. As Figure 2.4 demonstrates, there were four major dialects: Northumbrian and Mercian, collectively known as Anglian, dominating the north, while the south was shared by West Saxon and Kentish. The dominance of the term *Englisc* probably reflects the early influence of the Anglian kingdoms, and the necessity of distinguishing the insular *Anglisc* from the continental *Saxones*. By the end of the Anglo-Saxon period, West Saxon had assumed the standard for the written form of the language, despite being used by a comparative minority. This prestige derived partly from the illustrious reign of King Alfred (871–99) and his vigorous policy of education.

Christianizing the heathen

In 597, a little over a century after the invasions, St Augustine of Canterbury arrived with a group of forty Christian monks entrusted by Pope Gregory the Great with the formidable mission of converting the Anglo-Saxons to Christianity. Despite their trepidation, the mission was favourably received by Æthelbert the king, who was baptized in the same year of Augustine's arrival.

Christianity had previously been brought to Britain in Celtic times, but much of that original influence had been destroyed or displaced by the invasions. It was now reintroduced from the north by missionaries from Ireland, such as St Columba, who brought Celtic Christianity to Scotland, and St Aidan, who converted Northumbria and founded the monastery of Lindisfarne in

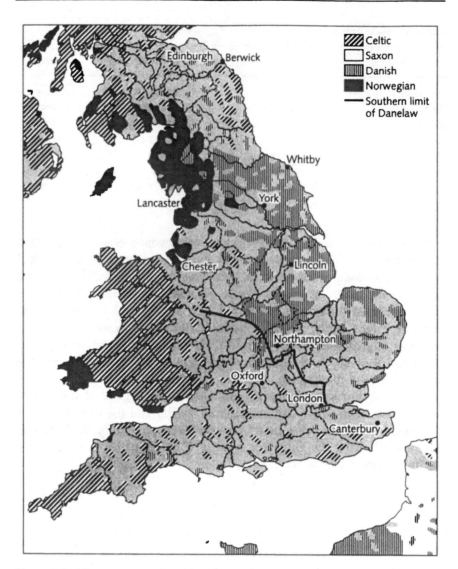

Figure 2.5   Place-names in the Old English period (after Leslie A. Haywood, 1959)

635. The subsequent fusion of Celtic and Mediterranean Christian traditions in Northumbria produced there a great flowering of scholarship and literature unrivalled in Europe. The outstanding scholars in this monastic tradition were Bede, his most distinguished pupil, Alcuin of York, chosen by Charlemagne to head his palace school, and Aldhelm of Malmesbury. England then provided the intellectual leadership of the West in the eighth century: as King Alfred

Table 2.7   Anglo-Saxon place-names

Anglo-Saxon (meaning)		⇒	Modern English form + example		
seax	Saxon		sex	–	Sussex
scir	shire		shire	–	Berkshire
ham	home		ham	–	Nottingham
tun	town		ton	–	Hampton
burg	fortification		burgh	–	Edinburgh
			borough	–	Middlesborough
			bury	–	Canterbury
ford	ford		ford	–	Oxford
brycg	bridge		bridge	–	Cambridge
leah	wood, glade		ley	–	Chorley
worþ	enclosure		worth	–	Worthing
feld	field		field	–	Macclesfield
ing	the sons of		ing	–	Buckingham

later noted, looking back to this great age with sadness in his preface to the *Cura Pastoralis*, 'people from abroad sought wisdom and learning here.'

The verbal record of this ancient Christian influence is embedded in Latin and Greek words which, like the early continental borrowings, no longer have their classical characteristics. Indeed, Jespersen noted (somewhat naively) that 'most of the loans were short words that tallied perfectly well with the native words and were easily inflected' (1962, pp. 30 and 39; see also Sheard, 1954, p. 155). The point is more that the original inflections were worn away to the extent that the words looked and sounded like natives. This becomes clear when one compares the Old English forms with their originals (Table 2.8).

The phonetic assimilation clearly took place early, and the words subsequently underwent the same sound-changes as native terms. For example, the transition from *biscop* to *bishop* follows the pattern of *scip* ⇒ *ship*, *scild* ⇒ *shield*, etc. Some of these words, for example *church*, had been borrowed long before Augustine's arrival, since the Germanic tribes had for centuries been visiting churches, 'not for the doctrine, but the treasure there', to paraphrase Alexander Pope. Hence the unusual survival of the word in preference to the standard continental term, Latin *ecclesia* and its derivatives, such as French *église*.

Pagan fossils

In many ways more interesting than the borrowings are the pagan fossils, words taken over from the heathen religions and given a new Christian gloss.

Table 2.8   Christian borrowings

Word	A–S form	Origin
church	cirice	kyriakon (G.)
minster	mynster	monasterium (L.)
priest	preost	presbuteros (G.)
monk	munuc	monachus (L.)
nun	nunne	nonna (L.)
abbot	abbod	abbas (L.)
bishop	biscop	episkopos (G.)
pope	papa	papa (L.)
angel	engel	angelos (G.)
devil	deofol	diabolos (G.)
school	scol	skhole (G.)

The early missionaries were obviously sufficiently shrewd and conciliatory to permit this form of conversion. For example, the two great festivals of the Christian calendar have pagan roots. *Easter* is clearly unrelated to the continental forms deriving from Latin *pasca*, such as French *Pâques*. The name in fact derives from the Dawn Goddess known in Northumbria as *Eastron*, cognate with Latin *Aurora*, a fertility goddess whose rites were celebrated in an ancient pagan spring festival. The dating of Easter is still determined by the vernal equinox, and much of the symbolism still reflects, albeit now in the form of confectionery Easter eggs and rabbits, the mystery of fertility. Interestingly, in parts of the north of England, Easter eggs are called *Pace eggs*, the form *Pace* being derived from Latin *pasca*.

Bede noted as far back as the seventh century that *Yule* was the basic word for midwinter festivities among the Anglo-Saxons. Though now largely obsolete in the south, *Yule* is still more common than *Christmas* in the north of England and in Scotland. (The first recorded use of *Christmas*, incidentally, is only in the twelfth century.) *Yule* was, no doubt, brought by the Saxons from the continent, where related forms are the basic term among the Scandinavian peoples. The Viking settlements established later in the north of England would have used the related Old Norse form *yol*. Its ultimate origin has never been explained, though Partridge tentatively relates it to *cold*. The harvest festival, *Lammas*, derives from the native term *hlaf* meaning 'bread', while *halig* 'holy' and *halga* 'a saint' were preferred in *Halloween* and *All Hallows Church* to *saint*, from Latin *sanctus*. *Hallowed* still survives, of course, in the Lord's Prayer.

Rituals often have revealing roots. *Bless* has unexpectedly gruesome origins, A-S *bletsian* originally meaning 'to sprinkle with blood', from the root *blot*, 'a bloody sacrifice', reflecting a ritual of blood being sprinkled by the pagan priest to confer magical powers on the faithful. A rare word used by Hamlet's father to express his horror at being murdered, *unhouseled* (I. v. 77), in a state of mortal sin, derives from Anglo-Saxon *husl*, which originally meant a pagan sacrifice, but which was converted to mean the Sacrament.

The names and titles of the divine are similarly significant and cover a whole range of roles. *God* is in origin a pagan word with roots in the rite of sacrifice, not a revealed term. A related Anglo-Saxon term, *Metod*, was converted from its heathen sense of Fate or Judge to the Christian meaning of Creator, a sense also rendered by *Scyppend*, rooted in *sceapan* 'to shape, create'. The miraculous powers of Christ concentrated in the later word Saviour, were in Anglo-Saxon times rendered by the term *Hælend*, 'the Healer'. Many of the secular titles were simply absorbed. They included *Drihten* and *Frea*, both meaning 'lord', *Weard*, 'protector, guardian', *Wuldorfæder* 'father of glory' and so on.

The most obvious pagan fossils are, of course, our names of the days of the week, all of which derive from Classical and Scandinavian deities, or supposed planetary influence:

Monday	Monandæg	the Moon
Tuesday	Tiwesdæg	Tiw, Scan. god of War
Wednesday	Wodnesdæg	Woden, Scan. supreme deity
Thursday	Thorsdæg	Thor, Scan. god of War
Friday	Frigedæg	Frige, Scan. goddess of Love
Saturday	Sæternesdæg	Saturn
Sunday	Sunnandæg	the Sun

Interestingly, an eighth-century Latin-Anglo-Saxon glossary in the library of Corpus Christi College, Cambridge, glosses Mercurium as Woden and Mars as Tiig, a variation of Tiw.

There was an initial resistance to some of the new terms, a hostility to innovation which we shall encounter regularly in this history. Thus *baptize* was not accepted, the more starkly physical term *dyppan* 'to dip' being preferred. Latin *trinitas* was similarly rejected in favour of the native term *þrynes* 'threeness'. Greek *euaggelion* was literally translated into *god spell*, 'good news'. *Boda*, 'a messenger', was preferred to Greek *angelos* and *bodian* 'to give a message' was used instead of Latin *praedicare*, to preach. Though *biscop* was adopted, the senior office was termed *heahbiscop*, not *arcebiscop*, just as *engel* generated the mixed form *heahengel*. Such hybrids became numerous:

priesthood	preost + had, 'state'
bishopric	biscop + rice, 'kingdom'
Christendom	cristen + dom, 'state'

It might be argued that the considerable survival of pagan fossils indicates that the conversion was more superficial than genuine. In the nature of things, it is difficult to assess the degree of spirituality on the basis of outward forms. For example, the spectacular Sutton Hoo treasure now housed in the British Museum has been identified as the burial regalia of Redwald, King of East Anglia, who died *c.*625. He was notorious for the duplicity of religious practices, offering pagan sacrifice in a sanctified church, and even the form of his burial shows a mixture of pagan and Christian practices. This momentous transition of world-view is powerfully evoked by Jorge Luis Borges in his imaginative vignette, 'The Witness' (*Labyrinths*, 1962, p. 279):

In a stable which is almost in the shadow of the new stone church, a man with grey eyes and a grey beard, lying amidst the odour of the animals, humbly seeks death as one would seek sleep. . . . The man sleeps and dreams, forgotten. He is awakened by the bells tolling the Angelus. In the kingdoms of England the ringing of bells is now one of the customs of the evening, but this man, as a child, had seen the face of Woden, the divine terror and exultation, the crude wooden idol hung with Roman coins and heavy clothing, the sacrifice of horses, dogs and prisoners. Before dawn he will die, and with him will die, and never return, the last immediate images of these pagan rites; the world will be a little poorer when this Saxon has died.

The Anglo-Saxon tongue

The language of the Anglo-Saxons forms part of the West Germanic branch of the Indo-European family, comprising German, Dutch, Frisian, Danish, Swedish, Norwegian and Icelandic. We have seen this relationship partly demonstrated in the discussion of base words at the outset of this chapter. Anglo-Saxon was a virtually pure language, in its own terms a *clene tunge*, apart from the admixture of the continental Latin borrowings and those resulting from Christian influence. Mary Serjeantson has listed some 250 words, both religious and secular, borrowed between 650 and the end of the Old English period (1935, ch. 2). Henry Bradley counted 400 such basic forms (1904, p. 82). But even these numbers are a small sample when set against an Anglo-Saxon vocabulary of some 40,000 words capable of expressing a wide range of things, concepts and tones.[6]

Although the great majority of the surviving words now belong to the base register, this situation has largely come about because of the special status subsequently accorded Norman-French, Latin and Greek. Before the Norman Conquest Anglo-Saxon was, obviously, the dominant language and had its own diversity of registers. In addition to the expected lexicon of base terms, words such as *eorðe* 'earth', *wæter* 'water', *sæ* 'sea', *land* 'land', *fæder* 'father', *modor* 'mother', *treow* 'tree', *hyll* 'hill', *fot* 'foot', *hand* 'hand', *muð* 'mouth', *toð* 'tooth' and thousands more, there was a whole vocabulary exclusively used for poetry (which we shall discuss later) and a surprisingly extensive lexicon of technical terms.

An obvious feature of Anglo-Saxon was its capacity for **compounding**, something we now regard as distinctive of the Germanic languages. For example, *orthodoxy* is rendered in Modern German as *Rechtgläubigkeit*, 'the quality of proper belief', *armchair* as *Grossvaterstuhl*, 'grandfather's chair' and so on. Sometimes this tendency for compounding seems to be carried to excess: the *Guinness Book of Records* (1986) cites *Rechtsschutzversicherungsgesellschaften* as being the longest word in German: (broken down it means 'insurance societies for legal protection'). As might be expected, Anglo-Saxon showed this Germanic characteristic to a notable degree. Thus 'medicine' was rendered by *læcedom* or *læcecræft* ('leechdom' or leechcraft'), 'astronomy' by *tungolcræft* ('star knowledge'), 'religion' by *godcunddom* ('the state of the knowledge of God'), 'dropsy' by *wæterseocness*. In these example we can see the concept being reduced to different elements and rendered literally. (In fact, of course, the Latin and Greek terms *medicine* and *astronomy* are also compounds, but now tend to be thought of as units.)

Some of the base words are compound metaphors similar to those of poetry. Thus *hymn* was conveyed by *lofsang* ('song of praise'), *body* by *flæschama* 'flesh home', *skeleton* by *banhus* 'bone house'. Similar in origin are everyday words like *garlick*, from *gar*, 'a spear' and *leac*, 'a leek', *rainbow*, from *regen*, 'rain' and *boga*, 'a bow', *husband*, from *hus*, 'house' and *bonda*, 'dweller', *daisy*, from *dæge*, 'day' and *eage*, 'eye', *woman*, from *wif*, 'wife' and *mann*, 'man'. More mundane is *buter flege* ('butterfly'), so called euphemistically because its excrement resembles butter.

The vocabulary could be extended in ways with which we are now familiar, namely by the use of prefixes like *un-* and suffixes like *-ful, -ness, -hood, -th, -ship*. Thus the base form *treowe*, 'true' could be extended to *untreowðfulnesse* 'untruthfulness', and abstract nouns like modern *manhood* and *scholarship* similarly formed. Verbal prefixes included *be-*, as in *betroth, befriend* and *behead*; *fore*, in the sense of 'before', as in *forewarn, foretell* and *foresee* and *for*, with a negative sense, as in *forget, forbear* and *forbid*. In addition to those already mentioned, the main Anglo-Saxon suffixes were *-dom*, as in *kingdom, freedom* and *Christendom*; *-ling*, a diminutive found in *duckling, darling* and *nestling*; *-ster*, originally feminine, as in *spinster, brewster* and *baxter*, but subsequently used of either sex as in *gangster, songster* and *punster.*

Grammatical fossils

As was explained briefly in chapter 1, Anglo-Saxon was a **synthetic** or **inflected** language in which the grammatical function of a word was conveyed chiefly by its **inflections**, or functional endings, rather than by **auxiliaries** and **word-order**, devices with which we are now familiar. The inflectional system was developed not only in nouns and verbs, as is still the case, but in adjectives and articles as well. Some of these forms lasted for centuries after the Anglo-Saxon period before dying out. Examples would be those endings in verbs such as giv*est* and lov*eth*. There were other distinctive forms. For example, we now have only one form for 'you', which can be singular or plural or ambiguous. But we are familiar with the forms *thou* and *ye*, which previously distinguished singular and plural, but are now regional or biblical, and survived as archaic or poetic variants up to Victorian times.

In grammatical terms *love* is classified as a **weak verb**, since it forms its past tense by means of a dental suffix (*d* or *t*). *Ride* on the other hand, is a **strong** verb, since it forms its past tense by means of a change in the stem vowel: *ride* ⇒ *rode*. As is the case with Modern German, Anglo-Saxon had many highly developed strong verbs. Over the centuries, in line with the simplification of English grammar, their number has been reduced, from about 400 to fewer than 100.

Interestingly, some verbs have maintained both varieties of past forms, but with semantic differences. Thus *hung* is now the general term but *hanged* has the special sense for the death penalty; likewise, *melted* is used generally, but *molten* is specialized in its application to metals, glass and substances which melt at high temperatures. However, *seethed* and *sodden*, which were originally cognate forms of the verb 'to boil', now have quite different meanings. Among nouns, we also have cases of more than one plural form, also showing semantic difference: thus *brothers* is the general term, but *brethren* has a special religious application.

Sound and sense in the Germanic base

In our discussion of semantics in chapter 1, we observed the important difference between the 'transparent' quality of the native Germanic element of English and the more abstract, opaque quality of the borrowed Latin and Greek elements. We also noted Saussure's axiomatic observation on 'the arbitrary nature of the sign' (1966, p. 67). Native English lexis contains many interesting examples of **onomatopoeia** in which sound seems to symbolize or echo sense. In his charmingly honest dialectical fashion, Saussure met his own generalizations with matching objections: he himself conceded that 'Onomatopoeia might be used to prove that the choice of the signifier is not always arbitrary. But [he continues] onomatopoeic formations are never organic elements of a linguistic system.' Though some words 'may strike certain ears with a suggestive sonority,' a comparison with their Latin roots shows this to be 'a fortuitous result of phonetic evolution' (1966, p. 69).

Saussure's discounting of onomatopoetic formations as never being 'organic elements of a linguistic system' has been one view in a considerable and enduring debate.[7] It can be countered by the observation in the *Oxford Etymological Dictionary* that the initial combination *wr-* is to be found 'occurring in many words implying twisting or distortion'. These words form a considerable group, including *wrangle, wrap, wreathe, wrench, wrest, wrestle, wriggle, wring, wrinkle, wrist, writhe, write, wrought* and *wry*. All are derived from Anglo-Saxon, and one should bear in mind that originally the 'w' was sounded, so that one really had to get one's tongue round the first two consonants in a form of sound symbolism. Other corroborating evidence is to be found in the initial combination *sp-*, in which the physical act of enunciation is integral to the meaning of, for example, *spew, spit, spatter, splutter* and *spurt*. Likewise, in *bulb, bleb, blubber* and *blister*, the bilabial plosives suggest roundness, while *snide, snake, sneak, snarl, sneer* and *snigger* all describe unpleasant actions, qualities or things. The very act of articulation of the initial consonants seems to invite a grimace. There is also the historical curiosity that modern *sneeze* and *snort* were originally *fneeze* and *fnort*, from A-S *fnesan* and ME *fnort*, altogether more spectacularly echoic renditions of their respective actions, before their pronunciation was modified by a misreading of *f* as f.

The implications of these instances lead, not in the direction of arbitrariness, but towards onomatopoetic 'universals' at the primitive stage of language. However, Saussure rightly insisted that 'we can speak of law only when a set of facts obeys the same rule, and in spite of certain appearances to the contrary, diachronic events are always accidental and particular' (1966, p. 93).

The lower registers

We know virtually nothing about Anglo-Saxon colloquialisms, slang or taboo. Although there are references to *sceandword*, meaning words which are 'vile, foul, opprobrious or abusive', the surviving literature is of such a high moral tone as to exclude Anglo-Saxon street-talk. While Old Norse had a strong tradition of 'flyting' or the fine art of savage competitive insult, this genre seems not to have survived in the Old English period, though it thrives later.

When we turn to the Anglo-Saxon words which are now regarded as either grossly impolite or taboo, we must first correct the popular misconception that the 'four-letter' words (as they have been called since 1934) are synonymous with 'Anglo-Saxon'. As figure 1.7 shows, the only truly Anglo-Saxon four-letter words on an etymological and historical basis are *arse*, *shit* and *turd*, since *piss*, *fart*, *fuck* and *cunt* are first recorded centuries later, and the last two have disputed origins.

Looking at the usage of these terms in Anglo-Saxon, we find that *ears* ('arse') is used fairly freely, as it tended to be through to Modern English. Thus *ears-ende* is used for 'buttocks' and one term for 'anus' is *ears-þerl*, literally 'arse-hole'. *Earsling* meant 'backwards', the opposite of modern *headlong*, which used to be *headling*. We may compare the subsequent phrases *arsey-versy* or *arse over tip*. Less widely used is *scitan*, the ancestor of *to shit*, which should phonologically have become *shite*. This form is found in Johnson's *Dictionary*, but is how regional, being found in a number of dialects, affected or facetious.

In an interesting article, 'An Outline History of Euphemisms in English', Robert Burchfield points out that most of the Anglo-Saxon synonyms for 'latrine' or 'privy' are based on the notion of 'going' or 'sitting' . . . (In Enright (ed.), 1986, p. 20).

Terms for the genitalia are also quite generally used. The most striking of the male terms is *wæpen*, the metaphorical extension of *weapon*. Thus a male child is glossed as a *wæpened-cild*, while 'the male sex' is *wæpened-cynn* and *wæpened-mann* means 'male', a sense which extends even to plants. A related metaphorical use is *geweald*, meaning 'power' or 'potency'. Less specific terms for the genitals are *gesceapu* ('a shape, or something shaped') and *getawa* ('instruments'); more recognizable is *lim* ('limb') for the penis, found in the description of Noah's drunkenness as *lim-nacod* ('limb-naked'). The most specific term is *teors*, later 'tarse', which died out in the eighteenth century. A tantalizing aphrodisiac recorded in the Anglo-Saxon *Leechdoms* prescribes as follows: 'Smear the penis and the testicles (*hærþan*); then he will have great pleasure.'

The main word for the female genitalia, on the other hand, is A-S *gecyndlic*, intimately related through its stem *cynd* to the notion of nature and procreation. Thus A-S *gecynd* covers the senses of 'nature', 'kind', 'gender', 'generation', 'nakedness' and 'offspring'.

Burchfield lists among the synonyms for sexual intercourse *hæmed* (literally 'homed'), *wif-gemana* ('companionship or conjunction with a woman') and two related compounds which include *lac* meaning 'play' as in Modern English *loveplay*, namely *hæmedlac* and *wiflac* (1986, p. 2).

As we can see, virtually all the Anglo-Saxon sexual words have died out or developed different senses. However, two insulting terms from a fairly rich field referring to prostitutes, namely A-S *hore*, subsequently *whore*, and *cwene*, subsequently *quean*, have survived, although *quean* is now archaic.

The Scandinavian Invasions

The Anglo-Saxons had been living in England in relative peace for some three centuries when they began to be disturbed by their restive northern relatives. The annal in the *Anglo-Saxon Chronicle* for the year 787 mentions the arrival of three ships, and the occupants killing a reeve who tried to compel them to visit the royal manor. These are described as 'the first ships of the Danes to come to England'. Within a few decades whole fleets and armies came, staying not just for the summers but for years. Within a century this minor visitation and its attendant skirmish was to become a full-scale invasion carried out by redoubtable marauders skilled in sailing and ferocious in battle. They were part of a great Viking expansion which extended in all directions, across the Atlantic to Greenland and America, eastwards to the Caspian and southwards to the Mediterranean. Their language, Old Norse, belonged, together with Anglo-Saxon, to the same western branch of the Germanic family, so that base words had the same roots, but different inflections.

The term *Dene* ('Dane') was used generically in the English records to refer to these Scandinavian invaders, though the influx was more complex. As is shown in figure 2.6, the Danes themselves, accompanied by some Swedes, tended to proceed 'southabout', attacking the east and south of England, while the Norwegians preferred to sail 'northabout', making landfalls in the Shetlands, the Orkneys, the Hebrides, Scotland, Cumbria and Ireland. As the Vikings proceeded to destroy monasteries and raid churches throughout the land, so the term *hæþen* 'heathen' was increasingly applied to them. The poet of the *Battle of Maldon*, celebrating the brave resistance of the men of Maldon in Essex against a Viking host in 991, refers to the enemy as *wæl-wulfas* 'slaughterous wolves'. The terms *raid* and *ransack* are Norse, while *Viking* itself derives alternatively from Old Norse *vik* meaning 'a creek' or Old English *wic*, 'a settlement', found in *Greenwich*, *Keswick* and many other place-names. *Wicing-sceapa*, meaning 'Viking marauder', is found in Anglo-Saxon glossaries dating from the eighth century. Over the years *wicing* acquired increasing emotive force and hostility; it is glossed by Ælfric as *pirata*, 'pirate'.

Since the Vikings did not write their own memoirs and histories, the records of their activities come exclusively from their enemies and victims. These accounts often make dramatic reading. Their first incursions are presaged by supernatural omens, set out in this alarming annal in the *Anglo-Saxon Chronicle* for the year 793:

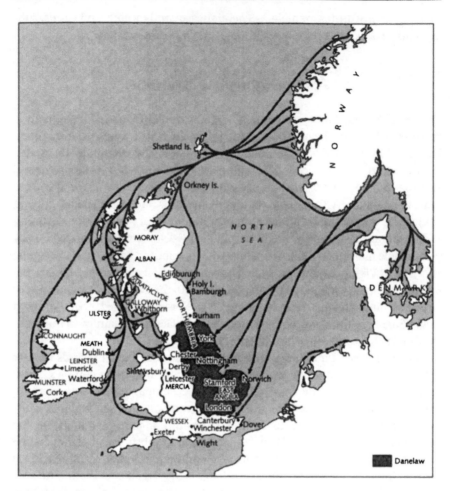

Figure 2.6   The Scandinavian invasions

> In this year terrible portents appeared in Northumbria, and miserably afflicted the inhabitants; these were exceptional flashes of lightning, and fiery dragons were seen flying in the air, and soon followed a great famine, and after that in the same year the harrying of the heathen miserably destroyed God's church in Lindisfarne by rapine and slaughter. (From the Parker Chronicle)

This entry, with its terrifying portents and their cruel fulfilment, casts the Vikings in the role of demonic forces especially intent, like some monstrous Antichrist, upon the destruction of Christ's kingdom on earth. This view prevailed, being indelibly recorded in the jeremiad sermons of Wulfstan, Archbishop of York from 1002 to 1023. Nor was it based simply on xenophobia, which is often accentuated by the catalysts of martial invasion and religious competition. Simeon Potter well summarizes their devastations:

> The light of learning was extinguished in Northumbria by the Scandinavian Vikings who sacked Lindisfarne in 793, who plundered Bede's own monastery at Jarrow in 794, and who put an end to the monastic schools in the north in 870. (1966, p. 27)

In 1012 a Viking host savagely murdered Ælfheah (later Alphege) Archbishop of Canterbury, who refused any ransome to be paid for him; in the words of the Laud Chronicle, 'they pelted him to death with bones and the heads of cattle.'

In recent years there has been an attempt to rehabilitate the Vikings under the slogan of 'traders, not raiders', or by claiming that their armies were not bent on large-scale destruction, but were small and efficient, simply intent on ecclesiatical pillage since, as heathens, they knew no better, and churches were traditional sources of treasure. These attacks on churches created a sense of crisis out of proportion to their real extent. As Peter Sawyer has put it: 'once the prejudices and exaggerations of the primary sources are recognised, the raids can be seen not as an unprecedented and inexplicable cataclysm, but as an extention of normal Dark Age activity, made possible and profitable by special circumstances.' (See Peter Sawyer in Campbell (ed.), *The Anglo-Saxons*, 1991, p. 144.) This is not the place to enter into this controversy. Suffice it to say that to most people 'normal Dark Age activity' essentially endorses the traditional barbaric image of the original period, which has not been greatly modified.

Figure 2.7 gives some idea of the intensity and range of the invasions. By the late ninth century the Viking threat seemed irresistible. The *Anglo-Saxon Chronicle* for 851 refers to a fleet of 350 ships, which would be more than a match for most British navies since. As the harrying and plundering of the land continued, a desperate prayer grew up: 'From the fury of the northmen, good Lord deliver us.' The answer to the prayer came in the form of Alfred, King of Wessex from 871 to 899, the only English king to be called the Great. He countered the Viking dominance of the seaways by founding the navy; he mobilized the army, and in 878 inflicted a notable defeat on the Vikings at Edington. Alfred would dearly have loved to expel the Danes, but by this time they had formed many permanent settlements in the north-east of the land. Consequently, in terms of the treaty of Wedmore (878) between Alfred and Guthrum, he had to settle for a form of apartheid whereby he ceded sovereignty to the Vikings over an area called the Danelaw to the north-east of the Watling Street, the old Roman road from London to Chester. This very

Figure 2.7 Viking raids on England and Western Europe (after M. Kirkby, *The Vikings*, Phaidon, 1970)

substantial portion of the country became a Viking homeland in which their language and customs predominated. (*Danelaw* itself meant an area where the Danish law held sway.)

This political arrangement clearly had major linguistic consequences, many of which are still apparent. We can distinguish three major processes:

the displacement of basic Anglo-Saxon terms by Norse equivalents; the establishment of Norse terms regionally in the Danelaw; and the semantic changes undergone by surviving Anglo-Saxon terms which have adopted the meaning of the Norse cognate.

When we consider the linguistic evidence of the Viking settlement, the probability of a large and aggressive incursion can hardly be disputed. Some 1400 place-names of Scandinavian origin occur in England. Of these some 600, containing the Old Norse element *by*, meaning a town or a settlement, are crucial: the familar examples are *Derby, Rugby, Whitby, Denby* ('town of the Danes') and *Grimsby* (*Grim*, meaning 'fierce' being a significantly common Scandinavian name). Figure 2.8 shows the concentration of such names, as well as what are called *Grimston hybrids* since the first element is Scandinavian and the second Anglo-Saxon. In parts of Yorkshire 75 per cent of the place-names are of Norse origin. The major areas of Danish settlement are Yorkshire, Derbyshire, Nottinghamshire, Lincolnshire, Leicestershire and Norfolk, while the Norwegian colonies occur more in the north-west, in Cumberland, Westmorland and north Lancashire. Table 2.9 shows some typical Norse elements in place-names.

In addition, there were Norse terms to do with admnistration and the social structure: the *Ridings* of Yorkshire derive from Norse *þriding* meaning 'a third part', and within regions there were *wapentakes*, areas from which chieftains could count on so many armed men who voted by a show of weapons.

Equally interesting are the regional variants of many base-words. Researchers have shown that the descendants of the Norse form still survive in the Danelaw, while the descendants of the Saxon alternative are still to be found in the south and the south-west. The example of *rick/stack* is shown in figure 2.9 (from the *Word Geography of England*). The **isoglosses** are imaginary lines revealing the boundary of usage. Time and again the Norse term will be found in the heart of the Danelaw:

Old Norse	Anglo-Saxon
stithy	anvil
slape	slippery
to clip	to shear
to lake	to play
stee	ladder
to teem	to pour
mun	must
lugs	ears
gallows	braces
lad	boy
lass	girl

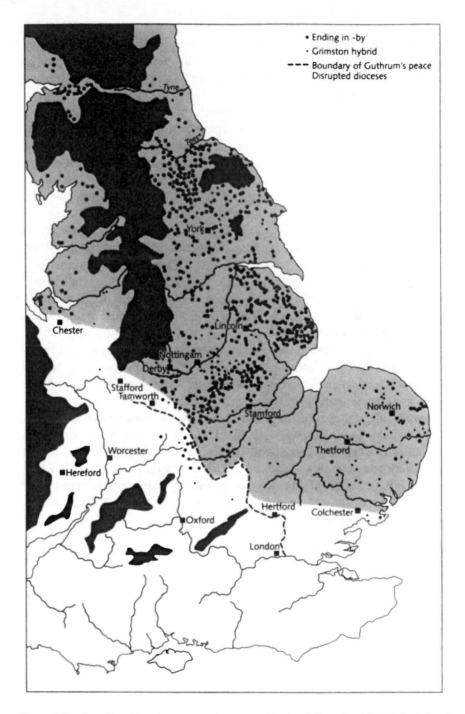

Figure 2.8 Scandinavian place-names in eastern England (from David Hill, *An Atlas of Anglo-Saxon England*, Blackwell, 1981, p. 45)

Table 2.9 Norse elements in place-names

Old Norse form	meaning	example
beck	a brook	Troutbeck
fell	a hill	Scafell
garth	a yard	Applegarth
gill	a ravine	Garrigill
keld	a spring	Dunkeld
toft	homestead	Lowestoft
thorp	farmstead	Bishopsthorp
thwaite	clearing	Bassenthwaite

In many ways the survival of variants is to be expected. What is unusual to the point of being remarkable is the extent to which Norse forms, which were in the nature of things regional, have penetrated to the common core of English lexis and grammar, displacing the Anglo-Saxon equivalents. We can show the process as it affected the basic verbs 'to die' and 'to take':

	Central	Subsidiary	semantic change
Old English:	A-S	*steorfan*	'to die'
⇒ ⇒ ⇒	ON	*deyja*	'to die'
Middle English:	*deye*	*sterve*	'to die'
Modern English:	*die* ⇒ ⇒ ⇒ ⇒ ⇒ ⇒ ⇒ ⇒ ⇒		*starve*

	Central	Subsidiary	semantic change
Old English:	A-S	*niman*	'to take'
⇒ ⇒ ⇒	ON	*taka*	'to take'
Middle English:	*take*	*nime*	'to take'
Modern English:	*take* ⇒ ⇒ ⇒ ⇒ ⇒ ⇒ ⇒ ⇒ ⇒ *numb*		

Most notable are the basic pronouns *they*, *their* and *them*, which displaced *hie*, *hiera* and *him*, which were becoming ambiguous. Other Norse terms which have become central are the following:

verbs: *are, call, die, take, cut, drag, ransack, smile, trust, thrive, cast* and *want*.
adjectives: *wrong, loose, ill, odd, flat, rugged, ugly, dirty, sly* and *low*.
nouns: *law, root, anger, bank, birth, crook, scab, skill, sky, steak, egg, bag, knife, axle* and *window*.

Names for parts of the body include *calf, leg, skin* and *skull*, while those for relationships include *husband, fellow* and *thrall*.

As we can immediately see, these are among the commonest words in the language, and are of the same character as the cognate native wordstock, having the same knotted and gnarled phonetic quality and the same blunt

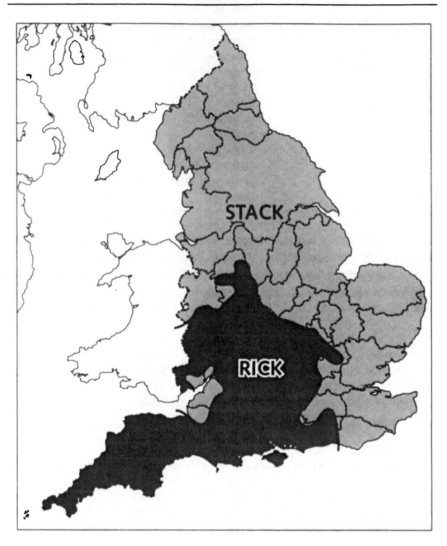

Figure 2.9 The regional distribution of ON *stack* and OE *rick* (from H. Orton and N. Wright, *A Word Geography of England*, Academic Press, 1974)

strength. They suggest that the Anglo-Saxons and the Norsemen interacted as equals and had much in common in their social structures, ethical norms and occupations. The term *law* stands out as having notable institutional force and reflects the Norse discipline and respect for order. The similarities between many of the base words are such that, had there not been written records of Anglo-Saxon before the Scandinavian invasions, it would be difficult, if not impossible, to identify the roots of many of the terms.

There were, however, phonetic differences between Anglo-Saxon and Old Norse, shown, for instance, in the following doublets:

Old Norse	Anglo-Saxon
skirt	shirt
scrub	shrub
kist	chest
kirk	church
dike	ditch
hale	whole

The first five examples show that the Norse forms maintained the *velar* form (articulated by stopping the flow of air by means of the *velum* or soft palate), whereas the Anglo-Saxon doublets use the *palatal* consonant, in which the air is forced between the tongue and the hard palate at the top of the mouth. In the cases of *kist/chest and kirk/church* there are no semantic differences, but *shirt* and *skirt* (which both used to mean 'a short garment') have since diverged considerably, as have *scrub* and *shrub*, *ditch* and *dike*.

A considerable number of Norse words begin or end with the combination *sk*. Apart from *sky*, *skull* and *skirt*, already mentioned, there are *skate* (the fish), *skerry*, *skid*, *skill*, *skillet*, *skim*, *skip*, *skittish*, *skittles*, *skua*, *skulk* and the verbs *bask* and *busk*.

Also distinctively Norse in their origins are those names ending in *-son*, such as Jackson, Gibson and Robinson. These originally had a literal sense, so that the famous Norse bard or *skald*, Egil Skallagrimsson was the son of Skallagrim, while his son would be Egilsson, and so on.

Notably revealing are the semantic changes undergone by native terms as a result of the Norse influence of cognate forms. Thus Anglo-Saxon *dwellan* meant 'to lead astray', but under the influence of Old Norse *dvelja*, 'to live', it took on the sense of 'dwell'. An equally central term, Anglo-Saxon *bread* meant 'a fragment', but it took on the modern sense of 'bread' under the influence of Old Norse *brauð*. Similarly Anglo-Saxon *dream* meant 'joy, revelry', but took on the sense of 'dream' under the semantic influence of Old Norse *draumr*, which had that meaning.

There are hardly any written records of Old Norse in the Anglo-Saxon period, so that many of the Scandinavian loan-words first appear in written form during the Middle English period. In some ways this is strange, since the great saga tradition of Iceland does not seem to have impinged on the Danelaw, which had no literary tradition.

As the maps of place-names in figures 2.5 and 2.8 show, Norse names are to be found outside the Danelaw, indicating that the political boundary could not contain the Vikings. In the eleventh cenury their dominance over the demoralized English became virtually complete when Knut, anglicized as Canute, already successor to the throne of Denmark, became King of England and of Norway. However, Canute continued to reside in England and English was spoken at his court. Had he not died at the age of forty-two, the Scandinavian supremacy would probably have resulted in Norse becoming the dominant language in western Europe.

The Survival of Anglo-Saxon

As we have seen, Anglo-Saxon still occupies the core of the lexis, together with some Latin and Norse elements from the Old English period. But this is not to say that all the original Anglo-Saxon core has survived. We can get a sense of the proportion of what has survived, often in fossilized form, and what has not, by analysing a fairly common piece of prose, namely the parable of the Prodigal Son in Anglo-Saxon. We shall not get involved in the complexities of the phonetics and grammar: this will be more an exercise in hunting the fossils. We need to recognize, however, the three unfamiliar Anglo-Saxon characters used in spelling: *æ* called 'ash' represents the 'a' as in *cat*, while þ ('thorn') and ð ('eth') represent 'th' in *thin* or *that*.

The parable of the Prodigal Son in Anglo-Saxon

Sōðlice sum mann hæfde twēgen suna. Þā cwæð se gingra tō his fæder, 'Fæder, sele mē minne dǣl minre æhte þe mē tō gebyreþ.' Þā dǣlde hē him his ǣhte. Đā æfter fēawum dagum eall his þing gegaderode se gingra sunu, and fērde wrǣclice on feorlen rīce, and forspilde pǣr his ǣhta, libbende on his gǣlsan. Þā hē hīe hæfde ealle āmierrede, þā wearð micel hungor on þǣm rīce, and hē wearð wǣdla. Đā fērde hē and folgode ānum burgsittendum menn þæs rīces; ðā sende hē hine tō his tūne þæt hē hēolde his swīn. Đā gewilnode hē his wambe gefyllan of þǣm bēancoddum þe ðā swīn ǣton; and him man ne sealde.

The length signs are editorial and not in the original A-S texts.

In order to grasp the meaning of this ancient text, let us start with a simple transliteration of the passage, following its original word order:

Truly a certain man had two sons. Then said the younger to his father, 'Father, give me my share of the inheritance which to me falls.' Then gave he him his share. Then after a few days all his things gathered the younger son and went touring to a far country, and wasted there his share, living in luxury. When he had wasted everything, then there was a great famine in that country and he became destitute. Then went he and worked for a citizen of the country; then sent he him to his farm that he might look after his pigs. Then wished he his stomach to fill with the husks which the pigs ate; but to him no man gave (no one gave him any).

Let us now examine the first 100 words of the Anglo-Saxon text (up to *wambe*) and see what forms have survived. Those which are clearly identical or reasonably similar in form and meaning are surprisingly few, a mere 14, namely: *mann, menn, to his, he, him, me, on, æfter, þing, sende, eall, hungor* and *swin*.

There is a larger group of words which have also survived, but intervening changes in phonetics, spelling, grammar and semantics obscure their relationship with their present forms. They are: *hæfde* (had), *twegen* (two), *suna* (sons), *gingra* (younger), *fæder* (father), *sele* (give), *minne* (my), *dæl* (share), *dælde* (distributed), *feawum* (few), *gegaderode* (gathered), *eall* (all), *ferde* (travelled), *feorlen* (distant), *þær* (there), *libbende* (living), *micel* (great), *folgode* (followed), *anum* (a) and *heolde* (keep). These amount to some 20 words.

Finally there are words which have died out long ago, or become archaic or undergone such extreme semantic and other changes that they are not recognizable as fossils without special training. They are: *cwæð, þa, soðlice, se, þe, hie, þæs, hine, æhte, gebyreþ, wræclice, rice, forspilde, gælsan, amyrede, wearð, wædla, burgsittendum, tune, gewilnode* and *wambe*. This group comes to some 21 words.

The last two categories are not entirely discrete. Thus the form *cwæð* is the ancestor of EME *quoth*, now obsolete, the initial consonant being rendered in a simple phonetic fashion. A number of semantic changes are apparent: *sele* and *sealde* derive from *sellan* meaning to 'give' ⇒ *sell*; *tune* means 'farm', 'settlement' ⇒ *town*; *wambe* means 'stomach' ⇒ *womb*.

Our finding, then, is that of an admittedly small but fairly straightforward sample, a fifth or 20 per cent of the words have died out, but over a third have survived as clear or obscure descendants.

Language, literature and the word-hoard

Centuries before, the Germanic tribes had been described by the Roman historian Tacitus in his *Germania* (AD 97–98) in terms which especially eulogized their stern military code and the admirable loyalty to the death which bound them into a ferocious and formidable force. More than once Tacitus observes that 'As for leaving the battle alive after your chief has fallen, *that* means lifelong infamy and shame' and 'Men have often survived the battle only to end their shame by hanging themselves afterwards' (chapters 14 and 6). Although one is aware that Tacitus is inclined to partiality, praising the pristine vigour of the noble German savage to the detriment of the decadence of contemporary Rome, the Anglo-Saxon poetry written nearly a thousand years later endorses the same inflexible warrior code.

There were two notable features of Anglo-Saxon society which underscore the importance accorded to language. The first is the almost sacred quality of the verbal bond between people. The poetry celebrates in battle and all manner of conflicts the heroic qualities of such loyalty, singling out for special scorn those whose word is not their bond. A key term for this tightly knit group was *cynn*, the ancestor of *kinsman* and *next of kin*.

The second feature is the concern that language should be used sparingly and properly in a laconic, disciplined fashion. Many gnomic poems (those offering 'saws' of familiar advice) stress that one should not unburden oneself uncritically. The poem called *The Wanderer* offers the common exhortation: 'A wise man must be patient, not over-passionate nor over-hasty of speech . . . A man must bide his time, when he boasts in his speech, until he knows well in his pride whither the thoughts of the mind will turn' (lines 65–72). It does not seem entirely fanciful to see in this prescription the beginnings of the 'strong silent type' and the 'stiff upper lip', the value accorded to being discreet and reserved.[8]

The content of Anglo-Saxon poetry was surprisingly various. A number of these forms show the primitive potency of word-magic, namely charms, spells, leechdoms or folk remedies. All of these derived their power from being spoken, while the Scandinavian runes, being written in their special alphabet, called the *futhorc*, generated potency in inscriptions. Other forms, such as the riddles, explore the teasing suggestiveness of language with wry humour and irony. More formal and institutional are the saints' lives, religious allegories, battle poems, elegies, and poems celebrating the lives of heroes. Yet stylistically the work is remarkably homogeneous, having the same sombre tone and high seriousness.[9]

Some 30,000 lines of Anglo-Saxon poetry have survived the accidents of fire, fervour and the jakes. It is a sobering thought that *Beowulf*, an epic poem which constitutes over one-tenth of this corpus, exists in a unique charred, beer-stained manuscript, very nearly consumed by the catastrophic fire which destroyed much of the great store-house of ancient literature, Sir Robert Cotton's library, in 1731. Though written in West Saxon, the poem celebrates the exploits of a Swedish prince who comes to the rescue of a beleaguered Danish kingdom, kills two marauding monsters, returns home to become king, and then dies destroying a dragon which is attacking his own realm. That summary makes it sound like 'a wild folk tale', but this single work, laboriously copied by two scribes in the late tenth century, gives us a unique picture of the heroic age, its unflinching courage, dignified, even courtly manners, formal eloquence, understated irony and faith in the midst of hopelessness.

Remarkably, a considerable proportion of the Anglo-Saxon lexis was exclusively poetic. Specifically, some 600 words in *Beowulf* are unique to that text. To explain these poetic high frequencies we need to understand the constraints and the creativity in which this poetry was produced.

Formally Anglo-Saxon poetry was totally different from post-medieval English poetry. First it was built on an intricate *alliterative* scheme whereby the *initial* letters harmonized, rather than the traditional *rhyme* scheme with which we are familiar. (Although the word *rhyme* existed in the language as *rīm* it meant 'to count'.) This scheme required that in a given line at least two words had to alliterate. For example, when the Vikings charge across the water at Maldon, the poet catches the moment in these lines, in which the alliterating letters are italicized:

Wodon þa *w*æl-*w*ulfas, for *w*æter ne murnon.
Charged the slaughterous wolves, for the water not caring
*W*icinga *w*erod, *w*est ofer Pantan
[the] Viking host, west across the Panta [river]
Ofer *sc*ir wæter, *sc*yldas wegon
across the shining water, shields carried
Lidmen to *l*ande, *l*inde bæron.
pirates [came] to land, shields carried.

The transliteration (which is necessarily wooden) gives one a sense of the repetitive, cumulative and metaphorical quality of the poetry: in these four lines the enemy is described in three different ways, namely *wæl-wulfas* 'slaughterous wolves', *Wicinga werod*, 'Viking host' and *lidmen*, 'pirates'. As one can imagine, the demands of the alliterative scheme tested the poet's vocabulary considerably, so that he had to ransack the word-hoard for a suitable term. Alternatively, he could make one up by means of compounding (which we have already discussed) or by metaphor. Anglo-Saxon poetry developed a fair number of these in the form of **kennings**, a Norse term for condensed compound metaphors. Table 2.10 shows some of the more common ones.

We may note that *swordplay* is still in use, while *whale's way* was used by John Masefield in his poem 'Sea Fever'. As we shall see in chapter 7, the kenning has remained a vital force in word formation, though not as a formal poetic device.

Given the convention of reticence, a more remarkable feature is that poetic ability was apparently not confined, as in modern times, to a gifted few. There were pre-eminent bards or *scops* (a word rooted in *sceapan*, 'to shape or create'), who were the guardians of the word-hoard and masters of the ancient traditions. But there is suggestive evidence that on occasion anyone could produce a 'party piece'. A famous story is told by Bede of Cædmon, an illiterate

Table 2.10 Kennings

kenning	literal sense	meaning
woruld-candel	world-candle	sun
mere-hengest	sea-horse	ship
famig-heals flota	foamy-necked floater	ship
beado-leama	battle-flame	sword
hwæles weg	whale's way	sea
swanrad	swan's road	sea
sweord pleg	swordplay	battle
wæl stowe	place of the dead	battlefield

Northumbrian cowherd who was suddenly blessed with inspiration to produce a hymn of praise to God. As Bede tells the tale, Cædmon was ashamed of his poetic incapacity: 'often at a feast, when there was considered to be an occasion for celebration, so that all in order had to sing to the harp, whenever he saw the harp approaching him, Cædmon would get up in embarrassment and go to his house' (trans. Shirley-Price, 1960, pp. 245–6). The mention of the harp is one of several indicating that the poetry was sung or perhaps chanted: the basic words for 'poem' are, significantly, *sang* or *leoð*, related to German *lied*. There seems to be little doubt that Cædmon's was a singular disability. In *Beowulf*, various warriors contribute their songs, although there are individuals 'specially gifted with eloquence' who produce occasional praise poems extempore. Furthermore, we know that during the Scandinavian supremacy, the great Norse *skald* or poet, Egil Skallagrimsson, visited the court of Æthelstan, the first King of all England, and performed before him. Skaldic verse was produced extemporaneously, although it was highly complex.

Cædmon's hymn provides an illuminating example of Anglo-Saxon poetic techniques, since it consists in the main of a series of eight kennings and epithets (capitalized in the poem) evoking the various qualities of God:

> Nu we sculon herigean   heofonrices Weard
> *Now we must praise   Heaven's Guardian*
> Meotodes meahte   ond his modgeþonc
> *The Lord's might   and his powerful thought*
> weorc Wuldorfæder,   swa he wundra wæs,
> *The work of the Father of glory,   his wonders*
> ece Dryhten,   or onstaelde
> *The Eternal Lord   created in the beginning*
> He ærest sceop   eorðan bearnum

He first created   the earth for men
heofon to hrofe,   halig Scyppend
With heaven as a roof   the holy Creator
Þa middengeard   monncynnes Weard
Then the world   the Protector of mankind
ece Dryhten,   æftertede
the eternal Lord   fashioned afterwards
firum foldan,   Frea ælmihtig
the earth for men,   the Almighty Lord.

Interestingly, none of these epithets has survived, and one might add that the modern equivalents for 'God' are more limited in their range. Notice how the modern translation uses *Lord* for three different Anglo-Saxon terms. Cædmon's hymn was a major text in its own right and so was written down in a number of dialect versions. Although all of them conform to the same basic text, the individual word-forms differ widely.

As we have seen, lexical structure reflects certain social preoccupations. In these precarious times common place-names like *burg* denote a place of fortification. Likewise, the Anglo-Saxon name for the people of Kent was *Cantware*, the second element of which comes from A-S *werian*, 'to defend'. Two of Cædmon's epithets for God are *heofonrices Weard*, 'Guardian of the Kingdom of Heaven', and *monncynnes Weard*, 'Protector of mankind'.

Perhaps the most striking lexical concentrations in Anglo-Saxon reflected the profound martial ethic of a society in which the notions of 'man' and 'warrior' necessarily overlapped. Some thirty-six terms are to be found in this field, including plain terms like *guma, cempa, wiga, wigend, oretta, dreng, freca* and *hyse*. (Of these only *guma* has survived, quite unbelligerently in *bridegroom*.) Others are made up of compounds such as *garberend*, 'spear-bearer', *sweordfreca*, 'sword warrior', *lindwigend*, 'shield fighter' and *wælwulf*, 'slaughterous wolf'. There is an exlusively poetic hoard made up of *byrnwiga, rinc, hæle, hæleð, beorn, eorl, þegen* and *secg*. (Of these both *eorl* and *þegen* are still with us, the first as *earl* and the second as archaic *thane*). It would not be possible to rival this lexical richness by stretching the resources of the Modern English vocabulary, even by the inclusion of low-register terms like *bloke, chap, fellow, cove, chum, geezer* and so on. There are, similarly, some thirteen synonyms for 'battle' and eleven for 'sword'. We can also infer that this concentration partly derives from the exigencies of the alliterative scheme.

Being a migratory people gifted at sailing, the Anglo-Saxons had a vocabulary with a great stock of terms for the sea. As J. A. Sheard justly observed, 'There is perhaps hardly an Old English poem which does not mention the sea in one way or another, and several are largely, if not entirely, connected with the sea' (1954, p. 132). Indeed, *The Wanderer* and *The Seafarer* exude an intense wanderlust, a yearning for the sea even in wintry danger. Within the word-hoard there are about two dozen plain terms for 'sea' and many more compounds and figurative expressions emphasizing variously its tranquillity, its violence, its danger and so on. These amount to well over fifty terms; when combined with a similar number for 'ship', one realizes the semantic concentration of this field.

Let us by way of conclusion consider a minor passage from *Beowulf* (lines 210–28) describing what would be a routine crossing from Sweden to Denmark. It still conveys an unmistakable sense of exhilaration. It uses a whole range of kennings for 'ship' and it provides us with another useful passage to analyse for terms which have survived, even in this remarkably intricate verbal art-form:

> Fyrst forð gewat; flota wæs on yðum,
> *Time passed on; the bark was on the waves,*
> bat under beorge. Beornas gearwe
> *the boat under the cliff. The prepared warriors*
> on stefn stigon, – streamas wundon
> *onto the prow stepped, – the currents pushed*
> sund wið sande; secgas bæron
> *the sea against the sand; men carried*
> on bearm nacan beorhte frætwe,
> *into the bosom of the ship shining armour,*
> guð-searo geatolice; guman ut scufon,
> *splendid war-gear; the men pushed out,*
> weras on wil-sið wudu bundenne.
> *heroes on their eagerly sought journey [in the] braced timbers.*
> Gewat þa ofer wæg-holm, winde gefysed
> *It departed over the wavy sea, driven by the wind*
> flota fami-heals, fugle gelicost,
> *the foamy-necked ship, just like a bird*
> oðþæt ymb an-tid, oþres dogores
> *until at the right time the next day*
> wunden-stefna gewaden hæfde
> *the curved prow had travelled so far*
> þæt ða liðende land gesawon
> *that the travellers saw land*
> brim-clifu blican, beorgas steape,
> *the shining sea-cliffs, the steep promontories,*
> side sæ-næssas; þa wæs sund liden,
> *the great sea-headlands; then was the sea crossed,*
> eoletes æt ende. Þanon up hraðe
> *the sea-journey at an end. Then up quickly*

> Wedere leode   on wang stigon,
> *the Geat people on land leapt*
> sæ-wudu sældon;   syrcan hrysedon,
> *made fast their ship; their armour rang*
> guð-gewædo;   Gode þancedon
> *the coats of mail; they thanked God*
> þæs þe him yþ-lade   eaðe wurdon.
> *that for them the sea paths had been easy.*

The first thing which strikes us is the great number of compounds, ten out of ninety-four words. This makes us realize that the notion of a 'word' was very different for an Anglo-Saxon poet. (The previous quotation from Cædmon's hymn showed five compounds out of forty-two words.)

Making allowances for spelling and grammatical inflections, we may list the following twenty-six forms as obvious or recognizable ancestors of current words: *forð, wæs, bat, under, on, streamas, wundon, sund, wið, sande, ut, wudu, ofer, winde, oþres, hæfde, þæt, land, gesawon, clifu, steape, æt, ende, up, Gode, þancedon.*

The following twelve words are also survivors, but are less recognizable. They are glossed by the modern form for ease of recognition, even though other terms are more appropriate in translation: *flota* ('floater'), *bæron* ('bore'), *beorhte* ('bright'), *scufon* ('shoved'), *bundenne* ('bound'), *fugle* ('fowl'), *gelicost* ('like'), *dogores* ('days'), *wunden-stefna* ('wound-stem' i.e. 'curved prow'), *sænæssas* ('sea-ness'), *hraðe* ('rather'), *gewædo* ('weeds'). Surprisingly, this poetic extract shows a higher rate of survival than did the prose passage, since some 38 per cent of the words have survived. However, many of them have undergone notable semantic changes.

Conclusion

The concentration of Anglo-Saxon in the core vocabulary is still dramatically evident. It makes up what Murray called the 'nucleus or central mass of many thousand words whose "Anglicity" is unquestioned'. As we noticed in chapter 1, both the evidence of spoken word counts and the analysis of major authors shows that the core of common words is derived from Anglo-Saxon.[9]

The durability, indeed the tenacity, of this core thus remains a permanent feature of the language, partly because the Anglo-Saxons constituted the majority of speakers, even under the subsequent Norman overlordship. There is no doubt that the base register remains that of immediate recourse, as is shown in *help, food, come here! go away!* and so on. The emotive quality of the Germanic roots of the language is also a notable feature of the lexicon. Thus *heart, hearth, home, love, lust, yearn, hate, loathe* and *weep* convey a more intense feeling than their Norman French or Latin counterparts. Finally, as we shall note in our last chapter, long after Britain's demographic conflicts have passed, the Anglo-Saxon core is resuscitating itself in thousands of new forms.

Notes

1 Tom McArthur has a useful article, 'English in tiers', showing how the three word-stocks, Germanic, Romance and Greek, contribute to various word-fields, e.g. *skinny, subcutaneous* and *dermatitis* (*English Today*, July 1990, pp. 15–20).

2 Such breakthroughs in phonetic archaeology were not universally acclaimed. Sir Walter Raleigh, Merton Professor of English Literature at Oxford, insisted a century ago that the study of English 'needed to be freed from the slavery of philology and phonology, [especially] the hunting of hypothetical sound-shiftings in the primeval German forests' (in Potter, 1937, p. 238).

3 On semantic richness see David Crystal (1987, p. 15); on words for snow see Geoffrey Pullum, *The Great Eskimo Vocabulary Hoax* (University of Chicago Press, 1991).

4 The semantic derogation of the conquered is evidenced in *caitiff, vassal* and *slave*. See Ullmann (1962), pp. 231–2.

5 Archaeological evidence has also made its contribution. According to James Campbell: 'It has become plain that there were indeed strong connections between Kent and Jutland' (1991, p. 30). However, on the time-scale, Martin Biddle has noted that 'far from there being a complete break between Roman Britain and Anglo-Saxon England, the new [archaeological] evidence shows that the roots of the English settlements were being planted while Britain was still part of the Empire' (in D. M. Wilson (ed.) *The Archaeology of Anglo-Saxon England*, London, 1976, p. 79).

6 Dieter Kastovsky gives the figure of 3% borrowing in his chapter on 'Semantics and Vocabulary' in vol. I of *The Cambridge History of the English Language* ed. R. M. Hogg (1992), p. 294.

7 For an account of the debate, see Ullmann (1962, pp. 80–115).

8 Beowulf clearly epitomizes this ideal of modesty and courage: lion on the batlefield, lamb in the hall.

9 In his preface to *A Saxon Treatise* (1623), William de l'Isle showed unusual pride in the versatility of the ancient language: 'What Englishman of understanding is there, but may be delighted to see the prety shifts [ingenious improvisations] our tongue made with her own store, in all parts of learning, when they scorned to borrow words of another?' (cited in Mitchell, 1995, p. viii).

3

THE NORMAN ELITE AND
THE NEW LANGUAGE OF
POWER

Then Duke William sailed from Normandy to Pevensey, on the eve of Michaelmas [28 September]. As soon as his men were fit for service, they constructed a castle at Hastings. When King Harold heard this, [having just defeated the invading Norwegians at Stamford Bridge on 20 September] he gathered together a great host and came to oppose him at the grey apple tree, but William came upon him unexpectedly before his army was set in order. Nevertheless, the king fought against him most resolutely with those men who wished to stand by him, and there was great slaughter on both sides. King Harold was slain, and Leofwine his brother, and earl Gurth his brother, and many good men. The French had possession of the place of slaughter, as God granted them, because of the nation's sins.

Anglo-Saxon Chronicle 1066

Thus are the fateful events of 1066, in which William the Bastard became William the Conqueror, summed up (somewhat partially) in the Laud manuscript of the *Anglo-Saxon Chronicle*. (William's title did not change overnight, of course: an anonymous fourteenth-century chronicler still used William's disreputable title, moralistically noting that 'William bastard of Normandy deposed Harold, which was a villainy.') In the nature of things, the *Chronicle* focuses on the transfer of power at the top of the hierarchy rather than the effects on the common people. From the point of view of the royal family, the Norman Conquest was not such a radical change, since Edward the Confessor was born of a Norman mother and spent many years in refuge at the Norman court during the rule of the Danish kings (1016–42). Furthermore, the Normans themselves were not in origin French, but part of the Scandinavian diaspora which started in the eighth century, Hrolf the Ganger (also known as Rollo the Rover) having been ceded Normandy in 912. In the subsequent century and a half they had assimilated the French language and the local customs.

However, for most of the upper echelons and for England at large the Norman Conquest heralded a shift of power as complete as the Anglo-Saxon invasions, though without a mass demographic upheaval. P. H. Reaney reminds us that 'the victors at Hastings numbered little more than some 6000 men' (1964, p. 192). Consequently, the Normans did not drive out the Saxons as the Saxons had expelled the Celts. Coming as a ruling caste, they simply destroyed and supplanted the Saxon aristocracy, taking over all positions of power. By 1072 only one of the twelve earls of England was an Englishman (Sheard, 1954, p. 199). By 1086 (the year of the *Domesday Book*, a comprehensive inventory of the ownership of English estates) 'only about eight per cent of the land remained in the hands of the erstwhile Anglo-Saxon aristocracy' (Douglas and Greenaway, 1953, p. 22). They established their rule by building castles with Saxon labour but garrisoning them with Norman men-at-arms. English bishops and abbots were replaced by Normans: only two Anglo-Saxon bishops outlived William.

Most significantly, the Normans established their rule in their own tongue, which became the new language of power and prestige, very much as English subsequently became the language of status in the British Empire. William dutifully set himself to learn English at the age of forty-one, but gave up in the face of other demands. Of course, Latin continued to be the language of the Church and of scholarship, and we must remember that Anglo-Norman or Norman French had its roots in Latin, but had mutated way from the parent stock, as had the other Romance languages. But for three centuries English ceased to be the official language of the land, surviving only as the speech of a largely dispossessed people. These unusual features of linguistic separation and status were emphasized in the verse history written *c.*1300 by the chronicler known as Robert of Gloucester:

> Þvs com lo engelond, in to normandies hond.
> *Lo, thus came England into Normandy's hand.*
> & þe normans ne couþe speke þo, bote hor owe speche.
> *And the Normans then could speak only their own language*
> & speke french as hii dude at om. & hor children dude also teche.
> *and spoke French as they did at home, and also taught their children it*
> so þat heiemen of þis lond. þat of hor blod come,
> *so that noblemen of this land, descended from them*
> holdeþ alle þulk speche. þat hii of hom nome.
> *all keep to that same speech that they received from them*
> vor bote a man conne frenss. me telþ of hime lute.
> *for unless man knows French, people take little account of him*
> ac lowe men holdeþ to engliss. & to hor owe speche 3ute.
> *but low people keep to English, and to their own language still.*

ich wene þer ne beþ in al þe world contreyes none.
I think that in the in the whole world there are no countries
þat ne holdeþ to hor owe speche. bote engelond one.
that do not keep to their own language, except for England alone.
(*Rerum Britannicarum Medii Aevi Scriptores*. Rolls Series no. 86)

As the Saxons fled from 'the place of slaughter' and as the news of the invasion spread, so the new Norman vocabulary of power surely followed rapidly in their wake. One imagines that basic Norman terms like *war*, *peace*, *tax*, *castle*, *prison* and *power* would soon have made their presence felt among the native population. They certainly discovered that *castel*, which in Anglo-Saxon meant 'a fortified village' was being superseded by *castle*, which in Norman French meant 'a stone-built fortress'. However, so complete was the dominance of the new linguistic regime that very few transitional manuscripts survive. Consequently, some scholars, arguing on the basis of the first recorded instances of the new vocabulary, claim that the Norman-French terms took more than a century to infiltrate into English, and that the main influx took place only from 1250 onwards. (See, in this respect, Jespersen (1962, p. 87), Baugh (1965, p. 214), Nist (1966, p. 151), Burgess (1992, p. 199) and Burnley (1992, p. 431).) However, this apparent time-lag is manifestly unlikely in view of the overall dominance of the Norman overlords, and would seem to be a feature of the source of the lexical evidence, necessarily dependent on the survival of manuscripts, rather than a reflection of the actual facts of speech on the ground.

We can test this view in relation to Robert of Gloucester's text: applying our word survival test, we note that of the ninety-six words in this passage, about 75 per cent are now recognizable survivors. This shows quite a dramatic shift from the Anglo-Saxon passages previously analysed in chapter 2. Yet the infiltration of French words is still very limited, the sole example being *countrey*: Robert of Gloucester prefers *speche* to *language* and *heiemen* to *nobles*.

As we have seen, the *Anglo-Saxon Chronicle* provides us with an invaluable record of the history of these turbulent times. After the Conquest the number of manuscripts diminishes to a single thread in the form of the chronicle written by the monks at Peterborough in Northamptonshire. Even this came to an end with the annal for 1154. As it records the events after the Conquest, the work consequently becomes a linguistic as well as a historical record. In the annal for the year 1137, for instance, we find the following French terms recorded for the first time: *tresor*, 'treasury', *Canceler*, 'Chancellor', *prisun*, *justice* and *tenserie*, 'protection money'. These were the harbingers of a whole new Norman vocabulary of power.

The Norman Conquest led to an enormous enrichment of the English vocabulary.[1] This was because the French loan-words differed greatly in reference and in focus from the Anglo-Saxon stock and the loans from the Vikings, which had come in at grass-roots level, dealing with everyday objects and experience. The Norman vocabulary came down the hierarchy of power from a ruling caste speaking a foreign Romance language quite alien to a population speaking two related Germanic languages, Anglo-Saxon and Old Norse. The point is well illustrated if we imagine the situation of a sheriff seeking some outlaw. In answer to his question 'Where is Egbert?' he might get the following reply in Anglo-Saxon:

He stag his hors and rad to his freondes hus.
('He mounted his horse and rode to his friend's house.')

If the pursuit were in the Danelaw, the reply would be in Norse:

Hann steig hans hross ok reið a hans frænda hus.

However, if the reply was in French it would be entirely different, principally in vocabulary, but also in grammar and syntax:

Il a monté son cheval et il est allé à la maison de son ami.

(This last reply is, of course, in modern French, but the same points of difference would apply to Anglo-Norman.) We can see that with a certain amount of goodwill and determination, the speakers of Anglo-Saxon and Old Norse could understand each other, since they would be communicating through similar Germanic root-words, even though the phonetic and inflectional differences would still stand as obstacles. However, there would be no possibility of either of them communicating with a French speaker, since they would have no linguistic link whatever. In view of this social and linguistic cleavage and the fact that the Saxons and Norse speakers were always greatly in the majority, it is not surprising that the language which eventually survived was in essence Anglo-Saxon, but with a great admixture of French words which had become established since the Conquest. The various categories whereby the Normans defined themselves form the basis of the following discussion.

Virtually every aspect of the lexis shows Norman supremacy. The following illustrations are full, but not totally comprehensive, since one does not wish to weigh down the reader with imposing word-lists. The vocabulary of law, always a clear reflector of power, provides a convenient starting-point. While the key term, *law*, as well as *by-law* and *thrall*, are Norse, the Norman dominance is unmistakable, reflected in a whole array of terms, such as *court, justice, judge, jury, suit, sue, plaintiff, defendant, accuse, plea, felony, crime, gaol, assize, session* and *damage*. The inverted French world-order (in which the adjective follows the noun) is still apparent in *Attorney General, court martial, fee simple* and *letter patent*. Simeon Potter reminds us that when the Queen signifies assent to an Act of Parliament, she still uses the French formula 'La Reyne le veult' ('The Queen wishes it') (1963, p. 35). The phrase *real estate* maintains the old semantic force of French *real* meaning 'royal', still current in *real tennis*.

It should not be assumed, on the basis of this lexical evidence, that Saxon England had lacked these legal procedures, for the Germanic peoples had a highly developed sense of law.[2] (The basic all-purpose word *thing* was in origin a legal term for a case or a dispute; it formed the base of the Althing, the Icelandic Parliament, which is the oldest in Western Europe.) But after the Conquest the vocabulary of law was largely removed from the native population. The old direct and familiar native terms were replaced by new opaque equivalents, a general model in the development of professional language in English. This shift becomes apparent when one compares the language of the Anglo-Saxon Laws with the terminology which has subsequently become established: thus *baernenne* 'burning' was displaced by *arson*, *geþeoft* 'theft' by *larceny*, *firen* by *crime*, *sacu* by *suit*, *scyldig* by *guilty*, and *bigamy* by the amusingly direct *twiewifing* ('two-wifing').[3] Similarly, the Saxon *witenagemot* ('the meeting of wise men') was replaced by the Norman *parliament*, and the Saxon *shire*, previously administered by an *eorl* or a *scirgerefa* (*shire reeve* ⇒ *sheriff*), was replaced by the Norman *county*, which in Anglo-Norman was 'the domain or territory of a count'.

The division of titles

Titles provide a telling semantic reflection of the Conquest. The Normans took over several of the Saxon titles, notably *king* and *queen*, *lord* and *lady*, but imported a considerable array, as can be seen in the following table:

Anglo-Saxon	Norman
King	
Queen	
	Prince
	Duke
	Marquess
Earl	Countess
Lord	
Lady	
	Viscount
	Baron

Knight

        Squire
        Franklin

Sheriff

        Bailiff

Reve

        Sergeant

Yeoman

        Page
        Groom

Churl   Villein
        Serf

This configuration shows the origin of the titles unambiguously, but the actual situation on the ground was more complicated. Several of the titles, notably *baron*, were applied to a variety of ranks. Others gained formal recognition only centuries after the Conquest. There are problems of translation. For instance, the title *duke* (applied, as we have seen at the beginning of this chapter, to William the Conqueror) was first formally conferred upon the Black Prince in 1337. The *OED* notes, in this respect, that 'From the Conquest till Edward II, *ealdormann* or *eorl* was rendered by *comes*, and *dux, duc, duk* was known only as a foreign title. Even William and Robert are known to the Old English Chronicle only as "earls" of Normandy.' Anglo-Saxon *eorl* was applied to a wide range of people, but it achieved promotion after the Conquest, displacing Norman *count*, perhaps because the Normans recognized in the English term an echo of the Norse term *jarl*, a viceroy or 'underking'. Thus *eorl* and *countess* form a unique bilingual pairing in the hierarchy. A speculative explanation for *count* never being accepted as an English title is its embarrassing phonetic proximity to *cunt*, first recorded c.1230. (The feminine form *cuntesse* was an early borrowing, dating from 1154.)

The dominance of the Normans is also shown in words which establish and define their regime, such as the terms of respect, like *master* and *dame*. Related words are *maistrie* (mastery), *command, order, rule, serve, obedience, discipline, force, fealty, allegiance, homage* and *danger* in its Old French sense of 'power, authority', before it subsequently developed the meaning of 'ability to inflict harm'. Much of the modern vocabulary of finance, an essential arm of authority, derives from the Normans: hence *account, balance, budget* (etymologically 'a small bag'), *dues, exchequer* (from the chequered floor on which the small bags were moved around), *debt, fine, levy, price, receipt, revenue, tax, interest, rent, cash* and *treasury.*

The Norman presence is, predictably, most visible in the overt vocabulary of power, such as that of the law and administration, which we have been dis-

Table 3.1   The Norman vocabulary of power, religion and the arts

power	war	religion	chase	art	fashion	architecture
court	battle	service	sport	image	garment	tower
crown	arms	saint	falcon	design	appparel	vault
authority	assault	miracle	quarry	beauty	dress	column
parliament	enemy	clergy	quest	figure	train	transept
government	armour	sacrifice	retrieve	romance	robe	cloister
justice	castle	grace	track	paint	mantle	chamber
state	lance	mercy	scent	music	gown	pillar
office	siege	faith	lure	verse	cloak	aisle

cussing, but is equally remarkable in the fields of war, religion, the chase, the arts, architecture and fashion. The small but potent sample arranged under these categories in table 3.1 gives a sense of Norman authority and refinement.

We notice that almost the whole basic vocabulary of the visual arts comes into the language from Norman French: in addition to the terms listed above are *colour, sculpture* and *melody*. So does the vocabulary of fashion and the more stately garments. To these may be added costly materials *satin* and *taffeta*, and the rarest furs, such as *sable, ermine* and *squirrel*, signifying rank. The exclusivity of these materials was endorsed by various ordinances preventing the lower classes from wearing them.

Hunting, or the chase, to name it by its Norman equivalent, contains a particularly interesting word-stock. Although most of the terms listed above under *chase* have filtered into the general vocabulary, there were many others defining the procedures and rules in this elaborate ritual. There were *lymers* (French *limiers*) who went out with hounds (also called *lymers*) on a leash to detect the whereabouts, quantity and quality of the game. There were terms for all the varieties of hounds (for instance, *alaunts, harriers* and *kenets*) as well as for the dozens of different horn-calls, of which the *retreat* (French *retrét*) is the most familiar survivor. *Quarry*, listed above, derives from Old French *curé*, from *cuir*, 'leather, hide', referring to the habit of rewarding the hounds by means of feeding them the intestines of the hunted animal on its hide. From falconry there were the specialist terms *jesses*, for the leather straps fastened round the bird of prey's legs, and *seeling* (from Old French *cil*, 'eyelash'), meaning to stitch up the eyes of the bird during training. *Mews*, now fashionable properties in London, started out with a humbler purpose, albeit with royal associations. A *mew* (French *mue*) was a cage in which hawks were kept while moulting. Hence 'to mew' meant both 'to moult' and 'to put in a cage'.

Curiously, the plural form *mews* arose only in the fourteenth century, used of the royal stables at Charing Cross in London, so called because they were built on the site where the royal hawks had previously been mewed.[4]

The religious word-stock, deriving largely, as we have seen, from Latin borrowings of the Anglo-Saxon period, was further extended by terms such as *pray, charity, passion, altar, saviour, sepulchre* and *absolution*. Many of the terms of our moral vocabulary were brought into the language, such as *conscience, charity, lechery, gluttony, avarice, treachery, loyalty, valour, virtue, duty, proud/pride* and a key medieval term **mesure**, meaning 'moderation'.

However, equally important were the terms defining a courtly stylishness, such as *gentil* ('noble' or 'well bred'), *gentillesse, curteis* and *curteisie*, in origin related to the manners and refinement befitting a court. This panache was combined with an unmistakable sense of *joie de vivre*, found in words like *pleasure, pleasant, pleasing, joy, gay, ease* and *comfort*.

It goes without saying that the Norman overlords lived in large imposing structures which carried the names of *palace, castle, mansion, manor* and *estate*, as opposed to the plainer Saxon terms *house* and *homestead*. Virtually all the terminology of the medieval castle is Norman French, many of the terms still having an alien timbre. The list includes *barbican, bastion, garderobe, ward, causeway, moat, motte, bailey, rampart, dungeon, palisade, portcullis, battlements, crenellations, embrasures, merlons* and *machicolations*. Similarly, the basic weapons of combat, *sword, spear, shield* and *helmet*, are Saxon, but the Norman warrior's body was in effect redefined with French terms for armour, namely *visor, gauntlet, cuisse, greave, vambrace, rerebrace, crinet, peytral*.

The culture of the horse

As the Bayeux Tapestry clearly shows, the Norman invaders brought horses with them in considerable numbers across the Channel, despite the obvious logistical difficulties. 'The Anglo-Saxons used the stirrup [A-S *stig-rap* meaning 'mounting rope'],' writes Lynn White, Jr, in his interesting study, *Medieval Technology and Social Change*, 'but they did not comprehend it: for this they paid a fearful price' (1962, p. 28). For the Normans had developed the art of mounted warfare, and their use of cavalry proved decisive at Hastings. Here Saxon *eorl* and *ceorl*, combining to form the traditional *scyld-burh* or 'shield wall', were cut down in terrible numbers. The Norman practitioners of mounted shock combat, often landless younger sons, rose to be a new class, the knights, taking their name, curiously, from A-S *cniht*, meaning simply 'a boy', as the cognate German term *knecht* still does. Other terms of rank rooted in the status of the horse are *marshal* (etymologically 'the boy who looks after the mares') and *constable*, from Latin *comes stabuli*, literally 'the count of the stable'.

We should also recall that the root of *chivalry* lies in French *cheval*, a horse, though we would not necessarily concur with the claim that 'It is impossible to be chivalrous without a horse,' made by Arthur Denholm-Young (1948, p. 240). This remark, probably made for its etymological wit, is countered by the sterling example of Beowulf (who is never seen on a horse) but is a model of honour, courtesy, courage, selflessness and modesty. The French culture of the horse and of mounted combat is apparent in the *tournament*, introduced into England by Richard the Lionheart, with its attendant vocabulary of *joust* and *lists*, the latter now a mundane word. From the Normans come such terms for the variety of horses as *palfrey, stallion, charger* and *ambler*, as well as basic equestrian words like *spur, lance, caparison* and *mace*. Unsurprisingly, we find that many of the terms for parts of the horse are of French origin; they include *coronet, croup, ergot, loin, muzzle* and *pastern*. While *saddle* itself derives from Anglo-Saxon, the *cantle*, the *pommel* and the *panels* carry French names.

Heraldry arose in the mid-twelfth century from the necessity of armoured knights being able to identify themselves in battle or in tournaments. Being essentially aristocratic in origin, almost the whole vocabulary (of several hundred terms) is derived from French and has remained so. If we confine our-selves to the colour terms, we find *argent* for 'silver', *gules* for 'red', *sable* for 'black', *vert* for 'green' and *purpure* for 'purple'.

The sociology of food

Food provides perhaps the most striking sociolinguistic division between Saxon and Norman, since the master/servant relationship was demarcated by differ-ing word-stocks: the animal in the field or on the hoof retained its Anglo-Saxon name, but when slaughtered for the overlord's table it was transmogrified into Norman:

sheep	mutton
ox	beef
pig	pork, bacon, gammon
calf	veal
deer	venison
boar	brawn
fowl	poultry

This distinction, not found in other languages, is carried down to the finer points of butchery, the choicest cuts like *haunch, joint, cutlet* being French, while the humbler portions, such as *brains, tongue, shank* were Saxon.[5] *Capon* and *bacon* were actually borrowed before the Conquest. While *breakfast* is Saxon, *dinner, supper, banquet* and *feast* are French. (*Lunch* is an oddity, the term having appeared only in the sixteenth century meaning 'a slice or hunk of food'.) The status of the hot meal is shown in the French monopoly of virtually all the modes of cooking: *boil, broil, roast, grill* and *fry*. Dishes, culinary refinements and spices with French names are *soup, potage, sauce, dessert, mustard, cream, ginger, liquorice, flan, pasty, claret* (originally *claré*, meaning 'clear'), *biscuit* (meaning literally 'twice cooked') and *wastel*, cognate with *gâteau* and meaning 'made with the finest flour'. All this suggests that the Saxon cuisine must have been a sorry affair.

The ritual and the personnel involved in a medieval feast are amazing to us now. At the top of the household hierarchy was the *steward* (ironically in origin a 'sty ward'), followed by a *marshal* (already mentioned), a *sewer* (whose curious name is derived from French *essuyer/essayer*, meaning a taster), a *pantler* in charge of the *pantry* (originating in *pain*, bread), a *butler* (from *bouteille*, a bottle), and an *ewerer*, in charge of the laundry and linen. Lower down were *scullions, blackguards, spit-boys* and *pot-boys*.

If we go back to a fifteenth-century cookery book we find the dominance of French terminology to be quite remarkable, as can be gauged from this delectable recipe, in which the French terms are set out in italic:

Oystres in grauey

Take *almondes*, and *blanche* hem, and grinde hem and drawe þorgh a *streynour* with wyne, and with goode fressh broth into gode mylke, and sette hit on þe fire and lete *boyle*; and cast therto *Maces, clowes, Sugur, pouder* of *Ginger*, and faire *parboyled oynons mynced*; And þen take faire *oystres*, and *parboile* hem togidre in faire water; And then caste hem ther-to. And let hem *boyle* togidre til þey ben ynowe; and *serve* hem forth for gode *potage*.

Today, with food a matter of interest among the sophisticated, *cuisine*, whether traditional, regional or *nouvelle*, is but one of many French terms to do with gastronomy now assimilated into English. Others will be found in figure 3.1, 'a historical menu'. (Food names contain a number of surprises, notably the antiquity of fashionable items, such as *cous-cous* (in Florio, 1598), surpassed by *polenta*, first recorded *c.*1000 in Ælfric's translation of the Bible.)

The terms for trades show a similar sociolinguistic division between the names of the materials and the tradesmen:

wood	carpenter
stone	mason
cloth	tailor
arrow	fletcher
beard, hair	barber
meat	butcher

	Food	Drink
	pesto salsa sushi	
	tacos quiche schwarma	
	pizza osso bucco	Chardonnay
1900	paella tuna goulash	
	hamburger mousse borscht	Coca Cola
	grapefruit éclair chips	soda water
	bouillabaisse mayonnaise	
	ravioli crêpes consommé	riesling
1800	spaghetti soufflé bechamel	tequila
	ice cream	
	kipper chowder	
	sandwich jam	seltzer
	meringue hors d'oeuvre welsh rabbit	whisky
1700	avocado pâté	gin
	muffin	port
	vanilla mincemeat pasta	champagne
	salmagundi	brandy
	yoghurt kedgeree	sherbet
1600	omelette litchi tomato curry chocolate	tea sherry
	banana macaroni caviar pilav	coffee
	anchovy maize	
	potato turkey	
	artichoke scone	sillabub
1500	marchpane (marzipan)	
	whiting offal melon	
	pineapple mushroom	
	salmon partridge	
Middle	venison pheasant	muscatel
English	crisp cream bacon	rhenish (rhine wine)
	biscuit oyster	claret
	toast pastry jelly	
	ham veal mustard	
	beef mutton brawn	
	sauce potage	
	broth herring	
	meat cheese	ale
Old	cucumber mussel	beer
English	butter fish	wine
	bread	water

Figure 3.1   A historical menu

Similarly, *ploughman, shepherd, cowherd, fisherman, smith, wright, miller* and *baker* are Saxon, while *farmer* is French, as are *butler, cutler, draper, farrier, joiner, turner, grocer* and *cooper* (a barrel-maker).

If we take a lexical field that is less subject to political or social influence, such as the names for common birds, we find the Norman influence to be less marked. Of forty-six bird names, those of French origin make up about a third. Several of these have aristocratic associations, namely *eagle, falcon* and *osprey*, but most are now common, namely *cuckoo, heron, pigeon, jay, robin, magpie, curlew, plover, jackdaw, martin, petrel, mallard* and *grebe.* Against these are the much more numerous Saxon flights of *swallow, sparrow, lark, duck, goose, hawk, swan, owl, dove, starling, thrush, finch, gannet, nightingale, blackbird, linnet, woodpecker, kingfisher, rook, raven, crow, wren, wagtail, swift, kite, stork, crane, moorhen* and *seamew.* (*Gull* is of Celtic origin, while *tern* comes from Norse.) A similar division is apparent in the names for common trees. While the *chestnut,* the *laurel,* the *plane* and the *poplar* derive from French, they are greatly outnumbered by the trees with ancient Saxon names: *alder, ash, aspen, beech, birch, box, elm, fir, hazel, holly, ivy, linden, maple, oak, thorn, willow* and *yew.*

Lexical status and centrality

In bringing this section to a close, we have observed that Norman French never became the language of the majority. Consequently, in most lexical areas the effect of the Conquest was to create a separation of registers, whereby the Norman term occupied associations of superiority, prestige and courtliness, while the Saxon became the humbler, general-purpose word. The following sample illustrates the point:

clothes	dress
holy	saintly
help	aid
lonely	solitary
homely	domestic
feed	nourish
begin	commence
hide	conceal
clean	pure

The difference is perhaps best summed up in the marked distinctions between the *hearty welcome* of Anglo-Saxon and the *cordial reception* of Norman French.

As we have seen, it is something of a truism that 'many of the French loan words reflect . . . cultural and political dominance' (Barber, 1964, p. 161). A great number of the Norman borrowings are nouns. Since the Conquerors did not share a common Germanic ancestral language as the Saxons and the Scandinavians had, these borrowings did not extend to the central grammatical forms, such as Norse *they* and *are.* However, the phrase *used to* steadily replaced Anglo-Saxon *ywoned* in the course of Middle English. While many of the Norman terms describe innovations or define upper-class aspects of experience and objects, it is important to realise how comprehensively the new French vocabulary displaced basic native terms for ordinary things. For example, *language, people, face, spirit, stomach, vegetables, fruit, table, chair, curtain, touch, action, air, age, season letter, place, point, piece, number, quality, sound, substance, form, dozen* and *second*. Furthermore, many terms penetrated the semantic core of the word-stock. These include *able, active, aim, allow, apply, approach, arrive, beast, blanket, blue, brave, calm, change, claim, close, common, coy, cry, cover, cushion, defy, cruel, desire, easy, fresh, fault, furniture, grain, hour, join, labour, large, manner, matter, marriage, nice, noise, obey, ocean, order, pain, pass, pleasure, poor, proper, push, refuse, reply, safe, save, special, state, strange, subtle, sure, travel, turn, use* and *usual*. As we can see, these have lost their old associations of rank and become some of the commonest words in the language.

Perhaps the most remarkable group of these basic borrowings is that for family relationships: *father, mother, brother* and *sister* are derived from Saxon roots, but French *uncle, aunt, nephew, niece* and *cousin* displaced their native equivalents. (Dr Johnson noted that the Anglo-Saxon term *eame*, 'uncle', was 'still used in the wilder parts of Staffordshire', his home county.) We should bear in mind that among the Germanic peoples the uncle–nephew relationship was especially strong, the nephew having the interesting Anglo-Saxon name *sweostorsunu* ('sister's son') of which the German cognate *schwestersohn* still survives.

The theme of the land, by which we introduced chapter 2, provides an illuminating aspect with which to conclude this section. There are comparatively few place-names of Norman origin, but they are revealing of the new rulers' positive attitude. A striking example provided by P. H. Reaney is that 'The name of the Essex vill of *Fulepet* "fithy hollow" was replaced after 1086 by the more attractive French name Beaumont "beautiful hill"' (1964, p. 193). The kinds of French names used suggest that this was more than a cynical piece of real-estate substitution. The two words for 'beautiful', namely *beau* and *bel*, figure prominently, as in *Beauchamp, Beaulieu, Beaufort, Beaumaris, Beaudesert, Belmont, Belsize, Belchamp* and dozens of less obvious derivatives. Plainer French terms which have become place-name elements are *mount, grange, market* and *park*. Other names were changed less drastically, the French family name simply being added to the traditional place-name, as in *Ashby de la Zouche* and *Melton Mowbray*.

This feature of sophisticated cultivation is apparent in such contrasts as Anglo-Saxon *grass* vis-à-vis Norman-French *lawn* and *garden*, Anglo-Saxon *field* vis-à-vis Norman French *park*, Anglo-Saxon *spring* vis-à-vis Norman French *fountain*. However, so great was the Norman influence that many of the commonest terms, now lacking any patina of class, derive from them. Such base-words are *country, river, forest, valley, lake, flower, coast, cloud, mountain* and *village*. These words now seem to epitomize the English countryside.

Middle English: Diversity and Richness

The radical linguistic effects of the Norman Conquest generated a new kind of English, which historians of the language call Middle English; it lasted in broad terms from *c.*1100 to *c.*1500. During this time the major foreign influences of the Conquest and the Scandinavian invasions were assimilated, so that by the end of the period there emerged a recognizable form of Early Modern English. Initially these influences led to diversification, breaking up what had been the reasonably standardized form of West Saxon. As we have seen, the whole new vocabulary of Norman power was transmitted throughout the country in an alien language, thereby creating a stratified linguistic separation between the rulers and the ruled. Anglo-Norman was in essence a class dialect dissemi-nated from London down the chain of authority. On the other hand, the Norse influence was demotic, occurring at grass-roots level, though concentrated in the north and the east, thus having considerable effects on those regional dialects. What is in many ways remarkable is that English not only survived, but re-established itself as the national tongue after being displaced as the official language for three centuries. The hybrid vocabulary of Middle English amounted to approximately 100–120,000 words, but the proportion of the native content as against the foreign obviously changed during the period.

Although there was no clear standard, regional differences started to become for the first time the object of adverse comment and satire, which sug-gests the beginning of a notional standard. By the end of the period the East Midland dialect had begun to assert itself as the dominant form, especially through the rise of the London Chancery standard, in which official docu-ments were produced. The invention of printing accelerated these tendencies, making standardized spelling a *desideratum*. As varieties became accentuated in print, so the search for a standard consisting of 'correct' forms became one of the major concerns of Early Modern English.

The diversity of forms

But this is looking ahead. One of the most obvious features of Middle English was the diversity of forms for quite common words. As James Milroy has put it, 'The most striking fact about Middle English is that it exhibits by far the greatest diversity in written language of any period before or since' (1992, p. 156). This diversity raises real problems about the definition of 'a word' in the period, for the instability of spelling affected grammatical inflections. Whereas in Anglo-Saxon the infinitive of the verb had ended in *-an* and the past tense plural had ended in *-on*, in Middle English both functions came to be conveyed by *-en*. Similarly, the well-defined singular noun inflections of *-u*, *-a* and *-e* in Anglo-Saxon became eroded to the ubiquitous final 'e', the most distinctive feature of Middle English. Nor were these simply regional differences. In a single manuscript of the *Peterborough Chronicle* written by the same scribe the form for *were* is written *wæron*, *uuaren* and *waren*. In the West Saxon of Old English the standard form had been *wæron*.

Around 1415, quite late in the period, a scholar producing a concordance for Wycliffe's translation of the Bible commented on the lexical variation and diversity of spelling:

> In Englisch as in Latyn, ben wordes synonemus, that is to seie, manie wordis betokenynge [meaning] oo [one] thing, as *kirk* & *churche*, *clepe* & *calle*, *yive* & *give*, *bigyle* & *deceyve* & *defraude*. And sumtyme suche wordis varyen or diversen al oonly in oo lettre, as *flax* & *flex*, *invie* & *envie*, *lomb* & *lamb*. (Kuhn, 1968, p. 271)

One curious confusion was caused by the ancient runic character called 'thorn' and written þ which we briefly encountered in chapter 2. This symbolized those sounds which we now represent by *th*, so that A-S *þisse* was the old form of *this* and *þreo* was the ancestor of *three*. As written in Anglo-Saxon manuscripts it looked appropriately like a thorn, with a long vertical stroke and a small angular wedge at its top. However, as it was phased out in Middle English in favour of 'th', scribes became less familiar with the character and it started to be written more like a *y*, a practice which was carried over into printing by William Caxton and his successor, Wynkyn de Worde.[6] It finally survived as an erroneous form of *y* in the word *ye*, properly meaning *the*, still preserved in the quaintly archaic style *Ye Olde Tea Shoppe* and other similarly named institutions which seek to trade on the traditions of the past.

Another interesting area of confusion which occurred in the transition from Old to Middle English, after the demise of the West-Saxon scribal tradition and before spelling again became fixed, concerned the article 'a' (then *an*) and words beginning with a vowel or an 'n'. Thus the Old English for 'an adder' was *an nædre*, but it was later mistakenly thought to be *an ædre* through wrong division, and the error became institutionalized. Other examples of common words are:

A-S nædre	⇒	adder
ME nompere	⇒	umpire
ME norange	⇒	orange

ME napron	⇒	apron
A-S eft	⇒	newt
ME eke name	⇒	nickname

These kinds of mistakes are quite understandable when people are not literate or when a spelling tradition breaks down. As we can see, the mistakes occurred in both directions, the *n* being added to some words and taken away from others. We shall return to the matter of diversity in our discussion of dialects.

The main lexical feature, the French influx, continued throughout the period. During this time there was, naturally, some demographic change. By the end of the reign of Henry II, there had been something of a merging of the two peoples: the *Dialogus de Scaccario*, written in 1177, comments on a shift in this respect: 'Now that the English and Normans have been dwelling together, marrying and giving in marriage, the two nations have become so mixed that it is scarcely possible today, speaking of free men, to tell who is English, who of Norman race' (Sheard, 1954, p. 203).

Some French words were borrowed twice, in different forms: the Norman-French terms brought over as a result of the Conquest were in time joined by **doublets** from Central or Parisian French, which was establishing itself as the standard. (Doublets are etymological twins which have pursued different phonetic routes.)

catch	chase
cattle	chattle
wage	gage
warden	guardian
warranty	guarantee
reward	regard
launch	lance

The semantic difference between several of these pairs is striking. The shift of meaning between *catch* and *chase* is substantial (and crucial for the participants). That between *cattle* and *chattle* shows the development of a quite different notion of property, while those between other pairs, such as *reward* and *regard*, *launch* and *lance* are equally notable. These remind us of the steady shifts of meaning undergone by the same words in different speech communities, as we shall see in our discussion in chapter 6 of British and American English. Other changes in the list are marginal (e.g. *warranty/guarantee*). The first two instances also remind us of the Norse origins of the Normans, since they have the same velar characteristic seen in Norse *kirk* as against Saxon *church*, etc. Here the initial consonant in the Norman form is velar, while the Central or Parisian equivalent is palatal.

Naturally, the great Norman-French lexical influx took centuries to complete, as the native population familiarized itself with the alien terms. During this time there grew up the habit of pairing a French word with the native synonym as a form of glossing. The practice is seen in 'cherité þat is luve'; 'desperaunce þet is unhope'; 'lecherie þet is golnesse'; 'ignoraunce þet is unwisdom', examples from the *Ancrene Riwle*, 'The Rule of Recluses' written *c*.1220. Chaucer uses a similar method in his *Prologue* when he writes that the lordly, idle Monk objected to having to 'swinken with his handes and laboure' (line 186), and that the Franklin, a noted *bon viveur*, insisted on his sauces being 'poynant and sharp' (line 352).

Chaucer and the creative use of registers

The pre-eminent exponent of the varieties of Middle English was Geoffrey Chaucer (*c*.1340–1400). Although he was born the son of a vintner, Chaucer spent most of his life in or around the courts of Edward III and Richard II. He travelled to Europe on various diplomatic missions and probably met Petrarch and Boccaccio, whose works influenced him. Yet as he developed as a writer, Chaucer moved further away from continental models, preferring to draw on his extensive human experience as a senior civil servant and to explore the potential of English. He was uniquely qualified both as a sociolinguistic observer and a stylist to create a diversity of literary worlds.

The old cliché describing Chaucer as 'the father of English literature' is manifestly untrue, both in its chauvinist assumptions of paternity and because (as we have partly seen) there was a great tradition of literature before him. But of all writers before Modern English, Chaucer is the one author who certainly exploited the vocabulary in all its richness. Centuries before the appearance of the first dictionary, the whole gamut of registers, from the most rarefied intellectual terms to the most vulgar and obscene, is to be found in his work. In terms of Murray's diagram of varieties, the whole diversity of the lexis is in Chaucer. A small sample includes *maat*, an Arabic word meaning 'dead' or 'defeated' (the second element of *checkmate*), *dulcarnoun*, 'a puzzle', many technical terms, such as *solsticium*, *declinacioun*, *orizonte*, *emysperies* and *almykanteras* from his 'Treatise on the Astrolabe'. We find the full range of so-called 'Anglo-Saxon' four-letter words: *ferte, erse, pisse, shiten, queynte* and *swive*, meaning 'to copulate', which predates the arrival of *fuck* around 1500, and which thrived from the Middle Ages onwards before suffering a curious demise around the death of Queen Victoria. His use of dialect we shall discuss later. There is also a wonderful range of demotic ejaculations, such as *tee hee!*, *owgh!*, *ha ha!* and *weilalwei!* (the last from Anglo-Saxon). Many of these are blasphemous, such as *bi cokkes bones* ('by God's bones!') gruesomely evoking the agony of the Crucifixion. The drunken gamblers in the *Pardoner's Tale* supply a whole hideous lexicon of this idiom:

> 'By Goddes precious herte,' and 'By his nayles,'
> And 'By the blood of Christ that is in Hayles' [as a holy relic]
> Sevene is my chaunce, and thyn is cynk and treye!' [five and three]

This variety of profanity astonishes us because we think of the Middle Ages as a period of strict ecclesiastic control and censorship.[7] In fact, Henry VIII of England was the first European monarch to limit the freedom of expression by publishing a list of banned books in 1529. Yet as we read the *Miller's Tale* and the *Wife of Bath's Prologue*, we have the sense of hearing the authentic uncensored ring of everyday speech. Chaucer's achievement is the more remarkable when we recall that he was a great poet working in complicated verse forms. The first commoner to be buried in Westminster Abbey, he was praised by his peers, both English and European, as 'a noble rethor' ('a fine rhetorician') and 'the first finder of our fair language' (Hoccleve).

The older view that Chaucer was a great innovator in the introduction of French words is now questioned. Generally speaking, the proportion of French borrowings in his work averages out at about 12 per cent (Serjeantson 1935, pp. 149–50), which is rather less than his contemporaries John Lydgate and William Langland. Nor is the famous view of Dryden (1700) that 'from Chaucer the purity of the English tongue began' entirely true.[8] For Chaucer's linguistic subtlety, apparent in so many creative ways, is seen in his telling juxtaposition of registers in the portraits which make up that remarkable cavalcade, the pilgrims described in the *General Prologue* to the *Canterbury Tales*. Chaucer deploys special concentrations of the word-stock with revealing pointedness. In describing the professional figures, like the Doctor and the Sergeant at Law, he fills the portraits with the special jargon of their callings in the form of a façade which seems impressive but hides an undeniable rapacity. The same is true of the devious Merchant.

But his creative ingenuity goes further. Thus the crude, cunning and resolutely unsophisticated Miller is created, not simply defined, in all his sheer oafish physicality through a remarkable massing of ancient, earthy, animalistic Saxon and Norse words, which in the following extract are italicized:

> *The Millere was a* stout *carl for the nones;*
> *Ful byg he was of* brawn, *and eek of bones,*
> *That proved well, for over al ther he cam*
> *At wrastlynge he wolde have alwey the ram.*
> *He was short-sholdred, brood, a thikke knarre.*

> *Ther nas no dore he nolde heve of harre,*
> *Or breke it at a rennyng with his heed.*
>
> (lines 545–52)

The Miller is made up of almost 100 per cent 'local content', lexically speaking. Even the two French borrowings, *stout* and *brawn*, do not stand out as obvious aliens, but harmonize with the knotted and gnarled native word-stock.

His antitype among the pilgrims takes the form of the Prioress, an absurdly affected and worldly nun created out of French clichés, entirely appropriate to an aspiring *grande dame* of the Church, more concerned with style than content:

> And sikerly she was of greet *desport*,
> And ful *plesaunt* and *amyable* of *port*,
> And *peyned* hire to *countrefete cheere*
> Of *court*, and to been *estatliche* of *manere*,
> And to ben holden *digne* of *reverence*.
> But, for to speken of hire *conscience*,
> She was so *charitable* and so *pitous*
> She wolde wepe, if that she saugh a mous
> Kaught in trappe, if it were deed or bledde.
>
> (lines 137–45)

Here the proportion of French terms rises to well over 30 per cent, if we exclude the last two lines, where there is a calculated anticlimax or bathetic descent from the language of religion to the trivial sentimentality of weeping over a dead mouse. The concentration of Gallic terms is especially ironic, since by the 1390s French was no longer the language of power, but was somewhat *passé*.[9] Madame Eglentine, whose name is more suited to that of a lady in a French romance than an English nun, has studiously cultivated a parochial but useless form of the language spoken only in England:

> And Frenssh she spak ful faire and fetisly [punctiliously]
> After the scole of Stratford atte Bowe
> For Frenssh of Parys was to hire unknowe.
>
> (lines 124–6)

In the lexical context of these two portraits, Chaucer's ideal Knight gains added moral and verbal significance, since it is a balanced blend of Saxon solidity and French courtliness. His key qualities are:

> Trouthe and *honoure* fredom and *courteisie*
>
> (line 46)

The magical verse romance, *Sir Gawayne and the Grene Knight*, uses an appropriately high proportion of French terms (around 20 per cent), in keeping with its courtly content. On the other hand, another of Chaucer's notable contemporaries, William Langland, whose satire in *Piers Plowman* was more bitter, has some caustic observations on the pretentious use of French, for example, by those who insist on their food being

> *chaud* and *plus chaud* for chilling of hir mawe [stomach].
> (Passus B, VI 313)

But Langland also mobilizes low diction to show his contempt for the idle monk who apes the aristocracy

> with an hepe of houndes at his erse, as he a lorde were.
> (Passus C, VI 161)

An even more powerful use of the low register is found in Chaucer's resounding four-letter word in his portrait of the ideal Parson, in which he registers his protest against corrupt clergy:

> And shame it is, if a preest take keep [take note],
> A shiten shepherde and a clene sheep.
> (lines 503–4)

Making a similar comment on the charlatanism of the effeminate Pardoner, the Miller uses equally coarse language:

> I wolde I hadde thy coillons [balls] in my hond. . . .
> They shull be shryned in an hogges toord!
> (lines 952–5)

The high and the low

Chaucer has many surprisingly modern qualities, not least among which are his psychological insight, his irony, which was recognized only from the mid-nineteenth century, his use of the **persona** or 'mask' assumed for narrative purposes, and an extraordinary awareness of **idiolect**, or specially individuated language which defines and reveals character through speech. *The Canterbury Tales* is a *tour de force* of this creativity. In this masterpiece we find tales with concentrations of courtly diction (the Knight and the Franklin), the colloquial and the obscene (the Miller and the Wife of Bath), the sermonizingly religious (the Parson), the archaic (Chaucer himself), the scientific and tech-nical (the Doctor and the Canon's Yeoman), the foreign (the Clerk), and one remarkable juxtaposition of all these varieties (the Nun's Priest). This virtuoso performance applies all the rhetorical tropes to a trivial farmyard episode in a mock-serious fashion, but combines passages of herb-lore, of heraldic magnificence, of dense philosophical jargon, of epic similes and vigorous couplings.

Yet this description is slightly schematic, since many of the narratives carry lexical surprises. The Miller's own tale, parodying the elevated courtly romance of the Knight, is a crude celebration of the physical which almost ostentiously parades all the taboo terms: *queynte* ('cunt'), *swyve* ('fuck'), *pisse*, *fart*, *ers* and *toute* ('arse'). Yet, surprisingly it also contains outrageous parodies of the Song of Songs, introduced when an admirer of the adulterous young wife (who is making love to her student lodger) propositions her *sotto voce*:

> 'What do ye, hony-comb, sweete Alisoun,
> My faire bryd, my sweete cynamome?'
> (lines 3698–9)

Likewise, the Wife of Bath refers to her genitalia with an exuberant range of register: the coyly euphemistic *thinge*, the directly taboo *queynte*, the stylishly French *bele chose* and the pseudo-scholarly *quoniam*.

The term *Chaucerian* now implies coarse vitality and that which is ribald, risqué or 'naughty', qualities which would certainly surprise his admiring con-temporaries, and derive largely from equating Chaucer the author with his creations. That aside, the author seemingly equates low language and class in the phrase 'cherles termes' (used in the *Reeve's Prologue*, line 3917). He like-wise apologizes in advance for the crudity of the Miller's tale by saying that the teller is a *cherl* and told a 'cherles tale'.[10] Yet those who use obscene language in their tales, namely the Miller, Reeve, Wife of Bath, Merchant, Friar and Sum-moner, are not 'churls' in the social sense, but show rather a moral crudity or a desire to shock.

However, it is important to realize that the coarse and even the obscene parts of the lexis then thrived literally in the street. *Cunt* is first recorded *c*.1230 in the startling London street name *Gropecuntlane*. (It was later changed to *Magpie Lane.*) *Shitteborowlane* was a London street name recorded in 1272, before it was euphemized to *Sherbourne*. There were numerous *Pissing Alleys* and a certain period of time was commonly termed a *pissing while*.[11] Similarly, the *dandelion* with its French heraldic assocations in 'dent du lion', has a coarser English name *pissabed*, given on account of the flower's diuretic qual-ities. Crude country names for the heron were *shitepoke* and *shiterow*. A certain

Randulphus acquired *c.*1202 the soubriquet *Scitebroc* ('the Shit-breech') and in the same period *shit-worde* was a common term for low language. Most amazing is the rural name of the windhover, glorified in Hopkins's poem, namely the *windfucker*. Common sayings of the medieval period are 'A drunken cunt needs no porter' and 'Every man thinks that his fart be sweet.' Something worthless was typically 'not worth a fart'. Even in our 'liberated' modern times, such currency is no longer given to common things.

Semantic change

Chaucer is unique among his contemporaries in being explicitly aware that language, its conventions and idioms change with time:

> Ye knowe ek [also] that in forme of speeche is chaunge
> Withinne a thousand yeer, and wordes tho [then]
> That hadden pris, now wonder nyce and straunge
> Us thinketh them.
>
> ['. . . and words which previously had prestige, now seem odd and unfamiliar to us'.]
>
> (*Troilus and Criseyde*, Book II, lines 21–4)

He is also adept at making semantic points with the subtlety we associate with Shakespeare and modern authors. For as we read the *Prologue*, we become aware, not just of the revealing deployment of different word-stocks, but of the pointed way Chaucer uses certain key ethical terms which were then at a semantic crossroads to illustrate the differing values of his pilgrims. For example, *worthy* is used five times of the *verray parfit gentil Knight* ('the genuine perfect noble knight') with apparent sincerity, but is elsewhere applied with invariable irony. Similarly *bisynesse*, *profit* and *winne* are used in both neutral and materialistic senses of different pilgrims. For instance, *winne* is used of the Knight in the traditional sense of achieving victory: ˙

> At Alisaundre [Alexandria] he was when it was *wonne* [taken].
> (line 51)

However, a quite different capitalist sense is starting to emerge. The rapacious Doctor profits from the human disaster of the Black Death:

> He kepte that he *wan* in pestilence [made out of the Plague].
> (line 442)

and he has a cynically efficient arrangement with 'hise apothecaries' whereby

> ech of hem made oother for to *wynne* [profit].
>> (line 427)

The Pardoner seeks 'To *winne* silver' by his hellfire sermons and 'over the top' hard-sell techniques:

> Myne handes and my tonge goon so yerne [energetically]
> That it is joye to se my bisynesse.
>> (*Pardoner's Tale*, lines 398–9)

Here *bisynesse* has the major sense of 'hyperactivity', but also anticipates 'stage business'. The Parson, by contrast, leads a life of virtuous diligence:

> To drawen folk to hevene by fairnesse [a beautiful example]
> By good ensample, that was his *bisynesse* [preoccupation].
>> (lines 519–20)

The traditional use of the term *profit* was found in medieval English in the phrase *the common profit*, i.e. the general good or the common weal. However, the modern sense of 'private profit' or 'making a profit' is pointedly applied by Chaucer to the materialistic ecclesiastics, such as the Friar (in line 249).

This technique of self-consciously making the reader aware of the different play of semantic nuance is frequently apparent in Chaucer's text. To take but one example, at the end of the *Knight's Tale*, the tragic death of the young knight Arcite is lamented by the victim in these poignant words:

> 'What is this worlde? What asketh men to have?
> Now with his love, now in his colde grave
> Allone, withouten any compaignye.'
>> (lines 2777–9)

However, within a few minutes, according to the illusion of the text, as the Miller's following tale of cynical adultery starts to unfold, his philandering 'hero' Nicholas is described in the very same terms:

> A chambre hadde he in that hostelrye
> Allone, withouten any compaignye.
>> (lines 3203–4)

In the first context the line enhances the terrible isolation of death, while in the second *compaignye* takes on a more cynical sexual sense.

Chaucer is also the first author to comment explicitly on linguistic affectation, of people changing their style of speech for some motive, usually for profit or self-advancement. Thus his avaricious Friar is a practised seducer who chats up would-be female clients:

> Somwhat he lipsed, for his wantownese,
> To make his English sweete upon his tonge;
> ['He lisped a little, out of affectation,
> To sweeten his English on his tongue;']
>   (lines 264–5)

This interesting comment shows that the lisp was not seen as a speech defect, but as an affected attempt to be charming. The Prioress sings the divine service

> Entuned in hir nose ful semely
> ['Intoning it in her nose most becomingly']
>   (line 123)

The rapacious Pardoner, a fourteenth-century spiritual confidence trickster, eagerly anticipates the opportunity of a lucrative sermon:

> He moste preche and affile his tonge
> To wynne silver, as he ful wel koude;
> ['He would preach and polish his tongue
> To make money, as well he knew how.']
>   (lines 712–13)

Middle English dialects

Since English had been supplanted as the language of power, it was left largely to its own devices, with the result that notions of a standard or a 'correct' form started to dissolve. By the end of the Old English period the West Saxon dialect had been used as the written standard all over the land. Although in the years immediately after the Conquest English was used for royal proclamations, it was soon supplanted by Latin and Anglo-Norman.

In the fourteenth century John of Trevisa wrote simply of 'Southeron, Northeron and Myddle speche' (Strang, 1974, p. 160). The dialect distribution of Middle English was more complicated than that of Anglo-Saxon times and can be said to have a traditional description and a revised version. In the tra-

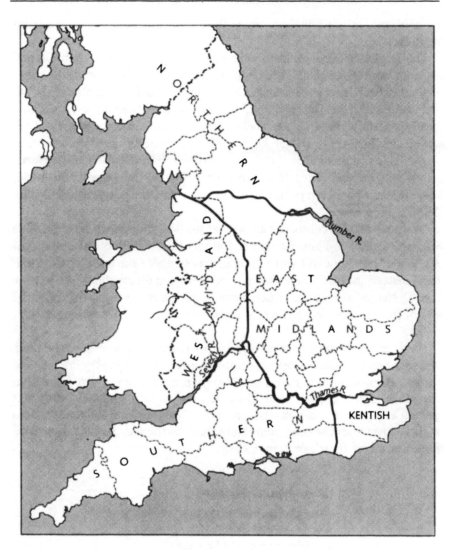

Figure 3.2 Middle English dialects

ditional description the broad varieties derived from Anglo-Saxon naturally continued, but are categorized under different names. If we compare figure 3.2, showing the spread of Middle English dialects, with figure 2.4, depicting the disposition of their Anglo-Saxon predecessors, we see these clear continuities: Kentish has become South Eastern, West Saxon has become Southern and Northumbrian has become Northern. However, there has been one major change: Mercian has split into East Midland and West Midland, reflecting the developments in the Danelaw, where Old Norse has become the dominant language.

This is the traditional picture, but research, notably by Angus McIntosh and his team working on the Middle English Dialect Survey, has shown the situation to be much more complicated, although the main features dividing north and south still hold. The traditional method of distinguishing a dialect is to specify certain features of the spelling, sounds, grammar, vocabulary, idiom and so on which are characteristic of it. The methodology used in the revised version is to concentrate on spelling and graphic features alone, and to focus on a limited number of key items in manuscripts from the period 1350–1450. These findings have been published in the *Linguistic Atlas of Late Middle English* (1986).

McIntosh and his colleagues found that particular items which are held to be characteristic of a given dialect commonly turned out not to be restricted to a limited area, but will also appear in areas outside the traditional boundaries. Instead they found a 'complex of overlapping distributions' (1986, vol. 1, p. 4). Nevertheless, the traditional configuration is still used, mainly for the sake of convenience. See, in this respect, Milroy (1992, p. 160) and Lass (1992, p. 34).

Some Middle English texts exist in manuscripts written all over the land. One such was the dour fourteenth-century moral poem called *The Prick of Conscience*, which survives in over a hundred manuscripts, amazingly more than any other Middle English poem. In them the various regional features of spelling and grammar are clearly apparent. If we take four different versions of three lines from the poem and relate them to the four regions they came from, we can see these variations clearly.

1 *South-West (Devonshire)*

He schal saye thanne ry3t to cristene man
Was neuer non be-fore his tyme be-gan
Bote falsly crist he wol hym calle

2 *Northern*

He sall say yat na right cristen man
Was neuer be-fore yis tyme began
Bot fals anticristes he sall yaim call

3 *Eastern (South Lincolnshire)*

He shal seie þat no cristene man
Was bifore þat his tyme began
And falce cristene he shal hem calle

4 *Southern (Wiltshire)*

He schal seiþ þt no cristen man
Neuere by fore hys tyme by-ganne
Bote false antecristes he schal hym kalle.

In these twenty-odd words we can see a surprising number of marked regional
variants. Some of these are derived from the altered meaning of the text, but
most relate to spelling and grammar. A number of basic words like *shall*, *before*,
false and *say* have marked differences. We note that thorn (þ) is starting to be
confused with *y*: the Northern manuscript has *yat* for *þat*. More significantly,
this text has *yaim* (for *þaim*, the ancestor of *them*) whereas all the other texts have
the older forms beginning with 'h'. It also has *sall*, whereas the rest have forms of
shall. The South-Western text, uniquely, has a double negative (in *neuer non*).

However, most Middle English manuscripts are unique or are found in few
versions. Their place of origin can be detected by their dialect. *Sir Gawain and
the Green Knight* exists only as Cotton Nero X and has strong features of the
northern part of the West Midland area. William Langland's *Piers Plowman*
exists in many manuscripts but derives from the southern part of the West
Midland area. Although these two locales are only about a hundred miles
apart, the two varieties are very distinct.

Chaucer was also the first author to exploit dialect differences in a creative
fashion. In the *Reeve's Tale*, a dirty story of low cunning and farcical bed-
hopping in the Cambridgeshire fens, two university students seek to gull a
shrewd and proverbially dishonest miller who has been taking advantage of
the illness of their manciple or college bursar. With sharply ironic misapplica-
tion of courtly terms, the Reeve, a master of theft himself, comments on the
rapacious miller of his tale:

> . . . therbiforn he stal but curteisly
> But now he was a theef outrageously.
> (lines 3997–8)

Stressing their northern dialect, the two students (John and Alayn) pretend to
be a couple of country bumpkins. In the following extract the northern forms
and uses are glossed in square brackets:

> 'Oure manciple, I hope [expect] he wil be deed
> Swa werkes [so ache] ay the wanges [molars] in his heed
> And forthy is I [therefore am I] come, and eek Alayn
> To grinde oure corn and carie it ham [home] agayn.'
> (lines 4029–32)

In the speech of John and Alayn we note that the Southern forms (*home, goes, both*) representing the sound 'oh', are replaced by *ham, gas, bathe*, representing the sound 'ah' which is the descendant of the Anglo-Saxon long vowel and is still heard in the north in forms like *hame* for 'home' and *bane* for 'bone'. Chaucer clearly exaggerates this feature in places for comic effect, as when John declares:

> I is ful wight, God waat, as is a raa.
> ['I am as vigorous, God knows, as is a roe']
> (line 4086)

The Scandinavian influence emanating from the Danelaw affected not only the core vocabulary but some basic grammatical forms, discussed briefly in chapter 2. Thus in every aspect the forms of the language are being diversified. The point is perhaps most simply illustrated by the comparison of the basic pronouns:

Modern	**I**	**she**	**they**
Northern	Hi	scho	þai
E Midland	Ic/hic	hoe	he
W Midland	I	hue	heo/ha
Southern	Ich/Ihc	he/heo/ho	hie/ho/heo

As we can see immediately, there was a lot of confusion and overlapping of the 'she' and 'they' pronouns in the East Midland, West Midland and Southern dialects. This, no doubt, explains the initial acceptability and subsequent dominance of the Northern forms deriving from Old Norse, the ancestors of 'she' and 'they', which spread southwards from the Danelaw and have subsequently become standard. They had the essential advantage of not being ambiguous. See the map of the forms of 'she' in Bloomfield and Newmark (1963, p. 221).

When we look at the usage of Chaucer, who came from Kent but lived most of his life in London, we find that he has adopted some, but not all of the Scandinavian forms.

Modern	**I**	**she**	**her**	**they**	**their**	**them**	**are**
Chaucer	I, ic	she	hire	they	hire	hem	ben

This shows that not all the Scandinavian forms which were to become standard had yet filtered through to the south-east.

The Re-establishment of English

The lifetime of Chaucer (c.1340–1400) saw a major shift in the linguistic balance of power in the land as English started to reassert itself. The first signs were attempts to maintain French artificially by prescription and by threat. Such desperate remedies are a sure indication that a language is falling out of use. A fourteenth-century statute required the students at Oxford to construe and translate in both French and English 'lest the French language be entirely disused'; similar prescriptions by various Oxford colleges (Exeter in 1322, Oriel in 1326) proscribed the use of English in student conversation. A parliamentary decree of 1332 required the aristocracy 'to teach their children the French language that they might be more able and better equipped in their wards' (Baugh, 1965, pp. 165–6). Nevertheless, in 1362 the Chancellor opened Parliament for the first time with a speech in English, and in the same year the *Statute of Pleading* required that thenceforth all legal procedings were to be in English, because of the 'great mischiefs' ('serious abuses') occurring as a consequence of incomprehension of the French language in the law courts. In 1399, when Henry Bolingbroke ascended the throne as Henry IV, he was the first English-speaking king of England since Edward the Confessor. His predecessor, it should be remembered, was called Richard of Bordeaux, in honour of his birthplace.

The re-establishment of English as the official language did not mean that English terms were reinstated for public functions. It would not have been practical or reasonable to resuscitate, for example, the Anglo-Saxon *witengemot* in place of *parliament*, the established term, since it had fallen out of use. The same was true of many such archaic words. In fact, the process accelerated the borrowings from French into those many areas where English had acquired semantic vacuums. This is another explanation for the point discussed earlier about the period of maximum borrowing from French.

These changes in the statute book and in the courts were significant, but took time to take full effect: 'Law French' continued in use until it was finally abolished in 1731. An interesting insight into the problems of bilingual education had been given by Ranulph Higden, a monk in the Benedectine abbey of Chester, in his *Polychronicon*, a vast history of the world in Latin (c.1327). He had complained that:

> This apayrynge [corruption] of þe burþe tunge is bycause of tweie þinges; oon is for children in scole aȝenst þe vsage and maner of alle oþere naciouns beeþ compelled for to leue hire [their] owne langage, and for to construe hir lessouns and here þinges in Frenshe, and so þey haueþ seþ [since] the Normans come first in

to Engelond. (*Polychronicon* II. 159, in the version of Trevisa, cited in Baugh, 1965, p. 179)

Higden concedes that French still retains some prestige: 'vplondisshe men wil liken hym self to gentil men and fondeþ wiþ greet besyness for to speke Frensce, for to be more i-tolde of' ('country bumpkins will ape the nobility and with foolish affectation pretend to speak French, in order to be thought of more highly'). But when John of Trevisa came to translate this passage over half a century later, he added the observation that things had changed somewhat by then (1385), though not entirely for the better:

in alle þe gramere scoles of Engelond, children leueþ Frensche and construeþ and lerneþ in Englische. . . . here [their] auauntage is, þat þey lerneþ her gramer in lasse tyme þan children were i-woned to do [used to]; disauauntage is þat now children of gramer scole conneþ [know] na more Frensche þan can hir lift heele [their left heel does]. . . . Also gentil men [the nobility] haueþ now moche i-left for [have largely stopped] to teche here children Frensche. (*Polychronicon* II. 159, in Baugh, 1965, p. 179)

We notice that Trevisa uses a considerable proportion of French and Latin terms, such as the earlier forms of *school, usage, manner, nations, compelled, language, advantage* and *gentle*, though in most cases the spelling reflects a French pronunciation.

The change from Middle to Early Modern English was broadly achieved by about 1500. If we compare the works of Chaucer, Langland and Lydgate, all of whom wrote in the late fourteenth century, with Malory a century later, we can see the change clearly. It seems best to use prose extracts, since the special conventions and diction of poetry tend to complicate comparisons. In the following relatively straightforward passage from Chaucer (*c*.1390) we can get only the gist of the passage, being constantly aware of the obstacles of spelling, grammar and semantic change. Lexically there are concentrations of classical terms (which are italicized):

Thy name is Melibee, that is to seyn [say], 'a man that drinketh hony.' Thou hast ydronke [drunk] so muchel hony of sweete *temporeel richesses*, and *delices* and *honours* of this world, that thou are dronken and hast forgeten Jhesu Crist thy *creatour*. Thou ne hast nat doon hym swich [such] *honour* and *reverence* as thee oughte, ne thou ne hast nat wel ytaken kep [taken care] to the wordes of Ovide, that seith, 'Under the hony of the goodes of the body is hyd the *venym* [venom] that sleeth the soule.' (The Tale of Melibee, in Robinson, 1957, p. 178)

However, in Malory's *Mort Darthur* (*c*.1485), the language of the moving lament for Lancelot is markedly more familiar to us. Lexically it has less classical content, since Malory is celebrating an ancient tradition of heroism, the lion in the battle-field and the lamb in the hall:

> 'Ah Sir Launcelot,' he said, 'thou were head of all Christian knights, and now I dare say,' said Sir Ector, 'thou Sir Launcelot, there thou liest, that thou were never matched of earthly knight's hand. And thou were the *courteoust* knight that ever bare shield. And thou were the truest friend to thy lover that ever bestrad [straddled] horse. And thou were the truest lover of a sinful man that ever loved woman. And thou were the kindest man that ever struck with sword. And thou were the goodliest person that ever came among *press* [concentration] of knights. And thou was the meekest man and the *gentlest* that ever ate in hall among ladies. And thou were the sternest knight to thy *mortal* foe that ever put spear in the *rest*.' (Book XXI, chapter 13)

This is in the version published by William Caxton, the first printer in England, who set up his press in Westminster in 1476. Though Caxton was essentially an editor rather than an author, his influence on the language has been such that he is regarded as the pivotal figure between Middle English and Early Modern English. One of the reasons that the Malory passage seems so modern is because of Caxton's editing. The contemporary Winchester manuscript of Malory's masterpiece is virtually identical in wording, but has older spellings such as *hede, Crysten, erthely, lovar, jentyllest* and *curtest*, which is a most unfortunate version of *courteoust*.

The notion of a standard

Chaucer, in bidding farewell to the great work of his middle years, *Troilus and Criseyde*, showed his authorial apprehensiveness in sending his 'litel bok' out into an uncertain linguistic world:

> And for ther is so gret diversite
> In Englissch and in writyng of oure tonge,
> So prey I God that non myswrite the,
> Ne the mysmetre for defaute of tonge.
> (Book V, lines 1793–6)

In the face the 'great diversite' of English, Chaucer prays that his text will not be wrongly transcribed ('myswrite'), nor have syllables wrongly added or taken away ('mysmetre'). But he makes no comments about what is considered right.

It is in John of Trevisa's translation of Ranulph Higden that we find one of the first pointedly adverse comments about regional differences in English. (We should bear in mind that Trevisa was a Cornishman who spent most of his working life as vicar of Berkeley in Gloucestershire):

> All the speech of the northerners, particularly at York, is so abrupt, piercing, harsh and outlandish ['scharp, slyttyng and unshape'], that we southerners can barely understand it. I believe this to be because they live near to strangers and foreigners with alien speech, and the kings of England always live far away from that region. . . . The reason why they keep to the south rather than to the north may be that the south has better arable land, more people, finer cities, and more profitable ports. (Nash, 1992, p. 7)

As Walter Nash (1992, p. 7) pertinently points out:

> Although this passage does not explicitly use the phrase 'the King's English', it strongly implies the concept. . . . The standard is where the king is; but the king is where he is for mainly economic reasons. Urban life, commerce and a high density of population, all have their influence on the location of the court, and the court has its influence in the shaping of a standard language.

The uniform format of print accentuated regional differences, which had seemed quite natural in the previous manuscript culture in that scribes wrote and spelt as the words sounded to them in their various parts of the land. Caxton articulated forcibly the problems of dealing with disparate forms in his famous prologue to the *Eneydos* (c.1490):

> And certaynly our langage now used varyeth ferre from that whiche was used and spoken when I was borne, for we Englysshemen ben borne under the domynacyon of the moone, which is never stedfaste, but ever waverynge: wexynge one season and waneth and dyscreaseth another season.
>
> And that comyn Englyssche that is spoken in one shyre varyeth from another. In so moche in that in my dayes happened that certayn marchauntes were in Tamyse [Thames] for to have sayled over the see into Zelande [Holland]. And for lacke of wynde thai taryed atte forlond [offshore] and wente to lande to refreshe them. And one of theym named Sheffelde, a mercer, came into an hows and axed [asked] for mete [food] and specially he axyd after eggys. And the goode wyf answerede that she coude speke no Frenshe. And the marchaunte was angry for he also coude speke no Frenshe, but he wolde have hadde egges; and she understoode hym not. And thenne at laste another sayd that he wolde have eyren; then the goode wyf sayd that she understood hym wel. Loo! what sholde a man in thyse dayes now write, 'egges' or 'eyren'? Certaynly it is harde to playse every man bycause of dyversitie and chaunge of langage.

Caxton's amusing anecdote shows both the problem and his frustration. The point of comic confusion is that *eggys* would have been more current in the north of England, *eyren* more common in the south. However, Caxton did not make it clear what he regarded as the standard. In terms of the larger lexical picture, he was generally fairly conservative, preferring established words. We note that the foreign terms are more common in the opening paragraph, namely *certaynly, langage, used, varyeth, domynacyon, season, dyscreaseth* and *comyn*. The story itself if told in a plain register, the only foreign terms being *marchauntes, refreshe, mercer, specially* and *playse*. Norman Blake has noted that Caxton's 'own vocabulary was not very extensive and it appears that he did not go out of his way to enrich it. His own prose contains few examples of first occurrences in English' (1973, p. 32).

Caxton also contributed to the bourgeois notion of 'language which is fit to print'. As we have seen earlier in this chapter, language we would regard as coarse and obscene thrived in common sayings and names. Although he made no overt comment about the propriety of such language in print, there are signs of Caxton's wielding the blue pencil. In the Winchester manuscript of Malory's *Mort Darthur* we read of the suffering of Lancelot as a truncheon is drawn out of his side: 'And [he] gave a great shriek and a grisly groan, so the blood burst out, nigh a pint at once, that at last he sank down upon his arse, and so swooned down, pale and deadly' (from 'The Fair Maid of Astolat', in *The Works of Sir Thomas Malory*, 1947, vol. III, p. 1074). In Caxton's version *arse* is edited out and the decent variant *buttocks* takes its place.

Caxton's successor at the press, Wynkyn de Worde, was less prudish, publishing in 1511 *The Demaundes Joyous* a collection of riddles, many of which were coarse:

QUESTION: What beast is it that hath the tail between her eyes?
ANSWER: It is the cat when she licketh her arse.
QUESTION: What time of the year bereth a goose most feathers?
ANSWER: When the gander is upon her back.
QUESTION: Which is the cleanliest occupation that is?
ANSWER: That is a dauber [plasterer]; for he may neither shite nor eat till he hath washed his hands.

(ed. Wardroper, 1976, pp. 19, 24, 22)

However, a comparison with the French source shows that de Worde or his compiler 'rejected a a great number of obscene and scatalogical riddles' (1976, p. 4).

Towards the end of the Middle English period, South-Eastern English, especially that around London, came to be regarded as the 'good' or 'proper' English. This development reflected the centralization of authority in the capital. John H. Fisher has shown that 'The dialect that came to serve as a new written standard was that of London, the political and economic centre of the country' (1974, p. 81). (The same forces promoted Parisian French and Castilian Spanish.) An important factor in this development was the rise of the London Chancery standard, an official 'house style' used by scribes for bureaucratic functions such as proclamations. These documents show increasing standardization of spelling. However, as we shall see in the following chapter, it was in Tudor and Elizabethan times the notion of a correct or Standard English – an essential feature of the modern language – started to develop clearly.

Latin and the lexical balance

Much of the previous discussion has focused on the interplay between French and English, since Middle English is very much concerned with the initial dominance of French, its establishment as the language of power and prestige and its subsequent displacement by English as the official language.

However, Latin continued to be the language of the Church, of the law and of administration. For Chaucer's dissolute Summoner, when in an alcoholic stupor, 'would speak no word but Latin', the language of the ecclesiastical court, incomprehensibly mouthing the phrase *questio quid iuris* ('What is the law [on this point]?'). The Prioress has engraved on her improperly ostentatious brooch the dictum *Amor vincit omnia* ('Love conquers all'), an ingenious ambiguity inviting the question of exactly what sort of love drives her. The simoniac Friar uses the solemn but meaningless tag *In principio* to dramatize his begging performances. The corrupt Pardoner uses as the seminal text for his pseudo-sermon the tag *radix malorum est cupiditas* ('covetousness is the root of all eivls'). The Parson's genuine but grimly comprehensive sermon on the Seven Deadly Sins is set out with Latin headings. These instances show that Latin had a genuine, almost mystical power.

Langland's *Piers Plowman* is full of scriptural quotations in Latin, such as *Non reddas malum pro malo* ('Do not repay evil with evil' (Passus B. VI 59)). These stand out against his generally plain Saxon register:

> In an hot hervest whenne y hadde myn hele [health]
> And lymes [limbs] to labory with, and loved wel fare
> And no dede to do but to drynke and slepe.
> (Passus C. VI 7–9)

Yet the language was genuinely current. In places Langland switches from English to Latin and back again in a single line:

> *Non de solo* y sayde, 'for sothe *vivit homo*
> *Nec in pane et in pabulo*; the *pater noster* witnesseth.'
> (Passus C. VI 87–8)

Some authors were trilingual. John Gower's *Confessio Amantis* ('The Confessions of a Lover') is actually written in English; his *Vox Clamantis* is in Latin, and his *Miroure de l'Omme* is in French. Translation was not a one-way process. The *Ancrenne Wisse* was written first in English in the early thirteenth century for a community of nuns in Herefordshire: it was soon translated into French and into Latin. Later in the period, scholars like John of Trevisa spent most of their lives translating Latin works into English. There were also anonymous 'macaronic' lyrics, so termed because they were written in both Latin and English: these ingenious works date from the thirteenth century, while as late as the fifteenth some lyrics are written in Latin, French and English.[12]

Throughout the period, therefore, Latin words continued to be absorbed. Some of these have retained their alien inflections, like *gratis, alias, abacus, incubus, genius, prima facie, et cetera, memento* and *limbo*, which is not so with earlier borrowings like *cheese, wine, pound* and *inch*. But thousands show assimilation, like *abject, allegory, frustrate, history, homicide, innumerable, malefactor, polite, scripture, solar* and *superabundance*. Such words came in from many sources. For example, John Wycliffe, an ardent reformer of the Church, insisted that Holy Writ should be available in the vernacular, and produced his translation of the Bible *c.*1388. Yet 'Wycliffe and his associates are credited with more than a thousand Latin words not previously found in English' (Dellit, 1905, p. 38, cited in Baugh, 1965, p. 222).

The growth in Latinate lexical content is apparent in Chaucer and Gower, and the tendency increases in the fifteenth century. This reaches its zenith in a self-consciously rarefied Latinized poetic diction often used in poems praising the Virgin Mary. In Chaucer's *Prioress's Tale*, written *c.*1390, we find such words as *sapience* ('wisdom') and *benygnytee* ('generosity'). But about a hundred years later, William Dunbar's 'Ballad of Our Lady' has a remarkable concentration of such diction. (The foreign words are italicized):

> Haile! *sterne superne*. Haile! in *eterne*,
>   In Godis sicht to schyne.
> *Lucerne* in derne, for to *discerne*
>   Be *glory* and *grace divyne*;
> *Hodiern, modern, sempitern*;
>   *Angelicall regine* . . .

> *Empirce* of *pris, imperatrice,*
> Bricht, *polist, precious* stane;
> *Victrice* of *vice,* hie *genetrice*
> Of Jesu, Lord *soverayne*;
> *Oratrice, mediatrice, salvatrice*
> To God gret *suffragene.*
> *Ave! Maria, gracia plena*
> *Haile! sterne, meridiane . . .*

(lines 1–22)

This kind of extremely rarefied diction is called **aureate**, itself a high-register work for *golden*, probably coined by John Lydgate (*c.*1370–1450). The context of worship is vital, since the aureate words are used like precious gems celebrating the Virgin in an emblematic verbal art-form like an icon. The style should not be condemned as simply artificial, bookish and ostentatious, even though many of these words have not survived. (The notable exception is *modern*, used here for the first recorded time.) However, historically aureate diction represents the highest proportion of classical borrowing (57 per cent in this extract) ever achieved in English literary history.

The major lexical consequence of the steady infiltration and assimilation of Latin words was that by the end of the Middle English period the language had acquired synonyms on three levels in virtually all semantic fields:

Anglo-Saxon	Norman French	Latin/Greek
rise	mount	ascend
help	aid	assistance
fair	beautiful	attractive
book	volume	text
foe	enemy	adversary

There are many such examples, some of which are set out in our opening chapter (p. 5). The Latin influx meant that the proportion of native content as against borrowed elements changed steadily through the Middle English period. In Early Middle English it is estimated that the lexicon consisted of 91.5 per cent native content; by later Middle English this proportion had fallen to 78.8 per cent (Dekeyser 1986, in Blake (ed.), 1992, p. 432). Nevertheless, this is still a high proportion.

This shift brings us to the theme of our next chapter, the great efflorescence of the vocabulary as a consequence of printing, and the various tensions generated by this lexical expansion through borrowing.

Notes

1 A very different view was expressed a century ago by the Professor of Modern History at Oxford, E. A. Freeman, in *The Norman Conquest* V. 247: 'This abiding corruption of our language I believe to have been the one result of the Norman Conquest which has been purely evil.'

2 One must always distinguish between words, things and institutions, and bear in mind the comment of A. C. Baugh: 'Much nonsense has been written on the relative merits of the Teutonic and Romance elements in the English vocabulary' (1951, p. 225).

3 This matter is taken up in chapter 4, pp. 220 ff.

4 A full treatment of medieval hunting practice is to be found in John Cummins's study, *The Hound and the Hawk* (1988).

5 See, however, Robert Burchfield's comments in his study *The English Language* (1985), p. 18.

6 Caxton did not have the character for 'thorn' in his fonts, having learnt the art of printing on the Continent and imported his equipment.

7 A fuller treatment of profanity in Chaucer is to be found in my study *Swearing* (1991).

8 Alexander Gill took the eccentric opposite view: 'Up to this point foreign words were unheard of in the English language, but then about the year 1400, Geoffrey Chaucer, star of ill-omen, rendered his poetry notorious by the use of Latin and French words' (*Logonomia Anglica* (1619) Part II, p. 84).

9 When visiting the English court in 1395, Jean Froissart registered surprise at the currency of French there.

10 This suggests that *cerl* was losing or had lost its old social sense in A–S *ceorl* and was acquiring its moral sense, which still survives in *churlish*.

11 Langland uses a shocking liturgical variant when Gluttony 'pissed in a potel a *pater noster* while' (Passus B. V 348).

12 Here is the beginning of a trilingual fifteenth-century lyric:

> A celuy que pluys eyme en mounde,
> Of alle tho that I have founde
> Carissima.

('To the one I love most in the world, most dear of all those that I have found.')

4

THE LEXICAL EXPANSION OF THE RENAISSANCE: EXUBERANCE AND RESTRAINT

Our language is improued aboue all others now spoken by any nation, and become the fairest, the nimblest, the fullest; most apt to vary the phrase, most ready to receive good composition, most adorned with sweet words and sentences, with witty quips and over-ruling Prouerbes: yea, able to expresse any conceit whatsoeuer with great dexterity, weighty in weighty matters, merry in merry, braue in braue.

William de L'Isle, preface to *A Saxon Treatise* (1623).

The linguistic environment of the Renaissance was characterized by the qualities of exuberance, expansion, experiment, exploration, individualism, above all a creative excitement, even a ferment. This great humanist movement is rightly seen as a rebirth or rejuvenation (although the term *renaissance* was coined only in the mid-nineteenth century in relation to this period). These positive attitudes and characteristics strike us as being clean contrary to the modernist perception of society and language as being in a state of exhaustion or decline, articulated, for example, by T. S. Eliot.

Interestingly, this 'rebirth' was achieved by renewed contact with the ancient classical culture of the west by means of a technical innovation. The primary factor which proved the catalyst for this growth was the introduction of printing into England. William Caxton had set up his press in Westminster in 1476, but his successor, Wynkyn de Worde, who took over the business in 1491, was so active and successful that by the time he died in 1534 he had published some 800 books, an amazing achievement, considering the laborious technology of early printing. Many of these were translations of classical works. So rapid was the increase in the rate of printing during the Renaissance that over 20,000 titles had appeared in English by 1640. It is hard for us now to recapture that excitement, encapsulated in the anecdote (related by George Steiner) of the great humanist scholar, Desiderius Erasmus, who 'bent down in a muddy lane ecstatically when his eye lit upon a scrap of print, so new was

146

the miracle of the printed page' (1969, p. 46). We now tend to associate print with T. S. Eliot's image of 'newspapers in vacant lots', part of what is old and discarded, the detritus of modern urban squalor.

The main features of Early Modern English which concern us were a rapidly expanding vocabulary, the growing notion of a standard form of the language and increased grammatical flexibility in words. As one can see, these developments worked against each other, some in the direction of change, others towards stability or fixity, and this led to conflict. Printing played two opposing roles. It helped stabilize spelling and thus encouraged the development of the notion of a standard. But it also became the vehicle for great lexical expansion, since words no longer travelled with peoples, individuals or in manuscripts, but were broadcast in first editions.

New words entering the language from classical and overseas origins became widely debated, so that the state of the language, especially the structure of the lexis, became for the first time the object of controversy. In vigorous exchanges attitudes of national pride, chauvinism and xenophobia became strongly apparent. Printing undoubtedly gave writers a new sense of power, deriving from the great circulations now attainable, so that controversialists started to stretch the semantic parameters of words. This became a period of contention in which words were used as weapons: long words were wielded like clubs; others like rapiers. High register was juxtaposed with low to great effect. New words were often made up extempore in the heat of battle.

The period saw the first prescriptions of a standard located in the vicinity of the capital, and the first 'traditional' dictionary was published in 1604. This was a rudimentary work explaining 'hard words' or difficult classical terms. However, 'canting' dictionaries, recording the cruder and less stable energies of underground argot had started to appear fifty years earlier. This initial lexicographical division, between standard works explicating 'correct' usage and those focusing on 'substandard', 'coarse' or 'slang' usage, continued for centuries, as we shall see in the following chapter.

These two styles, the literary and the demotic, were not then as far separated socially as might be supposed. To use the analogy of fashion, the image of Queen Elizabeth is that of a brilliant icon (to whom everybody knelt) and that of her courtiers is likewise quintessentially elegant, in their brocade doublets, their ruffs, their hose exhibiting their shapely legs, their dainty high-heeled shoes and their flamboyant codpieces. But Elizabeth, although a courtly and diplomatic woman, also 'swore like a man' and made coarse jokes (Hughes, 1991, p. 103). King James's correspondence with his favourite Buckingham contained four-letter words.[1] Yet laws against swearing were instituted in 1606, mainly to try to curb the practice on the stage. Even more amazing was the resurgence of 'flyting', or elaborately crude swearing matches in which the fine art of savage insult was exhibited (mainly in the north) by notable Scots poets such as Dunbar and Kennedy, King James V and Sir David Lindsay. Though these scurrilous and scatalogical tirades may originally have been delivered extempore, they became literary works.

Two very different publications gave the language a new status, authority and sense of recognition throughout the land. These were *The Book of Common Prayer* (1549) and the The Authorized Version of the Bible commissioned by King James, published in 1611 and still the preferred choice in many churches.

The major literary development was the great efflorescence of the drama, which became the vehicle for the whole diversity of registers, from the abstrusely classical, the foreign, the 'diction of common life', as Dr Johnson was to call it, regional and dialect forms, as well as bawdy. However, censorship came with the institution by the ill-named Master of the Revels in 1574, since plays had to be read aloud for his approval or censorship before staging. Consequently, bawdy was no longer open, as it had been in Middle English, but was increasingly conveyed through word-play, a thriving mode of the times.

Let us return to some of the themes mentioned in our overview. In terms of spelling, the problems of diversity were reduced but not entirely solved by the coming of printing. Shakespeare famously spelt his own name several ways, and Queen Elizabeth, a great scholar in her own right, used many phonetic, seemingly illiterate renditions of common words, for example *offen, hed, ment, frend, wiche, yt, cosin* and *Godz*. She finishes a letter to Lord Burghley in 1572 with an interesting word division: she writes that the letter can serve as a warrant since it is 'all written with my none hand'. C. L. Barber gives a similar example as late as 1693, taken from Scripture: 'This is my nowne sone, in whome I take delighte' (1972, p. 201). The form *ye* was erroneously used for *the* up to the mid-seventeenth century: Lady Catherine Dyer, in her epitaph for her husband (1641) writes:

> Mine eyes wax heavy and ye day growes cold.
> (line 11)

Thus our modern linguistic state, in which a word has a stable form, had yet to be reached.

As we noted in chapter 1 in the section 'Words as Mobile Forms' (pp. 17–18), the steady erosion of inflections which had taken place in Middle English meant that words were no longer bound to particular grammatical categories, but were free to be used in various ways. Thus a word like *champion*, which had been a noun since the thirteenth century, was used as a verb for the first time by Shakespeare in *Macbeth* (1605): 'Come Fate, and champion me to the utterance' (III. i. 71). This process is termed **conversion** or 'zero derivation', a more opaque formulation which means that the new word does not derive from a separate root. One fruitful source was words ending in Latin *-atus*, originally the inflexion of the past participle of the verb. Thus when Macbeth speaks of his 'initiate fear' he means 'that which has just begun' (III. iv. 142). In time such words began to be used as verbs in the way we now use *initiate*, for example, *generate* and *speculate*. Other forms of conversion can be be seen in the following line from *King Lear* (1605), in which Lear denounces his daughter Cordelia for publicly embarrassing him, rejecting her as

> **Dowered** with our curse and **strangered** with our oath.
> (I. i. 203)

Here *dowry* and *stranger* have for the first time been converted into verbs, with powerful dramatic and ironic effect. While neologisms are technically achievable at any stage of the language, conversion became possible only after the loss of grammatical inflections. Prior to that, words were limited to particular functions. Thus if Shakespeare had lived in the Middle Ages, he would not have been able to convert words from one function to another as he did with such remarkable facility and invention.

Let us turn to the growing notion of a standard. About a century after Caxton's querulous comments about the diversity of English, George Puttenham included in his major study, *The Arte of English Poesie* (1589), a most important chapter in Book III, 'Of Language'. Unlike most of his predecessors, Puttenham was prescriptive in selecting the preferred variety, that which was 'natural, pure and the most vsuall of all this countrey'. His prescription was for a variety of Southern English: 'ye shall therefore take the vsuall speach of the Court, and that of London and the shires lying about London within lx. [sixty] myles, and not much aboue' (1869, p. 157). This has proved remarkably enduring, in that South-Eastern English is still broadly regarded as the standard. Puttenham was also quite proscriptive about the varieties of English which the poet should avoid, articulating views similar to those expressed by Thomas Wilson before him, as we shall see. These were archaisms and regional forms:

> Our maker [poet] therfore at these days shall not follow *Piers plowman* nor *Gower* nor *Lydgate* nor yet *Chaucer*, for their language is now out of vse with vs: neither shall he take the termes of Northern-men, such as they vse in dayly talke,

whether they be noble men or gentle-men, or of their best clarkes, all is a matter:
nor in effect any speach vsed beyond the river of Trent, though no man can deny
but that theirs is the purer English Saxon at this day, yet it is not so Courtly nor
so currant as our Southerne English is, no more is the far Westerne mans speach
... (1869, pp. 156–7)

The concession that Northern English is the truer successor of 'English Saxon'
is unusual for its time. But Puttenham is equally prescriptive about the preferred social dialect:

neither shall he follow the speach of a craftes man or carter, or other of the infe-
riour sort, though he be inhabitant or bred in the best towne and Citie in this
Realme, for such persons doe abuse good speaches, by strange accents or ill
shapen soundes, and false ortographie. But he shall follow generally the better
brought vp sort. (Cited in Barber, 1976, p. 38)

Although Puttenham claims that 'we are already ruled by th'English Dictionaries and other bookes written by learned men' (1869, p. 157), there were
as yet no dictionaries in the modern sense of the term. The first of these was
Robert Cawdrey's *Table Alphabeticall of Hard Vsual English Words*, published
in 1604. Indeed, the first dictionaries of any sort were, somewhat ironically,
canting dictionaries dealing with underworld slang, and they were surprisingly numerous. Among these works were Thomas Harman's *A Caveat or
Warening for Commen Cursetors vvlgarely called vagabones* (1567) and Robert
Greene's *Notable Discovery of Coosnage. Now daily practised by sundry lewd
persons, called Connie-catchers, and Crosse-biters* (1591). Some of these authors
had considerable literary reputations, but nevertheless publicized the varieties
of underground language, the argot of the criminal classes. We shall discuss
these various works in greater detail in the following chapter in the section
'A Short History of the Dictionary' (pp. 248–75).

However, a number of authoritative works had recently appeared, attesting
to the new identity of the English language. Puttenham would probably be
referring to works such as Thomas Wilson's *The Arte of Rhetorique* (1553),
John Hart's more quaintly titled study, *An Orthographie, conteyning the due order
and reason, howe to write or paint thimage of mannes voice, most like to the life and
nature* (1569), William Bullokar's eponymous study *Bullokar's Booke at Large,
for the Amendment of Orthographie for English speech* (1580) and Richard Mulcaster's *Elementarie* or *The first Part of the Elementarie, which entreteth chefelie of
the right Writing of our English Tung* (1582). As their titles suggest, these were
essentially prescriptive works concerned principally with orthography or
correct spelling.

Nevertheless, regional varieties were increasingly publicized. In his *Henry V* (1599), Shakespeare juxtaposes the major national dialects in the figures of Fluellen the Welshman, Jamy the Scotsman and Macmorris the Irishman. In a play which has considerable chauvinist, even triumphalist *élan* in its glorification of the famous English victory over the French at Agincourt, these fiercely competitive British nationalisms strike a slightly discordant note. Although the stage presences are sometimes rendered comic in their dialectal speech, they bristle with ancient regional loyalties and hostilities to the spreading authority of England and English.

English was already expanding into the 'New World', with outposts being established in America, the Caribbean and West Africa. We shall trace the lexical consequences of this expansion in chapter 6.

The expanding vocabulary and the Inkhorn Controversy

As was mentioned in the opening overview, the expansion of the vocabulary came from two major sources: the classical languages and what was called 'oversea' language. The first source was the result of the intellectual enquiry of the Renaissance; the second was the consequence of England becoming a major maritime power. This commercial expansion resulted in foreign borrowings from various European languages, although the words often came from more distant roots.

Thus from French came such naval, military and other words as *pioneer* (1523), *brigantine* (1525), *colonel* (1548), *machine* (1549), *gauze* (1561), *volley* (1573), *cartridge* (1579), *rendezvous* (1591), and such artistic words as *rondeau* (1525), *scene* (1540), *grotesque* (1561) and *hautboy* (1575; literally 'high wood', the predecessor of the *oboe*).

The Spanish influx was also rich, including general terms such as *galleon* (1529), *armada* (1533), *cannibal* (1533), *negro* (1555), *potato* (1565), *tornado* (1566), *cask* (1557), *renegade* (1583), *comrade* (1591), *anchovy* (1596), *sherry* (1597), *banana* (1597), *spade* (in cards; 1598), *booby* (1599) and *bravado* (1599).

From Italian came such general words as *artichoke* (1531), *artisan* (1538), *ballot* (1549), *carnival* (1549), *partisan* (1555), *magnifico* (1573), *signor* (1577) and *mountebank* (1577). More military are *pistol* (1550), *cavalier* (1560), *squadron* (1562), *bandolier* (1577), *escort* (1579) and *musket* (1587). The great literary and artistic influence of Italy is shown in such borrowings as *sonnet* (1577), *pastel* (1578), *stanza* (1588), *canto* (1590), *madrigal* (1588), *fugue* (1597) and the theatre words *buffoon* (1594) and *zany* (1588). Virtually the whole specialized vocabulary of architecture comes from Italian. Thus *cornice*, *frieze* and *pedestal* date from 1563, when they appeared in Shute's *Architecture*.

They were followed by *pilaster* (1575), *piazza* (1583) and *stucco* (1598). Two etymological curiosities are *milliner* (1529) from *Milan* and *pall-mall* (1568), originally a game played in an alley (the present *Pall-Mall* dates from 1656).

This brief survey gives us a sense of the flavour and range of the borrowings, but how does one put a number on the volume? It is now possible to quantify the actual expansion of the vocabulary by means of the *Chronological English Dictionary* (*CED*) (1970). In this most useful resource, the data of the *Shorter Oxford English Dictionary* (*SOED*) is rearranged on the basis of linear time, instead of the traditional random system of the alphabet. The annual increment of new words and meanings is recorded in annals. Since the *CED* is based on the *SOED* and not on the compendious *OED*, it does not give the whole lexical picture. And it must now be conceded that even the *OED* has been shown to be less than completely reliable in recording the huge lexical influx of the Renaissance. Students should note, in this respect, Jurgen Schäfer's major study, *Documentation and the OED: Shakespeare and Nashe as Test Cases* (1980). However, against these objections it should be noted that many of the first usages listed in the *OED* have a short life, and the *SOED* in the nature of things, records those which have become established in the language.

These qualifications aside, the *CED* shows that in the course of a mere century, the annual increment of new words and meanings rose some sevenfold, from an average increment of about fifty in 1500 to an astonishing peak of approximately 350 in 1600; thereafter the rate of increase shows a decline. These developments are represented graphically in figure 4.1.

In a valuable article, 'Shakespeare's Classical Neologisms', (1982, in Salmon (ed.), 1987, pp. 207–28) Bryan A. Garner tabulates the number of neologisms from 1500 to 1649 in twenty-year segments:

1500–1519	1104
1520–1539	2704
1540–1559	2955
1560–1579	3341
1580–1599	5110
1600–1619	5192
1620–1639	2824
1640–1659	3717

Although Garner's data are taken straight from the *CED* and he does not distinguish between degrees of neologism, they show how the rate of increase rises sharply up to 1600–20 and then declines. A detailed analysis by the present writer shows that a high proportion of this huge influx comprised classical and foreign neologisms. For example, of the 2755 additions recorded in

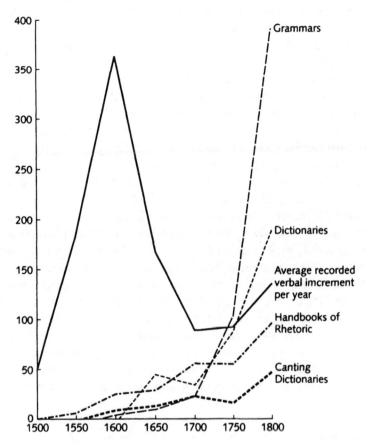

Figure 4.1 The expansion of vocabulary, dictionaries, etc.

the *CED* between 1600 and 1609, 38.5 per cent or 1063 are Latin or Greek in origin.

This wave of new words obviously caused some unbalance and stress in the linguistic economy and in the speech community, provoking comment and dispute as scholars and writers aligned themselves into factions which variously welcomed, rejected or cautiously accepted the verbal newcomers. This linguistic contretemps, or storm in an inkwell, is known in the history of the language as the Inkhorn Controversy. The participants have been categorized by Charles Barber in his excellent study, *Early Modern English*, as the Neologizers, the Purists and the Archaizers (1976, pp. 79–100). The harmlessly neutral inkhorn (used for carrying ink in powder form) was invoked as an emotive term of scorn to denigrate 'hard' or 'dark' words, as opaque or obscure neologisms were then termed. This usage is first recorded in the works of a noted polemicist, John Bale, in 1543, and is well exemplified by Puttenham in his *English Poesie* (1589) when he observed that '*irreuocable, irradiation, depopulation* and such like . . . were long time despised for inkehorne termes' (Bk II, ch. xii[i], 1869, p. 130).

Today innovation is regarded as a favourable quality, but in Elizabethan times *innovation* and *innovator* had essentially critical meanings denoting sinister subversion of the status quo. Thomas Norton, in *Calvin's Institutes* (1561) observes that 'A desire to innovate all things . . . moveth troublesome men,' while Richard Hooker records in his *Ecclesiastical Politie* (1597) that a certain person was traduced 'as an authour of suspitious innouation'. Indeed when the term *neologism* itself was coined, two centuries later, *c.*1800, it invariably invoked hostility: in 1841 Disraeli thundered against 'The vicious neologist, who debases the purity of English diction by affecting new words or phrases'.

The Purists vehemently rejected foreign borrowings as being alien contaminations which were in themselves *dark*, i.e. 'obscure', to native speakers. In this respect they had some right on their side, since, as we have seen, virtually all instances of malapropism involve the incorrect, ignorant use of classically derived terms. This foreign influx, they argued, if allowed to continue unchecked, would weaken the native linguistic economy and bankrupt it. Equally hostile to 'oversea' language or continental borrowings, they advanced chauvinist arguments of patriotic purity. It was during this ferment that the notion of 'the King's English' was first formulated, by Thomas Wilson in this polemical passage from his popular and comprehensive treatise, *Arte of Rhetorique* (1553):

Plaines [plainness] what it is
Emong al other lessons, this should first be learned, that we never affect any straunge [foreign] ynkehorne termes, but so speake as is commonly received, neither sekyng to be ouer fine, nor yet liuyng ouer carelesse, usyng our speache as most men do, & ordryng our wittes, as the fewest haue doen. Some seke so farre for outlandishe English, that thei forget altogether their mothers language. And I dare swere this, if some of their mothers were aliue, thei were not able to tell what they say: & yet these fine Englishe clerkes [scholars] wil saie thei speake in their mother tongue, if a man should charge them with counterfeityng the kynges English. Some farre jorneid jentlemen at their returne home, like as they loue to go in forrein apparell, so thei wil pouder their talke with oversea language. He that commeth lately out of France will talke Frenche English & neuer blushe at the matter. Another choppes in with Angleso Italiano [English Italienated]. (Book III, 1982, pp. 325–6)

Wilson's chauvinist tirade is one of the opening salvos in the Inkhorn Controversy. We notice how skilfully he plays off the 'home' Saxon register against the artifical and the foreign terms, making them sound stilted and pretentious: 'some farre jorneid jentlemen'; 'love to go in forrein apparell'; 'thei wil pouder their talke with oversea language'; 'talke Frenche English & neuer blushe'; 'another choppes in with Angleso Italiano.' Wilson's views were still considered sufficiently topical to be quoted (without acknowledgement) half a century later in the preface to Cawdrey's *Table Alphabeticall* in 1604. Another participant, Sir Thomas Chaloner, who translated Erasmus's *Praise of Folly* in 1549, weighed in with heavy sarcasm:

> Such men therfore, that in deede are archdoltes, and woulde be taken yet for sages and philosophers, maie I not aptlie calle theim fooleosophers? . . . to poudre theyr bokes with ynkehorne termes, although perchaunce as unaptly applied as a gold rynge in a sowes nose . . . and if they want suche farre fetched vocables, then serche they out of some rotten Pamphlet four or fyve disused woords of antiquitee therwith to darken the sence unto the reader . . . (Cited in Baugh, 1965, pp. 261–2)

The argument for linguistic patriotism was turned into a simple dogmatic precept by Sir George Gascoigne (1542–77): 'the most auncient English wordes are of one sillable, so that the more monasyllables that you use, the truer Englishman you shall seeme, and the lesse you shall smell of the Inkehorne' (cited in Hussey, 1982, p. 13). Undoubtedly the most extreme Purist was Sir John Cheke, who despite being the first Professor of Greek at Cambridge, strenuously opposed loan-words in a letter appended to Sir Philip Hoby's well-known translation of Castiglione's *The Courtier* (1561):

> I am of this opinion that our own tung should be written cleane and pure, vnmixt and vnmangeled with borowing of other tunges, wherein if we take not heed by tijm, euer borowing and neuer payeng, she shall fain to keep her house as bank-rupt.

We can see the awkwardness of Cheke's studied preference for the native term *tung* (in place of the classical equivalent *language*) and his attempted restoration of *cleane* to its old, general sense which would include 'pure'. Cheke's policy of exclusion of foreign terms was carried to extremes in his translation of St Matthew's Gospel, where he actually coined such quaint and unfamiliar native formations as *moond* for 'lunatic', *crossed* for 'crucified', *freschman* for 'proselyte', *foresayer* for 'prophet' and *gainrising* for 'resurrection'.[2]

The Neologizers, contrariwise, regarded the classical register as containing the embellishments of literary civilization, without which English would be impoverished. George Chapman, the distinguished translator of Homer, argued in his dedication to *Ovids Banquet of Sence* (1595) against plainness and simplicity: 'That Poesie should be as perviall ['clear'] as Oratorie, and plainnes her speciall ornament, were the plaine way to barbarisme.' Chapman's use of the odd nonce-word *pervial* shows his unashamed relish for the recherché term. An equally ironic instance is the scholarly Ben Jonson's prescription in *Discoveries* (1641) that 'the chief virtue of style is perspicuity' (by which inkhorn term he also meant 'clarity').

Whereas the Purists stigmatized foreign terms for being *dark*, the Neologizers regarded the state of the language without them as being *barbarous*, a key term in the controversy meaning 'Unpolished, without literary culture; pertaining to an illiterate people'. The first recorded quotation (from 1526) runs: 'My wytte is grosse . . . and my tonge very barbarouse.' Fascinatingly, this term which now means 'uncivilized' derives from a linguistic emphasis; the original meaning of *barbarism* was: 'the use of words or expressions not in accordance with the classical standard of a language'. This sense (recorded from 1579) soon extends to mean 'a foreign or non-classical word or idiom'. We shall find a similar emphasis in the sense of *barbarian*, discussed in the introduction to chapter 6.

Although the most memorable exchanges of the Inkhorn Controversy are the tirades of the extremists, there were notable moderates who preferred 'the middle way' of judicious borrowing. The most famous and discriminating was Sir Thomas Elyot, who in his treatise on education (a word he coined) called *The Boke of the Governour* (1531) introduced such neologisms as *dedicate, animate, encyclopaedia, frugality, metamorphosis, modesty, persist* and many others. He sensibly followed the practice established from Middle English of pairing neologisms with established words and phrases to make the newcomers comprehensible. Examples of this practice are: '*animate* and give courage'; '*education* or bringing vp of noble children'; '*persist* and continue'.

What makes Elyot virtually unique in his contentious times is his acute perception that to introduce a new term is to disturb an existing semantic field by displacing synonyms which are already established. We see his grasp of the problem in his justification for the introduction of *maturity*, 'wherevnto we lacke a name in englisshe':

> Wherefore I am constrained to vsurpe a latine worde callyng it *Maturitie*: whiche worde though it be strange and darke / yet . . . whan ones brought in custome / shall be as facile to vnderstande as other wordes late commen out of Italy and Fraunce / and made denizens amonge vs.
>
> *Maturum* in latine may be enterpreted ripe or ready: as frute / whan it is ripe / it is at the very poynte to be gathered and eaten. Therefore that worde maturitie is translated to the actis of man / that whan they be done with such moderation / that nothing in the doinge may be sene superfluous or indigent / we may saye / that they be maturely done: reseruyng the wordes ripe and ready

to frute and other thinges separate from affaires / as we have nowe in vsage. And this do I nowe remember for the necessary augmentation of our langage. (Cited in Barber, 1976, p. 80)

Fascinatingly, Elyot has described *in advance* the separation of registers which has, in fact, subsequently taken place between the native term *ripe* and the borrowed Latin word *maturity*. The borrowed term has acquired an abstract intellectual register, while the native term has moved into a more concrete physical register. Thus we would not speak of 'a ripe man' or 'a ripe judgement' any more than we would of 'a mature mango' or a 'a mature crop'. Caxton, however, had written half a century earlier of London children who 'at their ful rypyng' were 'chaff for the moste parte'.

Richard Mulcaster, Headmaster of Merchant Taylors' School and later of St Paul's, also a moderate and a utilitarian, wrote of the two motives for borrowing at a time of great lexical influx:

the latest terms which [the English language] boroweth daielie from foren tungs, either of pure necessitie in new matters, or of mere brauery [out of pure ostentation], to garnish itself withall. (Cited in Barber, 1976, p. 81).

Charles Barber has observed the shift in attitudes which occurred in the late sixteenth century: 'Before 1575, everybody agrees that English is barbarous; after 1580 there is a whole chorus of voices proclaiming that English is eloquent' (1976, pp. 76–7).

Where did the major Elizabethan authors align themselves in the Inkhorn Controversy? The answers are individual, not general. Just as they had quite different notions about human nature and about literary art, so they produced totally different kinds of language. Consequently, they took up quite different positions, more by example than via overt manifestos. Dr Johnson commented perceptively on how these authors in their different ways enriched the vocabulary and enlarged the capacities for expression:

If the language of theology were extracted from Hooker and the translation of the Bible; the terms of natural knowledge from Bacon; the phrases of policy, war and navigation from Raleigh; the dialect of poetry and fiction from Spenser and Sidney; and the diction of common life from Shakespeare, few ideas would be lost to mankind, for want of English words, in which they might be expressed. (Preface to his *Dictionary*, 1755)

We may not agree entirely with all of Johnson's emphases, for we shall find that Edmund Spenser (1552–99) used an archaic vocabulary for his *Faerie Queene* (1590–6), whereas Christopher Marlowe (1564–93) and John Milton

(1608–74) preferred a highly classical word-stock. Ben Jonson (1572–1637) wrote in both a classical vein and in a coarser, demotic, topical idiom. William Shakespeare (1564–1616) was the exponent of the greatest range of lexis. However, before dealing with the literary authors, it is valuable to study the different lexical modes used by other authors of the period in spiritual, religious, philosophical and polemical texts.

Lexical Variation in Elizabethan Prose

The period was noted for a number of major spiritual texts. The *Book of Common Prayer* (1549) was largely attributable to Archbishop Cranmer. In the midst of fierce liturgical and ritualistic differences the work set out, as it puts it in the preface, 'to keep the mean between the two extremes', since some 'be so addicted to their old customs' and again on the other side, some be so new-fangled, they would innovate all things'. Such strong language was entirely typical of the times: *new-fangled*, which we tend to think of as a modern formation, had been in use as a critical term since the time of Chaucer. As we noted in chapter 1 in relation to the Marriage Service, the *Book of Common Prayer* stays close to the lexical roots of the tongue. Here is one of many such instances, from the Burial of the Dead:

> Man that is born of a woman hath but a short time to live, and is full of misery. He cometh up, and is cut down, like a flower; he fleeth as it were a shadow, and never continueth in one stay.
> In the midst of life we are in death: of whom may we seek for succour, but of thee, O Lord, who for our sins art justly displeased?

Here *misery, continueth, justly, succour* and *displeased* are from French, but they have long been assimilated into the lexical core. Elsewhere are the movingly simple phrases 'O death, where is they sting? O grave, where is they victory' and 'Earth to earth, ashes to ashes, dust to dust, in sure and certain hope of the Resurrection to eternal life'.

In many ways more famous were two major translations of the Bible. The King James or Authorized Version (1611) has become one of the great monuments of English prose, combining sonority and simplicity in a potent fashion. The work was a remarkable example of collaboration, since it was the product of four committees which met in different parts of the land to carry out the command issued by King James in 1604. However, they were greatly assisted in their task by previous achievements, notably that of William Tyndale (*c.*1492–1536).

Like Wycliffe before him, Tyndale was fearlessly committed to reforming the Church and to translating the Bible into the vernacular as a form of spiritual liberation for the common people. Today the translation of the primary spiritual text into the vernaculars seems a self-evident priority, but at the time of the Reformation the availability of the Word of God was at the heart of the struggle between received or dogmatic authority and individual interpretation. Having received no support from the Bishop of London, Tyndale travelled to Germany, where his translation was published in 1525 in the face of vehement opposition in England, where it was actually banned.

Tyndale tersely rejected the usual arguments that English was unsuitable for translation in his treatise *The Obedience of a Christian Man* (1528): 'They will saye it can not be translated into oure tonge it is so rude. It is not so rude as they are false lyers' (in Barber, 1976, p. 71). He was arrested, imprisoned, tried, strangled and burnt at the stake in 1536. Some sense of the suppression of the possession of Holy Writ in print and in the mother tongue can be gauged from the proclamation of Henry VIII in 1546: 'From henceforth, no man, woman or person . . . shall have, take, or keep in his possession the text of the New Testament of Tyndale's or Coverdale's translation in English' (Foxe, 1732, V, p. 565).

A brief extract from the Parable of the Prodigal Son (St Luke 15: 11–17) in Tyndale's translation gives a sense of his work. The italicized words are of classical origin:

> And he sayde: a *certayne* man had two sonnes, and the yonger of them sayde to his father: father geve me my *parte* of the goodes that to me belongeth. And he *devided* unto them his *substance*. And not longe after, the yonger sonne gaddered all that he had to geder, and toke his *jorney* into a farre *countre*, and theare he *wasted* his goodes with *royetous* lyvinge. And when he had spent all that he had, ther arose a greate derth thorow out all the same londe, and he began to lacke. And he went and clave to a *citesyn* of that same *countre*, which sent him to his felde, to kepe his swyne. And he wold fayne have fylled his bely with the coddes that the swyne ate: and no man gave him.
>
> Then he came to him selfe and sayde: how many hyred *servauntes* at my fathers, have breed ynough, and I dye for honger.

Tyndale uses the lexical core of the language to the fullest possible extent, actually decreasing slightly the degree of foreign borrowing in comparison with the Wycliffite version produced in the fourteenth century. This is a natural part of his intention to reach the widest possible audience: only eleven out of the 158 words in the passage, or 7 per cent, are from Latin or French sources. In describing the extravagance and decadence of the Prodigal Son's lifestyle, he coins the arresting phrase *royetous living*, deriving from the old sense of OF *riot*, which was 'debauchery' or 'dissipation'.

The King James translators made liberal use of Tyndale's work, which by then had become an institution. Simeon Potter observes that 'One third of the King James Bible of 1611, it has been computed, is worded exactly as Tyndale left it' (1963, p. 53). We find, for instance, the replication of the phrases *took his journey into a far country, riotous liuing* and *when he came to himself*. They likewise drew extensively on the Anglo-Saxon core of the word-stock, although this leads to instances of semantic change (viewed from the modern perspective) such as: *falleth, farre* (country), *mighty* (famine), *ioyned* (*himself*).

Between these two works came another monument of Elizabethan prose, the theologian Richard Hooker's *Of the Lawes of Ecclesiastical Polity* (1593) a classic expression of the old medieval synthesis of natural and ecclesiastical law. In the passage which follows, Hooker describes what we would now regard as an ecological nightmare, the human consequences of a breakdown in the laws of nature:

> Now if *nature* should *intermit* her *course*, the leaue altogether, though it were but for a while, the *obseruation* of her own Lawes; if those *principall* and Mother *Elements* of the World whereof al things in this lower World are made, should lose the *qualities* which now they haue; if the frame of that Heauenly *Arch erected* ouer our heads should loosen and dissolue it selfe; if *Celestiall Spheres* should forget their wonted *Motions* and by *irregular volubilitite turne* themselues any way as it might happen; if the Prince of the Lights of Heauen, which now as a *Giant* doth run his vnwearied *course*, should as it were through a *languishing faintnesse* begin to stand and *rest* himselfe; if the Moone should wander from her beaten way, the times and *seasons* of the yeere blend themselves by *disordered* and *confused mixture*, the Winds breathe out their last gaspe, the Clouds yeeld no Raine, the Earth be *defeated* of heauenly *Influence*, the *Fruits* of the Earth pine away as Children at the withered brests of their Mother, no longer able to yeeld them *reliefe*; what would become of Man himselfe whom these things now doe all *serue*? (In Muir (ed.), 1956, p. 117)

Lexically Hooker combines the qualities of a solemn, elevated, religious tract with the plain style of a sermon. Thus the weighty high-register Latinizations like *intermit, observation, celestial spheres, irregular volubilitie, disordered and confused mixture* (which are italicized in the passage and which make up about 15 per cent of the total) are juxtaposed with the plainest terms. The main stylistic feature of the passage is its magnificent periodic sentence. This has a compendious Elizabethan quality, encapsulating in the microcosm of the syntactic structure the whole world-view of harmonious elements in the divinely ordained macrocosmic hierarchy and their relationship with the world of man.

Hooker's style of rhetorical elaboration using the classical register can be traced back to Cicero and forward through Milton, Johnson and Gibbon.

As we have partly seen, Elizabethan controversies were carried on in a robust personal style. A powerful example of a less academic tirade is Gabriel Harvey's portrait of Robert Greene (1592), a notoriously dissolute and scurrilous minor talent of the times. (Greene (1558–92) himself is the source of the first reference to Shakespeare as a dramatist, dismissing him in a curmugeonly fashion as 'an upstart crow beautified with our feathers . . . in his owne conceyt the onely shake-scene in a countrey'.)

> I was altogether vnacquainted with the man, & neuer once saluted him by name: but who in London hath not heard of his dissolute, and licentious liuing; his fonde disguisinge of a Master of Arte with ruffianly haire, vnseemely apparell, and more vnseemelye Company: his vaineglorious and Thrasonicall brauinge: his piperly Extemporizing, and Tarletonizing: his apishe counterfeiting of euery ridiculous and absurd toy: his fine coosening of Iuglers, and finer iugling with cooseners: hys villainous cogging, and foisting; his monstrous swearinge, and horrible forswearing; his impious profaning of sacred Textes; his other scandalous and blasphemous rauinge; his riotous and outragious surfeitinge; his continuall shifting of lodginges; his plausible musteringe, and banquetinge of roysterly acquiantaunce at his first comminge: his beggarly departing in euery hostisses debt; his infamous resorting to the Banckeside, Shorditch, Southwarke, and other filthy hauntes: his obscure lurkinge in basest corners. (In Muir (ed.), 1956, pp. 28–9)

Harvey relishes mixing pretentious classicism (as in *dissolute, licentious, unseemly, apparell, extemporizing*) with underground slang, the argot especially associated with Greene, such as *coosening, iugling, cogging* and *foisting*, which denote various kinds of cheating. (We shall encounter Greene's underground dictionaries in the following chapter.) By repeatedly using forms ending in *-ing* Harvey suggests Greene's habitual but diverse criminality. The phrase 'his vaineglorious and Thrasonicall brauing' ('his conceited and over-the-top posturing') carries an eponymous reference to Thraso, the character of a braggart soldier in the Roman comedian Terence's play *Eunuchus*. Against this the phrase 'his piperly Extemporizing and Tarletonizing' is typical of the polemical creativity of the time. *Piperly* and *Tarletonizing* are nonce-words, the first suggesting that Greene was a low-grade entertainer, the second that he was an imitator of Robert Tarleton, a famous comic actor and the favourite clown of Queen Elizabeth.

The capacity to juxtapose the high and the low word with wounding power or rhetorical persuasion is one of the hallmarks of Elizabethan lexis. Thus Sir Philip Sidney, perhaps the truest embodiment of the Renaissance man, criticizes the 'mungrel tragi-comedy' of the times, while Sir Thomas Overbury satirizes the hypercritical man in amusingly contemporary terms: 'London-bridge is the most terrible eyesore to him that can be' (in Dover Wilson, 1944, p. 203). Donald Lupton comments that actors 'are as crafty [skilful] with an old play as bawds [prostitutes] with old faces' (ibid., p. 210). Stephen Gosson notes that 'The ground-work of comedies is love, cozenage [deception] flattery, bawdry [filth], sly conveyance of whoredom,' whereas the response to tragedy is ignoble:

> The beholding of troubles and miserable slaughters that are in tragedies drive us to immoderate sorrow, heaviness, womanish weeping and mourning, whereby we become lovers of dumps [depression] and lamentation, both enemies of fortitude. (in Dover Wilson, 1944, pp. 205–6).

The new custom of smoking tobacco generated some notable responses. John Earle's description of a tobacco merchant contrasts registers in a superbly satirical fashion, contriving to end each clause with bathos: 'His shop is the rendezvous of spitting, where men dialogue with their noses, and their communication is smoke' (in Dover Wilson, 1944, p. 147). King James I's famous fulmination 'A Counterblast to Tobacco' (1604) warns the would-be smoker that he 'shall be filthily corrupted with an incurable stink', and finishes in the mode of a hellfire sermon:

> A custom loathsome to the eye, hateful to the nose, harmful to the brain, dangerous to the lungs, and in the black stinking fume thereof nearest resembling the horrible Stygian smoke of the pit that is bottomless. (in Dover Wilson, 1944, p. 149)

The vigour, extravagance and polemical power with which lexical resources were mustered in the Renaissance have probably never been surpassed. However, a prose stylist of a very different kind and intention was Francis Bacon, Baron Verulam and Viscount Saint Albans. (1561–1626), a great statesman (though he retired in disgrace), as well as a highly influential philosopher. Bacon was generally impatient with the current controversies about language, commenting acerbically in his major work, *The Advancement of Learning* (1605): 'Here therefore is the first distemper [abuse] of learning, when men study words and not matter' (1902, p. 191). In this comment, cited as the first Epigraph in this book, he was possibly giving a pointed riposte to Roger Ascham's contrary assertion: 'Ye know not, what hurt ye do to learning, that care not for wordes, but for matter' (*The Scholemaster*, 1582, cited in Blake, 1983, p. viii).

Around 1600 Ciceronian elaboration (splendidly crafted in Hooker) started to give way to the terse, succinct, epigrammatic but still balanced style of the Roman authors Seneca and Tacitus. This style was exemplified by Antony Bacon, brother of Francis, in his introduction to the first translation of Tacitus in 1591, where he advocated 'the most matter with the best conceyt [clearest thought] in the fewest words'. This style suited Francis Bacon perfectly. Ben Jonson, a man not given to idle praise, commented of his speech: 'No man ever spake more neatly, more pressly, more weightily, or suffered less idleness, in what he utter'd' (*Discoveries*, 1930, p. 37). We see the succinct style in virtually every sentence of the following essay, 'Of Studies' (1597):

> Studies serve for delight, for ornament, and for ability. Their chief use for delight, is in privateness and retiring; for ornament, is in discourse; and for ability, is in the judgment and disposition of business. For expert men can execute, and perhaps judge of particulars, one by one; but the general counsels, and the plots and marshalling of affairs, come best from those that are learned. To spend too much time in studies is sloth; to use them too much for ornament, is affectation; to make judgment wholly by their rules, is the humour of a scholar. They perfect nature, and are perfected by experience: for natural abilities are like natural plants, that need proyning [pruning] by study; and studies themselves do give forth directions too much at large, except they be bounded in by experience. Crafty [powerful] men contemn studies, simple men admire them, and wise men use them.

Lexically, Bacon does not confine himself to the Saxon vocabulary: rather he realizes the potent capacity for dignified abstraction in the classical register and uses it to great effect. If we analyse the passage, we find that out of 148 words, some 52, or a remarkable 35 per cent are classical borrowings. But they are not inkhorn terms. They are common classical words, which is why Bacon seems so modern, seems almost to have been writing a hundred years ago, not four hundred. Bacon becomes a model for the terse style taken up later by Thomas Hobbes in his own century and by Ernest Hemingway and George Orwell in this. He was also a pioneer in scientific thought and was intensely interested in the language of science, a theme which we shall explore a little later.

Almost at the opposite pole, stylistically and lexically, was Robert Burton's *The Anatomy of Melancholy* (1621). This too was a classic of its kind, a huge study of the condition which we would normally now call depression or melancholia. It is often regarded as one of the 'old books', that is, not an empirical view of human behaviour but a compendium crammed with folk-lore, old wives' tales, mumbo-jumbo and classical tags:

A most incomparable delight it is so to melancholize, and build castles in the air, to go smiling to themselves, acting an infinite variety of parts, which they suppose, and strongly imagine they represent, or that they see acted or done: *Bland[um] quidem ab initio*, saith *Lemnius*, to conceive and meditate of such pleasant things, sometimes, *Present, past or to come*, as *Rhasis* speaks. So delightsom these toyes are at first, they could spend whole days and nights without sleep, even whole yeers alone in such contemplations, and phantastical meditations, which are like unto dreams, and they will hardly be drawn from them, or willingly interrupt, so pleasant their vain conceits are, that they hinder their ordinary tasks and necessary business, they cannot address themselves to them, or almost to any study or imployment, these phantastical and bewitching thoughts so covertly, so feelingly, so urgently, so continually set upon, creep in, insinuate, possess, overcome, distract, and detain them, they cannot I say go about their more necessary business, stave off or extricate themselves, but are ever musing, melancholizing, and carried along, as he (they say) that is led round about an Heath with a *Puck* in the night, they run earnestly on in this labarinth of anxious and solicitous melancholy mediations. (In Ure (ed.), 1956, pp. 195–6)

Burton uses a great range of vocabulary, juxtaposing high-register words like *incomparable, phantastical, ruminate, melancholize* and *labarinth* with plain words like *toyes, things, stave off* and idioms like *build castles in the air*. In places he sounds like a thesaurus, bookishly setting out rows of synonyms, as in the observations that 'these phantasticall and bewitching thoughts . . . set upon, creep in, insinuate, possess, overcome, distract and detain them.' Although Burton writes about the condition and its symptoms in a suggestive fashion, he lacks the clarity and syntactical discipline of Bacon. His vast sentences have simply too many words, wandering, drifting, repeating, convoluting until they finally crawl to an exhausted conclusion.

Spenser

Before turning to the major dramatists of the period, we should consider one poet, Edmund Spenser (1552–99), who is remarkable for exploiting a special variety of lexis, namely the archaic. Spenser's masterpiece, *The Faerie Queene*, was written in the last decade of the sixteenth century. In it he sought to recreate the lost world of medieval chivalry and its traditions. Since the language had changed so fast over the previous two centuries, even Chaucer's work was not properly accessible to him, but he contrived, nevertheless, to imbue his poem with a medieval atmosphere by using a predominantly archaic vocabulary.

Although Spenser's work does have an antique air, in truth few of his notable archaisms are previously current English words. He coined *elfin, gride,* 'to pierce' and *bellibone*, 'a fair maid', from French *belle et bonne*; he also created two portmanteaux, namely *wrizzled* out of *wrinkled* and *grizzled*, and *scruze* out of *screw* and *squeeze*. But he misinterpreted *yond* to mean 'fierce' in Chaucer's line 'egre as is a Tygre yond in Ynde' ('fierce as is a tiger *far away* in India' in the *Clerk's Tale*, line 1134). Similarly, a number of amusing errors combined in the genesis of one of his most enduring phrases, *deeds of derring do*: Chaucer's original reference was to Troilus *dorrying don* ('daring to do'), which was subsequently misprinted as *derrynge do* and misinterpreted by Spenser as a compound noun, meaning 'daring action, chivalry'. This pseudo-archaism was resuscitated by Sir Walter Scott in *Ivanhoe* in 1820 as 'a deed of such derring-do', and has since become an old-fashioned literary cliché. His most notable coinage, *blatant*, is described with a sense of astonishment by the *OED* as 'apparently invented by Spenser' to describe a monster, 'the blatant beast'. For centuries the term meant 'loud, noisy, clamorous' (possibly from its supposed etymology in French *blattant*, meaning 'bleating' or 'crying'). Since about 1900 it has become established in its modern sense.

Contemporary judgements take very different views on the success of his enterprise. 'Spenser, in affecting the ancients, writ no language,' was the trenchant dismissal of Ben Jonson, while Sidney criticized him for 'framing his style to an old and mystic language'. Spenser's friend 'E.K.' (possibly Edward Kirke) used the kind of patriotic argument which we have witnessed in the Inkhorn Controversy: '[Spenser] laboured to restore, as to theyr rightfull heritage such good and naturall English words, as haue ben long time out of vse and almost cleane disherited.' (The same writer criticized those who have 'made our English tongue a gallimaufray or hodgepodge of all other speeches'. These comments come from the preface to *The Shepheardes Calendar*.)

The ironic circumstance that Spenser actually invented archaisms by what is technically catachresis or the erroneous use of words should not obscure the significant point that over time these words have become well established through currency. They clearly filled a semantic gap.

The Play's the Thing

Although there had been a long tradition of religious and morally edifying drama (termed respectively the miracle and morality plays) the first public playhouse in England was built only in 1576. This proved the catalyst for what Gamini Salgado has rightly called 'the greatest efflorescence of dramatic writing England has ever seen' (1980, p. 37). The conditions of the Elizabethan stage, though difficult to reconstruct with total accuracy now, were generally primitive. To compensate for these inadequacies, a whole new linguistic medium was created. On a bare stage with minimal properties and effects with which to build up a sense of theatrical illusion, the great dramatists, Shakespeare especially, created an extraordinary diversity of experience and range of characters exclusively through the medium of individuated language, worlds of words in which their creations could philosophize, agonize, laugh, suffer and die. In the following discussion we shall trace the lexical contributions and creativity of the three major dramatists of the time, Marlowe, Shakespeare and Jonson, especially in relation to classical borrowing, as the drama evolved.

Marlowe's mighty line

Shakespeare's great contemporary, Christopher Marlowe (1564–93), created in a short but brilliant *tour de force* of a career a whole new notion of character and style. Being a product of both King's School, Canterbury and Corpus Christi College, Cambridge, Marlowe had a natural propensity for the classical register. From 1587, when he introduced Tamburlaine, his first hero, without apology or compromise, as

> Threatening the world with high astounding terms,
> (Prologue, line 5)

greatness of speech became a *sine qua non* of the Elizabethan dramatic hero. The Prologue to *Tamburlaine the Great*, more an artistic manifesto, is immediately and openly derisive of the banal contemporary style of 'jigging veins of rhyming mother wits' (line 1). Marlowe's 'mighty line' (as Ben Jonson called it in the Shakespeare First Folio verses) was the perfect vehicle for the colossal ambitions of his hubristic heroes who tested the boundaries and shook the foundations of traditional order with nonchalant charisma. The ancient tomes of the Cambridge libraries flowered anew, generating potent classicisms in the most entrancing lines. Bookish vocabulary (italicized in the speeches below), studied inversion and artificial cadence are everywhere apparent in the magniloquent declamatory Marlovian style:

> *Nature*, that fram'd us of four *elements*,
> Warring within our souls for *regiment* [rule]
> Doth teach us all to have *aspiring* minds.
> Our souls, whose *faculties* can *comprehend*
> The *wondrous architecture* of the world,
> And *measure* every wandering *planet's course*,
> Still climbing after *knowledge infinite* . . .
> (*Tamburlaine*, Part I, II. vii. 18–24)

> Was this the face that launch'd a thousand ships,
> And burnt the topless towers of *Ilium?*
> > (*Dr Faustus*, V. i. 96–7)

> Cut is the branch that might have grown full straight,
> And burnèd is *Apollo's laurel* bough . . .
> > (V. iii. 1–2)

But at moments of ultimate crisis a plainer diction emerges for a moment:

> Why, this is hell, nor am I out of it . . .
> > (*Dr Faustus* I. ii. 76)

> Now, Faustus, hast thou one bare hour to live . . .
> > (V. ii. 132)

> My God, my God, look not so fierce upon me.
> > (V. ii. 185)

> O soul, be changèd into little water drops,
> And fall into the ocean, ne'er be found:
> > (V. ii. 183–4)

Yet the high register refuses to be entirely dislodged, as when Faustus seeks to escape his doom:

> You stars that *reigned* at my *nativity,*
> Whose *influence* hath *allotted* heaven and hell
> Now draw up Faustus like a foggy mist
> Into the *entrails* of yon *labouring* cloud.
> > (*Dr Faustus*, V. ii. 155–8)

> See, see, where Christ's blood streams in the *firmament!*
> > (V. ii. 144)

Marlowe's style was as original as his heroic conception, and epitomized the excitement, exploration and experiment of the Renaissance. As Roma Gill has put it well, 'The proud-paced verse of *Tamburlaine* stormed the English stage' (1967, p. xi). However, as the elevated medium for the epic drama of a mono-maniac, even for the self-styled 'Scourge of God and Terror of the World,' it contained an inherent predictability in diction which invited ultimate monotony. It was, no doubt, the uncritical preference for polysyllabic classicism over blunt Saxon which lay behind Ben Jonson's satirical comments about the current fashion for 'foot-and-half-foot words' in the prologue to *Everyman in His Humour* (acted in 1598, with Shakespeare in the cast). He also coined the amusingly grotesque form *un-in-one-breath-utterable.* In this play, we are pointedly told, artificial diction and far-fetched action will be eschewed for 'deeds and language such as men do use' (line 21).

Furthermore, Marlowe's vocabulary, for all its resonant impact, is seldom original in a strict sense. Like Milton, he creates a magnificently sonorous 'organ voice' out of a predominantly classical word-stock, but he is not remarkably innovative in terms of verbal creation or borrowing. Arresting words in the previously quoted extracts, such as *regiment, faculties, architecture, topless, nativity, entrails* and *firmament* impress us because we do not expect to hear them on the stage, except, perhaps, from a formal figure like a Prologue. But most of them had been in the language for at least a century. Of this list only *topless* is a Marlovian coinage, a suitably original form expressive of boundless ambition. A detailed study of *Tamburlaine*, Part I, yields a sample of just over a dozen neologisms. They are mainly high-register forms such as *excruciate, pro-rex, retorqued* and *valurous*, or foreign borrowings, such as *carbonadoes, basso* and *ebon*, reflecting the themes of power and opulence. Several are only technical neologisms, qualifiying by virtue of prefixes or suffixes. They include: *engirt, fleshless, lustless, resistless, reflexing, royalise* and *unaffrighted*. However, *incensed* and *cheer up* anticipate the first recorded instances in the *OED*.

The classical component

The old academic controversy concerning the rival claims of Shakespeare and Marlowe to the authorship of Shakespeare's work could have been dispensed with had the participants focused more closely on lexical and stylistic analysis of the 'rival' authors, especially on the degree of the classical component. This is notably higher in Marlowe than in Shakespeare, who had 'small Latin and lesse Greeke', according to Jonson's account of his education in the First Folio verses. Indeed, the old debate derived in large measure from the snobbish assumption that someone with Shakespeare's limited education could not have produced his magnificent works.

Although he was able to exploit the classical register with remarkable effect, Shakespeare does not intimidate his audience with a Marlovian profusion of classical names. For example, *Ilium* and *Apollo*, natural elements of Marlowe's idiom, figure little in Shakespeare's text. In the whole Shakespearean canon there are only two references each to Aurora, Cynthia, Gorgon and Styx, and only single references to Charon, Hermes and Atlas. Often a tactful paraphrase is preferred to Marlowe's thunderous name-dropping: thus Charon is alluded to as 'that grim ferryman which poets write of' (*Richard III*, I. iv. 46). Indeed, where classical allusions do appear, it is usually in satirical or comic contexts (IV. 76). An early and unsubtle use is Bottom's rant in 'Ercles' vein' in *A Midsummer Night's Dream* (1594–6):

> And Phibbus' car
> Shall shine from far
> And make and mar
> The foolish Fates.
> (I. ii. 38–41)

A more developed overblown style is used in the Player's speech and in 'The Murder of Gonzago', the play within the play in *Hamlet* (1603–5):

> Full thirty times hath Phoebus's cart gone round
> Neptune's salt wash and Tellus' orbèd ground . . .
> Since love our hearts, and Hymen did our hands,
> Unite commutual in most sacred bands.
> (III. ii. 145–50)

This kind of inflated, turgid or inappropriately lofty language attracted two contemporary labels, namely *bombast* and *fustian*; both terms were originally applied to material, *fustian* being a coarse, thick cloth, *bombast* cotton wool or padding. Thomas Nashe satirized in 1589 'the swelling bumbast of a bragging blanke verse', while Marlowe himself has a clown in *Dr Faustus* complain that the hero 'speaks Dutch fustian' (IV. 76). The Player's speech in *Hamlet* (II. ii) is an excellent example of *bombast* or *fustian*.

A typically revealing contrast between Shakespeare and Marlowe is to be found in the references to Pythagoras in these two passages:

> Ah, Pythagoras' *metempsychosis* – were that true,
> This soul should fly from me, and I be changed
> Unto some brutish beast.
> (*Dr Faustus*, V. ii. 172–4)

Even in his desperate straits, Faustus' 'scholarism' remains part of his mind-set, so that 'Pythagoras' *metempsychosis*' (the doctrine of the transmigration of souls) is not only mentioned in this dire spiritual crisis, but even glossed as a tantalizing hypothesis for escape. Contrariwise, in *Twelfth Night*, when 'Sir Thopas the curate' (the fool Feste in disguise) comes to visit Malvolio, meanly kept as 'the lunatic' in a cell, the pagan doctrine is explained but also roundly mocked in a cruelly comic scene riddled with ironies:

FESTE: What is the opinion of Pythagoras concerning wild fowl?
MALVOLIO: That the soul of our grandam might happily [possibly] inhabit a bird.
FESTE: What thinkest thou of this opinion?

169

MALVOLIO: I think nobly of the soul, and no way approve his opinion.
FESTE: Fare thee well: remain thou still in darkness: thou shalt hold the opinion of Pythagoras ere I will allow of thy wits, and fear to kill a woodcock, lest thou dispossess the soul of thy grandam. Fare thee well.

(IV. ii. 56–66)

Malvolio remains well and truly trapped in a 'Catch 22' situation: his orthodox Christian convictions will, in this absurd situation, keep him in 'the dark house' of the insane, his only possibility of escape being via the espousal of what is, from a Christian point of view, a piece of pagan mumbo-jumbo. But the salient point for our purposes is that the references to Pythagoras are used in an 'inclusive' fashion, so that the audience can share the scholastic joke, not be alienated by it.

Caroline Spurgeon's convincing differentiation between the imagery of Shakepeare and Marlowe serves equally well as a description of their respective vocabularies:

> Thus, to give the simplest kind of example, with Shakespeare [images of] nature (especially the weather, plants and gardening), animals (especially birds), and what we may call everyday and domestic, the body in health and sickness, indoor life, fire, light, food and cooking, easily come first; whereas with Marlowe, images drawn from books, especially the classics, and from the sun, moon, planets and heavens far outnumber all others. (1935, p. 13)

In the case of Shakespeare, the greatest (and most popular) writer of the times, it is notoriously difficult to infer from the diversity of perspectives in his plays his own views on anything. We may treat him in three basic ways: via the comments of his contemporaries; via his own dramatized comments on the language issue; and lastly, by his actual lexical contribution to the language of his time.

His contemporary, Francis Meres, in his *Palladis Tamia* (1598) mentions Shakespeare and Chapman as being among the poets by whom 'the English tongue is mightily enriched, and gorgeously invested in rare ornaments and resplendent abiliments', singling out especially 'Shakespeare's fine filed phrase' (cited in Salmon (ed.), 1987, pp. 15–16). This assessment focuses only on the most overtly literary aspect of his creativity. We recall the opposing emphasis from Dr Johnson, who stressed Shakespeare's contribution to 'the diction of common life'.

Though Shakespeare himself made no authoritative statement on the controversy, which was in any case much less of a burning question when he became a playwright, his dramatic examples show an essentially balanced position. His sonnets, written in the 1590s, show less linguistic originality than his plays, but have many comments on exaggerated or high-flown language, notably number 130, 'My mistress' eyes are nothing like the sun', which ends with a typically simple claim:

> And yet, by heaven, I think my love as rare
> As any she belied with false compare.

A contempt for affectation is consistently apparent. We find it in the sentiments of Mercutio in *Romeo and Juliet* (1597): 'The pox of such antic, lisping, affecting fantasticoes; these new tuners of accent . . . these fashion-mongers, these pardon me's' (II. iv. 27, 32). There is a clear hatred of the high-register hyperbole exploited by Regan's professed claim to be 'alone felicitate in your dear highness' love' in *King Lear* (I. i. 77–8). In the Watch scenes in *Much Ado About Nothing* (1598), Shakespeare realizes the comic potential of malapropism: those nominally in authority, Dogberry and Verges, are absurdly inarticulate and confused in their instructions, using *comprehend* for *apprehend*, *vigitant* for *vigilant*, *vagrom* for *vagrant*, and so on (III. iii). Yet they uncover the conspiracy of Don John.

In *Love's Labour's Lost* (1594–5), the play which most makes language an explicit issue, sharper satire is aimed at Don Armado and Holofernes. The former, 'a fantastical Spaniard', uses absurdly affected language, living up to his reputation as 'a man of fire-new words': 'So it was [he writes in a letter], beseiged with sable-coloured melancholy, I did commend the black-oppressing humour to the most wholesome physic of thy life-giving air; and as I am a gentleman, betook myself to walk' (I. i. 229–32). Holofernes, a pedant who speaks like a thesaurus, is equally ridiculous, describing Don Armado thus:

> *Novum hominem tanquam te.* His humour is lofty, his discourse peremptory, his tongue filed, his eye ambitious, his gait majestical, and his general behaviour vain, ridiculous, and thrasonical. He is too picked, too spruce, too affected, too odd, as it were, too peregrinate, as I may call it. (V. i. 12–16)

Holofernes is also an orthographer, an extreme stickler for 'correct' spelling, even to the point of creating unpronounceable forms:

> I abhor . . . such rackers of orthography, as to speak *dout*, fine, when he should say *doubt*; *det* when he should pronounce *debt*, – d, e, b, t, not d, e, t: he clepeth [calls] a calf *cauf*; half *hauf*; neighbour *vocatur* [is said] *nebour*; neigh abbreviated *ne*. This is abhominable (which he would call *abominable*).[3] (V. i. 18–24)

(Chaucer and his contemporaries had used such unaffected spellings as *doute*, *dette* and *receite*; the sixteenth-century orthographers had pedantically insisted on 'correcting' the forms by adding the 'b' and 'p' to make them conform etymologically to Latin *dubitum*, *debitum* and *receptus*. Holofernes now insists on the pronunciation conforming to the new forms.) While Don Armado and Holofernes display their absurd affecta-tions in mutual incomprehension, two minor characters provide a comic commentary:

> MOTH: They have been at a great feast of languages, and stolen the scraps.
> COSTARD: O they have lived long in the alms-basket of words. I marvel thy master hath not eaten thee for a word, for thou art not so long by the head as *honorificabilitudinitatibus*.
>
> (V. i. 30–4)

However, the play contains the nearest thing to a linguistic manifesto in Berowne's earnest but slightly stilted protestation to Rosaline:

> O! never will I trust to speeches penn'd
>   Nor to the motion of a school-boy's tongue,
> Nor never come in visor to my friend,
>   Nor woo in rhyme, like a blind harper's song,
> Taffeta phrases, silken terms precise,
>   Three-pil'd hyperboles, spruce affectation,
> Figures pedantical; these summer flies
>   Have blown me full of maggot ostentation:
> I do forswear them; and I here protest,
>   By this white glove, – how white the hand, God knows, –
> Henceforth my wooing mind shall be express'd
>   In russet yeas and honest kersey noes;
>
> (V. ii. 403–14)

The evocative imagery of rich materials in 'taffeta phrases, silken terms precise' epitomizes the brilliant but showy surface which the 'maggot ostentation' undermines. These are set off against *russet*, 'a coarse homespun woollen cloth of reddish-brown, grey or neutral colour, formerly used for the dress of peasants and country-folk', and *kersey*, 'possibly named from the village of Kersey in Suffolk', denoting 'a plain, coarse cloth woven from long wool'. Shakespeare's figurative uses of both terms in this passage are first recorded instances. Although this speech does in many ways prefigure the development of his own style from hackneyed embellishment to daring simplicity, it is full of self-irony and self-parody, to the point of excess. And, as we shall see, in moments of tragic passion and stress, the most rarefied diction suddenly bursts forth in fire-new words from the furnace of his poetic imagination and the further reaches of a compendious word-hoard. However, highly literary terms form only one aspect of Shakespeare's linguistic creativity. As we shall see, he was also remarkably adept in juxtaposing classical and native elements within the language.[4]

The Marlovian idiom, with its magniloquent language, colossal conceits and hubristic challenges, both upstaging and subverting traditional mythology, inspires an operatic unreality. The death of Tamburlaine's beloved queen Zenocrate, for instance, provokes in him a public display of hubris at once frantic, magnificent and deeply classical. He will punish the Fates, no less:

> What, is she dead? Techelles, draw thy sword,
> And wound the earth, that it may cleave in twain,
> And we descend into th' infernal vaults,
> To hale the Fatal Sisters by the hair,
> And throw them in the triple moat of hell,
> For taking hence my fair Zenocrate.
> (*Tamburlaine*, Part II, II. vii. 18–24)

Even Tamburlaine's own death-line is a sonorous fiat:

> Tamburlaine, the scourge of God must die. [*Dies*]

Against this, King Lear's heart-rending cosmic question at his daughter Cordelia's death reflects the true depth of personal agony in its cruelly simple terms:

> Why should a dog, a horse, a rat, have life,
> And thou no breath at all?
> (V. ii. 308–9)

Ben Jonson represents an interesting lexical split between the classical and the basic. His wide-ranging critical comments entitled *Timber or Discoveries* (1641) are larded with Latin tags, and the marginal comments are also in that language. He refers off the cuff to the whole range of classical personages with an easy familiarity, typically calling Cicero *Tully*, anglicized from his full Roman name of Marcus *Tullius* Cicero. The same is true of many of his hundreds of poems: even his most famous lyric, 'Drink to me only with thine eyes' contains the classical reference 'But might I of Jove's Nectar sup'. He wrote two tragedies based on classical heroes, *Sejanus* (1603) and *Catiline* (1611). But his urban comedies plumb the corruption and vitality of city life, celebrating the vigour and flamboyance of popular speech.

In both his plays and poems Jonson relishes a bawdy vein of savage direct-ness, castigating (in a slightly voyeuristic way) the sexual mores of 'the ser-vants of the Groine' of his hypocritical times:

> Adulteries now, are not so hid, or strange;
> They're grown Commoditie upon Exchange.

Jonson consistently presents human relationships in crude animalistic images and lexis:

> How much did Stallion [Sir Stud] spend
> To have his Court-bred fillie there commend
> His Lace and Starch? And fall upon her back
> In admiration, stretch'd upon the rack
> of lust, to his rich Suit and Title, Lord?
> ... she must lie down: Nay more,
> 'Tis there civilitie to be a whore.
> ('An Epistle to A Friend', lines 47–54)

The same poem has phrases like 'a saut [randy] Lady Bitch' and 'pound a Prick'. Most of the four-letter words are to be found in Jonson, several in the scatological poem, 'The Famous Voyage' (1614), which mentions 'the grave fart, late let in Parliament' and the discharging into a sewer of a 'merdurinous load' a unique lexical combination of French *merde* ('shit') and Latin *urine*.

Shakespeare's magisterial contribution was many-faceted. He not only con-tributed more new words and idioms to the language than any other writer, he was also unique in his exploitation of the whole gamut of the lexicon, crea-ting diverse verbal effects, magniloquent, trivial, tragic, ridiculous, absurd and even 'amphoteric', to use a recherché but ingenious term from chemistry meaning 'producing completely opposed reactions simultaneously'. (A power-ful example is the storm scene in *King Lear*, in which Lear's words inspire a sense of tragic horror, but are juxtaposed with those of the Fool, which produce an antithetical sense of farce.) No play of his is lacking in some criti-cal awareness or exploration of the potentialities of the language. He created extraordinarily individuated languages for his characters, and wove through many of his plays motifs of the key words, such as *honest* in *Othello*, *nature* in *King Lear*, *revenge* in *Hamlet* and *ambition* in *Macbeth*. A careful reading of these plays means having to examine the problematic meanings and nuances in these words.

His mastery of juxtaposed registers is remarkable, and is developed as an essential part of the mind-set of his heroes, as we shall see. But at moments of dramatic crisis Shakespeare's language encapsulates the experience, by the

most amazingly rarefied diction, often set against words of terrifying simplicity. A classic case is Macbeth's reaction when gazing upon his blood-
stained hand after murdering his King Duncan:

> This my hand will rather
> The multitudinous seas incarnadine,
> Making the green one red.
>
> (*Macbeth*, II. ii. 62–4)

The archaism *multitudinous* and the classical neologism *incarnadine* are of the
highest scholarly register, both used here for the first time, whereas 'Making
the green one red' is the language of a child. So is Lady Macbeth's recollection
of the hideous murder: 'Who would have thought the old man to have had
so much blood in him?' is her pitiful question (V. i. 42–4). Terrible moments,
like that in *King Lear* when the blinded Gloucester is given a letter to read, are
articulated in the simplest, burning words:

> Were all the letters suns, I could not see.
>
> (IV. vi. 143)

Shakespeare did not, therefore, entirely accept Jonson's realistic prescription of 'deeds and language such as men do use'. While his comic creations
certainly used this kind of medium, in his tragedies he explored the sufferings
of extraordinary characters in the extremity of 'passion' in its old sense of 'suffering'. For in depicting their catastrophic fall, Shakespeare sought to human-
ize the ambitions, passions, terrors and style of his heroes. This involved
reducing them in scale from Marlowe's supermen, modulating their utterances so that they were not beyond the pale of human experience, but still
retained an unmistakably arresting and extraordinary quality. In Shakespeare's 'ultimate lines', the simplest, plainest words burn on the page:

> She's dead as earth.
>
> (*King Lear*, V. iii. 263)
>
> Tomorrow and tomorrow and tomorrow.
>
> (*Macbeth*, V. v. 19)
>
> To be, or not to be: that is the question.
>
> (*Hamlet*, III. i. 56)
>
> A little water clears us of this deed.
>
> (*Macbeth*, II. ii. 68)
>
> Yet here's the smell of the blood still.
>
> (*Macbeth*, V. i. 55)

I am dying, Egypt, dying.
(*Antony* and *Cleopatra*, IV. xii. 18)

William Shakespeare

The life of England's greatest (and most popular) dramatist has a surprising number of gaps, into which legends and hypotheses have been fitted. He was born at Stratford-on-Avon in 1564, the son of a prosperous glover who appears to have been illiterate, since he signed documents with a mark. William probably went to the local grammar school, but was not a university man as were Marlowe, Greene and Nashe. According to his great friend and fellow dramatist, Ben Jonson, Shakespeare had 'small Latine and lesse Greek'. At the age of eighteen he married Anne Hathaway, eight years his senior, six months before the birth of their daughter, Susanna. Two years later were born twins, Judith and Hamnet, his only son, who died at the age of eleven. It is uncertain what Shakespeare did between 1585 and 1592, when he appeared in London on the fringe of the new theatrical companies as an obscure actor and aspiring playwright.

Between 1591 and 1611 Shakespeare wrote some thirty-seven plays (regarded as the *canon*) whose genuineness is as undisputed as their excellence. They cover all the major genres, comedy, tragedy and history, as well as a new form, romance, which has tragic potential but a comic conclusion. In addition to the atonishing creative feat of producing a new play at least every six months, he collaborated in other plays, as was common, and wrote two long narrative poems, *Venus and Adonis* and *The Rape of Lucrece*, as well as a substantial sequence of 154 sonnets. Within Shakespeare's theatrical company were Richard Burbage, the greatest tragic actor of his time, and two famous clowns, Will Kempe and Robert Armin. The company (of which Shakespeare was a shareholder) rose in stature and patronage, becoming first the Lord Chamberlain's Men and then the King's Men. In his own lifetime and partly through his excellence, the theatre was transformed from a marginal, dubious enterprise to a great national institution appealing to all classes.

Shakespeare retired to Stratford in about 1612, a wealthy man, bought the most expensive house in the town, reportedly 'lived at a £1000 a year' and died in 1616. Because of the absence of modern laws of copyright, he did not publish his own plays in his own lifetime, since rival acting companies would then have used them. Consequently, corrupt pirated texts of *Hamlet*, *King Lear* and many other plays appeared in the early 1600s. Curiously and sadly, none of his plays exists in his own manuscript: they were published in 1623 as the First Folio edition (an 'authorized version, so to speak) edited by two of his actor colleagues, John Heminges and Henry Condell. (A sample page, from *Hamlet* appears as figure 4.2) They emphasized his truth to nature and his extraordinary powers of composition: 'Who, as he was a happie imitator of Nature, was a most gentle expresser of it. His mind and hand went together: And what he thought, he vttered with that easinesse, that wee haue scarse receiued from him a blot in his papers' ('To the great Variety of Readers'). In his lines of tribute appended to the First Folio, Ben Jonson, a notoriously cantankerous man not given to idle praise, has left us a memorable contemporary estimate of Shakespeare's remarkable facility as a literary artist and his capacity to replicate and even enhance nature:

> Nature her selfe was proud of his designes,
>   And joy'd to weare the dressing of his lines!
> Which were so richly spun, and wouen so fit,
>   As, since, she will vouchsafe no other Wit.
> (lines 47–50)

Shakespeare's linguistic originality

A considerable portion of this chapter will focus on the work of Shakespeare as a microcosm of the expanding potential of the language, both lexical and semantic. Although all his work is categorized as 'literary', we shall find in it all these major features:

> high register and common creations
> oversea language
> regional and class dialects
> phrases which have become part of common currency
> conversion
> individuated character language
> word motifs
> word-play
> bawdy

Let us start with the global question: how many words did Shakespeare use? Various educated guesses have been made, ranging from 15,000 to 30,000 words. The higher figure is given in *The Story of English* (1986) and presumably derives from Marvin Spevack's *Complete and Systematic Concordance to the Works of Shakespeare* (1968–80), which gives a total of 29,066 different words. The answer is largely dependent on the definition of a *word*, more especially whether derivative forms should be counted separately from head-words. For example, *discandy* is a clear nonce-word used in *Antony and Cleopatra*, but is

With turbulent and dangerous Lunacy.

Rosin. He does confesse he feeles himselfe distracted,
But from what cause he will by no meanes speake.

Guil. Nor do we finde him forward to be sounded,
But with a crafty Madnesse keepes aloofe:
When we would bring him on to some Confession
Of his true state.

Qu. Did he receiue you well?

Rosin. Most like a Gentleman.

Guild. But with much forcing of his disposition.

Rosin. Niggard of question, but of our demands
Most free in his reply.

Qu. Did you assay him to any pastime?

Rosin. Madam, it so fell out, that certaine Players
We ore-wrought on the way : of these we told him,
And there did seeme in him a kinde of Ioy
To heare of it: They are about the Court,
And (as I thinke) they haue already order •
This night to play before him.

Pol. 'Tis most true:
And he beseech'd me to intreate your Maiesties
To heare, and see the matter.

King. With all my heart, and it doth much content me
To heare him so inclin'd. Good Gentlemen,
Giue him a further edge, and driue his purpose on
To these delights.

Rosin. We shall my Lord.   *Exeunt.*

King. Sweet *Gertrude* leaue vs too,
For we haue closely sent for *Hamlet* hither,
That he, as 'twere by accident, may there
Affront *Ophelia.* Her Father, and my selfe (lawful espials)
Will so bestow our selues, that seeing vnseene
We may of their encounter frankely iudge,
And gather by him, as he is behaued,
If t be th'affliction of his loue, or no,
That thus he suffers for.

Qu. I shall obey you,
And for your part *Ophelia*, I do wish
That your good Beauties be the happy cause
Of *Hamlets* wildenesse: so shall I hope your Vertues
Will bring him to his wonted way againe,
To both your Honors.

Ophe. Madam, I wish it may.

Pol. *Ophelia*, walke you heere. Gracious so please ye
We will bestow our selues : Reade on this booke,
That shew of such an exercise may colour
Your lonelinesse. We are oft too blame in this,
'Tis too much prou'd, that with Deuotions visage,
And pious Action, we do surge o're
The diuell himselfe.

King. Oh 'tis true:
How smart a lash that speech doth giue my Conscience?
The Harlots Cheeke beautied with plaist'ring Art
Is not more vgly to the thing that helpes it,
Then is my dee de, to my most painted word.
Oh heauie burthen!

Pol. I heare him comming, let's withdraw my Lord.
                                             Exeunt.

Enter Hamlet.

Ham. To be, or not to be, that is the Question:
Whether 'tis Nobler in the minde to suffer
The Slings and Arrowes of outragious Fortune,
Or to take Armes against a Sea of troubles,
And by opposing end them : to dye, to sleepe
No more; and by a sleepe, to say we end
The Heart-ake, and the thousand Naturall shockes

That Flesh is heyre too? 'Tis a consummation
Deuoutly to be wish'd. To dye to sleepe,
To sleepe, perchance to Dreame; I, there's the rub,
For in that sleepe of death, what dreames may come,
When we haue shuffel'd off this mortall coile,
Must giue vs pawse. There's the respect
That makes Calamity of so long life :
For who would beare the Whips and Scornes of time,
The Oppressors wrong, the poore mans Contumely,
The pangs of dispriz'd Loue, the Lawes delay,
The insolence of Office, and the Spurnes
That patient merit of the vnworthy takes,
When he himselfe might his *Quietus* make
With a bare Bodkin? Who would these Fardles beare
To grunt and sweat vnder a weary life,
But that the dread of something after death,
The vndiscouered Countrey, from whose Borne
No Traueller returnes, Puzels the will,
And makes vs rather beare those illes we haue,
Then flye to others that we know not of.
Thus Conscience does make Cowards of vs all,
And thus the Natiue hew of Resolution
Is sicklied o're, with the pale cast of Thought,
And enterprizes of great pith and moment,
With this regard their Currants turne away,
And loose the name of Action. Soft you now,
The faire *Ophelia?* Nimph, in thy Orizons
Be all my sinnes remembred.

Ophe. Good my Lord,
How does your Honor for this many a day?

Ham. I humbly thanke you : well, well, well.

Ophe. My Lord, I haue Remembrances of yours,
That I haue longed long to re-deliuer.
I pray you now, receiue them.

Ham. No, no, I neuer gaue you ought.

Ophe. My honor'd Lord, I know right well you did,
And with them words of so sweet breath compos'd,
As made the things more rich, then perfume left :
Take these againe, for to the Noble minde
Rich gifts wax poore, when giuers proue vnkinde.
There my Lord.

Ham. Ha, ha: Are you honest?

Ophe. My Lord.

Ham. Are you faire?

Ophe. What meanes your Lordship?

Ham. That if you be honest and faire, your Honesty
should admit no discourse to your Beautie.

Ophe. Could Beautie my Lord, haue better Comerce
then your Honestie?

Ham. I trulie : for the power of Beautie, will sooner
transforme Honestie from what it is, to a Bawd, then the
force of Honestie can translate Beautie into his likenesse.
This was sometime a Paradox, but now the time giues it
proofe. I did loue you once.

Ophe. Indeed my Lord, you made me beleeue so.

Ham. You should not haue beleeued me. For vertue
cannot so innocculate our old stocke, but we shall rellish
of it. I loued you not.

Ophe. I was the more deceiued.

Ham. Get thee to a Nunnerie. Why would'st thou
be a breeder of Sinners? I am my selfe indifferent honest,
but yet I could accuse me of such things, that it were better my Mother had not borne me. I am very prowd, re-
uengefull, Ambitious, with more offences at my becke,
then I haue thoughts to put them in imagination, to giue
them shape, or time to acte them in. What should such
                                                       Fel-

Figure 4.2   Hamlet in the authorized version: the Shakespeare First Folio (1623)

derogately in the same category or merely an extension of *derogate*? If one were to consolidate the forms *derogation, derogatory* and *derogately* under the root-word *derogate* and extend the principle to all other words and derivatives, the total would fall to some 20,000 words. But this is surely putting too much emphasis on the root and not enough on subsequent growths. The general rule is to take the individual head-words in the *OED*, which lists all the forms separately.

The figure of 30,000 words is not remarkable when compared with modern authors, but is astonishing when compared with estimates of contemporary texts, which are some 4000 words for the Authorized Version of the Bible and some 8000 for Milton, who was an immensely learned classicist. Furthermore, a more detailed assessment is needed of Shakespeare's original contribution to the language of his own time, which will include original words that have not survived.

As we saw in chapter 1, linguistic originality covers a variety of degrees, from coining a totally new word or **neologism**, to the less radical mode of simply adding a prefix or suffix; in between lies the process of **conversion**, or extending the grammatical function of a word, from a noun to a verb or vice versa. Linguistic originality has obviously to be tempered by a degree of comprehension. The writer of a scientific treatise can assume a learned readership, whereas a dramatist is limited in the degree of originality available by the necessity of communicating with a fairly diverse audience. In Elizabethan times this extended from the educated and sophisticated grandees who occupied the 'gods' down to the groundlings who stood on the sand around the apron stage and who, in the acerbic view of Hamlet, were 'for the most part capable of nothing but inexplicable dumb-shows and noise' (*Hamlet*, III. ii. 12–14).

Nevertheless, Shakespeare showed a consistent, even an increasing desire to experiment with the resources of the language. No play of his is lacking in linguistic originality. Indeed, he would appear to go to the limits with some of his high-register creations, such as *incarnadine, assassination* and *assubjugate*, which are neologisms, and *unseminared, discandy* and *unprovoke*, which are extensions by means of prefixes, as well as such conversions of traditional noun forms to verbal uses as in *companion, beggared* and *palates*. However, these represent only one segment of an astonishingly rich sample. There are many original uses which do not challenge comprehension severely, such as *But me no buts, fob off, take your time* and so on.

Shakespeare's linguistic originality has been praised as much as his remarkable psychological insights, the subtlety of his imagery and his mastery of dramatic form and technique. Some of the earlier judgements, such as this are by George Gordon in his study, *Shakespeare's English* are fulsome, but seemingly impressionistic:

Shakespeare was to do what he liked with English grammar, and drew beauty
and power from its imperfections. In the rankness and wildness of the language
he found his opportunity, and exploited it royally, sometimes tyrannically. (1928,
p. 17)

In similar vein Henry Bradley wrote in his minor classic, *The Making of English*:
'Unrivalled in so many other ways, Shakespere [*sic*] has no equal with regard
to the extent and profundity of his influence on the English language' (1904,
p. 229).

How original was Shakespeare from a linguistic point of view? In these days
when bardolatry (the uncritical praise of Shakespeare) is very much under suspicion, how can we arrive at some reliable assessment of his originality?
Perhaps the simplest, fairest and soundest method is to consider Shakespeare's
contribution in terms of the new words and senses recorded in the annals of
the *Chronological English Dictionary (CED)*, which we discussed earlier in this
chapter. On the basis of this authority we find that Shakespeare's coinages do
indeed form a remarkably high proportion of contemporary innovations.
Thus, for the year 1602, a total of some 250 new words and meanings
are listed in the *CED*. Of these, 43 (or an astonishing 17.2 per cent) are
directly traceable to *Hamlet*. By the same process, of the 349 new words and
meanings recorded for 1605, the combined contributions of *Macbeth* and *King
Lear* total 45 items or 12.8 per cent. (The breakdown shows *Macbeth* to be
the richer contributor, with 27 new words and meanings, as against 18 for
King Lear.)

These striking statistics give a reasonably reliable quantification of
Shakespeare's remarkable contribution to the word-stock of his own time.
Overall it would not be extravagant to assess this contribution at around 10
per cent of the current new words and meanings entering the language. They
demonstrate his peerlessly original qualities in linguistic creativity and corroborate the earlier, impressionistic judgements. Furthermore, research into
the tragedies as a group shows a steady increase in originality with time, as he
developed from the melodramatic but comparatively unchallenging language
of the early works to the strikingly impressive linguistic creativity of the
mature tragedies.

These data, impressive as they are, clearly do not give us the whole picture,
since the *CED* is based on the word-stock of the *Shorter Oxford English Dictionary*, not the compendious *OED*. When more detailed analysis is brought to
bear on this vast word-hoard, the number of Shakespearean original uses rises
dramatically. For example, the number of original instances in *Hamlet* alone
increases from the figure of 43 mentioned above to ±150. For *Macbeth* it rises

from 27 to over 110. In the discussions and analyses of the individual plays, therefore, it will be necessary to amplify the data of the *CED* with that of the *OED*.

However, it should be borne in mind that many of the first usages listed in *OED* had short lives. In his article on 'Shakespeare's Latinate Neologisms', Bryan A. Garner claims 'that 31 per cent of Neologisms have not survived' (1982, in Salmon (ed.), 1987, p. 156). This is not simply because Shakespeare coined unusual words in a pedantic fashion (*pedant* and *pedantic* being two of his coinages). It is rather because he created pedantic characters, or those who liked to play with language, or those who 'put on the style' in a humorous or cynical fashion. Thus the drunken Porter in *Macbeth* says of the effect of drink that it 'provokes and *unprovokes*' lechery (II. iii. 33), clearly making up the form *unprovokes* for the moment. In *Othello* the cynical villain Iago uses a deliberately pretentious form in the phrase '*exsufflicate* and blown surmises' (III. iii. 182). Edmund, the villain of *King Lear*, rejects astrological notions, creating two original formations in one little speech: 'Sfoot! I should been that I am had the *maidenliest* star in the firmament twinkled on my *bastardizing*' (I. ii. 147–9). Such formations are genuine 'nonce-words', created for the occasion. Of necessity, few passed into the mainstream of the language.

More than 600 Latinate neologisms are listed in the article by Garner. Of these over 200 are to be found in the mature tragedies, namely *Hamlet*, *Macbeth*, *King Lear*, *Othello*, *Coriolanus*, *Troilus and Cressida* and *Antony and Cleopatra*. *Hamlet* leads the field with 53 neologisms, closely followed by *Troilus and Creassida* (49), after which come *King Lear* (30), *Othello* (28) *Coriolanus* (22) and *Macbeth* (20). (We should bear in mind that *Macbeth* is by far the shortest of the tragedies, having 2349 lines as against *Hamlet*, the longest with 4042. Another play which, as expected, features in this grading is *Love's Labour's Lost* with 33 items, many of them high-register words used in a satirical fashion. Interestingly, *Antony and Cleopatra*, Shakespeare's most poetically creative play, has only 12, since many of the creations are too rarefied to have become a permanent part of the word-stock.

Many of these Latinate neologisms are extremely rare words like *assubjugate*, *corresponsive*, *concupy*, *deceptious*, *embrasures*, *multipotent*, *oppugnancy*, *repured* and *untent*. This is largely to be expected, for the reasons just given. But, very surprisingly, about one-fifth are common words. Here is a sample of just 60 of them:

accommodation	addiction	admirable	amazement	arbitrate
assassination	castigate	comply	compulsive	consign
counterpart	denote	discontent	dislocate	domineering

educate	epileptic	exhale	exposure	fashionable
fixture	frugal	gallantry	generous	hostile
impair	impede	investment	invitation	luggage
majestic	manager	mimic	misquote	monumental
mutineer	negotiate	obscene	operate	overpay
pious	posture	performed	prophetic	proposer
protester	reliance	restoration	retirement	reword
sanctimonious	savagery	supervise	survivor	torturer
traditional	tranquil	unlicensed	unreal	useful

Oversea language

Although Shakespeare certainly satirized the ostentatious use of 'oversea' and 'classical' language, he was unafraid of the previous strictures made by the Purists, and used a surprising number of foreign terms. As always, he had specific motives for these special lexical effects. Some are used to create an exotic atmosphere: for instance, in *Othello* when Iago comments cynically on Othello's appetite for Desdemona: 'the food that to him now is as luscious as locusts [carob fruit] shall to him shortly be as bitter as coloquintida [the colocynth or bitter-apple]' (II. i. 350–2). In his speech to the Venetian senate, Othello himself tells of

> . . . the Cannibals that each other eat,
> The Anthropophagi and men whose heads
> Do grow beneath their shoulders.
> (I. iii. 143–5)

(As we shall see in chapter 6, both the name *Cannibal* and the practice are now known to be dubiously grounded, but the term would have had a notable impact.)

However, the potential of comic confusion is more commonly exploited, as when Sir Andrew Aguecheek asks helplessly: 'What is *pourquoi?* do or not do?' (*Twelfth Night*, I. iii. 97). In the same play Sir Toby Belch uses *Kickshaws*, a corruption of *quelque chose*, which had acquired the sense of a small sweet dish (I. ii. 124). Similar contexts surround *basta, diablo* and *palabras*.

In view of the general hostility to Spain in the period, one is surprised to find the following Spanish terms used for the first time by Shakespeare: *ambuscado, bandetto, barricado, bastinado, carbonado, hurricano*. The last is from the storm scene in *King Lear*, but the second last refers amusingly to disgusting foreign diets of 'adders' heads and toads carbonadoed' (*Winter's Tale* (V. iii. 267)).

Latin

One of the most famous tragic moments in all of Shakespeare is

> *Et tu Brute?* Then fall, Caesar! [*Dies*]
> (*Julius Caesar*, III. i. 77)

The grand death-line of Caesar is achieved by the unique and unexpected irruption of Latin into the English text, creating an epic 'moment in and out of time', as T. S. Eliot has called such an experience ('The Rock', VII). (Marlowe's text, by comparison, is full of Latin tags which are often more pedantic than dramatic.) Elsewhere Hamlet memorably contemplates the possibility of achieving *quietus*, using (for the first time) the Latin for 'peace' with its religious overtones (III. i. 75) in *requiem* and *requiescat in pace*.

Current common Latin terms used by Shakespeare include *autem*, *item*, *ergo*, *iota* and its Anglicized form *iot*, as well as *ergo* and its corrupted form *argal*. Being a man of the stage, he is the first writer to Anglicize *exit* (originally a stage direction for 'he/she goes'), in the famous comparison between life and theatre:

> They have their exits and their entrances.
> (*As You Like It*, II. vii. 141)

However, Latin is one of the principal vehicles of comedy and satire, as we shall see in the following section.

The diction of common life

Dr Johnson's emphasis on Shakespeare as exemplifying 'the diction of common life' seems surprising to us now, in view of the great volume of literary words we have been discussing, but it turns out to be a typically shrewd observation. For indeed, a remarkable number of common, native terms and idioms are first recorded in his plays. Part of the linguistic legacy of Shakespeare is made up of many felicitously phrased or highly-charged forms of literary language which have over time become reiterated phrases of received experience, part of the warp and woof of the language. Consider the following passage:

One must observe, *more in sorrow than in anger, that codes of sportsmanship are increasingly *more honoured in the breach than in the observance. There has developed, particularly in soccer, a regrettable degree of showmanship, with players seeking to *out-Gascoigne or out-Maradona each other, as if they were the *be-all and end-all of the game. Professional fouling now *beggars all description, the players tripping, diving, elbowing and butting as if *to the manner born. Despite all *the pomp and circumstance surrounding the Football Association's recent initiatives, the time has come to expel the ringleaders of dirty play at *one fell swoop.

This (slightly pompous) piece of made-up commentary contains eight idioms derived from Shakespeare, nearly all of them originally created at moments of high drama, but now reduced virtually to the level of cliché. They are the phrases beginning with an asterisk, *.

Most of these phrases have a literary air: few people would use them in conversation. But they are greatly outnumbered by those heard on a daily basis:

blinking idiot, breathe one's last, cheer up, crack of doom, do famously, fob off, foregone conclusion, foul play, full of sound and fury, good riddance, green-eyed monster, hoist with his own petard, household names, it's Greek to me, one's pound of flesh, a palpable hit, salad days, seamy side, small beer, there's the rub, tower of strength, what the dickens.

Most of these have been incorporated through the familiarity of Shakespeare's texts to the majority of people in the English-speaking world, so that the idioms have become part of their mind-set. The point is made by the apocryphal story of the lady who emerged from a performance of *Hamlet* saying how much she had enjoyed the play 'because it was so full of quotations'. On this point the reader should also see Bernard Levin's essay on the subject in *Enthusiasms* (1983, p. 99).

However, what is astonishing is the number of truly common, ordinary words which are first recorded in his works. These include:

amazement, barefaced, beetle (protrude), *blanket* (vb), *boggler, bump, buzz* (rumour), *critic, crop* (vb), *do* (copulate), *dwindle, fitful, foppish, foul-mouthed, gibber, hob nob, hubbub, humour* (vb), *humorous, hunch-backed, hurry, leak* (urinate), *leap-frog, lonely, pat* (right now), *pedant, puke, queasy, stealthy, unreal, weird.*

As F. P. Wilson rightly says, 'his instinct for what was permanent in the colloquial language of his day is stronger than that of any contemporary dramatist' (in Ridler (ed.), 1970, p. 92). Many filled their plays with the merely topical (which would have added spice at the time but makes them difficult to understand now). Shakespeare sensed what would endure.

Dialect

As we have seen, *dialect* includes forms of the language which are distinctive both regionally and socially. In his founding work, *A Shakespeare Glossary* (1911), C. T. Onions stated that it was part of his plan 'to show the relation of the poet's vocabulary to that of the dialects of the Midland area, and in particular the dialect of his own county, Warwickshire' (1958, p. iv). Among these words are local variants for common items, such as *ballow* for 'cudgel', *batlet*, a wooden bat for beating the washing, *gallow* meaning 'to frighten', *muss*, a local game, *pash* for 'smash', *potch* for 'thrust', *tarre* meaning 'to provoke', *tun-dish* for 'funnel' and *vails* for 'perks'. Two dialect words used in emotional moments are Malvolio's bitter complaint that he has been made 'the most notorious *geck* ['fool'] and gull' and Macbeth's horrified comment that Banquo's Ghost is 'blood-*boltered*', meaning clotted or matted with blood. The oddest word in this group is *mobled* ('muffled'), used in *Hamlet* of the Trojan Queen Hecuba in her frantic grief.

This is not a large sample, and a number of scholars, including G. D. Willcock (1934) and Hilda Hulme (1962) have argued that Shakespeare seems to have left his native Stratford dialect behind when he moved to London. However, in her study, *Explorations in Shakespeare's Language*, Hulme shows that Shakespeare used a number of dialect terms in instances which antedate those first recorded in the *OED*.

As one would expect, Shakespeare was very sensitive to the social nuances of the language of his times. To take but one example, Onions comments on the word *humour* 'The excessive use of this word in fashion in Shakespeare's time is often ridiculed by him.' He was quite prepared to use underground criminal argot and *déclassé* words. When the clown Autolycus, 'a snapper-up of unconsidered trifles' in *The Winter's Tale*, uses the words *doxy* and *dell*, vagabond or thieves' slang for 'a beggar's mistress', these are in keeping with his character. However, in a very different context, that of *King Lear*, Edgar, the fugitive honest son of Gloucester, adopts the disguise of Poor Tom, an 'abram man' or counterfeit madman. In this role he uses *angler* meaning 'pole-fisher' and other underworld terms. As S. Musgrove points out in a useful article, 'Other Jacobean dramatists used canting material freely – Jonson in *The Gypsies Metamorphosed*, Dekker in *The Roaring Girl*, Beaumont and Fletcher in *The Beggars' Bush*, Brome in *The Jovial Crew* – but they are straightforward and unsubtle as compared with Shakespeare. Their comic intention is obvious, and they usually translate the jargon directly' (in Salmon (ed.), 1981, pp. 10–11).

Underground bawdy and profanity

The diction of common life included crudities which would have surprised Dr Johnson. John Florio, a noted literary figure of the times, defined Italian *fottere* in his *Worlde of Wordes* (1598) as 'to iape, to sard, to fuck, to swive, to occupy', running through the whole gamut of copulatory registers with a typical Elizabethan exuberance. However, only the last of these words appears in Shakespeare. We have seen that in Middle English coarse language thrived in the street and in certain texts.

The reason for bawdy language going underground is fairly simple. From the time that the office of the cynically named Master of the Revels was established in 1576, plays were subject to scrutiny and routine censorship and institutionalized fines for infringements of linguistic decorum, or dealing with politically unsuitable subjects. These restrictions served, as they usually do, to encourage circumvention through enforced ingenuity. This no doubt explains what Norman Blake calls 'the sudden emergence [of word-play] in the Elizabethan period' (1983, p. 19).

The profusion of what are called 'minced oaths' which sprang up contemporaneously as a consequence of the laws against profanity on the stage is remarkable:

1598 *'sblood* (God's blood)	– Shakespeare, *Henry IV, Part I*, I. ii. 82.
'slid (God's eyelid)	– Shakespeare, *Merry Wives*, III. iv. 24.
'slight (God's light)	– Jonson, *Everyman Out of his Humour*, II. ii. 69.
1599 *'snails* (God's nails)	– Hayward, *Henry IV*, I. 19.
1600 *zounds* (God's wounds)	– Rowlands, *The Letting of Humours*, V. 72.
1601 *'sbody* (God's body)	– Jonson, *The Poetaster*, II. i. 91.
1602 *'sfoot* (God's foot)	– Marston, *Antonio's Revenge*, IV. iii. 126.

Many of these must originally have been in-jokes, which guyed the authorities and sailed provocatively close to the wind. Otto Jespersen long ago made a most perceptive observation on Shakespeare and religion:

> His reticence about religious matters, which has given rise to the most divergent theories of his religious belief, is shown strikingly in the fact that such words as *Bible, Holy Ghost* and *Trinity* do not occur at all in his writings, while *Jesus* and *Christmas* are found only in some of his earliest plays; *Saviour* occurs only in *Hamlet*. (1962, p. 203)

As Eric Partridge showed in his pioneering study, *Shakespeare's Bawdy* (1947), the circumvention of establishment restraints on coarse language was achieved by a complex variety of coded evasions and euphemisms. Prior to his book many of the more risqué or obscene puns were ignored, either because they were misunderstood or because it was felt inapposite to point them out in the work of the national poet. Partridge com-mented rather con-tentiously in the preface to his work: 'If Shakespearean criticism had not been for so long in the hands of academics and cranks, a study of Shakespeare's attitude towards sex and his use of the broad jest would probably have appeared at any time since 1918' (1947, p. vii).

Partridge convincingly demonstrates that great numbers of innocent common words contain sexual innuendoes. For example, in *Much Ado About Nothing*, the last word of the title is a coded sexual pun on 'an O thing' (= 'cunt'). The heroine Beatrice makes a bawdy comment on courting when she observes, early in the play, that 'With a good leg and a good foot, uncle, and money enough in his purse, such a man would win any woman in the world, if 'a could get her good will' (II. i. 15–18). Here the *double entendres* are *leg* (= 'penis'), *foot* (= *foutre* = 'fuck') and *will* (= 'sexual appetite').

Such sexual verbal fun, it might be argued, is partly to be expected in comedy. Yet in *Romeo and Juliet*, the flamboyant Mercutio's language is full of bawdy punning, clearly juxtaposed with Romeo's idealism. And Hamlet mer-cilessly pursues the genital meaning of *nothing* in his public degradation of Ophelia in the play scene (III. ii. 120–9):

HAMLET: Lady, shall I lie in your lap?
OPHELIA: No, my lord.
HAMLET: I mean, my head upon your lap?
OPHELIA: Ay my lord
HAMLET: Do you think I meant country matters?
OPHELIA: I think nothing, my lord.
HAMLET: That's a fair thought to lie between maid's legs.
OPHELIA: What is, my lord?
HAMLET: Nothing.

The savageness of Hamlet's word-play shows the attitude of cynical hatred epitomized in his earlier denunciation, 'Frailty, thy name is woman!'[5] Inci-dentally, Dr Johnson in his edition proposed 'country manners', which the Victorian scholar Malone rejected, in the style of his time: 'What Shakespeare meant to allude to, must be too obvious to every reader to require any explanation' (Hulme, 1977, p. 92) Malone's point is surely endorsed by the omission of the last five speeches in this exchange from standard school editions such as the Pitt Press Shakespeare, edited by A. W. Verity (from 1911).

Other common words which also carried sexual senses are *do* (copulate), *die* (experience orgasm), *stone* (testicle), *tool* (penis). One of Timon's deranged wishes is that children should 'do't in your parents' eyes!' (IV. i. 7). Ben Jonson, translating Petronius, has the Puritanical sentiment that 'Doing a filthy pleasure is, and short.[7] Lear, now insane, says 'I will die bravely, like a smug bridegroom' (IV. vi. 202). The Fool in *Timon of Athens* is 'sometimes like a philosopher, with two stones more than his artificial one' (II. ii. 115–16). *Tool* is used in the most astonishigly frank expression of xenophobic penis-envy in *Henry VIII*: 'Have we some strange Indian with the great tool come to court, the women so besiege us? What a fry of fornication is at the door!' (V. iv. 35–8).

Shakespeare is adept at using a foreign language with apparent naïvety as a vehicle for obscene puns. An ingeniously bawdy instance is the scene of earnest delicacy in *Henry V* where the French princess is inducted into the rudiments of English:

KATHARINE: *Comment appellez vous le pied et la robe?*
ALICE: De foot, *madame; et* de coun.
KATHARINE: De foot, *et de con? O Seigneur Dieu! ces sont mots de son mauvais, corruptible, gros, et impudique, et non pour les dames d'honneur d'user.*

(III. iv. 55–8)

The innocent English terms which so affront the Queen-to-be are, of course, the ultimate taboos in French, namely *foutre* ('fuck') and *coun, con* ('cunt'). Robert Greene had a few years earlier used *foutre* in the French exclamation 'foutre de se monde!' but Shakespeare was to go further, having Pistol, an outrageously uncensored character, simply take over *foutre* and denounce all and sundry with the variant *foutra*:

A foutra for the world and worldlings base!
(*Henry IV, Part II*, v. ii. 98)

The word was subsequently borrowed as *fouter, footer* and *foutling* in a much less vigorous, and therefore generally acceptable sense. The modern equivalent, *footling*, is entirely innocent.

Often scenes of apparent formal respectability are amusingly undermined by bawdy puns. A seemingly dry, but actually 'naughty' grammar lesson in *The Merry Wives of Windsor* provides an instance:

SIR HUGH EVANS: . . . What is the focative case, William?
WILLIAM: O *Vocativo*, O.
SIR HUGH EVANS: Remember, William: focative is *caret* [it is missing].
MISTRESS QUICKLY: And that's a good root.
SIR HUGH EVANS: 'Oman, forbear.

MRS. PAGE: Peace!
SIR HUGH EVANS: What is your genitive case plural, William?
WILLIAM: Genitive case?
SIR HUGH EVANS: Ay.
WILLIAM: *Genitive, horum, harum, horum.*
MISTRESS QUICKLY: Vengeance of Jenny's case! fie on her! Never name her, child, if she be a whore.

(IV. i. 53–65)

Here *case* carries the sense of 'genitals' and *horum* is a clear pun on *whore*. The comedy of this scene is enriched by Mistress Quickly's eager participation in underlining the sexual innuendoes and William's comment 'O Vocativo O'.

This brings us to the general topic of punning. 'Word-play was a game the Elizabethans played seriously,' Molly Mahood reminds us in her major study, *Shakespeare's Word Play*. She shows that puns are ubiquitous and that the average number in a Shakespeare play was no less than seventy-eight (1968, p. 164). Two famous incidents are John of Gaunt punning on his own name on his deathbed (in *Richard II*, II. i. 74) and Mercutio, wounded to death in *Romeo and Juliet*, commenting wrily: 'ask for me tomorrow, and you shall find me a grave man' (III. i. 104). Whether such behaviour is 'true to life' is debatable. It was certainly part of a heroic attitude to life, a nonchalance in the face of death or danger which was to be admired. Shakespeare, who probably did not even know of the unities as set out in Aristotle's *Poetics*, preferred to follow his own instinct.

Dr Johnson was clearly disapproving: 'The pun was to Shakespeare the fatal Cleopatra, for which he was prepared to give away the world' (in Mahood, 1968, p. 9). Obviously Johnson's views were governed by Augustan notions of decorum which regarded 'unity of tone' as being crucial, and any mixture of comic and serious elements as an inartistic disruption. As we shall see in the next chapter, these assumptions led Johnson to criticize a number of high dramatic moments where he felt that 'the diction of common life' was inappropriate. Today, we regard Shakespeare's instinct, less schooled by classical decorum, is being truer to human experience. Shakespeare's use of what D. S. Bland calls the 'ordinary' word in dramatic speeches is both powerful and effective, or in Bland's terms, 'vivid and arresting' (in Salmon (ed.), 1957, p. 55).

The bloody stage to theatre of the mind

The earliest Elizabethan tragedies showed a relentlessly crude reliance on spectacular stage violence rather than linguistic subtlety and originality to achieve dramatic impact. Shakespeare's own early works were very much in keeping with the mode of these 'tragedies of blood'. Within his *oeuvre* the point is made forcibly, though perhaps simplistically, when one compares his earliest tragedy, *Titus Andronicus* (1592–4) with his last two, *Timon of Athens* (1605–8) and *Coriolanus* (1607–8). To put it at its crudest, there is a general diminution in the body-count and the gruesomeness of despatch as we move from the early to the mature tragedies. *Titus Andronicus* represents the notorious nadir of crudity, a *grand guignol* medley of cannibalism, dismemberment, rape, murder, regicide, fratricide, infanticide and suicide. In all, some eight people die. It is as if Shakespeare the apprentice tragedian, like his contemporaries, regarded the audience as some monster which had to be fed with a regular diet of corpses, cruelty, insanity and macabre theatricality.

It is true that in *King Lear* and *Hamlet* many die: when Fortinbras enters the Danish court in the final act, he refers to the four corpses in hunting terms as a 'quarry' (V. ii. 378). Yet the last of the tragedies, *Coriolanus*, concerns only the fall of the hero, whose exploits are only briefly seen but copiously described. Although he is the war hero *par excellence*, the dramatic balance of the piece is away from action (apart from the battle of Corioli and the hero's final treacherous murder at the hands of Aufidius) and towards the energies of language: the play is a chorus of hectoring, ranting, manipulating, cajoling, abusing and cursing. In the case of *Hamlet*, a great deal of the play is taken up with the hero's self-analysis and violent execration, much philosophizing and agonizing. Even more extraordinary, *Timon of Athens* is technically without action (apart from Timon's mock feast of air and water), but is suffused with verbal energy. The hero does not even die, properly speaking, but fades mysteriously into the ambivalent state between earth and water, leaving behind a strange cursing epitaph.

As the hero's psyche replaces 'the bloody stage' as the arena of focus, so language replaces incident as the major generator of emotion. With every tragedy, the sufferings of the hero are articulated with language of increasing intensity, passion, subtlety and originality. The fury of Lear at 'filial ingratitude', of Coriolanus at the injustice of Roman politics and of Timon at Athenian ingratitude form violently articulate responses to what are, in the scale of human suffering, comparatively minor affronts and disappointments. But their heroic outrage is conveyed in awesome language which far outweighs the stilted, verbose, overtly rhetorical and obviously contrived verse which struggles to match the savageries of the early tragedies.

While it would be possible to give a survey of the whole of Shakespeare's work, this would require a full-length study. Thus it seems preferable to focus on certain key works with which the student is likely to be familiar and to analyse more closely the exploitation and extension of the language in detail.

The works chosen are *Macbeth, Hamlet* and *Antony and Cleopatra*. In these masterpieces of his maturity, we see Shakespeare creating 'worlds of words', verbal microcosms of extraordinary ingenuity and originality.

Lexical Diversity in the Major Tragedies

By common consent *Hamlet* is regarded as the richest of Shakespeare's tragedies, from philosophical, ethical and dramatic points of view. Less obviously, it is also intensely and overtly concerned with language, of which some aspects have already been discussed. It is truly a linguistic *tour de force*, with Shakespeare's command of the lexical diversity of Early Modern English shown in an astonishing range of characters and scenes. Virtually every character, even the most minor, is given some moment of holding the stage in his special style. These include the horrific disclosure of the Ghost; the plausible but devious statesmanship of the fratricidal King Claudius; the pompous discourse of Polonius; the bombastic rant of the Player; the fustian of the Play Scene; the crude down-to-earth comedy of the Grave-Diggers and the absurd affectation of the courtier Osric.

Hamlet himself matches this whole gamut of styles, displaying an astounding word-hoard. His role as hero, a philosopher and reluctant avenger in a revenge tragedy, is highly complex and enigmatic. He is a virtuoso performer in passion whose language reflects many contraries, notably his manic-depressive oscillations of mood in his anguished soliloquies. He uses brilliantly savage word-play in sharply critical observations on hypocrisy and linguistic fashion, licence and falsity. Ironically, in the horrific situation in which he finds himself, the world of words becomes something of an escape from which his dying line is a final quietus: 'The rest is silence.'

Clearly, a detailed discussion of the complexity of the language of *Hamlet* would require a whole book. What follows serves simply as an introduction to the linguistic richness of the play. A brief examination of the first scenes shows these qualities even in *Hamlet* without the prince. The play starts with an unexpected cry in the night and the entry of the catalyst of the whole action, the Ghost. This is never mentioned directly, being referred to by nervous evasions as *this thing, our fantasy, this dreaded sight, this apparition* and simply *it*.

The speeches of the watchers on the battlements of Elsinor, all of them minor characters, are remarkable for originality, suggestiveness of character, scholarly tenor and metaphorical density. (In the following discussion neologisms are shown in bold type.) Horatio's thoughtful but shrewd cast of mind is shown in an essentially high-register vocabulary stocked with legalisms such as **emulate** (adj.), **compulsative,** *forfeit, moiety; competent, gagèd* and *covenant.*

But he does not eschew vivid, earthy metaphors like *pricked on* and *sharked up*, which show Fortinbras' ambition unfavourably. His terms *post-haste and rummage* comment crisply on the invasion scare in the land. Yet a strikingly lyrical note emerges in the famous lines:

> But look, the morn in russet mantle clad,
> Walks o'er the dew of yon high eastern hill.
> (I. i. 148–9)

Even Marcellus is given two substantial poetic speeches. He likewise uses bookish terms like **invulnerable**, *majestic*, and *malicious*, as well as the more demotic nonce-word *takes*, meaning 'bewitches' or 'blasts', in the speech on the 'hallowed and gracious time' when evil is driven from the world (I. i. 163).

The practised insincerity and political acumen of Claudius are immediately apparent in the court scene (I. ii). His lengthy opening speech is a performance which skilfully covers, in measured and anaesthetic terms welded into highly elaborate syntactical structures, the various crises through which the Danish kingdom has passed: the sudden death of the elder Hamlet, the impropriety of his own hasty marriage to his brother's widow, and the threat from the young Norwegian prince, Fortinbras. Fortified by some heavy verbal artillery, Claudius's courtly communiqué is nevertheless delivered smoothly, as if by rote, and moves authoritatively through its awkward agenda, employing clichés and urbane phrases which console, flatter and unite: 'our dear brother's death' is used twice, 'your better wisdoms' are unctuously thanked for their support, and 'our sometime sister, now our queen', is elevated to a patriotic pillar in the nation of great Danes as

> Th'imperial **jointress** of this warlike state.
> (I. ii. 9)

Superficially, all appears well. But there are many subtle false notes. Claudius's speech is heavily stocked with artificial neologisms which are either opaque abstractions or polysyllabic pomposities designed to impress or intimidate. He starts out with **jointress** and *supposal*, terms which would obviously stand out and draw attention to themselves in the early 1600s. Claudius is 'putting on the style' in very much the same contrived fashion that Goneril and Regan do in the opening court scene in *King Lear*. We notice that there is no disturbing reference to the fact that the Danish economy is on a war footing: Fortinbras is wished away by a peremptory fiat: 'So much for him' (line 25). By Claudius's reiterated use of *we* and *our*, Shakespeare invites us to probe whether he is referring to the Danish council in an exercise of solidarity, or is simply assuming the royal 'we'. As the scene progresses, so Claudius increasingly asserts himself, moving from ambiguity to clear appropriation, even using the royal personification of 'the Dane' in line 44. However, in his evident anxiety to accommodate both grief and joy, thereby putting a good face on his unorthodox marital union, Claudius undermines his carefully crafted illusion of unity:

> . . . with a defeated joy,
> With one auspicious and one dropping eye,
> With mirth in funeral and dirge in marriage.
> (I. ii. 10–12)

Here the oxymoron (*defeated joy*) is followed by bizarrely conflicting images and muddled rituals of hideous tastelessness. It is this charade which Hamlet caustically exposes later in the most concrete terms:

> The funeral baked meats
> Did coldly furnish forth the marriage tables.
> (I. ii. 180–1)

Claudius's confident start of 'Therefore' is followed by a whole series of subordinate clauses with inapposite pairings which in this heavily burdened sentence contrives to suspend to the very last possible moment the embarrassing admission of '. . . taken to wife'.

The first resistance to Claudius's smooth progress comes, appropriately, from Hamlet, who enters the play with witty and bitter rejoinders very much in the vein of a truth-telling Fool:

> CLAUDIUS: But now, my cousin Hamlet and my son –
> HAMLET: A little more than kin and less than kind.
> CLAUDIUS: How is it the clouds still hang on you?
> HAMLET: Not so, my lord I am too much i' the sun.
> (I. ii. 64–7)

By his enigmatic word-play, Hamlet both subverts courtly *politesse* through veiled insult, and refuses to accept the idiom of superficial order and harmony. At the same time, he avoids being rudely confrontational in the manner of Cordelia in the opening scene of *King Lear* where she rejects Lear's loaded request for affection with the bald insulting riposte of 'Nothing'. The sticking-point is highly significant. Hamlet naturally bridles at Claudius's criticism of his mourning and his appropriation of the familiar (and familial) term *son*, since he is mortified at the ambiguous and distasteful relationship he now has with the King. His animus is contiually displayed in savage paradoxes about his 'uncle-father and aunt-mother', notably in the parody of biblical language about the mystical relationship of man and woman in marriage:

> Farewell, dear mother.
> CLAUDIUS: Thy loving father, Hamlet.
> HAMLET: My mother. Father and mother is man and wife; man and wife is one
> flesh; and so, my mother.
>
> (IV. iii. 51–4)

As if unwilling to be drawn into any kind of speech, Hamlet's opening lines in the play are short, sharp and bitter. When, however, his mother tactlessly implies that his grief might not be genuine, he is stung into a fierce parody of the hypocritical and overblown 'court style' stocked with high-register creations (shown in bold type):

> Seems, madam? Nay, it is, I know not 'seems'.
> This not alone, my inky cloak, good mother,
> Nor **customary** suits of solemn black,
> Nor windy **suspiration** of forced breath,
> No, nor the fruitful river in the eye,
> Nor the dejected **haviour** of the visage . . .
>
> (I. ii. 76–81)

These are overtly mocking, as empty and stilted as the hyperbole of the 'fruitful river in the eye', the outward show of exaggerated grief. Furthermore, Hamlet uses *customary* in a philologically subtle fashion, alluding to the word's etymology in *costume*, His outburst draws from Claudius a lecture of breathtaking hypocrisy on the propriety of mourning: he too draws heavily on the Latinized neologisms, **condolement, obsequious, retrograde** and **unprevailing**. At once insistent and showing a remarkable lack of tact, he reasserts his paternal role, claiming Hamlet as

> Our chiefest courtier, cousin and our son.
>
> (I. ii. 117)

The battle-lines have been drawn, morally, linguistically and stylistically, even before the Ghost's alarming revelations.

Hamlet father and son: revenge and salvation

The ghost of Hamlet's father is quite unlike the crudely melodramatic spooks which stalked the Elizabethan stage accompanied by fireworks and thunder and lightning. Shakespeare's creation is stately and dignified. As Marcellus says,

> We do it wrong, being so majestical,
> To offer it the show of violence.
>
> (I. I. 125–6)

Above all, 'the embassy of death', as Wilson Knight (1949, p. 17) well calls it, is mysteriously reticent until it unburdens itself to the Prince. A significant and ultimately unresolved ambiguity inheres in the terms applied to the creature by the hero:

> Be thou a spirit of health or goblin damned,
> Bring with thee airs from heaven or blasts from hell,
> Be thy intents wicked or charitable . . .
>
> (I. iv. 19–21)

Hamlet subsequently prefers the favourable interpretation, though as Dover Wilson has shown, the contemporary sense of *spirit* was more likely to be diabolical than benign.

The spirit's alarming disclosures are given in an expansive, elevated, regal style, with especially fluent bitterness shown in the treacherous fratricide it has endured. The elder Hamlet was, we gather, an impressive man of action, unlike his devious and manipulative brother: as Horatio recalls in a memorable vignette, 'in an angry parle [he] smote the **sledded** Polacks on the ice' (I. i. 63). Surely, however, the most striking part of the whole speech is its emphasis on the horrors of Purgatory, notably in the use of archaic religious vocabulary for the atonement it was denied:

> Thus was I, sleeping, by a brother's hand
> Of life, of crown, of queen at once dispatched,
> Cut off even in the blosssoms of my sin,
> Unhousel'd, **disappointed, unaneal'd**.
>
> (I. v. 74–7)

That last poignant line, made up of three words unused elsewhere by Shakespeare, contains a history of religious ritual. All three terms mean essentially the same thing, namely the deprivation of extreme unction before death, but they have a cumulative emphasis and convey a unique sense of strictly observed hallowed rites. *Unhouseled* is a rare resuscitation of the ancient term rooted in Anglo-Saxon *husl*, originally a pagan sacrifice, before it was converted to mean the Christian Eucharist. (The previous recorded instance is from Sir Thomas More in 1535.) *Unanealed* and *disappointed* are, more re-markably, Shakespearean coinages seemingly unused for over a century subsequently. This powerful line would have an arresting impact on a con-temporary audience. Furthermore, it obviously weighs heavily with Hamlet in the crucial scene after the play within the play, when he comes across Claudius seemingly at prayer and rejects the seemingly ideal opportunity as 'hire and salary, not revenge' (III. iii. 79).

The Ghost cries out, then, not simply for justice and redress for murder, adultery and incest. It is an awesome reminder of the importance of dying in a state of grace. Throughout the play we are reminded, more than any other, of the afterlife, the *reckoning*, the *audit*, and the true horror of dying in a state of mortal sin. The topic is treated with apparent flippancy when the gravedig-gers, in the course of exhuming Yorick to make way for Ophelia, bandy the legal terminology of *se offendendo* and reduce vital issues of salvation and damnation to the crudely physical point of whether the man goes to the water or the water goes to the man (V. i). It is most fully explored, with superb irony, in the prayer scene as Claudius, the villain, desperately seeks repentance for his 'limed soul' in the face of a judgement above, where, he acknowledges, 'there is no shuffling' (III. iii). And it emerges most pointedly when Hamlet, in a diabolical refinement of his own calculated murder of Rosencrantz and Guildenstern, insists in the forged death-warrant that they should be 'put to sudden death, / Not shriving time allowed' (V. ii. 46–7). *Shriving time*, which strikes us now as a curious archaism, is the last recorded usage in the *OED*.

This Christian complication creates profound tensions in what is, generi-cally, a revenge tragedy. The catalyst, the Ghost, admits that killing is 'murder most foul' even 'in the best' (I. v. 27). When Laertes says shockingly, that his wished revenge on Hamlet would be 'To cut his throat i' the church', the villain rejoins sanctimoniously, 'No place, indeed, should murder **sanctuarize**' using one of his typical Latinized neologisms (IV. vii. 127–8), Ultimately, in this tragedy of what Horatio calls 'purposes mistook', the whole of the royal house of Denmark is wiped out. Worse, all die in a state of·mortal sin. Even Hamlet, who said coldly of his callous treatment of Rosencrantz and Guildenstern, 'They are not near my conscience,' is not given another chance to repent for their murder. Their deaths are announced just after his own passing, actually interrupting Horatio's moving elegy of 'flights of angels sing thee to thy rest'. It is as if he has been denied 'shriving time' by his own creator.

Hamlet's word-hoard

With Hamlet dies an extraordinary mind which philosophizes on virtually every aspect of human existence, and a wonderful word-hoard. Horatio's final lament, 'Now cracks a noble heart,' describes in generous terms more the ideal Hamlet than the suffering and tormented prince enmeshed by evil whom we see in the play. Though Ophelia is generally less perceptive and reliable a judge of character, her premature 'obituary' at Hamlet's supposed madness conveys more justly the diversity of his talents and the tragedy of their loss:

> The courtier's, soldier's, scholar's, eye, tongue, sword;
> The expectancy and rose of the fair state,
> The glass of fashion and the mould of form
> The observed of all observers, quite, quite down!
>
> (III. i. 160–2)

The strangely compacted syntax of this heightened utterance foregrounds the point that Hamlet was the cynosure of the court and a peerlessly brilliant man of many talents. We see this diversity in his unique lexicon, which is predominantly academic and high-register, as one might expect, but includes an extraordinary range. In his famous speech of self-analysis he juxtaposes registers with astonishing facility, setting rarefied scholarly words against the commonest and crudest:

> I have of late – but wherefore I know not – lost all my mirth, foregone all custom of exercises; and indeed it goes so heavily with my disposition that this goodly frame, the earth, seems to me a sterile promontory; this most excellent canopy, the air, look you, this brave o'erhanging firmament, this majestical roof fretted with golden fire, why it appears no other thing to me but a foul and pestilent congregation of vapours. What a piece of work is a man! How noble in reason! how infinite in faculty! in form and moving how express and admirable! in action how like an angel! in apprehension how like a god! the beauty of the world! the paragon of animals! And yet, to me, what is this quintessence of dust? (II. ii. 312–29)

Furthermore, in the following lists, all the terms listed in the low, middle and high register (some forty-eight in all) are original:

Low register: 'as' es (a pun on *asses*), **buzz buzz, fishmonger, groundlings, honeying, jig-maker, lug the guts, saw** (a motion with the hand) **whored;**

Middle register: chapless, chop-fallen, candied, dizzy (vb.) **gain-giving, trippingly, ungored, unweeded;**

High register: apoplexed, batten, beteem, bourn, cerements, coinage, comingled [commedled Q2], comply, compulsive, concernancy, consummation, crimeful, definement, disasters [Q2], enseamed, escoted, excitements, extolment, inurned, inventorially, malefactions, occulted,

o'erleavens, o'eroffices, pregnant, proposer, reword, robustious, suspiration unpregnant;

Archaic register: clepe, rood;

Exotic register: bilboes, chanson, chopine, miching malicho, pajock, eisel;

Classical register: Alexander, Hercules, Hyperion, Mercury, Nemean lion, Nero, Niobe, Ossa, satyr, Vulcan;

Set phrases: antic disposition, cast of thought, caviare to the general, chameleon's dish, country matters, a falling off, galls his kibe, slings and arrows, something is rotten . . . , speak daggers, went to cuffs.

Hamlet without the prince

The extraordinary linguistic richness of the play is shown equally in the diversity of speech given to the other characters. Over fifty words (including all the high-register list) are original. Here is some sense of the range:

Low register: beetle (vb.), **drabbing, muddied,** hugger-mugger, **buzzers, dupped, pooh!, privates, tarre, tumble** (sexual);

Middle register: beggared, colour (vb.), **fretful,** sugar (vb.), painted (word), **sledded, upshot;**

High register: annexement, aslant, blastments, cicatrice, climatures, comart, commutual, compulsatory, compulsive, condolement, congruing, coted, credent, cunnings, demi-natured, distilment, enactures, encompassment, illume, implorators, incorpsed, jointress, operant, palmy, penetrable, pious, precurse, primy, ratifier, re-speaking, sanctuarize, sate, scrimer, strewments, survivor, unanealed, unimproved, unpolluted, unnerved, unprevailing, ventages;

Archaic register: Cock (God), gis (Jesus), down-gyvèd, unhouseled;

Exotic register: bissom rheum, cataplasm, crants, porpentine;

classical register: Lethe, Pelion;

Set phrases: primrose path, protest too much;

Special features (flexibility); the unseen good old man, dies of his own too-much.

Macbeth

'All art constantly aspires to the condition of music,' wrote the noted Victorian critic, Walter Pater, selecting the art in which form and content are least separable. On the basis of this analogy, it could be claimed that several of Shakespeare's mature tragedies can be understood as aspiring to opera, especially the Wagnerian conception of the 'total work of art' or *Gesamtkunstwerk*, which unites all the features of poetic drama, music, scenery and even dance. In *Macbeth* pre-eminently, theme, character, atmosphere, scene-settings, even the Wagnerian idea of theme music or *Leitmotiv*, are rendered by combining the resources of language and imagery into an organic whole of astonishing concentration and originality. Shakespeare achieved this remarkable feat by going even further than the creation of different kinds of language for the principal characters which we have seen in *Hamlet*. Though he had used this technique before, the synthesis he achieved in *Macbeth* shows the greatest skill and subtlety.

As Caroline Spurgeon (1935), George Wilson Knight (1949) and Wolfgang Clemen (1951) have shown in their various ways, *Macbeth* is a brilliantly well-made play, with key-words and patterns of imagery woven through its texture with such subtlety that they become part of the play's organic structure rather than poetic embellishments. Thus, to take one of the more obvious examples, the reiteration of *blood* and *bloody* more than forty times (in a total of some 2086 lines) is merely the outward statistic for a complex integral pattern in which the word takes on a diversity of symbolic meanings: these include 'death', 'life', 'kinship' and 'guilt'. Often meanings are ironically juxtaposed, as in Donalbain's bitter and suspicious observation after the murder of Duncan: 'The near in blood, the nearer bloody' (II. iii. 146–7). He thus rejects the traditional idea of the family as the source of unity, security and loyalty, for he means that 'next of kin are most dangerous since they have most to gain.'

Some idea of the play's linguistic creativity can be gauged by the fact that the first audience would have witnessed in the speeches of Macbeth alone over fifty new words and semantic extensions of existing terms. Most of these are found in his early, passionate, guilt-stricken soliloquies, as will be shown in subsequent analysis and discussion. Although one might expect this linguistic feature to be highly developed in the hero, it is not confined to him. A striking example is that moment of classic dramatic irony when Duncan and Banquo comment graciously on the tranquillity and security of Macbeth's castle at Inverness. Contrasting with the violent tension of the treachery plotted inside the castle, their speeches are notably lyrical, highly wrought with original effects and neologisms, highlighted in bold type:

> DUNCAN: This castle hath a pleasant seat; the air
> **Nimbly** and sweetly recommends itself
> Unto our gentle senses.
> BANQUO: This guest of summer,
> The **temple-haunting** martlet, does approve
> By his loved **mansionry** that the heaven's breath
> Smells **wooingly** here: no jutty, frieze,

Buttress, not **coign** of vantage, but this bird
Hath made his bed and pendent **procreant** cradle:

(I. vi. 1–8)

Confusion, equivocation and ambiguity in 'supernatural soliciting'

Macbeth has affinities to the schema of a morality play, as is shown in the relatively uncomplicated conflict of values, the comparative simplicity of characterization and the pointed disposition of a number of crucial terms, notably *blood, ambition, heaven* and *hell*. Although it is by far the shortest and fastest-moving of the tragedies, the play has various highly developed and special features in its language. Metaphorical density is, perhaps, the most striking, making some of the hero's agonized soliloquies almost impenetrable. Another is a reflection of the play's essential preoccupation with the supernatural, embodied in charms, spells and invocations which come weirdly true, though often in confused and distorted ways. Two of the key terms, *weird* and *equivocation*, are used in original ways. An extension of this 'weird' property of language in that several key terms do not 'belong' to an individual character exclusively, but become woven into semantic chains which are shared and echoed (often unconsciously) by a variety of characters, thereby intensifying dramatic irony. More will be said of this later.

Things, actions, qualities, even characters, are seldom referred to in their true nature. They are variously euphemized, denigrated, eulogized, exaggerated or avoided. We can see this process simply demonstrated in the schizophrenic variety of terms applied to the hero, reflecting both his social advancement and his moral decline from *brave Macbeth, valour's minion and Bellona's bridegroom* to *black Macbeth, hell-kite!, this fiend of Scotland, hell-hound* and *this dead butcher*. There is no neutral, objective assessment of Macbeth; that is left to the audience/reader to achieve in weighing up these extraordinarily diverse judgements.

Macduff, the ultimate avenger of Duncan and exorcizer of the 'hell hound', revives and sustains the religious perspective as it atrophies and dies in Macbeth. At the discovery of the murder, his language is so elevated in its sacred and spiritual terms that he is not immediately understood:

Most sacrilegious murder hath broke ope
The Lord's anointed temple and stole thence
The life o' the building!

(II. iii. 73–5)

It is he who applies all the diabolical epithets mentioned above to Macbeth, and he who simultaneously sanctifies Duncan and his Queen:

> Thy royal father
> Was a most sainted king; the queen that bore thee
> Oftener upon her knees that on her feet,
> Died every day she live'd.
>
> (IV. iii. 108–11)

Throughout the play the unnatural is as marked as the supernatural. Reinforcing the copious symbolic representations of disorder, so powerfully described by Wilson Knight (1949, pp. 145–7), are numerous verbal correlatives. The more obvious can be categorized as invocations of the unnatural such as 'Stars, hide your fires!', 'Come, thick night', 'Come fate into the list', and so on. In addition, there is a substantial vocabulary of strange negatives. These include such remarkable original formations as **unbend, undivulged unheeded, unmake, unmanned, unprovoke, unreal, unsafe, unsex, unshrinking** and **unspeak**, several of which are still arresting. Others in this category first recorded within some ten years of *Macbeth* are: *unattended, unbattered, unbecoming, unguarded, undaunted, unlineal* and *unwiped*.

The 'weird sisters' who open the piece epitomize the themes of equivocation and ambiguity, the interweaving of double meanings into a form of words. These themes and their 'weirdness' are sustained by the fact that the true nature of the Witches is never revealed. An audience unfamiliar with the play and therefore not having read the stage direction: *An open place. Thunder and lightning. Enter three WITCHES.* would necessarily be uncertain of their true moral status. Are they figures of Fate, as Macbeth believes, or do they simply know the future, or are they as Banquo believes, 'instruments of darkness' using the ambitious and the gullible to create chaos?

The play treats these issues experientially, starting with the shrewd scepticism of Banquo:

> . . . oftentimes, to win us to our harm,
> The instruments of darkness tell us truths,
> Win us with honest trifles, to betray's
> In deepest consequence.
>
> (I. iii. 123–6)

and finishing with the bitter experience of Macbeth:

> I pull/pall in resolution and begin
> To doubt the equivocation of the fiend
> That lies like truth
>
> (V. v. 42–4)

Fascinatingly, Macbeth's usage of the key term *equivocation* is recorded as original in the *OED*, although the term had been current with a wider meaning from the fourteenth century. He subsequently gives a masterly definition in a later speech, but then it is too late:

> And be these juggling fiends no more believed,
> That palter with us in a double sense:
> That keep the word of promise to our ear,
> And break it to our hope.
>
> (V. vii. 48–51)

The ambiguity of 'the weird sisters' derives from Holinshed, Shakespeare's primary source. Wisely, he does not resolve it, but derives maximum effect from his virtual resuscitation of the word *weird*. This term, much used in Anglo-Saxon as the noun *wyrd* meaning 'fate', had steadily fallen into disuse in Middle English, surviving chiefly in Northern texts. The *OED* notes: 'the later currency and adjectival use [are] derived from the currency in the story of Macbeth.' This fey northern word, which plays such a vital role in the tragedy, then fell again into disuse. It is an interesting poetic footnote, however, to record that the more recent senses of *weird* ('supernatural, uncanny, strange unusual, odd, fantastic') are first recorded in the poetry of Shelley and Keats. (This is part of a general tendency for Shakespeare's work to become a resource for subsequent literary usage.) In contemporary usage, of course, *weird* has become very common, especially in America, as has another of the play's coinages, *unreal*.

The language of the Witches is strangely simple, even childlike in its diction, its rhymes and its riddles, into which are woven the tantalizing potential of prophecy. Their sophistries become apparent only later. They generate several key words, such as *fair, foul, double* and *trouble*, which reverberate eerily through the play, almost infecting the speech of the other characters. Macbeth's opening line in the play is only one of several notably pointed ironic echoes:

> So foul and fair a day I have not seen.
> (I. iii. 38)

Banquo's comment on the prophecies has a strange, echoing dissonance:

> Good sir, why do you start, and seem to fear
> Things that do sound so fair?
>
> (I. iii. 51–2)

Even Duncan is unwittingly drawn into the jingling use of *trouble*:

> The love that follows us sometimes is our trouble,
> Which still we thank as love. Herein I teach you
> How you shall bid God 'eyld [reward] us for your pains,
> And thank us for your trouble.
>
> (I. vi. 11–14)

to which Lady Macbeth chimes in, with hypocritical unctuousness, precisely in the idiom of the witches:

> All our service,
> In every point twice done, and then done double . . .
>
> (I. vi. 15–16)

The Two Styles

Macbeth provides the example *par excellence* of the schizophrenic character, torn between murderous ambition for the 'golden round' with its horrifying problems of attainment, and the desire to be the loyal thane glorying in 'golden opinions'. Shakespeare consequently creates for him two quite diverse styles, public and personal. That of the public persona is plain, blunt and monosyllabic. His opening line – 'So foul and fair a day I have not seen' – is typically unimpressive, flat and ambivalently non-committal; it acquires its significance by being an unconscious echo of the Witches' opening chorus and is thus riddled with dramatic ironies, of which he is unaware. It prepares us for such resounding understatements as 'Twas a rough night' and 'This is a sorry sight,' astoundingly phlegmatic responses to the hideous events and experiences surrounding Duncan's murder. Mary McCarthy, a critic of great shrewdness, was so struck (perhaps so well deceived) by this public style that in her essay 'General Macbeth' she presented the ambitious, tortured thane as a simple soldier, banal and dour:

He is a general and has just won a battle; he enters the scene making a remark about the weather. 'So fair and foul [*sic*] a day I have not seen.' On this flat note Macbeth's character tone is set. 'Terrible weather we're having.' 'The sun can't seem to make up its mind.' A commonplace man who talks in commonplaces, a golfer, one might guess, on the Scottish fairways, Macbeth is the only Shakespeare hero who corresponds to a bourgeois type: a murderous Babbit, let us say. (1962, p. 229)

Though this view contains a grain of truth, it is manifestly superficial. It ignores entirely the inner Macbeth, who suffers bizarre hallucinations and bursts out in soliloquies rich in phantasmagoric imagery and extraordinary, rarefied diction, revealing a highly imaginative and poetic soul. The flat public style is largely a front. The irony of Lady Macbeth's rather patronizing lecture to her husband: 'look like the innocent flower, But be the serpent under 't' (I. v. 66–7) is that Macbeth does not need her advice; he is already expert at assuming the mask of dullness.

McCarthy also ignores the signal paradox that a man so literal-minded in many ways (notably in his interpretations of the Witches and their prophecies) should be so densely metaphorical in his own speech. Macbeth's imagination, anything but bourgeois, infuses the inanimate with life, depicting the abstract in vivid, extraordinary metaphors. Shakespeare catches the essence of his paranoia: the 'very stones prate of my whereabout', his 'fears in Banquo stick deep', his mind is 'full of scorpions'; in a weird moment, even the very 'light thickens' (an original use of the verb). So far from being 'commonplace' he is intensely aware of the loss of peace, innocence and security, the rich potential of life which he somnambulistically and tragically destroys.

Furthermore, so far from being a dull military man, he has that hallmark of the Shakespearean tragic hero, a remarkably diversified vocabulary which encompasses ranks of learned and intellectual words like *antidote, bounteous, catalogue, cloistered, commencing, disposition, equivocation, fantastical, hyrcan, incarnadine, ingredients, intelligence, intrenchant, multitudinous, navigation, nonpareil, parricide, pernicious, predominant, speculation, supernatural, treatise* and *vulnerable.*

Macbeth's language always reflects this schizophrenic quality, oscillating between high-register abstractions and direct, common terms as he is torn between recognizing the horrifying truth of his nature and his actions and the desire to euphemize them. Rather than face his deed by the use of plain words, he prefers evasions, but he does not resort to standard euphemisms as he seeks to accommodate 'the present horror of the time'. His first developed aside is stocked with a remarkable proportion of high-register terms (in italics), although it contains only one original usage (in bold type):

> [*Aside*] Two truths are told,
> As happy *prologues* to the swelling act
> Of the *imperial theme.* – I thank you, gentlemen. –
> [*Aside*] This *supernatural soliciting*
> Cannot be ill, cannot be good; if ill,
> **Why hath it given me** *earnest* of *success,*
> *Commencing* in a truth? I am Thane of Cawdor:

> If good, why do I yield to that *suggestion*
> Whose *horrid image* doth unfix my hair
> And make my **seated** heart knock at my ribs,
> Against the use of nature? *Present* fears
> Are less than *horrible imaginings*;
> My thought, whose murder yet is but *fantastical*,
> Shakes so my single state of man that *function*
> Is smothered in *surmise*, and nothing is
> But what is not.
>
> (I. iii. 127–42)

His tendency to use obscure classicisms becomes more emphasized as he approaches the crisis of the murder. Throughout the play he uses the plain word *kill* only once, not in relation to his victims: 'We have scotched/scorched the snake, not killed it' (III. ii. 13). As if reaching the perimeter of known and accepted language, he gropes beyond, using increasing numbers of rarefied original words (in bold type):

> If it were done when 'tis done, then 'twere well
> It were done quickly; if the ***assassination***
> Could ***trammel*** up the *consequence*, and catch
> With his *surcease success*; but that this blow
> Might be the **be-all** and the **end-all** here,
> But here, upon this bank and shoal of time,
> We'd jump the life to come. But in these cases
> We still have *judgement* here; that we but teach
> Bloody *instructions*, which, being taught, *return*
> To plague the *inventor*; this even-handed *justice*
> *Commends* the *ingredients* of our *poison'd chalice*
> To our own lips. He's here in double trust:
> First as I am his kinsman and his *subject*,
> Strong both against the deed; then, as his host,
> Who should against the murderer shut the door,
> Not bear the knife myself. Besides, this Duncan
> Hath borne his *faculties* so meek, hath been
> So clear in his great *office*, that his *virtues*
> Will *plead* like *angels* **trumpet-tongued** against
> The deep *damnation* of his **taking-off**;
> And pity, like a naked new-born babe,
> Striding the blast, or *heaven's cherubin*, horsed
> Upon the sightless *couriers* of the air,
> Shall blow the *horrid* deep in every eye,
> That tears shall drown the wind. I have no spur
> To prick the sides of my *intent*, but only

> *Vaulting ambition,* which **o'er-leaps** itself
> And falls on the other.

(I. vii. 1–28)

Macbeth's psychomachia or 'struggle of the soul' is revealed in the changes of register. The 'horrible imaginings' of the first eleven lines are suggested (but not defined) in the concentrations of opaque Latinisms and original formations. From 'double trust' the language becomes plain and simple, reflecting the uncomplicated call of duty incumbent upon the loyal thane. But from 'bear the knife myself' the terrifying images of damnation and revenge surge up in alarming metaphors and extraordinary, unique diction. It is this juxtaposition which impresses throughout the gruesome experience, as scholarly words like *palpable, sensible, instrument, ravishing, descended, addressed, pronounce* and *nourisher* are set off against the plain and stark: *I have done the deed; these hangmans hands;*[6] *stuck in my throat; they pluck out mine eyes.* The original formations come from all sources, rare and common: **heat-oppressed, dudgeon, curtained, alarum'd, stealthy, ravelled.**

At the discovery of the murder, Macbeth struggles vertiginously to keep control, seeking to exorcize his guilt as murderer while simultaneously keeping up the front of the loyal thane. His speeches of explanation contain bizarre images and shifts of register:

> from this instant,
> There's nothing serious in mortality,
> All is but toys:

(II. iv. 99–101)

> The expedition of my violent love
> Outran the pauser, reason. Here lay Duncan,
> His silver skin lac'd with his golden blood;
> And his gash'd stabs looked like a breach in nature
> For ruin's wasteful entrance: here the murderers,
> Steep'd in the colours of their trade, their daggers
> Unmannerly breech'd with gore:

(II. iv. 117-23)

John Middleton Murry brought out memorably the classic dramatic irony that, as Macbeth seeks to deceive, so he tells the truth: 'He intends the monstrous hypocrisy of a conventional lament for Duncan; but as the words leave his lips they change their nature, and become a doom upon himself' *Shakespeare*, (1936, p. 332). On these speeches Dr Johnson shrewdly observed: 'It is not improbable that Shakespeare put these forced and unnatural metaphors into the mouth of Macbeth, as a mark of artifice and dissimulation, to show the difference between the studied language of hypocrisy and the natural out-cries of sudden passion.' Mary McCarthy called them 'fustian' (1963, p. 236).

These acute observations can be corroborated by detailed lexical analysis, which clarifies and explains the effect of falsity which this speech evokes in sensitive readers. It is not, however, simply a piece of fustian; it is a skilfully wrought juxtaposition of high style, melodramatic overemphasis and banal-ity. The incongruity of lexical elements creates a whole series of false notes. Thus *expedition* and *refrain* are altogether too stilted and cerebral for this context, as is the curious original word, **pauser**. The haunting and magical line, 'Here lay Duncan, his silver skin lac'd with his golden blood,' forms a serene, iconic moment of stasis in which the heraldic terms *silver* and *golden* reflect the peace of death which Macbeth envies, rather than conveying the gruesome spectacle. The crucial terms describing the hideous crime, *gash'd stabs*, form a disturbingly awkward tautology, alongside which mundane words like *wasteful entrance*, *colours of their trade* and above all, *unmannerly*, seem absurdly out of place. It is hardly surprising that Lady Macbeth faints (or pretends to faint) at the conclusion of this passionate and strange farrago.

The pointed shift in the balance of power between Macbeth and his 'dearest partner in greatness' is directly reflected in the power and originality of their language. It is she who 'carries' him through the crisis of the murder with potent imperatives and original forms. Thereafter, as she loses control, her language wanes pitifully and Macbeth's becomes frighteningly robust. The turning point comes in Act III, where Macbeth takes the initiative in plotting the murder of Banquo and paternalistically excludes her in a new, confident language. Liberally stocked with neologisms, his speeches embrace evil in powerful symbolic metaphors reminiscent of Lady Macbeth's own earlier diabolical invocations:

> MACBETH: There's comfort yet; they are **assailable**;
>   Then be thou jocund. Ere the bat hath flown
>   His **cloistered** flight, ere to black Hecate's summons
>   The **shard-borne** beetle with his drowsy hums
>   Hath rung night's yawning peal, there shall be done
>   A deed of dreadful note.
> LADY MACBETH: What's to be done?
> MACBETH: Be innocent of the knowledge, dearest chuck,
>   Till thou applaud the deed. Come seeling night,
>   **Scarf** up the tender eye of pitiful day,
>   And with thy bloody and invisible hand
>   Cancel and tear to pieces that great bond
>   Which keeps me pale! Light **thickens**, and the crow
>   Makes wing to the **rooky** wood;

> Good things of day begin to droop and drowse,
> Whiles night's black agents to their preys do rouse.
> Thou marvell'st at my words: but hold thee still:
> Things bad begun make strong themselves by ill:
>
> (III. ii. 39–55)

The four last lines have the strange rhyming idiom of the Witches.

Macbeth becomes the classic type of paranoia, combining simultaneously delusions of grandeur and of persecution. His increasing isolation and irrationality are clearly visible in the invocation to 'seeling night', just quoted. Obsessed with the undefined 'great bond which keeps me pale', he envisions even night as an active force with a hand which is (impossibly) both 'bloody and invisible'.

One of the striking results of detailed lexical analysis is the extent to which the experience of fear is rendered by numerous original uses. For instance, when Macbeth is told that Fleance has escaped his murderous plot, these neologisms pour out in his paranoid reaction:

> Then comes my fit again: I had else been perfect:
> Whole as the marble, founded as the rock,
> As broad and general as the **casing** air
> But now I am **cabin'd, cribb'd** confin'd, bound in
> To saucy doubts and fears.
>
> (III. iv. 21–5)

The last line contains revealingly paranoid sentiments: 'doubts and fears,' the common lot of humanity, are regarded as 'saucy'. Often the context of fear generates original uses in related terms. This is true of the concluding couplet to Act III scene iv:

> My strange and **self-abuse**
> Is the **initiate** fear that wants hard use.

Macbeth's famous final speech starts with his numbed response to Lady Macbeth's death:

> She should have died hereafter:
> There would have a time for such a word.
> Tomorrow, and tomorrow, and tomorrow
> Creeps in this petty pace from day to day
> To the last syllable of recorded time:
> And all our **yesterdays** have lighted fools
> The way to dusty death.
>
> (V. v. 17–23)

The speech is an alarmingly clear expression of meaninglessness, of life as an empty succession of moments, as a charade, as a tale told by an idiot. Yet, apart from **yesterdays**, the lexis is flat and plain; it is the expression of a man who has murdered trust, destroyed his own moral sensibility, 'supped full of horrors' and now faces nothingness.

Shakespeare's Development of his Source:
Antony and Cleopatra

Antony and Cleopatra deserves special emphasis in any study of Shakespeare's language, since its richness of metaphor, symbolism and neologism make it the most remarkable expression of all the potentialities of the language of the time. However, it is one of the paradoxes of Shakespeare's creativity that virtually all his plays derive from well-defined sources from which he borrowed copiously, sometimes even verbatim, and yet a comparison with these sources invariably demonstrates his originality most forcibly. The two sources for which he evidently had considerable respect are Sir Thomas North's translation of Plutarch's *Lives* and Raphael Holinshed's *Chronicles of England, Scotland, and Ireland*. North is a primary and fundamental source for *Julius Caesar, Antony and Cleopatra* and *Coriolanus*, while Holinshed was a clear source for *Macbeth* and *King Lear*.

In order to acquire an insight into Shakespeare's relationship of indebtedness and creativity with these sources, let us compare the most famous 'purple passage' of all, the description of Cleopatra on the Cydnus, as found in North's Plutarch and as transformed by Shakespeare:

> she disdained to set forward otherwise, but to take her barge in the river of Cydnus, the poope wherof was gold, the sails of purple, and the owers [oars] of silver, which kept stroke in rowing after the sounde of the musicke of flutes, howboyes [oboes], citherns, violls, and such other instruments as they played upon in the barge. And now for the person of her selfe: she was layed under a pavilion of cloth of gold of tissue, apparelled and attired like the goddesse Venus, commonly drawen in picture: and hard by her, on either hand of her, pretie fair boyes apparelled as painters doe set forth the god Cupide, with little fannes in their hands, with the which they fanned wind upon her. Her ladies and gentlewomen also, the fairest of them were apparelled like the nymphes Nereides (which are the mermaides of the waters) and like the Graces, some stearing the helme, others tending the tackle and ropes of the barge, out of which there came a wonderfull passing sweete savor of perfumes, that perfumed the wharfes side, pestered with innumerable multitudes of people. Some of them followed the barge all alongest the rivers side: others ranne out of the citie to see her comming

in. So that in thend, there ranne such multitudes of people one after an other to see her, that Antonius was left post alone in the market place, in his Imperiall seate to geve audience. (1968, p. 262)

Against this we may set the entranced account ingeniously put into the mouth of the cynic Enobarbus, in which the original uses are highlighted in bold type:

> The barge she sat in, like a burnished throne
> Burn'd on the water: the poop was beaten gold;
> Purple the sails, and so perfumed that
> The winds were love-sick with them; the oars were silver,
> Which to the tune of flutes kept stroke, and made
> The water which they beat to follow faster,
> As amorous of their strokes. For her own person,
> It **beggar'd** all description: she did lie
> In her pavilion – cloth of gold of tissue –
> **O'er-picturing** that Venus where we see
> The fancy outwork nature. On each side her,
> Stood **pretty-dimpled** boys, like smiling Cupids,
> With divers-coloured fans, whose wind did seem
> To glow the delicate cheeks which they did cool,
> And what they undid did.
> AGRIPPA: O, rare for Antony!
> ENOBARBUS: Her gentlewomen, like the Nereides,
> So many mermaids, tended her in the eyes,
> And made their bends adornings. At the helm
> A seeming mermaid steers: the silken tackle
> Swell with the touches of those **flower-soft** hands,
> That yarely frame the office. From the barge
> A strange invisible perfume hits the sense
> Of the adjacent wharfs. The city cast
> Her people out upon her; and Antony,
> **Enthron'd** in the market-place, did sit alone,
> Whistling to the air; which, but for vacancy,
> Had gone to gaze on Cleopatra too,
> And made a gap in nature.
>
> (II. ii. 191–218)

Plutarch is a historian epitomizing what the French hisorian Alexis de Tocqueville categorized as the aristocratic mode of history, since vulgarized and popularized, somewhat ironically in the present context, as 'the Cleopatra's nose school of history'. His wonderfully vivid account of Cleopatra's theatrical appearance on the Cydnus shows a journalistic eye for colourful and opulent detail, emphasized in 'the poope wherof was gold, the sails of purple, and the owers [oars] of silver' and so on. His sentences (only six in the original) are dutifully stocked with factual matter. In North's version, this often leads to an overloading of the clauses, thus creating an unfortunate sense of diminuendo which dissipates the drama of the moment, notably in 'the musicke of flutes, howboyes [oboes], citherns, violls, and such other instruments as they played upon in the barge' and 'with little fannes in their hands, with the which they fanned wind upon her'. Plutarch's original, it should be noted, is much less ornate: 'urging [the barge] on with silver oars to the sound of the flute blended with pipes and lutes' and 'boys like Loves in paintings stood on either side and fanned her.'

Plutarch describes Cleopatra and her entourage in a manner which makes us very aware of artifice, contrivance and 'dressing up'. Hence the reiteration (not very skilful in North's version) of *apparelled*: 'apparelled and attired like the goddesse Venus'; 'apparelled as painters doe set forth the god Cupide'; 'apparelled like the nymphes Nereides'. We are party to the disguises by means of viewpoints which are simultaneously public and 'behind the scenes'. North's language is clear and direct, but does not engage us by means other than emphasis and repetition: he will use two or three epithets ('pretie fair boyes'; 'wonderfull passing sweete savor of perfumes') where Plutarch has one.

Although Shakespeare follows the order of Plutarch's description and borrows most of the detail, it would clearly be mistaken to take the view of Richard Farmer in the eighteenth century: 'Our Authur [sic] hath done little more than throw the very words of North into blank verse' (in Blake, 1983, p. 48). Shakespeare's description is obviously poetic in the highest sense, imbuing Cleopatra with magical and mythical qualities. Details are concentrated to give a sense of overpowering sensuality, exploiting the responses of all the senses. Instead of the bland sweep of Plutarch's prose, concentrations of metaphor, supernatural paradoxes and echoic sound effects pervade the passage, with emphases invariably falling on Shakespeare's original contributions, which are italicized in the following analysis. They are of two kinds, namely those changes which he has wrought upon North's translation, and those which are original to the language of the time.

The barge itself, like everything around Cleopatra, is endowed with amorous and seductive qualities, strikingly realized in the verbs and participles. Now 'like a *burnish'd throne*', it '*burns* on the water', the sails are *perfumed*, the tackle is *silken*, it *swells* tumescently to the *touches* of *flower-soft* hands, the winds are *love-sick*, the oars keep stroke 'to the *tune* of flutes', making the water 'to *follow faster, As amorous of their strokes*', the last term having obvious sexual associations. The shift of tense from past to present increases immediacy, and Cleopatra's impact is further increased by the power of simple verbs: 'a strange invisible perfume *hits* the sense,' so that 'the city *cast* her people out.' In a masterly coup, Cleopatra is not actually described at the climactic moment: she occasions the memorable phrase of poetic hyperbole, now a virtual cliché: she **'beggar'd all description'**, excelling not just Venus, but the poetic imagination: **'O'er-picturing** that Venus where we see / The fancy outwork nature.' Vividness and magical impossibility compete: a *seeming mermaid* steers, the fans of the 'pretty *dimpled* boys' *glow* the delicate cheeks which they *cool*, and 'what they *undid did*'. Out of the realm of magic, Antony is left ridiculously alone, *whistling to the air* which too was enticed, but could not suspend its natural function and make *a gap in nature*.

The conclusion, then, is that even where the source is most obvious and closely followed, Shakespeare enhances it with imagination, poetic transformation and linguistic originality.

Milton

Although John Milton (1608–74) was born nearly half a century after Shakespeare, his work represents the final flowering of the Renaissance. Probably the most learned man of his age, Milton's deep classical learning is highly apparent in his language. In his great epic poem *Paradise Lost* (1667) he sought to create 'Things unattempted yet in prose or rime', namely the cosmic and religious mysteries of Man's creation, loss of innocence and relations with God. He invoked, self-consciously, the 'Heavenly Muse' and was frankly elitist in his wish that he should 'fit audience find, though few'.

After pondering the possibility of writing his *magnum opus* in Latin, Milton decided to create a specially elevated form of English for his poem. He thus went broadly the same route as Marlowe before him, exploiting the magnificently sonorous and weighty quality of the classical elements of the lexis. Also like Marlowe, he created verse paragraphs, great building blocks of verse, although even individual lines convey the sound of his 'organ voice'. Thus Satan being cast out of heaven is conveyed by a powerful concentration of magniloquent classical terms:

> Him th' Almighty *Power*
> Hurled headlong flaming from the *ethereal* sky,
> With *hideous ruin* and *combustion*, down
> To bottomless *perdition*, there to dwell
> In *adamantine chains* and *penal* fire.
>
> (Book I, 44–8)

John Aubrey, the contemporary biographer, tells us that Milton composed the poem aloud, the tragic blindness which had afflicted him in middle age having made him more sensitive to the sound qualities of words. His blindness surely lay behind the invocation to Book III: 'Hail, holy Light, offspring of Heaven first born!' and the paradox of Hell being in a state of 'darkness visible'.

T. S. Eliot noted what he called Milton's 'auditory imagination', a compensation for his blindness. In an extraordinary example, when the fallen angels are turned into serpents, he exploits the classical element to create a brilliant special effect: the exotic snake-names are specially chosen to create sibilant sounds:

> Dreadful was the din
> Of hissing through the hall, thick-swarming now
> With complicated monsters, head and tail
> Scorpion and Asp and Amphisbaena dire
> Cerastes horned, Hydrus, and Ellops drear,
> And Dipsas
>
> (Book X, 521–6)

Milton's use of classical terms was understandably conservative, since he knew their original roots and meanings. Thus his most famous coinage, *Pandemonium*, was the literal name of the home 'of all the demons' in Hell, 'the high capital of Satan and his peers'; the term took on its present sense of 'a state of confusion or uproar' only about three centuries later. He similarly used *orient* to mean 'bright', *horrent* to mean 'bristling', *reluctant* to mean 'struggling', *complicated* (quoted in the passage above) to mean 'intertwined' and *sublime* to mean 'lofty' or 'raised aloft'. Possibly his learning inhibited his creativity, but a number of terms are first found in his work: one surprising example is *gloom* in the modern sense of 'darkness'; others include *horrent, impassive, irresponsible* and *anarch*, meaning, paradoxically, the ruler of Chaos.

However, at a time when spelling was becoming fixed, Milton showed considerable initiative in the direction of phonetic simplicity. In the manuscripts of his early poems and of Books I and II of *Paradise Lost* (which he wrote before he went blind) we find forms like *yee, mee, theefe, suttle, sovran, artic* and *iland*. But there are still some classical vestiges, such as *praesent, praepare* and *daemon*, as well as inconsistencies such as *vers/verse* and *music/musick*.

Milton's poetic vocabulary represents the furthest degree of Latinization that can reasonably be attained. His achievement was so great that his influence tended to intimidate some of his successors, and led others, such as Wordsworth and Keats, into unwilling imitation.

213

The Language of Science

Most of this chapter has focused on the great lexical expansion through the borrowing of classical and foreign words, especially those which are now designated as 'common' or 'literary'. However, the Renaissance also saw the growth of major scientific interest, with considerable borrowing of specialist terms from the classical languages and from Arabic.

We should be aware at the outset that most of our basic scientific vocabulary is borrowed from these sources, and that many of the terms had been absorbed into the language well before the Renaissance. *Science* itself dates from late ME, *c.*1340, when it still maintained its broad general sense of 'knowledge', derived from Latin *scientia*. Since then it has steadily acquired the more specialized sense of a discipline which rigorously follows systematic procedures of observation, experiment and deduction. Today the word is widely applied to a whole variety of fields, such as life sciences, human sciences, earth sciences and so on. Other essential terms defining the scientific method, with corresponding dates, are:

> *problem* (Greek) 1382
> *solution* (Latin) 1375
> *experiment* (Latin) 1362
>
> *idea* (Greek) 1531
> *method* (Greek) 1541
> *theorem* (Greek) 1551
> *theory* (Greek) 1597
> *diagram* (Greek) 1619
> *system* (Greek) 1638

The powerful influence of science as a way of thinking is shown by the fact that all these words are now common and have generalized meanings. Other terms, describing whole branches of knowledge, which entered the vocabulary from the medieval period onwards are:

> *astronomy* (Greek) 1205
> *arithmetic* (Greek) 1250 (in the erroneous early form *ars metric*)
> *medicine* (Latin) 1320
> *philosophy* (Greek) 1340
> *geometry* (Greek) *c.*1350
> *rhetoric* (Greek) *c.*1350
> *logic* (Greek) 1362
> *grammar* (Greek) 1362

Table 4.1 The growth in scientific terms

	astro-	bio-	geo-
Johnson's Dictionary (1755)	16	2	20
OED (1884–1928)	39	24	55
OED Supplement (1972–86)	15	38	20

chemistry (Arabic) 1605 (previously *alchemy* 1362)
astrology (Greek) 1375

algebra (Arabic) 1541
anatomy (Greek) 1541
geography (Greek) 1542
physics (Greek) 1589
mathematics (Greek) 1581
pharmacy (Greek) 1597

What is particularly striking about the time-structure of both sets of words is the notable gap of 150–200 years in each, between the late fourteenth century and the mid-sixteenth. This shows the essential stagnation between the medieval period and the Renaissance. We should be aware that several of the earlier terms in the second group are the names of the old medieval base syllabus of the *trivium* (logic, grammar and rhetoric) and the *quadrivium* (arithmetic, astronomy, geometry and music). The 'new generation' of terms, so to speak, forms the beginnings of the great growth of scientific enquiry which has continued ever since, generating a huge lexical expansion of specialized terms, most of them of classical origin. We can get some sense of the scale of this lexical growth when we consider table 4.1 concerning words beginning with *astro-*, *bio-* and *geo-*.

The lexical growth has not been consistent in all fields, as table 4.1 shows. The *bio-* compounds, which show the most vigorous expansion, include *biochemistry* (1881), *biophysics* (1892), *biopsy* (1895), *biosphere* (1899), *biometric* (1901), *biomechanics* (1933) and *bionics* (1960). In subsequent decades the expansion has continued with forms like *biodegradable, biofeedback, biofuel, biodiversity* and *biotechnology*.

Many of the recent words are opaque to laymen. However, let us consider a less rarefied word-field which has changed notably in character since the Middle Ages, namely that of medicine, especially as it relates to the human anatomy. This shows a development which we have partly seen in the earlier chapters, whereby native terms (which are generally transparent and readily comprehensible) have increasingly been displaced in professional language by opaque classical borrowings.

Professional Language: The Parts of the Body in Medical Lexis

Our human body, as defined by the polite native vocabulary, has notable concentrations and omissions. The head is well covered, with *head, hair, brow, eye, ear, nose, nostril, cheek, mouth, teeth* and *tongue* all being Anglo-Saxon words, as are *neck* and *back*. The upper and lower extremities are similarly served by *shoulder, arm, elbow, wrist, hand, finger*, and *leg, knee, heel, ankle, foot* and *toe*. As one would expect, the vital organs form part of the native core, namely *lung, heart, liver, kidney* and *bladder*, as do general terms like *blood* and *skin*. However, when we come to terms for the sexual or excretory organs and for bodily functions, there are notable gaps which are filled by either high-register technical terms or slang.

It was not always so. A study of medieval medical texts, such as the English translations of Lanfrank's *Cirurgery* ('Surgery') (*c*.1400) and *The Cyrurgie of Guy de Chauliac* (*c*.1425), shows us that core words now regarded as coarse and grossly impolite were previously acceptable as medical terminology. 'In wymmen,' we read in Lanfrank, 'þe necke of the bladdre is schort & is maad fast to the cunte' (1894, p. 172). We find even in Wycliffe's contemporary translation of the Bible the graphic term *arse-ropes* for *intestines*, a word whose coinage half a century later did not drive the variant term *arseguttes* out of use until the seventeenth century. *Arse* was of course, sufficiently acceptable in former times to be used in Shakespeare and Dr Johnson, while *guts* was employed without embarrassment by Sir Philip Sidney in his translation of the Psalms in 1580. (Sidney has 'My eyes, my guts, yea my soule, grief doth wast' for Psalm 31: 5, where the Authorized Version (1611) prefers *belly* and the Prayer Book *body*.)

Several native terms of basic physicality have become obsolete. When we read (in entries in the *OED*) that '[the urine] passith out by the ʒerde' (1379) or of the 'cancre of the mannes yerde' (1425), we are reminded (after a momentary confusion) that *yard* was a basic word for 'penis' in medieval times. Guy de Chauliac has sections on the 'passiouns of the yerde' and defines *priapisme* as 'the vnwilful stondynge [erection] of the ʒerde'. The main rival in medieval times was *tarse*, an older term deriving from Anglo-Saxon *teors*. Both terms had become obsolete by the nineteenth century, having been supplanted by classical *penis* and *phallus*. The definition of *penis* in its first recorded use in 1693 (in the translation of the second edition of *Blancard's Physical Dictionary*) is an interesting combination of the old and the new: '*Penis*, the Yard, made up two nervous bodies, the Channel, Nut, Skin and Foreskin.' In addition to this use of native *nut* for the *glans penis*, the old word for testicle was *stone*, recorded from the twelfth century, and carrying the usage marker in the *OED* of 'Obsolete, except in vulgar use, e.g. *stone-horse* for stallion and *stone-priest* for "a lascivious cleric".' Similarly, the old word for *copulate* was *swive*, recorded from Chaucer until it suffered a Victorian demise, shortly after this piece of quasi-medical advice recorded in 1896: 'Don't bathe on a full stomach: nor swive.'

Reference to the sexual organs was problematized by the fact that the term *sex* (recorded from the fourteenth century) tended to be used in a generalized way (e.g. 'the fair sex', also the *gentle, soft, weak, second* and even 'the *woman* sex'), rather than in the modern physiological and genital fashion, up until the seventeenth century. Hence the sexual organs are referred to by Guy de Chauliac as 'the membres of generacioun' or 'þe membres generatifes' (1971, pp. 526–7); he defines *hermafrodicia* as 'þe nature of double kynde' (1971, p. 529). Here we have an interesting use of two broad terms, *nature* and *kynde*, which also creates ambiguity. Both *kynde* and another highly generalized term, *shape*, had from Anglo-Saxon times been used more specifically to refer to the sexual organs: Ælfric's version of the drunkenness of Noah in *Genesis* 9: 23 runs: 'Sem and Iafeth . . . beheledon heora fæderes ȝecynd'; however, the previous verse has the term ȝesceapu. (As we saw in chapter 2, the word *lim* ('limb') was also used in this context.) These senses became obsolete in the course of the late Middle Ages, a late instance being 'Couer thy shap with some fly-flap,' an amusing injunction found in Skelton (1529).

Other bodily functions are described in low-register language: Guy de Chauliac writes of 'the crafte [power] of pissynge' (1971, p. 525), while Lanfrank offers the following prescription: 'If he [the patient] schite but oones a day, helpe him þerto . . . with clisterie' (1894, p. 12). All in all, it is a valid generalization to claim that all the available 'four-letter' words were used in medical contexts up to about 1500.

The point of the modern separation of registers according to a principle of decorum is most clearly illustrated in sexual terminology, on which C. S. Lewis made the trenchant observation that 'As soon as you deal with it [i.e. sex] explicitly, you are forced to choose between the language of the nursery, the gutter and the anatomy class' (in Tynan, 1975, p. 154). Historically what has occurred is that the old terminology has been driven out of accepted usage, either into obsolescence, the farmyard or the gutter. In the whole area of the genitalia there are no neutral terms like *arm, leg* or *head*.

As figure 4.3 illustrates, opaque classical nomenclature started to become current in this professional area, as in many others, in the sixteenth century.

Spleen *c*.1300
Palate 1382 Wycliffe
Stomach 14th century
Vein 14th century
Sperm 1386 Chaucer: Greek, to sow
Genitals 1390 Gower
Cell 1393 Gower
Artery 1398 Trevisa
Colon 1398 Trevisa
Diarrhoea 1398 Trevisa: ('a symple fluxe of the wombe')
Oesophagus 1398 Trevisa
Semen 1398 Trevisa: Latin *serrere*, to sow
Thorax *c*.1400 Lanfrank
Trachaea *c*.1400 Lanfrank: Greek *trachea*, rough (orig. 'rough artery')
Uvula *c*.1400 Lanfrank
Virus *c*.1400 Lanfrank
Testicle *c*.1425
Intestine 1425 Guy de Chauliac
Embryo 1477 (in Homer 'a young animal')
Muscle 1533 (Latin *musculus* diminutive of *mus*, a mouse)
Nerve 1538
Abdomen 1541 Copeland: 'the fat deposited round the belly'
Cartilage 1541 Copeland
Cavity 1541 Copeland
Fracture 1541 Copeland
Rectum 1541 Copeland
Ulna 1541 Copeland
Cranium 1543
Tendon 1543
Vulva 1548–77
Larynx 1578 Banister
Pancreas 1578 Banister: (Greek, sweetbread)
Scapula 1578 Banister
Skeleton 1578 Banister: (Greek, dried up) 1578; cf. A-S *ban-hus*
Scrotum 1597 Guillemeau
Phallus 1613 (Purchas, *Pilgrimage*)
Clavicle 1615 Crooke
Clitoris 1615 Crooke (Greek, ?to shut)
Coccyx 1615 Crooke: (Greek, cuckoo bone)
Epiglottis 1615 Crooke
Pelvis 1615 Crooke
Radius 1615 Crooke
Uterus 1615 Crooke
Vertebra 1615 Crooke
Gland 1631: from Latin *glans*, an acorn
Faeces 1639
Anus 1658
Saliva 1676
Cochlea 1688 (Greek, a spiral staircase)
Patella 1693 Blancard
Penis 1693 Blancard: (= Latin cauda, a tail)
Phalanges 1693 Blancard
Pharynx 1693 Blancard: (Greek, a chasm)
Tibia 1693 Blancard

Figure 4.3 The word-field of classical terms in anatomy, arranged historically, with major source works

Prior to that a fair number of common terms like *stomach, vein, genitals, artery, colon* and *virus* had come into the lexis, but we notice once more the gap in the time-structure between *c.*1400 and *c.*1540. Then we find specialized words coming into the vocabulary via particular publications. Terms like *abdomen, cartilage, cavity, fracture, rectum* and *ulna* appeared in 1541 in Robert Copeland's *The Questyonary of chirugery; larynx, pancreas, scapula,* and *skeleton* appeared in John Banister's *The History of Man* (1578) and *scrotum* in 1597. These were followed by *clavicle, clitoris, coccyx, epiglottis, pelvis, radius, uterus* and *vertebra,* first recorded in Helkiah Crooke's *Mikrokosmographia, A description of the body of man* (1615).

As one might imagine, there was a period of uneasy lexical cohabitation as the native and the classical elements contrived to divide the territory: this rivalry is epitomized in Robert Copeland's definition (1541) under *ulna*: 'the arme is deuided in thre great partyes. One is called vlna, the other lytel arme.' (This is a charmingly unexpected example of 'the excluded middle'.) As we have seen, *radius* emerged only in 1615, and the *humerus* arrived lexicographically nearly a whole century later in 1706, in John Kersey's updating of Edward Phillips's *The New World of English Words,* where it is tentatively defined as 'the shoulder; the shoulder-bone or first bone of the arm'. Clearly, by the sixteenth century we have moved into a quite different lexical world from that of Guy de Chauliac's translator, who wrote in a homely fashion of *the brayne pan, the rigge bone, the forked bone, the spawde bone, the canell bone* and *the rollynge bone* (1971, pp. 20–1), as well as *the priue stones* (1971, p. 511) for *testicles* and *coldnesse* for *frigidity* (1971, p. 527).

One must concede that a specific technical terminology is needed for certain physiological areas, for two reasons. First, native terms like *ankle, knee, shoulder, elbow* and *hip* tend to be general: classical terminology efficiently defines by breaking down these joints to their component parts. Thus native *hand* and *finger* are augmented by *digit* in 1644 and *metacarpal* in 1854.

Secondly, there is the factor of semantic instability, especially in the genital area. As the term *womb,* for example, made its extraordinary semantic transition from the early general sense of 'stomach' to exclusively feminine 'uterus', so *cod,* meaning a 'bag' or 'covering' made an opposite shift in the male sex to an ambiguous area incorporating both 'scrotum' and 'testicles', subsequently surviving only in *codpiece.* Chaucer's Pardoner uses the old senses in one of his hysterical outbursts: 'O wombe O bely, O stynkyng is thi cod' (*Pardoner's Tale,* line 206). When we encounter Dr Johnson's definition of the *pelvis* as being 'the lower part of the belly', we realize the imprecision of the terminology of this area. *Bowel,* from Late Latin *botellus,* 'pudding or sausage', moved from its early sense of 'intestine or gut' in the fourteenth century to the broad plural sense of 'vitals' in the sixteenth, and on to the vague poetic sense of the 'seat of compassionate and tender feelings' or the feelings themselves, a sense which lasted through to the nineteenth before fading way. Now only the medical sense survives. The term *nerve* has also undergone a major shift from its early physical sense of 'muscle' or 'sinew' in the sixteenth century, which included the sense of 'penis' recorded in 1662. Thereafter it moved via the neurological sense of the nervous fibres connecting muscles and brain in the seventeenth century, to its more subtle modern psychological meaning in *nerves* and *nervous*, which emerges in the nineteenth.

In concert with these changes, but less excusably, professional titles in medicine have changed. The ancient native term *leech* (which has no relation to the blood-sucking variety) gave way to the Latin *doctor*, which is in turn being replaced (especially in the United States) by Greek *physician* and *therapist*. Virtually all new fields of medicine style themselves in Greek terminology. Hence *psychiatry, gynaecology, orthodontics, otorhinolaryngology, gerontology, paediatrics, oncology* and so on. The only branch of medicine with an Anglo-Saxon name is *midwifery*, steadily being ousted by *obstetrics*.

Such changes partly inspired George Bernard Shaw's caustic observation that 'All professions are conspiracies against the laity,' found in the extended polemic which passes for a preface to his play, *The Doctor's Dilemma*, written in 1906 (1971, p. 72). Shaw's cynical remark contains a linguistic truth, namely that professional status and social distance between practitioner and layperson are notoriously maintained by linguistic barriers and by obfuscation. The ramparts of professional jargon, legal and medical especially, have been powerfully satirized and undermined over the centuries by such notable authors as Chaucer, Shakespeare, Ben Jonson and Dickens. Yet they remain intact.

The Language of the Law

Let us briefly consider the language of the law. The base term is, as we noted in chapter 2, a Scandinavian word, and considering the early practice, one is especially struck by the fact that the law was originally not in the hands of a profession at all. The ancient tradition is epitomized by the role of the Icelandic *lawman*, who recited the whole law from memory before the annual session of the Althing. Thereafter matters of dispute were settled by the parties concerned.

The earliest extant Anglo-Saxon legislation is found in the Laws of Ine, King of Wessex, promulgated between 688 and 695; they have a continuous and complementary relationship with those of Alfred (*c*.885–899).

These early laws are, unlike their successors, models of native simplicity and clarity:

> If anyone steals so that his wife and children do not know, let him pay sixty shillings fine. If he should steal with the knowledge of his family, then they should all go into slavery. A ten year old boy may be [considered] an accomplice to a theft. (*Laws of Ine* §7)

However, legal terminology acquired an alien register from the time when the Norman overlords used their standard practice of defining themselves and all aspects of their rule in their own terms. From the point of view of the native majority of the population, this meant that a foreign nomenclature was henceforth used to define offences which had previously been denoted by native terms. Thus the direct terminology used in the Anglo-Saxon laws, *aþbryce* ('oath-breaking'), *bærnette* ('burning'), *stale* ('stealing'), *gefeohte* ('fighting') were supplanted by *perjury, arson, larceny, assault*, etc., which were opaque or ambiguous or both. The point of obfuscation is nicely made in one of the earliest instances of malapropism, which occurs in the fourteenth-century poem, *Piers Plowman*, where a character evidently thinks that *restitution* means precisely its opposite, namely 'robbery' (B Text, ed. Skeat, 1886, p. 238).

A notable exception lies in what we now call 'capital crime': both *murder* and *manslaughter* are Germanic in origin, and have maintained the crucial distinction between intentional and unintentional killing. Generally, however, there consequently developed parallel vocabularies of broad, general, native words and specific alien technical terms: *wrong-doing vis-à-vis felony/ crime/delict; theft vis-à-vis larceny*. Furthermore, there is often confusion caused by competing definitions between the technical and the general senses in *libel vis-à-vis slander; assault vis-à-vis battery* and *rape; damage* and *damages; guardian* in its various senses, and so on.

Thereafter came the infiltration of law Latin in the form of numerous phrases like *habeas corpus, prima facie, quid pro quo, inter alia, in flagrante delicto, in fee simple. Culprit* represents an odd case of a word being invented for legal purposes and then abandoned.[7]

Critical comments on the voluminousness and unintelligibility of legal language have been *de rigueur* for centuries, as David Mellinkoff shows in his classic study, *The Language of the Law* (1963). He devotes two whole chapters to the necessity of making the law clearer and briefer: they are entitled, simply and appropriately 'Shorter' and 'More Intelligible'. The Plain English Campaign (founded in 1979) has continued to focus on the languages of medicine and the law.

Notes

1 The correspondence between King James and Buckingham is covered in N. Stone (ed.) *Makers of English History* (London 1967) p. 104.

2 A similarly alien vocabulary was devised by Ralph Lever, who in 1573 published a book on logic, which he termed *witcraft*. Lever devised odd native words for the basic Latin terms, namely *endsay* for 'conclusion', *saywhat* for 'definition', *shewsay* for 'proposition' and *naysay* for 'negation'.

3 Holofernes' etymology of *abominable* was common but is mistaken, since the word is rooted in Latin *omen*, not *homo*: thus *abominable* is the correct spelling.

4 The American poet John Crowe Ransom wrote an illuminating article on juxtaposed registers, 'On Shakespeare's Language' in the *Sewanee Review* (1947), pp. 181–98.

5 In his rejection of Ophelia, Hamlet uses a brilliant piece of word-play, since his famous advice 'Get thee to a nunnery' (III. i. 124) means alternatively 'become a nun' and 'go into a brothel' (the 'underground' sense of *nunnery*).

6 Macbeth's puzzling reference to 'hangman's hands' becomes gruesomely clear when one realizes that in Elizabethan times the punishment for treason was hanging, drawing (disembowelment) and quartering (dismemberment), all of which the hangman performed.

7 *Culprit* came about through an ignorant running together of Anglo-Norman *culpable* ('guilty') and *prit*, the old form of French *prêt*, 'ready'). A similar case from a biblical source is *helpmeet*, originally, in the Authorized Version of Genesis 2: 18 Eve is 'an help meet [suitable] for him' (Adam).

5

LICENTIOUSNESS, DECORUM
AND LEXICOGRAPHICAL
ORDER

When we see men grow old and die at a certain time one after another, from century to century, we laugh at the elixir which promises to prolong life to a thousand years, and with equal justice may the lexicographer be derided, who being able to produce no example of a nation that has preserved their words and phrases from mutability, shall imagine that his dictionary can embalm his language, and secure it from corruption and decay, and that it is in his power to change sublunary nature, or clear the world at once from folly, vanity and affectation.

Samuel Johnson, preface to his *Dictionary* (1755)

The second part of this chapter is concerned with the evolution of the dictionary from Elizabethan times to contemporary developments. However, it is important first to give a sense of the movement between phases of linguistic freedom and restraint as well as the different styles of lexis which became fashionable in this great span of time.

The Restoration was marked by extremes of licentiousness as the shackles of Puritanism were thrown off. In the course of the eighteenth century a conservative reaction predictably set in, expressing a desire for moderation, rationality and a preference for classical models and vocabulary. The period revealingly styled itself the Augustan Age, thus identifying itself with the original Roman era of the Emperor Augustus, which combined social stability with the flowering of great literary talent. The other term applied to the period was 'the Enlightenment', because of its concern for order and clear explanation. This took the form of two linguistic initiatives: one was to establish an academy to 'fix' the language, notably by Jonathan Swift and others; the other was to produce comprehensive, respected and respectable dictionaries, which materialized in the shape of the amazingly substantial volumes of Nathaniel Bailey and Samuel Johnson. The importance of scientific writing as a formative influence on modern English prose should also not be underestimated.

However, there was another side to the age, exemplified in the scatalogical verse of Swift, the bizarre, nonsensical novels of Laurence Sterne, and the emergence of a pornographic tradition, notably in the works of John Cleland.

Romanticism, that period which led up to and immediately followed the French Revolution (1789), was in turn a phase of liberation in reaction against the rationality and order of the previous age. Consequently, highly emotional, poetic and idealistic language became *de rigueur*, not simply among the major poets (William Wordsworth, Lord Byron, Percy Bysshe Shelley and John Keats) but in the prose of the period.

The Victorian period, which saw the major social changes of the Industrial Revolution and the extension of the franchise throughout the population, showed many of the schizophrenic qualities of the eighteenth century. Its authoritative aspect was apparent in the substantial works of the major authors. The latter part of the age saw the generation of the definitive dictionary in the form of the monumental *Oxford English Dictionary* by Sir James Murray and his team at Oxford (1884–1928). However, those who are termed 'the other Victorians' continued the pornographic tradition and the age also produced the first comprehensive thesaurus of foul language, *Slang and its Analogues* (1890) by J. S. Farmer and W. E. Henley. A more polite but interesting form of subversion of the 'high seriousness' of the Victorians was the emergence of the nonsense verse of Edward Lear and the beguilingly absurd works of Lewis Carroll. Few authors managed to straddle these extremes, though Dickens came closest to exploring the full diversity of register.

The student will find it useful and informative to study the semantic changes undergone by some of the key words of these periods: *Restoration, Augustan, Enlightenment, Romanticism, Victorian.*

Restoration licentiousness

The Restoration saw a descent into licentiousness and decadence as extreme as the Puritan restraint to which it was a reaction. These qualities were epitomized in the lifestyle of the restored monarch, Charles II, whose sexual promiscuity was proverbial. The King's Road (in Chelsea) derives its name from the frequency and the brazenness with which the monarch promenaded down it to make assignations with Nell Gwyn, the best-known actress of the Restoration theatre, who began her theatrical career selling oranges, amongst other favours, at the Drury Lane theatre. 'She retired from the stage at the age of nineteen to pursue a more lucrative career among the upper echelons of her erstwhile audience' (Salgado, 1985, p. 223).

The most famous (or notorious) literary figure in this respect is 'the most brilliant wit and the most accomplished rake' in the court of Charles II, namely the Earl of Rochester, who died of syphilis in 1680 at the age of thirty-three. Rochester flouted bourgeois prudery and linguistic censorship by writing freely about sex in poems which still surprise by their shocking frankness. Perhaps the first poet to pierce the façade of respectability built round the social life of the times, Rochester's work may be gauged from this sample from a poem called 'A Ramble in St James's Parke' (in central London):

> Much wine had past with grave discours
> Of who Fucks who and who does worse . . .
> When I who still take care to see
> Drunknenness Reliev'd with Leachery
> Went out into Saint James's Park
> To coole my head and fire my heart.
> But tho' Saint James has Honor on't
> 'Tis Consecrate to Prick and Cunt . . .
> And nightly now beneath [the] shade
> Are Buggeries, Rapes and Incests made:
> Unto this all-sin-sheltring Grove
> Whores of the Bulk, and the Alcove
> Great Ladies, Chamber Mayds, and Drudges
> The Ragg Picker, and the Heiress trudges;
> Carrmen, Divines, Great Lords and Taylors,
> Prentices, Pimps, Poets and Gaolers,
> Footmen, Fine Fopps, doe here arrive,
> And here promiscuously they swive [copulate].
>
> (lines 1–32)

As one can see, Rochester relishes the juxtaposition of religious or polite terms with the grossest 'four-letter' words, lexically symbolic of the reduction of all social classes to the same activity of sexual congress. Rochester was not alone in exploiting this vein: several of the literary figures of the time, including George Etherege, Lord Buckhust, John Oldham wrote bawdy and salacious verse.

With the reopening of the theatres and women actors being restored to the stage, the new Restoration comedy of William Congreve, William Wycherley and George Farquhar exploited risqué sexual situations in a witty and knowing fashion, but obviously could not use the most explicit language, preferring instead bawdy puns and *double entendres* which had been a staple from the time of Shakespeare. Furthermore, certain women writers, including Aphra Benn, Mary Pix and Mary Manley, came to the fore with plays which dealt with sexuality directly.

Restoration dandies also used the names of God and the Devil in all sorts of wittily decadent modes which would have been an affront to Puritan sensibilities. The Devil, of course, had been used in imprecations from the Middle Ages and continued to thrive in many idioms. In his play *Love and a Bottle* (1698), the dramatist George Farquhar makes comic capital out of the fashionable pronunciation of *zounds*, which, as we have seen, has a horrific origin in 'God's wounds', referring to the Crucifixion. An apprentice 'rake' (a decadent upper-class idler) called Mockmore is anxious to acquire the idiom of 'beau' or smart man about town. He asks his tutor Rigadoon:

> Pray what are the most fashionable Oaths in Town? *Zoons* I take it is a very becoming one.

But Rigadoon corrects him pointedly:

> Zoons is only us'd by the disbanded Officers and Bullies; but Zauns is the Beaux' pronunciation. (II. ii)

(A *bully* was then a prostitute's 'protector'.) The point of this exchange, of course, is that this fashionable pronunciation shows that *zounds* no longer has any literal meaning for this social set, despite having been used first only about 1600. Daniel Defoe, writing in 1712, castigates the indiscriminate use of profanity and foul language: 'at play 'tis G—d damn the cards; a-hunting, G—d damn the hounds; they call dogs sons of whores and men sons of bitches' (1951, p. 260).

Pepys

The notion that the Restoration was a sewer of iniquity and foul language is corrected by the remarkable *Diary* of Samuel Pepys (1633–1703). Written in his own secret shorthand code and not deciphered until 1825, this gives a candid record of Pepys's busy life as Secretary of the Navy, observer of court life, playgoer, musician and flirt in words he never intended to be read by anyone else. Pepys never ventures into the lexical underworld of Rochester. 'But,' as he comments on one occasion, 'to see how Nell [Gwynn] cursed, for having so few people in the pit, was pretty.' His enthusiastic effusions give us a sense of the fashionable words of the time: his wife's new teeth 'are indeed now pretty handsome', but she becomes 'heartily jealous' and 'mightily vexed' at Pepys being abroad with theatre ladies. The 'poor wretch' becomes 'mighty dull' but 'mad as a devil' when Pepys is out at the playhouse and the bookshop, leading to 'nothing but ill words between us all evening.' His reiteration of *mighty* is a fashion which has continued in America, but largely died out in

Britain. Asseverations come, as height be expected, in his records of the Plague and the great Fire of London, 'a horrid great fire', later 'a horrid, malicious, bloody flame, not like the fine flame of an ordinary fire' (2 September 1666). The Plague (usually called 'the sicknesse' in the early references) generates such comments as: 'But Lord! how sad a sight it is to see the streets empty of people and very few upon the Change!' (15 August 1665) and 'The Plague, blessed be God! is decreased' (15 November 1665).

The failing language

From the late seventeenth century through to the mid-eighteenth there developed an increasing anxiety about the way the language was changing, a feature which was interpreted as a sign of deterioration, and a feeling that something should be done to arrest this change or at least control it. Many of the major literary figures took this view, and they tended to look back nostalgically to older, more stable times. The poet Edmund Waller complained in 1664 that

> Poets that Lasting Marble seek,
> Must carve in Latin or in Greek;
> We write in sand . . .
> *(Of English Verse)*

It is interesting to see how these writers identified 'the golden age'. Dryden himself took the view that 'from Chaucer the purity of the English language began,' and he wrote of the Elizabethans as 'the giant race before the flood,' while Dr Johnson, when he came to write the preface to his *Dictionary* (1755), identified a later age:

> So far have I been from any care to grace my pages with modern decorations, that I have studiously endeavoured to collect examples and authorities from the writers before the restoration, whose works I regard as *the wells of English undefiled*, as the pure sources of genuine diction.

The quotation in italics comes from Edmund Spenser, who referred to 'Dan [master] Chaucer, well of English undefiled' in *The Faerie Queene* (IV. ii. 32). We should note in passing that this view that Chaucer or the Elizabethans represented a state of 'purity' in the language is a nostalgic fiction. As we have seen, Chaucer exploited the French register, but was equally disturbed about the confused state of the language (which was no longer 'pure'), and the Inkhorn Controversy was fought over precisely the issue of foreign or 'impure' elements coming into the language.

The idea of a formal body, an Academy, to legislate over the use of English, had been proposed early in the seventeenth century, without coming to fruition, and was mooted again by John Dryden in 1664. About the same time the Royal Society was formed, and Dryden, John Evelyn, Thomas Sprat and Edmund Waller were voted onto a committee 'for improving the English language'. Evelyn set out a detailed and ambitious proposal, including a 'lexicon of all the pure English words by themselves', but nothing materialized, probably because the main interests of the Society were scientific. Defoe proposed a similar Academy in 1697, as did Swift in his *Proposal for Correcting, Improving, and Ascertaining the English Tongue* of 1712. However, the desirability of such a body was increasingly questioned, most formidably by Dr Johnson, who commented on the proposal in his preface: 'if an academy should be established . . . which I hope the spirit of English liberty will hinder or destroy'. As we shall see, the first major dictionaries grew out of this anxiety at the state of the language and a determination to do something about it.

Decorum, Vulgarity and Obscenity

The dominant tenor of Augustan lexis is formal and classical, although we shall see a number of surprising intrusions from slang and obscenity. The age saw the emergence of a curiously artificial form of poetic diction whereby, for example, fish were referred to as 'the finny prey', birds became 'the feathered race' and a gun became 'a deadly tube'. This feature was especially notable in the work of Alexander Pope, from whom these examples are taken. Dr Johnson's preferences are very apparent in his writing and in his prejudiced critical response to the use of plain terms in moments of high drama, which is one of Shakespeare's most daring qualities. Let us consider Lady Macbeth's famous soliloquy:

> Come, thick night,
> And pall thee in the dunnest smoke of hell,
> That my keen knife see not the wound it makes,
> Nor heaven peep through the blanket of the dark,
> To cry, 'Hold, hold!'
>
> (I. v. 51–4)

Most modern editors and critics would be impressed by the savage directness and ruthless violence of the language, concentrated in *dunnest, hell, keen, knife, wound* and *blanket of the dark*. Johnson, however, in a trenchant commentary (which, curiously, misattributes the speech to Macbeth) contemptuously rejected precisely these features as debasing the dignity of the drama. Johnson's comments in *The Rambler*, number 168, give us a fascinating insight into the preferred register for high drama: 'Yet the efficacy of this invocation is destroyed by the insertion of an epithet [*dunnest*] now seldom heard but in the stable.' He continues: 'this sentiment is weakened by the name of an instrument used by butchers and cooks in their meanest employments; we do not immediately conceive that any crime of importance is to be committed with a *knife*.' Finally, he continues in characteristic vein: 'Macbeth proceeds to wish ... that he may, in the involutions of infernal darkness, escape the eye of Providence ... this is so debased by two unfortunate words, that ... I can scarce check my risibility, when the expression forces itself upon my mind; for who, without some relaxation of his gravity, can hear of the avengers of guilt *peeping through a blanket?*'

We can see, with the benefit of hindsight, that Johnson's judgement was unduly coloured by contemporary notions of decorum. Pope went further. In an innocent functional context in *Julius Caesar* where the conspirators meet at Brutus's house, we read, mystifyingly, in Lucius's speech as rendered in Pope's edition that

> Their——are plucked about their ears
> (II. i. 75)

Pope has here taken the most extreme recourse of editorial disapproval, namely expunction: yet the offending term, which Pope considered an affront to *Romanitas*, was *hats*.

But there was another side to the age which came out in a variety of forms. These included three quite different works by Swift: his scatalogical verse, his so-called *Polite Conversation* and his curious *Journal to Stella*, addressed to a society lady (Esther Johnson) but written in a curious baby language. In the first are his poems in the vein of Rochester, but less concerned with sexual congress and almost obsessed in exploring the less decent intimacies of female life. The climax to 'The Lady's Dressing Room' (1730) runs as follows:

> Thus finishing his grand Survey
> The Swain disgusted slunk away,
> Repeating in his am'rous fits
> Oh! Celia! Celia! Celia! shits!
> (lines 115–18)

(*Celia*, incidentally means 'the heavenly one': Swift took particular delight in using inappropriate classical names or poetic terms for sordid subjects.) Many of Swift's poems preserve the idiom of the street, seeming to have been written yesterday. Thus 'Corinna, Pride of Drury Lane', the lady of questionable occupation who forms the subject of 'A Beautiful Young Nymph Going to Bed' (1731) has

> No drunken Rake to pick her up
> No Cellar where on Tick to sup . . .
> (lines 5–6)

The *Journal to Stella* (1710–13) contains many pages written in this vein:

> I have been scribbling this morning, and believe shall hardly fill this side today, but send it as it is; and it is good enough for naughty girls that don't write to a body, and to a good boy like Presto [i.e. himself, *presto* in Latin meaning 'swift']. I thought to have sent this tonight, but was kept by company, and would not; and to say the truth, I had a little mind to expect one post more for a letter from MD [Madam Dingley, a code name for Esther Johnson] (19 September 1710).
>
> I was at a loss to-day for dinner, unless I would have gone a great way, so I dined with some friends that board hereabout as a spunger; . . . but we had a neck of mutton dressed *à la Maintenon*, that a dog could not eat (8 October 1710).

The *Journal* is very much like the transcript of intimate telephone conversations. Scholars have still not completely defined the relationship between Swift and Stella, but he writes very forward and knowing things like 'I wish I could put my cold hand in the warmest place about you' (5 February 1711). Idiomatic phrases abound, such as 'Here's ado and clutter!'; 'up a-dazy'; 'I have got a cruel cold'; 'it is a rainy ugly day'; 'I am a little piqued'; 'I am here in a pretty pickle'; 'she is pretty quiet now, but has a diabolical Temper'; and 'Presto's plaguy silly tonight an't he?' (i.e. 'ain't he?', a usage which lasted up to Victorian times). He also plays with literate conventions, referring to 'Rrrrrare Chelsea buns' and uses illiterate spellings such as 'nite'. He also enjoys the odd practical joke: 'The Duke of Buckingham's house [i.e. Buckingham Palace] fell down with an earth-quake and is half swallowed up. . . . An April fool, An April fool, oh ho young women' (1 April 1711). His amusingly ironic *Polite Conversation* (1738) explores the absurdities and excesses of upper-class social idiom.

There was even an Augustan antitype of Dr Johnson, in the form of one Captain Francis Grose, who produced in 1785 a vigorous and appealing *Dictionary of the Vulgar Tongue*. Although, as we have seen, dictionaries of underworld slang had existed since Elizabethan times, the great merits of

Grose's work are the wit and bawdy humour of the definitions, of which a sample is shown in figure 5.1.

More explicitly in the area of the bawdy are the pornographic writings of John Cleland, especially his *succès de scandale*, *Fanny Hill* (1737). (The title is itself a bawdy pun for the Latin *mons veneris*.) However, being eighteenth-century pornography, Cleland's works never use crude 'four-letter words', preferring suggestive metaphors and high-register Latinized terms, such as one finds in the following:

> I not only tightened the pleasure-girth around my restless inmate by a secret spring of suction and compression that obeys the will in those parts, but stole my hand softly to that store-bag of nature's prime sweets, which is pleasingly attached to its conduit pipe from which we receive them; there feeling, and most gently indeed squeezing those tender globular reservoirs; the magic touch took instant effect, quickened, and brought on upon the spur of the symptoms of that sweet agony, the melting moment of dissolution, when pleasure dies by pleasure, and the mysterious engine of it overcomes the titillation it has raised in those parts, by plying them with a stream of a warm liquid which is the highest of titillations, and which they thirstily express, and draw in like the hot-natured leech, which to cool itself tenaciously extracts all the moisture within its sphere of exsuction. (*Fanny Hill*, 1994, p. 106)

This description of sexual congress shows the unintentional comedy which arises from applying a scientific register to a vital activity. It reminds one of Gore Vidal's dismissive remark about Henry Miller's 'hydraulic approach to sex' (1974, p. 198).

Finally, the period shows the beginnings of the tradition of nonsense literature in the extraordinary novel by Laurence Sterne, *Tristram Shandy* (1760–7). Here is a sample:

Chapter XIV

—They are Socrates's children, said my uncle Toby. He has been dead a hundred years ago, replied my mother.

My uncle Toby was no chronologer – so not caring to advance one step but upon safe ground, he laid down his pipe deliberately upon the table, and rising up, and taking my mother most kindly by the hand, without saying another word, either good or bad, to her, he led her out after my father, that he might finish the éclaircissement himself.

Chapter XV

Had this volume been a farce, which, unless everybody's life and opinions are to be looked upon as a farce as well as mine, I see no reason to suppose – the last

but.we brought him back by a great blow on the head, which laid him speechless.

CRACKSMAN. A house-breaker. The kiddy is a clever cracksman; the young fellow is a very expert house- breaker.

CRAG. The neck.

CRAMP RINGS. Bolts, shackles, or fetters. *Cant.*

CRAMP WORDS. Sentence of death passed on a criminal by a judge. He has just undergone the cramp word; sentence has just been passed on him. *Cant.*

CRANK. Gin and water; also, brisk, pert.

CRANK. The falling sickness. *Cant.*

To CRASH. To kill. Crash that cull; kill that fellow. *Cant.*

CRASHING CHEATS. Teeth.

CRAW-THUMPERS. Roman catholics, so called from their beating their breasts in the confession of their sins. See BRISKET BEATER, and BREAST FLEET.

CREAM-POT LOVE. Such as young fellows pretend to dairy-maids, to get cream and other good things from them.

To CREEME. To slip or slide any thing into the hands of another. *Cant.*

CREEPERS. Gentlemen's companions, lice.

CREW. A knot or gang; also a boat or ship's company. The canting crew are thus divided into twenty-three orders, which see under the different words:

MEN.

1 Rufflers	9 Jarkmen, or Patricoes
2 Upright Men	10 Fresh Water Mariners, or
3 Hookers or Anglers	Whip Jackets
4 Rogues	11 Drummerers
5 Wild Rogues	12 Drunken Tinkers
6 Priggers of Prancers	13 Swaddlers, or Pedlars
7 Palliardes	14 Abrams.
8 Fraters	

WOMEN.

1 Demanders for Glimmer or Fire	5 Walking Morts
	6 Doxies
2 Bawdy Baskets	7 Delles
3 Morts	8 Kinching Morts
4 Autem Morts	9 Kinching Coes

CRIB. A house. To crack a crib: to break open a house.

To CRIB. To purloin, or appropriate to one's own use, part of any thing intrusted to one's care.

To FIGHT A CRIB. To make a sham fight. *Bear Garden term.*

CRIBBAGE-

Figure 5.1 Underground argot: a page from Francis Grose's *A Classical Dictionary of the Vulgar Tongue* (1785)

chapter, Sir, had finished the first act of it, and then this chapter must have set off thus.

Ptr..r..r..ing – twing – twang – prut – trut – 'tis a cursed bad fiddle. – Do you know whether my fiddle's in tune or not? – trut .. prut .. – They should be fifths. – 'Tis wickedly strung – tr..a.e.i.o.u. – twang. – The bridge is a mile too high, and the sound post absolutely down, – else – trut..prut – hark! 'tis not so bad a tone. – Diddle, diddle, diddle, diddle, diddle, diddle, dum. (*The Life and Opinions of Tristram Shandy*, 1948, pp. 292–3)

Sterne's extraordinary anarchic and self-deconstructive work is the most original in English literature, not least because it was written two centuries ago, in complete defiance of the contemporary ethos of Augustan Enlightenment. It subverts the traditional notion of literature as a coherent and harmonious artefact at every level, epistomological, structural, narrative, semantic and syntactic. The customary asssurances of art are replaced by an aleatory chaos in which everything is liable to chance. Instead of progressing, the plot radiates into circuitous irrelevances and shows endless regression. The ostensible narrative is invaded by the accidents, confusions and unmanageable trivia of the real world. Semantically, the work shows an infinite variety of register from the most intellectual and abstract terms (such as *éclaircissement*), down to the most primitive echoic level at which sound is simply and crudely replicated (such as *twing – twang – prut – trut*. Sentences sprawl, curl up, dissipate or suddenly stop. The element of play is also highly developed, the text being littered with asterisks, squiggles and doodles. The diligent reader in search of traditional 'meaning' is overtly assured of frustration: 'If I thought you was [sic] able to form the least judgement or probable conjecture to yourself, of what was to come in the next page, I would tear it out of my book.'

Scientific Naming in the Enlightenment

The eighteenth century also saw two initiatives typical of the desire for order which were to organize the system of naming the natural world for ever. The chaotic nomenclature of the plant and animal worlds were systematized by Carolus Linnaeus, subsequently Carl von Linné, Professor of Medicine and Botany at Uppsula University. In his *Systema Naturae* (1730 onwards) he organized plants, animals and minerals into classes, orders, genera and species, using a binomial system of Latin terms so that each item carried the name of its genus and species. Hence the lion is *Panthera leo*, the leopard *Panthera pardus*, and so on. He coined the term Mammalia for those creatures which suckle their young, designated Man as *Homo sapiens*, placing the species in a revolutionary fashion among the *Primates*, which include apes, monkeys and lemurs.

Linnaeus's *Species Plantarum*, the basis for modern systematic botany, was published in 1753, two years before Johnson's *Dictionary*. Here are some of his Latinized names for common flowers and trees:

buttercup	Ranunculus bulbosus
daisy	Bellis perennis
weeping willow	Salix babylonica

Although a fair number of the Linnaean terms, such as *rhododendron*, *clematis* and *chrysanthemum*, have become common names for garden plants, great numbers of traditional names continue in ordinary usage: we cannot imagine Wordsworth writing a poem about *Narcissus bulbocodium* rather than about daffodils. And we should not forget that many flowers have somewhat 'rude' common names: the *dandelion* with its fine French etymology in *dent de lion*, 'lion's tooth', has for centuries had the vulgar name of *pissabed* on account of its diuretic properties. The passage describing Ophelia's drowning in *Hamlet* refers to the flowers in her 'fantastic garlands' as including the suggestively phallic

> long purples,
> That liberal shepherds give a grosser name
> But our cold maids do dead men's fingers call them.
> (IV. vii. 170–2)

But because of its practicality and clarity, the Linnaean system of nomenclature continues to have international scientific currency.

The same century saw the beginnings of systematic scientific terminology in the French scientist Antoine Lavoisier's publication of the *Méthode de nomenclature chimique* in 1787. Using Greek roots he and his colleagues from the Académie des Sciences made up such words as *oxygène*, *nitrogène* and *hydrogène*. These terms are now widely used and have acquired some central metaphorical senses: Margaret Thatcher once explained that denying terrorist organizations press coverage was depriving them of 'the oxygen of publicity'.

The essential difference, therefore, between the original classical terms (like *radius* and *ulna* discussed at the end of chapter 4) and the modern terms is that the modern for us are artificial, being made up of classical elements, whereas the 'old' words are genuine. Yet many of the huge new crop have become current terms. These include *molecule* (1678), *protein* (coined by Mulder in 1838), *carbohydrate* (1869), *calorie* (via French 1870), *chromosome* (1897), *vitamin* (1913), *gene* (1913) and the terms of nuclear physics, such as the *proton* (1920) and the *neutron* (coined in 1899 but actually discovered in 1932). This theme is taken up in our concluding chapter in the section on the evolution of psychiatric terminology.

Romanticism: A Plainer Register

One of the common purposes of the authors who belonged to the Romantic movement was that of making literature more accessible to the people at large. William Wordsworth (1770–1850) wrote of 'a selection of the language really used by men',[1] and this simplified diction is clearly apparent in all the work of the Romantic poets, as we can see from some of the following famous lines. Here is Wordsworth reminiscing on the exhilaration of the French Revolution:

> Bliss was it in that dawn to be alive
> And to be young was very heaven.
> (*The Prelude*, XI, 108)

And here he enthuses on the prospect of London:

> Earth has not anything to show more fair.
> ('Upon Westminster Bridge')

Shelley (1792–1822) writes an invocation to the west wind which has a clear revolutionary meaning combined with a depiction of his own suffering:

> O wild West Wind, thou breath of Autumn's being . . .
> Oh lift me as a wave, a leaf, a cloud!
> I fall upon the the thorns of life! I bleed!
> O Wind
> If Winter comes, can Spring be far behind?
> ('Ode to the West Wind')

He rhapsodizes on the passing of time in the broadest terms:

> O world! O life! O time!
> ('A Lament')

Keats (1795–1821) celebrates the timeless beauty of the nightingale's song:

> Thou wast not born for death, immortal Bird!
> No hungry generations tread thee down;

The voice I hear this passing night was heard
In ancient days by emperor and clown.
('Ode to a Nightingale')

All these lines were written within forty years of Dr Johnson's death in 1784, yet we are aware of being in a very different verbal environment. The sense of rational control and restraint which was the hallmark of the Augustans has given way to what Wordsworth called 'the spontaneous overflow of powerful feelings' (*Lyrical Ballads*, ed. Sampson, p. 10). The impersonality of the previous age, in which works are invariably written in the third person, is replaced by highly personal effusions and exclamations. *O!* and *Ah!* are to be found all over Romantic poetry, as is the exclamation mark. Neither of these feature in the Augustan Age, although they abound in Shakespeare's text. Classical vocabulary has given way to very direct, simple diction. Dr Johnson, Pope and Swift would have found some of these lines embarrassing, even slightly ridiculous.

Several of the Romantics actually criticized Johnson's style. William Hazlitt (1778–1830) described it as 'walking on stilts' in an essay in a suitably named journal, *The Plain Speaker*. William Cobbett (1762–1835), also noted for his direct style, admired Johnson but commented ironically on 'the balance of that see-saw in which Dr Johnson so much delighted' (in Warner, 1961, p. 122). Coleridge (1772–1834) was, typically, more analytical and penetrating: 'Johnson's style has pleased many from the very fault of being perpetually translateable; he creates an impression of cleverness by never saying anything in a common way' (Lecture XIV, 1818).

Although Coleridge did not advocate simplicity of diction as strongly as Wordsworth did, his own poetry exemplifies it even more markedly. A study of 'The Rime of the Ancient Mariner' shows a very high proportion of native terms (even though the quaint title does not: 'The Poem of the Old Sailor' would be the plain equivalent, but would be very dull).

The fair breeze flew, the white foam flew,
  The furrow followed free;
We were the first that ever burst
  Into that silent sea.

Water, water, everywhere,
Nor any drop to drink.

Like one that on a lonesome road
Doth walk in fear and dread.
('The Rime of the Ancient Mariner', parts 2, 6)

In these eight lines only *breeze* and *silent* are not Anglo-Saxon in origin, but they nevertheless clearly belong to the base register. The poet who went furthest in this direction was William Blake (1757–1827), especially in his *Songs of Innocence* (1789) and *Songs of Experience* (1794). Blake sought a specially purified language to convey the experience of innocence:

> To see the World in a grain of sand,
> And Heaven in a wild flower,
> Hold Infinity in the palm of your hand,
> And Eternity in an hour.
>> ('Auguries of Innocence')

Here the abstractions *Infinity* and *Eternity* stand out against the simple natural diction. In other poems Blake sets the occasional classical term in the sharpest possible contrast to the plain register:

> Tiger! Tiger! burning bright
> In the forests of the night,
> What immortal hand or eye
> Could frame thy fearful symmetry?
>> ('The Tiger')

Here *symmetry* has an almost sinister quality because it seems so alien in the verbal context. A similarly menacing quality surrounds the terms in bold type in the following poem:

> O Rose thou art sick!
> The **invisible worm**
> That flies in the night,
> In the howling storm,
>
> Has found out thy bed
> Of **crimson** joy;
> And his dark **secret** love
> Does thy life **destroy**.
>> ('The Sick Rose')

Unlike the rationalists of the previous age such as Johnson, Blake wrote that 'energy is eternal delight!' and indulged in paradoxical syntactical arrangements, as when he described Love as having 'the human form divine' (in 'The Divine Image'). He is also very direct in his social criticism. Compare Wordsworth's celebration of London in the poem we have already glanced at, 'Upon Westminster Bridge', with Blake's view of the city as the victim of capitalist accumulation:

I wandered through each chartered street.

('London')

Perhaps his most famous comment on contemporary society lies in his piercing question on the social effects of the Industrial Revolution:

And was Jerusalem builded here
Among these dark Satanic mills?

('Jerusalem')

We can see that the special lexical choices ('chartered', 'Satanic') are carefully placed to achieve the greatest impact. The 'dark Satanic mills' were the new factories of industry where workers, who had previously been able to produce their goods at home by means of 'cottage industries' now became wage-slaves. They were indeed 'dark' because of the tax on windows, which was repealed only in 1851.

Byron (1788–1824) was in his lifestyle bohemian, outrageous and revolutionary, the most self-consciously Romantic of all the Romantic poets. However, in *Don Juan*, the striving for the sublime is replaced by satire in the form of deliberate anticlimax or bathos, and slipshod rhymes. Byron enjoys using inappropriate registers:

What men call gallantry, the gods adultery,
Is much more common where the climate's sultry.

But – Oh! ye lords of ladies intellectual,
Inform us truly, have they not henpecked you all?

In virtues nothing earthly could surpass her
Except thine 'incomparable oil', Macassar.

(*Don Juan*, I, xvii, xxii, lxiii)

The last couplet is an early instance of parodying the overblown language of advertising. The dedication of *Don Juan* makes fun of the traditional acts of literary piety to be found at the opening of long poems. Byron starts with the Poet Laureate:

Bob Southey! You're a poet – Poet Laureate,
And representative of all the race;
Although 'tis true you turned out a Tory at
Last, – yours has lately been a common case.

Coleridge's philosophical prestige is wittily reduced:

> Explaining Metaphysics to the nation –
> I wish he would explain his Explanation

In his short life (he died at the age of 26) Keats explored a great diversity of registers. He was strongly criticized by both *The Quarterly Review* and *Blackwood's Magazine* (in 1818) for using inappropriate diction. This view proved fairly tenacious, for in his major edition of 1905, Ernest de Selincourt commented in the course of his comprehensive Appendix 'On the Sources of Keats's Poetic Vocabulary':

> The vulgarisms of Keats's diction resolve themselves into the use of words, which, debased by trivial associations, or in themselves quite incompatible with genuine passion, should never be used in poetry; [and] the use of words to which he gives a meaning which they do not bear, except in slang or the loose language of a too familiar conversation. (1905, p. 572)

In the first group de Selincourt notes *elegant, giggle, tip-top, hist!*, the 'unfortunate remark' *Pallas is a dunce* and the description of the poet himself as a *blank idiot*; in the second category are the use of *jaunty* of a stream, *smitten* of love, and *treat* of something enjoyable (1905, p. 572). One critic noted the recurrence of *delicious* twenty times, and Robert Bridges called attention to the 'undue iteration' of *melting, fainting, swooning* and *panting*, no doubt because of their sexual associations.

Keats survived these early critical attacks and went on to write great odes in the few years remaining. In these he achieved remarkable evocations of sensuous experience by a singular choice of words. He was a tireless and assured reviser, as the different drafts of the odes show. In the following lines of the 'Ode to a Nightingale', the terms italicized replaced those set at the right, which appeared in the early draft of the poem:

> My heart aches, and a *drowsy* numbness *pains* / painful falls
>
> With *beaded* bubbles winking at the brim / clustered
>
> Where youth grows *pale and spectre-thin*, and dies / pale and thin and old
>
> I have been half in love with *easeful* death / painless

In perhaps the most romantic lines in the poem, Keats changes only two words, but transforms the effect:

Charm'd *magic* casements, opening on the foam / the wide
Of *perilous* seas, in faery lands forlorn. / keelless

Although Keats was clearly influenced by Spenser and Shakespeare in his use of a slightly archaic vocabulary such as *a-cold, amort, beldame, bruit, darkling, ebon, parle, pleached* and *ruddy* (of drops), he began to revert to an excessively classical style under the influence of Milton. This included features of vocabulary such as *argent, lucent, orbed* and *reluctant*; archaic inversions such as *palace bright, stride colossal, radiance faint, palpitations sweet, pleasures soft*; and balanced epithets in formulations such as *gold clouds metropolitan* and *lithe serpent vast*.

These are all found in *Hyperion*, the epic poem Keats worked on from April 1818 to September 1819, when he wrote to a friend, 'I have given up Hyperion . . . there are too many Miltonic inversions in it . . . English ought to be kept up' (letter to Reynolds, 22 September 1819). At the same period he wrote to his brother: 'The *Paradise Lost*, though so fine in itself, is a corruption of our language' (letter to George Keats, September 1819). Similarly, Wordsworth (who lived to the age of 80) fell under Miltonic influence when he came to revise his *Prelude* (first published in 1805) in the last years of his life. He now preferred such classical terms and phrases as *umbrageous coverts*, which are a far cry from 'the language of ordinary men'.

Another important lexical aspect of Romanticism was the resuscitation of regional dialects. These had tended to wither away with the establishment of the standard in Augustan times, but now they became rallying points of cultural identification. The major figure here is Robert Burns (1759–96) who was born in poverty as the son of a peasant, but became the major Scots poet. His collection *Poets Chiefly in the Scots Dialect* was published in 1787, a few years before Wordsworth and Coleridge's *Lyrical Ballads* (1798). Following the examples of Robert Fergusson, James Johnson and George Thompson, he revived and reworked a number of lyrical songs in Lallans, or the Lowlands dialect, which have become world-famous. Some, like 'Auld Lang Syne' ('For Old Time's Sake') have become part of British culture. All come from the base roots of the language; some have very few regional forms:

O, my Luve's like a red red rose
That's newly sprung in June;
O, my Luve's like a melodie
That's sweetly play'd in tune;

Others have several:

Wee, sleekit, cow'rin, tim'rous beastie
O what a panic's in thy breastie

Thou need na start awa sae hasty,
Wi' bickering brattle!

('To a Mouse')

Even from this brief sample of Romantic writing we can glean a number of key words associated with this remarkable literary movement: *wild, wander, sublime, divine, heaven, immortal, rapture, bliss.* We can also see that although Romanticism was chiefly a movement to bring literature back to its common roots, it generated a considerable lexical variety, including archaism, classical elements and dialect.

The Victorians

Attitudes towards language in the Victorian era resembled in many ways those of the Augustans. The traditional or 'official' language style was above all authoritative and controlled, marked by what Matthew Arnold called 'high seriousness',[2] a phrase which well described both the register and the tone. This was a highly 'normative' period when Standard English became clearly established, models of 'proper' usage abounded, and the great *Oxford English Dictionary* was planned and started to be produced. As Britain became a major imperial power, so its mission to colonize and educate the world gave English global prestige and made a standard form a necessity. Yet behind the formidable façade of rectitude and conformity which epitomizes the outward show of the Victorian age can be found the emergence of vital ordinary speech in novels and other records, and of less respectable verbal drives towards pornography, absurdity and even nonsense.

Although the age had these divisions, the dominant tone was that of public respectability. Queen Victoria made two famous comments which essentially sum up this quality, albeit from different points of view. 'We are not amused,' she objected sternly at a moment of unseemly levity. Yet she also complained that Mr Gladstone, the Liberal Prime Minister, spoke to her 'as if she were a public meeting'. The dominant tone of formality in Victorian prose is well conveyed by Lionel Trilling and Harold Bloom: 'Its voices are various in their intonations, some being reminiscent of the pulpit, some of the floor of the House of Commons, some of an Oxford lecture hall or senior common room' (1973, p. 5).

In both speech and writing the models of Dr Johnson and Gibbon were adopted once again. Lord Macaulay wrote a major *History of England* and a number of historical essays, one dealing with the impeachment of Warren Hastings, previously Viceroy of India, for mismanagement. Macaulay sets the scene of his trial in the House of Lords:

He looked like a great man, and not like a bad man. A person small and emaci-
ated, yet deriving dignity from a carriage which, while it indicated deference to
the court, indicated also habitual self-possession and self-respect, a high and
intellectual forehead, a brow pensive, but not gloomy, a mouth of inflexible deci-
sion, a face pale and worn, but serene, on which was written as legibly as under
the picure in the council-chamber at Calcutta, *Mens aequa in arduis* [a mind equal
to adversity]; such was the aspect with which the great Proconsul presented
himself to his judges. (1907, p. 635)

We note the high register and the balanced syntax: the last sentence, some
eight lines long, has ten pauses, highly reminiscent of Gibbon's *Decline and Fall
of the Roman Empire* (1776–88). Yet classical models did not reign supreme.
Thomas Carlyle, 'the Sage of Chelsea', used a quite idiosyncratic lexical
mixture:

Did not Paul of Tarsus, whom admiring men have since named Saint, feel that
he was 'the chief of sinners'; and Nero of Rome, jocund in spirit (*wohlgemuth*),
spend much of his time in fiddling? Foolish Word-monger and Motive-grinder,
who in thy Logic-mill hast an earthly mechanism for the Godlike itself, and
wouldst fain grind me out Virtue from the husks of Pleasure – I tell thee, Nay!
(*Sartor Resartus*, Book II, chapter 7)

Language and class

With the great social changes of the Victorian era, class differences became
less clearly defined in real terms, but they emerged in other forms. George Eliot
wrote in *Middlemarch* (first published in 1872, but set at the time of the great
Reform Bill of 1832) of certain established families who were 'conscious of an
inherent social superiority which was defined with great nicety in practice,
though hardly expressible theoretically' (chapter 23). As K. C. Phillipps points
out in his excellent and comprehensive study, *Language and Class in Victorian
England*, 'language was a principal, precise, pragmatic, and subtle way of
defining one's position and having it defined by others' (1984, p. 3). Many
modern notions about language and class derive from Victorian attitudes.

A significant factor influencing these linguistic class distinctions was the
advent of universal primary education in 1870. As we shall see, education
itself became a major theme in much Victorian fiction, as the natural regional
speech of children was discredited and the standard forms were imposed.
Furthermore, class differences were highlighted in various works stressing the
'correct' forms of language, such as W. H. Savage, *The Vulgarisms and Improprieties of the English Language* (1833), Samuel Lysons's *Our Vulgar Tongue*
(1868) and the anonymous volume, *Vulgarities of Speech Corrected* (1826). *A*

Plea for the Queen's English, published by Henry Alford in 1864, was highly successful, going through seven editions in twenty-five years. Such works obviously catered to a substantial market of people anxious to improve themselves linguistically.

One noted class marker of the times was the pronunciation of the letter 'h'. Both dropping the 'h' and intruding it were regarded as serious solecisms to be roundly mocked, and the feature was highlighted by spelling. W. H. Savage, in his previously mentioned study, *The Vulgarisms and Improprieties of the English Language* (1833), sought to preserve as many words with a silent 'h' as possible, giving a four-page list of them. He was equally scornful of those who, by false refinement, intruded the aspirate redundantly:

> The rustics attach their rough breathing indiscriminately to every letter capable of receiving it. We thus hear of *H-India, h-orthography, h'ell-wide, h'ebony, h'instinct, h'oxen,* lacerating at the same time their own larynx and afflicting the more delicate tympana of their metropolitan auditors by a cacophonous phraseology as nauseous as it is falsely imagined to be proper. (Cited in Phillipps, 1984, p. 137)

Dickens satirized this characteristic in the speech patterns of a number of characters, notably that of the odious hypocrite, Uriah Heep: 'I am well aware that I am the 'umblest person goin . . . my mother is likewise a very 'umble person. We live in a numble abode' (*David Copperfield*, chapter 16). Sam Weller talks of having 'hextra power' (*Pickwick Papers*, chapter 34). Dickens's contemporaries also allude to this feature. In *Pendennis* (1848–50), Thackeray has a minor character say deferentially: 'Artises [artists] come and take hoff [i.e. portray] the Church from that there tree – It was a Habby once sir' (Book I, chapter 15). George Gissing went as far as to write of his hero's 'struggles with the h-fiend' in chronicling the rise of Richard Mutimer in *Demos* (1886, p. 106).

More complex was the pronunciation of words ending in *ing*. H. C. Wyld, in his *Studies in English Rhymes* notes that 'down to the thirties of the last century, *-in* and not *-ing* was the almost universal pronunciation of among all classes of speakers – in fact, many thousands of excellent speakers never use any other form today' (1923, p. 112). A. S. C. Ross endorses this, noting that *-in'* for *-ing* (as in *huntin' shootin'* and *fishin'*) 'was undoubtedly once a U-indicator and still survives among a few U-speakers; among younger ones it seems, today, to be altogether dead' (1954, p. 39).

Other usages, now rejected as substandard or plain incorrect, were previously regarded as acceptable. One such (amazing to us now) is the use of *you was*: 'I have often heard my father say you was the finest Lord Lieutenant in

England' is a recorded utterance of George IV, no less (Phillipps, 1984, p. 68). Similar are the uses of *ain't*, and worse, *don't*, as in 'it don't matter now' (Thomas Hughes, *Tom Brown at Oxford*, 1861, chapter 16). The first of these, now regarded as an Americanism, can be used as an abbreviation of both 'is not' and 'has not'. We are surprised to hear upper-class speakers say things like 'We ain't safe in our beds' (Trollope, *The Vicar of Bullhampton*, 1870, chapter 3) or 'Ain't you pleased?' (Thomas Hughes, *Tom Brown at Oxford*, 1861, chapter 15).

Dickens

Charles Dickens (1812–70), the last great popular writer in English, began his writing career as a journalist and thus became involved in many of the social problems of the time. Since his father had been imprisoned for debt and the young Charles had been consigned to the cruel drudgery of a blacking factory at the age of 10, his interest in the plight of the poor and the working class was very personal.

Dickens went further than any of his contemporaries in replicating the ring of *idiolect* – individualistic speech – as well as commenting on the various uses to which language was put. While he uses these features to place people socially, he does not make the proscriptive judgements of Savage and Alford. Indeed, when using quite explicit sociolinguistic distinctions, such as when Estella openly mocks Pip's low-class terminology: 'He calls the knaves, Jacks, this boy!' in *Great Expectations*, chapter 8), the effect is clearly to generate sympathy for Pip and hostility towards Estella for her snobbbery.

Many of Dickens's characters have special hallmarks of expression. Mrs Gamp complains 'Don't squeege so' and refers to 'the very refuge [refuse] of society'. He uses idiosyncratic spelling to convey some of the special features. Sam Weller is a prime example of the Cockney interchange of 'w' and 'v', giving his name to a judge as 'Weller with a V'. When asked to explain this conundrum, 'Do you spell it with a "V" or a "W"?', he will not be drawn: 'that depends on the taste and fancy of the speller, my Lord,' replied Sam (*Pickwick Papers*, chapter 33). Though he is not a linguistic philosopher, Sam is in a profound sense right, in that names do have arbitrary careers in which their spelling is not entirely controlled. He has clearly acquired this particular phonetic ambiguity from his father, who advises him to 'be wery careful o' vidders all your life, specially if they've kept a public house, Sammy.' (chapter 20) and laments: 'Oh Sammy, Sammy, vy worn't there a alleybi?' (chapter 34). Although the spelling is often an amusing distraction, one consistently hears the ring of speech across 150 years: 'That 'ere young lady,' replied Sam. 'She knows wot's wot, she does' (chapter 37).

Many other examples of idiolect are to be found: Joe Parks is 'Rather a tough customer in an argeyment' (*Barnaby Rudge*, chapter 1); 'I am a lone lorn creetur' . . . and everythink goes contrairy with me, 'complains Mrs Gummidge in *David Copperfield*, chapter 3; in the same book a minor character is summed up in the formula ''Barkis is willin''' '; another observes that 'Orses and dorgs is some men's fancy.' Mrs Skewton in *Dombey and Son* has only a faint grasp of comparative religion: 'Say, like those wicked Turks, there is no What's-his-name but Thingummy, and What-you-may-call-it is his prophet!' (chapter 27). Joe Gargery finds a print of London 'drawd too achitectooralooral' (*Great Expectations*, chapter 27); 'I wants to make your flesh creep,' threatens the Fat Boy (*Pickwick Papers*, chapter 8); 'Sairey,' Says Mrs Harris, 'sech is life. Vich likeways is the hend of all things!' (*Martin Chuzzlewit*, chapter 29).

Dickens also shows how language can be exploited for special purposes. In places capitalization is used ironically for foregrounding: Mr Turveydrop is 'celebrated almost everywhere, for his Deportment' (*Bleak House*, chapter 14), while in the same book Mr Chadband declares 'the light of Terewth' (chapter 25). The puffery of advertising, both cynical and absurd, is also exposed: the 'United Metropolitan Improved Hot Muffin and Crumpet Baking and Punctual Delivery Company' features in *Nicholas Nickleby*, chapter 2, as an institution whose title has clearly grown as a makeshift agglomeration. In the same book Wackford Squeers's Academy is called, with only partial appropriateness, Dotheboys Hall. When Nicholas intimates that the title aggrandizes the reality, Squeers explains shamelessly: 'We call it a Hall up in London, because it sounds better, but they don't know it by that name in these parts. A man may call his house an island if he likes; there's no act of Parliament against that, I believe' (chapter 17). In his satire on bureaucracy in *Little Dorrit*, Dickens juxtaposes registers to highlight the inefficiency of the Circumlocution Office:

> If another Gunpowder Plot had been discovered half an hour before the lighting of the match, nobody would have been justified in saving the parliament until there had been half a score of boards, half a bushel of minutes, several sacks of official memoranda, and half a family vault of ungrammatical correspondence on the part of the Circumlocution Office. . . . Whatever was required to be done, the Circumlocution Office was beforehand with all the public departments in the art of perceiving – HOW NOT TO DO IT. (Chapter X)

Much satire is directed against the follies of Victorian education, especially its crude utilitarianism. The appalling case of Mr Gradgrind in *Hard Times* (who wanted 'nothing but facts') has been touched on in chapter 1. Mr Squeers in *Nicholas Nickleby* also sees vocabulary as the key to education, but in a bizarre fashion which puts words before reality. Introducing 'the first class in English spelling and philosophy', he explains: 'We go upon the practical mode of teaching, Nickleby, the regular education system. C-l-e-a-n, clean, verb active, to make bright, to scour. W-i-n, win, d-e-r, der, winder, casement. When the boy knows this out of book, he goes and does it. . . . When he has learnt that bottinney means a knowledge of plants, he goes and knows 'em. That's our system, Nickleby; what do you think of it?' (*Nicholas Nickleby*, chapter 8).

Linguistic chauvinism is also pilloried, especially prejudice against French: 'What's the water in French, sir?' '*L'eau*,' replied Nicholas. 'Ah!' said Mr Lillyvick, shaking his head mournfully. 'I thought as much. Lo, eh? I don't think anything of that language – nothing at all' (*Nicholas Nickleby*, chapter 16). In a notable scene in *Our Mutual Friend* the pompous and patronizing Mr Podsnap addresses an 'unfortunately born foreigner':

> "How Do You Like London?" Mr Podsnap now inquired from his station of host, as if he were administering something in the nature of a powder or potion to a deaf child; "London, Londres, London?"
>
> The foreign gentleman admired it.

Later, misconstruing a question, the unnamed 'foreign gentleman' refers to 'a Orse':

> "We call it Horse," said Mr Podsnap with forbearance. "In England, Angleterre, England, We Aspirate the 'H', and we say 'Horse'. Only our Lower Classes Say 'Orse!' "
>
> "Pardon," said the foreign gentleman; "I am alwiz wrong!"
>
> "Our Language," said Mr Podsnap, with a gracious consciousness of being always right, "is Difficult. Ours is a Copious Language, and Trying to Strangers."
> (Chapter 11)

Mayhew

Dickens had the freedom of fiction and of his own imagination in which to create a whole gamut of linguistic styles and lexical types. But many of his social observations are corroborated by a major philanthropic study of the times, Henry Mayhew's *London Labour and the London Poor*, first published in 1851. Mayhew (1812–87) both described and interviewed many of the vagrants and derelicts of the London underworld, and his work embodies a fascinating contrast between the formal high-register euphemism of the socially concerned Victorian pillar of society and the direct language of the street. Here is the beginning of his chapter on 'Park Women', which brings us back to the same social setting described in such a different register by Rochester at the opening of this chapter:

Park women, properly so called, are those degraded creatures, utterly lost to all sense of shame, who wander about the paths most frequented after nightfall in the Parks, and consent to any species of humiliation for the sake of acquiring a few shillings. . . . These women are well known to give themselves up to disgusting practices, that are alone gratifying to men of morbid and diseased imaginations. They are old, unsound, and by their appearance utterly incapacitated from practising their profession where the gas-lamps would expose the defects in their personal appearance, and the shabbiness of their ancient and dilapidated attire. (1983, p. 88)

Later on Mayhew records their experiences in their own quite different words:

"You call yourself a widow now," I said, "while before you said you were married and had seven children. Which are you?"
    "Which am I? The first I told you's the true. But Lor', I's up to so many dodges I gets what you may call confounded; sometimes I's a widder, and wants me 'art rejoiced with a copper, and then I's a hindustrious needlewoman thrown out of work and going to be druv into the streets if I don't get summat to do. Sometimes I makes a lot of money by being a poor old cripple as broke her arm . . . and when I gets home, we gets in some lush [drink] and 'as some frens, and goes in for a reglar blow-hout. . . ." (1983, p. 93).

Out of this medley of Victorian voices, let us conclude with one which gives an unexpected premonition of the semantic instabiity of modern times. The author of the 'Alice' books, namely Lewis Carroll, insinuated into his works of ingenious fantasy a number of sophisticated comments about the confusions and absurdities of logic and language. Carroll (1832–98), a remarkable Oxford mathematican, invented a playful pseudonym based on his real name, which was Charles Lutwidge Dodgson. He is the only author in English to have invented a lexical type, the *portmanteau* or *blend*, discussed in chapter 7. In addition, he made up other forms like *curiouser, un-birthday* and *uglification*. In a section of *Through the Looking-Glass* (first published in 1872), Carroll takes to its furthest limits the philosophy of nominalism, which regards meanings as simply arbitrary and conventional. Here Alice, who symbolises the innocent, unsophisticated normative reader, is bewildered by the dogmatism and semantic tyranny of Humpty Dumpty:

"I don't know what you mean by 'glory'," Alice said.
    Humpty Dumpty smiled contemptuously. "Of course you don't – till I tell you. I meant 'there's a nice knock-down argument for you!' "
    "But 'glory' doesn't mean 'a nice knock-down argument,' " Alice objected.
    "When *I* use a word," Humpty Dumpty said, in rather a scornful tone, "it means just what I choose it to mean, neither more nor less."

"The question is," said Alice, "whether you *can* make words mean so many different things."

"The question is," said Humpty Dumpty, "which is to be master, that's all."
(Chapter 6)

Carroll's profound absurdity provides a suitable point for us to turn from the complexities of language to the evolution of the dictionary, which seeks variously to reveal, to describe, to correct and to define the meanings of words.

A Short History of the Dictionary: Varieties of a Genre

'The history of the English dictionary' is a formulation which has tended to carry with it the assumption that 'the dictionary', like 'the grammar', has been essentially the same kind of work through its evolution. So it is, but only in a basic sense. Standard histories of the dictionary proceed on this assumption, tracing the growth of the type from Cawdrey's rudimentary work, *The Table Alphabeticall* (1604) via Johnson's magnificent opus (1755) to the monumental *Oxford English Dictionary* (1884–1928). The traditional view of the development of lexicography is of an evolution from prejudice to enlightenment, specifically shown in the gradual shift in policy from proscriptivism (emphasizing what is wrong) and prescriptivism (emphasizing what is right) to description (describing actual usage). A more inclusive and qualitative overview shows that 'the dictionary' is not so much a type evolving in size and sophistication, but a genre which broadens as it develops, more like the novel. Its history can be broadly divided into five different phases, some of which become recurring emphases.

For centuries the division of usage into the decent bourgeois standard and the less acceptable lower varieties of slang has been *de rigueur*. This split is notable in the history of the dictionary, where one finds a 'proper' tradition of Bailey (1728), Johnson (1755) and Murray et al. (1884–1928), and a 'canting', slang or underworld tradition (which is actually older) starting in Elizabethan times with works by Harman (1566), Greene (1591) and others, continued by Grose (1785), Farmer and Henley (1890–1904) and Partridge (1937), and is currently showing a resurgence, with a variety of works appearing virtually on an annual basis.

The lexical underworld

Within the English tradition the canting dictionaries can be regarded, significantly, as the first category in the field, dating from *c*.1552 and proving to be a thriving type, especially as the sixteenth century draws to a close. Although it may be claimed, with some justification, that they are not dictionaries in the strict sense, since they often contain a lot of anecdotal material, their broad aim and function is clearly the explication of the argot of the lexical underworld of Elizabethan times by means of a limited but detailed description of the low register. It is particularly interesting in the context of the Inkhorn Controversy that these early works should focus on an unfamiliar oral aspect of the mother tongue, not on the literary contributions of a foreign element of the lexis.

While the writers of canting dictionaries adopt an air of moralistic criticism towards the lifestyles of the idle poor and the confidence tricksters they describe, several show a clear sense of illicit enjoyment in describing this *demimonde*. One of the first in the field is *A manifest detection of the moste vyle and detestable use of Diceplay . . . a Myrrour very necessary for all yonge Gentilmen & others sodenly enabled by worldly abundance, to loke in* (1552). Though ostensibly a homily against dicing, this work describes the cheating practised in various opulent dens, explaining unfamiliar terms for the false dice, such as the *langret*, the dice with greater length along one axis; *fullans*, weighted dice; *gourds*, hollowed dice, and so on.

Canting works typically announce themselves in their own terms, thereby attracting the attention of the potential customer, whom the works profess to help. A notable example is *A Caveat or Warening, for Commen Cursetors vulgarely called Vagabones, set forth by Thomas Harman, Esquiere, for the utilitie and proffyt of his naturall cuntrey* (1566). In this work, the first to use the word *cant*, Harman broadly follows the pattern of John Awdeley's *The Fraternitie of Vagabonds* (1561), describing a whole rogues' gallery, with picturesque or ironic names such as a *prigger of prancers*, a horse thief, *Abraham men*, 'those who feign themselves to have been mad', and *Fresh-Water Mariners or Whipjacks*, those 'whose ships were drowned in the plain of Salisbury . . . [and] counterfeit great losses on the sea'. Being a country magistrate in Kent, Harman would certainly have come into contact with 'the unscrupulous activities of this vast army of wandering parasites', as Gamini Salgado refers to this underclass in his excellent and accessible collection, *Cony-Catchers and Bawdy Baskets* (1972, p. 10). In all some twenty-three such types are defined, often with the embellishment of anecdotes. The 'most notorious and wickedest' are even listed, and 'their usage of the night' is explicated by means of a glossary of about 100 words (in Salgado, 1972, p. 140). This section is introduced with a critical vehemence which smacks of protesting too much:

> Here I set before the good reader the lewd, lousy language of these loitering lusks and lazy lorels, wherewith they buy and sell the common people as they pass

through the country, which language they term pedlars' French, an unknown tongue only but to these bold, beastly, bawdy beggars and vain vagabonds, being half mingled with English when it is familiarly talked. (in Salgado, 1972, p. 146)

Some words in Harman's list are still current 400 years later, such as *booze* for drink and *drawers* for 'hosen'; others, like *prat*, 'a buttock', *to filch*, 'to beat' and *to niggle*, 'to have to do with a woman carnally', have stayed in the provenance of slang but changed their meaning.

The notorious Robert Greene entered the field with a number of canting works, initially one dated 1591 with the enticing title of *A Notable Discovery of Coosnage. Now daily practised by sundry lewd persons called Connie-catchers and Crosse-biters. Plainly laying open those pernitious sleights that hath brought many ignorant men to confusion. Written for the general benefit of all Gentlemen, Citizens, Aprentises, Countrey Farmers and yeoman, that may hap to fall into the company of such coosening companions.* After an anecdotal introduction, Greene gives out 'A Table of the Words of Art, Used in the Effecting These Base Villainies'. He sets out eight 'laws', as they are ironically termed, including *High Law*, '(robbing by the highway side)', *Sacking Law*, '(lechery)', *Crossbiting law*, '(cosenage by whores)' and *Cony-catching law*, '(cozenage by cards)'. A brief glossary for each category then follows. Thus, in Sacking Law:

> The bawd, if it be a woman, *a pander*;
> The bawd, if a man, *an apple-squire*;
> The whore, *a commodity*;
> The whore-house, *a trugging-place*.
> (In Salgado, 1972, p. 176)

Greene is not always as candid and informative as he might be: in the section under *Cheating Law*, '(play at false dice)', he lists the various names for false dice but tantalizingly does not explain them, simply concluding 'yet for some special reason herein I will be silent' (in Salgado, 1972, p. 176). He followed this work with *The Second Part of Cony-Catching* and *The Third and Last Part of Cony-Catching*. Both appeared in 1592, a year which also saw the publication of related works called *A Disputation, A Defence of Cony-Catching* and *The Black Book's Messenger*.

Canting dictionaries prove to be an important sociolinguistic phenomenon. It is significant that without these publications we would have very little evidence of the burgeoning tongue variously called *cant, pedlars' French* and so on, the clearly developed code language of the Elizabethan underworld. Three-quarters of the terms we have encountered in this brief survey are recorded as first instances by the *OED* in these canting contexts. (They are: *Abraham men, coosnage, connie-catchers, crosse-biters, to filch, fullans, langret, to niggle, prat, prancer* and *prigger*.) If we are to take Greene's first title (*A Notable Discovery of Coosnage*) literally, then it would appear as if this was, indeed, a new linguistic phenomenon. There seems to have been little sign of this underworld cant previously: Chaucer's *Cook's Tale*, for example, a text admittedly truncated because of its bawdy content, describes low life in London, but does not reveal signs of a particular argot.

To judge from the number of editions and reissues, canting dictionaries were very popular. They also prove to be an enduring type, generating similar works, notably Francis Grose's wonderfully exuberant *Dictionary of the Vulgar Tongue* (1785), which is set out in the traditional alphabetical format, but has entries full of wit and racy detail. It is particularly significant that as the production of the *OED* proceeded a century ago, Farmer and Henley were engaged in the vexatious process of producing their monumental opus of the lower register, *Slang and its Analogues* (1890–1904). The persistence of the canting variety of dictionary shows that pressure for recognition for the lower registers proves to be consistent, whether it is ignored, resisted or accommodated.

Explicating the classical register

The 'hard words' dictionaries are traditionally taken as the first dictionaries *per se* in, for example, such standard works as those of Starnes and Noyes (1946, p. 1), Wells (1973, p. 85) and McArthur (1986, p. 17). Gabriele Stein, in her definitive study, *The English Dictionary Before Cawdrey* (1985) does not mention the canting dictionaries.[3] The function of these works is the explication of opaque and unfamiliar classical terms by means of a limited treatment of the high register. Their emergence is a consequence of the wholesale borrowing of Latin and Greek terms which had been such a dominant feature of the lexical development of the sixteenth century and which, as we have seen, had in turn led to the Inkhorn Controversy.

Thomas Cawdrey is traditionally regarded as leading the field with his rudimentary work, which contained 2560 words, the *Table Alphabeticall of hard usuall English wordes* (1604). However, Noel E. Osselton has drawn attention to what may be an earlier, albeit an 'abortive attempt at starting an English-English dictionary' in the Bodleian Library. MS Rawlinson Poet. 108, dated *c.*1570 (in Hartmann (ed.), 1986, p. 175). The Rawlinson compiler shows a balance between learned and common words which is unusual for the time, and Osselton concludes that, had the work come to fruition, 'the English dictionary might very well have been more balanced in its vocabulary even from the start' (p. 183). Cawdrey pointedly uses a plain register to translate rarefied written Latinisms, stressing this point in his title: 'with the interpretation thereof by *plaine English words, gathered for the benefit & helpe of Ladies, Gentlewomen, or any other unskilfull persons'* (Cawdrey's emphasis). However, as Starnes and Noyes have shown, Cawdrey clearly drew on Edmund Coote's *The English Schoole-Master* (1586) for the compilation of his word-list, his definitions and even for his preface. Similar influence or 'inspiration' is to be found in the works of Cawdrey's immediate successors, John Bullokar's *An English Expositor* (1616) and Henry Cockeram's *The English Dictionarie* (1623), the first work in the tradition to use the term *dictionary* in its title.

The 'hard words' dictionaries clearly had more a genuine public-service function than that claimed by the canting variety, which is vitiated by a degree of sordid curiosity and even prurience in the ways of the underworld. Tom McArthur has argued that 'These men [Cawdrey et al.] possessed, it would appear, one consistent trait: they sought (in the spirit of both Renaissance and Reformation) to broaden the base of the educated Elect' (1986, p. 87). This view is persuasive, but perhaps a little naive, since all these works are clearly targeted towards a profitable niche market, one with a strong class element, namely those who lacked a classical education. There is an unmistakable tone of the hard sell in the title-pages. Thomas Blount's *Glossographia* (1656) is no exception, and as figure 5.2 shows, it lives up to its 'hard words' claim by including some of the rarest classical terms imaginable.

The usefulness and discrimination of the 'hard words' dictionaries requires some scrutiny. Although Cawdrey, Bullokar and Cockeram stress the function of their works as being to assist their readers in the understanding of 'hard' words, many of the chosen terms had been in the language for centuries. Nevertheless, they tended to treat these words as if they had just appeared, translating them in a literal fashion back to their etymologies, rather than in terms of their current meanings.

An extreme example of this literalism is Cawdrey's definition of one of the oldest 'Greek' words in the lexicon, *bishop*. The word had been in the language from Anglo-Saxon times in its modern ecclesiastical sense, and hardly needed defining, one feels, in 1604, but Cawdrey gives primacy to the literal Greek sense of *episkopos*: 'ouer-seer, or prelate'. Likewise, *benediction* is defined as 'praysing or blessing'; *translation* as 'altering, chaunging'; to *upbraid* as 'rise in one's stomach, cast in one's teeth'; *insult* as 'to triumphe, or vaunt ouer'; *passion* as 'suffering, grief' and *illusion* as 'mockery, jesting or scoffing'.

It would be unfair to isolate Cawdrey in this respect. All of these three early lexicographers show the same quality of literalism, which in the explication of words which had already been developing in the vernacular for decades or even centuries, is a form of semantic conservatism. *Martyr*, for instance, is related by all three to the notion of 'witness'; *tradition* is taken literally by all as a 'delivering'; *transcendent* as 'that which clymeth over' (Bullokar's definition, which

Illacerable (*illacerabilis*) that cannot be torn or rent in pieces.

Illachrymation (*illachrymatio*) a weeping or bewailing.

Illaqueate (*illaqueo*) to bind, snare or entangle.

Illatebration (*illatebratio*) a hiding, or seeking of corners.

Illation (*illatio*) an inference, conclusion, a reason or allegation that inforceth; a bringing in of a matter.

Illatration (*illatratio*) a barking against one.

Illecebrous (*illecebrosus*) that enticeth or allureth.

Illegitimate (*illegitimus*) unlawful, base-born, bastard.

Illepid (*illepidus*) without delectation or Grace, unpleasant.

Illicitous ⎫ (*illicitus*) un-
Illicite ⎭ lawful, without warrant.

Illigation (*illigatio*) an inwrapping or intangling.

Illimitable, that cannot be limited or bounded.

Illogical, not logical, not according to the rules of Logick.

Illucidate (*illucido*) to enlighten or give light, to cleer, or explicate cleerly.

Illuminous (*illuminosus*) without light.

Illusion (*illusio*) a mocking or scorning.

Illusory (from *Illusor*, a mocker) that mocketh or scorneth.

Illutible (*illutibilis*) that cannot be purged from filth.

Imbargo or **Embargo** (Span.) a stop or stay; an usual word among our Merchants, when their ships or Merchandizes are arrested upon any occasion.

Imbecillity (*imbecillitas*) weakness, feebleness. And some use the word *imbecillated* for weakened or enfeebled.

Imbellick (*imbellis*) unaccustomed to war, nothing manly, cowardly, *Feltham*.

Imber days, or **Imber weeks** (*quatuor tempora*) which weeks are four in the yeer, and anciently, Wednesday, Friday and Saturday in each fasted, according to these old Verses,

Post cineres, Pentec. post crucem, postque Luciam,
Mercurii, Venerii, Sabatho, jejunia fient.

That is, the next Wednesday after *Cineres* or *Ash-wednesday*, after *Pentecost*, i. *Whitsunday*, after holy-Rood-day, or the Exaltation of the Cross; and the next Wednesday after St. *Lucies* day in *Decem-*

ber. See *Ember*.

Imbibe (*imbibo*) to receive in. to drink in.

Imbibition (from *imbibo*) a drinking or receiving in.

Imbossement. See *Embossement*.

Imbosses

Figure 5.2   Hard words: classical rarities in Thomas Blount's *Glossographia* (1656)

is representative); *ventricle* as 'the stomach'; *disciple* as 'scholler' (from Cawdrey) and *anarchy* as 'when the land is without a prince, or governour', also from Cawdrey. The modern Hobbesian sense, which describes the likely effects rather than the cause, had already been recorded from 1539.

In places the definitions lapse into eccentricity and error. Cawdrey defines *phantasie* as 'imagination', but *fantastique* as 'conceited, full of deviles'; *akecorn* is, simply, 'fruit'; *incend*, presumably through confusion of the prefix, is tendered as 'clime up, or mount up', and *interlace* as 'mire'. *Theology* is charmingly rendered as 'divinitie, the science of living blessedly for ever'. Cockeram in his turn defines *phylologie* as 'love of much babbling', which is probably more of a clumsy literalism than an irony. Inconsistencies or inaccuracies in spelling are not rare: Cawdrey sanctions the obsolete, corrupt forms *orphant* and *gnible* (the latter perhaps by analogy with *gnaw*); *vlgar* slips past the proof-reader. Cockeram assures surprised readers that *urinate* means 'to dive or swimme vnder water', a literal perpetuation of Classical Latin.

The 'comprehensive' and authoritative dictionary

As the linguistic fashion changed from exuberance to correctness, so the lexicographical emphasis changed from 'the most refined and difficult words'[4] to one of inclusiveness. Nathan Bailey, the first to attempt this wider field with his *Universal Etymological English Dictionary* (volume I, 1721; volume II, 1728),[5] claimed still more for his *Dictionarium Britannicum* of 1730: it is subtitled 'a more complete Universal Etymological English Dictionary than any extant'. Etymologies, first seriously attempted by Blount in 1656, are considerably elaborated, but definitions are, for the most part, general.

Bailey's densely packed title-page endorses the claim to inclusiveness, stressing that the work will explain 'hard and technical words, or Terms of Art, in all the ARTS, SCIENCES, and MYSTERIES following'. Over sixty fields of knowledge are then listed, including 'Catoptricks', 'Chyromangy', 'Dioptricks', 'Hydrostaticks', 'Optacousticks' and 'Pyrotechny'. Bailey's word-list generally reflects this technical compendiousness: thus *wreath* has four entries, one general, one from architecture, one from heraldry and one from hunting; *writ*, similarly, has six entries. A great merit of Bailey's work is that it preserves some remarkable curiosities, such as *wulfeshefed* i.e. wolf's head.[6] Whereas Johnson asserts that the letter 'x' 'begins no word in the English language', Bailey lists no less than forty such words, many of them admittedly very rare and of tenuous Englishness.[7] But his definitions are often banal: *write* is defined rather lamely and tautologically as 'to enter any thing down in writing'.

Dr Johnson was certainly influenced by Bailey: according to Sir John Hawkins, an early biographer of Johnson, 'an interleaved copy of Bailey's dictionary in folio' was used by Johnson as 'the repository of certain articles' culled from his own reading (McCracken, 1969, p. 338). But although Johnson was indebted to Bailey's work, he was selective: David McCracken has shown that 'Under the letter L Johnson included 394 words not found in Bailey's work, but he omitted 909' (p. 339). Though Bailey was in some ways more erudite, Johnson's work became immediately the pre-eminent authoritative standard.

Johnson's magnificent preface shows the evolution of his linguistic philosophy. In it he addresses the intelligentsia and the literati of the nation, not the general public, and his attitude is largely elitist and chauvinist. He announced that he would use only 'writers of the first reputation' and, as Robert Burchfield reminds us, Johnson's is the only English dictionary compiled by a writer of the first rank (1985, p. 87). Like most of the 'choice and master spirits of the age', Johnson was highly sensitive and extremely concerned about 'corruptions' in a language which was seen as being in a state of decline. In a memorably pessimistic aphorism, he remarked that 'tongues, like governments, have a natural tendency to degeneration.' In this view he was broadening the observation of Pope in *An Essay on Criticism*:

> Our sons their fathers' failing language see,
> And such as Chaucer is, shall Dryden be.
> (lines 482–3)

In Johnson's time, of course, prescriptive and proscriptive linguistic attitudes were dominant, because of this fatalistic sense of decay and decline which permeated thinking in language matters. His original stance was strongly prescriptive, very much in the manner of a linguistic Newton come to impose order on unruly philology:

> When I took the first survey of my undertaking, I found our speech copious without order, and energetick without rules: wherever I turned my view, there was perplexity to be disentangled, and confusion to be regulated.

We notice that he uses *energetic* in a clearly negative sense, implying that energy should be controlled or channelled. His later position is more complex, both resigned and determined. Suspicious of academies, aware of the futility of trying to 'enchain syllables', and scornful of the lexicographer 'who shall imagine that his dictionary can embalm his language', Johnson is yet urged to his task by that profound, clairvoyant pessimism which illuminates his greatest work.

Jonathan Swift, whose thinking was often more acutely political than that of his contemporaries, had asserted political causes for linguistic decay. In his

A Proposal for Correcting, Improving and Ascertaining the English Tongue (1712) he posited this causation, identifying the causes as the 'Enthusiastic Jargon' (religious fanaticism) of the Cromwellian Commonwealth and the 'Licentiousness which entered with the Restoration' (Swift, 1957, p. 10). Swift's mode of confronting those impurities and 'barbarisms' was, typically, by means of ironic parody in letters to *The Tatler*. In one of these in 1710 he urged the editor, Richard Steele, 'to make use of your authority as Censor, and by an annual *index expurgatorius* expunge all words and phrases that are offensive to good sense, and condemn all those barbarous mutilations of vowels and syllables'.

Johnson was quite specific about the detrimental causes and he was the first lexicographer to employ usage labels to highlight abuses. In his view there were four: the French influence, high society, low society and commerce. 'The great pest of speech,' he asserted, 'is frequency of translation.' This process surreptitiously imported hundreds of words and, worse, dozens of idioms. Johnson's particular *bête noire* was the French influence which, if it continued unchecked would, in his view, 'reduce us to babble a dialect of France'.

Johnson's xenophobia or Francophobia was in many ways a continuation of the Purism exhibited by Sir John Cheke, Ralph Lever and Thomas Watson in the Inkhorn Controversy. But his hostility was not an individual quirk: it was shared by many of his contemporaries, notably Joseph Addison, who in 1711 had written an essay in *The Spectator* deriding the absurd excesses of French influence, and seriously suggesting some form of linguistic control.

Johnson clearly acted out his hostility to French terms by excluding many from his dictionary, an aspect which has generally been ignored.[8] French words seem to have been more fashionable during the earlier part of the eighteenth century than when Johnson was compiling his dictionary. An analysis of the *Chronological English Dictionary* reveals an average recorded influx of at least half a dozen words per year during the reign of Queen Anne (1702–14), after which the flow is reduced to a trickle. I am referring here to words which have an obvious French timbre, like *coterie, ennui, connoisseur* and *casserole*, not to terms like *nationalist* and *civilization*, which – though borrowed from French – have more clearly visible Latin roots.

Words excluded by Johnson (with the earliest *OED* citation) are:

corsage (1481)	champagne (1664)	riposte (1707)
sou (1556)	faux pas (1676)	debris (1708)
bourgeois (1564)	cortège (1679)	clique (1711)
esprit (1591)	contretemps (1684)	beau monde (1714)
unique (1602)	picturesque (1703)	reconnoitre (1714)
spa (1626)	casserole (1706)	bouquet (1716)

hauteur (1628)	cutlet (1706)	roulette (1734)
concierge (1646)	meringue (1706)	vampire (1734)
façade (1656)	envelope (1707)	coterie (1738)
ennui (1732)[9]		

Johnson, always a pragmatist, did not aim at a wholesale exclusion of French terms. But he did try to prevent the fashionable acceptance of those which, in his linguistic model, represented for him the qualities of 'false refinement and declension'. Thus *trait* is accepted, but with the hostile comment 'scarce English'. *'The sublime,'* Johnson grudgingly admits, 'is a Gallicism, but now naturalized,' whereas *cajole* is simply, 'a low word'. *Voiture* and *role* are recorded but, paradoxically, judged to be 'not in use'. His general antipathy to borrowings which he regarded as unnecessary is summed up in this passage:

> The words which our authors have introduced by their knowledge of foreign lan-
> guages, or ignorance of their own, by vanity or wantonness, by compliance with
> fashion, or lust of innovation, I have registered as they occurred, though com-
> monly only to censure them, and warn others of the folly of naturalizing useless
> foreigners to the injury of the natives.

Johnson also employed the condemnatory usage labels of 'a low word' or 'cant' to discourage the use of a fair number of words. He often invoked the criterion of etymology, so that a word without respectable roots was regarded as an ill-bred parvenu. The case of *banter* has already been discussed. Some words regarded as 'low' by Johnson still have a colloquial register: they include *bamboozle, budge, coax, flush* (in the sense of temporarily rich), *fuss, glum, job, sham, spick and span, squabble, swop, tiff, touchy, traipse* and – depending on one's attitude to the work ethic – *gambler*. Others similarly labelled, however, seem eminently respectable, such as *belabour, doff, dumbfound, ignoramus, sensible, simpleton* and *to volunteer*.

His policy towards the perpetually flourishing but generally unstable language of the underworld or cant was broadly one of straight exclusion. Ironically, as we have seen, these were the very words which had occasioned the earliest dictionaries of all, recording and explaining to a curious bourgeois populace the meanings of such terms as *cove, beak* and *fence*. These terms of the underground establishment were at least a century old by Johnson's time and are still heard today, more in some circles than in others.

At the opposing end of the register, Johnson admitted many classically derived words which Albert C. Baugh regards as having 'a very questionable right to be regarded as belonging to the language' (1959, p. 327). Noah Webster even believed that the inclusion of such recherché terms as *assation, ataraxy, conclusible, detentition, incompossibility, indigitate* and thousands of others jeopardized the *Dictionary's* right to be a 'safe standard of writing' and perhaps even constituted a 'corruption of the English Language' (in Baugh, 1959, pp. 327–8). The significant contribution of Webster, the founding father of American lexicography, is discussed more fully in chapter 6. Johnson himself had a predilection for longer classical terms, which were then in fashion, and this is reflected in some of his definitions, such as the following:

net:	Anything reticulated or decussated, at equal distances, with interstices between the intersections.
smoke:	The visible effluvium, or sooty exhalation from anything burning.
cough:	A convulsion of the lungs, vellicated by some sharp serosity.
fit:	A paroxysm or exacerbation of any intermittent distemper.

Writing which shows such a concentration of classical vocabulary has accordingly been given the stylistic label of 'Johnsonese'. There is a revealing instance where Johnson transposed a plain diary entry into a far more pompous style when it was published as a journal. In its original form the entry ran as follows: 'A dirty fellow bounced out of the bed in which one of us was to lie.' In the journal this is changed substantially: 'Out of one of the beds on which we were to repose, there started up at our entrance a man black as a Cyclops from the forge' (Warner, 1961, p. 120). We can see here that not only has the register been transformed, but the word order is also highly artificial.

Though the adjective *Johnsonian* now denotes alternatively commonsensical wit or polysyllabic elegance in syntax, it would be misleading to see him as solely biased towards classical derivations, for he included without comment several of the four-letter words (though Bailey was the only contemporary editor to challenge the taboos of the time by including all). In addition he accepted such low register terms as *haggle, hatchet-faced, hen-pecked, huff, jail-bird, noodle, numskulled, oaf, pettyfogger, piddle, swig* and *titbit* without demur. Of the terms previously discussed from the canting dictionaries, Johnson included six out of eighteen. These are liberal inclusions from a man who regarded the 'fugitive cant' of the 'laborious and mercantile part of the people' as 'unworthy of preservation'.

Johnson's *Dictionary*, in keeping with the sense of decorum of the time, did not include the grossest of the 'four-letter' words, though there are amusing definitions and quotations for *fart, piss* and *shit*. The point of omission is ironically made in the following contemporary anecdote. Johnson was in the habit of visiting two society ladies:

He called on them one day soon after the publication of his immortal dictionary. The two ladies paid him due compliments on the occasion. Among other topics of praise, they very much commended the omission of all naughty words. 'What! my dears! then you have been looking for them?' said the moralist. The ladies, confused at being caught, dropped the subject of the dictionary. (*Oxford Book of Literary Anecdotes*, 1975, 84)

Johnson was also the first lexicographer to perceive that affectation in the higher echelons of society contributed to semantic decay. This took the form of exaggerated or melodramatic applications of serious words to trivial contexts. He was diagnosing what is today called *verbicide*, as C. S. Lewis applied the term of Oliver Wendell Holmes, or *weakening*. Johnson's condemning term was the adjective 'ludicrous'. It is found in *desperately* as in 'she fell desperately in love' from Addison's *Spectator*. Similarly, in *abominable*: 'in low and ludicrous language, it is a word of loose and indeterminate censure.' *Anthropophaginian* is a 'ludicrous word, formed by Shakespeare from *anthropophagi* for the sake of a formidable sound'. Within this area of exaggeration he detected a particular syndrome of feminine affectation. These words he simply condemned as 'women's words'. *Frightful*, he noted, was 'a cant word among women for anything unpleasing'; *flirtation* in the sense of a 'quick sprightly motion' is similarly categorized, while *horrid* in women's cant is 'shocking; offensive; unpleasing'. The echoes can still be heard in fashionable suburbs or other locales of in-group chatter.

It is very easy to dismiss Johnson's Gallophobia as an academic or nationalist tic and to reject his ostracism of 'low' and 'ludicrous' usage as the inflexible prescriptivism of an authoritarian age. But even in our times, with their increasingly descriptive ethos, whether eager or grudging in its acceptance of popular usage, one can only admire Johnson's broad, acute and prescient analysis of the insidious effects of commerce:

Total and sudden transformations of a language seldom happen; conquests and migrations are now very rare: but there are other causes of change, which though slow in their operation, and invisible in their progress, are perhaps as much superiour to human resistance, as the revolution of the sky, or intumescence of the tide. Commerce, however necessary, however lucrative, as it depraves the manners, corrupts the language.

Johnson is, of course, describing here a subtle shift in values and in the credibility of many terms, not a clearly isolated group of key words. One is dealing more with a syndrome than with an influx, with a cynical convention of exaggeration on the part of the advertiser and a cynical connivance on the part of the reader or customer.

As he wrote in *The Idler* of 1759:

> Advertisements are now so numerous that they are very negligently perused, and it is therefore become necessary to gain attention by magnificence of promises, and by eloquence, sometimes sublime and sometimes pathetic. Promise, large Promise is the soul of an Advertisement.

Johnson perceived that advertising was even in his time acquiring that convention of incredibility which is now dignified by the legal loophole of 'legitimate puffery'. Though he might be shocked at the extent of the 'hypnotic mendacities of the mass media' (Steiner, 1969, p. 261) and of the institionalized illiteracy of advertising, he had perceived their root causes.

Johnson's great work has a number of outstanding merits. It is the first attempt to produce a dictionary on historical principles, that is to say, the senses of individual words are arranged in the historical order of their emergence, with supporting quotations. Furthermore, the meanings are separated with a fine sense of discrimination. Johnson's astonishingly wide reading provided the material on the first count, and his acute semantic intelligence is everywhere apparent on the second: he was able, for instance, to distinguish 134 different meanings in the word *take*, a quite amazing feat. A third merit, perhaps the most significant, is the clarity and force of its definitions. Some notable example are:

animal: A living creature corporeal, distinct, on the one side, from pure spirit, and on the other, from mere matter.

ass: An animal of burden, remarkable for sluggishness, patience, hardiness, coarseness of food, and long life.

mince: To walk nicely [precisely] by short steps; to act with appearance of scrupulousness and delicacy; to affect nicety. [Johnson defines *niceness* as 'superfluous delicacy or exactness.']

prude: A woman over nice and scrupulous, and with false affectation.

puberty: The time of life when the two sexes begin first to be acquainted.

punster: A quibbler; a low wit who endeavours at reputation by double meaning.

shrew: A peevish, malignant, clamorous, spiteful, vexatious, turbulent woman.

tawdry: Meanly shewy; splendid without cost; fine without grace; shewy without elegance.

It is difficult to believe that Johnson produced this huge work almost single-handedly, since it contains the definitions of over 40,000 words illustrated by some 114,000 quotations. A sense of its scale, complexity and thoroughness can be gained from the page shown in figure 5.3. Furthermore, he completed

His beard they have fing'd off with brands of fire ;
And ever as it blaz'd they threw on him
Great pails of puddled mire to quench the hair.
My mafter preaches patience, and the while
His man with fciffars nicks him like a fool. *Shakefpeare.*
    Breaks watchmen's heads, and chairmen's glaffes,
And thence proceeds to nicking fafhes. *Prior.*

3. To fuit, as tallies cut in nicks.
    Words nicking and refembling one another, are applicable
to different fignifications. *Camden's Remains.*

4. To defeat or cozen, as at dice ; to difappoint by fome trick
or unexpected turn.
    Why fhould he follow you ?
    The itch of his affection fhould not then
    Have nick'd his captainfhip, at fuch a point. *Shakefpeare.*

NICKNA'ME. *n. f.* [nom de nique, French.] A name given in
fcoff or contempt ; a term of derifion ; an opprobrious or con-
temptuous appellation.
    The time was when men were had in price for learning ;
now letters only make men vile. He is upbraidingly called
a poet, as if it were a contemptible nickname. *Ben. Johnfon.*
    My mortal enemy hath not only falfely furmifed me to be
a feigned perfon, giving me nicknames, but alfo hath offered
large fums of money to corrupt the princes with whom I
have been retained. *Bacon's Hen. VII.*
    So long as her tongue was at liberty, there was not a
word to be got from her, but the fame nickname in derifion.
                        L'Eftrange.

To NICKNA'ME. *v. a.* To call by an opprobrious appellation.
    You nickname virtue vice ;
    For virtue's office never breaks men's troth. *Shakef.*
    Lefs feem thefe facts which treafons nickname force,
    Than fuch a feaf'd ability for more. *Denham.*

To NI'CTATE. *v. a.* [nicto, Latin.] To wink.
    There are feveral parts peculiar to brutes, which are want-
ing in man ; as the feventh or fufpenfory mufcle of the eye,
the nictating membrane, and the ftrong aponeurofes on the
fides of the neck. *Ray.*

NIDE. *n. f.* [nidus, Lat.] A brood : as, a nide of pheafants.

NIDGET. *n. f.* [corrupted from nithing or niding. The opprobrious term with which the men was anciently branded
who refufed to come to the royal ftandard in times of exi-
gency.] A coward ; a daftard.
    There was one true Englifh word of greater force than
them all, now out of all ufe ; it fignifieth no more than abject, bafeminded, falfe-hearted, coward, or nidget. *Camden.*

NIDIFICA'TION. *n. f.* [nidificatio, Latin.] The act of building nefts.
    That place, and that method of nidification, doth abun-
dantly anfwer the creature's occafions. *Derham.*

NI'DING. *adj.* [from nið, Saxon, vilenefs.]
    Niding, an old Englifh word fignifying abject, bafe-minded,
falfe-hearted, coward, or nidget. *Carew.*

NIDO'ROUS. *adj.* [nidorous, from nidor.] Refembling the fmell
or tafte of roafted fat.
    Incenfe and nidorous fmells, fuch as of facrifices, were
thought to intoxicate the brain, and to difpofe men to de-
votion ; which they may do by a kind of contriftation of
the fpirits, and partly alfo by heating and exalting them. *Bac.*
    The figns of the functions of the ftomach being depraved,
are eructations either with the tafte of the aliment, acid,
nidrofe, or foetid, refembling the tafte of rotten eggs.
                      Arbuthnot on Aliments.

NI'DOROSITY. *n. f.* [from nidorous.] Eructation with the
tafte of undigefted roaft-meat.
    The cure of this nidorofity is, by vomiting and purging.
                      Floyer on the Humours.

NIDULA'TION. *n. f.* [nidulor, Latin.] The time of remaining in the neft.
    The ground of this popular practice might be the com-
mon opinion concerning the virtue prognoftic of thefe birds,
the natural regard they have unto the winds, and they unto
them again, more efpecially remarkable in the time of their
nidulation, and bringing forth their young. *Brown's V. Err.*

NIECE. *n. f.* [niece, niepce, French ; neptis, Latin.] The
daughter of a brother or fifter.
    My niece Plantagenet,
    Led in the hand of her kind aunt of Glofter. *Sha. R. III.*
    While be thus his niece beftows,
    About our ifle he builds a wall. *Waller.*

NIGGARD. *n. f.* [niggr, Iflandick.] A mifer ; a curmud-
geon ; a fordid, avaricious, parcimonious fellow.
    If thou do, then let thy bed be turned from fine gravel to
weeds or mud. If thou do, let fome unjuft niggards make
wents to fpoil thy beauty. *Sidney, b. ii.*
    Be not a niggard of your fpeech. *Shakef. Macbeth.*
    Serve him as a grudging mafter,
    As a penurious niggard of his wealth. *Milton's Poems.*
    Be niggards of advice on no pretence ;
    For the worft avarice is that of fenfe. *Pope on Crit.*

NI'GGARD. *adj.*
1. Sordid ; avaricious ; parcimonious.

One fhe found
With all the gifts of bounteous nature crown'd,
Of gentle blood ; but one whofe niggard fate
Had fet him far below her high eftate. *Dryden.*

2. Sparing ; wary.
    Moft free of queftion, but to our demands
Niggard in his reply. *Shakefpeare's Hamlet.*

To NI'GGARD. *v. a.* [from the noun.] To ftint.
    The deep of night is crept upon our talk,
    And nature muft obey neceffity ;
    Which we will niggard with a little reft. *Shakefpeare.*

NI'GGARDISH. *adj.* [from niggard.] Having fome difpofition
to avarice.

NI'GGARDLINESS. *n. f.* [from niggardly.] Avarice ; fordid
parcimony.
    Niggardlinefs is not good hufbandry, nor generofity, pro-
fufion. *Addifon's Spectator, N°. 443.*

NI'GGARDLY. *adj.* [from niggard.]
1. Avaricious ; fordidly parcimonious.
    Where the owner of the houfe will be bountiful, it is not
for the fteward to be niggardly. *Hall.*
    Love is like a penurious god, very niggardly of his oppor-
tunities : he muft be watched like a hard-hearted treafurer.
                      Dryden's Spanifh Friar.
    Why are we fo niggardly to ftop at one fifth ? Why do we
not raife it one full moirety, and thereby double our money ?
                        Locke.
    Providence not niggardly but wife,
    Here lavifhly beftows, and there denies,
    That by each other's virtues we may rife. *Granvil.*
    Tiberius was noted for his niggardly temper ; he ufed only
to give to his attendants their diet. *Arbuthnot on Coins.*

2. Sparing ; wary.
    I know your mind, and I will fatisfy it ; neither will I do
it like a niggardly anfwerer, going no farther than the bounds
of the queftion. *Sidney.*

NI'GGARDLY. *adv.* Sparingly ; parcimonioufly.
    I have long loved her, followed her, ingrofs'd opportu-
nities to meet her ; feed every flight occafion that could but
niggardly give me fight of her. *Shakef. M. W. of Windfor.*

NI'GGARDNESS. *n. f.* [from niggard.] Avarice ; fordid parcimony.
    All preparations, both for food and lodging, fuch as would
make one detect niggardnefs, it is fo fluttifh a vice. *Sidney.*

NIGH. *prep.* [nyh, Saxon.] At no great diftance from.
    They fhone
    Stars diftant, but nigh hand feem'd t'other worlds. *Milton.*
    Nigh this recefs, with terror they furvey,
    Where death maintains his dread tyrannic fway. *Garth.*

NIGH. *adv.*
1. Not at a great diftance.
    The day of the Lord cometh, for it is nigh at hand. *Jo. ii. 1.*
    He was fick nigh unto death. *Phil. ii. 27.*

2. To a place near.
    He drew nigh, and to me held,
    Ev'n to my mouth, of that fame fruit held part
    Which he had pluck'd. *Milton's Paradife Loft, b. v.*
    I will defer that anxious thought,
    And death, by fear, fhall not be nigher brought. *Dryd.*

NIGH. *adj.*
1. Near ; not diftant ; not remote.
    The loud tumult fhews the battle nigh. *Prior.*

2. Allied clofely by blood.
    He committed the protection of his fon Afanes to two of
his nigh kinfmen and affured friends. *Knolles.*
    His uncle or uncle's fon, or any that is nigh of kin unto
him of his family, may redeem him. *Lev. xxv. 49.*
    His fifter a virgin, that is nigh unto him. *Lev. xxi. 3.*

To NIGH. *v. n.* [from the particle.] To approach ; to advance ; to draw near.
    Now day is done, and night is nighing faft. *Hubberd.*

NI'GHLY. *adv.* [from nigh the adjective.] Nearly ; within a
little.
    A man born blind, now adult, was taught by his touch
to diftinguifh between a cube and a fphere of the fame metal, and nighly of the fame bignefs. *Locke.*

NI'GHNESS. *n. f.* [from nigh.] Nearnefs ; proximity.

NIGHT. *n. f.* [naht, Gothick ; nihte, Saxon ; nuit, Fr.]
1. The time of darknefs ; the time from fun-fet to fun-rife.
    The duke of Cornwall, and Regan his dutchefs, will be
here this night. *Shakefpeare's K. Lear.*
    In the morning he fhall devour the prey, and at night di-
vide the fpoil. *Gen. xlix. 27.*
    Pharaoh rofe up in the night. *Exodus xii. 30.*
    They did eat and drink, and tarried all night. *Gen. xxiv. 54.*
    Let them fleep, let them fleep on,
    'Till this ftormy night be gone,
    And th' eternal morrow dawn ;
    Then the curtains will be drawn ;
    And they waken with that light,
    Whofe day fhall never fleep in night. *Crafhaw.*
                           Dire

Figure 5.3   Dr Johnson on great words and small (1755)

it in a mere seven years, seated on a chair with only three legs, and with the assistance of but six amanuenses, or copiers of quotations from many source-books. (The equivalent French dictionary took forty scholars forty years, and the editors of the great *OED* took twenty-five years to produce the first fascicle and a further forty-three years to bring it to completion.) Johnson managed this enormous and painstaking enterprise in addition to producing a considerable number of other literary works. As he put it memorably, the *Dictionary* was 'written with little assistance of the learned, and without any patronage of the great; not in the soft obscurities of retirement, nor under the shelter of academick bowers, but amidst incovenience and distraction, in sickness and in sorrow'. This last phrase alludes to the death of his wife Tetty in 1752, a loss which brought on 'extreme agitation and melancholy of the blackest and deepest kind' (Bate, 1977, p. 273).

Johnson's *Dictionary* also exemplifies very clearly a point often forgotten, namely that dictionaries are written by people. They thus have failings and prejudices. There were errors in etymologies and in definition, while in places a certain partiality showed through. For example, Johnson mistakenly defined *pastern* as 'the knee of an horse', when it is, in fact, the part between the fetlock and the hoof. When asked by a lady to explain the error, he confessed with resounding simplicity, 'Ignorance, madam, pure ignorance.' The etymology of *nickname* in the sample page is inaccurate. Both *windward* and *leeward* are given the same definition although their meanings are opposite. He erroneously informed his readers that *camp-fight* was 'an old word for *combat*', that the butterfly is so named 'because it first appears at the beginning of the season for butter', that the porpoise is 'the sea hog' and that the stoat is 'a small stinking animal'. Some of his definitions are notoriously partial. Being no friend of Scotland, he defined *oats* with irony as 'A grain, which in England is given to horses, but in Scotland supports the people.' Having been wretchedly treated by his patron, Lord Chesterfield, he clearly took a personal revenge in defining *patron* as 'Commonly a wretch who supports with insolence, and is paid with flattery.' Furthermore, he must surely have had some undefined person in mind when he added to his definition of *pension* the comment: 'In England it is generally understood to mean pay given to a state hireling for treason to his country.' He defined *excise* simply and popularly as 'a hateful tax'.

In their assessment of Johnson's achievement, James Sledd and Gwyn Kolb note Johnson's inclusion of 'sesquipedalian monstrosities', but they conclude:

> The conventional verdict, in general, is obviously sound: it took the historical linguistics of the nineteenth century to make a better Dictionary than Johnson's. (1995, p. 32)

When the assessment is extended to the matter of Johnson's effect on the subsequent history of the language, the question becomes very complex. George McKnight took the view that the *Dictionary* 'accomplished much that it had been intended an Academy should accomplish. Toward the accomplishment of Swift's plan [of "fixing" the language] . . . it made a long stride' (1968, pp. 375–6). Kenneth Wimsatt regards Johnson's work as 'a public instrument of the highest authority for shaping the language after 1755' (1948, p. ix), and with this view Starnes and Noyes are in qualified agreement: 'Indeed in many ways Johnson's *Dictionary* did effect lasting improvements in the language' (1946, p. 273). However, none of these writers really substantiate their generalizations, or even specify areas of influence, which is unfortunate.

As Sledd and Kolb have acutely observed, 'those who say that Johnson shaped the language often mean by "language" only the vocabulary' (1955, p. 184). They point out, in addition, that statements about linguistic influence 'are more likely to be made by men of letters than by philologists; and linguists, at least in the United States today, too often dismiss them with an impatience which only prolongs misunderstanding' (1955, p. 33).

A clear example of such a limited, linguistically oriented response is found in Ronald A. Wells's study *Dictionaries and the Authoritarian Tradition*:

> To say, then, that a dictionary has 'shaped' the language, is to elevate the artificial written language over the natural spoken one, and the lexicon over the more fundamental considerations of phonology, morphology, and structure. In short, it is to misconstrue the very nature of language itself. (1973, p. 95)

Wells concludes:

> The desire to stabilize language, then, and the notion that the dictionary can be the means to achieve that end, have been linked in our culture since the late seventeenth century. To modern thinking, however, the attempt to achieve conscious control of language is futile, for it is only by continuing adaptation to the needs of men that the language can fulfill its function. (1973, p. 95)

What is strange about this last statement, and what would have made it almost absurd to Johnson, is the implication that linguistic stability is not, apparently, to be regarded as one of 'the needs of men'. Such a view is manifestly inadequate. Language, like any human institution, fulfils the opposing needs for rigour and for flexibility, for constraint and for freedom. As he made abundantly clear in his preface, Johnson was poignantly aware of sociolinguistic forces outside his control. To be sure, prescriptivism was the current linguistic philosophy of the eighteenth century, just as relativism has become fashionable in this. But, ever since the grammar and the dictionary rose to popularity in the eighteenth century, the market for works of linguistic guidance has never slackened. This fact alone seems important, since it strongly suggests that the mode of correctness, of conformity, still meets an important need, even in the face of disagreement among authorities over what the correct form might be.

Johnson's *Dictionary* may have been overrated in his own time, since a standard was felt to be lacking, and Johnson supplied it with the Augustan virtues of strong-minded intelligence, sanity, clarity and wit. There were then few who could knowledgeably cavil at the deficiencies of his etymology, his bias, his ignorance of 'Teutonick', for the great integrating philological discoveries of the nineteenth century lay far ahead. And even when the fine monument of the *OED* took shape, Johnson's contribution, particularly the magisterial intelligence and felicitous exactitude of his definitions, was often acknowledged by a simple bracketed capital J.

The following anecdote may serve to reveal Johnson's authoritative influence and some of the dangers of the essentially parasitic mode of lexicography:

> Johnson received from some unknown source a letter deriving the word 'curmugeon' from *coeur méchant*, or wicked heart – a wild enough guess, which pleased the doctor so much that he adopted it in his *Dictionary*, giving due credit to 'unknown correspondent'. Twenty years later, Dr Ash preparing a dictionary of his own, was struck by this gem, and transferred it to his own pages. But, wishing all the glory of the discovery for himself, he gave no credit to Johnson, and informed a wondering world that 'curmugeon' was formed from *coeur*, 'unknown', and *méchant*, 'correspondent'. (*Oxford Book of Literary Anecdotes*, 1975 pp. 82–3)

The encyclopaedic tendency of the dictionary can be traced as far back as Bullokar (1616). His entry under *Dolphine* is typical:

> A fish friendly to man, and especially to children; the Females of this fish, have breasts like to women, which are stored with milke.

Lore of all kinds was incorporated into subsequent works. John Ray's *Collection of English Proverbs* (first published in 1670) was extensively, and sometimes abruptly, used by Bailey, and the conclusion of Johnson's lengthy entry under *elephant* shows that even his strong-minded scepticism was susceptible to tall stories:

> In copulation the female receives the male lying upon her back; and such is his pudicity, that he never covers the female so long as any one appears in sight.

And in the case of the camelopard, few people would recognize the animal from this description:

> An Abyssinian animal, taller than an elephant, but not so thick. He is so named, because he has a neck and head like a camel; he is spotted like a pard, but his spots are white upon a red ground. The Italians call him *giaraffa*.

Even before Johnson the compendious quality of the dictionary is given a pragmatic emphasis, with an appeal, sometimes discreet, sometimes blatant, being made to those who, through swift upward mobility, have not had the benefit of a classical education. These qualities are evidenced in the popular work of Thomas Dyche and William Pardon: *A new general English dictionary: peculiarly calculated for the use and improvement of such as are unacquainted with the Learned Languages . . . To which is prefixed, A Compendious English Grammar . . .* Derivations and etymologies are entirely omitted; difficult words are, however, accented 'to prevent a vicious pronunciation'. First issued in 1735, the work ran to seventeen editions by 1794. A few years later a predictable modification is made: size is reduced, and *The Pocket Dictionary or Complete English Expositor* makes its appearance in 1753. To achieve condensation and comprehensiveness:

> many modern Words are introduc'd, which are not to be found in other Dictionaries; and to make it more concise and portable, such Words are omitted, as being neither properly English, not ever used by good Authors, would only serve to mislead and embarrass the Learner.

Such words are further described, in the commendatory letter which does service as a preface, as 'all obsolete, bad, low and despicable words'. A 'compendious' grammar is included, as well as 'an History of the English Language', a feature first found in Bailey (1721). The work is described, not very candidly, as being 'entirely new'.

With some shrewdness, the claim is made that it is 'design'd for the Youth of both Sexes, the Ladies and Persons in Business'. In terms of promotional language and tactics, the major works of Johnson and Bailey show much greater restraint and chastity. The severe classicism of Johnson's title-page admits only a quotation from Horace and a referential statement of content and policy. Alongside it John Wesley's *The Complete English Dictionary* (1753) has the tone of a tout:

> Explaining most of those Hard words which are found in Best English Writers; by a Lover of Good English and Common Sense. NB The Author assures you, he thinks this is the best English DICTIONARY in the world.[10]

The Oxford English Dictionary

The latter part of the nineteenth century was a period of enormous lexico-graphical activity, in which the varieties of the language were accumulated and recorded with astonishing industry by some remarkable individuals. In addition to the steady production of the *OED*, the period saw the first publica-tion of the *English Dialect Dictionary* edited by Joseph Wright in six volumes (1898–1905), John S. Farmer and W. E. Henley's *Slang and its Analogues, Past and Present*, in seven volumes (1890–1904) and Joseph Bosworth and T. N. Toller's *Anglo-Saxon Dictionary* (1898). The first of the thematic dictionaries, *Roget's Thesaurus*, described in its preface as 'a desideratum unsupplied in any language', was first published in 1852.

The *New English Dictionary on Historical Principles* or *NED*, subsequently the *OED*, is acknowledged to be the monumental achievement of comprehensive lexicography on historical principles. Its production represents a triumph of patience, industry, rigour and determination in the face of numerous setbacks. The project was initiated by the Philological Society, which proposed a radi-cally new methodology by resolving shortly after its foundation in 1842 that the evidence should be re-examined and re-collected. This involved setting up a committee to collect words not listed in existing dictionaries. Yet it was con-ceded that for pragmatic considerations absolute historical comprehensiveness had to be limited, in that the work should exclude all writings before 1250 except in so far as they provide evidence for words in use after that date. When the editorship passed to Frederick Furnivall upon Herbert Coleridge's prema-ture death, he recognized that it was in turn necessary to produce reliable edi-tions of texts existing in manuscript. These initiatives resulted in the Early English Text Society and the Chaucer Society. When James A. H. Murray, a Scottish autodidact and schoolmaster, was appointed as the first editor proper in 1879, he took over nearly two tons of accumulated material. In terms of the original agreement with Oxford University Press, the work would take ten years and would consist of 6400 pages in four volumes. In fact it took forty-five years and consisted of 15,487 pages in twelve volumes.

Whereas all the dictionaries up to and including Johnson's had been largely the product of individuals, the *OED* was, perforce, more of a collaboration between Murray and the subsequently appointed joint editors, Henry Bradley, William Craigie and C. T. Onions. The group had a range of backgrounds which went some way to accommodating the point which Murray famously noted in his preface: 'No one man's English is *all* English.' Bradley was from Lancashire and had acquired his considerable scholarship while working as a clerk in a cutlery firm. Craigie was a Scot, a classics graduate of St Andrews and Oxford. Onions was a teacher from the Midlands with an external degree from the University of London.[11] Yet Murray was the real driving force of this enormous undertaking, until his death in 1915, when he had reached *turn down*. By then he had, incredibly, edited some 7207 pages, or nearly half the work. Hence the appellation of 'Murray's dictionary', used by an earlier generation.

However, as Robert Burchfield has shown, the group was by no means a real team, since they worked independently at two different sites and generally corresponded via the Oxford University Press rather than directly. Burchfield quotes a long and fairly acrimonious letter from Murray to Craigie criticizing various articles for being 'not in accordance with the principles and method of the Dictionary' (in Bailey, 1987, p. 17). Richard Bailey has noted the significant difference between Murray's famous diagram of the different registers of English and that of his successor, the editor of the *Supplement*, Robert Burchfield, who in his first preface, represented in pyramid form the division of labour in the process of editing (in Bailey, 1987, p. 2).

Although the *OED* saw itself obliged to include 'all the "Common Words" of literature and conversation', it was inhibited by the Victorian attitudes of its historical origins, when, it should be remembered, obscenity was a legal offence. In a letter to Murray (3 June 1891) Farmer wrote: 'I have had no alternative but to bring an action of breach of contract against my first printers, which breach they admit, but plead justification on ground of obscenity of such words as range themselves under "C" and "F".' Farmer went on to ask if a letter Murray had written to him on 'his own difficulties' with these words might be used in the action, concluding: 'I am in a small way fighting your own battle in advance.' As figure 1.11 showed, his work has a stupendous variety of synonyms for copulation. Murray himself was, by all accounts, a liberal thinker, but he was very sensitive to decorum, as is highly apparent in the comment on *bloody*:

> In general colloquial use from the Restoration to *c.*1730; now constantly in the mouths of the lowest classes, but by respectable people considered 'a horrid word', on a par with obscene or profane language and usually printed in the newspapers (in police reports, etc.) 'b—y'.

He consequently felt constrained to exclude the most egregious of the 'four-letter' words. However, as the present writer has noted elsewhere, inconsistencies inevitably crept in:

> Curiously, the taboos were not rigorously observed in the *OED*. Readers could be thoroughly informed on *masturbation* and the extraordinary history of *bugger*. But *fuck* was excluded, though a place was found for *windfucker*, also known as a

fuck-wind, more politely a *windhover* or *kestrel*. While Hopkins celebrated the *windhover*, George Chapman could use *windfucker* in the Preface to his *Iliad*, without embarrassment. *Cunt* was similarly excluded, though the underground euphemism *coney* (pronounced and often spelt *cunny* in earlier times) was fully revealed and illustrated by jaunty verses such as: 'All my Delight is a Cunny in the Night' (1720). The pronunciation altered, the Dictionary speculates, through 'a desire to avoid certain vulgar associations with the word [unprinted] in the *cunny* form'. *Condom* was excluded (one of the voluntary readers felt that it was 'too utterly obscene' for inclusion), though it was well documented in the eighteenth century, as can be seen from the witty entry from Francis Grose's *A Classical Dictionary of the Vulgar Tongue* (1785). (Hughes, 1988, p. 28)

Foul language and obscenity may be regarded as something of a special case, reflective more of the linguistic mores current at the time of the dictionary's production than its comprehensiveness *per se*. However, one historical period of which recent scholarship has found coverage to be lacking in its documentation and dating is that of Early Modern English, a time of enormous lexical and semantic growth. In a number of studies, notably *Documentation in the OED: Shakespeare and Nashe as Test Cases* (1980) Jürgen Schäfer cites omissions, misdatings and other errors and even goes so far as to make the following judgemental comments: 'Quite apart from misdatings characteristic of the early *OED* letters, many words and senses were arbitrarily omitted' (in Bailey, 1987, p. 67). However, when proposals were developed for a comprehensive *Early Modern English Dictionary*, the enormous scale of such a work became apparent: 'When Professor Fries developed sample pages some fifty years ago, he found to his dismay that his labors would result in a work larger than the chronologically more comprehensive dictionary' (in Bailey, 1987, p. 71). E. G. Stanley has shown that in places the *OED*'s treatment of the Old English evidence 'falls short of the ideal' of tracing the usage back to the earliest records (in Burchfield, 1987, p. 21).

Generally speaking, of course, the *OED* is justly esteemed as a byword of lexicographical excellence. Ever since it appeared, the dictionary has been regarded as 'the final authority on the English language in law courts, government bureaus, scholarly debates, newspaper offices and publishing houses' (Ehrlich et al., in McArthur, 1986, p. 131). A sense of comprehensiveness and erudition can be gained from the page reproduced as figure 5.4. Many of the omissions referred to were made good in the subsequent four volumes of the *Supplement to the OED* edited by Robert Burchfield (1972–86). As Edmund Weiner has well shown:

The atmosphere of many parts of the *Supplement* certainly contrasts with that of the first edition of the main *OED*. Opening a volume at random, one can

Figure 5.4   Murray's monument: a page from the *OED* (c.1905)

encounter a series of severely scientific terms, such as *spirogyra, spiroidal, spiro-lactone, spironolactone,* rubbing shoulders with pungently demotic phrases: *spit and sawdust, to go for the big spit, the dead spit of;* alongside them, clusters of markedly foreign terms: *Sprechgesang, spreite, sprezzatura, springar;* ephemeral, rather ludicrous expressions, like *Spock-marked, squalorology, Squaresville, squattez-vous;* name of artifacts, many proprietary: *Staybrite, Stechkin, Steinway, Steinwein, Stelazine, Sten;* and words, or meanings of words, that until recently were unprintable: *slit, slot, spunk, suck off,* and so on. (in Ricks and Michaels (eds), 1990, pp. 492–3)

The *Supplement* also perforce reflected the global role that English has come to assume in the twentieth century. Both sequences were consolidated into the second edition of the *OED* in 1989; three years later a CD-ROM version appeared. All the Oxford dictionaries, the *Shorter,* the *Concise,* the *Pocket,* continued to be distillations of the original work, begun in the Victorian era, until the publication of the *New Oxford Dictionary of English* or *NODE,* in 1998. But comprehensiveness of the kind originally envisaged by the founding fathers of the *OED* is now recognized as a goal unachievable in a single work. The extent of the English language, both in time and variety, is too great. Consequently, dictionaries of regional English and period dictionaries of English have become the order of the day.

The modern varieties

In the last phase of this brief history, broadly covering the period since 1960, concise standard dictionaries have become the dominant type, although 'the dictionary' has broadened to the point of becoming a genre. As the word-field is divided in numerous ways, specialist dictionaries have proliferated.

As we have seen, concise dictionaries of a sort have been in existence for some two centuries. Within the modern era, however, the Oxford University Press took an important initiative in 1906 by commissioning the Fowler brothers (Henry and Francis) to produce the first *Concise Oxford Dictionary* (*COD*) which was intended to be a distillation of the *OED.* In his article, 'A Concise History of the *COD*', Robert E. Allen comments:

The structural resemblances are very great, and the historical treatment of the *OED* has left a very definite mark on the layout of entries in the smaller work right up to the current edition, where archaic and historical senses continue to receive a prominence due rather to their *OED* sources than to convenience or logical sequence. (in Hartmann, 1986, p. 1)

The Fowlers completed the work in the five years forecast, despite the fact in this period they 'overtook' the parent *OED*, which had reached the letter R by 1911, when the *COD* was in press.

Since then the market for concise dictionaries has become very competitive, and several works have come to be generated more on the basis of corpora of current usage than on historical principles. Thus the Collins series is now based on COBUILD, a corpus initiated in 1980 by collaboration between Harper Collins and the University of Birmingham, while the *Longman Dictionary of Contemporary English* is based on the British National Corpus, a collaboration between the universities of London and Lancaster.[12]

The change in compilation has significant effects on the whole process of definition, in that popular usage becomes the core of the definitions, not exclusively written and historical meanings, as has traditionally been the case. We may use two definitions of *bastard*, one from the *Concise Oxford Dictionary* (*COD*) (1982) and the other from the *Longman Dictionary of Contemporary English* (*LDOCE*)(1995) to illustrate this shift. The *COD* entry runs broadly as follows:

> **Bastard** *a. & n.* 1.*a.* born out of wedlock, illegitimate; (of things unauthorized, hybrid, counterfeit; (Bot. and Zool.) closely resembling another species. 2.*n.* a bastard person; (*colloq.*) a disliked or unfortunate person or thing.

The *LDOCE* lists the term among the most 3000 most frequently spoken words and gives a very different emphasis in its definition:

> **bastard** 1 *slang* an offensive word for someone, especially a man, who you think is unpleasant. 2 *spoken* an insulting or joking word for a man. 3 *BrE* something that causes difficulties or problems. 4 *old-fashioned* someone whose parents were not married when they were born.

The difference in the senses given primacy in the two definitions is significant, and reflects the contrary attitudes deriving from literary or written contexts and oral usage. Asked for a definition of *bastard*, most educated people would probably follow the sequence of the *COD*, but they would, no doubt, concede that the first meaning given by the *LDOCE* is now dominant. It is now very rare to come across *bastard* used in its traditional, literal sense of 'a child born out of wedlock'. As *bastard* is now too judgmental, *love-child* is becoming a common euphemism.

Dictionaries dealing with the sciences continue the hard words tradition, although, of course, they also deal with unfamiliar concepts. The Oxford

University Press now publishes a range of over twenty volumes dealing with chemistry, biology, physics, literary terms and many other topics.

Those dealing with the lexical underworld and obscenity continue the tradition of the canting dictionaries. For decades this field was dominated by Eric Partridge, with his major studies, *Slang* (1933–), *A Dictionary of Historical Slang* (1937–) and *Shakespeare's Bawdy* (1947). The neglected area of American slang, often with a focus on the drug culture, started to be covered in works like Harold Wentworth and Stuart Berg Flexner, *A Dictionary of American Slang* (1960), a major study, and J. E. Schmidt, *Narcotics, Lingo and Lore* (1959), Bruce Rogers, *The Queen's Vernacular* (1962), Eugene Landy, *The Underground Dictionary* (1970), Clarence Major, *Dictionary of Afro-American Slang* (1970) and Robert A Wilson, *Playboy's Book of Forbidden Words* (1972). This tendency has continued unabated in recent decades. Among the works dealing with this area are: Judith S. Neaman and Carol G. Silver, *A Dictionary of Euphemisms* (1984), Hugh Rawson, *A Dictionary of Euphemisms and Other Doubletalk* (1981), James McDonald, *Dictionary of Obscenity, Taboo and Euphemism* (1988) and Lawrence Paros, *The Erotic Tongue* (1988).

Dictionaries of neologism proliferate, as new words become more acceptable. Recent publications in the field are Simon Mort, *Longman Guardian New Words* (1986), Sarah Tulloch, *The Oxford Dictionary of New Words* (1992 and 1995), Jonathan Green, *Neologisms* (1991). Such works obviously seek to record neologisms, buzz-words and other manifestations of language as fashion in the knowledge that standard dictionaries cannot keep abreast of the incessant flow of new terms into various semantic fields.

Global varieties of English continue to generate new volumes. In America the cachet established by Noah Webster continues in the form of the house of Merriam Webster, with major editions of *Webster* being produced in 1934 and 1961. H. L. Mencken's thematic dictionary, uncompromisingly titled *The American Language* and running through four editions from 1919 to 1936, has become a unique, maverick institution. The *Dictionary of American English* was issued from 1935 to 1944, and the first volume of the *Dictionary of American Regional English* appeared in 1985. Other ground-breaking works were William A. Craigie's initiation of *A Dictionary of the Older Scottish Tongue* (1938 onwards), W. Great and D. Murison, *The Scottish National Dictionary* (1931–76), F. G. Cassidy and R. B. Le Page, *Dictionary of Jamaican English* (1967), W. Ramson, *The Australian National Dictionary* (1988), P. Silva et al., *A Dictionary of South African English* (1996) and H. W. Orsman (ed.) *The Oxford Dictionary of New Zealand English: A dictionary of New Zealandisms on historical principles* (1998). Most of the standard English dictionary houses now have consultants to advise on global varieties of English and select lists of regional terms for general of special editions.

Jürgen Schäfer wrote fulsomely in 1987 that, lexicographically speaking, 'An international division of labour seems inevitable', given the revolutionary changes being wrought by computers' (Bailey, 1987, p. 72). Indeed, several of the most recent works are the product of electronic technology and such co-operation. However, two major period projects have been slower in coming to fruition. *The Middle English Dictionary* was initiated in 1925, started to appear in 1952, but has still not reached completion. The *Old English Dictionary*, initiated in 1969, has produced two computer-generated concordances of the entire corpus of Old English, but the main work has still to be published. However, a *Thesaurus of Old English* has been produced by Professors Jane Roberts and Christian Kay (1995).

Dictionary policy has become a much more contentious and publicized matter. Certainly the most notable publishing event in this regard was the publication of *Webster III* in 1961. This provoked a bitter national controversy about lexicography and the role of the dictionary, essentially because of the policy of removing the traditional usage labels 'colloquial' and 'informal', replacing them with the terms *nonstandard, substandard* and *slang*. However, it was more the descriptive policy in applying these labels which generated hostility. Of the many points on which the controversy turned, perhaps the usage comment on *ain't* generated the most ire. Whereas the second edition had categorized it as 'dialect or illiterate', the third attempted a fuller description, but only of the oral usage: 'Though disapproved by [sic] many and more common in less educated speech, used orally in most parts of the United states by many cultivated speakers, esp. in the phrase *ain't I*.' This and other similar usage notes which adopted an oral rather than a written standard were criticized by a great number of academics and commentators as adopting a policy of permissiveness *or laissez-faire*. As Robert Burchfield has written, 'Through reviews and editorials, many critics deplored what they regarded as an abdication of the dictionary's responsibility to foster good English' (McArthur (ed.), 1992, p. 1104). The whole controversy became the subject of a casebook edited by James H. Sledd and Wilma R. Ebbitt, *Dictionaries and THAT Dictionary* (1962).

The significance of this 'Inkwell Controversy' essentially derived from the perceived expectation of the dictionary as semantic authority on the one hand and the role of the literati, as custodians of linguistic tradition, on the other. When the dictionary ceased to be an authority, the custodians rebelled. By contrast, the *OED Supplement*, edited by Burchfield, was received with a general chorus of praise. It significantly adopted a more prescriptive policy, but from the standpoint of what Burchfield referred to in the preface to the first volume as 'British written English'.

It would be a mistake, however, to regard the Webster stable as having a purely descriptive policy. *Cunt* was included but *fuck* was not, demonstrating both outdated prudishness and an inconsistent recording of the relative currency of the two terms: after centuries of being taboo, *fuck* has become more widely used in colloquial speech in America, especially in the bizarre incestuous form *motherfucker*, while *cunt* has retained its ancient unmentionable quality. A new proscriptivism emerged in a policy of selective expunging adopted by David B. Guralnik, editor in chief of *Webster's New World Dictionary*, second college edition (1970). Guralnik justified the exclusion of words like *dago, kike, wog* and *wop* in the following way: 'It was decided in the selection process that this dictionary could easily dispense with those true obscenities, the terms of racial and ethnic opprobrium, that are, in any case, encountered with diminishing frequency these days.' Burchfield, rightly, makes a point of specifically rejecting what he calls 'Guralnikism', the racial equivalent of 'Bowdlerism'. This policy of 'verbal sanitization' is, however, continued in the *Oxford American Dictionary*, and is a revealing instance of the influence of social change upon lexical status.

This tendency has since developed into that mode of euphemism termed politically correct language, which avoids, not simply traditional ethnic slurs, but most embarrassing subjects, referring, for example, to slums as 'informal settlements' or drug addiction as 'substance abuse'. Henry Beard and Christopher Cerf produced a not entirely facetious dictionary of such usage in 1992. The topic is discussed more fully in chapter 8.

Overtly ideological and propagandist works have entered the field. Raymond Williams's *Keywords* (1976), while heavily dependent on the *OED*, gave certain terms an ideological slant, commenting, for instance, on *educated* that 'There is a strong class sense in this use, and the level indicated by *educated* has been continually adjusted to leave the majority of people who have received an education below it.' Casey Miller and Kate Swift's *Handbook of Non-Sexist Writing* (1981) went further, claiming, for example, that 'All forms of the word *fellow* can be used sex-inclusively' and that '*Fathering* has acquired the meaning of "caring for or looking after someone", previously ascribed only to *mothering*.' A more extreme work, *A Feminist Dictionary*, edited by Cheris Kramarae and Paula A. Treichler (1985), makes no pretence at objective definition or accurate description, most of the entries being simply radical comments by feminists, for example the 'definition' of *brother*: 'A male who has a close relation to another. A term which is not a symbol of universal human kinship, when it ignores generations of sisters.' These latter examples manifestly do not reflect current usage, but fall under the category of what C. S. Lewis called 'tactical definitions' (1960, p. 17), being more in the realm of wish-fulfilment than fact, designed more as 'consciousness-raising' strategies than descriptions.

Although the notion of authority is increasingly questioned in academic discourse, the status, potency and importance accorded the dictionary remains largely undiminished in modern times.[13] It is commonly found in more households and offices than, for example, sacred texts, and it is surely more frequently consulted. What may be called the less traditional dictionaries, such as those just discussed, obviously seek to appropriate the status and importance accorded 'the dictionary' by claiming the title. However, the manifold varieties of the modern dictionary show that all such works are clearly in demand, particularly in the context of modern linguistic 'anomie' or normlessness.

Notes

1 From the famous preface to the *Lyrical Ballads* (1798), added to the second edition in 1800 (ed. Sampson, 1940, p. 8).

2 Matthew Arnold's famous phrase comes from his essay 'The Study of Poetry' in Trilling and Bloom (eds) (1973, p. 245).

3 Starnes and Noyes relegate canting lexicography to an appendix in their study (1946, pp. 212–27).

4 From the enticing subtitle of *Cocker's English Dictionary* (1704). The authorship is clearly suspect, Cocker having died in 1676.

5 Bailey's vol. II has problematic status, being more in the nature of a supplement.

6 Bailey's definition of this originally Saxon term runs: 'i.e. Wolf'e Head. The Condition of an outlaw'd person, who, if he could not be taken alive, might be killed, and his Head brought to the King.'

7 Examples are: *xenia* (two meanings), *xeraphium, xerasia, xerophagy, xiphion, xoana, xylon, xystarcha* and *xystos*.

8 Cf. E. L. McAdam and George Milne, *Johnson's Dictionary: A Modern Selection* (London, Gollancz, 1963) and Susie I. Tucker, *Protean Shape* (London, Athlone Press, 1967).

9 Evelyn uses *ennui* earlier, in 1676, in his *Diary*.

10 Although Wesley's name did not appear on the title-page, there seems to be little doubt of his authorship.

11 The allocation of the different letters of the alphabet to the editors is set out in the preface to the first *Supplement* (1833), pp. xvii–xix.

12 The British National Corpus is a consortium consisting of Oxford University Press, the Longman Group, Chambers, Harrap, Unit for Computer Research on the English Language (Lancaster University), Oxford University Computing Service and the British Library Reseach and Development Department. It comprises 90 million words of written English and 10 million words of transcribed spoken English. The *LDOCE* also used the American English component of the Longman Lancaster Corpus of Spoken American English. Adam Kilgarriff has a useful article, 'Putting Frequencies in the Dictionary' in *International Journal of Lexicography*, 10, no. 2 (1997), pp. 135–55.

13   The competitive market for guides to English usage continues to expand, with works being marketed by Oxford, Cassell, Chambers, Harrap and Penguin. *Authority* is a key selling word on front covers, as in 'The New Authority on English Usage' (*The Chambers Guide to Grammar and Usage*, 1997), and 'The Acknowledged Authority on English Usage' (*Fowler's Modern English Usage*, rev. ed., 1996).

6

THE LEXICAL INTERCHANGE OF IMPERIALISM

And who in time knowes whither we may vent
The treasure of our tongue, to what strange shores
This gaine of our best glory shall be sent
T'inrich vnknowing Nations with our Stores?
Samuel Daniel, Musophilus (1599)

At the outset it is important to have an overall awareness of the different ways in which English-speaking communities grew up in various parts of the globe, since these circumstances clearly affected attitudes towards the home country and the mother tongue. Despite Daniel's sentiments, the first settlements in America derived from the diverse motives of commercial expansion and religious refuge. Australia was originally settled as a penal colony for transported convicts, the intention being to get them as far away from Britain as possible. British interests in the West Indies were primarily focused on plantations worked by prisoners from Europe, slaves from West Africa and indentured labour from the East Indies. The Cape Colony was originally annexed for strategic reasons during the Napoleonic Wars and then settled by farmers sponsored by the British government.

Thus the founding populations were of very different social character. Furthermore, they left Britain at different stages in the development of English: the earliest ventures took place in the reign of Queen Elizabeth, but the flood-tide of emigration occurred in the reign of Queen Victoria. More than a century and a half elapsed between the Pilgrim Fathers of Massachusetts (1620) and the founding felons of Botany Bay (1788), and a further thirty years passed prior to the coming of the 1820 settlers to South Africa. During that time, as we have seen, the language had changed in many ways. Furthermore, attitudes towards the home country were similarly varied. The bitter conflict leading up to the American Declaration of Independence in 1776 naturally had the linguistic consequence that the American variety of English began to acquire its own sense of identity and independence. By that time there was considerable hostility towards the English monarchy, whereas one of the 1820 settlers in the Cape had the glowingly patriotic plan for a town called Angloville and the erection of 'a Colossal Monument of our beloved Sovereign King George the fourth, expressing the natural feeling we must ever have for our native and beloved country' (G. M. Theale (ed.), *Records of the Cape Colony*, 1902, vol. XII, p. 131). All the main global varieties of English other than the American have developed in states which have continued to maintain an allegiance to Britain through the agency of the Commonwealth.[1]

Varieties of English

Varieties are differentiated from the source by phonetic, lexical, grammatical, syntactical and idiomatic features. Furthermore, within a given variety scholars have posited categories: cultivated, general and broad are those applied to Australian English, while conservative, respectable and extreme have been used of South African English. The distinctiveness of a variety is largely governed by three factors, namely time, indigenous cultural influences and status, a problematic concept which involves both the number and the political power of the speakers of a given variety. Thus American English is the most developed variety, followed by Caribbean English, Indian English, South African English, Australian English, New Zealand English, Canadian English and so on. Isolation from other varieties can also be a factor, as we have already seen in the case of Icelandic *vis-à-vis* the other Germanic languages. Contrariwise, proximity between varieties obviously influences distinctiveness. Thus Canadian English has largely fallen under the dominant influence of American English and has few distinct features, apart from the French influence in Quebec; the same is true of New Zealand English *vis-à-vis* Australian English. On the other hand, South African English has many distinctive features, being more isolated and having drawn quite extensively from Afrikaans, the newest of the Germanic languages, and the indigenous black languages.

Attitudes towards varieties change with time and the developing power relations between societies. One can distinguish three main stages. Initially users of the home 'standard' regard the colonial varieties with a sense of superiority and contempt as inaccurate, exemplifying solecisms and vulgarities to be condemned. The varieties then become the object of ridicule and satire, their features being exaggerated and amusingly distorted. Eventually there may be an acceptance, at first grudging and then even willing. Once this acceptance is established, features of the 'variety' are borrowed and imitated in a sincere fashion.

Sometimes the second stage takes the form of 'institutionalized' satire, such as Peter Sellers's parodies of Indian English or the similar use of Australian English or Strine by 'Barry McKenzie' (see pp. 301–2). An interesting role in the process of a variety establishing itself is that of the native writers. Speakers are often unconscious of the fact that they are speaking a variety, so that in many cases it is the writers who publicize the variety. Primary amongst these have been Mark Twain for American English, Afferbeck Lauder and Barry Humphries for Australian English, Rawbone Malong and Jenny Hobbs for South African English. Most of these names are pseudonyms. 'Mark Twain' was the *nom de plume* of Samuel Langhorne Clemens; 'Rawbone Malong' is a phonetic rendition in a South African accent of Robin Malan, while the identity of 'Afferbeck Lauder' remains a mystery. The time scale is also significant: Mark Twain's major work, *The Adventures of Huckleberry Finn* came out in 1885; Barry Humphries and Robin Malan produced their works in the 1960s.

American English provides a good example of increasing acceptance. About a century ago British attitudes towards this variety were generally in the first category, i.e. condescending and dismissive. By the Second World War the second phase was nearing completion: the acceptance of American English was accelerated by the stationing of many US troops in the British Isles. However, residual British hostility to American variants in the vocabulary is well summed up by Professor John W. Clark:

> some at least of the differences most frequently found appear to give many Britons special pain and hence attract their special attention – appear to impress them not merely as foreign, but as ugly, and not merely as ugly, but as crude and ill-bred and bumptious. (in Vallins, 1954, p. 174)

In the past couple of decades, with the rise of American cultural imperialism, especially through the dominance of the media of film and television, British English has been increasingly influenced by the American variety. Many institutions, notably the BBC, have shown modifications towards the American model. Some examples are given in chapter 7.

Contrariwise, Japanese English or Japlish and Indian English are often exploited for ridicule, despite the fact that Japan has become a world power and Indian English is spoken by millions. The correlation between language borrowing and status is also exemplified in the 'New Britons', immigrants from the Caribbean, India and Pakistan. They have had minimal lexical influence on English. It is noteworthy that the term most closely associated with the

Pakistani immigrants is, regrettably, *Paki-bashing*, while from the Caribbean the main borrowings have been fairly specific musical terms, such as *mento, ska, yanga* and the Rastafarian cultural group of *ganja, dread, dreadlocks* and *Jah*.

The Colonial Experience

It is a commonplace that expansionist cultures tend to be chauvinist and exclusive, assuming themselves to be 'superior', 'normal' and 'civilized', regarding the colonized cultures as 'inferior', 'aberrant' and 'barbarous'. These attitudes are reflected in the vocabulary. We have seen that when the Anglo-Saxons dominated England, they described the aboriginal Welsh tribes as *wealas* or 'foreigners', and that this term deteriorated semantically to denote various kinds of immorality. The usual vocabulary used by the colonizers of the natives consists of terms such *savage, barbarian* and *primitive*, or religious terms such as *heathen, infidel* and so on. During the modern period, when colonialism and progress have alike become suspect, these words have either developed neutral senses where this is possible (as in *native*), or fallen into comparative disuse (as in *savage* and *barbarian*). A historical perspective demonstrates the chauvinist relativity of *barbarian*, since it was used successively of those who were 'non-Hellene', then 'non-Roman', then 'non-Christian', then of 'one of a nation outside Italy'. Other factors have contributed to the diminished usage, of course. The study of anthropology has encouraged a respectful awareness of the complexity of social and linguistic systems which so-called 'primitive', 'savage', 'barbarian' 'natives' have evolved. Heightened awareness and increased unpopularity of racism have, furthermore, had the effect of self-censorship, driving the more emotive or critical words underground or out of use.

However, the dynamic can be varied. In the nineteenth century an older civilization, the Chinese, applied the sense of 'barbarian' to the English (using the character 'I'). We shall see that the early Arab traders referred to the black tribes of Southern Africa as *kaffirs*, i.e. 'infidels'; subsequently certain Muslim princes in India were to use the term to describe the English, and that in time the English themselves were to follow this practice and apply the term, in a more disparaging sense, to a broader group of African people. A key term in this respect is *cannibal*, from Spanish *Canibales*, a variant of *Carib, Caribes* (the root of *Caribbean*), a fierce nation inhabiting the West Indies who were reputed to be cannibals or *anthropophagi*. When Columbus was first told of these people (in Cuba), he recorded the name as *Canibales*, but supposed (erroneously) that the first element related to the Eastern title *Khan*. Nevertheless, the association between *Canibales* and *Caribbean* grew up. A further interesting complication is the growth of the related name *Caliban*, used by Shakespeare for a sub-human, semi-savage character in his play *The Tempest* (1610), set on an imaginary island in the Atlantic. The term *barbarian* provides an important link with another colonialist attitude, namely linguistic xenophobia, shown in a desire to mock or belittle a foreign language, making it approximate to infantile babbling. *Barbarian* is a Greek form related to Latin *balbus*, 'stammering', a derisive imitation of the 'primitive' languages encountered. *Hottentot* similarly means 'stutterer' or 'stammerer', 'originally applied to the people on account of their clicking speech', later deteriorating to 'a person of inferior intellect or culture'.

Another significant lexical feature was the dominance of the 'pure' category of the white race, shown in the terms for those of impure breeding. Thus *mulatto*, recorded from 1595, referred to a person with one black and one white parent; the term derives from Portuguese and Spanish *mulato*, a diminutive of the word for a mule, itself a half-breed of a male ass and a female horse. A *quadroon* is a person of one-quarter black descent, and an *octoroon* is a person of one-eighth black descent. Numerous derogatory terms such as *half-caste*, *chi-chi* and *griffe* reinforce this category.

The expansion of English occurred at a time when England, eclipsing Spain as the dominant European nation, was beginning to see itself as a growing world power. The New World excited different reactions in writers. John Donne's erotic poem, 'To his Mistris Going to Bed' (*c.*1598) combines passion and geographical exploration in a way which now seems quaint:

> O my America! my new-found-land,
> My kingdome, safeliest when with one man mann'd,
> My Myne of precious stones, My Emperie [Empire],
> How blest am I with this discovering thee!
> (lines 27–30)

Donne, like all Elizabethans, loved to pun: he here uses *discover* in the dual sense of 'uncover' and 'find', and there are two other probable puns in the lines. On the other hand, the noted sonneteer Samuel Daniel speculated in 1599 (in the epigraph to this chapter) on the theme of the spread of English in grand, confident terms, asking:

> What worlds in th'yet vnformed Occident
> May come refin'd with th'accents that are ours?
> (*Musophilus, or a general defence of learning.* 1599)

Even more remarkable in its confidence in the spread of English is the speech at the climax of Shakespeare's *Julius Caesar* (also 1599), when Cassius, in an admittedly egotistical reflection, exults in his moment of enduring drama as Caesar is assassinated:

> How many ages hence
> Shall this our lofty scene be acted o'er,
> In states unborn and accents yet unknown.
> (III. i. 111–13)

Naming the New World

The first explorers and merchants, like earlier historians, spoke of the 'discovery' of the 'New' World as if that world had no existence prior to the arrival of the colonial powers. Like Adam in the garden of Eden, they took upon themselves the role of naming the places and creatures they encountered. They accordingly named (actually renamed) places in terms of their expectations and the cultural values of their mother country. Thus the earliest European explorers, the Vikings (who reached America in the tenth and eleventh centuries) called the new continent Vinland, since it bore grapes. Incidentally, their naming practices were not entirely naive: in the *Greenland Saga* we are told that 'Eric the Red named the country he had discovered *Greenland*, for he said that people would be much more tempted to go there if it had an attractive name' (*The Greenland Sage*, chapter 1).

However, the application of the term *Indian* to the 'West Indies' and to the indigenous population of the Americas is a notable misnomer, since it is based on the assumption that Columbus and his companions had circumnavigated the globe, arriving at the East Indies, which was their desired destination. Although it was subsequently accepted that this was not so, the original nomenclature of 'Red Indian', the 'West Indies' and so on was retained. The first recorded use of *Indian* in relation to America occurs in 1618, applied simply to 'Indian tobacco'. In recent decades a corrective naming process has been initiated whereby *Indian* is being replaced by *Native American* and *West Indian* by *Caribbean*. But some errors are simply too large and entrenched to be corrected. The name *Canada* is also a misnomer: when the early explorer of the new territory, Jacques Cartier, asked the indigenous Iroquois Indians the name of the land, they thought that he was enquiring about their settlement, so they said 'canata', which meant in their language 'a village'.

The naming of the various landscapes, flora and fauna shows a similar mixture of improvisation and error. The *giraffe* was originally called the *camelopard*, a curious hybrid name for this strange creature (Dr Johnson's dictionary entry was quoted in the previous chapter on p. 265.) The early settlers at the Cape referred to *wolves*, by which they meant *hyenas*, and some even adopted *seacow* (from Afrikaans) for *hippopotamus* (literally 'river horse' in Greek). From the same source they borrowed words for the differing terrains, such as *veld*, *boland* and *platteland*. The Australian settlers, on the other hand, expanded the simple word *bush* to mean virtually the whole hinterland, probably from the colonial Dutch use of the word. Anthony Trollope noted in 1873 that 'Nearly every place beyond the influence of the big towns is called "bush", even though there would not be a tree to be seen.' The other distinctively Australian landscape word, *outback*, started as two words with a literal meaning: 'the trail led "out back"'; the sense of 'the interior', as in 'the Out Back', later 'the outback' is first recorded in 1907. *Paddock* and *station* are also used in a special fashion in the continent. An intriguing puzzle still surrounds the origins of *kangaroo*. Although Captain Cook and Joseph Banks recorded the word as the Aborigine name of the animal, a later explorer, Watkins Tench, asserted that the natives of Port Jackson used the name of Patagaran, adding this note: 'The name Kanguroo was unknown to them, for any animal, until we introduced it.' Some authorities have even suggested that *kangaroo* means 'I don't know.'

Thus names also have a life of their own: it is ironic that a comparative late-comer in exploration, Amerigo Vespucci, should have provided the name of *America*, rather than Christopher Columbus. (However, neither of them actually set foot on the continent.) Vespucci, who claimed to have sighted the mainland of South America in 1499, called it, appropriately, Mundus Novus (New World); his own name was given to the continent in 1507 by the German geographer Martin Waldesmüller. Only recently has the prior claim of the Icelander, Leif Eriksson, and the name *Vinland* been seriously entertained.

The first linguistic landfall

The first English settlement in the New World was not auspicious. In 1584 two ships chartered by Sir Walter Raleigh made landfall on the coast of North Carolina near an island named Roanoke, part of the territory which Raleigh had named Virginia in honour of Queen Elizabeth. After a promising start, conflict developed between the settlers and the local Algonquin Indians: in 1590 a mission to the colony found no trace of the settlers except an empty palisade. The mystery of their disappearance has never been solved.[2]

Raleigh (who had not actually been on the expeditions) remained confident of the enterprise, writing to Sir Robert Cecil in 1602: 'I shall yet live to see in it [the New World] an English nation' (McCrum et al., 1986, p. 97). Four years later another expedition consisting of three ships arrived at Chesapeake Bay (near modern Washington) and moored off an island which they named Jamestown, after the new English king. Under the resourceful and determined leadership of Captain John Smith, the new settlement survived and expanded along the coast, bringing the English tongue permanently to the edge of the vast continent.

The Pilgrim Fathers, religious refugees mainly but not exclusively of a Puritan persuasion, established a colony at Plymouth, Massachusetts, in 1620. (They had intended to land in Virginia, but finished up further north at Cape Cod.) The majority of these early settlers hailed from East Anglia and the south-eastern counties of England, especially from Essex, Lincolnshire, Nottingham, Kent and the London area. Naturally, they gave themselves a home from home with names such as *New England, New York, New London, New Hampshire, Boston, Cambridge,* and so on. Massachusetts (named after an Indian tribe) contains the counties of *Berkshire, Hampshire, Worcester, Essex, Middlesex, Norfolk* and *Plymouth.* By 1675 some forty English names had been given to towns founded in America (Wakelin, 1988, p. 142). Classical and exotic names also came to figure, such as *Athens, Cairo, Crete, Hannibal* and *Memphis* as well as the ubiquitous instances of *Newcastle, George, Victoria* and so on.

Unsurprisingly, the English of the settlers started to absorb native American terms for flora, fauna and cultural artefacts: among these are *wigwam, totem, tomahawk, papoose, moccasin, igloo, kayak, hickory, pecan, chipmunk, moose* and *terrapin.* Often words were modified from their original form in the process of borrowing. Captain John Smith's *Journal* records modern *cockroach* as *cacarootch,* from Spanish *cuccuracha,* and *racoon* as *raughroughoons.* Similarly *opossum* became simplified to *possum, seganku* became *skunk* and *isquontersquash,* from Narraganset *askutersquash,* meaning 'vegetables eaten green', became plain *squash.*

Some established English words underwent semantic changes early: *pond* was extended to larger expanses of inland water like lakes; *creek* was used of a stream rather than an inlet from the sea. Other topographical terms were brought into play. They included *swamp, ravine, hollow* and *bluff.*[3]

However, the settlers, who were essentially conservative, also preserved many words which have passed out of use in the mother tongue. The best known is *fall* for *autumn.* In fact, *fall* was a comparatively new usage, supplementing the traditional term *autumn* (which came into the language with the Norman Conquest) from around 1545, usually in the phrase *the fall of the leaf.* It maintained a diminishing literary currency in England up to the nineteenth century. Similarly, the use of *guess* in the sense of 'suppose' or 'imagine': the phrase 'I guess' is used as far back as Chaucer. Likewise, *dumb* for 'stupid':

William Tyndale was the first of several religious controversialists to use the word in this sense when he denounced 'the byshop of Rome [i.e. the Pope] with his domme traditions'. Other terms which have become American variants are:

bug (insect)	*plumb* (utter)	*rooster* (cock)
raise (rear)	*hog* (pig)	*gotten* (got)
junk (rubbish)	*mad* (angry)	*skillet* (frying-pan)
trash (rubbish)	*closet* (cupboard)	*kettle* (saucepan)

The new nation

The idea of the new nation was fundamentally grounded in language. The essential ideology of America, idealistic, democratic, egalitarian and progressive, comes from the Founding Fathers and is enshrined in the great public documents, the Declaration of Independence and the Constitution. (All these capitalized terms have an institutionalized, mythic force in the United States.) The statements have the clarity of the Enlightenment and a sense of noble purpose which is romantic and inspiring. By contrast, as Sidney Low observed of the British Constitution, 'We live under a system of tacit understandings. But these understandings themselves are not always understood' (1914, p. 12). Many of these 'understandings' amount to traditional deference, the antithesis of equality and democracy. Similarly, whereas 'the United Kingdom' has always been something of cipher combining a loose affiliation of ancient kingdoms, some of which are showing distinct signs of restiveness and independence, 'these United States' were linked by a common ideology, purpose and loyalty from the beginning. Although a sense of strong national identity was created, the actual words *nation* and *national* were eliminated from the Constitution.

The new variety

The divergence between American English and the home variety was accelerated by the Declaration of Independence in 1776. Indeed, a number of histories of the English language see this date as a watershed: Robert Burchfield called his relevant chapter in *The English Language* (1985) 'The Disjunctive Period: 1776 to the Present Day' and the *Cambridge History of the English Language* similarly uses the date as a marker between Early Modern English and Modern English.[4]

Even in 1756, Dr Johnson had written of an 'American dialect', using the term in a derogatory fashion, but in 1789 the founder of American

Table 6.1   Webster's simplified spelling

Etymology	British spelling	American spelling
color (Lat.)	colour	color
labor (Lat.)	labour	labor
defensa (Lat.)	defence	defense
kentron (Gk.)	centre	center
theatron (Gk.)	theatre	theater
programma (Gk.)	programme	program
katalogos (Gk.)	catalogue	catalog

lexicography, Noah Webster, who then styled himself 'Jun. Esquire', argued in his *Dissertations on the English Language* that 'numerous local causes' and America's being 'placed at a distance from Europe . . . will produce, in a course of time, a language in North America, as different from the future language of England, as the modern Dutch, Danish and Swedish are from the German, or from one another' (pp. 22–3).

The designation of the *American Language* was first recorded in 1802, in the US Congress, while in 1806 Webster used the form *American English* in his first dictionary, called *A Compendious Dictionary*. In this work his original innovatory flair was subsequently tempered by local opposition. However, in 1828 Webster produced his major work, *An American Dictionary of the English Language*, the first of a series of works which was subsequently to carry his name after his death in 1843. The major successors were the second edition, published in 1847, and the controversial third edition, *Webster's New International Dictionary*, published in 1961 and discussed in the previous chapter (pp. 273–4).

Influenced by the indefatigable Benjamin Franklin, Webster first embarked on an enterprise of simplifying orthography in the direction of a more phonetic spelling system. He advocated such simplified spellings as *color* for *colour*, *labor* for *labour center* for *centre*, *theater* for *theatre* and the removal of the cumbersome silent consonants in *through, though, catalogue* and *programme*. The simplified forms appeared first in his highly patriotic and popular *American Spelling Book* (1783), subsequently in his *American Dictionary of the English Language* (1829), and have since become established.

Although such simplified spellings are often regarded as 'illiterate' and castigated as such, the criticism is frequently invalid, since in many cases Webster was merely advocating a spelling closer to the etymological root as well as simpler in form, as is shown in table 6.1.

Of these seven examples, the first three indicate a return to etymological roots; the second two are more of a divergence from them, while in the last two Webster was seeking to avoid the French influence which had generated the English forms. Similarly, in preferring *check* to the English spelling *cheque*, Webster was guided by the semantic root, as the *OED* confirms.

Webster was only partially successful in his enterprise, in that several of the silent consonants he excluded have since been resuscitated. (Thus *thru* and *tho* are frowned on, and hundreds of Webster's discriminatory spellings of 1828 have been rejected by subsequent editors.) However, he was highly influential, both as an independent thinker advocating a new variety of the language, and as an authority seeking to apply logical principles in restoring words to their etymological roots.

Various visitors to America in the nineteenth century commented on the language, usually in a critical fashion: Charles Dickens noted in 1822 the American nasal drawl, especially outside Boston and New York, and the use of 'doubtful' grammar. (Students will find his *American Notes* of interest.) Mrs Frances Trollope found many faults in her study, *The Domestic Manners of the Americans* (1832). She claimed that she seldom heard a correctly pronounced sentence, and found the style of a Presbyterian service in Ohio 'extravagantly vehement, and offensively familiar in expression . . . the sermon had considerable eloquence but of a frightful kind' (1927, p. 15). She commented that the conversation of the military company on a Mississippi steam-boat 'was entirely political, and the respective claims of Adams and Jackson to the presidency were argued with more oaths and more vehemence than it had ever been my lot to hear' (1927, p. 15). Captain Frederick Marryat (1839) noted that 'it was remarkable how debased the English language had become in such a short time in America' (Flexner, 1976, p. 9).

As Henry Steele Commager has rightly observed, 'Many, if not most, of those who wrote about America came here with a closed mind, came not to learn but to confirm preconceived notions. They assumed – naturally enough – that the Old World was the norm and interpreted every deviation from that norm as quaint, vulgar and eccentric' (1946, p. x). However, the most illuminating observer of the character, institutions and language of America was Alexis de Tocqueville, a young French aristocrat who in 1835–40 produced a major work, *La Démocratie en Amérique*, translated as *Democracy in America*.

Tocqueville begins his chapter XVI, 'How American Democracy has Modified the English Language' by stressing that 'It is not, then, to the written, but to the spoken language that attention must be paid' (1945, p. 64), observing the consequence that 'Among such a people the majority lays down the law in language as well as in everything else' (1945, p. 65).

Developing his radical insight of how fundamentally democracy affects language, Tocqueville observes: 'In aristocracies language must naturally partake of that state of repose in which everything else remains. Few new words are coined because few new things are made. . . . The constant agitation that prevails in a democratic community tends unceasingly, on the contrary, to change the character of the language' (1945, p. 65). 'Besides', he continues, 'democratic nations love change for its own sake, and this is seen as much in their language as in their politics. Even when they have no need to change words, they sometimes have the desire' (1945, p. 65).

Tocqueville finishes with one of his major prescient emphases:

> I shall not leave this topic without touching on a feature of democratic languages that is more characteristic of them than any other, [namely] a taste and sometimes a passion for general ideas . . . displayed by the continual use of generic terms or abstract expressions. . . . This is the great merit and the great imperfection of these languages.
>
> Democratic nations are passionately addicted to generic terms or abstract expressions because these modes of speech enlarge thought and assist the operations of the mind by enabling it to include many objects in a small compass. A democratic writer will be apt to speak of *capacities* in the abstract for men of capacity and without specifying the objects to which their capacity is applied. (1945, p. 69)

As usual, Tocqueville analyses the mental style which lies behind the verbal form:

> These abstract terms which abound in democratic languages, and which are used on every occasion without attaching them to any particular fact, enlarge and obscure the thoughts they are intended to convey; they render the mode of speech more succinct and the idea contained in it less clear. But with regard to language, democratic nations prefer obscurity to labour. (1945, p. 69)

Tocqueville would seem to be describing in advance a tendency in American political rhetoric since labelled *gobbledygook*, *Pentagonese* and for a while termed *Haigese*, after General Alexander Haig, who gave new meaning to the slogan 'Dont be Vague, ask for Haig.' As Secretary of State, Haig became so notorious for his ambiguous and unclear language that he was awarded the US National Council of Teachers of English annual Doublespeak award.

Less obviously, one notices the highly artificial, abstract form of 'robotspeak' used by American Law Enforcement Officers (i.e. Police) in forms such as: 'I have visual contact' for 'I can see' and 'the suspect is approaching.' Perhaps the strangest examples are 'Affirmative' and 'Negative', which when spoken on a crackly telephone line are dangerously close phonetically in a way that plain 'Yes' and 'No' could never be. The officer in charge of the sad case of the infanticidal Mrs Susan Smith used a similar form of spokesmanese: 'She is being incarcerated in another location,' rather than 'She is in prison elsewhere.' But in less formal contexts terms like Tocqueville's *capacities* are frequently encountered: a person suffering from an 'eating disorder' said: 'I have problem with portion control.'

With his typically fine sense of irony, Tocqueville brings this generalized discussion to a very concrete conclusion: 'An abstract term is like a box with a false bottom; you may put in it what ideas you please, and take them out again without being observed' (p. 70).

After Noah Webster, the single authority who did most to establish the independence of the American variety of English was Henry Louis Mencken, always known as H. L. Mencken. A journalist who worked for the *Baltimore Sun*, he produced in 1919 his major work (over 600 pages long) with the uncompromising title, *The American Language*, and proceeded to produce further editions in 1921, 1923 and 1936, culminating in two *Supplements* in 1945 and 1948. Mencken wrote in a trenchant, humorous and ironic style, and conveyed the essence of American English with indefatigable detail. Though not without bias, he was far more outspoken than his contemporaries about where the centre of gravity lay in the relative claims of the two varieties for supremacy:

> I think I have offered sufficient evidence in the chapters preceding that the American of today is much more honestly English, in any sense that Shakespeare would have understood, than the so-called Standard English of England. (1948, p. 608)

He also quotes, with some effect, William McAlpine, who used a simple majoritarian argument: 'When two thirds of the people who use a certain language decide to call it a *freight train* instead of a *goods train*, they are "right"; and the first is correct English and the second a dialect' (1948, p. 608). Mark Twain had put the same point with equal trenchancy in *Pudd'nhead Wilson's Journal* (1894), using a financial model: 'The King's English is not the King's. It is a joint stock company and Americans own most of the shares.' Yet Mencken was no uncritical champion of American English, noting that 'The early Americans showed that spacious disregard for linguistic nicety which has characterized their descendants ever since' (1936, p. 117).

George Bernard Shaw is said to have made the much quoted remark that 'Britain and America are two countries separated by a common language.' Of the numerous differences between the two varieties, David Crystal has noted:

'There is no definite survey of all the differences between American English and British English. The only safe statement is that there are far more of them than are usually recognised' (1988, p. 246). He proceeds to give a substantial list under the main linguistic categories.

Grammatical differences (which partly impinge on lexical differences) between the two varieties are more numerous than most people realize. There is a great tendency in American English to use adjectival forms as adverbs, as in 'He's *real* good' for 'He's *really* good.' Similarly, 'I feel good' as opposed to 'I feel well.' The double negative is more acceptable than in British English: upon his re-election in 1984, President Reagan jubilantly assured the electorate: 'You ain't seen nothing yet!', using a form of words which no British politician would. The perfect tense, as in British 'I have just eaten,' indicating that the action is completed, becomes in American the plain past tense 'I just ate.' Similarly, 'I haven't seen it yet' in the British variety would be 'I didn't see it yet' in the American equivalent. Two rare strong verbs are also to be found in American English: namely *dove* for *dived* and *snuck* for *sneaked*. Different conventions surround the use of articles and prepositions. Some of the American usages are becoming current in British English. They include: *different to/than* rather than *different from*, the increasing use of prepositions with certain verbs, as in *to meet with* or *to speak with* a person, and *to free up*, and the increasing omission of them with other verbs, e.g. *to agree* a proposal or *to protest* a measure.

Consider the following two versions of a news report:

A Secretary of State Warren Christopher is expected to protest the arrest of Human Rights Activist Kim Su Long, detained Friday by Chinese authorities.

B The Secretary of State, Mr Warren Christopher, is expected to protest against the arrest of the Human Rights Activist, Mr Kim Su Long, who was detained on Friday by the Chinese authorities.

The first is in the American style, the second is in the British. Even in this fairly simple sentence, there are at least six variations. Thus, in a number of ways American English shows more condensation. Shorthand statements such as 'No problem!' 'Sure thing' 'No way!' and 'I want out!' abound. The following two versions make the point:

A Under no circumstances would I have taken the position. The manager was not to be trusted, and in addition his organization was under police investigation.

B No ways was I going to take the job. The boss was not to be trusted plus the cops were checking his outfit.

Table 6.2 Lexical alternatives in British and American English

British	American	British	American
car	auto (mobile)	trousers	pants
petrol	gas	tights	pantyhose
gear lever	shift	underpants	knickers
mudguard	fender	shorts	underpants
bonnet	hood	garter	suspender
windscreen	windshield	waistcoat	vest
generator	dynamo	vest	undershirt
silencer	muffler	zip	zipper
boot	trunk	dinner jacket	tuxedo
hoot (vb)	honk	telephone (vb)	call
pavement	sidewalk	taxi	cab
nappy	diaper	cot	crib
shop	store	chemist	drug store
tin	can	drawing pin	thumb tack
dust bin	trash can	lorry	truck

Yet in other ways, as we have partly seen under the headings of Register and the comments of Tocqueville in the preceding pages, Americans have a penchant for the longer, high-register word. Mencken himself noted the slightly absurd inflation of common terms, such as:

greengrocer – vegetable executive
hairdressing salon – tonsorial parlour
rat-catcher – vermin exterminator

Lexical alternatives

We have already noted some of the main early semantic changes, which concerned the same word acquiring two different meanings on different sides of the Atlantic. Over time the natural development was for lexical distinction, namely for different words to grow up (or be invented) for the same thing. Many of these are technical, as is shown in those terms in table 6.2 concerning components of the motor car and other items.

This list does not claim to be complete. The student will be able to add other pairs of alternatives and be able to make some deductions about the difference of lexis and register.

Black English

By the time of the abolition there were some four million black slaves in America, concentrated mainly in the southern states: it should be remembered that Georgia and the Carolinas were originally British colonies. Words which derive from the African languages the slaves originally spoke are *buckra*, first 'master' then 'white man', *dashiki*, a loose fitting shirt, *juke*, to misbehave, go on pub crawls, *sambo*, *tote*, *voodoo* and the food words *ockra*, *goober*, *gumbo* and *yam*.[5]

Although Black English was originally a **basilect** (a variety lacking prestige) and the object of satire, it has, according to J. L. Dillard, been a major formative influence on Southern English in America through the forms of Plantation Talk. Celia M. Millward points out that Black English is not a regional dialect, but 'an ethnic and socieconomic variety of the language, defined by the social position and education of its speakers' (1989, p. 330). But, as David Crystal reminds us, 'The history of Black English in the United States is complex, controversial and only partly understood' (1988, p. 237).

A surprising number of terms which have become colloquial Americanisms originated in 'jive talk', the language used by black jazz musicians of the 1930s. (*Jazz* itself, first recorded in New Orleans in he 1870s, has throughout its history been intimately associated with blacks, especially from 1917, when jazz bands became a major feature of New York life.) Cab Calloway, a popular bandleader, recorded in 1938 what he called 'the first glossary of words, expressions and general patois employed by musicians and entertainers in New York's teeming Harlem'. In his list were:

beat exhausted	*latch on* get wise to
cat swing musician	*mellow* all right, fine
chick girl	*pad* bed
groovy fine	*sharp* neat, smart
have a ball enjoy yourself	*square* unhip person
hip wise, sophisticated	*stache* hide away, secrete
jam improvised swing music	*yeah man* an exclamation of assent

Black English has become the medium of political solidarity, especially from the 1960s. Among words which had a distinctly political meaning in the period are *nitty gritty*, *rap*. Peviously *brother* and *homeboys* (those who had served prison sentences together) started to take on this ethnic exclusivity, which became overt in forms like *Black Power* and *Black Panther* (both from 1966). Derogatory terms for whites include *ofay* (1926), *peckerwood* (1930s), *honkey* (1950s) and *WASP* (an acronym for White Anglo-Saxon Protestant)

(1960s). As often happens with 'out groups' or those who have been discriminated against, the groups adopt the stigmatizing names. The extract of the following poem, 'Nigger Talk', shows this robustly:

> Na white talk dis.
> It is coon, nignog sambo wog talk.
> Mikey Smith (1984)

English in the Caribbean: Pidgins and Creoles

English was brought to the Caribbean by the owners of sugar plantations, by slave labour from West Africa and by indentured workers from the East Indies. The lucrative trade-route which formed the origin of this development is known as the Atlantic Triangle. Ships would embark from the thriving ports of Bristol and Liverpool in England for West Africa, where they would barter cheap goods and trinkets for slaves. Those that survived the horrific conditions of the journey across the Atlantic would then be sold as plantation labour in the West Indies or America in exchange for sugar, molasses and rum for the home market. The trade, which began in the seventeenth century, was abolished in Britain in 1807 and in the United States in 1865.

The slave trade generated forms of pidgin English at the points on the base of the triangle and introduced Black English into the United States. English thus came to the Caribbean in very different forms, since only the plantation owners were first-language speakers. To this day the varieties of the language termed Caribbean creole are varied and complex. Furthermore, the language is spread in an arc of some 2000 miles containing numerous islands in a generally Hispanic-speaking environment, from Trinidad, only seven miles off the coast of Venezuela, to the Bahamas, not far distant from Florida. Trinidad is influenced by Spanish, French creole and Indian traditions, while Barbados and Jamaica have strong English traditions.

Before proceeding, we should be clear about what is meant by the terms **pidgin** and **creole**. A *pidgin* is a makeshift, rudimentary, hybrid, contact language which grows up as a means of communication between communities which do not understand each other's language and have no common language.[6] It is mainly a simplified nucleus of a language in which most of the vocabulary is, as might be expected, drawn from the language of the dominant group.

The term *pidgin* derives from the Chinese pronunciation of *business*, and survives in the phrase 'that's your pigeon,' meaning 'that's your business,' but is not generally understood as such, since *pidgin* has been wrongly 'corrected' to *pigeon*. Pidgin English grew up in the nineteenth century as a medium of communication between the Chinese and the English in the trading ports of China and the Straits Settlements. To call a pidgin a 'language' is not strictly accurate, since it has no native speakers, nor is it a complete system of communication, being principally concerned only with certain commodities and concepts. The grammar is greatly simplified to single cases and tenses: thus *mi kam* ('me come') means 'I come', 'I am coming' or 'I came.' Among the various English-based pidgins are Tok Pisin (Pidgin Talk) used in Papua New Guinea, Hawaii Pidgin English and Korean Bamboo English. The earliest recorded pidgin was Sabir, a Mediterranean nautical trading language dating back to the Crusades, but now extinct. Its name derives from Portuguese *sabir*, 'to know', and it seems to have generated a number of base words, such as *savvy*, 'to know' (from *sabir* itself) and *picanin*, *picaninny* from *pequeño*, 'small', still found in English-based pidgins and creoles in the Caribbean and the Pacific.

When a pidgin becomes the principal native language of a group, it becomes a *creole*, a word which evolved from the Portuguese *crioulo*, from the verb *criar*, 'to nurse or breed'. *Crioulo* came to mean, revealingly, an African slave born in the master's household, a sense first limited to Brazil, but then extended to the Caribbean. Once the slaves had been cut off from their home speech, they would perforce use pidgin (English, French, Spanish or Portuguese) to survive. But their children would develop the use of the language in a creolized form, taking in disparate elements from their linguistic environment. Thus Caribbean creole has an English base, whereas Haitian creole is French-based. English-based creoles have grown up at many points of trade and colonization. Among them are Aku in Gambia, Krio in Sierra Leone, Kamtok in Cameroon, Bajan in Barbados, Trinbagonian in Trinidad and Gullah in North America.

An expected consequence of Empire has thus been the growth of pidgins throughout the world. In her study, *Modern Englishes: Pidgins and Creoles* (1984), Loreto Todd distinguishes no less than thirty-one varieties of English pidgins and creoles, principally located in West Africa, the West Indies and the Pacific. Less predictable is the interesting mixture of registers: in a number of these varieties, what would be regarded as swear-words in 'Standard English' (broadly conceived) are used as inoffensive general terms. The most prevalent of such terms in Papua New Guinea Tok Pisin [Talk Pidgin] is *baga*, from *bugger*, meaning simply and generally 'a man' in its noun form and 'destroy' as a verb. It has generated *lesbaga* ('lazy bugger') and the highly generalized verb *bagarap*, from 'bugger up', defined in its intransitive uses as 'break, become impaired, have an accident happen to, become exhausted or injured, disintegrate'; the transitive variant *bagarapim* encompasses the senses 'to destroy, break etc., rape, render useless'. Other surprisingly central words are *bulsitim* (from 'bull-shit', meaning 'to deceive or cheat' and the general use of *sit* ('shit') to mean 'residue', as in *sit bilong faia* for 'ashes' and *sit bilong lam* (lamp) for 'soot'. *As* (from *arse*) is similarly very generalized, including the senses 'buttocks, bottom, stump, underlying cause, place of origin, underside, rear', while *baksait* means 'back' or 'rear' and not 'buttocks'.

Although the precise circumstances of the origins of Tok Pisin are uncertain, it is known that from the late nineteenth century Papuans worked as indentured labourers in Queensland and thus acquired Queensland Plantation Pidgin English. The central location of these derogatory terms in the lexis indicates, as Loreto Todd puts it, that 'the local people were disparaged by their overseers' (1984, p. 253). They also remind us of the truism that all linguistic use is a matter of convention. For the native speakers, these 'strong' terms have been defused, just as for Standard English speakers *gorblimey!* and *he gets on my wick* are not shocking since the original meanings of the phrases ('God blind me!') and ('He gets on my prick') are now quite opaque. Pidgins shock and amuse outsiders because the separation of registers formalized in most varieties of English is consistently violated: slang and taboo terms jostle and rub shoulders with polite words without any sense of incongruity. Thus, in Cameroon Pidgin, the basic bodily vocabulary consists of *anus* which is technical, *bɛlɛ* ('belly') and *bobi* ('bubby', 'breast'), which are informal, *pis* and *shit*, which are vulgar.

In her excellent study on Caribbean verse, Paula Burnett brings out both the roots and the richness of the varieties:

> The vernaculars of the English-speaking Caribbean show strong African influence in their syntax and intonation, although they are based on an English vocabulary, with some influence from the other European languages of the region, Portuguese, Spanish, French and Dutch. Words of African origin can be counted in hundreds, although they often have a cultural significance out of proportion to their numbers. (1986, p. 26)

We must remember that Barbados was settled in the 1620s and Jamaica not long after. Consequently, there are interesting phonetic relics and curiosities like *ax*, the old form for 'ask' and *baas*, the older form of 'boss'. In words ending in *-ing* there is universal substitution of the *-ng* sound, resulting in pronunciations such as 'mornin', 'blowin' and 'goin'. This, too, is also a relic of older speech. *Buss* survives as an old word for 'kiss', while other old forms are *cuss* for *curse* and *nuss* for *nurse*. These forms show that local pronunciations have become institutionalized in spellings to a far greater degree than in other varieties of English.

From the West African origins of the first speakers there are other phonetic signs, such as the following substitutions:

'b' for 'v', as in *eben* for *even, bickle* for *victuals* and *fabour* for *favour*;
'd' for 'th', as in *bredda* for *brother, madda* for *mother fedda* for *feather* and *doah* for *though*.

Other forms which reveal features of pronunciation are *do'* for *door, ting* for *thing, tink* for *think, teata* for *theatre, tief* for *thief, pays* for *peas*. While some of these suggest that Caribbean English is non-rhotic, in fact there is a division between the varieties: those of Jamaica, Barbados and Guyana are **rhotic** (i.e. the 'r' is articulated in all positions) while most of the others are not. Other special features include the intruded 'h': *hact* for 'act', *Hinglan* for 'England' and *hoat* for 'oath'.

Semantic specializations include: *bite*, 'small amount of money' or 'job', *bitty* for 'money', *caution* for 'warn' and *lick* for 'hit' or 'beat'. Other cultural specializations are shown lexically in *obeah* for 'witchcraft', *duppy* for 'ghost', *dashiki*, a loose, African-style shirt, *buckra* for 'white person or people' and the Rastafarian terms: *ras*, 'holiness', *ganja*, 'marijuana' and *dread*, 'awesome'.

Caribbean poetry has become a serious site of struggle for the language variety with strong political overtones. In her study, Paula Burnett divides the poetry into an Oral tradition and a Literary tradition. While this division is common, the Oral tradition usually comes to an end (indeed is brought to an end) by the Literary tradition. However, in Caribbean poetry there has been a significant resurgence of the Oral tradition. Especially in the form of dub poetry (so called because it is dubbed on to Reggae music), it has become an overtly politicized expression of linguistic independence. Here are to be found many phonetic spellings, such as *caff* for *cough, chap* for *chop, cloaz* for *clothes, fiah* for *fire* and *soja* for *soldier*.

Other features include French borrowings: *corbeau*, a turkey-vulture, from the French word for a crow, *collobree* from French *colobri*, a humming-bird, *fete*, a party, from French *fête* and *picong*, biting, sharp, from French *piquant*. There are also similarities to Black American English, seen in *gwaan* for 'go on'; cf. *gwine* for 'going' and *ketch* for 'catch'. Other borrowings are: *roach* for *cockroach* (from Spanish *cuccuraca*), *pickney*, 'child' from Portuguese *pequena, roti*, unleavened Indian bread, and *sangria*, wine and fruit juice, from Spanish *sangria*.

Given this diversity in usage, the definition or 'placing' of Caribbean English is problematic. While Standard English is the ostensible official 'higher norm', it is not really apparent on the ground. Similarly, *dialect* is not a favoured term, in view of the varieties within the notional dialect. The writer Edward Brathwaite has championed what he terms 'nation language' which, as Paula Burnett observes, 'is a worthy attempt to get round this, but doesn't seem to be taking over in popular usage' (1986, p. xxv). She prefers the less contentious term *vernacular*. The issue is of what language to write in, 'proper English' or this 'vernacular'. Two Caribbean poets sum up their different choices, Grace Nichols emphasizing the 'new' tongue:

> I have crossed an ocean
> I have lost my tongue
> from the root of the old one
> a new one has sprung
> ('Epilogue')

Derek Walcott, on the other hand, is a brilliant exponent of the old tongue. Where others might dismiss the 'language of imperialism', as being an ugly relic, Walcott distinguishes between the Empire and the linguistic legacy:

> It's good that everything's gone, except their language,
> Which is everything.
>
> ('North and South')

Australian English

The founders of the English-speaking community in Australia were predominantly 'marinated' or transported convicts. According to Sidney J. Baker, 'Between 1788 and 1868 nearly 160,000 convicts were shipped to Australia from Britain' (McLeod, 1963, p. 103). It has been estimated that within two generations of the arrival of the First Fleet in Botany Bay, 'a staggering 87 per cent of the Australian population were either convicts, ex-convicts or of convict descent' (McCrum et al., 1986, p. 288). Indeed, in 1837 James Mudie coined an ironic new social classification, *felonry*, to describe the social make-up of the colony. However, one must realize that judicial sentences in England tended to be extremely harsh: the novelist Henry Fielding (who was also a magistrate) creates an episode in *Joseph Andrews* (1742) in which a young lad who has just performed a charitable act is 'written out' of the novel in the following way: 'This fine young man was shortly afterwards transported to Australia for stealing a loaf of bread.'

The distinctive dialect of the convicts was a criminal argot called *flash*, a term for underworld slang which had been current in England from around 1750. A Captain of the Marines, Watkin Tench, in his *Complete Account of the Settlement at Port Jackson*, commented on this linguistic feature as early as 1793:

A leading distinction, which marked the convicts on their outset in the colony, was the use of what is called 'flash', or 'kiddy' language. In some of our early courts of justice, an interpreter was frequently necessary to translate the deposition of the witness, and the defence of the prisoner. This language has many dialects. (Cited in Hornadge, 1980, p. 78)

James Hardy Vaugh, a thrice-transported convict, compiled a glossary of the argot and published it in his *Memoirs* in 1819 under the title of *A New and Comprehensive Vocabulary of the Flash Language*. Vaugh defined *kiddy* (mentioned above and commonly defined as a 'professional thief') as 'a thief of the lower order, who . . . dresses in the extreme of vulgar gentility'. The term was probably related to *kid* meaning 'to deceive', which is included in the vocabulary, together with *grub* ('food'), *lark* ('fun' or 'sport'), *to queer*, ('to spoil'), *new chum* ('newly arrived prisoner'). Also included is *cove*, a term recorded in Elizabethan thieves' slang for 'man'. One of the most distinctive flash words to have passed into the mainstream of Australian English is *swag*, which now refers to the bundle of personal belongings carried by an itinerant worker or *swagman*. However, it was defined by Vaugh as 'any booty you have just obtained'. (This term too was transported from the mother country, where it had meant 'stolen goods in general' since *c.*1785.) From this criminal provenance emerged another distinctively Australian term of insult, a *bludger*. Originally meaning a street bully or prostitute's pimp, it has become extended through army usage to mean a parasite, idler, skiver or freeloader.

Other common terms in Australian English which have underworld or low-class origins in England are *mate* and *nark*. Consider this comment on *mate*: 'The term a coster or low person applies to his friend or companion. "Me and my mate did so and so" is a common phrase wth a low Londoner.' The observation is made by John Camden Hotten in his *Dictionary of Modern Slang, Cant, and Vulgar Words* in 1859. *Cobber* has its origins in English dialect; so do *dinkum*, 'genuine', 'reliable', *larrikin*, a hooligan, *wowser*, a killjoy and *dunny*, the common term for the lavatory. *Tucker*, the general word for food, derives from English *tuck*, as in *tuck in* and *tuck shop*.

In this society where servitude was the norm, the term *free* acquired a special status, being applied in categories like *free convict* (i.e. one who had been emancipated or freed from penal servitude) and also to those who had never been convicted, such as *free emigrants*, *free settlers* and *free natives*. Transportation ceased only in 1868, so that for three-quarters of a century there was a steady supply of convicts. However, the proportion of settlers increased, so that by 1851 the make-up of the speech community had altered to such a point that the proportion of convicts to free immigrants was roughly 60 per cent to 40 per cent. As in America, there seems to have been little separation of registers on the basis of social class in Australia. Within half a century of Captain Arthur Phillip's founding of the first penal colony in 1788, Edward Gibbon Wakefield observed in his *Letter from Sydney*:

> Bearing in mind that our lowest class (the convicts) brought with it a peculiar language, and is constantly supplied with fresh corruption, you will understand why pure English is not, and is unlikely to become, the language of the colony . . . . Terms of slang and flash are used, as a matter of course, from the gaols to the Viceroy's palace, not excepting the Bar and the Bench. No doubt they will be reckoned quite parliamentary, as soon as we have a parliament. (Cited in Hornage, 1980, p. 76)

This situation still largely applies. Although scholars use three general categories, namely *Broad*, *General* and *Cultivated*, 'The most marked feature of the Australian accent is its homogeneity' (*OCEL*, 1992, p. 92). On the point of register the editors of the *Australian National Dictionary* (1988) make the observation that 'Australian English allows easy movement between formal and informal usage.' They continue with a somewhat unexpected statement of policy:

> It should be clear from the citations if a word belongs mainly in colloquial use or to the slang of a particular group, and equally clear if it is for some reason taboo in some contexts. Labels like *coarse, colloq., derog.,* and *slang,* which tend unnecessarily to categorize, have therefore been omitted. (p. vii)

The work also notes that there is little regional variation in terminology, apart from terms used for flora and fauna and 'the names given to glasses of beer' (p. viii).

An interesting lexical feature of Australian English is the comparative paucity of native terms. There was an early intake of Aborigine words describing the distinctive fauna: these included *dingo* (1788), *koala* (1798), *kookaboora* (1834), *wombat* (1798) and *kangaroo*, discussed earlier. Terms for special artefacts, such as the *boomerang* (1825) and the *woomera* (1798) were also early borrowings, as was the call *cooee* (1790). But as relations with the Aborigines deteriorated, so the borrowings dried up: thus the wanderings of the Aborigines were called *walkabout* (1910) and the mythological past of the people is termed *the dreamtime* (1896), both words being translations rather than borrowings. Curiously, the two best-known terms of Australian origin to have been incorporated into global English are *boomerang* as a verb and *walkabout* as a royal perambulation among the people.

Although the majority of the population is now urbanized, the raising of cattle and sheep has generated a variety of terms. One of the first was the use of the verb *squat* in the special sense of 'to occupy Crown Land in order to graze livestock, a practice sanctioned from 1836 by the introduction of a licensing system' (*AND*). From this root grew *squatter* (1837), *squattage* (1845), *squatterdom* (1855) and the curious formation *squattocracy* (1845). Among the various terms for territory are *stations* (ranches), *runs* (tracts for grazing), *brush*, *bush* and *scrub*. The various farmers are termed *graziers*, *stockmen*, *drovers*, *overlanders*, *rouseabouts* (general hands) and *jackaroos*, well-connected learner farmhands.

Freedom from restraint has proved an enduring characteristic of Australian English. One of the first writers to comment on the astonishing currency of the word *bloody* in the settlement was Alexander Marjoribanks, in his *Travels in New South Wales* (1847, p. 57). By noting the fact that a bullock driver used the word twenty-five times in a quarter of an hour, Marjoribanks was probably not the first to be sufficiently impressed to record the performance of an Australian native speaker giving tongue. No doubt the currency of the word reflected the convict origins of the settlers, for Francis Grose observes in his *Dictionary of the Vulgar Tongue* (1785) that *bloody* was 'a favourite word used by thieves in swearing'. Other contemporary commentators referred to it as 'the crimsonest of adjectives' and 'this odious word' (Hornage, 1980, pp. 141–2). The *OED* entry (originally in a fascicle published in March 1887) makes the following class comments on the usage: 'In general colloquial use from the Restoration to *c*.1750; now constantly in the mouths of the lowest classes, but by respectable people considered "a horrid word", on a par with obscene or profane language, and usually printed in the newspapers (in police reports, etc.) "b—y".'

Things were different in the outback, and by the end of the century the term was starting to acquire the sobriquet of 'the great Australian adjective'. (On 18 August 1894, the *Sydney Bulletin* referred to *bloody* as 'the Australian adjective'.) The sensational use of the word in *Pygmalion* elicited an amusingly laconic comment in the Sydney *Bulletin* of 30 July 1914: 'I see how a bloke in the old dart named Shaw has wrote a play and makes a tart say "bloody".' In a significant judgement given in the Sydney Divorce Court on 22 June 1942, Mr Justice Halse Rogers held that 'the word *bloody* is so common in modern parlance that it is not regarded as swearing' (Hornadge, 1980, p. 144). Wakefield's prophecy about the word becoming parliamentary has been amply fulfilled. In 1970 a Member of the House of Representatives announced: 'I never use the word "bloody" because it is unparliamentary. It is a word I never bloody well use' (Hornadge, 1980, p. 145). Equally interesting is the Australian speciality of integrating the adjective into an adjoining word as in *kangabloodyroo*, a practice recorded as far back as 1908. The process, which shows that the word has lost all semantic force and is being used as an enclitic for the purposes of syncopation, has proved very fruitful. *Bastard* is another instance of a strong term used with greater frequency in Australian English. The precise tone is often ambivalent, including not just the derogatory, but feelings of compassion ('the poor bastard') and even affection or praise ('he's a good bastard').

The emergence of Australian English

In the early decades of this century, 'Banjo' Paterson and Henry Lawson recorded and publicized much of the common Australian parlance and idiom. However, Australian English ceased to be self-deprecating and part of what is termed there 'the cultural cringe' only in the 1960s. There is an amusing anecdote which supposedly defines this cultural moment. In November 1964 the English author Monica Dickens was autographing copies of her latest book in a Sydney bookshop when a woman approached with a copy, handed it to her and said 'Emma Chisit'. Whereupon Miss Dickens inscribed the volume 'To Emma Chisit' and signed the book. 'No,' said the woman, realizing a misunderstanding, 'Emma Chisit?' (i.e. 'How much is it?').

When this inter-dialectal confusion was reported in the newspapers, Australian readers identified enthusiastically with the woman, and a fashionable craze for phonetic renditions of the local argot and idiom ensued, especially in the columns of the *Sydney Morning Herald*. These and others were published in two collections, *Let Stalk Strine* by 'Afferbeck Lauder' and *Aussie English* by John O'Grady. Both were published in May 1965; *Let Stalk Strine* ('Let's Talk Australian') went through seventeen impressions in one year. Strine is a manifestation of the shift in status in the variety from reticence to exhibitionism. It came of age in amusing renditions such as the following:

Strine	Translation
Naw shaw	North Shore
sag rapes	sour grapes
air fridge	average
hair bat	how about
stewnce	students
Sinny	Sydney
tiger look	take a look
split nair dyke	splitting headache
nerve sprike tan	nervous breakdown

The last three examples illustrate one of the most prominent features of Australian pronunciation, namely the vowel in *take* being sounded as *tike*. This shows the enduring influence of the Cockney or London English of the founding community.

The major exponent of Strine in the wider Anglophone culture has been the stereotyped fictional figure of Barry or 'Bazza' McKenzie, the creation in 1963 of the humorist Barry Humphries, who describes him as 'a pastiche figure'. His vocabulary is borrowed from a diversity of national types, and words like "cobber" and "bonzer" still intrude as a sop to Pommy readers, though such words are seldom, if ever, used in present day Australia' (1988, p. 134). The lexis of this satirical institution has revealed limited foci evoked in charmingly picturesque metaphors which have gained a considerable currency. The vast majority of the terms concern urination (*drain the dragon, point Percy at the porcelain* and *syphon the python*), defecation (*strangle a darkie*) and vomiting (*technicolour yawn* or *liquid laugh down the great white telephone*). Sexual activity is similarly alluded to by means of humorously graphic (and uncomplicatedly chauvinist) figures of speech, copulation being rendered variously as *sink the sausage* and *spear the bearded clam*, alternatively by means of coy euphemisms (*to feature, exercise the ferret* or *dip the wick*). *Flog the lizard* or *jerking the gherkin*) are the preferred terms for masturbation.

The use of Cockney rhyming slang is fairly common: thus *mulligatawny* is pedantically glossed as 'in a a state of heightened sexual erethism', i.e. 'horny', while *to take a Captain Cook* is 'to look' and a state of extreme thirst is melodramatically rendered as being *as dry as a kookaburra's khyber*. McKenzie shows, furthermore, a typical prissiness in taboo genital areas, as is shown by the saying 'dry as a nun's nasty' for 'to be quite thirsty'. Yet, curiously, both *naughty* and *nasty* are ancient euphemisms, which McKenzie and his Fellowmen of Oz are merely perpetuating long after their disappearance in the homeland. *Naught* and *naughty* used to have a strong sense of 'wickedness' or 'evil', but the phrase *to do naught* is clearly used with sexual innuendo as far back as Shakespeare's *Richard III* (I.i. 98–100). (For a further discussion of the sexual sense of *naughty*, see my study *Swearing*, 1988, pp. 175–80.) Both *naught* and *naughty*, as well as *have a naughty*, have become the speciality of Australian and New Zealand English, where they are applied even to marital intercourse, long after *naughty* has become trivialized in relation to its old strong sense. *Nasty* is less easily traced, but under *C**t*, Grose observes, presumably with a pun, that the word is 'a nasty word for a nasty thing'.

The tradition of vigorous and picturesque idioms in Australian English shows little sign of atrophying. For example, *rare as rocking horse manure*, *rare as hen's teeth* or to be unable *to blow the froth off a glass of beer* are self-explanatory, but less obvious are *to bang like a dunny door* (to copulate frenetically) and *as flash as a rat with a gold tooth* (highly dubious character, deriving from *flash*, mentioned at the beginning of this section). Some derive from the history of the land: the bandit and folk hero Ned Kelly has his memorial in condemnatory phrases such as 'They're a bunch of bloody Ned Kellys' or 'Who said Ned Kelly was dead?' Others have no obvious source: *to come the raw prawn* is to try to deceive someone. Some of the most common expressions of surprise are *stone the crows!* and *my word!* In addition to the various forms of swearing mentioned above are *my oath!* or, more predictably, *my bloody oath!* Many abbreviations or **hypocoristic** forms are found, as in *barbie* for *barbecue*, *garbo* for *garbage collector*, *journo* for *journalist*, *smoko* for *smoking break* and *arvo* for *afternoon*. (The *AND* even lists *sarvo* for *this afternoon*.) Sometimes these suffixes are simply added to short words, as in *tin* ⇒ *tinnie*, *brick* ⇒ *brickie*, 'bricklayer' and *school* ⇒ *schoolie*, 'schoolteacher'. Other distinctive terms are: *barrack* to shout or jeer at players in a game, *chook*, a chicken and *furphy* 'a rumour or false report', originally circulated in the First World War by drivers of water carts manufactured by J. Furphy and Sons.

Indian English

English was brought to India by trading companies early in the seventeenth century. It became the language of colonialism and was gradually accepted as that of the elite. Prior to independence in 1947, there was understandable hostility to it, and subsequently a policy was envisaged to establish local official languages in the various regions. However, with the subsequent partition of the country, there emerged competition between the main native languages, and the role of English then changed to one of neutrality. Consequently, it has been accepted as the practical official language of the state.

There is considerable variety in competence with corresponding terminology. The **acrolect** or highest variety is usually termed educated Indian English, which is very close to RP. There is a considerable variety of **basilects**, variously termed *Boxwallah English*, *Butler English*, *Bearer English* or *Kitchen English* and *Babu English*. There are also many regional varieties.

Since English has been on the continent for such a very long time, great numbers of words have entered the common global vocabulary: the *OED* lists some 900.[7] Some of these have come via Portuguese, for instance, *ayah*, *caste*, *bamboo*, *curry* and *mango*. Of the more direct borrowings, several are terms of status or esteem, among them *pundit*, *sahib*, *mogul*, *guru* and *yogi*. Others, like *ayah*, denote occupations, e.g. *sepoy* and *dhobi*. Several, such as *bungalow*, *cheetah*, *chintz*, *godown*, *jodhpurs*, *juggernaut*, *mulligatawny*, *tiffin*, *dekko*, *pukkah* and *chit*, have become so common that to many people they no longer seem to be foreign words, apart from the indications in some of the spellings.

Many of these words passed into Army slang and thence back 'home'. Of these the most interesting was *Blighty*, 'England' or 'home', from Hindustani *bilayati*, meaning 'foreign', specially 'European'. Two specialized terms which have taken root in Indian English but are no longer current in British English are *stepney* for a spare tyre and *dicky* for the boot of a car (transferred from the back seat of a carriage).

Many observers have commented on the quaint mixture of registers which is a notable feature of Indian English: 'I am bubbling with zeal and enthusiasm to serve as a research assistant'; 'Land is a well of honeyed ambrosia. In order to get at it we need buckets – buckets of intellectual capacity' (Mehrotra, in Millward, 1989, p. 342). Literary archaism is also found in conversation: someone will be *of tender years* rather than *young* and a friend may have visited *thrice*.

English in South Africa

Because of the essentially conflictual nature of South African history, the terms for the major population groups have seldom been neutral. It seems prudent, therefore, to start with the matter of names. The first European settlers at the Cape of Good Hope referred to the indigenous hunter-gatherers as *Boesjemens (Bushmen)*, the pastoralists as *Hottentoos* or *Ottentots (Hottentots)* and the mixed farmers as *Caffres (Kaffirs)*. All of these words acquired derogatory overtones and then hostile denotations. *Hottentot* is a Dutch term recorded in 1652 in the *Diary* of Jan Van Riebeek, the first Governor of the Cape, and explained by Olfert Dapper in his *Beschryvingh der Afrikansche Gewesten* (1670) 'as a word meaning "stutterer" or "stammerer", applied to the people on account of their clicking speech'. Two later explorers took a similar view of the Bushman language, saying 'So it is not without reason that it has been said of them that they cluck like turkeys' (Pettman, 1985, p. 2). To this Dampier (in 1697) added the hilariously implausible, but revealing explanation that 'Hottentot . . . is the name by which they call to one another . . . as if every one of them had this for his name.' *Hottentot* was borrowed into English and by the eighteenth century had deteriorated to mean 'a person of inferior intellect or culture', becoming quite a common term of insult: one Nicholas Amherst commented of Oxford in 1726 that he 'was surprized to find a place . . . so much renown'd for learning, fill'd with grey-headed novices and reverend Hottentots'. This sense the *OED Supplement* records, but pointedly rejects: 'This derogatory sense, which was based on a failure to understand an alien culture, appears now to be very rare.' The word still survives in South African English in this sense in the form *hotnot*, 'an offensive mode of address or reference to a coloured person' (*DSAE*).

Kaffir comes from quite a different source, namely, Arabic *kafir* meaning 'infidel', 'heathen' or 'unbeliever' (from the Muslim point of view). The term was widely applied to foreigners: a letter of 1799 records that 'Tippoo Sultan wished to drive the English Caffres out of India.' But even before the Dutch settlement at the Cape, Richard Hakluyt had noted in 1599 that Arabs were trading from Mozambique 'to Caffraria to trade with Cafars', referring to the area and the tribes of the Eastern Cape. When Thomas Pringle observed, in

1834, that 'the Kaffers are a tall, athletic and handsome race,' he would seem not to have been concerned about the name itself, but in 1847 William Shaw commented that the term was 'not used by the natives themslves . . . The Border Kaffirs know that the white nations apply the term to them, and many of them regard it as a term of contempt' (DSAE). Since then the term has intensified as an insult to the point that since 1976 its use has been grounds for *crimen injuria*.

Consequently, the modern scholarly vocabulary for the three groups involves substitution. The relevant terms are *San* or *Khoisan* for Bushmen, *KhoiKhoi* for Hottentot and *Africans* for Kaffirs. The pastoralists called themselves *KhoiKhoi* and called the Bushmen *San*; *Khoisan* is a coined word, which would originally have included the Africans (see Thompson, 1990, p. 55). As the Dutch settlement of the Cape grew, so the names *Afrikander*, subsequently *Afrikaner* developed, derived from the Dutch *Afrikaan*. A subsequent legacy of hostility between the English and the Afrikaners has led to the the term *boer*, meaning 'farmer' or 'settler' in Afrikaans, being used by both the English and the Africans as a term of opprobrium for Afrikaners. They in turn referred to the English as *uitlanders* ('foreigners'), *rooineks* ('rednecks') or *khakis*, the latter two terms deriving from the Boer War (1899–1902).

Prior to the discovery of minerals, South Africa was historically viewed as a place of strategic rather than intrinsic importance by the great colonial powers. The first Portuguese explorers, Bartholomew Dias (1488) and Vasco da Gama (1497) found their reception by the Hottentots too hostile to entertain the scheme of founding an outpost as they were to do in Mozambique and their other East African ports. Though they gave the Cape of Good Hope its name, they tended to give it a wide berth. The Dutch originally developed the Cape from 1652 as a staging post for their fleets *en route* to and from the Far East. In 1795, in the course of the Napoleonic Wars, the British annexed the Cape Colony (as it had then become) in order to curtail French influence in the East; in the course of the next few years the Cape was returned to the Dutch (1802), recaptured (1806) and finally given to the British as part of the terms of the Congress of Vienna (1814).

The major influx of English speakers came as the 1820 settlers. They were sponsored by the British government by means of a grant of £50,000 voted by Parliament the previous year to encourage some 4,000 settlers to farm land earmarked in the Eastern Cape Province, also known at the time as Caffraria. They were given assisted passages and 100 acres of land; in addition, another 1000 settlers came at their own expense. This was not an entirely altruistic exercise, since there was considerable unemployment and disaffection at home. Furthermore, the strategy or 'hidden agenda' was to use the settlers as a buffer between the warlike Xhosa tribes and the British colonial authority. Some ten years previously, Colonel Richard Collins had recommended, indeed, that 'All intercourse between the settlers and the Caffres should be scrupulously prevented' (Thompson, 1990, p. 54). A sense of border hostility is sharply evident in the comments of Lieutenant-General Sir John Cradock's report after a punitive expedition: 'I am happy to add that in the course of this service there has not been shed more Kaffir blood than would seem necessary to impress on the minds of these savages a proper degree of terror and respect' (Thompson, 1990, p. 55).

The majority of the 1820 settlers had no farming experience, but were urban artisans. Consequently they tended to spread out from the Eastern Cape. The speech community was not dominated by a particular group, as the founding settlement in Australia was by Londoners. Out of 1658 families, 460 (or 27 per cent) came from London, 147 (or 9 per cent) came from the home counties, 263 (or 16 per cent) came from the south and south-east; 412 (or 25 per cent) came from Scotland, mainly the Highlands, and 147 (or 10 per cent) came from Ireland. (Detailed records are to be found in G. M. Theale (ed.), *Records of the Cape Colony*, volume XII, PP. 263–5, printed for the Government of Cape Colony, 1902.) There was a subsequent English-speaking settlement in Natal from 1848. The discovery of diamonds at Kimberley in 1868 and then of gold on the Witwatersrand in 1886 attracted a further major influx from the British Isles, America and Europe.

Although English is spoken as a first language by less than 10 per cent of the population, it is the language of power and prestige. Despite deriving from such a diversity of original speakers, South African English has acquired an accent almost as distinct as that of American and Australian English. The major phonetic influence and the obvious lexical feature of South African English is the considerable degree of borrowing from Afrikaans. The Afrikaners constitute some 55 per cent of the white population and Afrikaans has a stronger claim to being a *lingua franca* throughout the land. In addition a fair number of words have been taken in from the indigenous black languages, and a few terms have survived from Portuguese and from Malay, as a consequence of the activities of the Dutch East India Company. These record in essence the semantic and lexical consequences reflecting the clash and coexistence of cultures, as well as colonialism and social engineering. They are terms which Georges Matoré has labelled *mots témoins* or 'witness words'.

The landscape, especially that of the arid interior, has had a profound formative influence on its peoples, who have given it a distinctive set of names, an aspect movingly caught by the poet Jeremy Cronin:

> To learn how to speak with the voices of the land,
> To parse the speech in its rivers, . . .

To trace with the tongue wagon-trails,
Saying the suffix of their aches in -kuil, -pan, -fontein
In watery names that confirm
The dryness of their ways.

('The Voices of the Land')

Following the course of the Voortrekker pioneers, who trekked away from British authority into the interior, Cronin uses three of many Afrikaans words for water in *kuil* 'water-hole', *pan*, a hollow in which water accumulates, and *fontein*, 'fountain'. Woven from other languages into the texture of the land are *karoo*, the dry plateau of the interior, from Hottentot (Khoikhoi) *garo*, 'a desert', *donga*, a dry eroded watercourse, from Nguni-*donga*, 'a washed-out ravine' and *bundu*, wild bushland, from Shona *bundo*, 'grassland'.

Several animal names now survive only in remote sources: thus the Khoi word for a lion, *xami*, survives only in place names like Gamka and Gamma; *eland*, from the Dutch and Lithuanian word meaning an elk, has replaced the Khoi word! *khani*, surviving only in *Kannaland*; *oryx* derives from Greek *orux*, a stonemason's hammer, from the similarity in the shape of the horns.

These lexical features show one perennial aspect of South African English, namely its almost omnivorous capacity to absorb words from other cultures. From these distant tributaries a few words like *trek, veld, kraal, inspan, commando* and *koppie* have flowed into the mainstream of English. Most of these reached a wider audience as a consequence of news coverage of the Boer War (1899–1902). Closely related to the war were the verb to *maffick*, meaning to celebrate uproariously, as people did on receiving the news of the relief of the siege of Mafeking in 1895, and to be *stellenbosched*, to be retired to a rural backwater where one's mlitary incompetence could have no serious effects. *Trek* now exists in a whole variety of forms such as *pony-trek* and *trekkie*, which originally meant a small group of trekkers, but has for some twenty years meant an enthusiastic follower of *Star Trek*.

There are many other indigenous terms which have not crossed the water or the Limpopo. Some of these are very ancient, but are words heard on a daily basis:

From Bushman (now Khoisan):
gnu from Koisan *nqu*,
kudu from Khoisan *kudu*.

From Hottentot (now Khoikhoi):
gogga, an insect,
dagga, cannabis,
kaross, clothing made of skins.

From Portuguese:
kraal, enclosure, cluster of huts, from Portuguese *corral*.

brinjal, aubergine, from Portuguese *berinjela*, egg plant,

mealie or *mielie*, maize, Indian corn from Portuguese *milho*, millet.

From Malay:

sosaties, kebab,

bredie, stew,

bobotie dish of curried minced meat,

compound, labourers' quarters, from Malay *kampong*.

From Nguni, a group of African languages and peoples including the Zulus, the Xhosa, the Swazi and the Ndebele:

songololo a millepede, from *ukusonga*, 'to roll up',

muti, medicine, from Zulu *umuthi*, 'plant, medicine',

indaba, (a) a problem, as in 'Well, that's your indaba'; (b) conference or meeting, as in 'We had better have an indaba to sort this out.'

bonsela, a present or bonus, from Zulu *ibhanselo*, a gift,

fundi, an expert, from Nguni *umfundisi*, a teacher.

From Afrikaans there are a great numbers of words. Perhaps most revealing are the many familial terms, such as *ouma*, grandmother, *oupa*, grandfather, *boet*, bother, *oom*, uncle, *tannie*, aunt, though the last two can be used as titles of respect for the elderly. The most common other words are:

bakkie, a light truck,

biltong, dried meat,

braai, a barbecue,

dinges, 'thingumabob',

dop, a 'shot' of spirits,

dorp, a small 'one-horse' town,

erf, the legal term for a plot of land,

dwaal, a state of confusion or brown study,

joll, a party, to have a good time,

pap, porridge, from Dutch *pap*, soft; also English *pap*, soft food,

skrik, a shock,

snoep, mean, tight-fisted,

veldskoen, leather ankle-boots,

voetsek, 'Go away!' commonly addressed to dogs, insulting if said to people; also as a verb 'I told him to voetsek.'

voetstoots, 'as it stands', a Roman Dutch legal term covering 'all defects, latent or patent'.

A few words come from India:

larney, classy, showy, posh (origin disputed),

breyani, a spiced dish similar to curry, from *biriyani*,

sjambok, a whip, from Urdu *chabuk*, though probably via Malay *tjambok*.

Several common English words are used in special senses:

> *bond*, mortgage,
> *stay*, in the sense of 'live': 'We stay in Cape Town.'
> *café*, meaning 'corner shop', 'grocer',
> *cadenza*, a fit: 'When she saw the bill, she had a cadenza.'
> *geyser*, hot-water boiler,
> *globe*, electric light bulb,
> *grief*, trouble.

Various common locutions are derived from English:

> *shame*: (a) an expression of sympathy: 'shame, he broke his leg'; (b) an expresion
>   of endearment: 'shame, what a cute little baby.'
> *howzit* ('how is it?'), a common greeting,
> *ya well no fine*, a reluctant acceptance.

Others are of unknown origin:

> *tackies, takkies*, for plimsolls,
> *tickets*, the end, as in 'He swerved off the road, hit a tree and that was tickets.'

Curious cases exist of English words which have survived in South Africa but died out in their homeland. These include *china*, meaning 'friend' or 'chum', the Cockney rhyming slang half of *china plate* (= *mate*): 'He's my china,' or 'Look my china, don't cause trouble.' *Bioscope*, the obsolescent word for cinema, originated in England *c*.1900, but passed out of currency there in the 1930s. *Sarmies*, from *sarnies*, a northern dialect word for sandwiches, still thrives, as does *moffie*, a slang term for a male homosexual, which relates to *mophrodite*, a facetious form of *hermaphrodite*, used by the novelist Henry Fielding in *Joseph Andrews* (1742). Another special South African use is *robot* for 'traffic light', the original word having been coined by Karel Čapek in 1920. *Shebeen*, from Irish *sibin*, meaning an outlet for illicit liquor, has acquired wide currency, originally in the black 'townships', now in the smarter, traditionally white suburbs.

Recording the variety

In 1913 the Revd Charles Pettman published *Africanderisms*, 'a Glossary of South African Words and Phrases', a word-hoard running to nearly 600 pages. Many words in Pettman were considered too exotic to be included in even the most comprehensive of general dictionaries. The main successor was the *Dictionary of South African English* (ed. Jean Branford), first issued in 1978 with subsequent editions in 1980, 1987 and 1991. There are, in addition, South African editions of major English dictionaries, such as those from Oxford and Collins. The *Oxford Dictionary of South African English on Historical Principles* (1996) was compiled at the Dictionary Unit at Rhodes University in Grahamstown under the editorship of Penny Silva, and is now the definitive work, a single volume about the size of one tome of the *OED*, listing some 6,000 headwords.

It has become customary to apply to South African English a tripartite categorization similar to that used of Australian English (Cultivated, General, Broad), namely 'Conservative', 'Respectable' and 'Extreme' (Lanham and Macdonald 1979, p. 30). Conservative South African English is phonetically virtually indistinguishable from British RP, since its speakers belong to an elite which has been taught at private schools by teachers from England, often followed by Oxbridge educations.

Especially in the 'Extreme' category is to be found a distinctive variety of English. It was recorded a few years after the emergence of 'Strine'. The first local equivalent, a collection of distinctive idioms, was *Ah big Yaws?* ('I beg yours,' i.e. 'I beg your pardon?') under the pseudonym of 'Rawbone Malong' (Robin Malan), published in 1972 with the subtitle of *A Guard to Sow Theffricun Innglissh*. The book follows the same scheme as the 'guides' to Strine, rendering everyday idioms into humorous phonetic spelling:

Ah spah wirth ma luttle ah (I spy with my little eye),
Gimmia chorns (Give me a chance),
Come more fit (Come off it),
Porti Paulli Tix (Party politics),
Yowsisorf Paulmint (Houses of Parliament).

A few years later the novelist Jenny Hobbs started an enormously popular magazine column featuring one Blossom Broadbeam, whose idiolect was a very accurate, albeit stereotyped, rendition of Broad South African English. In it are to be found many local lexical features: 'My boet [brother] is a skinny okie [bloke] of fifteen with sticking out ears and chorbs [pimples] and a sense of yumour what schemes [thinks] putting a six-foot mole snake under your bed is darem [really] the biggest larf in town . . . Ouma smaaks [likes] good graze [food], giving advice and a leeker [enjoyable] loud argument (1979, pp. 5–6). Perhaps the best-known of the satirical exploiters of the varieties of South African English on the stage is Pieter-Dirk Uys, who like Barry Humphries, has developed a stage *alter ego*, Evita Bezuidenhout, with similar success.

A published collection of five plays by Athol Fugard has such a range of demotic usage that it requires a glossary of some 300 terms, mainly Afrikaans. This is partly because Fugard's chosen milieu is the working class or under-class: hence there are calques like *boggerall*, spelling variants like *blerry* and *bladdy* for 'bloody', intensive adjuncts such as *ek sê!* ('I declare'), directly physical terms such as *kaalgat* ('bare-arsed' for 'naked'), exclamations like *Jislaiik!* ('Jesus!') and *Here!* ('Lord!'). Yet even in Cultivated South African English, borrowing from Afrikaans is a notable feature: executives with Oxbridge educations are quite likely to use Afrikaans terms like *poep* for 'fart' or *kak* for 'shit', and so on.

South African English has many other distinctive idiomatic features, lexical alternatives or semantic extensions. These include the following:

The omnipresent interrogative particle *hey?*, always added at the end of a phrase or sentence: 'We're having a lekker time, hey?'
The frequent vocative use of *man*, applied to either sex and even to children: 'Don't worry, man, it could have been worse.'
The use of *with* without the usual accompanying pronoun in phrases such as *are you coming with?*
The use of *is it?* as a general expression of incredulity or surprise: 'We lost the rugby.' 'Is it?'

A frequent use of diminutives is also obvious: 'Just give me a seccie [second] while I get my cossie [swimming costume], some ciggies [cigarettes] and few dumpies [beers].' The suffix *-ie* derives from Afrikaans *-tje*, found in *naartjie*, a tangerine. In most cases it is no longer regarded or used as a diminutive, notably in *wheelie*, to spin the wheels of a car by acceleration, and *uee/uie* for a U-turn. This feature is shared by many global varieties, discussed in chapter 7 (pp. 355–6).

Many everyday phrases show the influence of Afrikaans:

'Everything will come right' (translation of Afrikaans 'Alles sal reg kom').
'Let's *make a plan* to meet next year' (translation of Afrikaans '. . .'n plan maak.'
'*Hang yong* [Hell, man], but you're clever, hey?'
'President de Klerk *was thrown with a stone*' (i.e. a stone was thrown at President de Klerk: used by the Minister of Foreign Affairs, R. F. 'Pik' Botha on televi-sion, 28 March 94.)
'*Did you got* [have you got] a licence for this TV?'
'I'm in a hurry. I don't want to go *just now* [in a little while]. I want to go *now now* [immediately].' This is also an aspect of the psycholinguistic tendency of procrastination (p. 63 n. 8).

The first two examples fall into the Conservative and Respectable categories, while the rest belong to that of Extreme.

The lexical impact of apartheid

Of all the world forms of English, the South African variety has suffered the stigma of semantic engineering whereby political strategies have been formulated in a specialized vocabulary, usually of a euphemistic type. Lexical substitution and shifts of register were the special feature of forty-six years of Nationalist Party rule (from 1948 to 1994), designed to enforce the policy of *apartheid* or racial separation through a whole semantic structure of factitious statutory definitions. Thus were generated the racist definitions of *group* (= race) in the Group Areas Act (1950), of *pass* and *reference book* (= permit) in the Pass Laws (1952), of *location* and *township* (= segregated black urban area) and *homeland* (= segregated black rural area) recorded from 1963.

Several of these terms and meanings pre-dated the implementation of apartheid. (The term itself is first recorded *c.*1917, but became the rallying cry and electoral slogan of the Afrikaner Nationalists in the 1948 election which brought them to power.) However, the most notorious semantic effect of the policy was the criminalization of miscegenation via the distortion of the term *immorality*, which the Immorality Act of 1927 defined as 'illicit carnal intercourse between Europeans and natives'. The designation of the indigenous population in official laguage also underwent various shifts. The traditional term *native*, previously pejorative from a Eurocentric point of view, started to acquire pre-emptive political associations and was replaced by *Bantu*, the Nguni word for 'people', but was frequently applied ungrammatically to individuals (as in 'he is a bantu'). Thereafter the curious term *plural* had a brief career, *black* being introduced into legislation only in 1978. (It is noteworthy that the terms *coloured* and *non-white*, often thought of as clear cases of the semantic engineering of apartheid, both have earlier American usages, dating from 1760 and 1921 respectively.)

As overseas disapproval and sanctions mounted, so the South African government renovated or remodelled the policy of *apartheid* at intervals in new semantic outfits: *apartheid* (which was itself a substitute for the older paternalistic term *baasskap*, 'domination'), was replaced by *separate development* from 1955, then *multinationalism* from 1971, then *plural democracy* from 1978, then *vertical differentiation*. The policy of apartheid was finally declared 'dead' in 1989. This aspect of South African English is a classic case of 'Orwellian' semantics, normally associated with totalitarian language control. (We note in particular the shift in register from strong, clear root words to increasingly vague polysyllabic classical terms.) However, the British, too, have their shameful contribution in the form of *concentration camp*, recorded from 1901, the brain-child of Lord Kitchener during the Boer War. In order to deprive the Boers of the support of their families, the camps were set up to detain Boer women and children.

The new South Africa

Since 1991, with the release of Nelson Mandela from jail, and especially since 1994, when the African National Congress won the first democratic election, South Africa has been in a phase of 'normalization', whereby the nation is being redefined in the terms of realistic global currency. During this short time many new lexical items have come into usage. Among them are *the rainbow nation* (coined by Mandela in his first speech as a free man), terms referring to the change of social structures, such as *transformation* and *rationalization* and those referring to the uplifting of the disadvantaged, such as *affirmative action*, *delivery* and *Masakhane*, the name of a campaign meaning 'Let us build together.' Other new key words are *redress*, *transparency* and *accountability*. The older militaristic terms from the period of the *struggle* for liberation, such as *comrades*, *cadres* and *necklace* (in its horrific local sense of 'to kill by placing a burning tyre over the victim's head') are giving way to civilian terms like *structures*, *civics* and *civil society*. An interesting recent lexical item is *bosberaad*, meaning a meeting in an isolated venue to break a political deadlock, derived from Afrikaans *bos*, bush, and *beraad*, a council.

As is to be expected, a number of words from African languages have come into currency with these political changes: the most prominent of the struggle phase was *amandla* ('power'). More recent are *ubuntu*, a spirit of humanity and social responsibility, the name of the South African soccer team, *bafana bafana* ('the boys, the boys') and less permanently, the name for the national rugby team, *amabokoboko*, since *springbok* is regarded by some as too closely associated with the past. In the new dispensation the whole definition of *African* is undergoing a series of semantic revisions. A shift in the balance of ideological power is shown in the increasing currency of derived forms such as *africanist*, *africanize* and *africanization* on the one hand, and *Eurocentric*, i.e. concerned with traditional European culture and norms, on the other.

Terms of status

In bringing this chapter to a conclusion, let us focus on one aspect of the lexical aftermath of the establishment of British rule in alien parts. This was brought about by *governors*, *viceroys*, *district commissioners* and so on. However, one understandable feature of the post-colonial period and the coming of a democratic dispensation is the obsolescence of the traditional Eurocentric terms of rank, notably *king* and *queen*.[8]

This 'lexical vacuum' has been filled by an amazingly heterogeneous vocabulary of exotic terms, nearly all of them the legacy of colonialism. They include *baas, big wig, big cheese, boss, bwana, chief, high up, honcho, memsahib, mogul, mugwump, nabob, pasha, sahib, sultan, supremo, tai-pan* and *tycoon*. A few have been borrowed from European languages, such as *czar* and *führer*, and in recent decades the traditional terms *baron* and *lord* have been recycled, but generally in critical formations like *land baron* and *druglord*. (*Randlord* was a similar compound denoting a mining magnate of Johannesburg at the turn of the century, and is recorded in the British press from 1904.) This field of terms has, of course, many registers, allowing a writer to show respect or openly criticize the person in power.

Notes

1   Richard W. Bailey's study, *Images of English* (1991), discusses many of the issues of the globalization of English in an interesting and provocative fashion.

2   Michael Foss's *Undreamed Shores* (London, 1974) studies what he calls 'England's wasted empire in America'.

3   Fuller discussions of these lexical points can be found in H. L. Mencken, *The American Language* (1919–48), S. B. Flexner (1976) and Bill Bryson, *Made in America* (1994).

4   Not all histories emphasize this split. See, for example, Georges Bourcier, *An Introduction to the English Language* (1978) and Dennis Freeborn, *From Old English to Standard English* (1992).

5   A fuller collection is to be found in Clarence Major's *Juba Jive* (1994).

6   However, note Walter Nash's insistence that 'a pidgin language is not simply a ramshackle dialect with a go-as-you-please grammar and a few bits and bobs of baby talk' (1992, p. 176). Both the Bible and the works of Shakespeare have been translated into pidgins. The betrayal of Christ in Matthew 26: 75 is rendered thus in the King James version of 1611: 'And Peter remembered the words of Jesus, which said unto him, "Before the cocke crow, thou shalt deny me thrice." And he went out and wept bitterly.' In the Bislama pidgin of the New Hebrides the version is: 'Nao Pita i tingabaot tok ia we Jisas i bin talem long em, i se 'Taem rusta i no singaot yet, yu, be bambae yu save haidem tri taem, se yu no save me.' Nao em i go aofsaid, em i kraekrae tumas' (in Freeborn, 1992, p. 207).

7   The major glossary is *Hobson-Jobson*, over a thousand pages long, compiled and published by Henry Yule and A. C. Burnell in 1886. The curious title refers to the process of assimilation whereby foreign terms are altered to fit the speech and spelling conventions of a borrowing language. An example is *juggernaut* for Sanskrit *jagannatha*.

8   The common American first name *Earl* is a curiously undemocratic exception.

7

LEXICAL VARIETIES IN MODERN AND CONTEMPORARY ENGLISH

The period 1963–72 was particularly rich in new words. . . . It started with the death of President Kennedy and has been an age of violence and rapid change. . . . Vocabulary is a index to a civilization, and ours is a disturbed one. That's why so many of the new words deal with war, violence, drugs and racism, and not so many with peace and prosperity.

Clarence Barnhart, *Dictionary of New English since 1963* (1973)

In this chapter we shall initially be concerned with the linguistic consequences of colonialism and imperialism. These have affected not just the structure of the lexis, the major theme of the following chapter, but also the notions of 'the English language' and 'Standard English' by shifting the centre of gravity from Britain towards its former colonies. We shall also trace the increasing exploitation of the language as a resource for mass persuasion in the mediated varieties of journalism, advertising and propaganda, of which the most extreme manifestations take the form of semantic engineering. In addition we shall consider the notable features of novelty and experimentation found in modern literature, and the constraints of censorship. The first part of the chapter will discuss these broader, formative influences, while the second will deal with modern lexical varieties *per se*.

At the turn of the century the territorial extent of English was generally confined to the British Isles, the British Empire and its former colonies. There was little dispute (outside the United States) that South-Eastern English, the standard since the fourteenth century, was the pre-eminent model. Linguistic usage was largely governed by a strong sense of conformity and decorum. At the Scriptorium in Oxford the laborious semantic reconstruction of the language, the *OED*, had reached the halfway point under the aegis of James Murray. The academic study of English had been evolving at University College and King's College, London, for over half a century, but the Oxford English

School had been founded only in 1894, after bitter controversy during which the subject was derided as being mere 'chatter about Harriet' and of having insufficient weight without the cumbrous obscurity of Germanic philology.[1]

The academic study of the language and its literature are now highly developed and fragmented into specialisms. The previous limitation whereby 'English Literature' was considered to be the literature of England (usually with a strong sense of its being the bearer of the cultural heritage of the race) has in most academic departments given way to a broader definition of literature written in English. As the faculty of language as a transparent medium reflecting the truth is increasingly questioned, so are the traditional logocentric foundations of knowledge. In some theoretical persuasions, notably deconstruction, the text is increasingly displaced from its traditional centrality, and the older certainties of meaning are exploded: 'the meaning of meaning is infinite implication,' wrote Jacques Derrida (*Writing and Difference*, 1978, p. 25). If that is so, some might respond, why is the meaning of Derrida's assertion so clear? We shall return to the languages of theory in our concluding chapter.

Expanding Englishes and the Problem of the Standard

The most obvious sociolinguistic fact is that in the course of this century Modern English has rapidly acquired the status of a world language. While this development might have seemed predictable as a consequence of imperialism, the spread of English has been unexpectedly accelerated since the withdrawal of the British imperial influence from newly independent states. This development has thus been quite the opposite of the symbiosis between the Roman Empire and the Latin language: the retreat of the legions and Roman authority allowed the European vernaculars to flourish and expand into the resulting linguistic vacuum. In many Commonwealth states, contrariwise, English has been chosen in the post-colonial era on political grounds as a 'neutral' language in preference to competing indigenous languages. Such a situation has obtained in Ghana and Nigeria. The attempt to make Hindi the official language of India upon independence in 1947 proved unacceptable to many non-Hindi states and has been put into abeyance. English is consequently used for many official purposes, as it is in several erstwhile British colonies in Africa. In the former Communist countries of Eastern Europe, English has gained prestige as the language of liberation. Still less predictable has been the increasing growth of English in Western Europe, in post-communist Russia and in Japan. As a consequence of these developments, English, now the first language of over 300 million people, is used as a second language by over 1000 million people across the globe. The rapid expansion of American influence and its effects on the lexical core of English will be taken up in the following chapter.

There is an interesting paradox that although the spread of English into the present Commonwealth states was initially accelerated by the discouragement of the local vernaculars, varieties of Commonwealth literature mainly concerned with the colonial and post-colonial experience have since developed in English. The most admired Caribbean poet, Derek Walcott from St Lucia, encapsulates powerfully the division of his loyalties between two aspects of imperialism, his slave history and the English language:

> Where shall I turn, divided to the vein? how choose
> Between this Africa and the English tongue I love?
> ('A Far Cry from Africa', 1962)

Walcott's work is notably suffused with European and English literary culture (unlike that of most modern English and American poets) as well as with dialect and patois.

The natural consequence of this spread of English has been the increasing diversity of global varieties, which have been revealingly termed *Englishes* in recent times. (The modern usage of the plural seems to date from a collection called *World Englishes*, published in 1985.) These varieties are, in the nature of things, more apparent in spoken forms than in written. Yet the best-selling authors of popular fiction, no less than those short-listed for the annual Booker Prize in Britain, are writers born or bred in all parts of the world. In the latter category are the names of Anita Desai from India, V. S. Naipaul from Trinidad, Doris Lessing from Zimbabwe, Salman Rushdie from India, Nadine Gordimer and J. M. Coetzee from South Africa, Kazuo Ishiguro from Japan, Timothy Mo from China, Keri Hulme from New Zealand and Ben Okri from Nigeria. Letters to the editors of local English newspapers in, say, Penzance, Dublin, Glasgow, Boston, Sydney, Auckland and Bombay continue to be written in essentially the same language by writers who would, almost certainly, encounter considerable difficulties in oral communication over the telephone because of divergences in accent, lexis, grammar and idiom. Today, with the development of fissiparous varieties of American English, Caribbean English, Australian English, Indian English, as well as varieties of Asian and African English, it is hardly an exaggeration to claim that on the ground a state of mutual incomprehension is fast approaching. Comparisons are naturally invited with the previous world language, Latin, which fragmented and evolved into the Romance languages. We shall return to this theme.

The Varieties of Mediated English

Modern English now exists not only in world varieties, but in functional varieties of mediated English, such as journalism, advertising and promotional language, which have become increasingly demarcated and resilient, developing their own lexis, idioms and conventions of usage.

At the turn of the century the main division in English journalism was between the 'quality' press, embodied in *The Times* and the *Manchester Guardian*, and the 'popular' press, exemplified by the *Daily Telegraph*, the *Daily Express* and the *Daily Mail*. Although there were differences in content between the categories, differences in style were marginal. However, in 1903 Lord Northcliff launched the first 'tabloid' newspaper in the form of the *Daily Mirror*. Marketed as the 'first picture-newspaper', it became in 1911–12 the first newspaper to attain a circulation of a million. The successful combination of banner headlines (pioneered by Pulitzer in America), sensationalism, high-impact photography and low-register language has made the rise of the tabloid the major trend in modern journalism: the genre currently occupies over 60 per cent of the British newspaper market. The successful launch of a new quality newspaper, *The Independent*, in 1986 was the first initiative for decades marking a reversal of this trend.[2]

Whereas earlier forms of journalism employed formal register, syntax and grammar, their modern equivalents exhibit a mixture and juxtaposition of register as well as flexibility and experimentation in word-formation. The point is often made that the English press, through its variety of news-style and choice of register, reflects the class-system. Thus the 'quality' papers generally favour the higher register, while the 'popular' and tabloid incline markedly towards the lower. The differing styles are simply illustrated by comparing the headlines of different newspapers on a given day, especially when they relate to the same story. The visit of the Soviet cosmonaut, Major Gagarin, to London in 1961 elicited the following range of journalistic responses:

The Times:	CHEERING CROWDS HALT MAJOR GAGARIN
The Guardian:	HERO'S WELCOME FOR MAJOR GAGARIN
Daily Telegraph:	GAGARIN LUNCH WITH QUEEN
Daily Mail:	SHAKE! 2000 TIMES
Daily Express:	FANTASTICHESKY
Daily Herald:	LONDON GIVES LITTLE YURI THE BIG HAND
Daily Worker:	A REAL HERO'S WELCOME
Daily Mirror:	RADY VAS VIDJETJI ['PLEASED TO SEE YOU']
Daily Sketch:	GA-GA OVER GAGA

(Raymond Williams, *Communications* (1970), pp. 71–2).

As this sample shows, 'headlinese' (first recorded in an American reference in 1927) tends to be most developed in the popular and tabloid categories. The headlines of the *Times* and the *Guardian* approximate to the vocabulary and syntax of ordinary speech, simply anouncing the event; those of the *Mail*, *Express*, *Mirror* and *Sketch* use 'foregrounding' techniques of the unfamiliar and incongruous to gain attention.

Whereas the register employed by the 'quality' press has traditionally been more abstract and classical, that of the 'tabloids' has favoured high-impact, low-register words to add 'drama' and 'colour'. Thus terms like *confrontation* or *disagreement* are replaced by *clash, row, battle* or *fight*; *criticize* is eschewed for *blast, slam, slate* or the odd phrasal verb *hit out at*; an *investigation* becomes a *blitz*, a *probe* or a *swoop*, while *power* is physically characterized as *punch, clout, muscle, bite* or even *teeth*. Underworld slang from America (as in *scam, heist* and *bust*) is also increasingly encountered. Terms are often deployed as flexible units to create the most potent combination of impact and ambiguity, as in SHOCK PROBE ROW. The tabloids are less bound by traditional taboos over 'strong' or 'bad' language, using demotic idioms like 'DON'T BE SO BLOODY RUDE' (the *Daily Mirror* criticising Mr Khrushchev's boorish behaviour at the United Nations on 17 May 1960). 'MURDERING BASTARDS!' was a tabloid headline denouncing the IRA's assassination of Lord Mountbatten on 27 August 1979. Recently the unashamedly illiterate has surfaced in forms such as *We wuz robbed, loadsamoney, wotalotigot, Dontchalovem!* and *Geddit?*

However, over the past three decades, this traditional distinction of registers has narrowed as there has been a considerable degree of 'levelling down'. As the following examples show, the importation of American slang is a major feature: 'Breast beats bottle in quest for brainy babies'; 'The buxom blond bimbette is absent from Ms Royalle's films'; 'she posed nude for art classes and started into light glamour or "cheesecake" modelling'; 'the male beefcake dancing team'; 'Eventual victory will depend on which faction commands the greatest common-room clout'; 'Assad revels in being cast as a good guy.' These are culled from copies of the *The Times* (January–February 1992). In similar vein are: 'The general's gung-ho remarks'; 'The Bush administration is planning to firm up its position as the front-runner'; 'President de Klerk's glitzy referendum campaign'. These examples come from broadcasts of the BBC World Service.

Another feature of the same process is to be found in the increasing use of puns in 'quality' journalism. *Time* magazine has regarded itself as unbound by any taboo in this regard for several decades, regularly amusing its readership with such items as 'It's Alimentary, mon petit!', 'Great Dane' (Hamlet) and 'Good Knight' (Sir Peter Ustinov) (*Time*, 29 October 1990). The British 'quality' press has taken some time to claim the same licence, shown in the following examples (all from *The Times*): 'Moore's the Pity' (on the British sculptor), 'Malice in Wonderland', 'Know your rites', 'close encounters on the high Cs' and 'Heirs and Graces'. Other, supposedly 'quality' journals have chimed in with 'Shore Thing', 'Collusion Course', 'Distance Lens Enchantment', 'Kitsch and Make-Up', 'Lingua Franker' and many others.

Largely as a legacy of British colonialism, there are now well in excess of 2000 English daily newspapers published worldwide (excluding international editions). However, the most distinctive mode of journalism outside the UK is that cultivated by *Time* magazine. It consists of an almost artificially wide range of registers designed to create maximum impact: 'You hear it before you see it. Clacker. Klickstick. Kabanger. No matter what you call it, it's the most ubiquitous and onomatopoeic toy in 20 years. . . . Competition for the cacophonous market share is reaching a peak' (*Time*, 29 October 1990, p. 47). The issue which covered President Clinton's eventual confession of an 'inappropriate' relationship with Monica Lewinsky carried a 400-word leader which wrote of Clinton's 'amazing pirouette', of 'national squirming about an anguishing investigation', of being 'newsy' and 'energizing', of 'ongoing fallout' and of offering 'a smart harbour amid the gales of punditry now in full force' (*Time*, 31 August 1998). Another typical hallmark of *Time* style is the use of sequences of adjectives compounded to create compactness, sharpness and journalistic 'colour': 'silver-haired, paunchy lothario, Francesco Tebaldi'; 'Zsa Zsa Gabor, seventyish, eight-times-married, Hungarian-born celebrity' (*Time*, 14 June 1976).

As with other aspects of culture, distinctions between 'high' and 'low' or 'serious' and 'popular' are being eroded. Nevertheless, these various journalistic varieties do constitute distinct forms of the language. One cannot imagine ordinary citizens using in their daily conversation such established journalistic idioms as 'Glory day for Tottenham' or 'World Cup fever grips Paris' or 'Superbitch hits town' or 'AIDS claims top film director.' Nor would they use such quaint archaisms as *Yule, slain, hustings* or *scribe*. Formations such as *new-look, see-through, lookalike, wannabe, lensman, weatherman* and *vocalist* are almost entirely confined to journalistic columns. However, another journalistic feature, namely the 'conversion' of nouns into verbs (e.g. *boost, splurge, mothball, corner, bulldoze, mushroom, broker* and *boom*) as well as of verbs and adjectives into nouns (e.g. *great, first, must* and *hopeful*) have now been accepted into general parlance. But, as the following examples show, journalistic practice often tests the limits of acceptability. A typical *Time* instance is 'this mature play-it-till-it-wears-out album' (4 January 1993, p. 56), while a less expected British example is: 'Anyone who has ever judged a literary award knows that bloody-minded disagreement and will-not-budge-an-inchism are the elements in which they take place' (*Times* leader, 26 September 1991).

Though there are distinctive features of journalism, one cannot identify a journalistic register as such, since the lexis is a mixture of neologism, archaism, conversion and compounding.

The language as a commodity

Advertising represents the most obvious form of linguistic capitalism, or exploitation of the language by vested commercial interests. In earlier times this process was confined to the creation of boosting copy. Dr Johnson's caustic observation in *The Idler* of 20 January 1761 that 'Promise, large promise, is the soul of an advertisement' long served to describe the major feature of the type, namely crass linguistic inflation, and still encapsulates the more blatantly overreaching. These are usually to be found in the luxury sector of the market, as in 'The best car/whisky/airline in the world'. Such extreme claims, though sanctioned by the American category of 'legitimate puffery', are usually counter-productive, being dismissed by the more discriminating as mere *hype* (a term coined *c*.1969). However, in the course of the century, a new area of semantic ambiguity has been exploited, namely *the weasel*. Coined in America at the turn of the century, a 'weasel word' subtly renders an apparently clear statement equivocal, as in: 'There's nothing just like X,' 'The better quality cigarette', 'Z makes it better for you' and similar 'open comparatives'. Since ethical constraints outlaw direct words like *cure*, sophistic alternatives such as 'symptomatic relief' move into the semantic vacuum.

The more recent form of exploitation concerns brand names, the creation of which has undergone a marked change of tactic. The older style (e.g. *Benson & Hedges, Dunhill, Huntley & Palmer* and *Ford*), reflected the names of the founding fathers and generations of goodwill. The new style is little more than verbal theft of the property of the speech community, the simple appropriation of positive terms, together with all their traditional denotations and connotations. Hence *Sunlight, Spring, Purity, Emotion, Pioneer* and *Cool*. Since there is obviously a limited number of such terms available, artificial hybrids like *Aquafresh, Oralfresh, Firehawk* and *Thunderbird* have been devised.

More explicit forms of self-fulfilling prophecy are found in cosmetic names like *Celebrity, Cover Girl, Agree* and the enthusiastically juvenile *Gee, Your Hair Smells Terrific!* This last at least represents a coherent enticement, unlike such 'omnibus' names as *Revlon Realistic Professional Formula Permanent Creme Hair Relaxer* or Estée Lauder's *Advanced Night Repair Protective Recovery Complex*, which are little more than a farrago of market-catching counters. Some political agenda or attitude is now often built in to brand names. Paul Johnson reveals a veritable cornucopia in the unlikely area of lavatory paper: 'Should it be Bio-degradable Nature, or Low-Grade-Waste Greencare, or Recycled

Environment-Friendly Revive, or Non-Chloric Bleached Nouvelle, or just old-fashioned Luxury Supersoft?' (*Spectator* 21/28 December 1991, p. 57).

A variation of this form of exploitation is the use of the slogan cliché. Previously slogans, like brand names, were implanted in the consumer's consciousness by ingenuity and repetition. Hence such stalwarts as 'Go well, go Shell,' 'Butter is better,' 'Top People Read the Times,' 'Drinka Pinta Milka Day' and 'Guinness is Good for you.' Today they increasingly take the form of embedded idioms which are simply pilfered. Of hundreds of citable examples, the following may serve: 'It's on everybody's lips' (Häagen Das ice cream) and 'Something to raise your spirits' (Teacher's whisky). The obvious pun is clearly designed as a winning ploy, especially useful in risqué situations such as: 'Australians wouldn't give a XXXX for anything else' (Castlemaine XXXX beer). Some, such as 'Meeting the Challenge' (Gulf Oil), seek to stress a corporation's supposed social responsibility. The industry itself, always anxious to improve its image, even claims a pseudo-democratic function in the slogan 'Advertising – the Right to Choose.'

A disturbing recent trend of aggressive illiteracy (presumably appealing to a fairly low common denominator) employs poor grammar and the destabilization of spelling. Hence such slogans as 'The Star Tells it like it is,' 'Honey, I just shrunk the mortgage,' and brand names such as *Eet-sum-mor*, *Ezkleen*, *Stafresh*, *kwikot*, *donut*, *tufpak*, *litemaster* and *carnu*. It is striking that advertisers, having exhausted, stultified and trivialized the vocabulary, increasingly rely on other, non-verbal forms of emotive communication, reducing the whole mosaic of human language to infantile gurgles, caveman grunts, snarls of rage and sighs of pleasure.

Literary Originality and its Limits: Modernist Experimentation

The artistic imperative to be original or creative is an essential part of the legacy of Modernism, that movement in the arts which occurred during the first three decades of this century. However, originality in the arts of language has not always been deemed a virtue, as we have seen. In medieval times the traditional and admired mode was more that of imitation, and even the spirit of liberation and exploration of the Renaissance did not prevent innovative practices from falling under some suspicion. Since language is essentially a communal form of communication, originality *per se* can, if unchecked, produce a labyrinth of private language, a solipsistic creation in which a profusion of perspectives and a plethora of styles, registers and neologisms leads to confusion. The limitations inherent in this extreme notion of originality are highly apparent in some Modernist works, especially those using the techniques of free association or 'stream of consciousness'. Within the movement there were, however, degrees of lexical originality.

The Modernist revolution announced itself by various propagandist techniques, involving a high degree of self-publicity and programmatic commentary, such as Ezra Pound's slogan, 'Make it New!' and his vulgarism' It is after all a grrrreat littttttterary period' (Phelps and Deane (eds), 1968, p. 89). The first of these had been anticipated by Flaubert's more elegant diktat: 'It faut être absolument moderne' ('It is necessary to be absolutely modern'). Much of T. S. Eliot's criticism carried an agenda for Modernism. In his essay on 'The Metaphysical Poets' he wrote: 'We can only say that it appears likely that poets in our civilization, as it exists at present [1921] must be *difficult*.' There was even the revolutionary desire to reshape history in such a way as to identify the crucial psychological moment at which modernism had been born. But on this point there was not total agreement: 'On or about December 1910 human nature changed,' declared Virginia Woolf. 'It was in 1915 the old world ended,' insisted D. H. Lawrence. More recently, critics have identified 1922 as the *annus mirabilis*, since it saw the birth of James Joyce's *Ulysses*, T. S. Eliot's *The Waste Land*, D. H. Lawrence's *Aaron's Rod*, Virginia Woolf's *Jacob's Room*, Eugene O'Neill's *Anna Christie* and 'Façade', a curious musical-cum-poetic drama resulting from the collaboration of the Sitwells and William Walton (cf. Bradbury and McFarlane (eds), *Modernism*, 1976, p. 33).

The most revolutionary notion was that the literary work was a self-contained verbal and symbolic microcosm not responsive to or responsible for the 'real world'. Indeed, the creation of cultural and linguistic pastiches (including foreign words and even opaque ideograms) severed the link between word and world. The problematic and paradoxical relationship betwen the two was encapsulated by Gertrude Stein in her famous conundrum: 'A rose is a rose is a rose.' It is notable that Modernist literature is perhaps best explicated by terms like *collage, pastiche, surrealism* and 'cubist fragmentation', the categories of contemporary art criticism. The techniques of the *roman fleuve* or 'stream of consciousness' novel led more in the direction of solipsism, disjunction and neurosis than towards social observation and rational analysis. Saussure's notion of language as a self-enclosed, autonomous system of signals became the model of the modernist text: As Samuel Beckett said of James Joyce, 'His writing is not *about* something; *it is that something itself*' (in Wynne-Davies (ed.), 1989, p. 272). Beckett's dictum is significant in that it stresses the independence of Modernist literature from the world around it. The insight may be broadened to show that literature is not necessarily 'about' its social context. From a different angle and at a later period, New Criticism stressed the autonomy of the text, Archibald MacLeish taking the extreme view that 'a poem should not mean but be' (Ronald Hepburn, in B. Ford (ed.), *The Present*, 1983, p. 495). Though it is customary by means of contextualization to trace correlations between social events and literary works, their separateness is equally obvious.

In recalling the Modernist revolution (as a means of partly explaining the current situation and discussing the status of a 'Literary' register) we may note that the experimentation of Eliot, Pound and Joyce was unashamedly elitist in its use of subtle cultural allusions, arcane vocabulary, disjunctive quotations and complexity of structure. While being self-consciously cosmopolitan and sophisticated, these authors eschewed traditional literary convention by juxtaposing high and low registers, familiar and rarefied diction to an outrageous extent. The idea of a literary text being a harmonious structure gave way to 'intertextuality', a pastiche of different literary traditions:

> London Bridge is falling down falling down
> *Poi s'ascose nel foco che gli affine*
> *Quando fiam uti chelidon* – O swallow swallow
> *Le Prince d'aquitaine à la tour abolie*
> These fragments have I shored against my ruins
> Why then Ile fit you. Hieronymo's mad again.
> Datta. Dayadhvam. Damyata.
> Shantih shantih shantih
>
>   (*The Waste Land*: conclusion)

This is an extreme example. But it should not distract us from the point that Eliot's English lexis is actually traditional: there is hardly a neologism in all of his serious work. But in *Old Possum's Books of Practical Cats* (1939) he indulges in such playful creations as 'ineffable effable effanineffable', 'ker-flip ker-flop', U-forms like 'gawn' and stage Cockney like 'horgan' with its intrusive aitch.

Pound was, initially, the more revolutionary, orchestrating 'the first heave . . . to break the pentameter', denouncing 'the crepuscular spirit of modern poetry', exploring the concentrated forms of Imagism, such as the Japanese *haiku*, and being recognized by Eliot as 'il miglior fabbro' ('the better workman') for his ruthless (and generally inspired) revision of *The Waste Land*. Always more explicit in his social comments, Pound violently denounced the horrific dishonesty and waste of war:

> Died some, pro patria,
>   non 'dulce' non 'et decor . . .'
> walked eye-deep in hell
> believing in old men's lies, then unbelieving
> came home, home to a lie.

> There died a myriad,
> And of the best, among them,
> For an old bitch gone in the teeth,
> For a botched civilization.
>   ('E. P. Ode pour l'election de son Sepulcre')

Though his unfinished *Cantos* have remarkable effects of cultural pastiche and stylistic ventriloquism, the raucous, vitriolic and slightly absurd voice of the propagandist and pamphleteer ultimately drowned that of the poet.

In his huge, myriad-worded work *Ulysses* (first published in 1922), James Joyce was more daringly original, juxtaposing registers to the furthest possible degree. In some thirty lines of the section called 'Ithaca' near the end of the book (1960 edition, pp. 870–1), two people in a state of post-coital bliss are described in a whole range of lexis. First come the geographical coordinates of the city of Dublin ('on the 53rd parallel of latitude, N. and the 6th meridian of longitude, W.'). Then follows an imprecise spatial location: the pair are in 'the proper perpetual motion of the earth through everchanging tracks of never-changing space'. The third description is a complex mixture: the postures are first geometrical ('right leg extended in a straight line'), but there is also a mythical element, The woman being compared with Gea-Tellus (Earth Mother), and an archaic, biblical register, as she is 'fulfilled, recumbent, big with seed'. Joyce used the language like a historical thesaurus, combining contemporary words like *snapshot* with archaic forms like *rereward*, describing conception as 'the manchild in the womb'. In the last section Joyce moves into the child's world of fantasy and fairy-tale. Starting with the folk-tale figure of Sinbad the Sailor, he develops the aleatory technique of Sterne, continuing with 'Tinbad the Tailor' and then proceeding with a series of alliterative absurdities ('Pinbad the Pailer and Minbad the Mailer') as the functional names become less recognizable, finishing with nonsensical and alien mismatches like 'Xinbad the Phthailer'. The fantasy ends with 'the bed of all the auks of the rocs of Darkinbad the Brightdayler'.

Though there is much sophisticated word-play in *Ulysses*, Joyce uses his knowledge of the history of the language in a profound way. In another section, the process of childbirth is symbolically reflected in the historical evolution of the language. Thus part of an early section runs: 'But sir Leopold was passing grave maugre his word by cause he still had pity of the terrorcausing shrieking of shrill women in their labour' (1960, p. 510).

Some Modernist creations call in question the validity of coinage or neologism. For instance, Joyce also coined such words as *oniony*, *fishgluey* and *scrotum-tightening* in *Ulysses*, and thousands more in *Finnegans Wake* (1939), but they have remained nonce-words floating in the tenuous limbo of Joyce's

text. Likewise, Gerard Marley Hopkins created such forms as *Amanstrength,
brickish, girlgrace, selfyeast, unchilding* and *unleaving,* all of which are virtually
unique, in spite of being accorded the cachet of an entry in the *OEDS.*

Less recognized but perhaps more successful were the creations of the
American poet, e.e. cummings (he insisted on the lower-case initials). His
lexical innovations were designed to create various effects, such as a sense of
innocence and spontaneity, a child's view of the world, as in this poem
celebrating spring:

> when the world is mud-luscious
> . . . and eddyandbill come
> running from marbles and
> piracies . . .
> when the world is puddle-wonderful.
> ('in Just-', 1923)

A more 'mature' version of the same theme opens paradoxically:

> Spring is like a perhaps hand
> (which comes carefully
> out of nowhere) . . .
> ('Spring is like a perhaps hand', 1925)

Eroticism is conveyed by the unexpected and the intensely inarticulate:

> . . . i like kissing this and that of you,
> i like, slowly stroking the, shocking fuzz
> of your electric fur, and what-is-it comes
> over parting flesh . . .
> ('i like your body when it's with your', 1925)

Cummings's originality does not falter when he deals with less promising
political themes:

> Huge this collective pseudobeast
> (sans either pain or joy)
> does nothing except preexist
> its hoi in its polloi
> ('of all the blessings which to man', 1944)

The last line is reminiscent of the highly popular American comic poet Ogden
Nash (1902–71), who routinely made up forms like *lobstertrician, Calypsoma-*

niacs or *Book-of-the-monther*, and jauntily 'rhymed' forms like *chillun* with *penicillun, kettle* and *popacatapetl, boys* and *avoirdupois.*

Although the Modernist movement proved to be highly influential for a period, it would appear in retrospect to have been what David Lodge crisply described as an avant-garde without a rearguard. Even the avant-garde did not show total solidarity to the cause. Joyce proved to be the most steadfast revolutionary of the original trio: in the sequence of his major works, *Dubliners* (1914), *A Portrait of the Artist* (1916), *Ulysses* (1922) and *Finnegans Wake* (1939), each creation is more experimental, eccentric, logomanic and polyglot than the previous. All the traditional notions of decorum, semantics and syntax are studiously violated, as can be seen from the brief extract from the opening of the *Wake*: 'Sir Tristram, violer d'amores, fr'over the short sea, had passencore rearrived from North Armorica on this side the scraggy isthmus of Europe Minor to wielderfight his penisolate war.' When he sent an early version of this 'prosepiece' (complete with key) to Harriet Shaw Weaver in 1926, he signed the letter 'Jeems Joker', an appropriate name for one who littered his work with literary wisecracks. He defined the desiderata of the writer essentially in terms of the outsider as being 'silence, exile and cunning'. Even as an undergraduate, Joyce had written in a pamphlet: 'No man . . . can be a lover of the true and the good unless he abhors the multitude; and the artist, though he may employ the crowd, is very careful to isolate himself' (Phelps and Deane (eds), 1968, p. 9).

It might be argued that in some respects the effect of Modernism was detrimental, alienating the ordinary reader, exaggerating the distinction between 'highbrow' and 'lowbrow' and marginalizing serious literature. The confusing and problematic experimentalism of Modernism created a minority audience, a coterie concerned with literary chic. Much Modernist poetry epitomizes that elitist notion of 'the poet's poet'. Invoking Joyce as the most steadfast exponent, one may note that in *Ulysses* he created the anomaly of 'the unread classic', while in *Finnegans Wake*, 'this crazy book,' as he himself called it, he achieved the ultimate paradox of 'the unreadable classic'.

Gentility and Savagery

A. A. Alvarez noted in 'Beyond the Gentility Principle', his controversial introduction to *The New Poetry* (1962), that from the time of Eliot's embourgeoisification, 'the whole movement of English verse has been to correct the balance experimentation had so unpredictably disturbed' (p. 21). One major exception was Dylan Thomas, who created rhapsodic responses to primal themes of death and sexuality, and exhilarating evocations of youth (notably in 'Fern Hill') running free 'down the rivers of the windfall light' and through 'the house high hay'. Alvarez diagnosed 'gentility' as being a form of English disease, a paralysing complacency preventing the post-war English poets from dealing with the really serious topics of the times, which he defined as 'mass evil' and the tenor of 'dominant public savagery' (p. 27), exemplified in the Nazi death camps and the threat of nuclear war.

The poet who perhaps violated the 'gentility principle' most trenchantly was Ted Hughes (1930–98), whose early collections celebrated 'nature red in tooth and claw,' closely observed and accurately rendered with a taut, thrilling dexterity. In a studiedly anti-Wordsworthian fashion, Hughes shows traditional pastoral settings that contain, not harmony, but the alarmingly precise machinery and lexis of war:

> Terrifying are the attent sleek thrushes on the lawn,
> More coiled steel than living – a poised
> Dark deadly eye, those delicate legs
> Triggered to stirrings beyond sense
> ('Thrushes', 1957)

'What is it,' Hughes asks, that gives these common or garden birds 'their bullet and automatic purpose?' The question is not really answered: skill in killing is simply a brute fact. 'Hawk Roosting' is a psychotic Browningesque soliloquy which directly projects savage political tyranny into the animal kingdom. Hawk boasts:

> I kill where I please because it is all mine.
> There is no sophistry in my body:
> My manners are tearing off heads –

The ending is uncompromising:

> My eye has permitted no change.
> I am going to keep things like this.
> ('Hawk Roosting', 1957)

Some critics identified Hawk as a manifestation of latent thuggery in British society, which Anthony Burgess was to portray so alarmingly and with such lexical creativity in *A Clockwork Orange* (1962).

Hawk is very much the ancestor of Crow, whose first collection, *Crow; From the Life and Songs of the Crow*, first appeared in 1970. Hughes widened the scope of his focus on violence and catastrophe into a metaphysical principle: the law of the jungle expands into a nightmare of cosmic chaos and confusion, embodied in the figure of Crow. In a gruesome parody of the Creation in which God is reduced to a blundering and incompetent Dr Frankenstein, Crow begets unwittingly all manner of horrors. The kindly parental discourse is set against feral energy:

> God tried to teach Crow how to talk.
> 'Love,' said God. 'Say, Love.'
> Crow gaped, and the white shark crashed into the sea
> And went rolling downwards, discovering its own depth.
>
> 'No, no,' said God, 'Say Love. Now try it. LOVE.'
> Crow gaped, and a bluefly, a tsetse, a mosquito
> Zoomed out and down
> To their sundry flesh-pots.
>
> ('Crow's First Lesson')

Inverting all the traditional motifs of Christian providence, Hughes presents the world as governed by a universal poltergeist with a keen sense of black, if not sick, humour:

> Cars collide and erupt luggage and babies
> In laughter
> The steamer upends and goes under saluting like a stuntman
> In laughter . . .
>
> The meteorite crashes
> With extraordinarily ill-luck on the pram
>
> ('In Laughter')

The apocalyptic vision which Hughes presents in his later work is, of course, different from what Alvarez had in mind. It is not man-made but God-made (in so far as there is a genuine divine principle in Hughes's mock theology and somewhat superficial metaphysics). In an interview with the *London Magazine* in January 1971, he described the work, not very helpfully, as being 'the songs that a Crow might sing. In other words, songs with no music whatsoever, in super-simple and super-ugly language.' But there remains the problem of creating a language appropriate to the mass suffering and bestiality of apocalyptic proportions which has been a gruesome monument of this century. Perhaps the incomprehensible scale of suffering and the unimaginable varieties of savagery render such experience inexpressible. Hughes, at any rate, does not really solve the problem; he simply creates bizarre and surreal effects by juxtaposing the experience of suffering with language which is either trivial or absurdly inappropriate.

The abrasive and violent tenor of Hughes's poetry was in some ways paralleled by that of his ex-wife, Sylvia Plath, whose collection *Ariel* caused a sensation when it was published in 1965, two years after her suicide. In 'Lady Lazarus' she wrote macabrely of her own suicide attempts, expanding the persona into an unkillable 'death-force' of Hiroshima and Dachau:

> Out of the ash
> I rise with my red hair
> And I eat men like air.

Two other poets with significantly differing lexis are Philip Larkin (1922–85), a university librarian who spent most of his life in Hull, and Seamus Heaney, an Ulsterman. Whereas the Moderns had been cosmopolitan and polyglot, 'the Movement' poets, a loose grouping of the 1950s, were parochial and demotic, studiously avoiding any tincture of 'the highbrow' or the elitist, indeed any kind of cultural affectation. Philip Larkin, who became the most famous, was notably dismissive of what he called 'myth-kitty' in 'Four Conversations' in the *London Magazine* (November 1964): 'to me the whole of the ancient world, the whole of classical and biblical mythology means very little, and I think that using them today not only fills poems full of dead spots but dodges the writer's duty to be original' (p. 72). This was an obvious riposte to the Modernist notion of 'the mind of Europe' arrestingly invoked by Eliot in 'Tradition and the Individual Talent' (1919).

Larkin fulfilled this manifesto admirably, marking a genuine return to the humble Wordsworthian definition of the poet as 'a man speaking to men' and using 'the language of ordinary men'. In 'Church Going' (1954), his major *fin de siècle* poem about the decline of religion, Larkin pointedly eschews the grand utterance, historical perspective, public statement and explicit symbolism of catastrophe found in an almost parallel work, Matthew Arnold's 'Dover Beach,' written *c*.1867, wherein 'the Sea of Faith' has ebbed and chaos is come again. Indeed, Larkin reflects the secularization of modern society by pointedly omitting the essential spiritual vocabulary of *faith, soul, divine*, etc., treating religion purely in terms of artefacts, of *lectern, pyx* and *roodlofts*. His poetic persona is an ironic compendium of agnostic confusions, aware of 'some brass and stuff / Up at the holy end', who, hatless, takes off his cycle clips in 'awkward reverence' and is almost reluctantly aware of the 'tense, musty, unignorable silence / Brewed God knows how long'. Whereas Arnold's poem had a compensating romantic commitment, 'Ah love, let us be true to one another,' Larkin's ends with a phlegmatic assertion that the church is 'A serious house on serious earth . . . If only that so many dead lie round.' The register is a subtle mixture of plain and specialized, ancient and modern, serious and ironic, essentially reflecting the traditional function and uncertain contemporary value of the institution. This 'cross of ground' holds an amalgam of *buttress, roodlofts, lectern, parchment, plate, pyx.* The decaying church is now, variously, the prey of 'some ruin-bibber, randy for antique', the haunt of 'dubious women' who 'pick simples for a cancer' and the passing object of idle interest for the vaguely curious, like himself.

However, Larkin's work is not entirely cool, lucid and ironic. In a less well-known poem, 'Faith Healing', he explores an unritualized modern form of religion. Dramatizing the moment of intense emotion at hearing the healer's call, Larkin makes use of a quite extraordinary term: 'and such joy arrives / Their thick tongues *blort*, their eyes squeeze grief' (my italics). *Blort*, which is virtually unrecorded, is a dialect word meaning 'to cry out inarticulately, like an animal'.

The poet of the grimy Welfare State, grinding urban existence and the little conforming man, Larkin nevertheless confounded what A. A. Alvarez had called 'gentility' by using a genuinely demotic idiom with far more daring than his 'angry' or 'underground' contemporaries. 'Ah, were I courageous enough,' his would-be rebel laments, 'To shout *Stuff your pension!*' in 'Toads' (1955). Sexuality is thrust at the reader, either in this coarse travesty of "Freudian" wisdom:

> They fuck you up, your mum and dad.
> They may not mean to, but they do.
>> ('This Be The Verse', 1971)

or in blunt comments on 'the sexual revolution':

> Sexual intercourse began
> In ninteen sixty-three
> (Which was rather late for me) –
> Between the end of the *Chatterley* ban
> And the Beatles' first L. P.
>> ('Annus Mirabilis', 1967)

Alone of contemporaries, he admitted into his poems a subject still largely taboo, what Lawrence had called 'the dirty little secret' of masturbation: 'Love again: wanking at ten past three' ('Love Again', 1979).

One of the most admired contemporary poets, Seamus Heaney, a Nobel laureate, is almost unique in his venerable probing of the ancient heritage of the tongue, digging down through the layers of the language to its roots, and vividly evoking the sharp clangour of the battle poetry of the Anglo-Saxon *scop* or poet:

> Bone-house:
> a skeleton
> in the tongue's
> old dungeons.
>
> I push back
> through dictions,
> Elizabethan canopies.
> Norman devices,
>
> the erotic mayflowers
> of Provence
> and the ivied latins
> of churchmen
>
> to the scop's
> twang, the iron
> flash of consonants
> cleaving the line.
>
> In the coffered
> riches of grammar
> and declensions
> I found *ban-hus* . . .
>
> ('Bone Dreams', from *North*, 1975)

As we saw in chapter 2, *ban-hus* ('bone-house') is a poignant Anglo-Saxon kenning for the body. However, in the very different vein of the public domain of the troubled Irish situation, Heaney acerbically dissects the clichés and the rhetoric 'of politicians and newspapermen':

> Who've proved upon their pulses 'escalate',
> 'Backlash' and 'crack down', 'the provisional wing',
> 'Polarization' and 'long-standing hate'.
>
> (from 'Whatever You Say Say Nothing')

Heaney here touches on the problem partly posited by Alvarez but directly articulated by George Steiner: 'What are the relations of language to the murderous falsehoods it has been made to articulate and hallow in certain totalitarian régimes?' (*Language and Silence*, 1967, p. 13). The inescapable point is that many writers up to the most recent times have tended to consider language from their own specialist and parochial needs. Indeed, Eliot and Pound have been criticized for using the language of racial prejudice. On the continent things were different: 'Can it be that Hitler has polluted the language of Nietzsche and Hölderlin?' asked Klaus Mann in a note in his diary in 1940. 'It can,' replied George Steiner (*Language and Silence*, 1967 p. 143). Theodor Adorno's response took the form of a succinct manifesto: 'After Auschwitz no poetry.'

Censorship and Modern Literature

A notable modern development concerning authority and literary language has been a marked decline in formal censorship, culminating in the abolition of the powers of the Lord Chancellor to censor plays in Britain in 1968. However, the banning of a number of literary works in the earlier decades of the century made them into *causes célèbres*. Whereas in previous centuries censorship was aimed primarily at preventing religious and political subversion, prosecutions in modern times have been principally concerned with obscenity or obscene libel. These punitive measures obviously had the effect of driving certain sexual terms underground and even affected the policy of inclusiveness of the *OED*. In his fine preface, Murray had spelt out his commitments: 'The lexicographer must include all the common words of literature and conversation, and such of the scientific, technical, slang, dialectal, and foreign words as are passing into common use' (p. xvii). Though he conceded that 'the lexicographer, like the naturalist, must "draw the line" somewhere', he made no explicit reference to obscenity. However, as we noted in chapter 5, there were notable instances of self-censorship in the *OED*.

The Indictments Act of 1916 facilitated prosecutions by admitting them on the grounds of subject-matter, no longer focusing on the intention of an accused author as necessarily being 'to poison the minds of divers of the liege subjects of our said Lord the King, and to raise in them lustful desires, and to bring the said liege subjects into a state of wickedness, lewdness and debauchery'. In that year D. H. Lawrence's novel *The Rainbow* was declared obscene, the publisher (Methuen) fined, and all existing copies of the book ordered to be destroyed. James Joyce's *Ulysses*, first published in Paris in 1922, was banned for alleged obscenity in England until 1936. Contemporary attitudes were well articulated by George Bernard Shaw, a liberal in most things, in his *Table Talk*: 'I could not write the words Mr Joyce uses: my prudish hand would refuse to form the letters.' In 1928 Lawrence published, privately in Florence, the work which was to become his *succès de scandale*, *Lady Chatterley's Lover*. Although its explicit sexuality met with almost universal critical opprobrium and official suppression in Britain, five pirated editions appeared on the continent and in America within nine months. The same year witnessed similar opposition to Marguerite Radclyffe Hall's novel about lesbianism, *The Well of Loneliness*. The book was declared obscene and banned (by a judge who declined to hear some forty witnesses), whereupon it was withdrawn by the publisher. It was reprinted in Paris, but the copies imported to Britain were seized and burned after the distributors were prosecuted.

The Obscenity Act of 1959 retained the old legal core, namely that a book was 'deemed to be obscene if its effect . . . [is] such as to tend to deprave or corrupt persons who are likely . . . to read it'. However, there were two significant relaxations in that it was required that the book should be judged 'as a whole', and that expert witnesses could be called to justify the book's contribution 'for the public good on the grounds that it is in the interests of science, art, literature or learning'. The change in the Act precipitated an important test-case in the form of the trial of the publishers of the unexpurgated edition of *Lady Chatterley's Lover*, namely *Regina v. Penguin Books* in 1960.[3] The defence called many prominent literary and academic figures. Their endorsement of the work's literary qualities and of Lawrence's attempt to 'redeem' the coarsest 'four-letter' words, *fuck* and *cunt*, was the principal reason for the publisher's victory. Within three months of the publisher's acquittal, the book had sold three million copies. Five years later, *The Rainbow* was prescribed for school study.

The *Chatterley* judgement was something of a watershed which encouraged in the succeeding decades a considerable upsurge of pornography, in the form of both magazines and literary works. *Fanny Hill* and *Memoirs of an Oxford Scholar*, written by the eighteenth-century pornographer, John Cleland, were reissued in the 1960s. (A passage from *Fanny Hill* was discussed in chapter 5.) Henry Miller's celebrations of bohemian life in Paris, combining moral nihilism and inexhaustible sexual energy, *Tropic of Cancer* and *Tropic of Capricorn*, originally published in Paris in 1934 and 1939 respectively, appeared in Britain in 1963 and 1964.

Partly as a consequence of the dwindling number of prosecutions, the state of contemporary linguistic mores with regard to 'foul language' (an elastic category which today admits profanity, blasphemy and obscenity) shows increasing laxness and permissiveness. Such language is not infrequently encountered in such unexpected contexts as the columns of the quality press, utterances by the royal family and in the Houses of Parliament, locales where such ejaculations would have been unthinkable in Victorian times.

Looking back at Lawrence's attempt to rehabilitate the four-letter words, Frank Kermode concluded that 'They can hardly be said to have acquired a tender, let alone a numinous quality' (1973, p. 123). While these words still undoubtedly provoke offence, especially among the elderly, attitudes of sophisticated boredom and ironic nonchalance are increasingly adopted by contemporary writers and commentators at what was previously considered outrageous and sensational. We have seen such attitudes in Larkin's casual use of obscene idiom in the previous section. Gore Vidal was more openly ironic: 'Because of Miller's hydraulic approach to sex and his dogged use of four-letter words, *Sexus* could not be published in the United States for twenty-four years' (1974, p. 198). David Lodge satirizes acutely in the following exchange the odd alliance (as well as the alienation) of opaque academic jargon and plain demotic idiom:

> "But doesn't it bother you at all?" Robyn said. "That the things we care so passionately about – for instance, whether Derrida's critique of metaphysics lets idealism in through the back door, or whether Lacan's psychoanalytic theory is phallogocentric, or whether Foucault's theory of the episteme is reconcilable with dialectical materialism – things like that, which we argue about and read about and write about endlessly – doesn't it worry you that ninety-nine point nine percent of the population couldn't give a monkey's?"
> "A what?" said Charles.
> "A monkey's. It means that you don't care a bit."
> "It means that you don't give a monkey's fuck."
> "Does it?" said Robyn, with a snigger. "I thought it meant a monkey's nut. I should have known: 'fuck' is much more poetic in Jakobson's terms – the repetition of the 'k' as well as the first vowel in monkey'. . . ." (1989, p. 217)

This passage juxtaposes registers in an extraordinary linguistic pot-pourri of a kind generally not encountered before the twentieth century, except in the pages of Sterne and Swift. Traditionally, 'literary' and 'common' languages have been distinguished by the principle of decorum positing a hierarchical model of 'high', 'middle' and 'low' actions with appropriate styles and lexis. This model, we recall, was that which Murray outlined and illustrated in the preface to the *OED*, discussed in chapter 1.

In the course of this century there has been a steady accommodation of the 'common' into the 'literary' language by means of a process of 'levelling down'. The diction of the major authors of the earlier decades, Galsworthy, Hardy, James and Conrad, approximated to the high register favoured by Dr Johnson, whereas that of a broad spectrum of their successors, such as Lawrence, Waugh, Updike, Burgess, Bellow and a host of post-modern and contemporary writers is very diversified. A highly erudite vocabulary is preferred by some writers, like John Barth, while others, such as Martin Amis, exploit more of a demotic idiom. Today, therefore, the notion of a literary language is difficult to define, since elements of the common and obscene language have been so readily absorbed into it, and partly because the definition of a literary work has now developed a variety of criteria. In a recent analysis of the the differing linguistic features of the fiction of Anita Brookner and Jeffrey Archer, Robert Burchfield posed the question of whether, as classic 'highbrow' and 'comparatively lowbrow' writers respectively, they wrote what he called 'Two Kinds of English?' (Ricks and Michaels (eds), *State of the Language*, 1990, pp. 356–66). We shall return to the problematic status of 'literary' language and the relationship of obscenity to the core in the next chapter.

Ideology and Orwellian Insights

The presence of the Greek root *logos* in *ideology* reminds us that many ideological notions are verbally impacted, having acquired a subsumed, traditional force. Although *ideology* had a general currency relating to ideas from the late eighteenth century, the modern politicized sense is well defined by the *OED* as 'A systematic scheme of ideas usually relating to politics or society, regarded as justifying actions, *especially one that is held implicitly*' (my italics). These 'compacted doctrines' as William Empson has called them (1977, p. 21) can grow up spontaneously, as have formulations like *free speech, free trade* and *the freedom of the press*. Others are simply collective sayings, such as 'safe as the Bank of England'. They can also be the creations of individuals, as the *Protestant work ethic, conspicuous consumption* and *civil disobedience* were the formulations of Max Weber, Thorstein Veblen and Henry Thoreau respectively. Propaganda in its semantic component concerns the fabrication of stereotypes and ideological formulations by mediated means. Hence 'the yellow peril', 'the Communist menace', 'the Popish Plot', etc. The more pernicious slogans thrive in extreme situations of war psychosis; hence the Nazi formulas of *Lebensraum*, the *Übermensch*, the Fatherland, 'the Final Solution' and so on. However, since the last war, the process of ideological engineering has continued in the democracies. 'Orwellian' substitutions, such as the Ministry of War being restyled the Ministry of Defence or the Ministry of Labour being restyled the Ministry of Productivity, are *de rigueur*.

'Orwellian' is the sobriquet which, of course, pays homage to the signal contribution of George Orwell (Eric Blair) to the understanding of ideology and propaganda.[4] In *Animal Farm* (1945), his satirical allegory on Stalinism, in *Nineteen Eighty-Four* (1949), his totalitarian dystopia, and in his major essay, 'Politics and the English Language' (1946), he dissected and parodied the distortions, evasions and euphemisms of propaganda with such masterful clarity that virtually no literate person in the West could claim to be innocent of the knowledge that much institutional language had been contaminated.

What Orwell realized and demonstrated with great clarity and force was that the classical element in the English vocabulary had a dangerous quality of polysyllabic prestige. These long and high-sounding words, because they were not understood, did not have a high currency and could therefore be manipulated to mean whatever those in power wished.

> Defenceless villages are bombarded from the air, the inhabitants driven out in the countryside, the cattle machine-gunned, the huts set on fire with incendiary bullets: this is called *pacification*. Millions of peasants are robbed of their farms and sent trudging along the roads with no more than they can carry: this is called *transfer of population* or *rectification of frontiers*. People are imprisoned for years without trial or shot in the back of the neck or sent to die of scurvy in lumber camps: this is called *elimination of unreliable elements*. (1958, p. 85)

We can see that this passage is written, in essence, in two registers, the plain, direct Anglo-Saxon ('people are shot in the back of the neck') which is transparent, set against the vague and polysyllabic ('elimination of unreliable elements') which is opaque. The lexis of the formulas is not an accident, nor a question of style, but a deliberate piece of political manipulation. It gives the illusion of orderly, almost scientific, administration. 'Such phraseology is needed,' he wrote, 'if one wants to name things without calling up mental pictures of them.'

He continues, using his potent mixture of a created 'set-piece', followed by lexical analysis:

> Consider for instance some comfortable English Professor defending Russian totalitarianism. He cannot say outright "I believe in killing off your opponents when you can get good results by doing so." Probably, therefore, he will say something like this:
>
> "While freely conceding that the Soviet régime exhibits certain features which the humanitarian may be inclined to deplore, we must, I think, agree that a certain curtailment of the right to political opposition is an unavoidable concomitant of transitional periods, and that the rigours which the Russian people have been called upon to undergo have been amply justified in the sphere of concrete achievement."
>
> The inflated style is itself a kind of euphemism. A mass of Latin words falls upon the facts like soft snow, blurring the outlines and covering up all the details. (1958, pp. 85–6)

In 'Politics and the English Language', Orwell was examining modes of deception; in *Nineteen Eighty-Four* he was to explore their institutionalization as a form of social control. The seriousness with which he took the whole matter of semantic engineering is apparent from the Appendix which is devoted the 'The Principles of Newspeak'. This is, in itself, an unusual refinement in work of ostensible fiction dealing with a vision of the future:

> The purpose of Newspeak was not only to provide a medium of expression for the world-view and mental habits proper to the devotees of Ingsoc [English socialism], but to make all other modes of thought impossible. . . . The word *free* still existed in Newspeak, but it could only be used in such statements as 'This dog is free from lice' or 'This field is free from weeds.' It could not be used in the old sense of 'politically free' or 'intellectually free'. (1972 edition, p. 241)

Orwell divided the lexis into three kinds: common, ideological or political, and scientific:

> *The A Vocabulary* consisted of the words needed for the business of everyday life – for such things as eating, drinking, working, putting on one's clothes, going up and down stairs, riding in vehicles, gardening, cooking, and the like. (1972, p. 242)

(Interestingly, this is largely the function of the Anglo-Saxon element in the language.)

> *The B vocabulary* consisted of words which had been deliberately constructed for political purposes. (1972, p. 244)
>
> *The C Vocabulary* was supplementary to the others and consisted entirely of scientific and technical terms. (1972, p. 246) [This is now largely the function of the Latin and Greek element of the vocabulary.]

The partial parallel with English lexical structure is apparent, namely the division between the core Saxon terms and the specialist classical component. The essential difference is in the B Vocabulary, which is the vital driving force in the system of semantic engineering:

> No word in the B vocabulary was ideologically neutral. A great many were euphemisms. Such words, for instance, as *joycamp* (forced labour camp) or *Minipax* (Ministry of Peace, i.e. Ministry of War) meant almost the exact opposite of what they appeared to mean. (1972, p. 247)

Orwell's insights have become seminal in the modern awareness of how language changes, especially in its lexical and semantic component. Considered from a historical perspective, it is clear that at the earliest stages of society, semantic changes are essentially symbiotic, reflecting broad social changes. Thus *free, noble* and *gentle* originally had class-bound aristocratic senses; with the breakdown of feudalism they acquired their modern generalized moral meanings. Similarly, the vocabulary of capitalism originally used broad trans-actional terms like *sell, fee, pay, purchase* and *finance* before employing lexical imports like *traffic, factory, nationalization, privatization, arbitrage* and *synergy*. With the development of media, especially mass media, it becomes possible for powerful vested interests to effect lexical and semantic changes. A striking example derives from the Protestant Revolution and its anti-Catholic propa-ganda, which generated a whole word-field of terms critical of Catholicism and the Pope (who was downgraded to the mere *Bishop of Rome*). They include:

papist (1521)	*papish* (1546)
popish (1528)	*papism* (1550)
popery (1534)	*popestant* (1550)
papistical (1537)	*popeling* (1561)
papistic (1545)	

The steadily increasing weight of deleterious suffixes is paralleled by more recent formations like *communistic, fascistic* and *racialistic*. Mediated changes in Communist propaganda show similar tactics, namely the vilification of the terms *bourgeois, capital,* etc., and the importation of the entirely alien term *proletariat*.

Once totalitarian control has been established over the media by an oli-garchy, the special refinement of 'Orwellian' change and semantic engineer-ing is a virtual formality. The post-revolutionary power struggle in Russia provided some spectacular examples. The cult of personality flourished as the leaders not only assumed mythic names like *Stalin* ('Man of Steel') and absurd totemic sobriquets like 'the Iron Soldier' and 'the Universal Genius', but also exploited these names as discrediting devices. Hence the emergence of *Trotskyite* (1919), *Trotskyism* (1925) and *Trotskyist* (1927); when Stalin started to assert himself via the euphemistically termed 'purges' and the show trials, *stalinism* became a term of condemnation overnight, in 1927, to be joined by *Stalinite* in the same year and *Stalinist* the next. Likewise the attach-ment of the mere labels *counter-revolutionary, fractionalist, revisionist* and *enemy of the people* became a virtual death sentence.

Subsequent developments include such entirely cynical usages as *pacification* and *liberation* to mean their opposites, i.e. 'subjection to a new tyranny'. The section on political language in South Africa in chapter 6 gave further examples. More disturbingly, the process continues in the democracies. Orwell's use of *pacification* was ironic, but by the 1960s it had become institu-tionalized, especially in American usage in the context of the Vietnam War, as 'a process (usually a military operation) designed to secure the peaceful co-operation of a population'. Perhaps the most potent ideological formula is that of *national security*, readily invoked by any government of the day to justify any cause or block any enquiry. Orwellian changes create in turn a specially modern experience, a disturbing sense of alienation from language, analogous to what Orwell analysed as 'doublethink', namely a simlutaneous sense of belief and scepticism, of naivety and complicity in the semantic fraud which is being perpetrated.

Some 'Orwellian' changes are surprisingly old: medieval purveyors became so unpopular as a result of their rapacious and dishonest habits that, according to a statute of 1360, 'the heinous term *purveyor* shall be changed and restyled as *achatour*.' The earliest recorded usage of the phrase 'detention under safe custody' is the application in 1570 to Mary, Queen of Scots; she was kept in this safe condition for nineteen years before being executed.

Orwell's insights continue to have relevance, even to expand semantically. In many societies in the latter part of the century Big Brother has been more than a fictional bogeyman. We have become aware, furthermore, of an expanding semantic field of 'official nonsense', incorporating such words as *officialese, mumbo-jumbo, blab-word, gobbledygook, doubletalk* and, of course, *newspeak* itself. A *Dictionary of Euphemisms and Other Doubletalk* was published by Hugh Rawson in 1981, followed three years later by Jonathon Green's *Newspeak: A Dictionary of Jargon*. A 'Semantic Field of Nonsense' is to be found in my *Words in Time* (1988, p. 235). *Newspeak* has become a burgeoning category, as we shall see in a later section, which will discuss the annual crop of formations using the -*speak* suffix to imply 'confusing or semantically angled language'.

Grammatical Aspects of Lexical Change

This section provides a bridge between the broader formative influences of literature, media and politics and the new lexical varieties. Although grammar and lexis are regarded as different linguistic categories, we have seen that changes in the grammatical inflection system have had both semantic and lexical results. Furthermore, actual or perceived deficiencies in the grammatical system have led to new lexical forms being devised.

Conversion

The main consequence of the reduction of inflections from the Middle English period onwards was, as we have seen, increasing semantic flexibility through conversion. In Modern English this process is now highly developed, more so in the American variety than in the British, being especially apparent in mediated language. Instances of new verbal extensions in American contexts (with the first recorded *OED* date) are *boost* (1848), *splurge* (1848), *engineer* (1873), *scoop* (1874), *bulldoze* (1876) and *boom* (1879). These surprisingly early dates show how well established the process is. It continues in forms like *author, fuel, host, message, mushroom, preface, power, showcase* and *obsolete*, for the most part originally nouns (and probably still thought of as being in that category) which have through journalistic practice developed usages as verbs and sometimes as adjectives as well. A recent addition is *high-five*, the congratulatory sporting gesture. A less expected development is the use of the adverb *nearly* as an adjective in 'the nearly man' (who almost achieves some distinction). Similarly adjectival forms like *hopeful* and *married* have in recent decades been used as nouns (as in 'the young hopefuls' and 'the newly marrieds'). New conversions now appear almost daily.

Other recent lexical forms are *obsess* (a verbal extension or 'back formation' of *obsession*) and *psych*, a similar extension from *psychology*, used in the compound forms *psych up* or *psych out*. Similarly *pervert* has generated the verb *to perve*, meaning to be sexually obsessed with someone. These have presumably grown up to fill a felt need for verbal forms in a particular lexical areas. Similarly, although adjectives have traditionally and commonly been created by the addition of *-y* (as in *fiery* and *chilly*), there is an increasing and almost random tendency to apply the ending to extended forms, like *outdoorsy* and *woodsy*. More traditional verbs have also been extended into new forms, as in the following passage:

> We stopped to buy some take-away food and were just passing the drive-in cinema when we saw the flashing lights of a police car. There had apparently been a drive-by shooting.

The reader will have noticed, because of their concentration, the use of the compound adjectives *take-away, drive-in* and *drive-by*. The first two forms can, of course, also be used as nouns: 'Let's get some take-away [or takeaway] and go to the drive-in.' This kind of flexibility is a very recent development, having occurred in the past decade or so. Other examples are 'a *come-hither* look' or 'to play *hard to get*'. However, the historical perspective shows us that the use of greatly compounded adjectives was already developed in Shakespearean language: Goneril denounces '*not to be endured* riots' (in *King Lear*, I. iv. 226), while Octavius criticizes 'the *neer-lust-wearied* Antony' (in *Antony and Cleopatra*, II. i. 38). Although this kind of extreme flexibility fell out of usage in the intervening centuries, it is coming back into fashion, particularly in journalism. A recent theatrical review wrote of the actor Antony Sher: 'He has abandoned tiresome look-at-me mannerisms' (*Daily Telegraph*, July 1995).

Problems with number: you and thou

Although *thou* and *thee* are still used in many regional dialects of England, as Trudgill shows (1990, p. 85), both forms have died out in the standard form of the language. The loss of *thou* has made *you* ambiguous, since it now has to cover both singular and plural functions. In many contexts this ambiguity can create problems. A dissatisfied customer in a department store may say 'You're not very efficient, are you?' intending to refer generally to the store's service, but the expression may be interpreted as an offensive personal complaint by the assistant to whom it is addressed. Consequently, to fill the lexical gap there has been a growth of *yous* as a non-standard plural. James Milroy comments that 'it is clear that for many Belfast speakers (and indeed for many speakers of Irish English generally), the pronoun *yous* (plural) is categorical, contrasting with *you* (singular)' (1992, p. 8). Peter Trudgill points out that *youse* is also part of the Merseyside dialect (1990, p. 85). In the US the forms *you'all* and *y'all* fulfil a similar function.

The inclusive masculine

The jocular grammatical precept is that 'Man embraces woman.' That is to say, there has been a traditional assumption that the masculine gender form also implies the feminine. This has led to a dominance of the male form in most official formulations, for example: 'A student wishing to change courses must ensure that *his* application form reaches the Registrar by . . .' Another notable instance occurred in the words uttered by the first astronaut on the moon: "A small step for Man: a great leap forward for Mankind."

Historically the practice is well documented. Dr Johnson regularly used the inclusive masculine, for instance in his self-deprecating definition of *lexicographer*: 'A writer of dictionaries; a harmless drudge; that busies *himself* with tracing the original, and detailing the signification of words.' He also referred to animals as 'he' rather than 'it'. One should also bear in mind that historically the form *its* emerges only after Middle English, the prior form being *his*. The famous first line of Chaucer's *General Prologue* runs: 'Whan that Aprill with *his* shoures sote' which is transliterated as: 'When April with *its* showers sweet.'

The *OED* places the emergence of the modern form *its* 'at the end of the sixteenth century', adding this note:

> With the gradual substitution of sex for grammatical gender in the concord of the pronouns, the indiscrminate use of *his* for male beings and for inferior animals and things without life began to be felt inappropriate.

About half a century ago Simeon Potter suggested that 'English would be improved as a medium of communication by the adoption of a common or epicene [dual gender] pronoun which might refer clearly and definitely to both male and female' (1963, p. 171). The logical alternative is to use the inclusive 'he or she' or 'his or her'. However, this duplication is not very elegant, especially in long formulations where the alternatives are repeated. Consequently, there arc signs of strain in the use of this inclusive singular: the desire to be inclusive but avoid *he/she* has led to the use of *their* as a non-standard singular. e.g. 'Would the person who left their pen behind after the test please collect it.' This is not such a recent development: 'Everyone has their level,' is found in Jane Austen's *Emma* (1816).

The first suggestion for a common gender pronoun, along the lines Potter mooted, was *ne*, put forward by the National Education Association of America in 1974 (Baron, 1986, p. 176). A number of feminists have recently suggested a new compacted form, namely *(s)he*. Generally speaking, such fundamental lexical alternatives for common words have not been accepted.

More pressure has been brought to bear on forms like *salesman* and *chairman*, where the *-man* suffix is increasingly regarded as improperly exclusive or invidious. (It should be understood that virtually all words ending in *-man*, such as *apeman*, *caveman* and so on, derive from Anglo-Saxon *mann*, the dominant sense of which was 'human being'. Even *woman* comes from Anglo-Saxon *wifmann*, in which *wif* is the specific sub-category and *mann* is the generic term for 'mankind'.[5] The modern debate, which is well documented in Dennis Baron's study *Grammar and Gender* (1986), has been complicated by arguments about the general appropriateness of the terms *woman* and *lady*, both of which have been in and out of fashion over the centuries. The increasingly accepted solution has been to use the gender-neutral term *person*. Historically *saleswoman* is recorded as far back as 1704, *saleslady* from 1855 and *salesperson* from around the turn of the century.

No doubt because of its greater status, *chairman* has occasioned more dispute. It is first recorded in 1654. Although *chairwoman* is instanced in 1699, the *OED* editors noted that it was 'hardly a recognized name'. *Chairperson* appeared *c*.1971 and occasioned considerable controversy. It was initially rejected from all sides: because it was not authentic, because it was not truly sex-neutral, being used 'when the chair is occupied by a *chairwoman*' (Copperud in Baron, 1980, p. 179) and by feminists like Mary Daly for 'obscuring women's existence and masking the conditions of our oppression' (in Baron, 1986, p. 179). Even less popular creations have been *chairone*, *chaircrone* and *chairmember*. Some American dictionaries have listed forms such as *adperson*, *anchorperson* and *businessperson*, which has led to the coinage of more obviously facetious forms such as *personhole*, *personslaughter*, *person-made* and *fireperson*.

These issues, arguments and attempts at lexical and semantic engineering are significant, because they derive from the recognition that language is a fundamentally formative social factor affecting world-view, ideology and gender roles.[6] We shall return to this issue in discussing politically correct language in our concluding chapter.

New Lexical Varieties and Forms

This section will focus on new lexical varieties created from the language's own resources, while the following chapter will trace the global lexical influx. Broadly speaking, many of these new 'native' varieties fall into three categories: kinds of **compounding, extension of existing forms** by the use of prefixes, suffixes and affixes, and kinds of **abbreviation**, of which the most prominent are: **portmanteaux, conflations, acronyms** and **diminutives**. Compounding continues to be the dominant category. The useful American collection *Fifty Years Among the New Words* (ed. J. Algeo), covering the half-century 1941–1991, gives a figure of 68 per cent for all compounds (1991, p. 14). However, some sense of the growth of the last categories (abbreviations, portmanteaux, acronyms and diminutives) can be gauged from comparing this source with more recent ones: *Among the New Words* has 12 per cent, the *Barnhart Dictionary of New English since 1963* (1973) has 15 per cent, a recent American collection of new words, *Trashcash, Fizzbos and Flatliners* (1993) has 17 per cent, while the first volume of the *Longman Register of New Words* (1989) has 20 per cent.

New Forms of Compounding

As we saw in chapter 1, English has throughout its history shown a capacity for compounding, which is a basic feature of the Germanic languages. It is natural that this tendency should continue, being evident in contemporary forms such as *road-rage, time-frame, wind-surf, think-tank, egghead, hard-core, downmarket, unbundling, street-wise, mindscape, heartland, psychobabble* and thousands of others. Even this brief sample shows that the dominant traditional model, consisting of two nouns, is now admitting numerous variations. In *Fifty Years Among the New Words* John Algeo notes, nevertheless, that 'About 90% of new compounds are nouns' (1991, p. 7). Furthermore, there is increasing flexibility of usage: whereas *hard core* is a compound noun denoting 'the dedicated members of a group', *hard-core* becomes a compound adjective referring, for example, to pornography. Similarly, *downmarket* could be used as an adjective in, say, 'a downmarket suburb', but the form could also take on the function of an adverb in 'the firm is going downmarket.' These examples also show that in contemporary usage compounds do not always carry the traditional sign of the hyphen: they may be hyphenated, 'free standing' or joined. By and large, the historical development tends to be: free standing ⇒ hyphenated ⇒ joined. A typical example is *grass roots* ⇒ *grass-roots* ⇒ *grassroots*.

Some of the more metaphorical modern compounds resemble the **kenning**, the compound metaphor which is a traditional feature of Anglo-Saxon and Old Norse poetry, discussed in chapter 2. Thus on the analogy of A-S *mere hengest* 'sea horse' = 'ship', we have the following modern creations:

> *air-head* = idiot
> *spin-doctor* = political analyst
> *sky-scraper* = very high building
> *sound-bite* = pithy statement for broadcasting
> *couch-potato* = television addict

These have, of course, a different tone from the typically poignant A-S kennings, such as *ban-hus*, 'bone-house' for 'body', but they follow a similar formula, requiring an imaginative leap to attain recognition. They also remind us that everyday speech is full of creative and graphic uses of metaphor. *Gob-smacked*, for example, means 'reduced to flabbergasted silence as though having been hit in the mouth', while a *handbagging* is 'a tirade of verbal abuse' administered by an aggressive woman, a picturesque stereotype owing something to the formidable Margaret Thatcher.

Flexibility of word-order is another feature of contemporary compounding. Thus in the traditional compound verbs *load up* and *size up*, the preposition comes last; these forms have now been joined by *upload* in its computerized sense and related inverted forms such as *down-size, front load* and *off-road*. Other forms showing more flexible use of prepositions are: *meltdown, hands on, up front, feed-back* and *lock-up* (for 'jail'). We find traditional word-order increasingly inverted in formulations like *day one, house beautiful, planet earth* and similar journalistic and promotional uses.

An increasing number of elements is also evident in contemporary compounding. Traditionally a compound has comprised two elements, but in recent decades forms such as *right-to-life* (i.e. anti-abortion) *in your face* (meaning 'aggressively direct or personal') and *to die for* ('highly desirable') are increasingly evident. This tendency can be quite developed in journalism, for example, 'we can be fairly sure that by 2010 their "touchy-feely, all-right-to-cry" ethos will have been supplanted' (*Spectator*, 21 March 1998, p. 25). Since there is a natural limit of tolerance over how many hyphens can be used without the forms appearing ridiculous, they are often dispensed with or reduced, as in: 'The fans are becoming frustrated over the on-again off-again visit of Michael Jackson' (*The Star*, 7 March, 1998).

Reduplicating varieties are also much in evidence, usually showing a degree of creativity or fun. Recent examples are *fun-run, toy-boy, kid-vid, nitty gritty, fat cat* and *aga saga*.

New compounding prefixes and suffixes

Prefixes and suffixes are increasingly drawn from a greater variety of stocks, or show increasing flexibilty in the use of traditional forms. Thus although the suffix *-able* has generated thousands of forms in the English lexis over the centuries, it is being used with greater flexibility in Contemporary English. Hence such forms as *doable, kickable, puttable, liveable* and facetious forms such as *gettatable* and *unputdownable*. The same is true of the *non-* prefix, previously found in many nouns and adjectives, such as *non-payment, non-existent* and *non-intervention*. In recent decades *non-* has become increasingly combined with verbal forms such as *non-skid, non-stick, non-stop* and *non-drip*. A similar development is the use of *no* in compounds such as *no go* (area), a *no-show* (a passenger missing a flight) and a *no no* (something taboo).

Modern English has dozens of words ending in *-ster*, such as *songster, youngster, mobster* and *trickster*. They seem to have nothing in common. However, as we go back into Old and Middle English, we find that many of these words referred to female agents. Thus Chaucer's rapacious and seductive Friar spends his time with 'tappesterres' (barmaids) and 'beggesterres' (beggarwomen) (*General Prologue*, lines 241–2). Complementary pairs like *baker* and *baxter, brewer* and *brewster* also show that originally the -ster forms applied to the female gender. However, the only modern survival which has a strict feminine denotation is *spinster*; the newer forms often suggest contempt for the occupation, as in *punster* (in Johnson), *rhymester, prankster, gangster* and *tipster*.

Other traditional prefixes which are being used in new ways are *anti-, pro-* and those to do with size, such as *extra-, super-, hyper-, mega-, mini-* and *micro-*. *Antichrist, anti-hero* and *anti-Semitic* are examples of typical earlier uses. However, as Hans Marchand points out, 'The 20th century has added the "defense" type' (1969, p. 143). This category refers to forms generated in World War I, such as *anti-aircraft*, and subsequent relatives, such as *anti-submarine*, followed by *anti-abortion, anti-crime* and *anti-freeze*, some of which may be used as independent nouns. *Pro-* is a much more recent form in its political sense, e.g. *pro-British*, which dates from the 1830s; recent developments are *pro-life, pro-choice, pro-democracy* and *pro-women*.

The emphasis on the extremes

The word *extraordinary*, first used *c*.1460, uses the prefix *extra* in its literal Latin sense 'out of' to mean 'out of the usual order'; it has subsequently generated many similar forms, such as *extra-marital*, *extra-territorial* and so on. In the seventeenth century, *extraordinary* came to be used as an adverb, as in 'extraordinary good', thus paving the way for modern usages such as *extra strong*, *extra clean* and so on. Very much the same development can be seen in *super-*, meaning originally 'over' or 'above', as in *super-abundant*. From the form *superman*, suggesting somebody quite unrivalled, have developed related compounds *supermarket*, *superhero* and *superpower*, as well as the simple emotive ejaculation *super*! With the general marketing tendency to stress size, so *mega*, originally meaning 'great', *hyper*, 'above' or 'beyond', and *ultra*, also 'beyond', have followed suit in forms like *hypermarket*, *megacity* and *ultra-thin*. *Extra*, *super* and *ultra-* have now become so potent as individual forms that they have been appropriated as brand names, while *mega* has acquired the sense of 'big' or 'important'. Such developments may seem strange to purists, but they show that these common classical forms have acquired a new semantic and lexical life in Modern English.

At the opposite end of the scale, *micro-* and *mini-* have been brought into play. They are much more recent, *micro-* developing out of scientific enquiry in the nineteenth century. Hence have grown whole fields of study such as *microbiology* and numerous terms for technical innovations such as *microfilm* and *microwave*. Remarkably, the *mini-* words have developed in a totally different fashion, the catalyst being the launch of the original *Mini* car by the British Motor Corporation in August 1959. Its compactness and originality of design caught the public imagination, so that the form *mini-* became a potent witness word, being exploited in a whole range of products. Most notable of these were the *mini-skirt*, the *mini-cab*, the *mini-bike*, indeed what *Punch* referred to satirically in 1964 as 'Mini-holidays, mini-cameras, mini-tellies'. The editors of the *OED Supplement* noted under *mini*: 'A prefix much in vogue in the 1960s. Only a selection of the virtually unlimited number of combinations is illustrated here.' The *Supplement* listed some sixty forms, many of them general terms such as *mini-budget*, which have survived. However, Simon Mort noted that the *mini-* prefix was 'virtually absent from the 1986 crop' (1986, p. v).

Traditional classical elements, such as *trans-* and *-ation*, while still a major source, have been joined by a whole new range of forms. Many of these are scientific and technical, such as *bio-*, *techno- tele-*, *nuclear-* and the suffix *-ware*. These have generated forms such as *bio-degradable*, *biofeedback*, *biodiversity*, *technofusion*, *techno-pop*, *tele-banking*, *teleshopping*, *telemarketing*, *nuclear device*

347

and *nuclear winter*. From the prototypical use of *software* in computing have developed *hardware, course-ware* and *group-ware*.

Various ideological and political programmes have recently made use of the prefixes *eco-, green-, pro-* and the suffixes *-free, -friendly*. The *eco-* forms have proliferated greatly, thanks to the growing interest in ecology, generating some fifty compounds (according to the *Oxford Dictionary of New Words* (1992 edition), the most common being *ecosystem, ecoclimate* and *ecotourism*, while the other prefixes are found in *greening, green tax, pro-choice, pro-life* and *pro-family*. Whereas *free* has over the centuries developed a powerful ideological position as an adjective in formulations such as *free speech, free trade* and *the free world*, the use of *free* as a suffix or second element in a compound has traditionally been less marked. It is found in general forms like *tax-free, carefree* and *trouble-free*. From the late 1970s it started to appear in dietary and environmental catchwords, such as *alcohol-free, cholestorol-free, lead-free* and *nuclear-free*. About the same time *user-friendly* became much used in computer jargon, generating relations like *reader-friendly*, and ecological forms such as *environmentally friendly* and *earth-friendly*.

With the accelerating emphasis on information as an accessible resource, we find new forms like *infotainment, infomercial* and *infotech*. Machines which can respond to information, computerized or other, are termed *smart* in the sense of 'intelligent', also apparent in *smart cards* and *smart bombs*. This usage has spread into *smart money*.

A term whose growth seems to indicate a regrettable degeneration in the tenor of modern times is *junk*. Its earliest sense (in the sixteenth century) was that of 'old rope', from whence the modern sense of 'rubbish' has grown. This has recently spread to *junk mail, junk food* and *junk bonds*, a high-risk investment. It has also generated *junkie* ('drug addict') and the verb to *junk*, interestingly paralleled by 'to rubbish' (*c.*1972) and 'to trash' (*c.*1970).

Two suffixes which encapsulate a sense of cynical criticism of certain kinds of jargon-filled contaminated institutional utterance or 'spokesmanese' are *-speak* and *-babble*. The first is derived from George Orwell's creation of Newspeak in his dystopia, *Nineteen Eighty-four* (1949), discussed in a previous section of this chapter. Hence arose the forms *adspeak, salespeak, airlinespeak, agentspeak, Femspeak, sportspeak* and *Haigspeak* (1981), this last deriving from General Alexander Haig's notorious capacity for obfuscation. (Haig was the US Secretary of State from 1981 to 1982; the obscurity of his pronouncements gained him the ironic recognition of the annual Alexander Haig Awards.) The novelist Kingsley Amis used the ironic form *creep-speak* back in 1960, while the latest formation (at the time of writing) is *Billspeak*, coined by *Time* magazine (31 August 1998, p. 14) to describe the evasions, weasel words, prevarications and ambiguities employed by President Clinton during the Monica Lewinsky scandal. Some -*speak* coinages are simply satirical, for example *Valspeak* or *Valley Girlspeak*, mocking the stereotypical usage of the San Fernando Valley in California, parodied in: 'Like, you know, who can predict about, you know, language? I mean, like, last year we got Valley Girlspeak' (*Family Weekly*, 9 January 1983, p. 5). The more overtly critical suffix -*babble* appeared in the 1970s in forms such as *eco-babble*, *psycho-babble* and *techno-babble*.

Abbreviations

Today we regard abbreviations, a major feature of modern lexis, as a completely natural and common part of the language. The point is simply made by considering the following statement:

> Being unable to hail a hansom cab in the rain, I took the omnibus to Streatham and had the misfortune to find myself seated between two passengers, one suffering from the symptoms of influenza, the other in an advanced state of intoxication from over-indulgence in some public house.

Such a passage is unlikely to have been written much after World War I. It is dated not only by the formal register but by the extended forms *hansom cab*, *omnibus*, *influenza* and *public house*. Today we use shorter forms like *plane*, *phone*, *fan* and *fax* without consciously reflecting that they are abbreviations of *aeroplane*, *telephone*, *fanatic* and *facsimile* respectively. Indeed, most of the abbreviated forms have become acceptable to such a point that it would be pompous and pedantic to use the longer originals. They mark a shift towards informality. However, this tendency, now greatly accelerating, is comparatively recent in the timespan of the language.

Old and Middle English did have have a highly developed convention of abbreviation. In order to save space on the manuscript material, which was vellum or parchment, made from the skins of calves or sheep and thus expensive, scribes started to use a series of conventional abbreviations called **diplomatics**. Common or familiar endings of words were omitted and signalled by a horizontal line. Hence Latin *destructum est* was rendered in the Old English period as *destructū ē*, *sanctus* as *stū* and *januarius* as *ianr*. These practices were carried over into the writing of Anglo-Saxon, so that *garum* was rendered as *garū*. More compact was the use of a symbol which looked like a '7' to signify 'and'.

These conventions died out in the course of the Middle English period, as the ancient scribal tradition was lost. The main survival was *þt* for *þæt*. Within the Early Modern English period the main forms of abbreviation concerned personal names, such as *Jas* for *James* and *Thos* for *Thomas*, and shortened forms of a few common words such as *tho'* for *although*, *wh'c* for *which* and the use of the ampersand (&) for *and*. These became quite popular, even in formal writing in the eighteenth and nineteenth centuries, but have since faded away.

Abbreviations became the object of adverse comment in the writings of Jonathan Swift in the early eighteenth century. He especially objected to the use of *mob* and *phizz*, shortenings of the full Latin formula *mobile vulgus* and *physiognomy*, as well as *rep* and *incog* for *reputation* and *incognito*, and even less drastically contracted forms like *drudg'd*, *fledg'd* and *rebuk'd*. In his typical fashion, Swift satirized this tendency in a letter to *The Tatler* (no. 238 in 1710). emphasizing the offending forms, which appear in italics:

Sir,
I *cou'dn't* get the things you sent for all about Town. – I *thôt* to *ha* come down myself, and then *I'd ha' brout' um* [I would have brought them]; but I *han't don't* [haven't done it], and I believe I *can't do't*, that's *pozz* [possible]. (Cited in Baugh, 1965, p. 313)

His objections, which were partly supported by Dr Johnson, proved to be largely ineffective. This is probably because abbreviation has become a natural and instinctive response to longer words, frequently used words and cumbersome formulas. Technical terms are a major source, especially in America, having generated in the past few decades *hifi*, *hitech*, *TV*, *slomo*, *CD*, *PC*, *VCR* and *fax*. As one can see, these are often rendered by phonetic spellings. General purpose terms include *OK*, *ID*, *demo*, *looney*, *fan*, *stroppy*, *perks*, *porno* and *aggro*. As was noted in the introduction (p. 36), many of these new shortened forms have become quite independent of their parents, developing both an altered meaning and a different register. One occasionally hears talk of 'the really fanatic fans', which originally would have been tautological, since *fan* is an abbreviation of *fanatic*. It is quite common for modern teenagers to use even more drastic, non-verbal forms like 'B4 I 4get How RU?' The American toy company has pandered to this code by calling itself 'Toys R Us', but with the 'R' dyslexically reversed.

Another sign of increasing informality is evident in the way traditional spelling is being undermined by the institutionalized illiteracy of advertising. Thus forms like *nite*, *lite* and *kwik* are attaining increased currency, having initially been confined to brand names and advertising copy. *Nite* is developing associations of excitement in *nite spot*, *nite life* and so on, leaving boring old traditional *night* behind. Similarly *lite* and *kwik* suggest slimness and energy through the brash cutting out of the silent consonants in the traditional spelling. There are also increasing numbers of forms such as *whodunnit*, *showbiz*, *dontcha* and *stunna* gaining currency. Whether these phonetic formations will eventually supplant the traditional conventions remains to be seen. However, the general trend in the modern development of the language has undoubtedly been in the direction of simplicity, and it is therefore likely that conventional spelling will follow suit. One should also note that there is an 'age separation' in this matter: teenagers and youngsters will often use forms like *thanx* and *howzit*. This was not the case a few decades ago.

American English has always been more hospitable to abbreviations than British English: abbreviations which have become current there in recent decades are *condo* for *condominium*, *rehab* for *rehabilitation*, *phenom* for *phenomenon*, *preemie* for *premature baby*, *promo* for *promotion* and *ex* for *ex-husband/wife*.

Conflations

Conflations are words generated by running together two or more forms, such as *ginormous* from *gigantic* and *enormous*, *fantabulous* from *fantastic* and *fabulous*, and *horrendous* from *horrific* and *tremendous*. They are slightly self-conscious vogue words. Another category is the lower-register rendition of colloquial speech, such as *innit?* from *isn't it?*, *helluva* from *hell of a* and *wannabe*, originally 'want to be', but now meaning 'an aspirant' as in 'a wannabe Madonna/Maradona', etc.

Portmanteaux

Lewis Carroll has the unusual distinction of creating an original category of word-formation, and adding a notable descriptive term to the vocabulary of English word-making, namely *portmanteau*. In *Through the Looking Glass* (first published in 1872) chapter 6, Humpty Dumpty explains to Alice some of the curious (or, in Carroll's coinage, 'curiouser') words found in the celebrated nonsense poem 'Jabberwocky': 'Well, "*slithy*" means "lithe" and "slimy." "Lithe" means the same as "active." You see it's like a portmanteau – there are two meanings packed up into one word.'[7] Carroll's portmanteau was thus a metaphorical extension of the portmanteau trunk (used for carrying clothes) which opens out into two halves. More technically, the portmanteau is a compound word in which both elements are incomplete or truncated.

Carroll's own portmanteaux were typically whimsical: in addition to *slithy* they included *mimsy* (assumed to be 'flimsy' and 'miserable') and *burble*, which Carroll explained in a letter, comprised *bleat*, *murmur* and *warble*, although the word is recorded from the fourteenth century, applied to water in the sense of 'to flow with a bubbling sound'. However, the most durable has proved to be *chortle* ('chuckle' with 'snort' in the middle). From these slight beginnings, numerous portmanteaux have sprung into existence. One of the first, coined in the 1890s as university slang, was the combination of *breakfast* and *lunch* into *brunch*. The great growth area has been in brand names or advertising counters, such as *ergonomic, hydrolastic* and *instamatic* which offer an attractive blend of apparent technological sophistication and mystification. In recent years we have seen similar creations in the form of *camcorder*, 'video camera' plus 'recorder', *advertorial* 'advertisement' in the guise of 'editorial material', *quasar, sensurround, sitcom* and *squarial*. The development of science-fiction creatures which are part human and part machine has generated *cyborg*, 'cybernetic' plus 'organsim' and *bionic*.

Although many portmanteaux have become a form of useful shorthand, some are made up of confusing and opposing elements, like *infotainment, edutainment, affluenza* and *infomercial*, so that their true meaning is not clear. Another recent exmaple in this category is *coopetition*, a mixture of *cooperation* and *competition*. But which way does the balance incline? The same problem is apparent in *stagflation*, a blend of *stagnation* and *inflation*.

Approximate portmanteaux (in which one element is complete) are *breathalyser, pantihose, cineplex, gorillagram, guestimate, identikit, sexploitation, televangelist, transputer, glitterati* and *youthquake*. As this list partly indicates, portmanteaux tend to grow in greater numbers in American usage: the collection *Fifty Years Among the New Words* (edited by John Algeo) lists hundreds of these forms, some quite familiar, such as *gasahol, slumlord, aerobat* and *simulcast*, but many which are more ingenious than practical, such as *gazunder* (*gazump + under*), *robomb* (*robot + bomb*), *radiobotage*, (*radio + sabotage*), *dramedy* *drama + comedy*), *plench* (*pliers + wrench*, *tenigue* (*tension + fatigue*) and *turkeyfurter* (turkey + frankfurter).

Political developments generate variations on a particular term. Thus *Watergate*, the name of a building in Washington which was the centre of a spying scandal in American politics in 1972, subsequently produced many forms, including *Waterbungler, Watergoof, Waterbugger* and *Waterfallout* (all listed in the Algeo collection). The suffix *-gate* then became an effective innuendo implying political irregularity or intrigue, generating *Oilgate* and *Muldergate* in 1978, *Cartergate* in 1980, *Irangate* in 1986, *Whitewatergate* in 1996 and *Monicagate* in 1998. The development of the European Community has produced even more forms, including *Eurocrat, Europarliament, Eurosceptic, Europessimism* and *Eurotunnel*. This will continue to be an obvious growth area. Less fertile, but effectively ironic formations are *Cocacolanization*, a term criticizing the wholesale assumption of American values, and *californication*, an equally hostile term rejecting urban sprawl and gross consumerism.

Several terms have yielded pseudo-suffixes. As *marathon* has become a more general-pupose term for anything taking a long time, so terms like *walkathon, spellathon, telethon* and *workathon* have been generated. Likewise *cavalcade* has produced *motorcade, aquacade* and even *aerocade*. An interesting variation has been the formation of *workaholic, chocoholic* and *shopaholic* from the base term *alcoholic*. The root is, of course, *alcohol*, but through ignorance of the etymology and wrong division, the form '-oholic' has acquired the associated meaning of 'addiction' and been added to *work, chocolate, shop* and so on.

All of these terms have been coined in the last thirty years, which gives some idea of the prevalence of portmanteaux. The compact, shorthand effect is pleasing to some (and suitably symbolic in, say, American forms such as *thruway*). But the element of play, at which Lewis Carroll excelled, is never far away. In recent years his own original term, *portmanteau*, has been superseded in many textbooks by **blend**.

Acronyms

An acronym is an abbreviation made up from the initials of other words and pronounced as a new word, Greek *akros* meaning in this instance 'high', referring to the capital letters usually employed. Although we now regard forms like NATO (for North Atlantic Treaty Organization) as common, the term *acronym* seems first to have been recorded in the journal *American Notes and Queries* only in 1943. Four years later acronyms were being referred to as 'Tomorrow's English', a prediction which even then was coming true.

The first acronym in English was *cabal*, a historical curiosity. At a time of intense political intrigue during the reign of Charles II, the term was used as a coded reference to a powerful political clique which operated secretly, a sense related to the word's ultimate roots in Hebrew *cabbala* and *cabbalistic*. The contemporary acronym was made up of the initials of the names of those who made up the clique: Clifford, Ashley, Buckingham, Arlington and Lauderdale. However, they were not the only members of the clique and they were not completely united in policy. Furthermore, the acronym shows that their identity was not secret. Nevertheless, *cabal* continues to have a thriving history.

Many common names for technical innovations are made up of acronyms, as can be seen from the following brief list:

radar	1941	*radio detection and ranging*
laser	1960	*light amplification by stimulated emission of radiation*
flak	1938	*Flieger abwehr kanone* ('anti-aircraft gun')
scuba	1952	*Self-Contained Underwater Breathing Apparatus*

Acronyms have become widely used as political and organizational names for a number of reasons. Many are simply useful abbreviations, such as UNESCO for 'United Nations Educational, Scientific and Cultural Organizaton' and *quango* for '*quasi* non-government organization'. However, political organizations have long realized the advantage of having a name which is compact and capitalized, such as SWAPO, 'South West African People's Organization'. In some cases the acronyms encode a name, for example, GESTAPO for *Geheim Statse Polizei*, or State Secret Police. This gives them an institutional force. It sems no accident that the secret services of many nations have such abbreviated code names: M15, NKVD, FBI, CIA, Politburo, Ogpu, Okhrana and KGB. For, as George Orwell shrewdly pointed out in *Nineteen Eighty-Four*, by abbreviating a name, one narrowed and subtly altered its meaning, by cutting out most of the associations which would otherwise cling to it'. He continued with this telling example:

> The words *Communist International*, for instance, call up a composite picture of universal human brotherhood, red flags, barricades, Karl Marx and the Paris Commune. The word *Comintern*, on the other hand, suggests merely a tightly-knit organization and a well-defined body of doctrine. . . . *Comintern* is a word which can be uttered almost without taking thought, whereas *Communist International* is a phrase over which one is obliged to linger at least momentarily. (1972 edition, pp. 247–8)

In recent decades acronyms have increasingly been devised with radical and arresting names designed as slogans to rally support for a cause. Examples are SCUM, 'The Society for Cutting up Men', DUMP, 'Disposal of Unused Medicines and Pills' and NOW, 'National Organization of Women'. The *Oxford Companion to the English Language* (edited by Tom McArthur, 1992) has an amusing section on creative acronyms:

> In 1987, during the compiling of the second edition of the *OED*, a system was created for examining and correcting text on computer screen. It was called *Oxford English Dictionary Integration, Proofing and Updating System*, partly so that it could be shortened to *OEDIPUS*. However, to avoid the kind of retribution inflicted on the original Oedipus, the editors called it *OEDIPUS LEX*. (p. 13)

Related to acronyms are **initialisms**, in which the terms abbreviating some word or phrase are treated as a new word. The initialism which has shown the most spectacular lexical and semantic growth is *OK*. There are many conflicting explanations for the origin of the form, which appeared quite suddenly in America in 1839. From being an expression of approval, the form rapidly expanded across the globe, often in the phonetic version *okay*, so that it can now be used as verb, adjective, adverb, indeed virtually any part of speech. Similar initialisms are *a.s.a.p.* ('as soon as possible'), *p.d.q.* ('pretty damn quick"), and (used by an earlier generation) *b.f.* ('bloody fool'). The euphemism seen in these last two examples sometimes extends to more coded usage amongst particular sections of the speech community. Thus *o.t.t.* is a generally upper-class initialism for 'over the top', an extension from theatre parlance to mean extreme or exhibitionist behaviour. More cliquish in its currency is *n.q.o.o.u* for 'not quite one of us'.

In recent decades there has been an enormous growth of these lexical types: the *Acronyms Initialisms and Abbreviations Dictionary* published by the Gale Research Company of Detroit contained more than 400,000 items in its eleventh edition (1987).

Diminutives

In this section we shall see that many suffixes originally indicating diminutives have greatly broadened in meaning, become all-purpose. The traditional markers of diminution are the suffixes *-ling* and *-let*, producing the forms *duckling, nestling, twinkling* and *booklet, circlet* and *streamlet* respectively. More recent are the endings *-ie* or *-y* (technically termed a 'hypocoristic suffix') added in words like *baby, daddy, puppy* and *laddy*, and the French-derived suffix *-ette* found in *cigarette, novelette* and *laundrette*.

The *-ling* forms are the oldest, found in Anglo-Saxon *earthling* (resuscitated in science fiction) and *hireling*. As one can see, these are not strictly diminutives, but in the course of Middle English the suffix became widely used to refer to the young of animals, as in *gosling, fledgling* and *fingerling* (a young salmon). However, by Early Middle English the suffix was being used in a derogatory fashion in forms like *fondling, weakling, underling* and *princeling*. Although *darling* means literally 'little dear', it provides a useful link between diminutives and affection, found in many forms like *sweetie, ducky, lovey-dovey* and *poppet*. The *-ette* suffix has expanded from strict diminutives, such as *dinette* and *kitchenette*, to a feminine denotation, most notably in *suffragette* (1906), *usherette, hackette* and *majorette*.

Perhaps the fastest-growing variety of diminiutives is the *-ie* form, used informally in *ciggie* for *cigarette, seccie* for *second*, as well as *veggie, cookie* and *brownie*. This feature is found in most varieties of global English: in American English *preemie* for *premature baby*, in South African and Australian English *cossie* for *swimming costume*, in Liverpudlian *sarney* and Lancashire *butty* for *sandwich*, as well as in Australian English *tinnie* or *frostie* for 'beer can' and *postie* for *postman*. The suffix is also used to indicate origin, as in *Yankee*, historically one from the North in the American Civil War, *Okie* (from Oklohoma), *Aussie* (from Australia), *Geordie* (from Newcastle), *Vaalie* (from the Transvaal in South Africa).

The suffix -ie has expanded into another area of word-formation, being found in a burgeoning variety of forms for social types, based on the *yuppie* prototype. *Yuppie* was originally an acronym for 'young urban professional' (often interpreted more as 'young upwardly mobile professional' generating the form *yumpie*, which survived only a few years). Coined in 1982, *yuppie* paved the way for many similar forms, such as the following:

yappie:	young affluent parent or young aspiring professional
buppie:	a black yuppie
guppie:	(British) a green yuppie; (American) a gay yuppie
yardie:	a member of a Jamaican or West Indian criminal gang
foodie:	a gourmet or food enthusiast
wrinklie:	(in young people's slang) a middle-aged or older person
crumblie:	(in young people's slang) an old or senile person

In addititon there are two acronyms:

woopie:	'well off older person'
dinkie:	'double income no kids'

As one can see, most of these have no strict diminutive meaning, although the original *yuppie* probably had a sense of 'diminutive contempt' found, for example, in the emotive use of *little*, recorded in the *OED* in senses 8 and 9. Similarly, the last two forms, *wrinklie* and *crumblie* also have the associated sense of 'a little old person'.

The -ie suffix, which also indicates affection in forms like *dearie* and *laddie*, has expanded into other semantic areas. These include political affiliation, e.g. *tankie* (a hard-line Communist) and the general forms like *weepie* for a maudlin or 'tear-jerking' film, *charlie* for 'a fool'.

Mainly in 'U' parlance are a number of forms with similar pronunciation, but differing spellings, e.g. *stiffy* for an engraved invitation card, *pressie* for 'present' and *soggies* for 'breakfast cereal'. Adjectival forms abound, such as *crummy, cushy, grotty, kinky, weedy, tatty, scruffy, shitty, shabby, dowdy, iffy, mingy, pokey, poncey, ropey, wobbly* and so on, not all of them clearly derived from a noun. Some of these are surprisingly old: *shabby*, derived from an obsolete verb *to shab*, meaning 'to cheat', has overcome the criticism by Dr Johnson as 'a word which has crept into conversation and low writing, but ought not to be admitted into the language'. Reduplicating relatives are *hanky-panky* and *hoity-toity*.

We can see that modern and contemporary English has clearly been more influenced by media interests, commercial and political forces than by literary innovation. However, as the last section has shown, many new lexical forms have derived from a general 'user-driven' impulse to make words simpler, shorter, more flexible and, dare one say it, more fun to use.

Notes

1 Stephen Potter's study, *The Muse in Chains* (1937), gives an acerbic account of the vexatious establishment of the Oxford English school. The jibe about Harriet refers to Shelley's unfortunate first wife, who committed suicide in 1816.
2 A fuller history of journalism is given in chapter 5 of my study, *Words in Time* (1988).
3 C. H. Rolph edited an interesting account, *The Trial of Lady Chatterley* (Harmondsworth, 1961).
4 It is a measure of Orwell's influence that the term *Orwellian* is recorded from 1950, the year after the publication of *Nineteen Eighty-Four*. In that year Mary McCarthy used the term in its dystopic sense, referring to 'the Orwellian future', while in 1952 *The Times* used the term in the sense of semantic substitution, alluding to 'two ugly Orwellian names'.
5 There is fuller discussion of the etymology (and pseudo-etymologies) of *woman* in chapter 1, pp. 25–6.
6 Among the important contributions to this controversy are Dale Spender, *Man Made Language* (London, 1980) and the review by Maria Black and Rosalind Coward in Deborah Cameron (ed.), *The Feminist Critique of Language* (London, 1990).
7 Readers wishing to appreciate Carroll's semantic and philosophical subtleties will be asssisted by Martin Gardner's edition, *The Annotated Alice* (Harmondsworth, 1965).

8

CHANGES IN LEXICAL STRUCTURE

The great energies of the language now enter into play outside England...
African English, Australian English, the rich speech of West Indian and Anglo-
Indian writers, represent a complicated polycentric field of linguistic force, in which
the language taught and written on this island is no longer the inevitable authority or
focus.

George Steiner, in the *Listener* (21 October 1965)

One cannot strictly write a 'conclusion' to the lexical history of a vital and changing social medium such as the English language, as one could for Latin. New words and new varieties keep appearing in current usage: *Monicagate* and *Billspeak* were just two neologisms which surfaced as this work was being written. Accordingly, this concluding chapter will identify some general trends which have occurred over the past thousand years or so; it will consider how the lexical structure of the language has changed, especially in relation to global borrowings, and will undertake a lexicological study of some major word-fields. After considering a workable definition of the core using current corpora, it will make some speculations about the future of the language in the light of present developments.

Broadly speaking, it would appear that from the time that the different dialects of English were brought to England, from the fifth century until the Norman Conquest, a period of some five centuries, the language changed comparatively slowly. One might note in this respect Bruce Mitchell's observation that 'the material changes which took place from the fifth to the eleventh century were far less dramatic and far less fundamental than those which have occurred since 1900' (1995, p. ix). Clearly we are reliant for such views on manuscript evidence, which is fragmentary and subject to the arbitrary accidents of survival. From the Norman Conquest to the lifetime of Shakespeare (1564–1616) the language changed very greatly in its lexis and its other components. By the end of the eighteenth century a clearly recognizable form of Standard English had been achieved, largely as a consequence of the influence of Dr Johnson's *Dictionary* (1755) and a number of successful prescriptive grammar books. These established a very powerful normative tradition which was strengthened by the discrediting of regional forms, which started to erode. In the half-century which has elapsed since the end of World War II, the language has undergone another period of rapid change. Incidentally, this period is demarcated 'World English' in David Graddol's study *The Future of English?* (1997, p. 7).

As we have seen, there are a number of factors accelerating this change. With the founding of the various English-speaking communities in the colonies, other varieties started to emerge and influence the mother tongue. Other forms have also started to assert themselves in their own regions. The consequence is that although there may be a worldwide Standard Educated English, the *koiné* or common language of scholars and journalists, great numbers of Englishes are emerging. Whereas in the past these varieties were distinguished largely on the phonetic basis of accent, now the whole range of linguistic aspects is more apparent.

As we saw in the previous chapter, over the past century or so another notion of variety has developed, that of mediated English. This has attained a currency in certain sectors of the press or broadcast media, although it is not really used by individuals in their various speech communities. Thus, whereas there was little difference between the style Dr Johnson used in an essay in *The Rambler* and in a personal letter (or even in his conversation, as reported by his biographer, James Boswell) there is now virtually no similarity between the style used by, say, an editor's writing in the popular press and in his personal letters. For example, such a person would be unlikely to write a personal communication, except in parody, in the following vein:

> The mother of all eyeball-to-eyeballs is exploding in the office over the shock horror sensation of the Clinton-Lewinsky romps in the Oval Office. The get-tough gang says 'Go for the jugular and rubbish him,' while the Old Guard wants a clamp on the dirt, insisting that our organ should be trumpeting family values. Dontchalovem! Scribes, hackettes and lensmen are all agog.

Furthermore, there is more similarity between the language used by the tabloid and the popular press worldwide, and in the network idiom of radio and television announcers in Britain and America, than there is between individuals in their various speech communities. Later in the chapter we shall return to these topics, but let us now turn to our main theme, that of lexical change.

Changes in the Core

In seeking to define and characterize the lexis of Modern English we are aware that the categories used by Murray are no longer simple or entirely fitting. It is appropriate, however, to start with his definition of the core: 'a nucleus or central mass of many thousand words whose "Anglicity" is unquestioned; they are the *Common Words* of the language.' This notion is still clearly true, but as the history of the English-speaking peoples has evolved, so there have been shifts in the political balance of power within the Anglophone group.

The increasing competition of regional varieties has meant that the notion of 'Standard English' has necessarily been revised. The relationship between the mother tongue and the Commonwealth varieties has changed, but remains complex and controversial. Certainly the most significant development has been the change in the dynamic of coexistence between English usage in the British Isles and in the United States. The views expressed in chapter 6 by Noah Webster, Mark Twain and H. L. Mencken are apposite here. This crucial change has inevitably had effects on the character of the lexical core.

Up to the middle of the twentieth century, discussions tended to focus on points of lexical and semantic difference, such as *pavement/sidewalk, boot/trunk, waistcoat/vest* and *dinner jacket/tuxedo*. A useful study in this respect is *British and American English since 1900* by Eric Partridge and John W. Clark (1951). In his prefatory remarks Partridge commented in a slightly defensive and reproving fashion: 'what right had I to ignore, as so many philologists throughout the British Empire have so long and successfully ignored, that branch of English which is spoken in the United States of America? Numerically considered in terms of its users, American English is more important than British English' (1951, p. 1). In the last two decades the balance of power between what are increasingly termed 'British English' and 'American English' has shifted markedly in favour of the American variety. This is, no doubt, a reflection of Britain's retreat from Empire and America's expanding geopolitical dominance, especially manifest in the growth of the Cable News Network (CNN) and what is sometimes termed 'cultural imperialism', notable in the forms of global popular culture generated by the scriptwriters of popular Hollywood films, television soap operas and sitcoms.

This influence can be simply demonstrated by the semantic pairings of the following base words, which show the increasing acceptance of the US forms and meanings (given first): *can/tin; mail/post; mad/angry; store/shop; hi!/hello!; fight/quarrel; moan/criticize* or *complain; pants/trousers; trailer/caravan*. In addition, there is the widespread adoption in the United Kingdom of such distinctive American idioms as *a whole new ball game, a ball park* (figure), a *stand-off, up-front, off the wall*, and the acceptance of *OK/okay* as any part of speech: *OK!*, *it's OK, he okayed the contract, he's an OK fellow, the car went OK*. The American tendency to prefer abstractions (noted by Tocqueville a century and a half ago) is apparent in the widespread use of terms like *facility* (as in 'mobile life-support facility' for *ambulance*) as well as *capability, utility, medication, relocation, finalization, affirmative* and *concertize*. The contrary tendency, of preferring low-register compounds, is apparent in the following examples (taken from BBC World Service broadcasts): 'the *long-running* [instead of *protracted*] dispute'; 'the *one-time* [instead of *previous*] mayor of New York'; 'the *pull-back* [instead of *withdrawal*] of troops from the Gulf'; 'the Israeli delegation failed to *show up* [instead of *arrive*].' Other uses of American idiom by the BBC are 'Mikail Gorbachev's *roller-coaster* trip through China' and 'Mrs Thatcher is accused of *railroading* policies through Parliament.' Also expanding in currency is the form of the subjunctive common in America, as in 'She asked that she not be identified' or 'We require that he leave immediately.' Interestingly, Simeon Potter noted as long ago as 1950 'the revival of the subjunctive . . . in America' (1963, p. 170).

How can we measure this shift in the centre of gravity in lexical fields? As we saw in chapter 5, the main new tool of lexicography and lexical analysis is the use of the corpus, the computerized body of words which can be used to analyse word-frequencies. Since the development of corpora is fairly recent, one cannot make valid comparisons over shifts in the past few decades. However, by analysing the treatment of central lexical items by the same dictionaries through different editions, it is possible to trace some important shifts.

Let us accordingly bring into play three editions of the *Longman Dictionary of Contemporary English (LDOCE)*. The first edition of the *LDOCE* (1303 pages) came out in 1978; the second (1229 pages) appeared in 1987 and the third (1668 pages) was published in 1995. The main innovations of the third edition were the use of the British National Corpus and the Longman Lancaster Corpus of British and American Speech, and the rating of words as being amongst the most frequently used in speech or writing. They were tagged by 'S' for 'Spoken' and 'W' for 'Written', followed by a figure indicating their frequency. Thus *alone* is tagged 'S2 W1', showing that it is among the 2000 most frequently spoken words but (interestingly) among the 1000 most frequently written words.

However, as Della Summers, the Director of Longman Dictionaries, commented (in a letter to the writer): 'There was considerable manual (or one could say intellectual!) intervention. It is amazing how raw basic frequency data actually is.' She cited a curious instance of using unedited data which resulted in another corpus rating *don* as one of the 700 most common words in English. This error probably arose from the name Don being included in the general frequency data.

Thus the database of a corpus clearly predetermines its findings. This is shown in the *LDOCE* treatment of American *ass* in relation to British *arse*. *LDOCE1* marked *ass* as 'Am E, taboo slang', while *LDOCE2* simply noted 'AmE for arse'. However *LDOCE3* tags *ass* as 'S2', i.e. among the 2000 most frequently spoken words, while the traditional British term *arse* does not merit any such rating. This is somewhat surprising from a British perspective, since it is hardly true of British speech. Likewise *pants* was defined in *LDOCE1* and *LDOCE2* as '1. BrE for "panties" or "underpants" 2. esp. AmE trousers', while *LDOCE3* rates *pants* as 'S3' and gives the American definition first, together with a graph showing the relative uses of both terms in both corpora. Similarly, both *shop* and *store* are rated 'S1 W1' by *LDOCE3*, whereas the British usage was given primacy in *LDOCE2*. Perhaps the most dramatic moves have been recorded by *buck* in the sense of 'money' and *call* in the sense of 'to telephone'. Both were marked 'esp. AmE' in *LDOCE1* and *LDOCE2*, but are rated 'S1' by *LDOCE3*. *Horny*, a distinctively American term meaning 'sexually excited', is not marked as such in *LDOCE3*.

The rapid assimilation of American forms reflects a notable change in the general attitude of English usage in the past century towards foreign words and idioms. Much greater acceptance now prevails, having superseded traditional attitudes of linguistic chauvinism and xenophobia. While the American influence is clearly predominant, the modern English vocabulary now reflects its worldwide usage much more clearly than previously. See, in this respect, David Crystal's comments in his recent study, *English as a Global Language* (1998, p. 138). Equally, English vocabulary continues to be borrowed wholesale by foreign languages.

Global Borrowings

As we have seen in previous chapters, Modern English has developed an almost omnivorous capacity to absorb words from exotic and alien sources, readily assimilating thousands of new and exotic words from all corners of the globe and from all levels of usage. A century ago this was not the case, foreign words being regarded with suspicion and colloquial usage being eschewed. Even a few decades ago letters to editors complaining of importations from America like *gimmick* and *schedule* appeared regularly in newspaper columns.

A typical instance signalling the shift is *mafia*, which was marked 'alien' in the original *OED* and given an entirely Italian/Sicilian definition. But that was nearly a century ago: today it is a common term so completely assimilated that it is applied to English cabals such as 'the Etonian/Foreign Office mafia'. There is even a humorous Welsh extension to *Taffia*. Two other assimilated terms from Italy are *ghetto* (originally the district in Venice which in medieval times was the centre of iron foundries, largely populated by Jews) and *paparazzi*, the plural of a word in the Umbrian dialect for a clam, metaphoricaly alluding to the opening and closing of photographers' shutters: its spread is largely owing to Frederico Fellini's filmic depiction of invasive photographers in *La Dolce Vita* (1959).

Today new words are no longer regarded as *parvenus* with suspicious backgrounds; they are fashionable.[1] They have the status, albeit ambiguous, of *buzz-words*. In 1953, when Paul S. Berg published his *Dictionary of New Words*, his fourteen-page introduction had a slightly apologetic air. As he charmingly put it, 'I suffered what I suppose must be the fate of all word-collectors: my hobby-horse ran away with me' (p. 5). Nowadays dictionaries of new words appear almost annually, and their *raison d'être* is assumed to be self-evident: their editors are more likely to be apologetic for not keeping up with the flood of neologisms. The principal recent collections are the *Longman Guardian New Words* (edited by Simon Mort, Longmans, 1986); *New Words*, edited by Jonathon Green (Bloomsbury, 1991); *The Oxford Dictionary of New Words* (edited by Sarah Tulloch (1992, revised edition edited by Elizabeth Knowles 1995), the three *Oxford Additions* volumes (edited by E. S. C. Weiner et al., 1993–), *Trashcash, Fizzbos and Flatliners* (edited by Sid Lerner, Gary S. Belkin et al., 1993) and *A Glossary for the 90s* (1998), by David Rowan.

Berg's collection contained about 2500 words, Mort's 'about 1000 words', Green's 'about 2000', Tulloch's also 'about 2000', the *Oxford Additions* 'about 3000' each and the last two about 1000 each. (The curious terms used in the title *Trashcash, Fizzbos and Flatliners* refer repectively to 'simulated money used in advertisements', an abbreviation of FSBO, i.e. 'for sale by owner', and 'a person who is dead' i.e. whose ECG graph is a flat line. The first edition of the Oxford new words collection used eleven icons indicating the provenance or area of origin of the terms, i.e. drugs, environment, business, health and fitness, lifestyle and leisure, music, politics, people and society, science and technology, war and weaponry, and youth culture. The second edition made a few significant modifications: it dropped the categories of 'war and weaponry' and 'drugs', but added 'arts and music' and 'computing', and changed 'youth culture' to 'popular culture'. The American collection used different categories, namely abbreviations, arts and entertainment, business and finance, causes and movements, computers, criminal and legal, environment, food and drink, health and medicine, international affairs, language, lifestyle and leisure, management marketing and organization, media, military, new products and services, politics, science and sports. Rowan dispenses with alphabetical order, collecting the words under similar headings.

These categories partly answer the questions: Why is there a need for new words? Where do they come from? What is their function? The need for neologisms derives from various motives. Certain fields of activity strive to maintain a sense of innovation: consequently they advertise themselves by means of a constant flow of neologisms. The world of fashion is the most obvious, drawing on a diversity of terms for new (or supposedly new) items. Hence *blouson, bustier, gilet, tanga* (previously *g-string*) and the like. Often items come back into fashion, but under different names: in Elizabethan times very fashionable women's shoes with high soles made of cork were called *chopines*; today they have come back into fashion, but are called *platforms*. Occasionally old terms, like medieval *tabard* and Algerian *zouave*, come to be recycled.

Another innovative field is that of computer technology, which has borrowed words like *file, icon, menu, mouse, programme, cut, paste* and *virus*, but has made up others like *mainframe, upload, online* and *input*. The *Longman Guardian* collection points out that 'the wealth of computer vocabulary which appeared in the principal dictionaries in the later 1960s (and which is now in extremely common usage) was largely coined towards the end of the 1940s' (1986, p. v). Even traditional areas of activity are enriched by neologisms: in this century we have seen the word-field of politics grow with the borrowing of terms like *apparatchik, apartheid, éminence grise, fatwa, jihad, dirigisme, perestroika, glasnost* and *revanchism*.

These copious borrowings suggest that the essential structure of the vocabulary of English has changed. Having been in origin a pure Germanic language, English had acquired by the Renaissance great lexical influxes of French, Latin and Greek. As we have seen, this tripartite arrangement of register has become a dominant feature of the lexis. However, specialized word-stocks have also been absorbed to define different activities. The basic terminologies of heraldry, fencing and ballet all come from French. Much of the lexis of music and virtually all that defining opera comes from Italian. Furthermore, as English has spread all over the world in the subsequent centuries, it has absorbed numbers of terms from outposts, so that it now has a heterogeneous word-stock. Consider the following narrative:

> When the blizzard started, we put on our parkas and balaclavas, had some whisky, and started to manoeuvre the yacht through the mammoth ice floes. We eventually made landfall, but our euphoria at being on *terra firma* was short-lived. As we were trekking across the tundra looking for a place to bivouac, a horde of bandits confronted us demanding cash. They ransacked our rucksacks. One of the thugs went berserk and we were scared that they might all run amok when they found nothing with which to traffick but bananas, chocolate and the alcohol.

This account (admittedy quite highly coloured) contains twenty-five words (or 27 per cent) from exotic or alien sources. Some sense of the scale of these borrowings can be gauged from the following list, which aims to be select, avoiding the merely 'exotic' and local, focusing on general words which have come into the mainstream of English:

African languages:	bundu, fundi, gnu, mumbo-jumbo, zebra
Afrikaans:	apartheid, commandeer, commando, inspan, koppie, trek
American Indian:	caucus, cockroach, hickory, moccasin, moose, mugwump, racoon, skunk, squash, toboggan
Arabic:	admiral, alcohol, algebra, alkali, amber, assassin, carafe, cipher, garble, ghoul, harem, hashish, kaffir, lackey, mask, mattress, monsoon, mosque, nadir, racket, saracen, sheikh, sofa, syrup, tabby, talc, tariff, tartar, zenith, zero
Australian:	aborigine, boomerang, walkabout
Caribbean:	buccaneer, canoe, guava, hurricane, reggae
Chinese:	chin-chin, chop-chop, ginseng, junk, kaolin, ketchup, kow-tow, litchi, tea, typhoon, wok, yen, zen
Czech:	gherkin, polka, robot, sable, vampire
Danish:	floe, jib
Dutch, *Flemish* and *Low German*:	brandy, cookie, drum, easel, grime, hunk, landscape, runt, skipper, sloop, smack, smuggle, yacht
Egyptian:	ammonia, labyrinth, oasis, sack
Eskimo/Inuit:	anorak, husky, igloo, parka
Finnish:	mink, sauna
French:	bastard, bigot, bizarre, blond, blouse, buffoon, charade, cry, debonair, disease, fashion, finish, fruit, garage, guillotine, lozenge, mediocre, moustache, patrol, police, restaurant, riot, silhouette, sobriquet, table, university, void
Gaelic	(General): bard, bog, brock, cairn, crag, dad, druid, galore, mog, shanty, whisk(e)y (Irish): banshee, blarney, brogue, colleen, leprechaun, shebeen, slogan, Tory (Scottish): caber, clan, glen, loch, plaid, trousers

	(Welsh): bug, coracle, cwm, eisteddfod, flannel, hwyl
German:	angst, blitz, flak, gimmick, gestalt, hamster, paraffin, poodle, rucksack, snorkel, strafe, waltz, yodel, zeppelin, zither
Greek:	analysis, biology, coma, crisis, diagram, dogma, euphoria, graph, hypothesis, hysteria, lexicon, mathematics, method, neurosis, problem, pylon, schizophrenia, science, stigma
Hawaiian:	aloha, hula, ukelele
Hebrew:	alleluia, camel, cherub, ethnic, jubilee, kibbutz, kosher, messiah, myrrh, paradise, pharaoh, rabbi, shibboleth
Hindi:	basmati, blighty, bungalow, chintz, choky, chutney, dinghy, dungaree, guru, kedgeree, loot, memsahib, pundit, raj, sari, sahib, shampoo, shawl, swami, thug, verandah, wallah
Hindustani:	bandana, bangle, bazaar, cushy, dekko, gymkhana, saffron
Other Indian languages:	chukka, polo
Hungarian:	goulash, hussar, paprika, sabre, tokay
Icelandic:	berserk, geyser, saga
Italian:	arcade, balcony, ballot, bandit, bravo, cameo, diva, fascist, fiasco, ghetto, jeans, lava, mafia, magenta, millinery, ninny, opera, paparazzi, piano, pizza, scampi, sonnet, soprano, timpani, traffic, volt, zany
Japanese:	bonsai, futon, haiku, hari kiri, honcho, judo, kamikaze, karate, kimono, mikado, sake, samurai, seppuku, soy, sushi, tofu, tycoon
Lithuanian:	birch, eland
Malagasy:	raffia
Malay:	amok, bamboo, caddy, gingham, gong, orang utan, prang, teak
Maori New Zealand:	haka, whakapohane, kia ora, kiwi, maori, pakeha
Mexican Indian:	avocado, cacao, chocolate, tomato
Norwegian:	fjord, lemming, ski, slalom
Persian:	arsenic, ayatollah, backsheesh, bazaar, caravan, cummerbund, khaki, lilac, pistachio, pilaf, pyjamas, shawl, sherbet, sofa, talc, talisman

Polish:	mazurka, polka, polonaise
Portuguese:	buffalo, caste, flamingo, marmalade, pagoda, palaver, pickaninny, port
Quechuan/Peruvian:	alpaca, guano, llama, pampas, quinine
Russian:	bistro, cossack, czar, disinformation, glasnost, horde, intelligentsia, kalashnikov, mammoth, molotov, perestroika, rouble, sputnik, steppe, vodka
Sanskrit:	candy, cheetah, indigo, juggernaut, jungle, jute, karma, pundit, swastika, yoga
Scots:	burn, canny, cosy, eerie, gumption, pony, raid, rampage, uncanny, wee, weird
Spanish:	banana, cannibal, canyon, cafeteria, capsize, cash, cigar, cockroach, cork, junta, machismo, macho, marijuana, patio, potato, rodeo, sherry, siesta, stampede, stevedore, supremo, tacos, tobacco, tomato, tortilla
Swahili:	bwana, safari, uhuru
Swedish:	gauntlet, ombudsman, slag, tungsten, weld
Swiss:	bivouac, chalet, chamois, muesli
Tahitian:	tattoo
Tamil:	catamaran, cheroot, coolie, mango, mulligatawny, pariah
Tibetan:	sherpa, yak, yeti
Tongan:	taboo
Turkish:	bosh, caftan, caviare, coffee, divan, fez, hummus, kiosk, scarlet, seraglio, sorbet, turban, yoghurt
Yiddish:	bagel, chutzpah, glitzy, kibbutz, kibosh, kosher, kugel, schmaltz, schlemiel, schlep, schlock, schmooze, schmuck, shemozzle, yenta

Word origins are not simple. While some terms like *sputnik* and *ombudsman* have clear origins, many have more complex sources. Borrowings such as these have often grown up in remote languages and then been brought into English by a 'carrier language' such as Portuguese, Spanish or French, used by the early European explorers and colonists. Such is the case of *verandah*, from Hindi *varanda*, brought into English via Portuguese.

Furthermore, within language families there are root stocks and subsequent growths. We noted in chapter 1 (p. 14) how Latin *discus* has given rise to *dish*, *desk*, *disc* and of course, *discus*. Many words in Hindi, Hindustani and the other Indian languages originate in Sanskrit, but often with different forms and meanings. Thus *juggernaut* derives its main sense in English from Hindi *jagannath*, but the ultimate root is in Sanskrit, *Jagannath*, the title of the god Krishna, derived from *Jagat* 'world' and *nathas* 'conqueror'. Similarly, English *pyjamas* derives from a compound in both Persian and Urdu meaning 'foot clothing', originally referring to loose drawers, while *khaki* originally meant 'dusty' or 'dust-coloured' in both these languages, before being applied to the material for uniforms.

This range covers, of course, only a fraction of the whole lexis, but the words are common. (It does not include the considerable and increasing degree of borrowing from American English, discussed in the previous chapter.) Many of the terms are simply witness words, i.e. names of things, and as such have no great cultural significance. In this respect we might consider the huge difference between *taboo* and *tattoo*, or that between *swastika* and *cheetah*, *ombudsman* and *bonsai*, *caucus* and *moccasin*. However, we noted at the end of chapter 6 that many of the new terms of status (*mugwump*, *tycoon*, etc.) have exotic origins. Assimilation depends on cultural familiarity: Japanese *karaoke* (literally 'empty orchestra') has 'caught on' in the West, but *karoshi* ('death from overwork') has not. Furthermore, the student will have noticed that while the majority of these words have remained static referential 'guest words', a few, such as *cash*, *loot* and *blitz* have become assimilated as loan words with new independent senses and functions, e.g. *cash-strapped*, *cash cow*, *blitzed*, *looter* and *looting*.

Most of the listed words are familiar to well-read people, who perceive that they are exotic words. But among recent borrowings there are many others with very uncharacteristic alien forms, such as *wa*, *gizmo*, *zap*, *skronk*, *sochu*, *zein*, *juku* and *zup*. By 'uncharacteristic alien forms', one means words that have unusual arrangements of vowels, such as final *-a*, *-i*, *-o* and *-u*. For example *narbo*, *dolo* and *Bubba*, as well as those which start or end with consonants which are rare in English, such as 'x' or 'z', for example *zein*, *zouk* and *zap*. Some of these words, like *gizmo*, 'an appliance', have gained currency, but most remain on the fringe, although all are listed in the American collection *Trashcash, Fizzbos and Flatliners* (1993).

However, the list not truly to scale. If it were, it would have to include hundreds of words from French, which 'continues to influence the English lexicon more than any other living language' (Millward, 1989, p. 281). Leaving aside such specialist vocabulary as that of culinary terms, much of the lexis of a sophisticated, literary tenor contains French words and phrases, such as *grandeur*, *hauteur*, *longueur*, *douceur*, *cachet*, *oeuvre*, *passé*, *blasé*, *éclaircissement*, *de nos jours*, *sang froid*, *déjà vu*, *avant garde*, *fin de siècle*, *au fait* and the splendid phrase, the *réponse d'escalier*, the witty remark or crushing rejoinder that one thinks of, but only after the event, when going down the stairs. Despite the anti-

Gallic strictures of Dr Johnson, many of these have acquired a thriving currency.

The same point about scale applies to the Greek component, but there is an important difference: words like *antibiotic, cholesterol, vitamin, schizophrenia, television, chlorophyll* and hundreds of modern scientific terms are made up of Greek elements, but they are not in origin Greek words in the way that *panacea, epidemic* and *epilepsy* are. Celia Millward points out the surprising fact that 'The classical vocabulary of English today is larger than the *total* known vocabularies of classical Greek and Latin because English has composed so many "new" Greek and Latin words' (1989, p. 281).

Nevertheless, the list shows that the notion of 'foreign' terms and attitudes towards them has changed. It can be supplemented by figure 8.1, 'Etymological sources of borrowings into English', which is quantitative. We can integrate them into our previous lexical tables of Anglo-Saxon, Norman French and Classical terms which demonstrated the difference of register between *hearty, cordial* and *cardiac* (see chapter 1, p. 15). We could then construct a complete schematic representation of the vocabulary, as in figure 8.2, 'Lexical history and register'. This scheme has the advantage of simplicity and clarity, but the disadvantage of a false equalization of scale, since, as we have seen, very few Celtic words have survived, but great numbers of Anglo-Saxon terms still thrive at the core of the lexis.

Generally speaking, these two schemes bear out the observations on 'Language and Power' at the end of chapter 1. Yet obviously all words do not stay stable over long stretches of time, since some become popular, some marginalized, some specialized, some obsolete, and so on. Thus *clout* in the sense of 'political power' was originally a Chicago term which came to prominence only in the 1964 US Presidential election, while *hump* (to copulate) was an underground slang term back in the eighteenth century. Let us consider a few other cases of mobility between categories:

Regional to common: OK, lorry, clout, bug, trek, weird
Classical to common: animal, area, basic, conversation, environment
Specialized to common: thing, saga, chemistry, stress, mess, stuff, guy
Central to obsolescent: sin, wrath, purity, soul, virginity, honour
Exotic to common: assassin, loot, flak, paparazzi, mafia, ghetto

With these considerations in mind, let us re-examine Murray's diagram of the disposition of registers in English (fig. 1.1, p. 3), which we discussed at the outset of chapter 1. How valid are these categories and this arrangement now, a hundred years after Murray's preface? The basic structure of the circle, with its core of common words and varieties of terms on the periphery, is obviously

Latin:	50,725	Tamil:	82
French:	37,032	Swiss:	65
Greek:	18,675	Hawaiian:	59
German:	12,322	Bengali:	48
Italian:	7,893	Carib:	48
Dutch:	6,286	Swahili:	47
Spanish:	5,795	Czech:	44
Norse:	4,430	Finnish:	42
Swedish:	3,438	Hungarian:	40
Portuguese:	3,130	Romanian:	40
Danish:	3,046	Burmese:	39
Provençal:	2,294	Mexican:	37
Frisian:	2,120	Manx:	37
Norwegian:	1,214	Tibetan:	35
Arabic:	958	Zulu:	33
Sanskrit:	873	Cree:	33
Icelandic:	819	Quechuan/	
Irish:	730	Peruvian:	29
Russian:	615	Bantu:	26
Flemish:	563	Bulgarian:	25
Persian:	536	Albanian:	25
Hebrew:	476	Basque:	24
Hindi:	426	Serbo-Croat:	23
Gaelic:	413	Malagasy:	21
Welsh:	365	Eskimo/Inuit:	21
Japanese:	343	Sicilian:	21
Catalan:	295	Lappish:	17
Chinese:	289	Tswana:	16
Afrikaans:	272	Korean:	12
Turkish:	265	Thai:	9
Malay:	253	Xhosa:	9
Maori:	231	Tahitian:	7
Celtic:	221	Iroquois:	7
Urdu:	210	Vietnamese:	6
Hindustani:	178	Tongan:	6
Yiddish:	133	Hopi:	4
Polish:	127		
Egyptian:	102		
Breton:	102		
Cornish:	95		

Source: *OED 2*

Figure 8.1 Etymological sources of borrowings into English

illuminating. But there would appear to be at least three major new structural factors. First, with the changed relations between British English and American and Commonwealth English, as well as the increasing hospitality to exotic words, how valid is the simple category of 'Foreign'? The discussions in this and the previous chapter suggest a different relationship. Secondly, is there much of a distinction between the categories of 'scientific' and 'technical'? More specifically, is 'scientific' superior to 'technical', as Murray places it?

Period/ Component		Register
Modern	∅∅∅	Mixed Exotic
Greek and Latin	∧∧∧ ΣΣΣΣΣΣΣΣΣΣΣΣΣΣΣΣΣΣΣΣΣΣΣΣΣΣΣΣΣΣΣΣΣΣΣΣΣΣΣΣΣΣΣ	Abstract Learned Technical Scientific
Norman French	ʃʃ	Courtly Refined
Scandinavian	ẚẚẚẚẚẚẚẚẚẚẚẚẚẚẚẚẚẚẚẚẚẚẚẚẚẚẚẚẚẚẚẚẚẚẚẚẚẚẚ	Basic
Latin (religious)	●●●●●●●●●●●●●●●●●●●●●●●●●●●●●●●●●●●●●●●	Common
Anglo-Saxon	ʄʄʄʄʄʄʄʄʄʄʄʄʄʄʄʄʄʄʄʄʄʄʄʄʄʄʄʄʄʄʄʄʄʄʄʄʄ	Neutral
Latin (trading)	εεεεεεεεεεεεεεεεεεεεεεεεεεεεεεεεεεεεεεεε	
Celtic		

Figure 8.2 Lexical history and register

Finally, what is the character of modern 'Literary' language and is it properly placed hierarchically above 'Common' language? We can understand that Murray's notion of a literary language would be based on the canon of English literature, notably Shakespeare, Milton, Dr Johnson, Jane Austen and the major Victorian authors. But today, if we take a sampling of modern poetry,

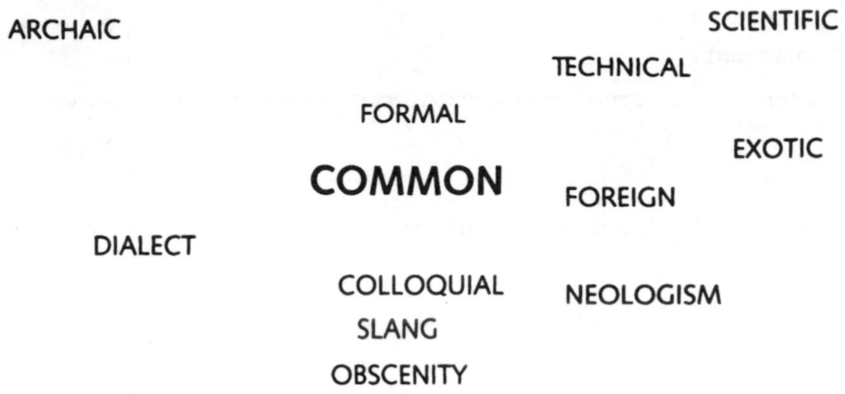

ARCHAIC   SCIENTIFIC

                                    TECHNICAL

                FORMAL

                                                    EXOTIC
              COMMON   FOREIGN

    DIALECT

                COLLOQUIAL   NEOLOGISM
                SLANG
                OBSCENITY

Figure 8.3 Murray's configuration revised

plays and novels, we find very little in the lexis that is distinctively 'literary'. Indeed, it is a common cause of complaint that much modern literature 'plumbs the depths' of the colloquial and the obscene with an unseemly thoroughness. The phrase 'the dignity of verse' and its assumptions of decency in subject-matter and language has little modern relevance. A notorious but revealing recent example was the award of the 1994 Booker Prize, the most prestigious English award for fiction. This was given, admittedly after considerable dissension among the judges, to James Kelman for his novel, *How Late it was, How Late*, which represented the confused and uncensored drunken maunderings of an alcoholic narrator speaking in Glasgow dialect with innumerable repetitions of the 'four-letter' words. This lexical feature became the main issue in the subsequent furore.

The point of change in literary register was starkly underscored by the simultaneous unofficial posthumous 'award' of the 1894 Booker Prize, a practice which has grown up in recent years largely out of protest against a perceived decline of standards in modern fiction. Out of a short list of George Moore's *Esther Waters*, George du Maurier's *Trilby*, Anthony Hope's *The Prisoner of Zenda* and Rudyard Kipling's *The Jungle Book*, the judges chose *Esther Waters*. The upshot of these observations is that there is no longer an exclusive category of 'Literary' language. It seems best to replace it by a less limiting term, namely 'Formal'.

If we were therefore to modify Murray's diagram in the light of modern developments, it would look more like figure 8.3. The most important symbolic shift in this diagram is that the top right-hand branch now includes all the opaque or non-native elements, namely Foreign and Exotic, Technical and

Scientific, arranged according to degree of remoteness. Archaic is introduced on the opposite branch, with Dialect placed on the same side, away from the foreign elements. Formal now replaces Literary. One problem concerns Neologism. Should it be a discrete category? If so, where should it be placed? The broader issue is whether it is possible to devise a scheme which combines registers and regional categories such as American and Commonwealth.

Various other configurations of the regional varieties of Contemporary English have been proposed, most of them using a circular scheme. One has a category of 'World Standard English' at the core. The reader will find them conveniently set out in David Crystal's *Cambridge Encyclopedia of the English Language* (1996, pp. 107–11). However, the model of a central core and a periphery essentially symbolizes the Victorian and Edwardian imperial world-view which obtained in Murray's time. Is it entirely appropriate when applied to modern global varieties? Some American and Commonwealth terms are central; others are not. But both categories have thousands of words in common. A very different configuration lies behind the view of Edmund Weiner that 'The English vocabulary is now federated rather than centralized' (in Ricks and Michaels, 1990, p. 501).

But, moving from the global to a more specific issue: how much validity does the concept of register still have? Clearly there are many technical and professional contexts (such as the law, medicine, user manuals and so on) where a particular kind of lexis must be used. But consider the following:

> Jake Shagger, the pop icon and darling of the hoi polloi, exuded his special brand of charisma and adrenalin at last night's rave-out at the shrine of heavy metal. His pelvic thrust and whirling dervish gyrations had the hormone-driven throng pulsing with ecstasy. The consensus among the faithful is that 'The Bonker from Blackpool' has still got a lot of bottle.

This colourful little journalistic piece contains examples of virtually every lexical category, combined in what the writer would probably call a 'postmodern thesaurus cocktail'. It could not have been written more than twenty years ago.

Words of the Century

The great interest in new words has manifested itself in increasing commentary on them. Authors like Philip Howard, John Ayto, John Silverlight, William Safire and Art Buchwald contribute regular newspaper columns on new words or new semantic extensions. Many of these treat lexis as an important kind of social evidence, as 'witness words' (reflecting material progress) or 'key words' (reflecting ethical change) to use the terms of George Matoré discussed in chapter 1. This approach was carried to an original conclusion by Collins Dictionaries in November 1997 when the house published a list of 'Words of the Century', allocating one significant word per year from 1896 to 1997. The Collins list, together with alternative suggestions for the past two decades supplied by Oxford English Dictionaries, is set out as figure 8.4, 'Words of the Century'.

As one can see, most of the lexical items are witness words or key words. However, the simplicity of a single annual choice is revealing of the ideology, values and location of the chooser. To make a simple point, *scrabble*, the chosen word for 1948, would seem trivial and highly 'Eurocentric' to a black South African, who would surely regard *apartheid* as more significant. Many would consider that two of the 'war words' chosen for 1943 and 1944, namely *dam busters* and *doodlebug* are too exclusively British. Others would regard *hooligan*, a word which suddenly sprang into prominence in 1898, as a more representative modern term than *krypton*, and would question the choice of *tupperware* for the momentous year of 1945. Similarly, many would wonder whether marginal (and largely forgotten) artistic movements, like Vorticism and Dada, merit their place in the crucial war years of 1914 and 1916. The student will find interest in many of the choices, in suggesting alternatives and in discussing the criteria on which 'representative' words are chosen.[2]

In bringing this section to a conclusion, we should be aware that, as in Elizabethan times, new words may stand out, but many have a short life. In the Collins list, *gamine, Cheka, chaplinesque, belisha, Montezuma's revenge* and the terms already discussed have largely faded away in general currency. In a few years' time the same will probably be true of *acid house, velvet revolution* and *alcopop*. In a useful article, 'Desuetude among new English words' in the *International Journal of Lexicography* (4 (1993), pp. 281–93), John Algeo argued that emphasis on neologisms has detracted from awareness of word-loss. His findings were that of new words recorded between 1944 and 1957, 58 per cent are no longer listed in unabridged dictionaries.

Lexical fields over time

The emphasis on new words, which by their very visibility have a high profile, can be misleading. Changes occur in word-fields which are not noticeable in even a century, let alone in an individual's lifetime. For example, the Anglo-Saxons counted their years in winters: a seven-year-old boy was *cnafa seofon wintra*. We would now use *summer* in such contexts. Since this change in con-

Collins Dictionaries:

1896	Radioactivity	1947	Flying saucer
1897	Aspirin	1948	Scrabble
1898	Krypton	1949	Big Brother
1899	Gamine	1950	Nato
1900	Labour Party	1951	Discothèque
1901	Fingerprint	1952	Stoned
1902	Teddy bear	1953	Rock 'n' roll
1903	Tarmac	1954	Teddy boy
1904	Fifa	1955	Lego
1905	Sinn Fein	1956	Angry young man
1906	Suffragette	1957	Psychedelic
1907	Allergy	1958	Silicon chip
1908	Borstal	1959	Hovercraft
1909	Jazz	1960	Laser
1910	Girl Guide	1961	Catch-22
1911	Air raid	1962	Montezuma's revenge
1912	Schizophrenia	1963	Rachmanism
1913	Isotope	1964	Moog synthesiser
1914	Vorticism	1965	Miniskirt
1915	Tank	1966	Cultural Revolution
1916	Dada	1967	Pulsar
1917	Cheka	1968	Fosbury flop
1918	Bolshie/Bolshy	1969	Moon buggy
1919	Fascism	1970	Butterfly effect
1920	Robot	1971	Workaholic
1921	Chaplinesque	1972	Watergate
1922	Gigoto	1973	VAT
1923	Spoonerism	1974	Ceefax
1924	Surrealism	1975	Fractal
1925	British Summer Time	1976	Punk rock
1926	Television	1977	ERM
1927	Talkie	1978	Test-tube baby
1928	Penicillin	1979	Rubik cube
1929	Maginot Line	1980	Solidarity
1930	Pluto	1981	SDP
1931	Oscar	1982	CD
1932	Neutron	1983	Aids
1933	Gestapo	1984	Yuppie
1934	Belisha	1985	Glasnost
1935	Alcoholics Anonymous	1986	Mexican wave
1936	Mickey Mouse	1987	PEP
1937	Surreal	1988	Acid house
1938	Nylon	1989	Velvet Revolution
1939	Walter Mitty	1990	Crop circle
1940	Jeep	1991	Ethnic cleansing
1941	Radar	1992	Clone
1942	Robotics	1993	Information superhighway
1943	Dam Busters	1994	National Lottery
1944	Doodlebug	1995	Road rage
1945	Tupperware	1996	Alcopop
1946	Bikini	1997	Blairite

Oxford Dictionaries:

1978	BMX, Teletext	1988	Lager lout
1979	Space Invaders	1989	Poll tax
1980	Reaganomics	1990	Global warming
1981	Walkman	1991	Citizen's charter
1982	Exocet	1992	Grunge, annus horribilis
1983	Star Wars	1993	Whitewater, Bobbitt
1984	Aids	1994	World Wide Web
1985	Yuppie	1995	Britpop
1986	Perestroika	1996	Ecowarrior, scratchcard
1987	Freemarket, Black Monday	1997	New Labour

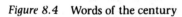

Figure 8.4   Words of the century

vention occurred duing the Middle English period, some would say that it represents Germanic gloom giving way to Gallic optimism.

As Andreas Fischer has pointed out (1994, pp. 79–95), the lexical field of terms for the seasons shows several changes over the centuries:

ModE	spring	summer	autumn/fall	winter
ME	?sumer	sumer	hervest	winter
EME	?	sumer	hervest	winter
OE	lencten	sumer	hærfest	winter

Surprisingly, only *summer* and *winter* have remained stable. The root of 'harvest' in the old name for autumn or fall seems simply appropriate to a previously agricultural age: although *autumn* is in origin an Old French word, it was actually rare before the sixteenth century. The name for 'spring' has been oddly unstable over time. (The Old English word *lencten* meant 'lent', which has quite different associations from the traditional notions of vivacity subsequently surrounding spring.)

In chapter 1 we considered the word-fields of pregnancy and madness as a way of understanding the varieties of register. Let us now turn to a more detailed lexicological study of a related topic, modern developments in the field of psychoanalysis, and a broader theme, the semantic field of war. The latter incorporates virtually every lexical type discussed in this book.

Words of War

The majority of wars nowadays are undeclared acts of concerted or randomly organized 'military intervention' or 'armed aggression', to use the standard euphemisms. 'Rebels', 'government forces', 'paramilitary units' and 'superpower surrogates' clash by night in bloody theatres of war which enact Matthew Arnold's prescient nightmare. States like modern Israel or Angola have been in a state of undeclared war or internecine conflict since their inception or independence. Today it is estimated that there about twenty-five of these conflicts grinding on in various states of attrition all over the world. One hundred years ago, by contrast, war was declared, open and defined as, say, the Crimean War (1854–5), the American Civil War (1861–5), the Franco-Prussian War (1870–1), the Spanish-American War (1898) and the Boer War (1899–1902).

The change in the style of war extends beyond the name to cover every aspect of the activity. The fundamental change in the form has been from the classic 'chequer-board' strategic set piece (conducted with elegance like a symphony or ballet, with different stages and movements) to the modern engagement which is ambiguous, confusing, part institutional, part guerrilla,

Anglo-Saxon	*bow, arrow, sword, shield, spear, fight, weapon*
Middle English	*castle, army, navy, battle, war, peace, enemy, fighter, ambush, armour, artillery, cross-bow, lance, pike, pole-axe, pike, hauberk, buckler, mace, gun, admiral, skirmish, archer, soldier, spy, chivalry (cavalry)*
1500	*trench, longbow, ordnance*
	redcoat, cannon, armada, harquebus, salvo, hussar
1550	*mortar, bomb, bombardier, pistol*
	petard, infantry, fireship, calibre, volley
1600	*grenade, musket, missile, rocket, carbine*
1650	*bayonet, blunderbuss, shell, recruit, grenadier*
1700	*armament, howitzer, salute (artillery), blockade, press gang*
1750	*uniform, civilian, manoeuvre, grapeshot*
	rifle, martinet
1800 Napoleonic	*guerrilla, torpedo, shrapnel, diehard*
1850 Crimean War	*balaclava, cardigan, raglan, jingoism*
	Gatling gun, machine gun, mine (naval), magenta, solferino, war widow, Maxim gun, mauser, Red Cross, tommy (Atkins), battleship, submarine, hand grenade
1900 Boer War	*concentration camp, khaki, maffick*
	hand grenade, submarine, destroyer, sam browne,
First World War	*tank, air-raid, bomber, fighter, strafe, depth charge, anti-aircraft, aircraft carrier, D-day, atomic bomb, camouflage, zeppelin, U-boat, flame-thrower, poison gas, rocketry, Hitler, scorched earth, total war*
Second World War	*blitz, flak, ack-ack, prang, fire bomb, doodlebug, guided missile, ground/air to air missile, bren, sten, snafu, napalm, nuclear bomb, warhead, ground zero, paratroop, G. I. Joe, holocaust, Quisling, Resistance*
1950	*Cold War, Iron Curtain, bazooka, silo*
Vietnam	*defoliation, air-support, pacification*
Falklands, etc.	*Exocet, heat-seeking missile, Stalin organ, neutron bomb, chemical warfare*
Gulf War	*collateral damage, friendly fire, smart bombs scud, patriot*
Bosnia	*ethnic cleansing*

Figure 8.5   The semantic field of war

clandestine, haphazard and (like much modern art) with no rules or framing conventions. The new style includes the notion of total war, hinted at by Clausewitz in his category of 'absolute war', initiated in modern times by General Sherman in his annihilating march to the sea in 1864, but formulated semantically later. It ruthlessly obliterates the distinction between military and civilian personnel, which had previously been scrupulously and chivalrously preserved. Indeed, *civilian* is a term which has definition only by virtue of its militarized opposite.

The accompanying 'Semantic Field of War' (figure 8.5) is a word-field built on the model of linguistic archaeology to illustrate the accumulated catalogue of principal terms over the centuries. Each new conflict reflects some refinement or increase in the capacity for slaughter as armies have changed in constitution from being feudal levies in medieval times, then professionals and finally conscripted civilians. The basic territorial impulse for war has also developed differing motives, being predominately religious in the Middle Ages, nationalistic in the nineteenth century and strategically expansionist in the twentieth.

Although the field contains many technical terms, it omits those no longer current, such as *arbalet, trebuchet, francisca, scramasax* and *pavise*, which were medieval terms. Many words (such as *shell, mine* and *tank*) are metaphorical extensions of common words; some, like *fighter* and *missile*, are specializations from within the field, as technology has evolved from earth via air to space. The more recent layers of the vocabulary corroborate the observation of Clausewitz that 'war is a mere continuation of policy by other means.' The dismaying richness of the field also bears out Eric Partridge's comment that 'War is the greatest excitant of new vocabulary' (1948, p. 115).

There is frequently a time-lag between word and thing. Thus *atomic bomb* was coined by H. G. Wells in 1914, though the first explosion took place at Alamogordo, New Mexico, in 1945. On the other hand, *spies, archers* and *soldiers* were obviously in existence long before the verbal borrowings from Norman French into Middle English. However, the terrible carnage at Magenta and Solferino (both fought in 1859) led to both terms being taken almost immediately into the language to mean 'blood-red' or maroon. (The untended suffering of the wounded at Solferino inspired the Swiss philanthropist, Jean Henri Dunant, to found the Red Cross.) Likewise, *refugee*, which has become a major 'war word' in modern times, emerged in 1688, exactly contemporaneous with the Revocation of the Edict of Nantes, which expelled Protestant Huguenots from France.

A seminal word in the development of the field is *guerrilla*, first recorded in one of Wellington's despatches in 1809 during the Peninsular War: 'I have recommended to the Junta,' he wrote, 'to set the guerrillas to work towards Madrid.' The advent of guerrilla tactics signalled the reversal of the expected dynamic in a war situation whereby the side with superior generalship and majority force would normally, in the long run, win. Now the 'host' nation refused to join force *en masse*, attacking sporadically and using Fabian tactics of attrition, knowing that time was ultimately on its side. Thus Napoleon, previously invincible, was unable to deal with the Spanish guerrillas, the British lost far more heavily to the Boers than they ever conceived possible (especially in the disasters of 'Black Week' in December, 1899) and the Americans met their catastrophe in the jungles of Vietnam.

One key to the success of guerrilla warfare is to prevent the invading force from being able to distinguish between soldier and civilian. Kitchener's drastic solution to this problem in the Boer War was the institution of the *concen-*

tration camp. Suitably styled in one of the first modern military euphemisms, the original camps were designed to cut off the Boer commandos from their people, their support and their supply lines by isolating the women and children. (This was combined with a severe variant of the 'scorched earth' policy by destroying the Boer farms.) It is estimated that 26,000 people perished in the camps, most of them under the age of 16, so that the policy and the institution became the object of considerable controversy. The 'Nazification' of the term *concentration camp* led to the preference for the substitutes *internment camp* and *relocation camp* in England and America.

The sartorial aspect of war makes itself apparent through various ironies. It seems unjust that commanders with such different talents and records as Wellington, Blucher, Cardigan and Raglan should have the eponymous memorial of boots, knitwear and cloaks. The bitterness of the Crimean winter, obviously a factor in the last two items, is more widely recalled in *balaclava*, which was also once military slang for a beard. The change in style of warfare necessitated a shift in the style of uniform from the brilliant and flamboyant to the drab and camouflaged. The red coat was phased out after the Crimea, since it was an obvious liability on the battlefield, although Wellington's unwavering 'thin red line' visibly disheartened many of his opponents. *Khaki*, deriving from an Urdu (ultimately Persian) word meaning 'dusty', began to see service from just before the outbreak of the Indian Mutiny in 1857. It acquired highly emotive overtones from the spirit prevalent at the time of the Boer War, and within a few months generated the phrases *khaki election, to vote khaki* and *khaki policy*.

A discussion of some of the philological curiosities can start with *blunderbuss*, which originates in Dutch *donderbus*, 'thunder box', so imprecise in its devastation that the perversion of the first element into *blunder* seems very appropriate. There is a touching air of dated chivalry in the *OED*'s comment: 'No longer in use in civilized countries.' In the related area of munitions are a number of eponyms: *shrapnel*, originally more like a mortar bomb, was named after its inventor, Lieutenant General Henry Shrapnel, and proved a decisive weapon in the Napoleonic Wars. Sir Hiram S. Maxim, the brothers Mauser and Dr R. J. Gatling developed more specific memorials in the field of weaponry, though the latter's is now downgraded to the mafioso *gat*. The *tank* was given its deliberately opaque name during December 1915 for reasons of secrecy during its manufacture. Perhaps the strangest etymology is that of *strafe*, dating from 1915 and originating in the German phrase *Gott strafe England* ('God punish England'), 'supposed to be a salutation in Germany in 1914 and the following years'. On a lighter note one is amused to read that in the British Army *bomb* was formerly pronounced [bum].

The field does not – for reasons of economy – put much emphasis on one of the endearingly human aspects of semantics, the capacity to defuse or disarm the terrifying with a familiar or intimate word. Thus *cheese-toaster* and *tooth-pick* were World War I euphemisms for *bayonet*, going *over the top* substituted for the horrors of a suicidally vulnerable advance in trench warfare, a *dogfight* denoted crucial aerial combat between fighters, and the friendly nicknames *Little Boy* and *Fat Man* were applied to the atomic bombs dropped on Hiroshima and Nagasaki respectively. Others of the numerous slang familiarizations are *scrambled eggs, doodlebug, whizz-bang, crump, dud, funk-hole* and *prang* (from Malay *perang*), still often accompanied by the oxymoronic *wizard*. Generally accepted terms of service origin are *grouse, juice, ace, conk out, zoom, hush-hush, foot-slog, kip, muck in, snaffle* and *clobber*.

Another technique of familiarization or 'cutting down to size' is the use of acronyms like *flak*, which is still current, but derives from the cumbersome Germanic original *flieger abhwehr kanone*, an anti-aircraft gun. Of similar origin, *awol* is still occasionally encountered, while *ack-ack, NAAFI, WAAF* and Wren are increasingly endangered species. A positively thriving formation of this kind is, however, that cynical observer of organized incompetence, *snafu* ('situation normal all fucked/fouled up'), recently joined by G.M.F.U. ('Grand Military Fuck Up').

Needless to say, one of the perennial growth areas in the field is the vocabulary of death. The fertility of this area derives from the general taboos governing the subject of death. The field ranges from the familiar slang phrases of metaphorical origin like *peg (peg it/out)* (from cribbage and croquet), *go for a Burton* (still disputed), *to hand in one's chips* (from gambling), *(to have) bought it, (to realize that) one's number is up*. Even in modern American military parlance, which is quite shocking in its explicitness (witnessed in verbally numbing films like *Platoon, The Killing Fields* and *Full Metal Jacket*), the most hardened veterans still use the euphemism *wasted* for *killed*. An alternative semantic strategy is the use of dysphemism, the cruelly direct phrase which is unflinching in its physicality and concreteness: *pushing up daisies* and *coming back in a Jiffy* (body bag) are, perhaps the starkest of these.

The mindless mental solidarity and belligerence which war situations foster (chillingly described by Thucydides in the fifth century BC) has produced two kinds of critical formulations: that of the *miles gloriosus* type like *chauvinist, jingoist* and *Blimp* on the one hand and the treacherous sell-out or enemy of the people like *Quisling* and Lord Haw Haw on the other. *Martinet* took about a century to become an unsympathetic byword in English for strict drilling and severe discipline, while *Hitler*, used satirically of a tyrannical figure, is recorded as early as 1934. *By Jingo!*, aptly described as a piece of 'sonorous nonsense' variously interpreted as conjurors' gibberish and a minced oath, became a bellicose rallying cry supporting Disraeli's Balkan policy of 'active intervention' in 1878. It rapidly spawned *jingoism, jingoist, jingodom* and the verb *to jingo*.

(*John Bullism* had a longer related currency throughout the nineteenth century.) Even the innocent ejaculation *hurrah!* became a fearsome rallying cry in Napoleonic times. Originally *huzza*, the word changed to reproduce French *houra*, from Russian *urá*, the shout of attack of the Cossacks, it came to symbolize and denote an attack. Marshal Bugeaud described the eerie imperturbability of 'the red English line, silent and motionless' in the face of the Old Guard. 'Then three formidable *Hurrahs!* terminated the long silence of our adversaries. With the third they were down upon us, pressing us into disorderly retreat.'

Institutionalized euphemisms, which form part of state propaganda, have been current even since Tacitus wrote in the first century BC, 'When they make a wilderness they call it peace' (*Agricola*, ch. 30). Anaesthetic terms like *casualties* and *losses* or the comforting emotive opacity of *making the supreme sacrifice* have been long entrenched. The newer, ominously 'scientific' terms like *eliminate, neutralize* and *exterminate* are notable here. The whole notion of 'loss' or 'retreat' is obviously surrounded by evasion and understatement in the military context. Hugh Rawson cites in his *Dictionary of Euphemisms* the instance of the Macedonian commander, Antigonus Gonatus, who in *c.*250 BC refused to admit retreating, describing the manoeuvre as a 'strategic movement to the rear'. George Orwell's ironic formation *pacification* has since become institutionalized and been joined by the Pentagonese terms *defoliation, armed reconnaisance, protective reaction* and *air support*.[3]

These techniques of 'semantic engineering' bring us to the shadow-line between war and terrorism, a boundary which is as large and disputed as the marches of medieval times. This whole area of terminology, and the philosophy which lies behind it, is really a field requiring a study in itself. *Terrorist*, born in the horrors of the Reign of Terror in France, has never lost its overtones of savagery, though few would now write with the moral denunciation of Edmund Burke in 1795: 'Thousands of those Hell-hounds called Terrorists'. It is, of course, a technique of terrorist movements to style themselves as 'armies' and to use quasi-military terms like 'fronts' or politically favourable counters like 'liberation' precisely to justify their tactics and propagandize their cause.

The styling or naming of wars is also important, since large propaganda benefits can accrue. Some are purely neutral and geographical, like the Hundred Years' War, the Vietnam War, the Korean War and so on. Others import logic and motive, such as the Wars of the Roses, the Crusades (to retrieve the Holy Cross) and the self-explanatory War of the Spanish Succession. Often these names contain retrospective rationalizations, like the War of Jenkins' Ear, in which the ear in question (excised from a smuggler) was made into a *casus belli* seven years after its loss. In older-fashioned English parlance the Kaiser's War and the Hitler War are still well established, but perhaps the most successful recent achievements in the propagandist style have been the Six Day War (reflecting the insulting ease of the Israeli victory) and the Yom Kippur War, recollecting the dastardly timing of the Arab invasion with obloquy. An ominous development in this respect has been the willingness to give political conflicts the status of a *jihad* or holy war.

For many people the most effective 'words of war' are contained in the oratory of Winston Churchill in the darkest moments of the conflict. They memorably showed the force of the plain style and the base register:

> We shall defend our island, whatever the cost may be; we shall fight on the beaches; we shall fight on the landing-grounds; we shall fight in the fields and in the streets; we shall fight in the hills; we shall never surrender. (4 June 1940)

The contributions of the twentieth century emerge as refinements in the gruesome. Principal among these has been the growth of terms anticipating mass death in a nuclear holocaust. The awesomely confident formations like *overkill, megacorpse* and *megadeath* (to denote a million dead) have become part of the strategic discourse since the last war. *Holocaust* itself reflects man's inhumanity to man by extending from the original Greek sense of 'a whole animal sacrifice' to 'a great slaughter or massacre' in the last century. Its application to the mass-murder of the Jews seems to date only from 1965. Genocide has been practised by many nations, though the word itself was coined only in 1944, in the War Crimes tribunal which brought the Nazis to justice. But perhaps the most notable semantic development in the face of these literally indescribable horrors has been the wholesale euphemization of the terminology of war into the neutral Latinizations of *defence, operations, devices, incidents, incursions, engagements* and *terminations.*

Mental Disturbance and Madness Updated

In the concluding section of chapter 4, we traced the evolution of two kinds of professional language, that of medicine and that of law. Let us now turn to the terminology of one of the 'new' professions, psychoanalysis. These terms, set out in figure 8.6, have traditionally been lacking in precision, mainly as a consequence of euphemism. The older terms were characterized by great semantic breadth even when not native: they included *natural, simple, silly, the vapours,* and a variety of terms involving the *nerves,* e.g. *nervous condition/ collapse,* etc. A surprisingly early example of a clearly foreign term is *mania,* recorded in Lanfrank: only in the seventeenth century is it joined by a first influx of similar classical terms such as *hysterical, melancholia, obsession,* and

Traditional	Specialization	Coinage
mania 1400		
maniac adj 1604 Cawdrey		
hysterical 1615		
hysteric (adj) 1657		
neurotic 1661		
	obsession 1680	
melancholia 1693		
psychology 1693		
neurosis 1776–84		
hysteria 1801		
psychosis 1847		
psychopathic 1847	*neurotic* 1847	
paranoia 1857		
paranoic 1857		
	neurosis 1871 Huxley	
	inhibition 1876 William James	
	psychomotor 1878	
katatonia 1883		
psychopath 1885		
psychotherapeutic 1890	*blocking* 1890 William James	
psychotic 1890		
dementia præcox 1891		
	trauma 1894	
	transference 1895 Freud	
		abreaction 1895 Freud
		psychoanalysis 1896 Freud
psychosexual 1897		
manic 1902		
psychotherapy 1904		
	complex 1907 Jung	
	rationalization 1908	
	defence mechanism 1909 Freud	*libido* 1909 Freud
	anxiety 1909 Freud	
	repression 1909 Freud	
	projection 1909 Jung	
ego 1910 Freud		
	regression 1910 Freud	
	sublimation 1910 Freud	
	obsessive 1911	
schizophrenia 1912		
schizophrenic 1912		
	displacement 1913 Freud	*id* 1917 Freud
	fixation 1913 Freud	*angst* 1922 Freud
		superego 1924 Freud
schizoid 1925		
	block 1931	
	manic depression/ve 1958	

Figure 8.6   The word-field of terms within psychology arranged historically

psychology itself. These drive out the old words like *wood, woodness*. The second wave of classical borrowings comes in the second half of the nineteenth century, which yields *psychosis, neurotic, paranoia, psychotic, psychopathic* and *psychotherapeutic*.

Two processes are notable in the evolution of the nomenclature: one is the degree of back-formation evidenced in several key terms. *Neurotic*, for example, is coined as a medical term in 1661 in the sense of a drug having a marked effect on the nervous system, especially a bracing one; the pathological sense of the adjective is defined by Webster in 1847 as 'a disease having its seat in the nerves'; *neurosis* itself emerged only in 1871 when T. H. Huxley made the distinction between *psychosis* and *neurosis*. Freud further refined the meaning by identifying *anxiety neurosis* in 1918. Similarly, *hysterical* precedes *hysteria* by nearly two centuries, while *psychopathic* precedes *psychopath* by nearly half a century. It is as if the discipline proceeded from the symptoms to an analysis of the given condition.

The second trend is specialization, classically evident in *obsession*, a term which would appear to encapsulate in its semantic development the history of psychiatric symptomatology and its interpretation. Its original meaning, recorded from 1513, is 'a siege, or the action of besieging'. This introduces the basic and enduring paradigm of the mental condition being conceived of in terms of attack and defence, resilience and breakdown, security and anxiety. A century later, from 1605, emerged the sense of 'the hostile action of the devil or an evil spirit in besetting any one'. By the end of the century, demonic possession had been replaced by a more rational explanation: 'The action of any influence, notion or "fixed idea" which persistently assails or vexes, esp. so as to discompose the mind'.

There were, however, 'false friends' in the existing terminology, notably the signal case of the 'etymological fallacy' which problematized the diagnosis of hysteria. Since the term is derived from Greek *hystera*, 'a womb', many early practitioners assumed that it was an exclusively female condition. The feminine association was reinforced by the sense of *mother* in the sense of 'womb', specially in the phrases *fits of the mother* (from c.1400) and *the rising of the mother* (from c.1527) to mean 'hysteria'. Thus in 1615 Crooke's *Body of Man* carries the definition: '*Hysterical* women, that is, such as are in fitts of the mother.' Yet we recall that in Shakespeare's tragedy, Lear describes the symptoms graphically: 'O how this mother swells up toward my heart!' (II. iv. 56). However, Freud had the greatest difficulty in persuading the more obdurate of his colleagues that hysteria could present itself in males.

There is also a notable difference in register between the first wave of modern psychological enquiry, epitomized by William James, and that of Freud and Jung in the second. James tends to give specialized meanings to established words, such as *blocking* (later *block*), *inhibition* and *obsession*. Huxley, in the same era, similarly extended the use of *neurosis* and *psychosis* from the provenance of pathology to psychology.

Freud predominantly, and to a lesser extent Jung, sought a more scientific and precise terminology which would be more exact because it was unshaped by semantic history, and would be within the ambit of their own legislation. They either resuscitated or redefined classical terms, just as William James had done in redefining *trauma* as an unhealed psychic wound. Freud added specialized meanings to *anxiety, ego, transference, regression, repression, displacement, fixation* and *sublimation* (originally a term from alchemy first recorded in Gower *c*.1390). Similarly, Jung used *complex* in a specialized fashion, famously of Oedipus and Electra, as well as extending the meaning of *projection*. Freud went further, coining *psychoanalysis* in 1896, *abreaction* in 1895, *libido* in 1909, and a special sense of *angst* in 1922. His famous tripartite division of the personality becomes the more interesting when one considers the evolution of the key terms: *ego* was given its Freudian specialization in 1910; *id* was formulated in 1917 in the course of Freud's correspondence with Groddeck, and *superego* was coined in 1924. The components of Freud's final duality in the personality were given such classical names as *eros* (first used by Freud in 1922) and *thanatos*, though it should be noted that Freud's own terms were *todestrieb* ('death instinct') and *todeswunsch* ('death-wish').

The predilection for arcane classical vocabulary was an extension of the process well established in medicine; it was the natural *koiné* of members of the intelligentsia, and was also probably designed to give the discipline the status it lacked. One should recall that the earliest sense of *psychotherapeutic* (1890) was 'the treatment of disease by "psychic", i.e. hypnotic influence'. Associations with mesmerism and occultism were common in the 1880s. (Before coining *psychoanalysis* in 1896, Freud had himself used the German formulation *psychische analyse*.) In this context, one can understand the coining of impressive formations like *katatonia* in 1883 and *dementia praecox* in 1891, this last by Pick, though much associated with Kraepelin (1899), later superseded by *schizophrenia*. As in medicine, status was achieved, but at the expense of clarity. Unsurprisingly, the term was subsequently (*c*.1944) retranslated back into layman's English as 'split personality'.

However, the fundamental problems of definition have not been resolved. The whole foundation of the discipline is essentially problematic, because neither patient nor therapist operates within the same clear parameters of evidence, symptoms, conditions and definitions as is the case in medicine: indeed, the evidence of the patient may be misleading or manipulative, as Freud recognized in his use of the term *transference*. This aspect has become a major focus in the work of Lacan and the neo-Freudian revisionists. The modern history of the discipline has been one of endless schism between 'druggists' and analysts, biologists and linguists. Lacan's dogmatic assertion that 'The unconscious is structured like a language' evoked Laplanche's riposte 'What linguistics? What language? And what Lacanianism' (1989, p. 41). Lacan 'eroticizes the language of "theory"', indulging self-consciously in provocative word-play, fabricating the evidence which Freud and his followers had detected as a key to the unconscious: hence Lacan's quasi-sexual use of *jouissance* and *conneries* (Bowie, 1991, pp. 199, 148, 151). More seriously, there seem to be no commonly agreed definitions of the major conditions. Above all, an essential aspect of the 'talking cure' is the crucially important area of ambiguity inherent in the use and interpretation of language in the process of analysis.

The enterprise of Freud and Jung, though worthy, has not been entirely successful, for another reason: the speech community has borrowed their terminology wholesale and used it with the unscientific latitude which the founding fathers sought to avoid. 'Terms not so long ago confined to specialists are handled familiarly by the laity: *moron, inferiority complex, mental age, . . . paranoid delusions, psychopaths.*' That comment was made in the *New Republic* in 1927. Since then the trend has accelerated. Furthermore, terms intended to be neutral have become universally unsympathetic. There is manifestly a fundamental difference in accepting the taboos which still surround the naming of terminal illnesses and the practice of callous labelling by means of the names of mental conditions. The interesting new factor here is the growth of politically correct language: its emphases have so far been on discriminatory terms concerning race, gender and 'normality' of physique: it remains to be seen whether it will have the effect of censoring the stigmatizing usage of psychological conditions.

Professional language

Professions traditionally take to themselves the powers of definition and self-styling. We have seen some examples of their appropriation of high-register titles, such as *therapist, gerontologist, gynaecologist* and so on. A spectacularly cynical example occurred in the year 1360, when royal *purveyors*, notorious for their corruption, were restyled by statute *achatours*. However, the exploited majority does have its recourse in the slower vengeance of semantic change: the word *cheat* derives from the dishonest practices of the medieval *escheators*; *quacksalver, quack, mountebank, charlatan* and *sawbones* all reflect critical views of unprofessional medical practitioners, most of them from the sixteenth century; *pettyfogging* and its variants have maintained the layman's view of the law from a similar distance in time; the contemptuously belittling term *headshrinker* is recorded from 1950, while *psychobabble*, expressing disdain for psychological jargon, has been in existence since 1976.

The problems of definition in these professional areas essentially replicate the model of the 'conflict of speech economies' posited by G. K. Zipf in 1949. Specialists prefer a wide range of precise terms; the public, contrariwise, prefers a small range of broad terms. It is hard to see what can be done about the split in the terminology. Despite calls for 'openness', one cannot imagine modern medical practitioners reverting to the direct demotic terms of medieval times.

When we consider the nomenclature of medicine and law (discussed in chapter 4) together with that of psychoanalysis, we can see that they represent differing models of interaction between the professions and the speech community across the register barrier. The older professions of medicine and law have managed, with the benefit of time, tradition and status, to maintain powers of definition and of obfuscation within their fields. While they may not have gained the total trust of the public, they have ensconced themselves as part of a professional establishment. On the other hand, despite a virtual epidemic of psychoanalysis, especially among the American bourgeoisie, there still seems to be a lack of sympathy for mental conditions, perhaps because they represent an affront to the Western ideology of success, and have yet to gain the status of socially acceptable disorders, and because of scepticism about the efficacy of psychiatric treatment. Consequently, this most recent discipline has yet to acquire the professional status of law and medicine – despite the illuminating contributions of magisterial figures – and has seen its terminology largely demystified and made more crude.

Postmodern theoretical discourse

We conclude this section with a brief discussion of another kind of professional language, that of literary criticism. The academic study of English has produced in recent decades many different approaches to both language and literature, increasingly framed in specialist vocabularies. The formation of canons of 'classic texts' and the complex evolution of modern literary theory do not fall within the scope of this book. Recently, however, theory has started to assume major importance in the discipline, with the text seen less as something 'given', and more the product of a variety of agendas, social, cultural, economic, psychological, sexual, sexist and linguistic. The various schools have developed, not only their special insights, but their exclusive vocabularies, so that the language of literary criticism is now of an altogether different order from that used by, say, Coleridge, Arnold and Bradley.

Traditional humanist criticism is comprehensible, but bedevilled by definitions of broad key terms such as *style, meaning, text* and *character*. Modern criticism followed three basic practices. The first has been the expanded use of traditional terms, as in *A Rhetoric of Fictions* or *A Grammar of Motives* by Wayne Booth, or Roland Barthes's assertion that 'culture in all its aspects is a language.' William Empson carried this approach further in his notable study, *Seven Types of Ambiguity* (1930), but T. S. Eliot used traditional vocabulary to generate entirely new abstract formulations such as 'objective correlative' and 'dissociation of sensibility'.

The second practice extends the vocabulary of the conceptual base, as the Structuralists have used Saussure's terminology of *langue, parole, signifier, signified, semiotic, syntagmatic* and *paradigmatic*, and the Marxists have used the terminology of *base, superstructure, reification, alienation, bourgeois* and so on. Postmodern theoretical discourse creates entirely new terms, such as Genette's *analepsis* and *focalization*, Barthes's *lisible* and *scriptible*, Derrida's *grammatology, logocentric, phonocentric*, and *différance*, and Bloom's *clinamen, tessera, kenosis, daemonization, askesis* and *apophrades*. The point hardly has to be argued that the development has been from the readily comprehensible to an array of opaque and alien terms obviously intimidating to the uninitiated.

A more recent development is the use of established forms in a highly flexible fashion. Up to a few years ago critics tended to use reasonably stablilized word-forms: thus a scholar might write of 'a critique of post-coloniality which deconstructs the culture of post-modernism'. While the specific meaning might not be clear to all, the general sense would be apparent to a fair proportion of readers, since the forms would at least be familiar and unambiguous. Today one is more likely to come across formulations using parentheses, alternative prefixes, capitalization and 'scare quotes' of this kind: 'a critique of the Other in (post) coloniality which de/reconstructs the "culture" of post-modernism'. Here the critical terms are rendered ambiguous or confusing or problematic. Such writing often seems an exercise in self-deconstruction which highlights the provisionality of language as a conveyer of meaning.

Politically correct language

Political correctness is premised on the philosophical observation that 'Men imagine that their minds have command of language: but it often happens that language bears rule over their minds.' That was not, as some might suppose, Benjamin Lee Whorf or Edward Sapir or Leonard Bloomfield in this century. It was the egregious Francis Bacon, writing in 1605. However, in recent times the notion that language represents a dominant ideology has become current in statements such as the following:

> Every language reflects the prejudices of the society in which it evolved. Since English, through most of its history, evolved in a white, Anglo-Saxon patriarchal society, no one should be surprised that its vocabulary and grammar frequently reflect attitudes that exclude or demean minorities and women. (Miller and Swift, 1981, p. 4)

Political correctness has in the past decade or so emerged as a major expression of radical attitudes towards a whole variety of social matters, such as culture, politics, education, the curriculum, gender and ethnic issues, especially the way that they are articulated and defined. The assumption that 'the dictionary' reflects the dominant ideology has some validity and can be supported by such quotations as the definition of *canoe* in the *OED*: 'used generally for any rude craft in which uncivilized people go upon the water ... savages generally use paddles instead of oars.' Intervention in language is thus crucial, since the aim is to achieve a whole series of redefinitions of roles, attitudes and programmes. It is, in effect, a form of semantic engineering which involves various kinds of lexical substitution.

These assumptions and tactics are not new. Simone de Beauvoir observed that '[Language] is inherited from a masculine society, and it contains many male prejudices. ... Women simply have to steal the instrument; they don't have to break it, or try *a priori*, to make it something totally different. Steal it and use it for their own good' (1972, p. 123). The question is whether it is possible for pressure groups to achieve such total control.

The earliest usage of the formula 'politically correct' has been traced back to the American New Left in the late 1960s, but the terminology itself probably originated from an English translation of Chairman Mao's *Little Red Book* (Cameron in Dunant (ed.), 1994, pp. 18–19). Although the phrase meant 'conforming to the party line or expectations', it was often used in an ironic and self-deprecating fashion in the early years of its currency. However, by the late 1980s political correctness had assumed a whole range of agendas and become a major area of debate, especially in America. On certain campuses attitudes hardened into programmatic forms with the introduction of both speech and behaviour codes, often on issues unconcerned with politics *per se*.

The terms which are particularly germane to this discussion concern ethnic groups, disabilities, material deprivations and criminal behaviour. Some of these have been the object of traditional euphemisms, for example, 'financially underprivileged' instead of *poor*. *Black*, which had previously been euphemized by terms such as *coloured* and *darky*, was now avoided as far as possible, even in instances such as *blackboard* and the *black* pieces in chess.[4] In parallel, *white* is increasingly replaced by the curious misnomer *Caucasian*.[5] In addition, other kinds of prejudice are highlighted by the suffix *-ism*: hence *ageism*, *classism* and *ableism*.

Extreme 'political correctionists' have gone further, supplying their own ideologically appropriate substitutions, using a choice of register which is sinisterly efficient: it is a mixture of curious hybrids like *lookism*, portentous classical labels like *phallocentric*, *gynophobic* and *logocentric* and the starkly direct. In one of the movement's most publicized ideological categorizations, 'the canon of traditional western culture', sketched by Professor John Searle (in the *New York Review of Books*, 6 December 1990, p. 34) as existing 'from, say, Socrates to Wittgenstein in philosophy, and from Homer to James Joyce in literature', is reduced to devastated impotence by being redefined as the provenance of 'dead white males', commonly abbreviated to *d.w.m.*, later extended and capitalized to 'Dead White European Males' (DWEMs). This offensive formulation cynically exploits not only the emotive force of the base register, but precisely the sexist and racist categorizations which the propagandists claim to condemn.

Typically, politically correct language avoids traditionally judgemental language, preferring an artificial currency of polysyllabic, abstract, euphemistic substitutions. Thus *drug addiction* is avoided, the preferred form being 'substance dependence', 'visually impaired' is preferred to *blind*, while 'sex worker' is the politically correct term for *prostitute*, as 'informal settlement' is for *shanty town*. Many of these have an eerie echo of the Orwellian formulations discussed in the previous chapter. Being artificial, they have virtually no currency in ordinary conversation and readily invite parodies.[6]

In a devastating rejection of this strategy of 'verbal uplift', Robert Hughes observed in his commentary on America, *Culture of Complaint* (1993):

> We want to create a sort of linguistic Lourdes, where evil and misfortune are dispelled by a dip in the waters of euphemism. Does the cripple rise from his wheelchair, or feel better about being stuck in it, because someone . . . decided that, for official purposes, he was 'physically challenged'? (in Dunant (ed.), 1994, p. 24)

These objections go right to the heart of the matter: changing the language does not solve social and political problems. However, it does change attitudes, which is the obvious intention of the political correctionists.

In the past two decades there have been successful campaigns to claim the word *gay* for 'homosexual' and to politicize *green* in the sense of 'environmentally beneficial'. In consequence established meanings as in 'a gay old time', have started to atrophy: Arthur Wimperis's line

> 'Cheer up cully!' you'll soon be dead!
> A short life and gay one!
> (*The Arcadians*, III)

now seems bizarre. A more recent development has been the use of the obverse tactic, namely to seek to reclaim the previously stigmatizing term *queer* by institutionalizing it in formulations like 'Queer Theory'. It would appear that pressure groups can make no more than mediated changes, some of them admittedly significant, as we have seen.

These developments have major implications for linguistic theory. Saussure notably took the view that although individuals might be able to create their own forms of *parole* or individuated 'speech acts', the *langue*, the whole linguistic system, was too vast to be manipulated by any set of vested interests because of the 'collective inertia towards innovation' (*Cours*, 1966, p. 73). 'Of all social institutions,' he declared, 'language is least amenable to initiative' (p. 74). Such a view was more plausible when he gave his lectures in Geneva in the first decade of the twentieth century, since the great national propaganda machines had not yet ground into action with their 'Orwellian' consequences. Today we know better and we know worse.

The four attitudes

We may distinguish between four attitudes towards language, especially towards keywords. The first is the traditional normative attitude, which regards language as a discipline, to be accepted and learnt in a basically conformist and uncritical fashion. The second we may call the attitude of awareness, perceiving that language uses us as much as we use language, and that languages derive from human and social forces. The third is militant, seeking strategic manipulations, such as the political names Irish Republican Army or Sinn Fein ('We Ourselves' in Irish) or the House Committee for Unamerican Activities. A variation of this tactic is the use of pressure to suppress pejorative senses, such as those surrounding *Jew* and *Palestinian* (as in the sixth edition of the *COD*). This is an extension of 'Guralnikism', covered in chapter 5. Last is the activist attitude, which seeks to reshape or reform exisiting words for some ideological purpose, such as *wimmin, herstory, misterectomy* and the like. In many ways these four stances reflect the evolution of attitudes towards lexis.

Redefining the Core

Throughout this study we have been using the term 'core' in a commonsensical fashion to describe the words which are the most common in speech and writing. But this begs the question of whose speech and writing? There are differences between the common words used by, say, Dr Johnson, Henry James and Ernest Hemingway. We have also seen in chapter 1 (p. 42) that the pro-portion of classical and native terms varies considerably with individual authors. These differences are influenced by historical change in the development of vocabulary, by convention and by individual style. There are also differences within the varieties of global English: thus *weird* would be a core word in American English, *bloody* would be a core word in Australian English, *trek* would be a core word in South African English, but would any of these be a core word in British English?

The aim, then, is to define the core of contemporary English on a basis which is not simply impressionistic, and then analyse the terms etymologically to build up a lexical profile. To my knowledge, such a project has not yet been undertaken, because of the problems of definition outlined in the previous paragraph. The closest approximation was the survey contained in *A General Service List of English Words*, edited by Michael West (1953). This gave data on semantic frequencies, arranged alphabetically, but was based solely on the OED and, as the editor put it, 'therefore tends rather to undervalue those items used more in speech than in writing . . .' (p. viii).

How can we define the lexical core of Modern English? As we have seen, the use of corpora by modern dictionaries, notably the *Longman Dictionary of Contemporary English* (*LDOCE*) (1995) gives us a statistical basis with which to work. We recall from the discussion earlier in this chapter (pp. 361–2) that this work includes American usage and identifies the most commonly spoken and written words, up to 3000 in each category. This resource thus allows for various concentrations of the definition of 'core'. It would be possible to use the widest definition by including any word tagged in either category. This would net about 5000 words, and would include, for example, *raffle, sir, technically* and *transition,* all of which are tagged 'S3' or 'W3'.

Where should one draw the line? For the purposes of this investigation, I decided to work with the 'kernel of the core' by confining the sample only to those words tagged as both 'S1' and 'W1'. This limitation has its problems in that some common words are inevitably excluded by being 'S1' but only 'W2' or 'S2' but 'W1'. This occurs where words are in competition in the same semantic field, as with *sick* and *ill.* On the other hand, it favours words like *party* and *thing,* which have many meanings. The limited core amounted to 600 words.

The project produced some interesting results suggestive of the values of modern society. Despite the limitation imposed, many 'social', organizational and business terms emerge in the core, for example *society, class, company, competition, relationship, commission, manage, manager, management* and *system.* The technical and materialist emphasis of modern society is also apparent in key words like *environment, energy, machine, material, produce, product, production, programme* and *science*. On the other hand, neither *heaven* nor *hell* are core terms; nor are central moral terms of the past, such as *false, fair, foul, honour, virtue, crime* or *evil*. Words reflecting lifestyle are revealing: inevitably *television, news, bar* and *club* are included, but *press, radio* and *film* are not; surprisingly neither *sex, sport* nor *goal* make the core, but *game* does. Curiously, neither *politics* nor *government* are core words, but *power* is. A shift in values is reflected in that *progress* is no longer a core word (as it certainly would have been a century ago), but *success* is.

Developing this ideological aspect, a comparison with Raymond Williams's notable collection *Keywords* (1976) is revealing of what might broadly be called 'political values'. Williams listed and discussed 109 key terms of great social and political significance. Only twelve of these achieved the current core, namely *art, city, class, common, community education, family, management, private, science, society* and *work*. Of the hundred or so which did not, many prove to be surprising omissions. Among them were: *charity, civilization, conservative, culture, democracy, equality, ideology, industry, labour, liberal, literature, radical, revolution* and *status*.

In this brief analysis it will have been noticed that many classical terms have now been incorporated into the core. This is surprising, since the limitation to 600 words obviously favours the basic native terms of grammar such as verbs, auxiliaries, prepositions and the essential vocabulary of nouns (such as *hand, tree, hair* and *friend*). An etymological analysis of the lexical core yields the following breakdown:

Anglo-Saxon	47%
Norman French	33%
Latin	12%
Norse	4%
Greek	2%
Other	2%

These findings are also surprising, on a number of grounds. First, the general informed expectation would be that the Anglo-Saxon element would be higher. in the region of 60–70 per cent (as it was with the authors analysed previously), especially given the weight of spoken corpora on a small sample like this. Secondly, the balance of elements in the breakdown is striking: if one were to combine the Norman French and the Latin percentages (on the reasonable grounds that Norman French is derived from Latin) they would amount to 45 per cent, almost equalling the Anglo-Saxon. Further, if one were to add the Norse to the Anglo-Saxon and the Greek to the Norman French and Latin, then the word-stock would divide virtually on a fifty-fifty basis between the Germanic elements and the classical.

This analysis shows then that the character of the core has indeed changed, as classical terms are increasingly assimilated. We are reminded of the prescient observation of Johnson in his preface: 'Our language, for almost a century, has, by the concurrence of many causes, been gradually departing from its original Teutonick character, and deviating towards a Gallick structure.'

The resuscitation of the core

It is clearly apparent that Modern English has become increasingly accepting of alien and exotic terms. Apart from the thousands of opaque scientific words derived from classical roots, there are many strange new terms which continue to bubble up in the current linguistic ferment.

Likewise, as we have seen, there continues to be a tendency to use pretentious high-register terms for a variety of motives and in various contexts. The desire to dignify or inflate is apparent, for example, in a football commentator remarking on a club's 'results-oriented philosophy', i.e. will to win, or its 'aerial defence', i.e. the skill of its defenders in the air. The motive to disguise some self-inflicted military disaster is apparent in opaque formulations like 'collateral damage' or the lethal 'uncontrolled liberation of a rotor blade' from a crashed helicopter. Likewise a sharp fall in stock-market prices is termed a 'technical correction'.

Yet, as we noted in chapter 7, the core continues to generate great numbers of new lexical terms and semantic innovations, such as *black box, grunt-show, wellness, hot seat, joblessness, street-wise, meltdown, fallout, up tight, laid back, video nasty, unbundle, off-road, headbanger* and *clean* in the sense of 'pure' and uncorrupt'. Core words tend to ramify semantically. Thus *beat* has over the centuries developed *beat off, beat down* and *beat up,* but has in recent decades generated the new forms *offbeat, downbeat* and *upbeat.* Even the basic prepositions have developed verbal senses, as in to *up* the price, to *down* a drink and, in the last few years, to *out* someone, meaning to name them publicly against their wishes as homosexual.

Furthermore, in recent decades there has been a notable trend to prefer a native form, often a compound, instead of an established classical word. Amongst these are *pull-back* (for withdrawal), *write-up* (for 'review'), *bad-mouth* (for 'criticize'), *know-how* (for 'expertise'), *know-nothing* (for 'ignoramus'), *low-life* (for 'scum'), *life-writing* (for 'biography') and *voice-over* (for 'commentary'). The tendency is extended to current phrases like *in your face* and *off the wall.* These examples also show the current tendency to translate established classical terms back into native roots. This is strongly evident in 'people power', often preferred to *democracy,* as a consequence of the uncritical overuse and cynical abuse of *democracy* by regimes which are often totalitarian in their political methods.

Obscenity and taboo

Another shift in the structure of lexis (which also relates to Murray's scheme) is the relationship between the core and slang and obscenity. While it is always problematic to establish norms in the mores of the spoken language, there is little doubt that traditional notions of decorum have shifted in written English, and that the lower registers have now established themselves closer to the core than in Murray's day. The previous discussions of journalism and literature endorse this point.

The analysis of obscene and taboo language has always been bedevilled by double standards, namely expressions of outrage on the one hand and apparently thriving usage on the other. Two recent publications have now clarified these two aspects of attitudes and usage. In 1991 the British Broadcasting Standards Council published a report, *A Matter of Manners: The Limits of Broadcasting Language* (edited by A. Hargreave). In the preamble it was stated that the Council (like the BBC) receives more complaints about 'bad language' (the Council's phrase) than about violence or any other form of offensive behaviour. It set out try to establish 'why in the face of such sustained criticism of bad language, does it continue to appear, without apparent justification, in a multitude of programmes providing, therefore, a potential source of offence to large numbers of people' (1991, p. 1). The Council set up a panel of carefully selected respondents, monitored their responses to a variety of programmes, extracts and lists of words, and the resulting research findings provided the basis of the Council's report.

One surprising finding was that more than 15 per cent of the panel of respondents did not know the words *motherfucker*, *cocksucker* and *tosser*. This is presumably because the first two terms are predominantly American in usage.[7] Nevertheless, these words were rated by the panel as among the four strongest and most offensive terms from a list of thirty-three such words, topped by the ancient taboo words, *fuck* and *cunt*. Fifth in this rating came *nigger*, the only racial epithet in the list. Notably, over half of the panel regarded traditional religious oaths such as *blast*, *damn*, *hell* and *God* as 'not at all' strong or offensive.

A demographic analysis of responses within the panel found that, generally speaking, women and older people rated bad language as more offensive than men and younger folk. However, younger people were more sensitive to racist epithets. A separate test exclusively comprising eighteen racist epithets showed a remarkable discrimination in ranking. The four terms ranked as most unacceptable by the panel were those referring to people of African or Asian descent, namely *nigger, wog, coon* and *paki*. The 'middle range' consisted of terms for continental or oriental people, namely *dago, chink, nip, kraut, frog, jap* and *honky*, the only word referring to white people. The 'most acceptable terms', i.e. the least unacceptable, according to the panel, were those described by the report as 'those words we shall call "national" descriptive words and refer to people from Wales, Scotland and Ireland', namely *mick, taffy, paddy* and *jock* (1991, p. 17).

A test comprising a mixture of sexist terms referring to women and homosexuals and to those suffering from disability and diminished intelligence produced similarly sharp discrimination. Of the ten terms used, *spastic* and *cripple* were rated by far the least acceptable, followed in descending order of acceptability by the homosexual terms *dyke, queer, poof* and *nancy boy*. Of the two terms referring to women, *slag* was third on the list but *bitch* second last. There were notable demographic differences within the sample, *slag* being rated as particularly unacceptable by women and older respondents, and the terms for homosexuals being regarded as more acceptable by younger men (1991, pp. 17–18). This test clearly shows a new and increased sensitivity to disability, since the terms *spastic* and *cripple* have long been current as derogatory terms. In their medical senses both words have now been replaced by more neutral terms, such as *cerebral palsy* and *disabled*. These changes, like those relating to racist epithets, relate to 'politically correct' language, already discussed.

Turning to lexicographical developments, as is made clear in chapter 5, there has been a considerable, but not an absolute, change in the policy of dictionaries so far as foul language is concerned. The ancient taboos have been largely removed, so that the 'four-letter' words now appear in most standard works, while dictionaries of slang and demotic language continue to appear on virtually an annual basis.

As we have seen, a valuable index of actual usage is provided by the *Longman Dictionary of Contemporary English (LDOCE)* (1995), since it 'tags' the 3000 most frequently used words in written and spoken English. Of what are termed the 'big six' (i.e. *fuck, cunt, shit, arse, fart* and *piss*), both *fuck* and *shit* are so rated in oral usage, *fuck* as S3 and *shit* as S2. Significantly *arse* does not gain a rating, but *ass* is marked S2, no doubt because of the American weighting in the corpora.

In popular culture there is no doubt that the 'four-letter' words have become more frequently used. Notable examples in the films of the past decade are *The Commitments* (1995), *Trainspotting* (1996), *Kids* (1997) and most of the films of Spike Lee, notably *Do the Right Thing* (1989). The hugely successful comedy *Four Weddings and a Funeral* (1993) virtually threw down a linguistic challenge in its opening sequence, in which the 'dialogue' consisted of the word *fuck* being reiterated four times. *Sliding Doors* (1998) similarly had the heroine repeating *shit* as her opening line.[8]

It is clear that a shift is occurring in the notion of the taboo. Although the word is often used in a slightly loose, broad fashion (as *obscene* was about a decade ago) the strict linguistic sense of *taboo*, namely 'that which is unmentionable', provides an excellent indicator of sensitivity. Traditionally *taboo* has meant that which cannot be uttered because it is ineffably sacred or unspeakably vile. Now, of course, only the second category applies. When we apply these notions to the present lexical situation, we can see that, generally speaking, religious referents and expletives are increasingly regarded as inoffensive, that sexual terms still have much resonance, but that the new area of genuinely potent taboo is race. Yet here, too, there is a double standard in that blacks can use the word *nigger* of their own group. Though such use is laden with complex ironies, it is partly to reclaim the word, partly to make a statement (as in the name of the rap group 'Niggers with Attitude') that they do not have the old subservient attitude which accepted the insult, and partly to highlight the race prejudice which still exists.

Anglicisms

One of the most obvious signs of the status of English as a global language has been the extent of borrowing of English terms or 'Anglicisms' into other languages. Just as English has become much more accepting of foreign and exotic words, so it has become a major lexical exporter. Similarly, attitudes towards Anglicisms have changed over the past few decades. The Académie Française has been a notable bastion seeking to maintain the purity of the French language by resisting the fashion for loan-words. It publishes annual lists of proscribed terms, a procedure which is largely ignored. Thirty years ago René Étiemble, Professor of Comparative Literature at the Sorbonne, fulminated against the wholesale importation of words like *call-girl, teenager, juke-box* and *supermarket*, declaring 'The French language is a treasure. To violate it is a crime. People were shot in the war for treason. They should be punished for degrading the language' (in Barnett, 1966, p. 17). Étiemble coined the ironic portmanteau *Franglais* for the new Anglicized French he detested.[9]

Today much French journalism is virtually written in Franglais. Words like *jobs, plan, shopping, rafting, dancing, jogging, hot, fans, porno, jet-lag, auto-stop, finish,* and *star* abound, together with bilingual compounds such as *super-maison, first class, groupe rock fifties, l'homme live jazz* and whole formulas, such as *les boys bands* and *SEA, SEX AND ZZZ*. (This sample is taken from a single issue of *Cosmopolitan* magazine for August, 1998.) European business terminology is now largely Anglicized: an edition of a German-language Swiss newspaper, *Tages Anzeiger*, published in Zurich (4 July 1998) is full of terms like *leasing partner, jobs, adverts, recycling, renovation, engagements, private banking, tools, supplement* and compounds like *microzoom, systemadministrator* and *small talk*. (One should bear in mind that traditionally German has avoided Anglicized forms, preferring to make up native forms like *Fernsehen* for *television* and *Autobahn* for *highway*.)

The basic international vocabulary of business and economics is now English, with local variants like *plan, blok, program, economou, politik, project, prosperita* and *ekologicke* appearing in Russian and Czech. The essential lexis of tourism is likewise made up of English words (many of them actually derived from French) such as *hotel, café, club, bar, buffet, pub, grill, lunch, foto, train* and *jet*.

The Future: Fragmentation or Diversification within a Common Frame?

Surveying these trends and changes in structure, the broad lexical question which presents itself is this: do the new Englishes represent dialects, i.e. regional variations, the recognizable offspring of one mother tongue, or have they developed to the point that they are independent forms, albeit with a clear familial relationship to the parent? The comparison which invites itself is with Latin, the previous world language. For centuries Latin existed in its different forms in the outposts of the Empire; then, gradually, this one tongue evolved into the Romance languages.

The comparison with Latin is useful since it reminds us of two considerations. The first is that Classical Latin survived as the language of the Church and of scholarship until this century, while the regional forms of the *lingua franca* became different vernaculars. In other words, there was a dual development, as the language of the intelligentsia and as that of the common people. (A similar case is the coexistence of Mandarin Chinese, the traditional governing language of the Chinese Empire, and the various other regional dialects.) Secondly, the only global medium before 1476 was handwriting, which necessarily reflected regional pronunciation. Today the global broadcasting networks form a force for standardization.

An influential view on these matters came in 1978 from Dr Robert Burchfield, Editor-in-Chief of the four-volume *Supplement* to the *OED*. In an essay entitled 'The Point of Severance: English in 1776 and Beyond', he noted that 'The two forms of English [American and British] slowly drifted apart, as languages tend to, when most of the speakers of one branch never actually meet or talk to most of the speakers of a geographically separated branch'

(1978, p. 131). He continued: 'I am equally sure that these two main forms of English ... are continuing to move apart, and that existing elements of linguistic dissimilarity between them will intensify as time goes on, notwithstanding the power of the cinema, TV, *Time* magazine and other two-way gluing and fuelling devices' (1978, p. 133).

The model of gradual separation, of languages slowly drifting apart, is well demonstrated by the original sources of English, the Indo-European family and the Germanic group (which were not sustained by a political force like the Roman Empire) and which now survive as the thriving independent entities of German, Dutch, Swedish, Norwegian, Icelandic and so on. At present it would appear that the new Englishes have not attained a full degree of differentiation and independence to be regarded as separate languages. As Burchfield wrote in the conclusion of his excellent study, *The English Language*:

> The multifarious forms of English spoken within the British Isles and by native speakers abroad will continue to reshape and restyle themselves in the future. And they will become more and more at variance with the emerging Englishes of Europe and of the rest of the world. The English language is like a set of juggernaut trucks that goes on regardless. (1985, p. 173)

Burchfield's final image is arresting in its suggestions of force and momentum. But there still remains the question of destination. Spoken English, as we have seen, has always been varied, even within the English-speaking portion of the small islands of Great Britain. But these variations have coexisted with the notion of an accepted *koiné* or standard.

Another major authority, Professor Sir Randolph Quirk, has consistently emphasized unity rather than diversity in what he terms variously Standard English or General Public English. By this he does not mean Standard English or Received Pronunciation as used in the narrow British context, but the *Gestalt* of recognizable spoken English used and respected by the BBC, by CNN, by world leaders in the West and in the Commonwealth, and by English-language newspapers around the world. A diagrammatic representation of what is called Global Standard English is to be found in David Crystal's *Encyclopedia of the English Language* (1995, p. 111).

The authors of *The Story of English* see the role of English as being less global and its state less fragmented:

> English is not about to become a universal lingua franca, as some have suggested; neither is it likely to splinter into a Babel of competing tongues, at least in a world of telefaxes and satellites. The most obvious future for English is at a powerful standardized international level coexisting with a localized, non-standard indigenous level. (McCrum et al., 1986, p. 394)

Persuasive as this argument is, it prompts the question of whether English can exist in these two states – of a universal standard and regional non-standard varieties – and still be one language.

The models cited earlier, of Classical Latin and the Romance vernaculars, and of Mandarin Chinese and other regional dialects, support such a potential 'bilingual' development on two strata. This seems to me to be the most likely scenario. As the previous section on 'Redefining the Core' indicated, the use of corpora in the study of English lexis shows that although there have been shifts in the elements which make up the core, these have not been substantial.

Literatures in different registers

As these final chapters have shown, the primary definitions of 'English', 'language' and 'literature' have undergone major revisions in the course of the twentieth century. The prediction made by I. A. Richards half a century ago has been amply verified: 'At countless points on the earth's surface,' he wrote, 'English will be the most available language – English of some sort' (1943, p. 120). Colin MacCabe observed in *Futures for English*, 'it is perhaps no longer appropriate to speak of English literature, but of a literature in broken English' (1988, p. 12).

Though the 'state of the language' reflects many destructive forces at work, and a host of competing varieties which invoke the notion of Babel, MacCabe's seems an unduly pessimistic prognosis for the literature, in view of the work of such elegant and creative stylists as Bruce Chatwin, Antonia Byatt, Julian Barnes, Tom Stoppard, Anita Brookner, as well as many American and Commonwealth writers who clearly belong to a great tradition. Current developments suggest that the 'bilingual' model of a Mandarin *koiné* and a regional patois applies to literature as well. We may conclude by exemplifying both of MacCabe's varieties in the 'oral' and 'literary' traditions of the poetry of the Caribbean. The two cited works have at their matrix the idea of language and cultural identity. The first voice rings with the raw anger of the rejected immigrant, using the savage argot of the underclass:

> sick to hear
> -SEND DEM BACK-
> black like me,
> vomit sounds an bad
> 'LICKS [beatings] in de POLICE VAN'
> for bad English
> -SEND DEM BACK-
> -SEND DEM BACK-

BLACK
like me
to land
BLACK LIKE ME
IN THAT LAND
OF HOPE AND
G-L-O-O-O-R-Y
(Delano Abdul Malik de Coteau, from 'Motto Vision 1971')

The passion of the second is deceptively measured, calmly tracing in the land-scape the long perspective of opposition and deprivation:

Wales

Those white flecks cropping the ridges of Snowdon
will thicken their fleece and come wintering down
through the gap between the alliterative hills,
through the caesura that let in the Legions,
past the dark disfigured mouths of the chapels,
till a white silence comes to green-throated Wales.
Down rusty gorges, cold rustling gorse,
over rocks hard as consonants, and rain-vowelled shales,
sang the shallow-buried axe, helmet and baldric
before the wet asphalt sibilance of tires.
A plump raven, Plantagenet, unfurls its heraldic
caw over walls that held the cult of the horse.
In blackened cottages with their stony hatred
of industrial fires, a language is shared
like bread to the mouth, white flocks to the dark byres.
(Derek Walcott, 1981)

Walcott's wonderful poem, like Seamus Heaney's 'Bone Dreams' discussed in the previous chapter, takes us back, past all the waves of invasion and dis-placement which we have traced in this history, to the simple Celtic life with its 'cult of the horse', before the coming of the English. We are given the vignettes of the Roman legions entering (with a sly pun on *Caesar/caesura* sym-bolizing 'the gap between the alliterative hills'). Then 'the shallow-buried axe, helmet and baldric' figure the retreat before the Saxons, followed by the arrival of the Plantagenet French and the social dislocation of the Industrial Revolu-tion. All that remains is an ancient, musical 'language . . . shared like bread to the mouth', as integral as the landscape. But the poem is written with all the rich resources which English has taken to itself in the past fifteen hundred years.

Notes

1 New words have been given more coverage in the United States in recent decades. The journal *American Speech*, founded in 1925, has contained a column 'Among the New Words' since 1941. See the collection edited by John Algeo.

2 Showing that the centrality of words depends on the values of the user, the satirical magazine *Private Eye* suggested a top six of *tit, bum, page three, corr, gotcha* and *bonk*.

3 The *New Yorker* of 8 May 1965 commented: 'We march to Vietnam under such bannerets as "escalate", "defoliate", "pacification", "counterforce concept", "controlled responses", "damage-limitation forces", "benevolent incapacitators", and "targeting lists".'

4 David Crystal notes some of the taboos against using the term *black* in his *Cambridge Encyclopedia of the English Language* (1995, p. 177).

5 *Caucasian* was coined by the German anatomist and anthropologist, Johann Friedrich Blumenbach, who in 1795 distinguished five races. Blumenbach's theories, based mainly on skulls, and positing degeneration rather than evolution, are now largely discredited, which makes the survival of the term *Caucasian* in official American terminology somewhat ironic.

6 One instance is *The Official Politically Correct Dictionary and Handbook* (1992), ed. H. Beard and C. Cerf. Another is James F. Garner's *Politically Correct Bedtime Stories* (New York, 1994), with such ironic sallies as 'The Prince was celebrating his exploitation of the dispossessed and marginalized peasantry by throwing a fancy dress ball' (p. 31) and ' "I am your fairy godperson, or individual deity proxy, if you prefer" ' (p. 32).

7 Commenting on the inclusion of some previously taboo terms in recent dictionaries, Frederic Raphael notes: 'The black provenance of *mother-fucker* is tactfully ignored everywhere' (*TLS*, 16 October 1998).

8 Such banal repetitions support Robert Graves's view of 'the imaginative decline of popular swearing' (1936, p. 165).

9 The Académie continues to be concerned about the purity of the language, as Dr Johnson was in the eighteenth century, whereas conservative attitudes in English tend to focus more on 'bad language' than foreign words.

APPENDIX

QUANTIFYING THE GROWTH OF THE ENGLISH VOCABULARY

The main source of numerical data for reconstructing the growth of the English vocabulary is the *Chronological English Dictionary* (*CED*, 1970) which, as we saw in chapter 4, is based on the *Shorter Oxford English Dictionary* (*SOED*, 1933 edn). Thus the figures in the graph in figure 1 are not comprehensive nor up to date, reflecting the catchment area of the *SOED*. The graph shows the annual increment of new words and meanings consolidated into decades. Thus the figure given for 1500 is the total recorded in the *CED* for the years 1500–9, and so on. This format is used to represent centuries of data in a manageable form. Some years ago I constructed a graph of the whole span of annual increments from 1300 to 1957: it turned out to be over 5 feet long! The advantage of the annual graph, however, is that it shows dramatically the lexical impact of particular publications, such as major dictionaries. The years of highest growth are 1598 (590) and 1611 (844).

The data show clearly that the lexical and semantic growth of the language is not constant, but develops in peaks and troughs. The decade graph consolidates the growth pattern into two major peaks: the first is from *c*.1550 to *c*.1630, with the sharpest growth in the Elizabethan period (discussed in chapter 4); the second is from *c*.1790 to *c*.1880, with strong growth in the Romantic period. The intervening trough covers the Restoration and Augustan periods, both notably conservative. For example, the dictionaries of Bailey (1721) and Johnson (1755) made only minor impacts. The plain global statistics for the 500-year span 1450–1950 yield a grand total of just over 60,000 new words or senses, or an average of 120 a year.

Clearly, however, there is doubt over the validity of the apparent decline from 1840 onwards, since we know from our basic observation that the vocabulary continued to grow vigorously from the Victorian period onwards. It would appear that the great enterprise of the *OED* (which was published from 1884 to 1928) did not focus on new words as much as on the semantic reconstruction of established words.

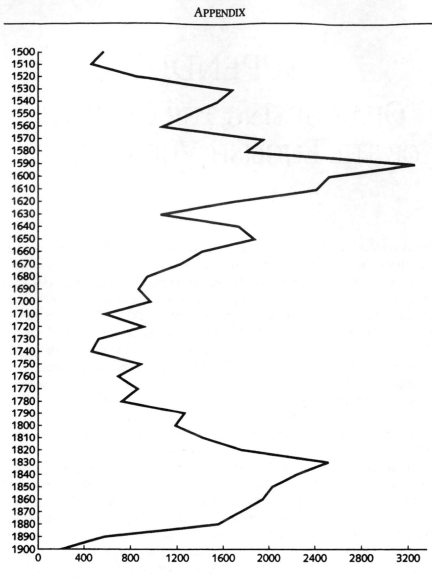

Appendix.1   The growth of the English vocabulary, 1500–1900

The *OED Supplement* (1972–86) had entries for some 57,700 main words, many of them newly recorded and exotic, though there were also numerous instances of ante-datings. Since the consolidation of the two sequences into the second edition (1989), a number of collections of new words have appeared, detailed in chapter 8, p. 363. The statistics given there as well as in *Fifty Years Among the New Words* (ed. John Algeo, 1991) indicate a tremendous surge in neologisms which is certainly rapid, but difficult to quantify accurately. The Algeo collection has approximately 7000 head-words covering the period 1941–91 and previously unrecorded. The total of words covered in these post-1986 sources is 16,000, but in the nature of such publications, there will be a certain amount of duplication.

BIBLIOGRAPHY

The bibliography is arranged in two sections: dictionaries (arranged chronologically) and other works (arranged alphabetically).

Dictionaries

1567: Harman, Thomas. *A Caveat or Warening for Commen Cursetors, vulgarely called Vagabones*. Early English Text Society, 9. London: [1869].

1591: Greene, Robert. *A Notable Discovery of Coosnage*. London.

1596: Coote, Edmund. *The English Scholemaster*. London.

1598: Florio, John. *A Worlde of Wordes*. London.

1604: Cawdrey, Robert. *A Table Alphabeticall . . . of hard usuall English words*. London: Edmund Weaver.

1611: Cotgrave, Randle. *A Dictionary of English and French*. London: Octavian Pulleyn.

1623: Cockeram, Henry. *The English Dictionarie*. London: Edmund Weaver.

1656: Blount, Thomas. *Glossographia*. London: Humphrey Moseley and George Sawbridge.

1658: Phillips, Edward. *The New World of English Words*. London. J. Phillips.

1721: Bailey, Nathaniel. *An Universal Etymological Dictionary*. London.

1730: ——*Dictionarium Britannicum: Or a more Complete Universal Etymological English Dictionary than any Extant*. London: T. Cox.

1755: Johnson, Samuel. *A Dictionary of the English Language*. London: W. Strahan.

1785: Grose, Francis. *A Classical Dictionary of the Vulgar Tongue*. London. Ed. Eric Partridge. London: Routledge, 1931, reprinted 1963.

1882: Skeat, Walter W. *A Concise Etymological Dictionary of the English Language*. Oxford: Clarendon Press.

1884–1928: Murray, J. A. H. et al. *A New English Dictionary on Historical Principles*. Oxford: Clarendon Press. [Later *The Oxford English Dictionary*.]

1890–1904: Farmer, John S. and Henley, William E. *Slang and its Analogues, Past and Present*. New York: Dutton. [Subsequently reissued as *A Dictionary of Slang*.]

1898–1905: Wright, Joseph. *The English Dialect Dictionary*. Oxford: Clarendon Press.

1898: Bosworth, Joseph and Toller, C. N. *An Anglo-Saxon Dictionary*. Oxford: Clarendon Press.

1913: Pettman, Charles. *Africanderisms*. London: Longmans Green.

1931– : Craigie, William A. et al. *A Dictionary of the Older Scottish Tongue*. Oxford: Oxford University Press and University of Aberdeen Press.

1933: Onions, C. T. and Craigie, W. A. *Supplement to the Oxford English Dictionary*. Oxford: Clarendon Press.

[1933–50]: Partridge, Eric. *Slang*. 3rd edn, 1960. London: Routledge & Kegan Paul.

[1937–61]: ——*A Dictionary of Historical Slang*. Abridged by Jacqueline Simpson, 1986. Harmondsworth: Penguin.

[1947]: ——*Shakespeare's Bawdy*. Reprint, 1968. London: Routledge & Kegan Paul.

[1958–61]: ——*Origins*. 3rd edn, 1977. London: Routledge & Kegan Paul.

1960: Wentworth, Harold and Flexner, S. B. *A Dictionary of American Slang*. New York: Crowell.

1961: Gove, Philip et al. *Webster's Third New International Dictionary*. Springfield, MA: Merriam.

1961: Franklyn, Julian. *A Dictionary of Rhyming Slang*. 2nd edn. London: Routledge & Kegan Paul.

1966: Onions C. T., with Friedrichsen, G. W. S. and Burchfield, R. W. *The Oxford Dictionary of Etymology*. Oxford: Oxford University Press.

1967: Cassidy, F. G. and Le Page, R. B. *Dictionary of Jamaican English*. Cambridge: Cambridge University Press.

1970: Finkenstaedt, Thomas, Leisi, E. and Wolf, D. *A Chronological English Dictionary*. Heidelberg: Carl Winter.

1970: Major, Clarence. *A Dictionary of Afro-American Slang*. New York: International Publishers.

1972–86: Burchfield, R. W. et al. *A Supplement to the Oxford English Dictionary*. Oxford: Clarendon Press.

1976: Flexner, Stuart B. *I Hear America Talking*. New York: Van Nostrand Reinhold.

1981: Rawson, Hugh. *A Dictionary of Euphemisms and Other Doubletalk*. London: Macdonald.

1982: Boycott, Rosie. *Batty, Bloomers and Boycott*. London: Hutchinson.

1984: Moss, Norman. *The British/American Dictionary*. London: Hutchinson.

1984: Neaman, Judith S., and Silver, Carole G. *A Dictionary of Euphemisms*. Hemel Hempstead: Unwin.

1984: Green, Jonathon. *Newspeak*. London: Routledge & Kegan Paul.

1984: ——*The Dictionary of Contemporary Slang*. London: Pan.

1985: Kramarae, Cheris and Treichler, Paula A. *A Feminist Dictionary*. London: Pandora.

1985: Smith, Christopher. *Alabaster, Bikinis and Calvados*. London: Huchinson.

1986: Eagleson, Robert D. (ed.). *A Shakespeare Glossary*. Oxford: Oxford University Press.

1986: Mort, Simon (ed.). *Longman Guardian Original Selection of New Words.* Harlow, Essex: Longman.

1987: Chapman, Robert L. *New Dictionary of American Slang.* London: Macmillan.

1988: Kirkpatrick, Betty (ed.). *Roget's Thesaurus.* Harmondsworth: Penguin. [First edition published in 1852]

1988: McDonald, James. *A Dictionary of Obscenity, Taboo and Euphemism.* London: Sphere.

1988: Ramson, W. (ed.). *The Australian National Dictionary.* Melbourne: Oxford University Press.

1988: Green, Jonathon. *The Slang Thesaurus.* Harmondsworth: Penguin.

1989: Rawson, Hugh. *A Dictionary of Invective.* London: Robert Hale.

1990: Ayto, John. *Bloomsbury Dictionary of Word Origins.* London: Bloomsbury.

1991: Mills, Jane. *Womanwords.* London: Virago.

1991: Green, Jonathon. *Neologisms.* London: Bloomsbury.

1992: Beard, Henry and Cerf, Christopher. *The Official Politically Correct Dictionary & Handbook.* London: Grafton.

1992: Tulloch, Sarah (ed.). *The Oxford Dictionary of New Words.* Oxford: Oxford University Press.

1993: Lerner, Sid, Belkin, Gary S. et al. *trashcash, fizzbos and flatliners.* Boston: Houghton Mifflin.

1994: Rawson, Hugh. *Devious Derivations.* New York: Crown.

1994: Major, Clarence. *Juba to Jive.* New York and London: Viking Penguin.

1995: Summers, Della (ed.). *The Longman Dictionary of Contemporary English.* 3rd edn. London: Longman.

1995: Roberts, J. A. and Kay, C. J. *A Thesaurus of Old English.* King's College Medieval Studies XI, London.

1996: Silva, Penny et al. (eds). *A Dictionary of South African English on Historical Principles.* Cape Town: Oxford University Press.

1998: Orsman, H. W. (ed.). *The Oxford Dictionary of New Zealand English.* Oxford: Oxford University Press.

Other Works

Algeo, John (ed.). (1991) *Fifty Years Among the New Words.* Cambridge: Cambridge University Press.

Alvarez, A. (1962) *The New Poetry.* Harmondsworth: Penguin.

Amis, Kingsley. (1997) *The King's English.* London: HarperCollins.

Anglo-Saxon Chronicle, trans. G. N. Garmonsway. (1954). London: Dent.

Ayers, Donald M. (1986) *English Words from Greek and Latin Elements.* Tucson: University of Arizona Press.

Bacon, Francis. (1605) *The Advancement of Learning.* London: Macmillan, 1902 reprint.

Bailey, Richard W. (ed.). (1987) *Dictionaries of English.* Ann Arbor: University of Michigan Press.

——(1991) *Images of English*. Ann Arbor: University of Michigan Press.

Bailey, Richard W. and Robinson, Jay L. (1973) *Varieties of Present-day English*. London: Macmillan.

Baker, S. J. (1945) *The Australian Language*. Sydney: Angus & Robertson.

Barber, Charles L. (1964) *The Story of Language*. London: Pan.

——(1976) *Early Modern English*. London: André Deutsch.

——(1993) *The English Language: A Historical Introduction*. Cambridge: Cambridge University Press.

Barfield, Owen. (1962) *History in English Words*. London: Faber. [First published in 1926.]

Barltrop, Robert, and Wolveridge, Jim. (1980) *The Muvver Tongue*. London and West Nyack: Journeyman Press.

Barnett, Lincoln. (1966) *The Treasure of Our Tongue*. London: Secker and Warburg.

Baron, Dennis. (1986) *Grammar and Gender*. New Haven: Yale University Press.

Barr, Ann and York, Peter. (1982) *The Official Sloane Ranger Handbook*. London: Ebury Press.

Batchelor, R. E. and Offord, M. H. (1982) *A Guide to Contemporary French Usage*. Cambridge: Cambridge University Press.

Bate, Walter Jackson. (1975) *The Life of Samuel Johnson*. New York: Harcourt Brace Jovanovich.

Baugh, Albert C. (1951) *A History of the English Language*. London: Routledge & Kegan Paul.

Beauvoir, Simone de. (1972) *The Second Sex*. Harmondsworth: Penguin.

Bede. (1960) *A History of the English Church and People*, trans. Leo Shirley-Price. Harmondsworth: Penguin.

Bernstein, Basil. (1971) *Class, Codes and Control*. London: Routledge & Kegan Paul.

Blake, N. F. (1983) *The Language of Shakespeare*. London: Macmillan.

Blake, N. F. (ed.). (1992) *The Cambridge History of the English Language*. Vol. II. Cambridge: Cambridge University Press.

Bloomfield, Morton W. and Newmark, L. M. (1963) *A Linguistic Introduction to the English Language*. New York: Knopf.

Borges, Jorge Luis. (1962) *Labyrinths*. Harmondsworth: Penguin.

Boswell, James. (1893) *Life of Johnson*. London: Macmillan. [First published in 1791.]

Bowie, Malcolm. (1991) *Lacan*. London: Fontana.

Bradbury, Malcolm and MacFarlane, James (eds). (1976) *Modernism*. Harmondsworth: Penguin.

Bradley, Henry. (1964) *The Making of English*. London: Macmillan.

Bréal, Michel. (1900) *Studies in the Science of Meaning*, trans. Mrs Henry Cust. London: Heinemann.

Brook, G. L. (1965) *English Dialects*. London: André Deutsch.

——(1973) *Varieties of English*. London: Macmillan.

Bryson, Bill. (1994) *Made in America*. London: Secker & Warburg.

Buckle, Richard. (1980) *U and Non-U Revisited*. London: Debrett/Futura.

Burchfield, Robert. (1978) 'The Point of Severance: English in 1776 and Beyond'. *Encounter*, June, pp. 129–33.

—— (1985) *The English Language*. Oxford: Oxford University Press.

—— (1989) *Unlocking the English Language*. London: Faber.

Burgess, Anthony. (1964) *Language Made Plain*. London: English Universities Press.

—— (1993) *A Mouthful of Air*. London: Vintage.

Burnett, Paula. (1986) *The Penguin Book of Caribbean Verse*. Harmondsworth: Penguin.

Burnley, David. (1992) *The History of the English Language: a source book*. London: Longmans.

Campbell, J. (ed.). (1991) *The Anglo-Saxons*. Harmondsworth: Penguin.

Cawley, A. C. (ed.). (1958) *The Wakefield Pageants in the Townley Cycle*. Manchester: Manchester University Press.

Chaucer, Geoffrey. (1957) *The Works of Geoffrey Chaucer*, ed. by F. N. Robinson. 2nd edn. Boston: Houghton Mifflin.

Chauliac, Guy de. (1971) *The Cirurgery of Guy de Chauliac*, [c.1363] ed. Margaret S. Ogden. Early English Text Society, no. 256. Oxford: Oxford University Press.

Cleland, John. (1969) *Memoirs of an Oxford Scholar*. London: Sphere.

—— (1986) *Fanny Hill: Memoirs of a Woman of Pleasure*. Harmondsworth: Penguin. [First published in 1749.]

Commager, Henry S. (1945) *Alexis de Tocqueville: Democracy in America*. Oxford: Oxford University Press.

Corson, David. (1985) *The Lexical Bar*. Oxford: Pergamon Press.

Crystal, David. (1987) *The Cambridge Encyclopaedia of Linguistics*. Cambridge: Cambridge University Press.

—— (1988) *The English Language*. Harmondsworth: Penguin.

—— (1995) *The Cambridge Encyclopaedia of the English Language*. Cambridge: Cambridge University Press.

—— (1997) *English as a Global Language*. Cambridge: Cambridge University Press.

Defoe, Daniel. (1957) *The Best of Defoe's Review*, ed. William L. Payne. New York: Columbia University Press.

Denholm-Young, N. (1948) 'The Tournament in the thirteenth century', in *Essays in Medieval History Presented to F. M. Powicke*. Oxford: Oxford University Press.

Derrida, Jacques. (1967) *Writing and Difference*, trans. Alan Bass. Chicago: University of Chicago Press.

Dillard, J. L. (1972) *Black English*. New York: Vintage.

Douglas, D. C. and Greenaway G. W. (eds). (1953) *English Historical Documents*. Vol. II. London: Eyre & Spottiswoode.

Dunant, Sarah, (ed.). (1994) *The War of the Words: The Political Correctness Debate*. London: Virago.

Elliott, Ralph W. V. (1974) *Chaucer's English*. London: André Deutsch.

Empson, William. (1977) 'Compacted Doctrines'. *New York Review of Books*, 27 October, pp. 21–2.

—— (1951) *The Structure of Complex Words*. London: Chatto & Windus.

Enright, D. J. (ed.). (1986) *Fair of Speech*. Oxford: Oxford University Press.

Evans, B. Ifor. (1959) *The Language of Shakespeare's Plays*. London: Methuen.

Fischer, Andreas. (1994) '"Sumer is icumen in": The seasons of the year in Middle English and Early Modern English', in D. Kastovsky (ed.) *Studies in Early Modern English*. Mouton de Gruyter, pp. 79–95.

Fisher, John H. and Bornstein, Diane. (1974) *In Forme of Speche is Chaunge*. New York: Prentice-Hall.

Ford, Boris. (ed.). (1983) *The Present* (Harmondsworth: Penguin).

Foster, Brian. (1970) *The Changing English Language*. Harmondsworth: Penguin.

Fowler, Roger. (1991) *Language in the News*. London: Routledge & Kegan Paul.

Freeborn, Dennis. (1992) *From Old English? to Standard English*. London: Macmillan.

Freeman, E. A. (1875–9) *The Norman Conquest*. Oxford: Oxford University Press.

Gibbon, Edward. (1796) *Autobiography* London.

Gill, Alexander. (1972) *Logonomia Anglica* [1610], ed. B. Danielsson and Arvid Gabrielson. Stockholm: Almquist & Wiksell.

Gordon, George. (1928) *The Language of Shakespeare*. London: Macmillan.

Graddol, David. (1997) *The Future of English?* London: British Council.

Graves, Robert. (1936) *The Future of Swearing and Improper Language*. London: Kegan Paul, Trench, Trubner. [Originally issued in 1927 as *Lars Porsena or The Future of Swearing*.]

Hargreave, Andrea Millwood (ed.). (1991) *A Matter of Manners? The Limits of Broadcasting Language*. London: John Libbey.

Hartmann, R. R. K. (ed.). (1986) *The History of Lexicography*. Amsterdam: John Benjamin.

Higden Ranulph. (1865–6) *Polychronicon* [1387], trans. John of Trevisa. London: Rolls Series.

Hobbs Jenny. (1979) *Darling Blossom*. Cape Town: Don Nelson.

Hogg, Richard M. (ed.). (1992) *The Cambridge History of the English Language*. Vol. I. Cambridge: Cambridge University Press.

Hornadge, Bill. (1980) *The Australian Slanguage*. North Ryde, NSW: Cassell Australia.

Howard, Philip. (1984) *The State of the Language: English Observed*. London: Hamish Hamilton.

——(1985) *A Word in your Ear*. Harmondsworth: Penguin.

Hughes, Geoffrey. (1988) *Words in Time*. Oxford: Basil Blackwell.

——(1991) *Swearing*. Oxford: Basil Blackwell.

Hulme, Hilda. (1962) *Explorations in Shakespeare's Language*. London: Longman.

Humphries, Barry. (1988) *The Complete Barry McKenzie*. London: Methuen.

Hussey, S. S. (1982) *The Literary Language of Shakespeare*. Cambridge: Cambridge University Press.

Jespersen, Otto. (1922) *Language, its Nature, Development and Origin*. London: Allen & Unwin.

——(1962) *Growth and Structure of the English Language*. 9th edn. Oxford: Basil Blackwell. [First published in 1905.]

Jones, Lyle V. and Wepman, Joseph. (1966) *A Spoken Word Count*. Chicago: Language Research Association.

Jonson, Ben. (1923) *Discoveries* [1641]. London: Bodley Head.

Joyce, James. (1960) *Ulysses*. London: Bodley Head. [First published in 1922.]

Joos, Martin. (1967) *The Five Clocks*. New York: Harcourt, Brace.

Keats, John. (1905) *Poems*, ed. E. de Selincourt. London: Methuen.

Kermode, Frank. (1973) *Lawrence*. London: Fontana/Collins.

Krill, Richard M. (1990) *Greek and Latin in English Today*. Bolchazy: Wauconda.

Kuhn, Sherman. (1968) 'The Preface to a Fifteenth Century Concordance', *Speculum*, 43, pp. 258–73.

Lakoff, Robin. (1975) *Language and Woman's Place*. New York: Harper & Row.

Lanfrank. (1894) *Lanfrank's 'Science of Cirurgery'* [c.1425], ed. Robert V. Fleischhacker. Early English Text Society, original series 102. London.

Langland, William. (1855) *The Vision of Piers Plowman*, ed. Walter W. Skeat. Oxford: Clarendon Press.

Lanham, L. W. and Macdonald, C. A. (1979) *The Standard in South African English and its Social History*. Heidelberg: Julius Groos.

Laplanche, Jean. (1989) *New Foundations in Psychoanalysis*. Oxford: Basil Blackwell.

Leith, Dick. (1983) *A Social History of English*. London: Routledge & Kegan Paul.

Lewis, C. S. (1960) *Studies in Words*. Cambridge: Cambridge University Press.

Lipka, Leonhard. (1990) *An Outline of English Lexicology*. Tübingen: Niemeyer.

Lockwood, W. B. (1975) *Languages of the British Isles Past and Present*. London: André Deutsch.

Lodge, David. (1989) *Nice Work*. London: Penguin.

Lorimer, James (trans.) (1984) *The New Testament in Scots*. Harmondsworth: Penguin.

Low, Sidney. (1914) *The Governance of England*. London: Unwin.

Macaulay, Lord. (1907) *Macaulay: Critical and Histrical Essays*. London: Dent.

MacCabe, Colin (ed.). (1988) *Futures for English*. Manchester: Manchester University Press.

Mahood, Molly. (1968) *Shakespeare's Wordplay*. London: Hutchinson.

[Malan, Robin]. (1972) *Ah Big Yaws?* Cape Town: David Philip.

Malory, Sir Thomas. (1947) *The Works of Sir Thomas Malory*, ed. Eugene Vinaver. Oxford: Oxford University Press. [1485].

Marchand, Hans. (1975) *The Categories and Types of Present-Day English Word Formation*. 2nd edn. München: C. H. Beck.

Marlowe, Christopher. (1965) *Doctor Faustus* [1584], ed. Roma Gill. London: Ernest Benn.

Matoré, George. (1963) *La Méthode en lexicologie: domaine francais*. Paris: Didier.

Mayhew, Henry. (1983) *London's Underworld*, ed. Peter Quennell. London: Bracken Books. [First published in 1851.]

McArthur, Tom (ed.). (1986) *Worlds of Reference*. Cambridge: Cambridge University Press.

——(1992) *The Oxford Companion to the English Language*. Oxford: Oxford University Press.

——(1998) *The English Languages*. Cambridge: Cambridge University Press.

McCarthy, Mary. (1962) 'General Macbeth' in *Macbeth*, ed. S. Barnet. New York: Signet Classics, pp. 229–40.

McCracken, David. (1969) 'The Drudgery of Defining: Johnson's Debt to Bailey's *Dictionarium Britannicum*', *Modern Philology* 66, pp. 338–41.

McCrum, R. et al. (1986) *The Story of English*. London: Faber/BBC.

McKnight, G. (1968) *The Evolution of the English Language*. New York: Dover.

McLeod, A. L. (ed.). (1963) *The Pattern of Australian Culture*. Ithaca, NY: Cornell University Press.

Mellinkoff, David. (1963) *The Language of the Law*. Boston: Little, Brown.

Mencken, H. L. (1919–36) *The American Language*. 4th edn. New York: Knopf. [First published in 1919.]

Mesthrie, Rajend (ed.). (1995) *Language and Social History: Studies in South African Sociolinguistics*. Cape Town: David Philip.

Michaels, Ian, and Ricks, Christopher (eds). (1980) *The State of the Language*. Berkeley, Los Angeles, London: University of California Press.

Miller, Casey and Swift, Kate. (1981) *The Handbook of Non-Sexist Writing*. London: Women's Press.

Millward, Celia M. (1989) *A Biography of the English Language*. Fort Worth: Holt Rinehart.

Milroy, James. (1992) *Linguistic Variation and Change*. Oxford: Basil Blackwell.

Mitchell, Bruce. (1995) *An Invitation to Old English and Anglo-Saxon England*. Oxford: Blackwell.

Mitford, Nancy. (1960) *Noblesse Oblige*. Harmondsworth: Penguin.

Muir, Kenneth (ed.). (1956) *Elizabethan and Jacobean Prose*. Harmondsworth: Penguin.

Murphy, John J. (1966) *The Book of Pidgin English*. Brisbane: Smith & Paterson.

Murray, Elisabeth K. M. (1977) *Caught in the Web of Words*. New Haven and London: Yale University Press.

Murry, John Middleton. (1936) *Shakespeare*. London: Jonathan Cape.

Nash, Walter. (1992) *An Uncommon Tongue*. London: Routledge.

——(1993) *Jargon*. Oxford: Basil Blackwell.

Nist, John. (1966) *A Structural History of English*. New York: St Martin's Press.

Orton Harold, and Wright, Nathalia. (1974) *A Word Geography of England*. London: Seminar Press.

Orwell, George. (1949) *Nineteen Eighty-Four*. Harmondsworth: Penguin (1972).

——(1958) 'Politics and the English Language' (1946), in *George Orwell: Selected Writings*, ed. G. Bott. London: Heinemann.

Partridge, Eric. (1933) *Words, Words, Words*. London: Methuen.

——(1948) *Words at War: Words at Peace*. London: Muller.

——(1963) *Swift's Polite Conversation* [1738]. London: André Deutsch.

Partridge, Eric and Clark, John W. (1951) *British and American English since 1900*. New York: Philosophical Library.

Pater, Walter. (1966) *Three Major Texts*, ed. W. E. Buchler. New York: New York University Press.

Phelps, Robert and Deane, Peter (eds). (1968) *The Literary Life*. New York: Farrar, Straus, Giroux.

Phillipps, K. C. (1984) *Language and Class in Victorian England*. Oxford: Basil Blackwell.

Plutarch. (1968) *Shakespeare's Plutarch*, ed. T. J. B. Spencer. Harmondsworth: Penguin.

Potter, Simeon. (1963) *Our Language*. Harmondsworth: Penguin.

——(1975) *Changing English*. London: André Deutsch.

Potter, Stephen. (1937) *The Muse in Chains*. London: Jonathan Cape.

Puttenham, George. (1896) *The Arte of English Poesie* [1589]. London: English Reprints.

Pyles, Thomas and J. Algeo. (1970) *The Origins and Development of the English Language*. New York: Harcourt, Brace.

Reaney, P. H. (1960) *The Origin of English Place Names*. London: Routledge & Kegan Paul.

Richards, I. A. (1943) *Basic English and its Uses*. London: Kegan Paul.

Ricks, Christopher and Michaels, L. (eds). (1990) *The State of the Language: 1990s Edition*. London: Faber.

Ridler, Ann (ed.). (1970) *Shakespeare Criticism*. Oxford: Oxford University Press.

Rochester, John Wilmot, Earl of. (1984) *Poems*, ed. Keith Walker. Oxford: Basil Blackwell.

Ross, Alan S. C. (1960) 'U and Non-U: an essay in sociological linguistics', in *Noblesse Oblige*, ed. Nancy Mitford. Harmondsworth: Penguin, pp. 9–32. [Originally 'Linguistic class-indicators in present-day English', *Neuphilologische Mitteilungen*, 1954.]

Rowan, David. (1998) *A Glossary for the 90s*. London: Prion.

Salgado, Gamini (ed.). (1972) *Cony-Catchers and Bawdy Baskets*. Harmondsworth: Penguin.

Salgado, Gamini and Thompson, Peter. (1985) *The Everyman Companion to the Theatre*. London: Dent.

Salmon, Vivian and Burness, Edwina (eds). (1987) *A Reader in the Language of Shakespearean Drama*. Amsterdam: John Benjamin.

Santayana, George. (1900) *Interpretations of Poetry and Religion*. New York: Scribners.

Saussure, Ferdinand de. (1966) *Course in General Linguistics*, ed. Charles Bally and Albert Sechehaye, trans. Wade Baskin. New York: McGraw Hill.

Schäfer, Jürgen. (1980) *Documentation and the OED: Shakespeare and Nashe as Test Cases*. Oxford: Oxford University Press.

Serjeantson, M. S. (1935) *A History of Foreign Words in English*. London: Routledge & Kegan Paul.

Shakespeare, William (n. d.) *The Works of William Shakespeare*, ed. W. J. Craig. Oxford: Oxford University Press.

Sheard, J. A. (1954) *The Words we Use*. London: André Deutsch.

Shirley, Frances A. (1979) *Swearing and Perjury in Shakespeare's Plays*. London: Allen & Unwin.

Sledd, James and Ebbitt, Wilma (eds). (1962) *Dictionaries and THAT Dictionary*. Chicago: Scott Foresman.

Sledd, James and Kolb, Gwyn A. (eds). (1955) *Johnson's Dictionary*. Chicago: Chicago University Press.

Spender, Dale. (1980) *Man Made language*. London: Routledge.

Spevack, Marvin. (1968) *A Complete and Systematic Concordance to the Works of Shakespeare*. Hidesheim: George Olms.

Spurgeon, Caroline. (1935) *Shakespeare's Imagery*. Cambridge: Cambridge University Press.

Starnes, de Witt T. and Noyes, G. (1946) *The English Dictionary from Cawdrey to Johnson*. Chapel Hill: University of North Carolina Press.

Steiner, George. (1969) *Language and Silence*. Harmondsworth: Penguin.

——(1975) *Extraterritorial*. Harmondsworth: Penguin.

Sterne, Laurence. (1948) *The Life and Opinions of Tristram Shandy*. London: John Lehmann. [First published in 1760–7.]

Stoppard, Tom. (1972) *Jumpers*. London: Faber.

Strang, Barbara. (1970) *A History of English*. London: Methuen.

Swift, Jonathan. (1925) *The Prose Works of Jonathan Swift*. London: G. Bell.

——(1957) *A Proposal for Correcting, Improving and Ascertaining the English Tongue*, ed. H. Davis and L. Landa. Oxford: Blackwell. [First published in 1712.]

——(1963) *A Complete Collection of Genteel and Ingenious Conversation*, ed. Eric Partridge. London: André Deutsch. [First published in 1738.]

Tacitus, Cornelius. (1964) *Tacitus on Britain and Germany*, trans. H. Mattingly. Harmondsworth: Penguin.

Thompson, Leonard. (1990) *A History of South Africa*. New Haven: Yale University Press.

Tocqueville, A. de (1960) *Democracy in America*, trans. Henry Reeve. New York: Knopf. [First published in 1825.]

Todd, Loreto. (1984) *Modern Englishes: Pidgins and Creoles*. Oxford: Basil Blackwell.

Trilling, Lionel and Bloom, Harold (eds). (1973) *The Victorians*. Oxford: Oxford University Press.

Trollope, Frances. (1927) *Domestic Manners of the Americans*. London: George Routledge. [First published in 1832.]

Trudgill, Peter. (1974) *Socioliguistics: An Introduction*. Harmondsworth: Penguin.

——(1990) *The Dialects of England*. Oxford: Basil Blackwell.

Tynan, Kenneth. (1975) *The Sound of Two Hands Clapping*. London: Jonathan Cape.

Ullmann, Stephen. (1951) *Words and Their Use*. London: Frederick Muller.

——(1962) *Semantics: An Introduction to the Science of Meaning*. Oxford: Basil Blackwell.

——(1964) *Language and Style*. Oxford: Basil Blackwell.

Upton, Clive and Widdowson, J. D. A. (1996) *An Atlas of English Dialects*. Oxford: Oxford University Press.

Vallins, G. H. (1954) *Better English*. London: André Deutsch.

Vico, Giambattista. (1948) *The New Science*, trans. Thomas G. Bergin and M. H. Fish. Ithaca, NY: Cornell University Press.

Vidal, Gore. (1974) *Collected Essays*. London: Heinemann.

Wakelin, Martin. (1988) *The Archaeology of English*. London: Batsford.

Wardroper, John (ed.). (1975) *The Demaundes Joyous*. London: Gordon Fraser.

Warner, Alan. (1961) *A Short Guide to English Style*. Oxford: Oxford University Press.

Webster, Noah. (1789) *Dissertations on the English Language*. Gainesville: Scholars' Facsimiles and Reprints (1951).

Wells, Ronald A. (1973) *Dictionaries and the Authoritarian Tradition*. The Hague: Mouton.

West, Michael (ed.). (1953) *A General Service List of English Words*. London: Longmans.

White, Lynn, Jr. (1962) *Medieval Technology and Social Change*. Oxford: Oxford University Press.

Whorf, Benjamin Lee. (1974) *Language, Thought and Reality*, ed. John B. Carroll. Cambridge, MA: MIT Press.

Williams, Raymond. (1976) *Keywords*. London: Fontana.

Wilson, John Dover. (1944) *Life in Shakespeare's England*. Harmondsworth: Penguin.

Wilson Knight, George. (1949) *The Wheel of Fire*. London: Methuen.

Wimsatt, W. K. (1948) *Philosophic Words*. New Haven: Yale University Press.

Wood, Frederick T. (1959) *An Outline History of the English Language*. London: Heinemann.

Wordsworth, William. (1959) *The Lyrical Ballads*, ed. G. Sampson. London: Methuen.

Wrenn, C. L. (1960) *The English Language*. London: Methuen.

Wyld, Henry Cecil. (1936) *A History of Modern Colloquial English*. 3rd edn. Oxford: Basil Blackwell.

Wynne-Davies, Marion (ed.). (1989) *The Bloomsbury Companion to English Literature*. London: Bloomsbury.

Zipf, G. K. (1945) 'The meaning-frequency relationship of words', *Journal of General Psychology*, 33, pp. 251–66.

——(1949) *Human Behavior and the Principle of Least Effort*. Cambridge, MA: Harvard University Press.

FURTHER READING

This is intended to be a compact, practical bibliography, directing the reader to the seminal or most useful works in a particular area. It covers general histories of the English language and particular topics.

General Histories of the English Language

Of the many works in the field, the student will find the following useful: C. L. Barber, *The English Language: A Historical Introduction* (previously *The Story of Language*), S. Potter, *Our Language*, R. W. Burchfield, *The English Language*, D. Crystal, *The English Language* and *The Cambridge Encylopedia of the English Language*, Dick Leith, *A Social History of English*, Celia M. Millward, *A Biography of the English Language*. Otto Jespersen, *Growth and Structure of The English Language*, now in its tenth edition, is still very stimulating. A. C. Baugh and T. Cable, *A History of the English Language*, is a longer study, while two collections of historical readings are J. H. Fisher and D. Bornstein, *In Forme of Speche is Chaunge* and D. Burnley, *The History of The English Language: A Source Book*. A useful general guide is T. McArthur (ed.), *The Oxford Companion to the English Language*.

Semantics, Register and Lexis

Of the various works by Stephen Ullmann, *Words and their Use* is the most compact, while Leonhard Lipka's *Outline of English Lexicology* is also useful. Mary M. Serjeantson's *A History of Foreign Words in English* is still the standard work, as is Hans Marchand, *English Word-Formation*. The following all have valuable historical emphases: O. Barfield, *History in English Words*, C. S. Lewis, *Studies in Words* and Geoffrey Hughes, *Words in Time*. The journal *English Today* has topical articles in this domain.

Dictionaries

The great *Oxford English Dictionary* (2nd edn, 20 volumes, also available on CD-ROM) is the indispensable resource for tracing the historical evolution of the vocabulary and the semantic histories of words. The two-volume *Shorter Oxford English Dictionary* is a useful abbreviation, while more practical works for general purposes are the single-volume *Concise Oxford Dictionary* and similar ones published by Collins, Longmans and Chambers. The principal dictionaries for American English are *Webster's Third New International Dictionary*, the *Random House Dictionary* and the *American Heritage Dictionary*.

More specialist dictionaries are *The Oxford Dictionary of English Etymology* and Eric Partridge, *Origins*. T. Finkenstaedt et al., *A Chronological English Dictionary* is a valuable resource for lexical change. *Roget's Thesaurus* has been revised many times, one of the best recent versions being that edited by B. Fitzpatrick. The standard work on the early history of the dictionary is D. W. T. Starnes and G. E. Noyes, *The English Dictionary from Cawdrey to Johnson*, while Jonathon Green's *Chasing the Sun* gives more insight into lexicographers. Further details of dictionaries, especially those of new words, are to be found in chapter 5 (p. 272) and chapter 8 (p. 363). The student will also find articles of interest in the *International Journal of Lexicography*.

Dialect

Since the publication of Joseph Wright's founding work, *The English Dialect Dictionary*, at the turn of the century, a number of vaulable studies have appeared. These include H. Orton and N. Wright's *An English Word Geography*, G. L. Brook, *English Dialects*, P. Trudgill, *The Dialects of English* and C. Upton and J. Widdowson, *English Dialects*.

Slang and Euphemism

The pioneering works were by Eric Partridge, *Slang* and *A Dictionary of Slang and Unconventional Usage*. More recent is Geoffrey Hughes, *Swearing*. The major early dictionaries were those of Francis Grose, *A Dictionary of the Vulgar Tongue*, and J. S. Farmer and W. E. Henley, *A Dictionary of Slang*. On euphemism see H. Rawson, *A Dictionary of Euphemism and Other Doubletalk* and D. J. Enright (ed.), *Fair of Speech*.

The Anglo-Saxon Period

Excellent introductions are to be found in Bruce Mitchell and Fred C. Robinson, *A Guide to Old English*, Bruce Mitchell, *An Invitation to Old English* and Richard M. Hogg (ed.), *The Cambridge History of the English Language*, vol. I.

Middle English

Similar to the above are J. Burrow and G. Turville-Petre, *A Book of Middle English* and Norman Blake (ed.), *The Cambridge History of the English Language*, vol. II. On Chaucer, see R. W. V. Elliott's *Chaucer's English*.

Early Modern English

A useful study is that of C. L. Barber, *Early Modern English*. On Shakespeare, see Ifor Evans, *The Language of Shakespeare's Plays*, Hilda Hulme, *Explorations in Shakespeare's Language* and S. S. Hussey, *The Literary Language of Shakespeare*. A Shakespeare Glossary, by C. T. Onions has been revised by R. D. Eagleson.

Modern English

Two collections dealing with a wide range of topics are C. Ricks and L. Michaels (eds), *The State of the Language*, the 1980s and the 1990s editions. Philip Howard has a number of collections of essays on contemporary usage. Suzanne Romaine (ed.), *The Cambridge History of the English Language*, vol. IV, covers the period 1776 to the present.

Englishes Abroad

On pidgins and creoles, see Loreto Todd, *Modern Englishes: Pidgins and Creoles*. Brief decriptions of regional varieties are to be found in Loreto Todd and John Hancock, *International English Usage*. More specific studies are S. B. Flexner's thematic collection of American usage, *I Hear America Talking*; P. A. Roberts, *West Indians and their Language*; G. W. Turner, *The English Language in Australia and New Zealand*; and C. Pettman, *Africanderisms*. The last major edition of Webster was published in 1961, while the past decade has seen the publication of W. Ramson (ed.), *The Australian National Dictionary* (1988), P. Silva et al., *A Dictionary of South African English* (1966) and H. W. Ormson, *A Dictionary of New Zealand English* (1998). Recent works dealing with the global future of English are David Crystal, *English as a Global Language* and Tom McArthur, *The English Languages*.

SUBJECT AND AUTHOR INDEX

WORD INDEX